Visual Basic 5

Developer's Guide

Anthony T. Mann

SAMS PUBLISHING

201 West 103rd Street
Indianapolis, Indiana 46290

SAMS Developer's Guide

To my dear wife, Alison, who has been instrumental in the success of this book. Without her love and unbelievable support, this book would not exist.

FIRST EDITION

International Standard Book Number: 0-672-31048-1

Library of Congress Catalog Card Number: 96-72078

2000 99 98 4 3

Interpretation of the printing code: the rightmost double-digit number is the year of the book's printing; the rightmost single-digit, the number of the book's printing. For example, a printing code of 97-1 shows that the first printing of the book occurred in 1997.

Composed in AGaramond and MCPdigital by Macmillan Computer Publishing

Printed in the United States of America

Publisher and President *Richard K. Swadley*
Publishing Manager *Greg Wiegand*
Director of Editorial Services *Cindy Morrow*
Managing Editor *Jodi Jensen*
Director of Marketing *Kelli S. Spencer*
Product Marketing Manager *Wendy Gilbride*
Assitant Marketing Manager *Rachel Wolfe*

Acquisitions Editor
Sharon Cox

Development Editor
Fran Hatton

Software Development Specialist
Brad Myers

Production Editor
Tonya R. Simpson

Copy Editor
Bart Reed

Indexer
Erika Millen

Technical Reviewer
Jeff Perkins

Editorial Coordinator
Katie Wise

Technical Edit Coordinator
Lynette Quinn

Editorial Assistants
Carol Ackerman
Andi Richter
Rhonda Tinch-Mize

Cover Designer
Alyssa Yesh

Book Designer
Gary Adair

Copy Writer
David Reichwein

Production Team Supervisors
Brad Chinn
Charlotte Clapp

Production
Ayanna Lacey
Polly Lavrick
Paula Lowell
Mary Ellen Stephenson

Indexer
Erika Millen

Overview

V Communications, Internet, and Intranet Building

VI Databases

VII Rapid Application Development

VIII Appendixes

Contents

III Enterprise-Specific Features

IV Controls and Containers

V Communications, Internet, and Intranet Building

Acknowledgments

I wish to thank the following people for their help and/or support:

Fran Hatton, Development Editor; Bart Reed, Copy Editor; Jeff Perkins, Technical Editor; and Tonya Simpson, Production Editor. I especially would like to thank Sharon Cox, Acquisitions Editor at Sams. Sharon has been very understanding and supportive during this process.

All of the numerous people who work "behind-the-scenes" to make this book possible.

All of the vendors that sent products and information to be placed on the CD-ROM.

My family, for putting up with me for six long months.

This book is made possible because my dear wife has once again put up with my relentless pursuit of success. To her, I owe the world!

About the Author

Anthony T. Mann is a consultant with Hall Kinion in Denver, Colorado. He currently is on contract with Cadis, Inc., based in Boulder, Colorado.

Mr. Mann is also the founder of SoftHouse, specializing in home/office X-10–based automation. For more information about SoftHouse, visit its Web site at `http://www.vbasic.com`.

Mr. Mann specializes in client/server development and finding real solutions to business problems. His experience ranges from small to large companies such as Philip Morris and Sara Lee. He has written two other books published by Sams, *Real-World Programming With Visual Basic* and *Real-World Programming With Visual Basic 4*. He was a contributing author to *Visual Basic 4 Developer's Guide*, and has written technical articles and spoken at Visual Basic conferences.

If you are interested in contacting Mr. Mann about contracting work or any issues about this book, you can reach him by e-mail at `tmann@vbasic.com`.

Tell Us What You Think!

As a reader, you are the most important critic and commentator of our books. We value your opinion and want to know what we're doing right, what we could do better, what areas you'd like to see us publish in, and any other words of wisdom you're willing to pass our way. You can help us make strong books that meet your needs and give you the computer guidance you require.

Do you have access to the World Wide Web? Then check out our site at `http://www.samspublishing.com`.

As the executive editor of the group that created this book, I welcome your comments. You can e-mail or write me directly to let me know what you did or didn't like about this book—as well as what we can do to make our books stronger. Here's the information:

E-mail: Chris Denny
`cdenny@mcp.com`

Mail: Chris Denny
Macmillan Computer Publishing
201 W. 103rd Street
Indianapolis, IN 46290

Introduction

Visual Basic has come a long way since its introduction in the early 1990s. I have enjoyed developing in Visual Basic and watching its progression through the years. It now has become very widely used and accepted by major corporations. There are currently over three million registered Visual Basic developers.

Microsoft has made many people rich with this product, including everyone from developers to third-party control providers. All of this is due to Bill Gates' vision of a Rapid Application Development (RAD) tool to make Windows development easy and productive.

Visual Basic 5.0 has made many improvements and enhancements over version 4.0. Chapter 1, "The Visual Basic Environment and Development Life Cycle," illustrates the new features of version 5.0, probably the most significant of which is the capability to compile your applications into native code and the capability to create ActiveX components.

You have chosen a very comprehensive book, which gives you the benefit of my years of experience as an author and developer. I have tried to make the information clear and concise to get you up and running in the shortest amount of time possible. Because this book covers many topics, covering each as in-depth as I would perhaps like to is not always possible. In many cases, entire books have been written on each of the topics presented.

Because many new technologies have emerged in a relatively short period of time, this book attempts to discuss many of them, as well as show examples for some of them. Every effort has been made to make sure that the data and information in this book is timely and accurate. However, the book was written with Visual Basic 5.0, Release Candidate 1 (RC1). For further information, refer to the Macmillan Computer Publishing Web site at `http://www.mcp.com`. The following are some of the topics and terminologies discussed throughout this book:

> Active Desktop: Term that describes the use of ActiveX technology on the client. This includes scripting, components, and dynamic HTML on the desktop.
>
> Active Server Pages (ASP): Server-side scripting that enables you to create dynamic Web pages.
>
> ActiveX: Components that utilize the ActiveX technology and can be developed in Visual Basic 5.0.
>
> ActiveX documents: Documents (such as Excel spreadsheets, Word documents, and PowerPoint presentations) that can be viewed in a browser.
>
> BackOffice: Microsoft family of server products that function behind the scenes and are transparent to the client application.
>
> Component Object Model (COM): Model that defines how components will be defined and interact with each other.

Denali: The technology that makes Active Server Pages possible.

Exchange Server: A BackOffice product that enables you to send, receive, and distribute e-mail messages.

HTML: HyperText Markup Language, used to show Web pages in a client browser.

Merchant Server: A BackOffice product that allows for online Web shopping.

VBScript: A scripting engine that allows for client- or server-side interactive dynamic Web pages.

Viper: Allows for the easy deployment of distributed applications.

This book not only discusses some of the key features of Visual Basic itself, but how to interface Visual Basic with the following:

- Access
- SQL Server
- Exchange Server
- Excel
- Word

Who Should Read This Book

This book is aimed at the intermediate to advanced-level user. In many cases, topics are discussed very thoroughly. Therefore, even if you are not at the intermediate level, you can still get much information and use out of those chapters.

How To Use This Book

The book is divided into the following seven parts:

- Part I, "Concepts," discusses many general key topics, such as classes, add-ins, testing, and debugging.
- Part II, "The Windows Execution Environment," discusses many topics that relate to Windows itself, including DLLs, multimedia, printing, files, and graphics.
- Part III, "Enterprise-Specific Features," has a section of chapters that discuss new features available only in the Enterprise Edition of Visual Basic 5.0. Such features include the Microsoft Transaction Server (code named Viper), remote data objects (RDO), and the Transact SQL Debugger (T-SQL).

- Part IV, "Controls and Containers," discusses many concepts related to components, objects, ActiveX controls, and collections. It shows how to create ActiveX controls in Visual Basic. It also discusses how to create collections.
- Part V, "Communications, Internet, and Intranet Building," is an important section for dealing with communications. It mainly focuses on Internet and intranet building, including an HTML primer chapter. The communication chapters focus on MAPI and TAPI.
- Part VI, "Databases," shows how to perform all-important database actions. Very few applications do not interface with a database in some way or other. It covers topics from general database concepts to SQL, ODBC, client/server, and Crystal Reports.
- Part VII, "Rapid Application Development," shows how to create real-world programs using the topics discussed throughout the book. Such applications include creating wizards, interfacing with Microsoft Office, developing MAPI and TAPI applications, as well as client/server development.

Conventions Used in This Book

This book uses certain conventions that make it easier for you to use.

- A `monospaced font` is used to identify program code.
- An *`italic monospaced`* font is used to identify placeholders in the code. Replace the placeholders with whatever specific values will help you utilize the code.

NOTE

Notes are used to call your attention to information that is important to understanding the material covered.

TIP

Tips like this are used to identify ways to do things more efficiently.

CAUTION

Cautions are used to help you avoid common problems you might encounter and to keep you clear of potential programming difficulties.

TRIED AND TRUE

Tried and True boxes contain advice from the experts. Pay attention to these, because they will help you avoid problems, give you helpful hints, and tell you proven ways to do things.

I

Concepts

1

The Visual Basic Environment and Development Life Cycle

The Visual Basic environment is fully integrated and supports the full development life cycle. Visual Basic fully supports all phases of the Windows software development life cycle—from design, to development, to deployment.

Visual Basic is a member of Microsoft's Visual Studio, which is a fully integrated suite of Visual tools that all have the same look and feel. The following products are part of the Visual Studio:

- Visual Basic
- Visual C++
- Visual J++
- Visual FoxPro
- Visual InterDev
- Developer Network

What's New in Version 5.0

There is a plethora of new features in Visual Basic, version 5.0, which make it the most comprehensive, robust, multitier client/server development language on the market. The next few sections list these features. As you go through this book, you will notice the New to Version 5.0 icon placed adjacent to all topics that cover new material related to version 5.0.

General Enhancements

Probably the most significant feature is the new native code compiler. This feature compiles programs into true executables, which have been rated as being up to 20 times faster than P-code in version 4.0. The new compiler gives many different options for optimizing your compiled code, as follows:

- Optimize for Fast Code
- Optimize for Small Code
- No Optimization
- Favor Pentium Pro
- Create Symbolic Debug Info
- Assume No Aliasing
- Remove Array Bounds Checks
- Remove Integer Overflow Checks
- Remove Floating Point Error Checks
- Allow Unrounded Floating Point Operations
- Remove Safe Pentium FDIV Checks

There is a new version of Visual Basic, called the Control Creation Edition (CCE). The CCE is used to create only ActiveX controls, not applications (DLLs or EXEs). It is used to deploy your ActiveX controls over the Internet or in any ActiveX-aware product.

Version 5.0 supports only 32-bit code. Therefore, you need to use it on the Windows 95 or Windows NT platforms. Versions 1.0, 2.0, and 3.0 were 16-bit only. Then, in version 4.0, you had the choice of compiling for 16-bit or 32-bit applications. The logical progression is to support only 32-bit applications, which is what version 5.0 does.

You can write wizards to automate the writing of code. A wizard is an application, applet, or add-in that guides you through a series of steps to perform a task. The wizard takes the results of the question you answer in each step to determine how it will perform the task. Version 5.0 makes creating these wizards very easy. In addition to the capability to create your own wizards, version 5.0 includes many new stock wizards.

A new repository was introduced to manage component models, or tool information models (TIMs). A TIM is an object model that you write for one or more software tools. It contains any or all of the major software components, such as properties, methods, events, collections, interfaces, and classes. In addition, a TIM describes the relationship between these objects. A repository is a new addition to version 5.0 that enables you to store TIMs.

CROSS REFERENCE

For more information about writing wizards, refer to Chapter 39, "Creating a Wizard Add-In." For more information about the new stock wizards, refer to Chapter 2, "Stock Wizards."

Visual Basic 5.0 is a very open environment that supports the Client/Server Architecture, ActiveX, Component Object Model (COM), and Distributed Component Object Model (DCOM). It also supports Open Database Connectivity (ODBC).

CROSS REFERENCE

For more information about the Client/Server Architecture, refer to Chapter 28, "Database Concepts," Chapter 32, "Visual Basic's Role in Client/Server Computing," and Chapter 42, "A Client/Server Application." For more information about ActiveX, COM, and DCOM, refer to Chapter 19, "Components and Objects" and Chapter 20, "ActiveX Controls." For more information about ODBC, refer to Chapter 30, "ODBC."

Visual Basic IDE Enhancements

The Integrated Design Environment (IDE) now is completely customizable to suit your needs. Just as with most Microsoft applications, you can customize the toolbars as well as some menu settings. The IDE also fully supports right-mouse clicks. You are able to move and dock windows and panels. These docking (and linking) windows help make productivity levels high.

IntelliSense

A new feature that Microsoft calls IntelliSense enables the system to react in real time to your coding. There are five basic IntelliSense features:

- QuickInfo
- Complete Word
- Data Tips
- List Members
- List Constants

QuickInfo is a feature that presents to you in a tooltip-like window the syntax of the procedure you are trying to code. This includes subroutines, functions, and API calls. It even goes one step further in that it will bold the specific parameter you are coding in real time.

Complete Word is a feature that automatically completes the word you are typing after you have typed enough characters to make the word distinct within the list of available words.

Data Tips is a very useful new feature that simply shows the value of the variable in a yellow tooltip format, similar to the way a tooltip will appear on a toolbar. To use this feature, simply place your mouse over the desired variable in break mode. You will see the value of the variable as a tooltip without needing to press any of the keys on the keyboard. This is a tremendous time-saving feature.

List Members is a feature that is used to simply list all of the properties or methods available to a given object. It is smart enough to present a current list, depending on the level of object orientation the cursor happens to be on. For example, if you have typed the name of an RDO object, as soon as you type the "." object identifier, you will see a list of available properties and methods available for that object. After you select one or type one in and then type another "." object identifier, you will again see a current list of properties and methods available for that object.

List Constants is a feature that works the same as the List Members feature, except that with this feature available constant values for properties are shown when you select a specific property. This greatly increases your coding speed because you no longer need to look up constants.

Other Features

Multiple projects can now be loaded into the IDE and treated as one. For example, you can have an OLE Server project and its client project loaded at the same time. This saves a tremendous amount of time for coding and debugging. This is true for all of the products in the Visual Studio. Before this feature, a developer had to load multiple instances of Visual Basic, which meant slower debugging and a larger amount of overhead.

Quick watches can now be implemented as easily as placing the cursor over a variable in design mode. You will see a tooltip-like yellow banner, called a DataTip, showing the current value of the variable.

Here's a list of some other enhancements:

- Breakpoints can now be toggled simply with a mouse click, showing the status in the code margin.
- Tabs can be created to group ActiveX controls in the toolbox any way you want.
- You can place bookmarks in your code for quick location. The bookmark shows in the code margin.
- Call stack markers are shown in the code margin.
- Setting the next statement is as easy as dragging the current line indicator in the code margin to a new line of code.
- Properties in the property window can now be manipulated alphabetically, or even by category.
- A new Locals window displays the values of all variables within the scope of the procedures in the call stack.
- The Object Browser has been enhanced to allow the developer to search for a class or member in a specific library or across all referenced libraries.
- A nice new feature is block comment and uncomment. With the click of a mouse button, all highlighted code will be commented or uncommented.

Aligning and formatting controls are now placed on the toolbar, so you can resize or realign controls at the touch of a button. These formatting options can be applied to one or more controls. To format multiple controls, simply make sure that you select them with the mouse before you choose a formatting option. Here are the possible actions:

- Align left
- Align right
- Align center
- Align top
- Align middle

- Align bottom
- Align to grid
- Make same size
- Size to grid
- Make horizontal spacing equal
- Increase horizontal spacing
- Decrease horizontal spacing
- Remove horizontal spacing
- Make vertical spacing equal
- Increase vertical spacing
- Decrease vertical spacing
- Remove vertical spacing
- Center in form
- Bring to front
- Send to back

The Visual Basic IDE model is now fully exposed so that you can create robust add-ins. Before version 5.0, you could create only limited add-ins.

Internet-Related Enhancements

Your existing Visual Basic applications now can be migrated to an ActiveX document, which enables your application to install and run from an Internet browser (such as Internet Explorer). This frees the developer from needing to know languages such as HTML or Java. However, the developer still needs to know Visual Basic.

Version 5.0 now enables you to create ActiveX controls, which were formerly know as OLE controls. ActiveX controls can contain these features:

- Property pages to group properties by functionality.
- Default properties so that you do not have to specify a common property.
- ActiveX bundle for multiple controls in one OCX file.
- Digital signatures to authenticate your control.
- Data awareness to bind to a database.
- Containers to house or serve as a parent for another control(s).
- Asynchronous property reading so that an Internet/intranet browser can download property settings even before the ActiveX control is downloaded.
- Visibility so that a control does not have to be visible.

- Licensing so that legal rights to controls can be protected.
- Object models to produce a hierarchical object model within a control.
- Transparent background to allow the lower z-order control to show behind the control. The z-order is the order from front to back in which the controls are graphically positioned.
- Multithreading for performance.
- Versioning to prevent the wrong version of the control from being used.
- In-process and out-of-process support (depending on your development needs). An in-process application, typically a DLL, runs in the same address space as the application that called it. For example, if application A calls DLL B, then DLL B runs in application A's address space. An out-of-process application, typically either an application or a DLL, runs in its own address space. For example, if application A calls application B, then application B runs in a separate address space from application A.
- Accessibility from 32-bit DCOM clients on an ActiveX server or from 16-bit clients using remote automation.

CROSS REFERENCE

For more information about ActiveX controls, refer to Chapter 20, "ActiveX Controls."

You use ActiveX controls to create compact, reusable components in your own applications or on your Web pages. You can also use them in a wide variety of products, such as Office, Visual J++, Visual FoxPro, and Visual C++.

Along with ActiveX controls, you can define property pages to help group properties in a logical order.

Deployment Enhancements

Your applications can now be deployed so that they are part of a server-based setup. This allows users on a LAN, WAN, or Internet/intranet to automatically install the application when the user clicks a hyperlink in an HTML document.

Visual SourceSafe 5.0 is included in the Enterprise Edition so that source code can be shared and maintained.

Distributed Component Object Model (DCOM) components on remote computers is supported both in the Windows NT and Windows 95 environments. At the time of this writing, DCOM could be downloaded from the Microsoft Web site at

`http://www.microsoft.com/oledev/olemkt/oledcom/eng/dleng.htm`

Code Generation Enhancements

Version 5.0 includes many new wizards that help with frequent tasks or actually generate code, based on a series of questions. Such wizards include the following:

- The ActiveX Control Interface Wizard builds the functionality of a control.
- The ActiveX Document Migration Wizard converts Visual Basic projects to ActiveX documents.
- The Application Wizard generates new applications.
- The Class Builder helps build public interfaces to classes.
- The Data Form Wizard develops bound forms.
- The Property Page Wizard builds property pages for ActiveX controls.
- The Setup Wizard distributes and deploys applications, ActiveX controls, and ActiveX documents.
- The Wizard Manager enables you to create new wizards.

CROSS REFERENCE

For more information about wizards, refer to Chapter 2, "Stock Wizards," and Chapter 39, "Creating a Wizard Add-In."

You now can create a multithreaded application for maximum speed, throughput, performance, and scalablility. Multithreading used to be very complex to implement, and therefore it was avoided. With ActiveX technology, components must be multithreaded for performance reasons. Implementing a multithreaded application is as simple as selecting the Unattended Execution option, which automatically handles scheduling of threads, dead locks, and contention.

Database Enhancements

There are many new database enhancements in version 5.0. Each is listed next.

- Data Access Objects (DAO) version 3.5 now achieves performance that rivals RDO.
- Stored procedures can now be called as intrinsic calls within the Visual Basic language, itself.
- Database creation can be automated with database schema and design tools. These tools can also simplify the creation of complex queries.

- Performance analysis can be achieved by testing and prototyping distributed applications using "what-if" scenarios.
- The capability to debug stored procedures has been added. This is an important new feature that will help increase your productivity.

CROSS REFERENCE

For more information about the stored procedure debugger, refer to Chapter 17, "T-SQL Debugger."

Language Enhancements

Many new enhancements were made to the Visual Basic language itself. Each is listed next.

- The new `Implements` statement allows Visual Basic to support polymorphism.
- Typed optional arguments are now allowed so that parameters of public and private procedures are optional. Also, you can set a specific datatype for these optional arguments.
- A new datatype (`ENUM`) is introduced to allow for enumerations. This is fully supported in the IntelliSense features of Visual Basic 5.0.
- The new `GlobalMultiUse` class enables you to write global procedures to be used across applications without needing to instantiate the class.
- You can now raise (or generate) your own events in your ActiveX control creation.
- The new `AddressOf` operator enables you to use callback API functions never before possible in Visual Basic.

CROSS REFERENCE

For more information about the WIN32 API, refer to Chapter 13, "Using the WIN32 API."

- New "Friend" properties allow objects to communicate in a familiar way without exposing those properties to the outside world.

The Development Life Cycle

The development life cycle can vary widely from company to company. There are different methodologies—some work well for some companies, others work for other companies. Therefore, this section is not intended to be a "bible" on the subject. It is intended to be used as a suggestion for some situations, and to get you thinking about how to develop and manage your software.

This section was put into the first chapter to get you thinking about the development life cycle as a whole so that you can consider it as you go through the rest of this book.

Determining User Requirements

One of the most important aspects of the development life cycle is to determine user requirements. More often than not, users don't know what they want. All they know is that they want "something else." That's why this stage is so important. If the users do not have a clear view of what's necessary, then the project will change along the way, unless you determine requirements in advance.

That's where a good analyst comes in. A good analyst will not only have enough insight and business knowledge, but usually a good technical background to suggest different options to the user. These options are usually based on the scope and goal of the project.

If the goal is to write a technically superior, state-of-the-art project, then you probably want to focus your effort on graphics, animations, voice response, and so on. If the goal is to replace a current system or develop a new one that is functional, but within a low budget, then these things will not matter as much.

If you were given all the time and money in the world, then you could hire as many developers and designers as needed to make the most technically advanced, functional product on the market. However, the scope is usually somewhere in the middle of the road.

Design

The first step after determining the user requirements is to design and develop a prototype. Documentation is key in this area. Documentation of each feature, scope, purpose, and benefit enables the user to determine whether this is really what is necessary. Often, documentation can take more time to create than the actual coding of the feature or application.

A prototype is often created in Visual Basic so that the user can visually see what the system will look like. A prototype is generally just a visual representation of the screen or screens, including all controls. This lets a user "walk through" the system, without a developer taking the time to write any code. The only code you might want to write is to open and close forms.

The documentation should include a list of all controls on the form and how each will interact with the user and system. This means listing every event that can be fired within a control. For example, you might only code the `Click()` event of a `cmdClose` command button. You would simply write this upon clicking the Close button, and a warning will be presented if the user has not saved records. On the other hand, you might decide to show what the warning dialog box will look like. This, of course, gives the user a better picture of what will happen, but it takes more time.

Development

After the users buy off on the prototype and design, it is time to start development. The rest of this book is devoted to helping you in the development stage, providing insight into many different Visual Basic-related areas. This section of the book also provides you with standard coding practices to follow as well as naming standards.

Coding Standards

To ensure ease in maintaining your code, it is advisable to use naming standards. Many large Information Systems (IS) organizations mandate use of corporate standards. Most of the time the corporate standards are adopted using those standards set forth by Microsoft Consulting Services. The need for standards apply to the following:

- Variables
- Object names

These items are discussed in the following sections.

NOTE

Please keep in mind that these naming conventions are by no means "law." They are suggestions and practices that many Information Systems (IS) departments use.

Variable Naming Conventions

Variable naming conventions deal with not only how you should name your variables, but also indicate the scope of your variables. For example, you should be able to determine the type and scope of any variable simply by glancing at it. Variable naming conventions follow this general syntax:

```
[g/m][a]tName
```

where all indicators before the variable name (prefix) are in lowercase.

- `[g/m]` is used only if the variable is declared as global (`Public`) or at the module level (`Private`). Omit this if the variable is used as local to a procedure.
- `[a]` is used only if the variable is an array. Omit this if the variable is not an array. *t* is the datatype of the variable, as follows:
  - `n` for integer
  - `c` for currency
  - `d` for double
  - b for boolean
  - `y` for byte
  - `l` for long
  - `g` for single
  - `t` for date
  - `o` for object
  - `s` for string
  - `v` for variant
  - `e` for enum
  - `u` for user-defined type
- *`Name`* is the name of the variable, which should be germane to the actual usage of the variable.

As an example, suppose you were using a variable that will be used in a local procedure to increment a count in a loop. Following these standards, you would declare the variable like this:

```
Dim nLoopcount As Integer
```

If you wanted to declare a module-level variable in the `(general) (declarations)` section that will be used as a string array to store last names retrieved from a database, you would declare the variable like this:

```
Dim masLastname(100) As String
```

If you were to declare a `Public` currency to hold sales tax, you would declare the variable like this:

```
Public gcSalestax As Currency
```

If you wanted to declare a constant in a BAS module to hold the sales tax rate, you would name the variable in uppercase and declare it like this:

```
Public Const ggRATE = 0.05
```

Note in this example that the rate is being used as a single datatype, even though it is not explicitly declared as such.

Object Naming Conventions

Object naming conventions are as important to objects, such as forms and controls, as variable naming conventions are to variables. Variable naming conventions follow this general syntax:

```
oName
```

where `o` is the object type. This is described in Table 1.1.

Table 1.1. Proposed object names and abbreviations.

Object Name	*Abbreviation*
3D check box	`chk`
3D command button	`cmd`
3D frame	`fra`
3D group push button	`psh`
3D option button	`opt`
3D panel	`pnl`
Animated button	`ani`
Check box	`chk`
Combo box	`cbo`
Command button	`cmd`
Communications	`com`
Data	`dat`
Data-bound combo box	`dbc`
Data-bound grid	`dbg`
Data-bound list box	`dbl`
Directory list box	`dir`
Drive list box	`drv`
File list box	`fil`
Form	`frm`
Frame	`fra`
Gauge	`gau`
Graph	`gra`

continues

Table 1.1. continued

Object Name	*Abbreviation*
Grid	`grd`
Horizontal scroll bar	`hsb`
Image	`img`
ImageList	`iml`
Key Status	`key`
Label	`lbl`
Line	`lin`
List box	`lst`
ListBox	`lsb`
ListView	`lsv`
MAPI	`map`
Masked edit	`mas`
Menu	`mnu`
Multimedia	`mci`
OLE container	`ole`
Option button	`opt`
Outline	`out`
Picture box	`pic`
Picture clip	`clp`
ProgressBar	`pro`
Remote Data Control	`rdc`
RichTextBox	`rtb`
Shape	`shp`
Slider	`sli`
Spin button	`spn`
SSTab	`tab`
StatusBar	`sta`
TabStrip	`str`
Text box	`txt`
Timer	`tmr`
Toolbar	`tbr`

Object Name	*Abbreviation*
Treeview	`trv`
Vertical scroll bar	`vsb`

`Name` is the name of the variable, which should be germane to the actual usage of the variable. As an example, if you had a form used to input employee information, you would name the form `frmEmployee`.

If you need to place a text box on a form that stores the last name, you would name the control `txtLastName`.

One final example is that if you need to place a combo box on a form that lists all possible last names, you would name the control `cboLastName`.

You will notice from Table 1.1 that there are some items duplicated, such as 3D command button and command button. If you want, you could name a 3D command button something like `3cb`, but usually, if a 3D command button is used at all, it is used everywhere throughout the project. This potentially means that there is no need to differentiate between the two different types of command buttons. Again, these prefixes are only suggestions. There is nothing carved in stone. The most important thing is that you maintain some sort of consistency. It is a good idea for all programming shops to either use this list or come up with some standards of their own.

Testing

Testing is an important part of the development life cycle. It is difficult to express in a couple of paragraphs how much testing is necessary. The amount of testing required is related to the size and complexity of the application. It can also be related to the size of the company. However, the optimum situation is to have a third party (other than the developers and designers) test the software, and compare it to the technical documentation.

Some smaller companies tend not to perform the amount of testing required—for example, they won't hire a QA (Quality Assurance) person or technical writer (to document and test) because they view these people as "not billable." Consequently, the quality will suffer to some degree. The degree of suffering will depend on how thorough the developers are who do the testing.

One of the main reasons to have someone other than the developers perform testing is that this person will be more objective. He or she will be able to test the application as a new user would. A developer will only concentrate on specific areas.

Delivery

After you have completed the amount of testing deemed required by your organization and have corrected any problems, you are ready for delivery. Delivery is sometimes referred to as "distribution" or "deployment." Delivery can take place in many forms. One is through the Internet or an intranet. Also, you can distribute internally throughout your corporation or even an external corporation. Finally, you could be distributing to a retail end user.

Regardless of the type of delivery, the Setup Wizard can handle it. It will generate the program required for the correct type of delivery.

CROSS REFERENCE

For more information about the Setup Wizard, refer to Chapter 2, "Stock Wizards."

Summary

Visual Basic 5.0 has many new features that enhance productivity and give capabilities never before possible. These new features range from full native compiling to creating ActiveX controls for use with your own projects or on the Web.

Many of the new features in Visual Basic 5.0 are discussed in much more detail throughout this book. For example, the use of the new stock wizards are covered in Chapter 2. Classes are discussed in depth in Chapter 3, "Classes." Integrating with the products in the Office 97 suite is discussed in Chapter 14, "Integrating with Office 97." ActiveX components are discussed in Chapter 19 as well as in Chapter 20. You learn how to create your own wizard in Chapter 39.

In addition, if you are using the Enterprise Edition, you learn its new features, such as Visual SourceSafe 5.0, in Chapter 15, "Visual SourceSafe." Remote Data Objects 2.0 is discussed in Chapter 16, "Remote Data Objects (RDO)." The Transact-SQL debugger is shown in Chapter 17. Finally, the Microsoft Transaction Server (code named Viper) is discussed in Chapter 18, "Microsoft Transaction Server."

As you read each chapter, keep in mind the new features listed herein, as well as the development life cycle and coding standards. Each of these will help to make you a more efficient developer.

2

Stock Wizards

You've probably noticed that Microsoft has been incorporating its wizard technology in all of its products over the last couple of years. Visual Basic version 4.0 included only one wizard: the Data Form Designer (DFD). Also, it was difficult to create your own wizards. However, version 5.0 incorporates six stock wizards, all of which are covered in detail throughout this chapter. Version 5.0 also makes it easier to create your own wizards. This is covered later in Chapter 39, "Creating a Wizard Add-In."

Wizards are essentially add-ins, which make your life as a developer much easier. That's because wizards can generate code, forms, projects, and automate many repetitive tasks. They ask a series of questions and build code or forms based on the results of those questions. The six stock wizards included in Visual Basic version 5.0 are shown in the following list with an indication of which edition each is included in (L for Learning, P for Professional, E for Enterprise, C for Control Creation):

- Application Wizard (LPE)
- Data Form Wizard (PE)
- ActiveX Document Migration Wizard (PE)
- ActiveX Control Interface Wizard (PEC)
- Property Page Wizard (PE)
- Setup Wizard (PE)

With the exception of the Setup Wizard, for any of these wizards to be available on your system, you must have installed them during the setup process and selected them by using the Add-In Manager. To do this, select Add-Ins | Add-In Manager from the Visual Basic menu.

CROSS REFERENCE

Visual Basic also includes two other wizards that are not covered in this chapter. The first is the Class Builder Utility. It is covered in Chapter 3, "Classes." The second is the Wizard Manager. It is covered in Chapter 39.

Notice the format, look, and feel of the wizards mentioned so far. Later in the chapter, you will create a wizard that uses the conventions of these stock wizards.

The Application Wizard

You use the Application Wizard to rapidly build a template, prototype, or application framework. You can run the Application Wizard in one of two ways. The first is by selecting the

Add-Ins | Application Wizard menu option. The second is by selecting the Application Wizard icon when you create a new project. The New Project screen is shown in Figure 2.1.

FIGURE 2.1.
The New Project screen.

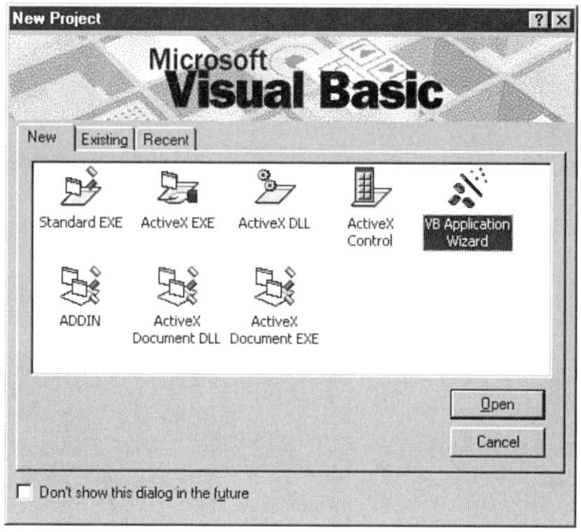

After you initiate the Application Wizard, successively clicking the Next button will present you with eight steps where you must answer questions. These questions are used to generate a project template specifically for your needs. These eight steps are described throughout the rest of this section. The first step is the Introduction screen, which describes the process briefly. You can disable this opening screen in the future by checking the "Skip this screen in the future" check box. Figure 2.2 shows this screen.

FIGURE 2.2.
The Introduction screen of the Application Wizard.

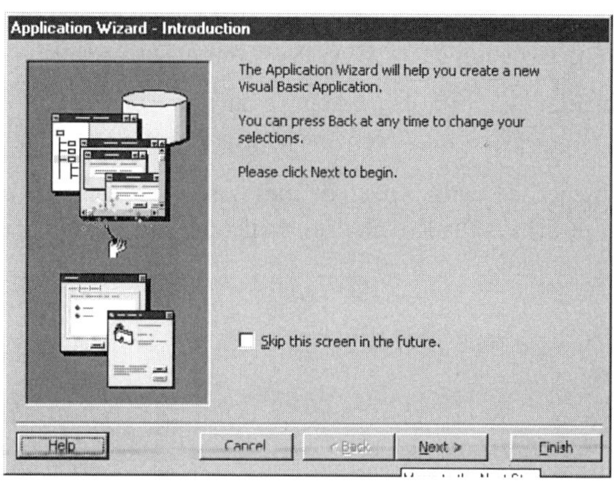

The second step, the Interface Type screen, defines the type of interface the application template will have. Figure 2.3 illustrates the three choices available, which are as follows:

- Multiple Document Interface (MDI)
- Single Document Interface (SDI)
- Explorer Style

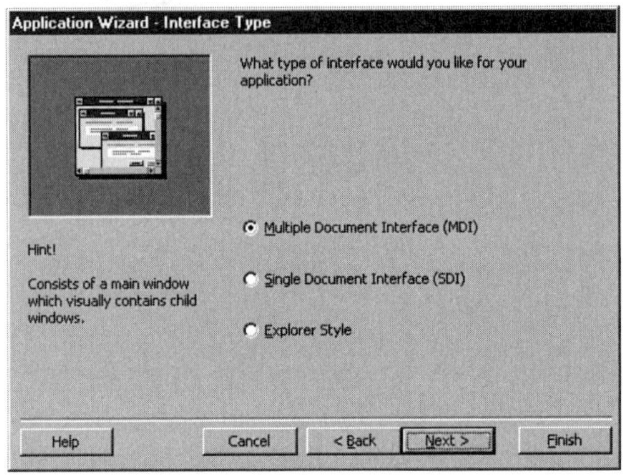

FIGURE 2.3.
The Interface Type screen of the Application Wizard.

Choose MDI applications if you need to have multiple client screens open at one time, with only one main parent screen acting as a container for those child screens. Such examples of this type of application include Microsoft Word and Excel.

Choose SDI applications if you need to have each screen operate independently. Such applications include Microsoft Notepad and Visual Basic, versions 1.0 through 4.0. Version 5.0 has the capability to configure whether to use an SDI or MDI interface.

Choose the Explorer Style if you want to have an SDI-type application, but with a hierarchical view of data or objects in a tree-view configuration.

The third step, the Menus screen, defines the type of menus the application template will have. Figure 2.4 illustrates the five choices available. The choices are as follows:

- File
- Edit
- View
- Window
- Help

FIGURE 2.4.
The Menus screen of the Application Wizard.

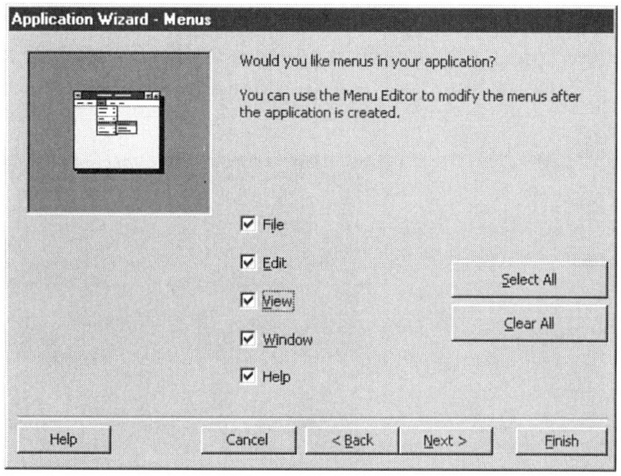

All options are available to MDI, SDI, and Explorer Style applications, except for the Window option. It is available only to MDI applications because only MDI applications enable you to cycle through windows, allowing the parent form to act as a container for those windows. Each one of these options, if checked, will be placed as a top-level menu item in your application.

The fourth step, the Resources screen, is used to specify whether a resource file will be included in the project. A resource file is used for localization, containing strings for different languages. Resource files are discussed in Chapter 10, "Writing Resource Files." If you want to include a resource file, you must select the Yes option button. This will enable the text box in which you must select the name of the resource file. Figure 2.5 shows what the Resources screen looks like.

FIGURE 2.5.
The Resources screen of the Application Wizard.

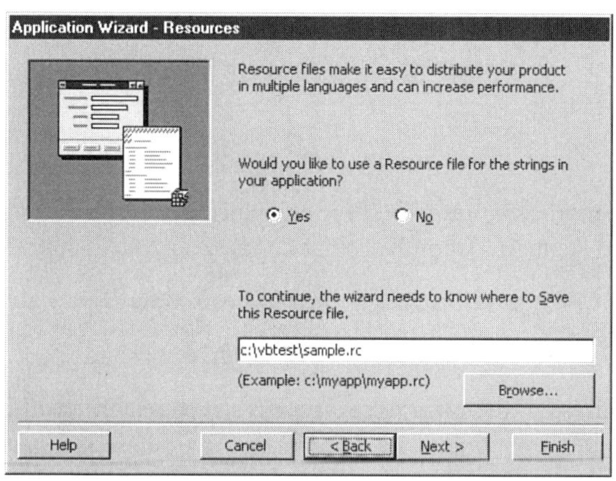

The fifth step, the Internet Connectivity screen, enables you to specify whether the application should enable Internet access. If it should, you can specify a default URL to use. Figure 2.6 shows what the Internet Connectivity screen looks like.

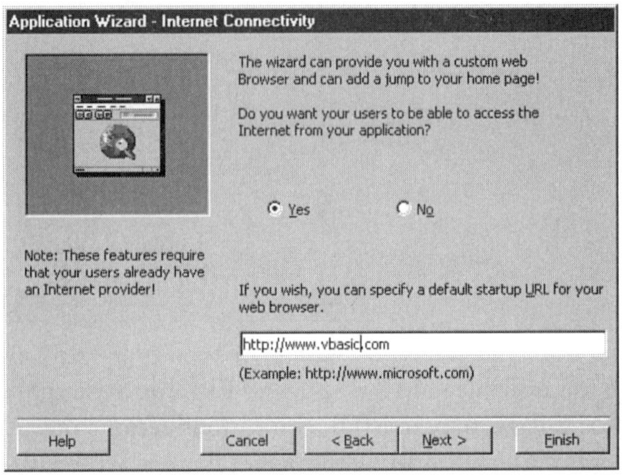

FIGURE 2.6.
The Internet Connectivity screen of the Application Wizard.

The sixth step, the Standard Forms screen, enables you to specify miscellaneous forms to be used in your application. You can choose from four stock options, or you can select an existing form template manually. Here are the four stock options:

- Splash screen at application start up
- Login dialog to accept an ID and Password
- Options dialog for custom settings
- About Box

Choose the Splash screen option if your application should show a logo form while the application is loading.

The Login dialog option builds a login and password form, commonly used in database access.

The Options dialog option will simply generate a form with a tab control, utilizing four tabs. These tabs are mainly templates that contain no code behind them.

The About Box option creates a form to be used to display about-type information.

Figure 2.7 shows the Standard Forms screen.

The seventh step, the Data Access Forms screen, enables you to build forms based on a database structure. This is similar to the Form Wizard described later in this chapter. You have two option buttons to choose from: "No, do not create forms from my database," or "Yes, create forms from my database." If you select the Yes option, you then must specify the type of database as well as the name of the database.

FIGURE 2.7.
The Standard Forms screen of the Application Wizard.

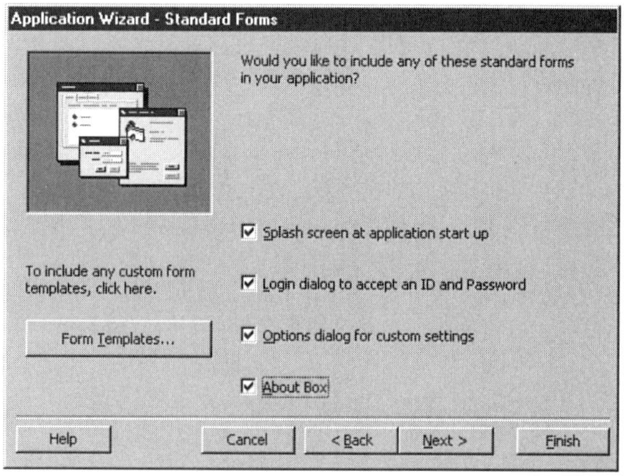

You have the choice of these types of databases:

- Access
- dBASE III
- dBASE IV
- dBASE 5
- FoxPro 2.0
- FoxPro 2.5
- FoxPro 2.6
- FoxPro 3.0
- Paradox 3.*x*
- Paradox 4.*x*
- Paradox 5.*x*

Figure 2.8 shows the Data Access Forms screen.

The eighth step, the Finished screen, simply enables you to name and create your new project. There are three pieces of information needed in this step. The first is what to name the application; simply choose a name. Project1 is the default project name.

The second is whether to create a summary report when your project is created. The default is Yes.

The third is a check box that specifies whether you would like the settings and choices you've made in all of the steps to be the default setting for future uses of the Application Wizard.

Figure 2.9 shows the Finished screen.

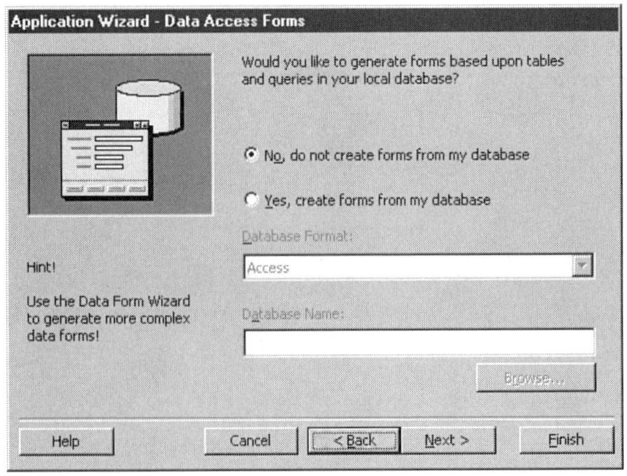

FIGURE 2.8.
The Data Access Forms screen of the Application Wizard.

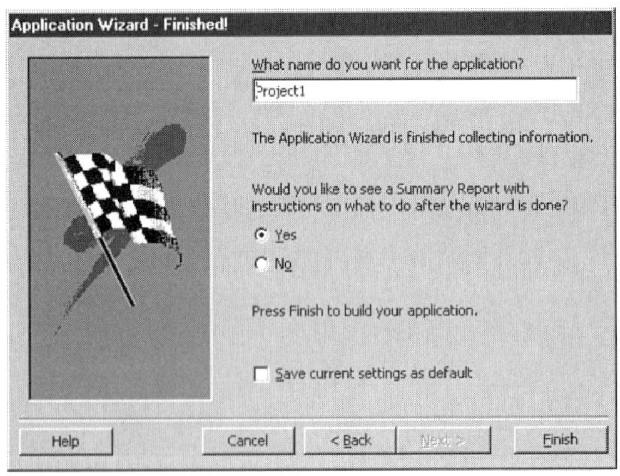

FIGURE 2.9.
The Finished screen of the Application Wizard.

You now have performed all the required steps for creating your application. Click the Finish button and watch your application be created.

Figure 2.10 shows how the finished application looks.

When the new project is created, if you have selected the Summary Report option in Step 8, you will see a dialog box that displays text similar to this:

```
Application Wizard Instructions:

The Application Wizard has finished creating your application.  Throughout the
project, you will find code comments indicating what you should do to add your
own functionality to the project.  Search for "TO DO" in the comments within
the project for more information.
What To Do Next

===============
```

```
You can save this report by clicking the "Save" button, or you can discard it
by clicking "Close".  Once you are returned to the Visual Basic environment,
run your application!  Press F5 or choose Start from the Run menu.

The Application Wizard has created the foundation for your application.  You
can begin by editing the project to fit your needs or you can run these other
Wizards to provide more functionality:

Data Form Wizard - Add more complex forms based upon your local or remote data
sources to your application.

Class Builder - Provide a rich object model for your application
using this tool.

ActiveX Document Wizard - Translate any of the forms in your application to
ActiveX Documents using this wizard.
```

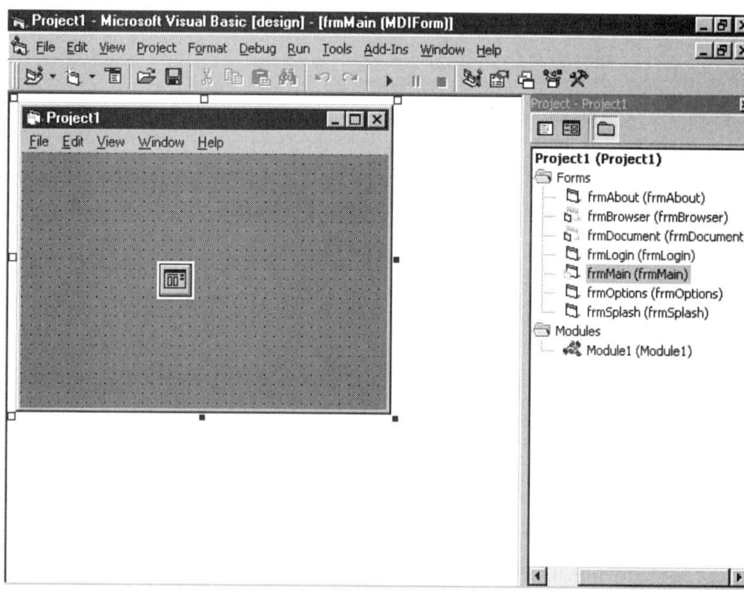

FIGURE 2.10.
Successful project creation using the Application Wizard.

The Data Form Wizard

You use the Data Form Wizard to rapidly build one form in an application that can provide data access based on tables and columns you specify from a database. This data access is provided through the use of a data control for a local database or a remote data control through a remote (ODBC) database. You can run the Data Form Wizard in one of two ways. The first is by selecting the Add-Ins | Data Form Wizard menu option. The second is by selecting the Project | Add Form menu option to bring up an Add Form dialog box. Select the VB Data Form Wizard option icon when you create a new project. The Add Form dialog box is shown in Figure 2.11. If you successively click the Next button, you will be presented with seven steps to complete the input process for this wizard.

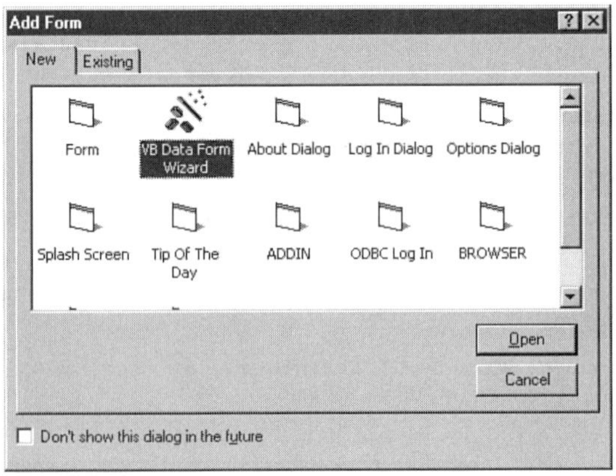

FIGURE 2.11.
The Add Form dialog box.

First, there is an Introduction screen, which you can disable by clicking the "Skip this screen in the future" check box. This screen is shown in Figure 2.12.

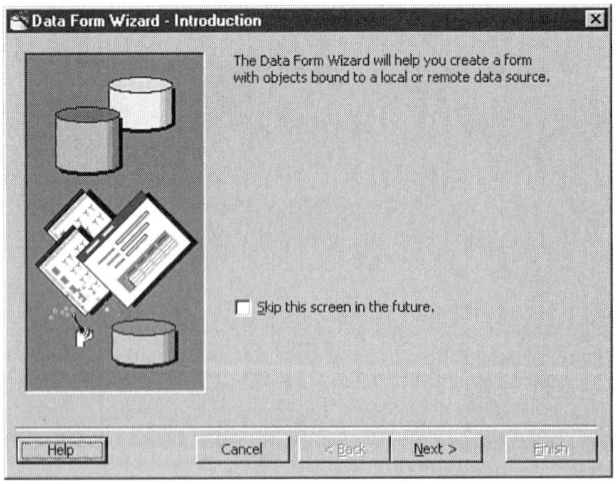

FIGURE 2.12.
The Introduction screen of the Data Form Wizard.

The second step, the Database Type screen, enables you to select the data source from which the form will be built. Figure 2.13 illustrates the choices available. Here's a list of the choices:

- Access
- dBASE III
- dBASE IV
- dBASE 5.0
- FoxPro 2.0
- FoxPro 2.5

- FoxPro 2.6
- FoxPro 3.0
- Paradox 3.*x*
- Paradox 4.*x*
- Paradox 5.*x*
- Remote(ODBC)

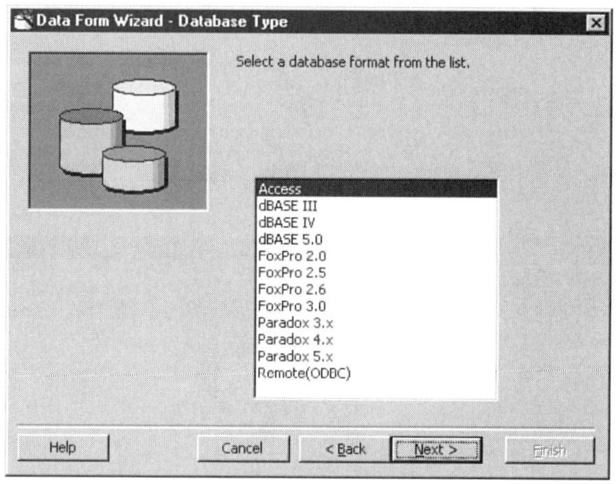

FIGURE 2.13.
The Database Type screen of the Data Form Wizard.

The third step, the Database screen, enables you to select the name of the database. This screen will look different depending on which type of data you selected in the Database Type screen. For example, if you selected Access in the Database Type screen, you will need to select the name of the `*.MDB` database. If you selected Remote (ODBC), you need to specify the connect string information.

Note that if you select the Remote (ODBC) option in the Database Type screen, you also must select from two other options. They are whether to use the data control or the remote data control. Figure 2.14 shows what this step looks like if you have selected the Access option in the Database Type screen.

In the fourth step, the Form screen, you select the format that will be used when the form is built. Figure 2.15 illustrates the available choices, which are as follows:

- Single record
- Grid (Datasheet)
- Master/Detail

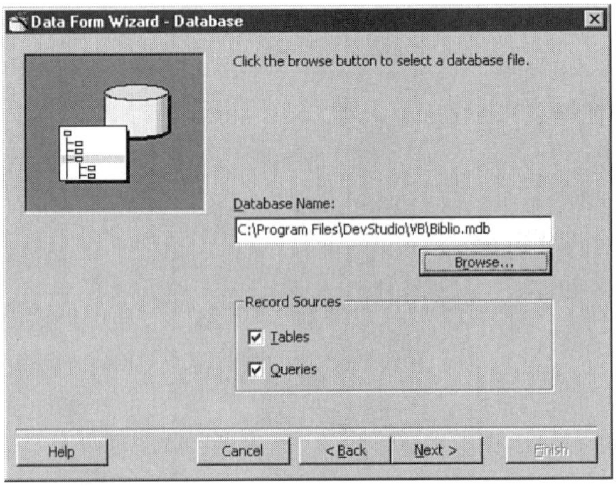

FIGURE 2.14.
The Database screen of the Data Form Wizard.

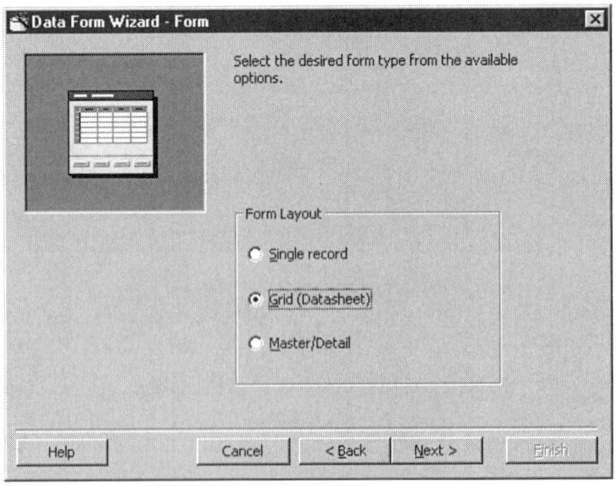

FIGURE 2.15.
The Form screen of the Data Form Wizard.

Choose the Single record option to see the data in a format that will present only one record on the screen at one time.

Choose the Grid (Datasheet) option if you want to present the data in a grid or spreadsheet format. All data available will be presented in the grid and editing will take place on the current row in the grid.

Choose the Master/Detail option if you would like to build a form in which you can choose a data item at the top of the screen and show a grid of data at the bottom of the screen. This enables you to manipulate a complex one-to-many relationship. The data source where the Master section comes from is different from that of the Detail section. See the following Note box.

The fifth step, the Record Source screen, enables you to specify not only which columns (fields) to show on the report, but also the order in which they will appear and how to sort the data. Figure 2.16 shows what this step looks like.

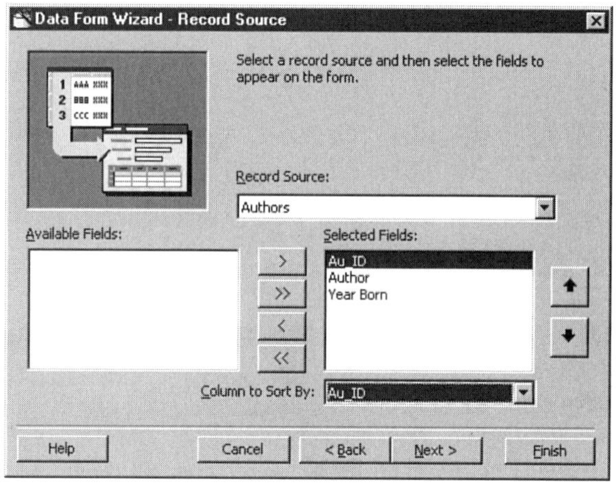

FIGURE 2.16.
The Record Source screen of the Data Form Wizard.

First, you must select the record source. The options presented in the list box are derived from the database selected in the previous step. After you select a record source, the Available Fields list box on the left will be populated with a list of fields from that table, query, or view. To select one or more fields, you must highlight them and click the buttons in the middle of the screen to move the fields to the Selected Fields list box on the right. You can also select a single item by double-clicking it. Then, you can reorder how the fields are placed on the form. The fields will be placed in the order shown in the selected list box. Therefore, if you need to reorder it, highlight the appropriate item and move it up or down by clicking on the up or down arrow. When all fields are in the correct order, you can choose how the records are sorted by selecting the field on which to sort in the Column to Sort By drop-down list. Note that the values in this field will be sorted in an ascending order.

NOTE

If you have selected the Master/Detail option, you will need to select the columns to view for the Detail section. You do this in another step. Also, when you specify the columns in the Detail section, you must specify how to link the columns in the potentially different tables for the Master and Detail sections. This will actually increase the number of steps from seven to nine.

The sixth step, the Control Selection screen, lets you specify which buttons will appear at the bottom of the form. It also enables you to choose whether the data control or remote data control (in the case of a remote data source) will be shown on the form. This allows for navigation between records. You have the choice of these types of buttons:

- Add
- Delete
- Refresh
- Update
- Close

Figure 2.17 shows what this step looks like.

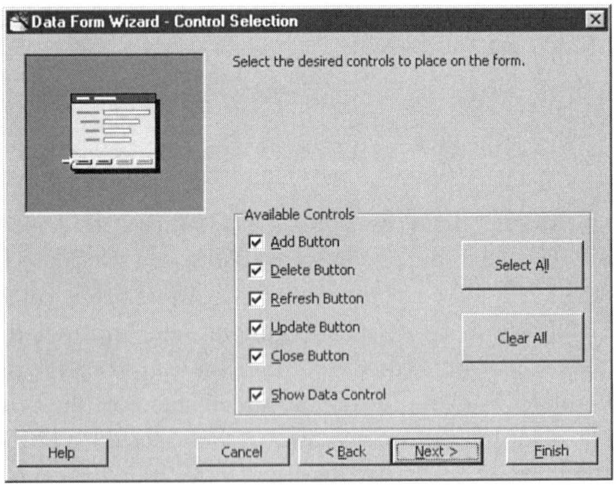

FIGURE 2.17.
The Control Selection screen of the Data Form Wizard.

The seventh step, Finished, simply enables you to name and create your new form. There are two pieces of information needed on this step. The first is what to name the form. Simply choose a name. By default, the prefix "frm" is followed by the name of the table, query, or view selected in the Database screen.

The second is a check box that specifies that you would like the settings and choices you've made in all of the steps to be the default setting for future uses of the Data Form Wizard.

Figure 2.18 shows the Finished screen.

You now have performed all the required steps to create your form. Click the Finish button and watch your form be created.

Figure 2.19 shows how the finished form looks.

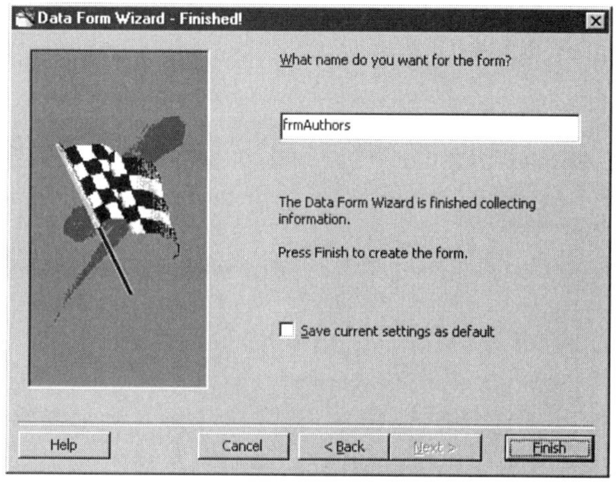

FIGURE 2.18.
The Finished screen of the Data Form Wizard.

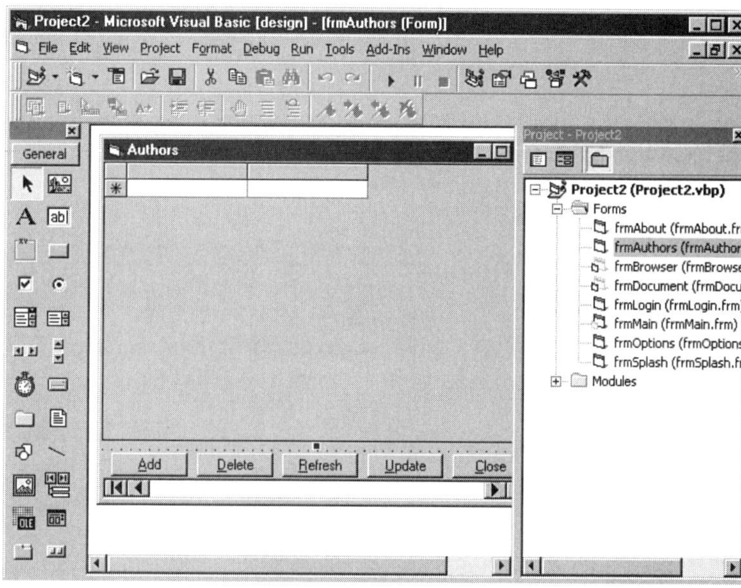

FIGURE 2.19.
Successful form creation using the Data Form Wizard.

The ActiveX Document Migration Wizard

You use the ActiveX Document Migration Wizard to help you migrate a form for use on the World Wide Web or in another Visual Basic application. Another way of thinking of ActiveX documents is to think of a way to have your Web browser view non-HTML documents. This can include Word, Excel, or even Visual Basic forms. To run the ActiveX Document Migration Wizard, select the Add-Ins | ActiveX Document Migration Wizard menu option. If you successively click the Next button, you will be presented with four steps to complete the input process for this wizard.

First, there is an Introduction screen, which you can disable by checking the "Skip this screen in the future" check box. This screen is shown in Figure 2.20.

FIGURE 2.20.
The Introduction screen of the ActiveX Document Migration Wizard.

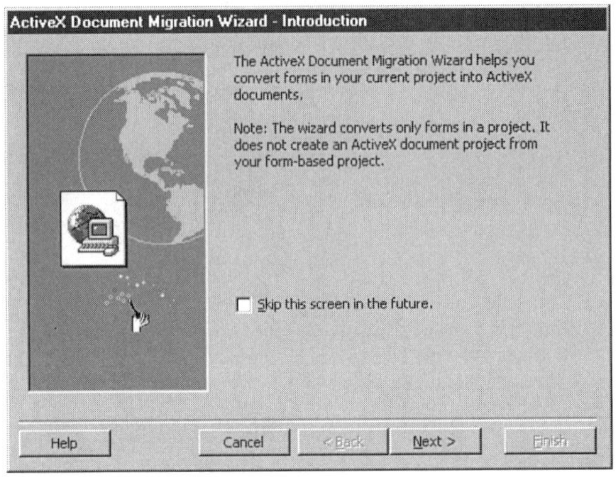

The second step, the Form Selection screen, enables you to select the form(s) that are to be migrated into an ActiveX document. The form must exist before you run the wizard. Figure 2.21 shows what this screen looks like.

FIGURE 2.21.
The Form Selection screen of the ActiveX Document Migration Wizard.

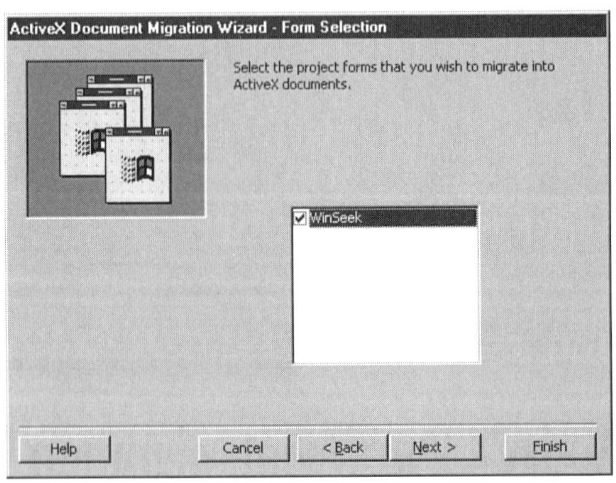

The third step, the Options screen, enables you to select from two options, both of which are check boxes. The first is "Comment out invalid code." Select this check box if you want form-specific code to be automatically commented out. These statements are not valid for ActiveX documents. Such code includes the following statements:

- `Show`
- `Hide`

- `Load`
- `Unload`
- `End`

The second option is "Remove original forms after conversion." This option will remove the form from the project in which it currently resides. You might want to do this if you intend to include the new ActiveX document in your project as an ActiveX document instead of a form. Figure 2.22 shows what this step looks like.

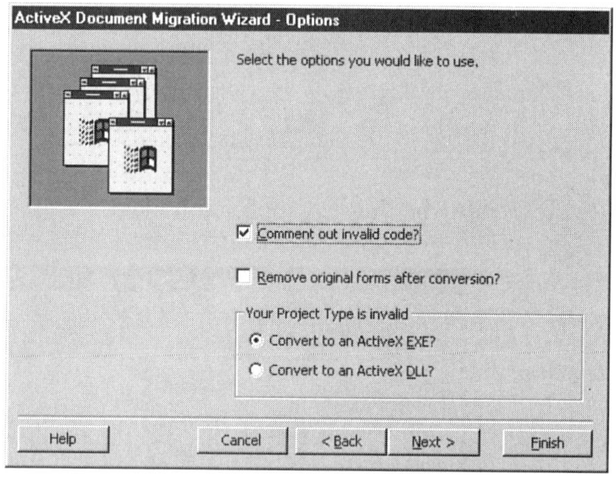

FIGURE 2.22.
The Options screen of the ActiveX Document Migration Wizard.

> **NOTE**
>
> If you see the message "Your Project Type is invalid" at the bottom of this step, then your project is not an ActiveX DLL or ActiveX EXE project. Your project will need to be one of these types to use the project as an ActiveX document. A standard EXE or DLL project will not enable you to run the wizard. Therefore, you are prompted whether you want to convert the format of the project to an ActiveX DLL or ActiveX EXE project.

The fourth step, Finished, simply enables you to name and create your new project. There are two pieces of information needed in this step. The first is whether to create a summary report when your project is created. The default is Yes. The second is a check box that specifies whether you would like the settings and choices you've made in all of the steps to be the default setting for future uses of the ActiveX Document Migration Wizard.

Figure 2.23 shows what the Finished! screen looks like.

You now have performed all the required steps for creating your application. Click the Finish button and watch your application be created.

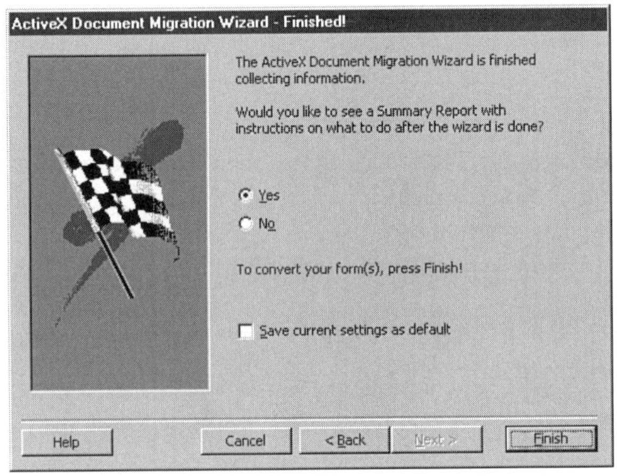

FIGURE 2.23.
The Finished screen of the ActiveX Document Migration Wizard.

Figure 2.24 shows how the finished application looks.

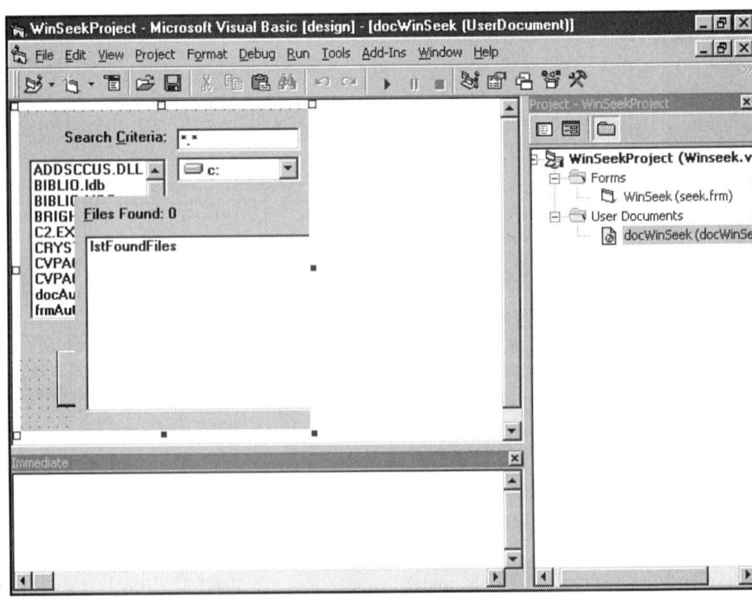

FIGURE 2.24.
Successful creation using the ActiveX Document Migration Wizard.

When the ActiveX document is created, if you have selected the Summary Report option in the Finished step, you will see a dialog box that displays text similar to this:

```
The ActiveX Document Migration Wizard has finished converting your forms.

What To Do Next
===============
```

```
ActiveX Document based applications provide a seamless way for Visual Basic
developers to create applications that run in-place in ActiveX Document
container applications, such as Microsoft Internet Explorer and Microsoft
Office Binder.

While a UserDocument is very similar to a standard Visual Basic form, there
are subtle differences. For example, with a standard form, there are methods to
show, hide, load, and unload forms. But because the UserDocument object's
display and lifetime are handled by the container, these methods don't apply.
Additionally, navigating between ActiveX documents typically requires using the
Hyperlink object.

To test your new ActiveX document in Internet Explorer:

1 Press F5 to run your project.

2 Switch to Internet Explorer.

3 On the File menu, click Open, and type in the name of the temporary .vbd file
created for your ActiveX document, then click OK.

4 You can then test and debug your project in the same manner as any other
ActiveX DLL or EXE project.

To test your new ActiveX document in Office Binder:

1 Press F5 to run your project.

2 Switch to Office Binder

3 On the Section menu click Add to display the Add Section dialog box. From the
list of ProgID's, double-click the ProgID of your ActiveX document.

4 You can then test and debug your project in the same manner as any other
ActiveX DLL or EXE project.

For a step-by-step lesson that teaches the basic principles of creating an
ActiveX document from scratch, see Chapter 5, "Creating an ActiveX Document,"
in "Creating ActiveX Components," in the Component Tools Guide, available in
the Professional and Enterprise editions.

For more details about ActiveX document creation, see Chapter 11, "Building an
ActiveX Document," in "Creating ActiveX Components," in the Component Tools
Guide, available in the Professional and Enterprise editions.
```

The ActiveX Control Interface Wizard

You use the ActiveX Control Interface Wizard to help you create the public interface for ActiveX controls. You must have at least one user control in your current project to run this wizard because the public interface (properties, methods, and so on) are being defined for the user interface that you already defined in the user control. For more information about user controls, refer to Chapter 20, "ActiveX Controls." To run the ActiveX Control Interface Wizard, select the Add-Ins | ActiveX Control Interface Wizard menu option. If you successively click the Next button, you will be presented with six steps to complete the input process for this wizard.

First, there is an Introduction screen, which you can disable by clicking the "Skip this screen in the future" check box. This screen is shown in Figure 2.25.

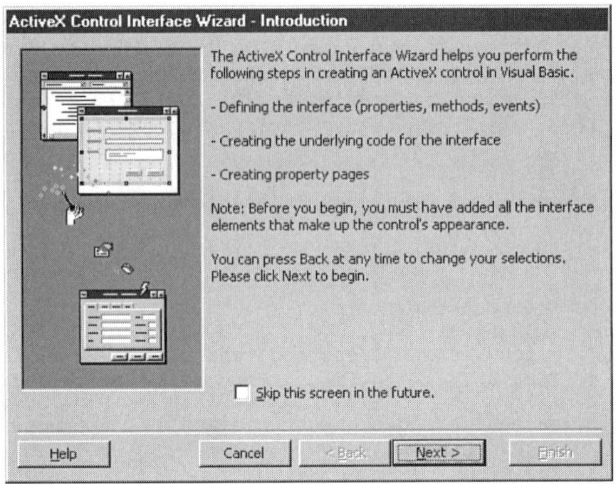

FIGURE 2.25.
The Introduction screen of the ActiveX Control Interface Wizard.

The second step, Select Interface Members, enables you to select the standard properties, methods, and events that will be automatically assigned to your interface. You select only the keywords in this step. You assign how they are mapped in the Set Mapping step later. Figure 2.26 shows what this step looks like.

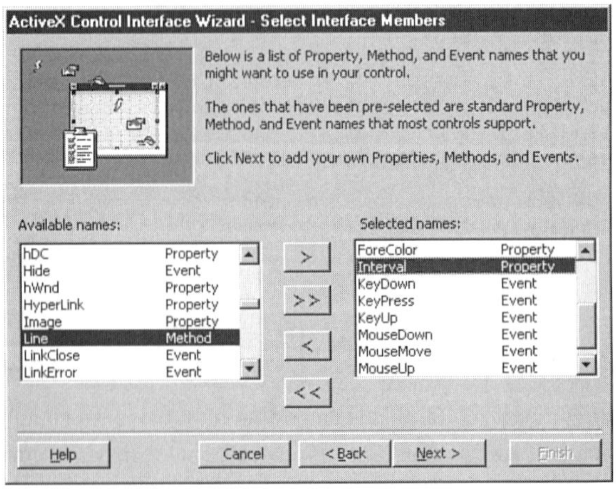

FIGURE 2.26.
The Select Interface Members screen of the ActiveX Control Interface Wizard.

The third step, Create Custom Interface Members, enables you to assign your own properties, methods, and events. You do this by selecting the New command button. Figure 2.27 shows what this step looks like, and Figure 2.28 shows what the screen looks like when you click the New command button.

FIGURE 2.27.
The Create Custom Interface Members screen of the ActiveX Control Interface Wizard.

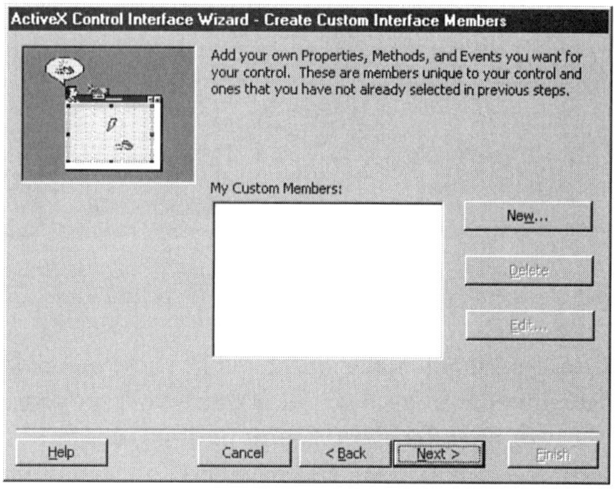

FIGURE 2.28.
ActiveX Control Interface Wizard—adding new properties, methods, and events.

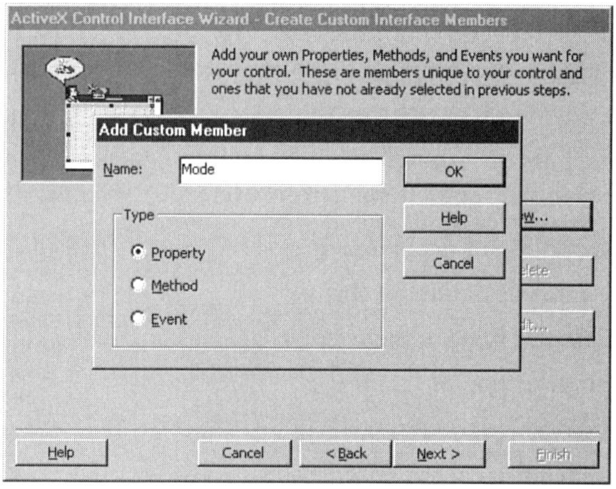

The fourth step, Set Mapping, enables you to map your standard (as well as custom) properties, methods, and events to specific methods of existing controls. Figure 2.29 shows what this step looks like.

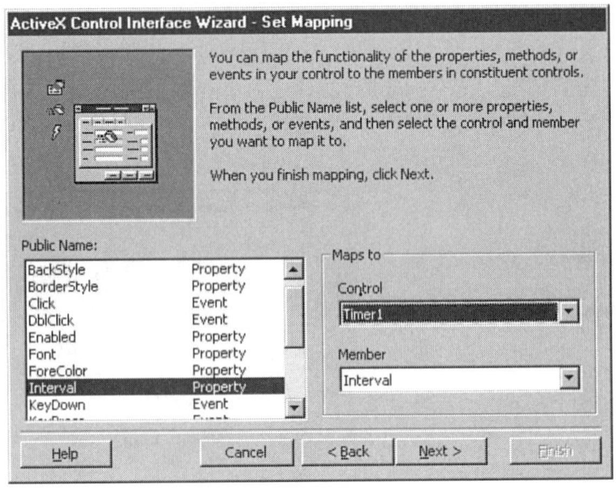

FIGURE 2.29.
The Set Mapping screen of the ActiveX Control Interface Wizard.

To use this screen, simply highlight the public name on the left and select the control in the user interface from the drop-down list on the right. Then assign it to a member of that control from the Member drop-down list. Continue doing this for each property, method, and event that you want to assign to a standard member.

For example, suppose you wanted your user control to have a `BackColor` property. If you wanted this `BackColor` property to set the `BackColor` property of a label shown in your user control, then you map the `BackColor` property of the user control to the `BackColor` property of the label control.

The fifth step, Set Attributes, enables you to assign any property, method, or event that was not mapped in the Set Mapping screen. Here are the values that can be assigned:

- A description of the member
- The datatype of the member
- The default value of the member
- Runtime attributes
- Design-time attributes
- Arguments

Because the members that you assigned are going to be the only public interface your applications will see, you expect them to be of a certain datatype with a default value. You also expect that they will behave a certain way during runtime and design time. That's why these values can be set on this screen. For more information about building user controls, refer to Chapter 20. Figure 2.30 shows the Set Attributes screen.

FIGURE 2.30.
The Set Attributes screen of the ActiveX Control Interface Wizard.

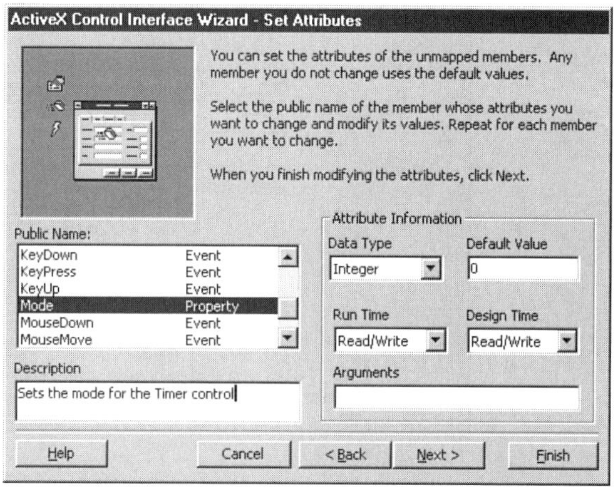

The sixth step, Finished, simply enables you to view a summary of the activity created by this wizard. Figure 2.31 shows this step.

FIGURE 2.31.
The Finished screen of the ActiveX Control Interface Wizard.

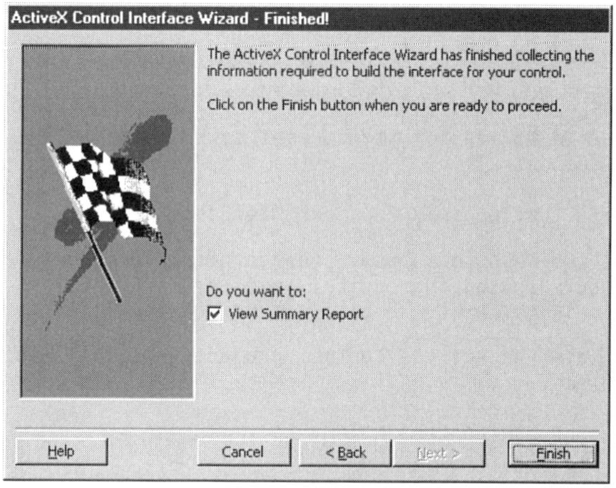

You have now performed all the required steps to create your ActiveX interface. Click the Finish button and the interface will be created. Figure 2.32 shows how the finished interface looks.

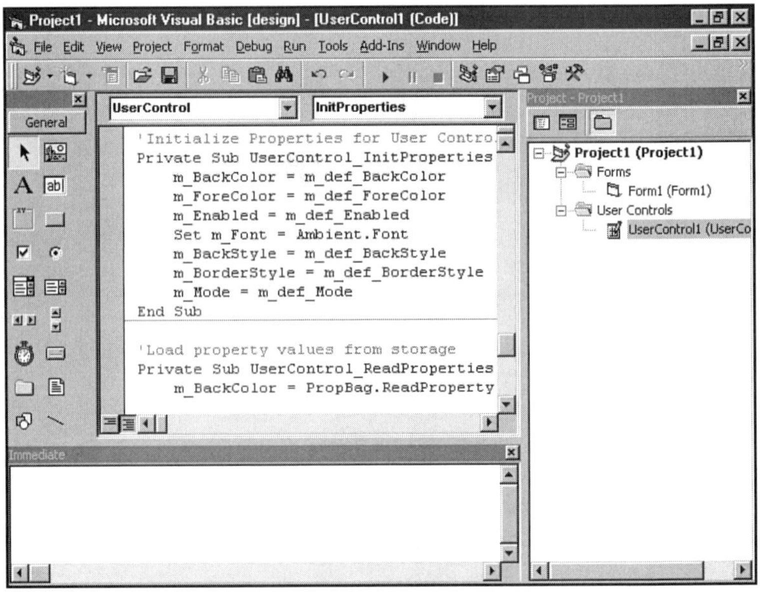

FIGURE 2.32.
Successful interface creation using the ActiveX Control Interface Wizard.

When the ActiveX interface is created, if you have selected the Summary Report option in the Finished step, you will see a dialog box that displays text similar to this:

```
Below is a To Do list of items required to complete the testing and debugging
of your UserControl.

A) Create a test program for your UserControl

There are two ways to set up a test program for your UserControl, depending on
whether you inserted the control in a Standard EXE, or created an ActiveX
Control project for it.

If you created an ActiveX Control project, the following steps will set up a
test program:

1)  Save your UserControl.

2)  Close your UserControl's designer, to put the control in run mode.

3)  If you haven't already created a test project, add a Standard EXE project
by selecting Add Project from the File menu.

4)  In the Toolbox, double-click your UserControl's icon to place an instance
of your UserControl on Form1, in the Standard EXE project.  You can move and
resize the control as needed.

5)  Save the project group. In later development and test sessions, you can
open both projects at once by opening the project group.

If you inserted the UserControl in an existing Standard EXE project,
follow these steps:
```

```
1)  Save your UserControl.

2)  Close your UserControl's designer, to put the control in run mode.

3)  In the Project window, double-click Form1 in the Standard EXE project, to
open its designer.

4)  In the Toolbox, double-click your UserControl's icon to place an instance
of your UserControl on Form1.  You can move and resize the control as needed.

B) Test your control's behavior at design time, and at run time.

1)  Select the control you placed on Form1 in the test project, and press F4
to open the Properties window. Verify that you can see and change the
properties you added to your control.

2)  Close Form1 and reopen it, and verify that the property values for your
control were correctly saved and retrieved.

3)  Double-click the control you placed on Form1, and verify that the
appropriate events appear in the right-hand (Procedure) drop down of the code
window.

4)  Add test code to the event procedures for your control.

5)  Add other controls, and put code in their event procedures to test the
run-time behavior of your control's properties and methods.

6)  Press F5 to run the test project, and test your control's run-time behavior.

You can modify your control by running the Wizard again, and selecting
your UserControl.

For more information on creating and testing ActiveX Controls, please read
Chapter 4, "Creating an ActiveX Control,"
and Chapter 9, "Building ActiveX Controls."

Chapter 6, "General Principles of Component Design," and Chapter 7, "Debugging,
Testing, and Deploying ActiveX Components," contain additional information
you may find useful.
```

The Property Page Wizard

You use the Property Page Wizard to help you create property pages for your user controls. Property pages can be very useful in organizing properties into logical groups. Property pages appear as an entry in the property sheet as a "Custom..." entry. When you click on the "..." you will see the property page. If you specify more than one property page, each will appear as its own tab. To run the Property Page Wizard, select the Add-Ins | Property Page Wizard menu option. If you successively click the Next button, you will be presented with four steps to complete the input process for this wizard.

First, there is an Introduction screen, which you can disable by clicking the "Skip this screen in the future" check box. This screen is shown in Figure 2.33.

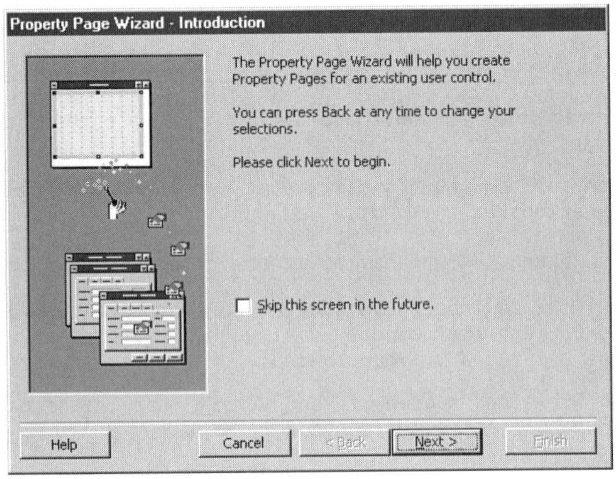

FIGURE 2.33.
The Introduction screen of the Property Page Wizard.

The second step, Select the Property Pages, enables you to add the property pages to be used with the specific user control. You can add multiple pages for use with your control. To add a new page, you can click the Add command button and type the name of the page. If you want to rename a page, simply click the Rename command button and type your new name. If you want to change the order of a specific page, click the appropriate page and then click the up and down arrows to place it in the desired position. Figure 2.34 shows what this step looks like.

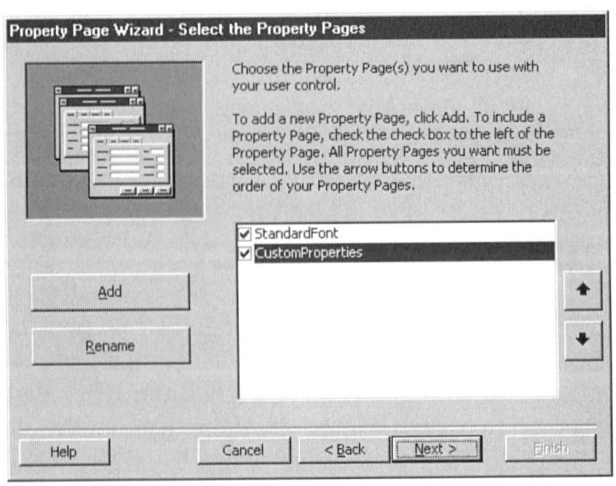

FIGURE 2.34.
The Select the Property Pages screen of the Property Page Wizard.

The third step, Add Properties, enables you to add the specific properties of a user control to the property pages defined in the previous step. You can assign a property in one of two ways. You can click the appropriate page to be used with the specific user control and then double-click the appropriate property. The other method is to click the specific property and drag-and-drop it on the property page. Figure 2.35 shows what this step looks like.

FIGURE 2.35.
The Add Properties screen of the Property Page Wizard.

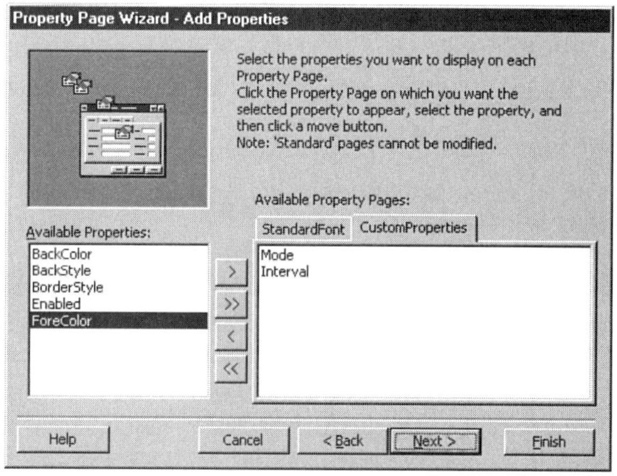

The fourth step, Finished, simply enables you to view a summary of the activity created by this wizard. Figure 2.36 shows what this step looks like.

FIGURE 2.36.
The Finished screen of the Property Page Wizard.

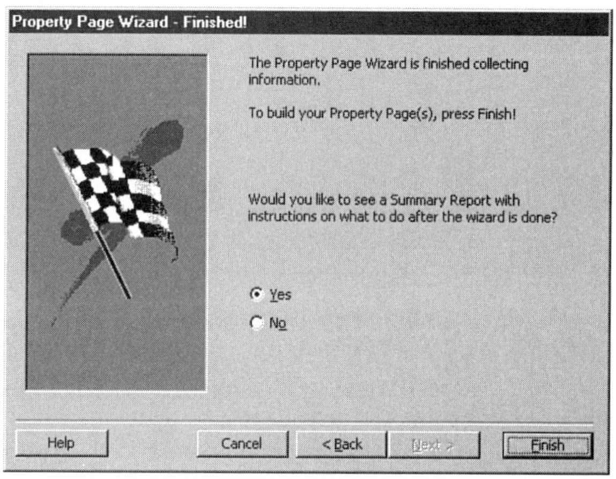

You now have performed all the required steps to create your property page. Click the Finish button and the property page will be created.

Figure 2.37 shows how the property page looks.

When you have created the property page, if you have selected the Summary Report option in the Finished screen, you will see a dialog box that displays text similar to this:

```
Property Page Wizard Instructions:

The Property Page Wizard has finished creating and modifying property pages.
Throughout the project, you will find code comments indicating what you should
```

```
do to add your own functionality to the project.  Search for "TO DO" in the
comments within the project for more information.

What To Do Next

===============

You can save this report by clicking the "Save" button, or you can discard it
by clicking "Close".
```

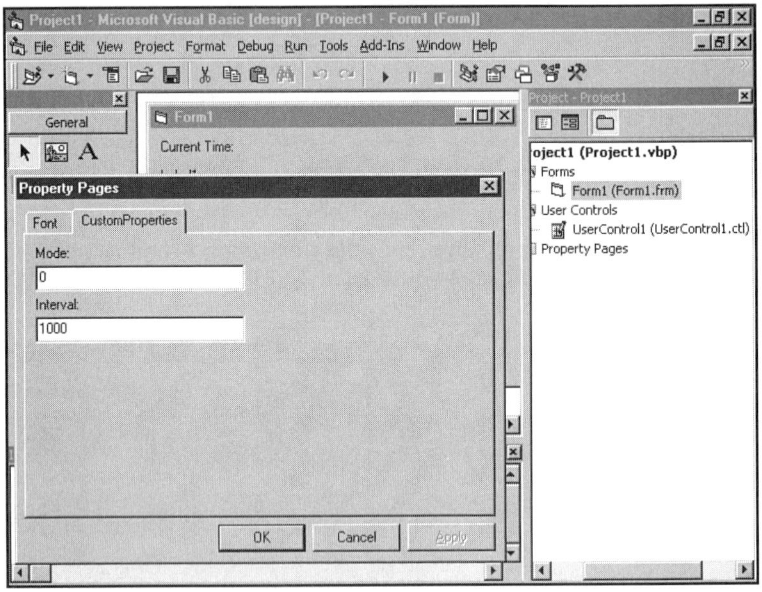

FIGURE 2.37.
Successful property page creation using the Property Page Wizard.

The Setup Wizard

You use the Setup Wizard to create distribution disks for your projects. The Setup Wizard looks at your project file (with a `*.VBP` file extension) and determines which files are necessary to distribute. It then compresses the files and places them on the disks. You have the option of creating a setup that deploys your project on a diskette, a single directory, or disk directories. A disk directory is a directory structure created on a hard disk that contains files which could be stored on diskettes at a later time. Furthermore, you have the option of creating a setup program or an automatic download program for use on the Internet. This section goes through the steps and issues involved in using this wizard. Again, the Setup Wizard is only included in the Professional and Enterprise editions of Visual Basic 5.0.

The Setup Wizard in earlier versions of Visual Basic has had some problems. The new version is much more stable. However, the Setup Wizard will not work in every case. For example, if your setup program not only must install files, but must update a database or needs more flexibility, you cannot use the Setup Wizard. You must either write the setup program yourself, possibly in Visual Basic, or use third-party setup programs. One such program is the Sax Setup Wizard, from Sax Software. There is a demonstration on the CD accompanying this book in the `\DEMO\SAX\SETUP` subdirectory.

You don't run the Setup Wizard by using the Add-Ins menu option (like other wizards in this chapter). To run the Setup Wizard, select the Application Setup Wizard menu option from the Visual Basic 5.0 Program Manager or Explorer group. If you successively click the Next button, you will be presented with eight steps to complete the input process for this wizard.

First, there is an Introduction screen, which you can disable by checking the "Skip this screen in the future" check box. This screen is shown in Figure 2.38.

FIGURE 2.38.
The Introduction screen of the Setup Wizard.

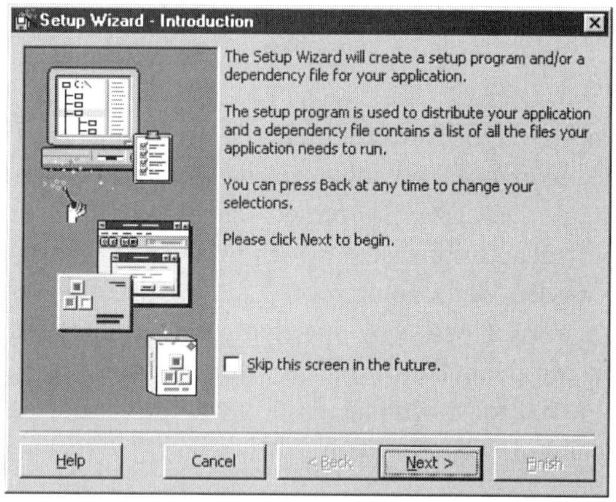

The second step, Select Project and Options, enables you to define the attributes of your setup program. These include the Visual Basic project (`*.VBP`) file. Alternatively, you can choose a Setup Wizard template (`*.SWT`) file, if you have previously saved a template. Another important option in this step is to instruct the Setup Wizard as to the type of setup you would like. You have three possible choices, which are shown in Figure 2.39. These choices are as follows:

- Create a Setup Program
- Create Internet Download Setup
- Generate Dependency File Only

Use the first option if you want to simply generate a setup program, having the wizard scan your `*.VBP` file for all dependencies and compressing all files for use with distribution. Creating a setup program gives you the option of generating a dependency (`*.DEP`) file with your application. This tells the setup program information about each specific dependency file to be included in your setup. It is advised always to select this option.

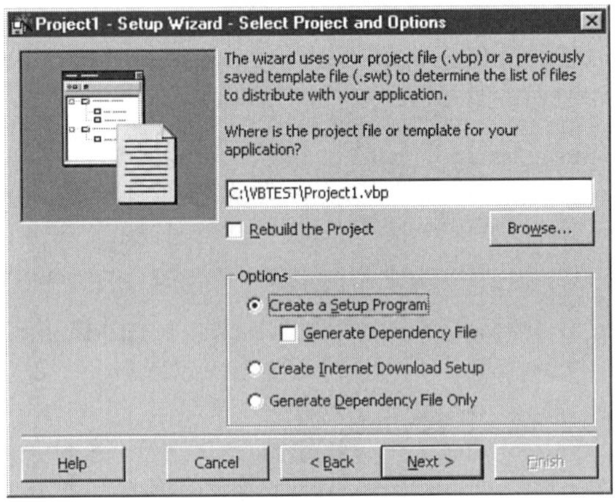

FIGURE 2.39.
The Select Project and Options screen of the Setup Wizard.

New to Version 5.0

The second option is to create an Internet download setup. This is a new feature that has never been included in any of the earlier setup wizards. To use this option, the project must be an ActiveX DLL, ActiveX EXE project, or ActiveX control. If you choose this option, you will be presented with an additional step, which instructs the Setup Wizard where to get the runtime components needed for the application. You have the option of downloading from the Microsoft Web site or of using a local copy, specifying the Internet URL or UNC. You can also leave this option blank and the default location will be used. The Setup Wizard will construct a single cabinet file (`*.CAB`) for download. Each `*.CAB` file contains all required files for setup, such as all ActiveX components.

One other aspect of this screen is that it enables you to stamp (or mark) your components as being safe for scripting and safe for initialization.

NOTE

Marking a component as being safe for scripting and initialization is required for any ActiveX component used in Internet Explorer, version 3.0 or higher.

Figure 2.40 shows what this additional step looks like.

The third step, Distribution Method, enables you to specify how you would like to distribute your application. Here are the three available choices:

- Floppy disk
- Single Directory
- Disk Directories

The first choice, Floppy Disk, is for generating one or more distribution diskettes.

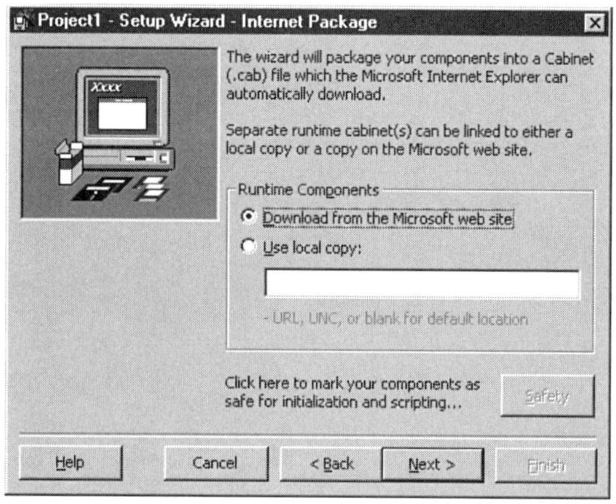

FIGURE 2.40.
The additional Internet Package screen of the Setup Wizard.

The second choice, Single Directory, is typically used for a network installation or a test installation. This type of distribution places all files into one directory on a drive that you specify.

The third choice, Disk Directories, is similar to the Single Directory option, except that each of the files is placed into a disk directory, such as `\DISK1`, `\DISK2`, and so on. This is useful when you have many diskettes to distribute but you don't want too many files in one directory (which is difficult to maintain).

Figure 2.41 shows the Distribution Method screen.

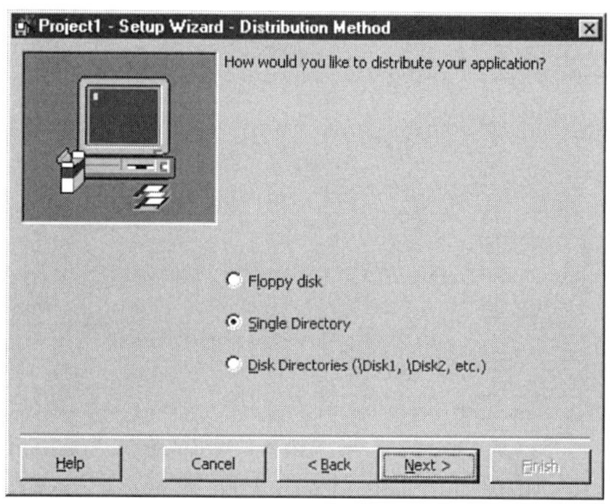

FIGURE 2.41.
The Distribution Method screen of the Setup Wizard.

The fourth step, Single Directory, simply enables you to specify the drive and directory on which the files will be installed. Figure 2.42 shows what this screen looks like.

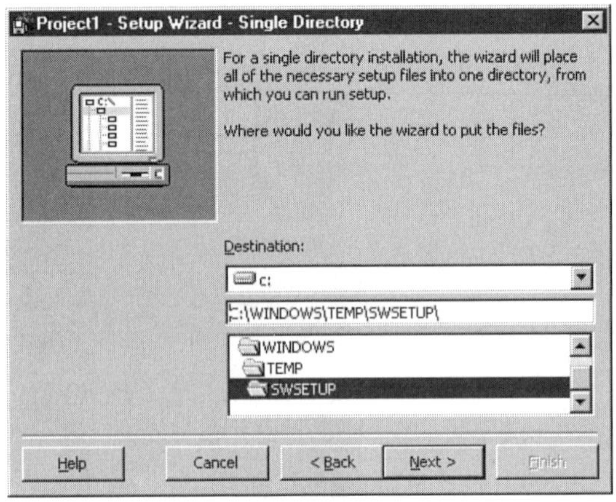

FIGURE 2.42.
The Single Directory screen of the Setup Wizard.

The fifth step, ActiveX Components, enables you to add either local ActiveX DLLs and ActiveX EXEs or Remote ActiveX components (VBRs). Simply click the Add Local or Add Remote command buttons to add the ActiveX component. Figure 2.43 shows what this screen looks like.

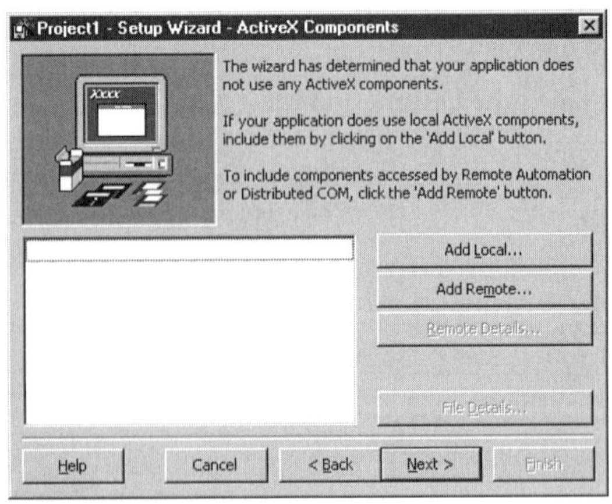

FIGURE 2.43.
The ActiveX Components screen of the Setup Wizard.

The sixth step, Confirm Dependencies, forces you to confirm the dependencies determined to be used by your application. If you do not want to use any of them, simply uncheck them and they will not be distributed on the disk(s). If you want to obtain details about a file before unchecking it, highlight the file and click the File Details command button. Figure 2.44 shows what this step looks like.

FIGURE 2.44.
The Confirm Dependencies screen of the Setup Wizard.

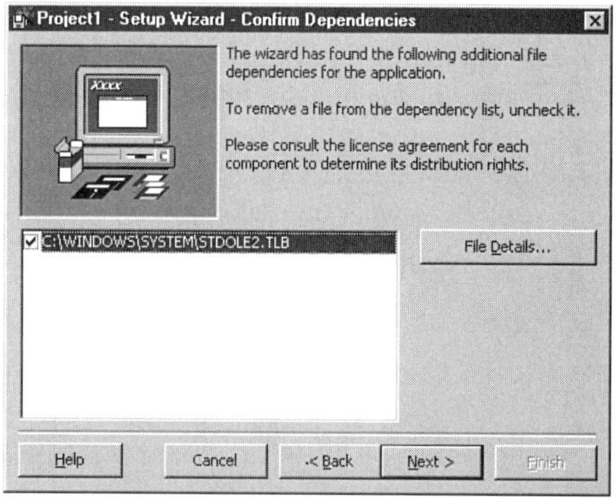

NOTE

If you do not have any additional dependencies necessary for your project, you will not see this step.

If you click the File Details command button, you will see a screen similar to Figure 2.45.

FIGURE 2.45.
The File Details dialog box of the Setup Wizard.

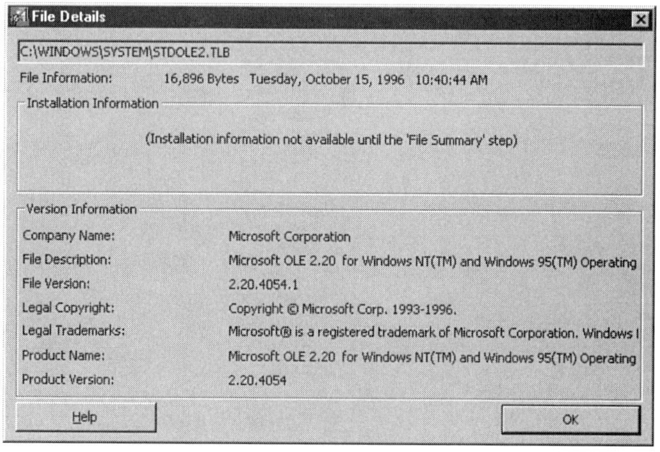

The seventh step, File Summary, forces you to confirm all files that will be distributed with your application. It shows the path and filename as well as what the file is a dependency of. You can see details about specific files by clicking the File Details command button. It shows details for the file, as shown in Figure 2.45. You can also choose Summary Details, which summarizes how many files will be distributed as well as how much disk space the uncompressed files will use. Although you do not know how much you will save in compression at this point, generally compressed files are one-third the size of the uncompressed files. However, you might notice individual files with smaller savings than this. Figure 2.46 shows what this step looks like, and Figure 2.47 shows what the dialog box looks like when you click the Summary Details command button.

FIGURE 2.46.
The File Summary screen of the Setup Wizard.

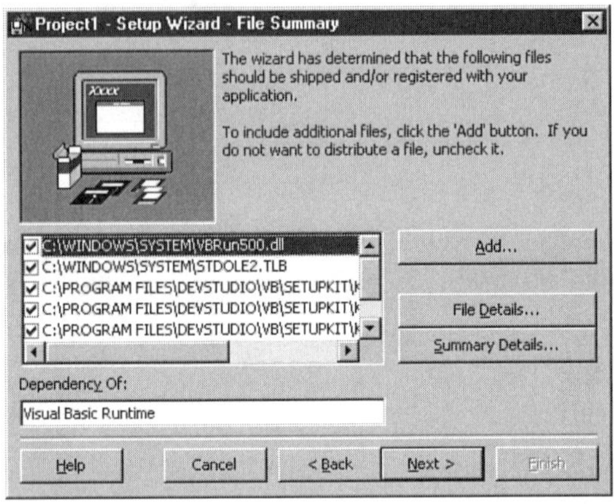

FIGURE 2.47.
The File Summary dialog box of the Setup Wizard.

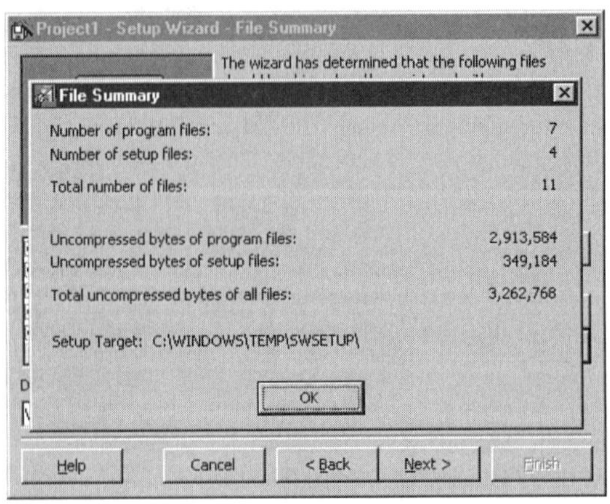

The eighth step, Finished, simply lets you save your template, if you want. The template will contain details about all choices made in the prior seven steps. Figure 2.48 shows what this screen looks like.

FIGURE 2.48.
The Finished screen of the Setup Wizard.

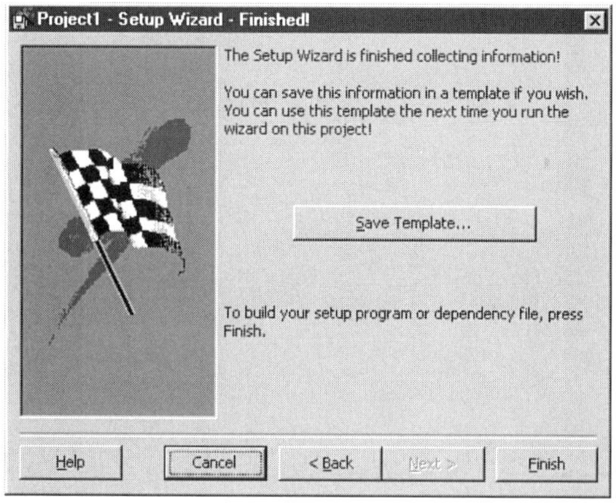

You have now performed all the required steps to create the setup program. Click the Finish button to actually create the setup program. As the setup is being generated, you will be shown a status of the compression of files.

Summary

Visual Basic 5.0 includes many stock wizards to help make your development tasks easier. Such wizards include the Application Wizard, Data Form Wizard, ActiveX Document Migration Wizard, ActiveX Control Interface Wizard, Property Page Wizard, and the Setup Wizard. Each of these were covered in this chapter. Visual Basic also includes two other wizards that are not covered in this chapter. The first is the Class Builder Utility, which is covered in Chapter 3. The second is the Wizard Manager, which is covered in Chapter 39.

3

Classes

Classes enable you to reuse code by creating code components. This chapter shows you how to create these components. A *class* is the basis for all objects in object-oriented programming. It enables you to create reusable code. Before version 4.0, there was no way to create a class, and therefore Visual Basic was not an object-oriented language—it was considered to be an object-*based* language. It is still not considered to be a true object-oriented language because even though you can create classes, another programmer cannot truly subclass a class you create. This is referred to as inheritance. It does, however, support polymorphism and encapsulation.

Inheritance is the ability to create a new object or class based on an existing object, which means that you can specify exactly how it is different from the parent object. For example, you not only can inherit the properties from an object, but you also can add other properties. *Polymorphism* is the concept of objects sharing characteristics from a base class, usually a common interface. This enables a developer to implement the methods and properties of that interface without knowing how the interface works directly. *Encapsulation* is the ability to wrap up, or encapsulate, different types of data and procedures into a single entity. This is probably the most common type of object-oriented programming.

Classes are useful, in part, because you can create multiple instances of the class. Assigning an object variable to the class is referred to as *instantiation*, which is the point at which the class is initialized and created. You can assign an object variable to an object in one of two ways. First, you can assign the object with *early binding*, which means Visual Basic assigns an association to the object as soon as it is declared because it is declared as being of a specific type. For example, assuming you had a class called `MyClass`, consider these two lines of code for early binding:

```
Private obj as MyClass
Set obj = New MyClass
```

The first line declares an object variable to be of a specific type. Then, on the second line, the variable is instantiated with a new instance of that class.

The second way to assign an object variable to an object is with *late binding*, which means Visual Basic does not assign an association to the object until it is used, not just declared. This is because it does not know what type of object to associate it with until it is instantiated. For example, again, assuming you had a class called `MyClass`, consider these two lines of code for late binding:

```
Private obj as Object
Set obj = New MyClass
```

The second line will create a reference to a new object called `MyClass`. Using this syntax, the code component will be reused every time it encounters the `New` keyword. Every class has any or all of the following associated with it:

- Properties
- Methods
- Events

To view which properties, methods, and events are available within a class, it is useful to use the Object Browser. You invoke the Object Browser by selecting the View | Object Browser menu option or by pressing the F2 key.

New to Version 5.0

One new feature of Visual Basic version 5.0 is the `Implements` statement. The `Implements` statement enables you to define one interface and have other classes use (or *implement*) that interface. Suppose you define the properties, methods, and events in a class module. The procedure of how to do this is discussed throughout this chapter.

Suppose this class is called `ClassA`. Then, for `ClassB` to implement the interface defined by `ClassA`, you would declare `ClassB` with this line of code:

```
Implements ClassA
```

Therefore, the preceding statement implements the interface designed in `ClassA`.

Creating Classes

You can create classes by selecting the Project | Add Class Module menu option. This brings up a dialog box in which you can choose the types of classes to add. There are three choices:

- Class Module
- VB Class Builder (only Professional and Enterprise editions)
- Add-In

These options make it easy, as with most features in version 5.0, to add classes. Figure 3.1 shows the dialog box that is displayed when you choose to add a class module.

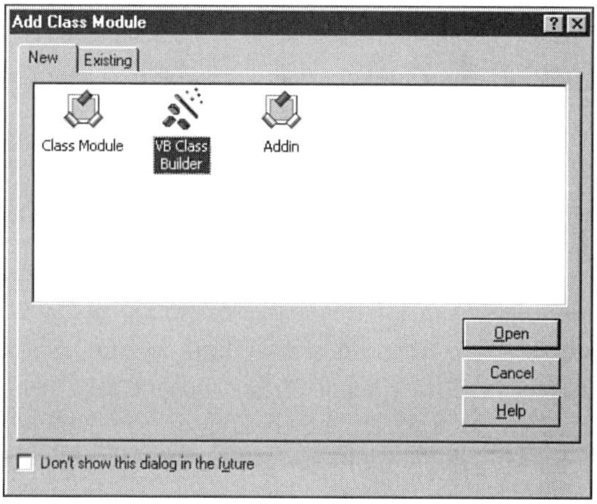

FIGURE 3.1.
The Add Class Module dialog box.

Class Module

The Class Module option makes it possible to add your own code manually. Some interfaces are so complex that it might not be advantageous to use a wizard to create the class. Also, some developers like to do everything manually. This makes them feel "in control." To write class modules manually, refer to the section "Coding Classes," later in this chapter.

VB Class Builder

The VB Class Builder is an add-in that makes defining a class's interface easy. This option is available only for the Professional and Enterprise editions of Visual Basic. This add-in can possibly save many hours of your time by prompting you on how the add-in should develop the interface. The VB Class Builder provides tabs and menu options that enable you to view and define your interface. (See Figure 3.2.)

FIGURE 3.2.
The VB Class Builder utility.

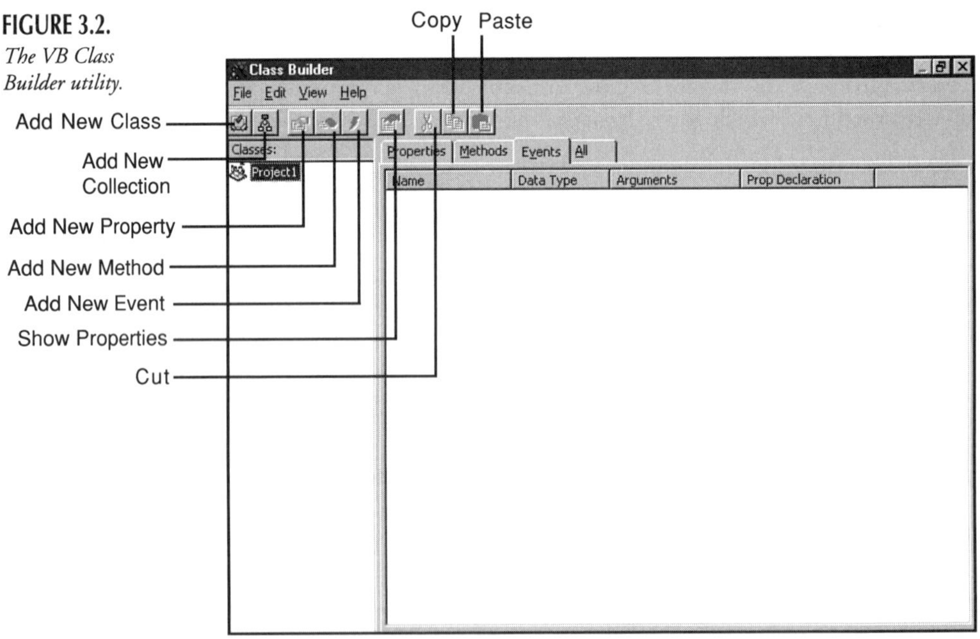

Suppose you wanted to create an order-taking system. In its simplest form, you would need to create two classes, one for the customers and one for the orders. The next step would be to rename the default `Class1` class by clicking on the name and then clicking the right mouse button and choosing the Rename option. Change the name to `Customers`. Note that the name of a class module must be less than 40 characters.

The `Customers` class needs to have the following properties with the shown data type:

Property	*Data Type*
`CustomerID`	Integer
`Name`	String
`Company`	String
`Address1`	String
`Address2`	String
`City`	String
`State`	String
`Zip`	String
`Phone`	String
`Fax`	String
`EMail`	String

To add a new property, select the File | New | Property menu option. Alternatively, you can right-click the appropriate class and choose the New | Property menu option, or, you can click the New Property toolbar button. Either option will enable you to define the new property. By default, the Properties tab is shown (see Figure 3.3).

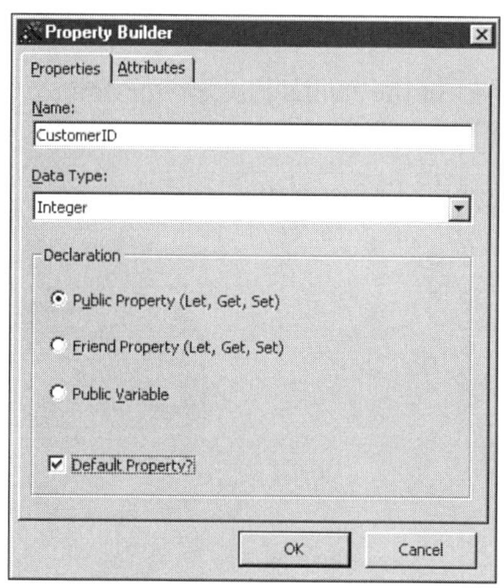

FIGURE 3.3.
The Properties tab of the Property Builder.

You must specify the name of the property. Using this example, type `CustomerID`, and then choose from the available datatypes. Here are the choices:

```
Byte
Boolean
Integer
Long
```

```
Single
Double
Currency
Date
String
Variant
Object
Collection
```

`Variant` is the default. In our case, choose `Integer`. Next, you must choose how to declare the property. Here are your choices:

New to Version 5.0

- Public Property—A property that will be exposed by your object to other interfaces that use objects.
- Friend Property—A property that is available for communication within objects but that is not exposed externally to the project.
- Public Variable—A variable that is available throughout the class but that is not exposed externally to the project.

Next, if this property is to serve as the default property, check the Default Property? check box. This means that if, in code, you do not refer to a property, but simply the class, this property will be used.

In this example, select the Public Property option to make the property available to other objects and environments that can access these objects.

The second tab on the Property Builder dialog box is the Attributes tab. It defines additional attributes, as shown in Figure 3.4.

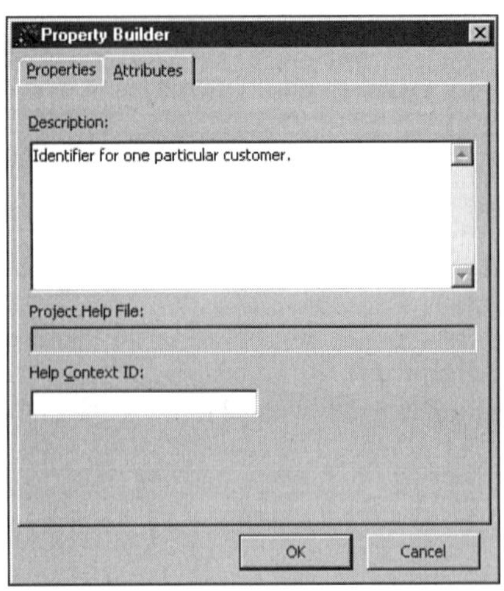

FIGURE 3.4.
The Attributes tab of the Property Builder.

These attributes are not functionally necessary. However, they do help to make the class complete. The Description field is used by the type library, which will be generated with the class. The Project Help File field is read-only. It shows the project's Help file, if one is assigned. Finally, in the Help Context ID field you should enter the Help Context ID if you have a topic assigned to the property inside the Help file shown.

Continue adding all the properties shown earlier. When you have added all the properties, the Class Builder main window will look as it does in Figure 3.5.

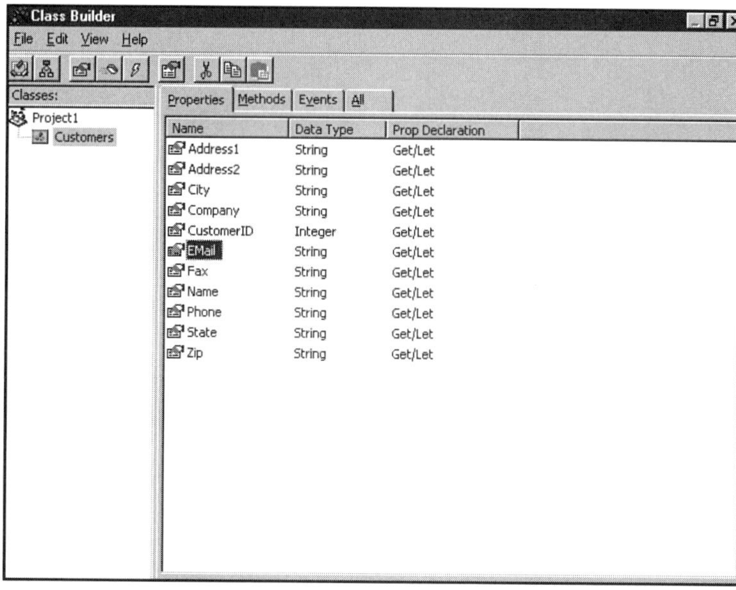

FIGURE 3.5.
The VB Class Builder with all properties added.

In addition to these properties, you will most likely need a couple of methods to perform some action within the class, such as the following:

- `Lookup`
- `Add`
- `Delete`
- `Update`

To add a new method, select the File | New | Method menu option. Alternatively, you can right-click the appropriate class and choose the New | Method menu option, or you can click the New Method toolbar button. This will enable you to define the new method. By default, the Properties tab is shown. This dialog box is shown in Figure 3.6.

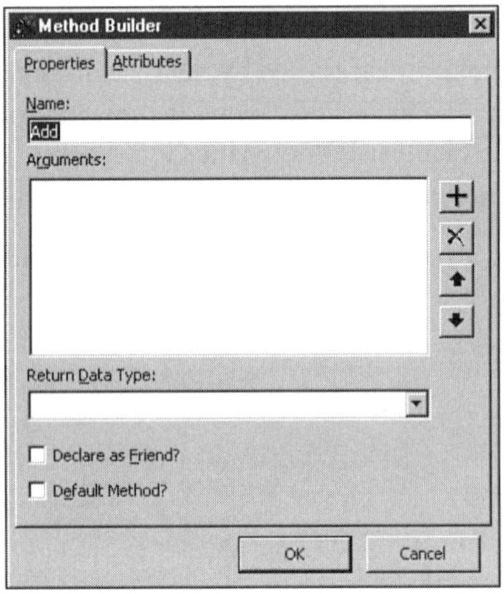

FIGURE 3.6.
The Properties tab of the Method Builder.

You must specify the name of the method. Using the earlier example, type `Lookup`, and then specify the arguments necessary for the method. Because you are going to be adding the customer whose attributes are specified as class properties, there is no reason to pass in an argument, so leave it blank. However, if you want to add an argument, click the + button. This enables you to add arguments and select data types for those arguments. When you have added the arguments you want, you can reorder them by highlighting each argument and clicking the up- and down-arrow buttons.

The next step is to choose the datatype that will be returned from the method, if applicable. Here are the choices:

```
(None)
Byte
Boolean
Integer
Long
Single
Double
Currency
Date
String
Variant
Object
Collection
```

(None) is the default. In this case, this is exactly what you want. Next, you must choose from one of two check boxes. The first is to declare the method as a Friend member. This means, as stated earlier, that the method will be made available internally to the other class modules in the project, but not externally to the outside world, including other interfaces that can use projects. This enables your classes to communicate with each other.

The second tab on the Method Builder dialog box is the Attributes tab. It defines additional attributes, as shown in Figure 3.7.

FIGURE 3.7.
The Attributes tab of the Method Builder.

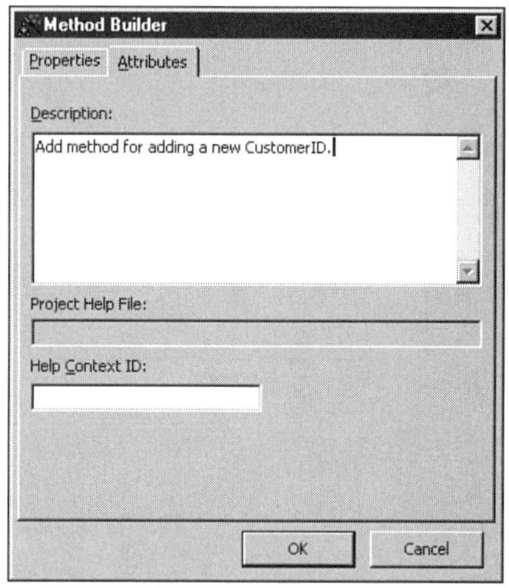

These attributes are not functionally necessary. However, they do help to make the class complete. The Description field is for use by the type library, which will be generated with the class. The Project Help File field is read-only. It will show the project's Help file, if one is assigned. Finally, in the Help Context ID field you should enter the Help Context ID if you have a topic assigned to the property inside the Help file shown.

Continue adding all the methods shown earlier. When all methods are added, the Class Builder main window will look as it does in Figure 3.8.

Finally, to make this class, you'll probably want to construct at least one event, such as ClassError.

To add an event method, select the File | New | Event menu option. Alternatively, you can right-click the appropriate class and choose the New | Event menu option, or you can click the New Event toolbar button. This enables you to define the new event. There are two tabs in the dialog box. The first is the Properties tab, which is shown in Figure 3.9.

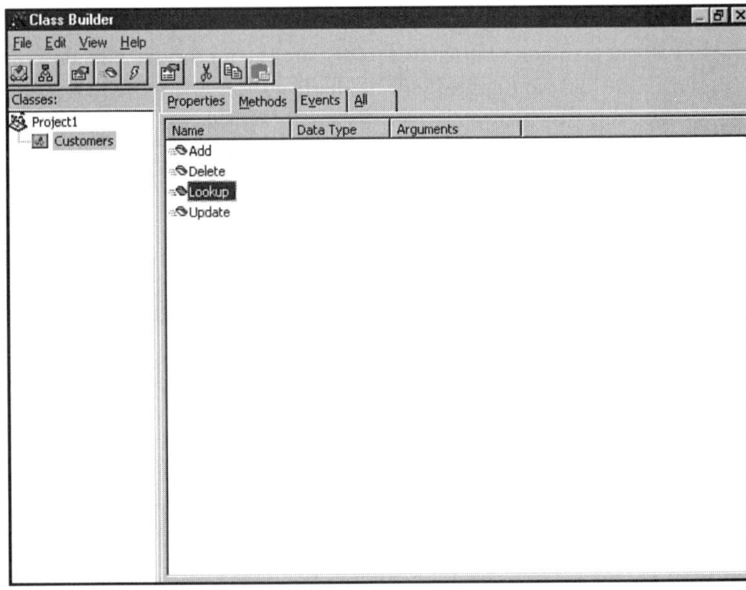

FIGURE 3.8.
The VB Class Builder with all methods added.

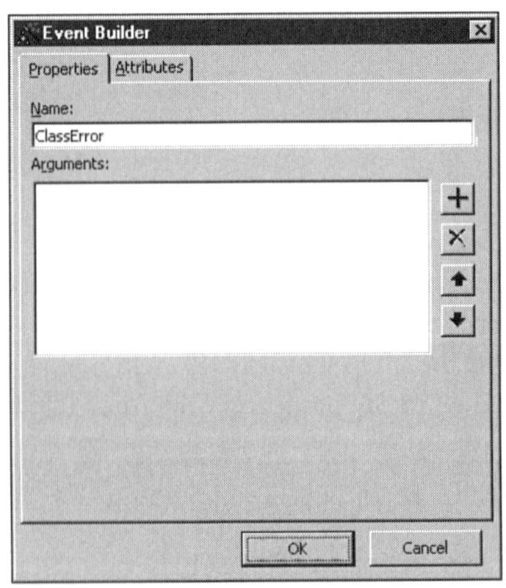

FIGURE 3.9.
The Properties tab of the Event Builder.

You must specify the name of the event. Using the preceding example, type `ClassError`, and then specify the arguments necessary for the event. Our event needs to have one argument, the error number. Therefore, name the argument `Err`. You add an argument by clicking on the + button. This enables you to add arguments and select datatypes for those arguments. Type `Err` for the name of the argument and select Integer for the datatype of the argument. After you have added the arguments you want, you can reorder them by highlighting the argument and clicking the up- and down-arrow buttons. Because you are using only one argument, you cannot reorder it.

The second tab on the Event Builder dialog box is the Attributes tab. It defines additional attributes, as shown in Figure 3.10.

FIGURE 3.10.
The Attributes tab of the Event Builder.

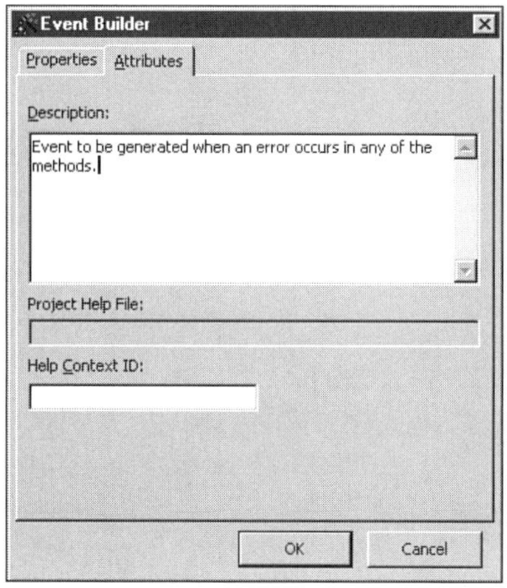

These attributes are not functionally necessary. However, they do help to make the class complete. The Description field is for use by the type library, which will be generated with the class. The Project Help File field is read-only. It shows the project's Help file, if one is assigned. Finally, in the Help Context ID field you should enter the Help Context ID if you have a topic assigned to the property inside the Help file shown.

Now that you have defined the `Customers` class, define the `Orders` class with the members shown in Table 3.1.

Table 3.1. Members that need to be added to the `Orders` class.

Properties	*Methods*	*Events*
`CustomerID` (Integer)	`Add`	`ClassError()`
`OrderNum` (Integer)	`Delete`	
`LineNum` (Integer)	`Update`	
`StockNum` (String)		
`Qty` (Integer)		
`Price` (Currency)		
`LineTotal` (Currency)		

There are several options available to the Class Builder utility. The first option is the properties of the class itself. The properties consist of two tabs: Properties and Attributes. To open the properties, either right-click the class name and select the Properties menu option or select the Edit | Properties menu option. This brings up the Properties tab in the Class Module Builder dialog box, as shown in Figure 3.11.

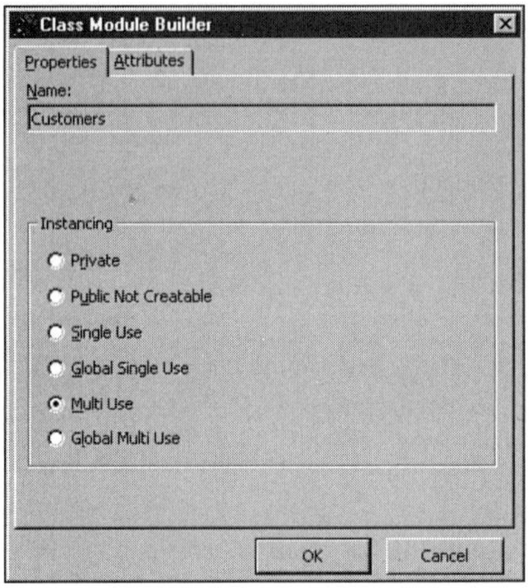

FIGURE 3.11.
The Properties tab of the Class Module Builder dialog box.

Here are the possible options:

- `Private`
- `Public Not Creatable`
- `Single Use`
- `Global Single Use`
- `Multi Use`
- `Global Multi Use`

These options are defined in the "Coding Classes" section, later in this chapter. The second tab in the Class Module Builder dialog box is the Attributes tab. It defines additional attributes, as shown in Figure 3.12.

These attributes are not functionally necessary. However, they do help to make the class complete. The Description field is for use by the type library, which will be generated with the class. The Project Help File field is read-only. It will show the project's Help file, if one is assigned. Finally, in the Help Context ID field you should enter the Help Context ID if you have a topic assigned to the property inside the Help file shown.

The second option available is the Class Builder Options dialog box. You invoke this by clicking the View | Options menu option. There are only two check boxes on this screen, as shown in Figure 3.13.

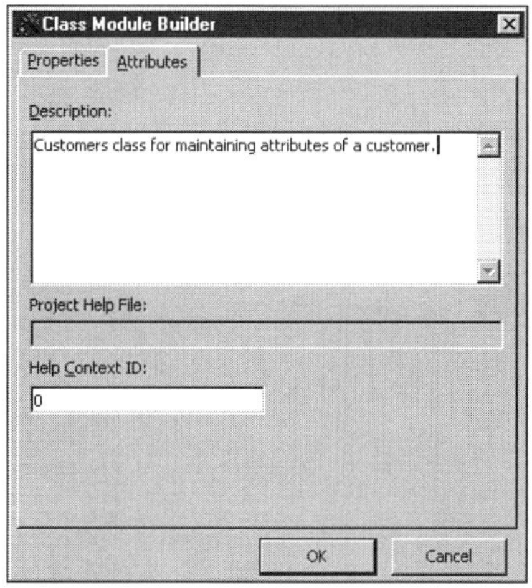

FIGURE 3.12.
The Attributes tab of the Class Module Builder.

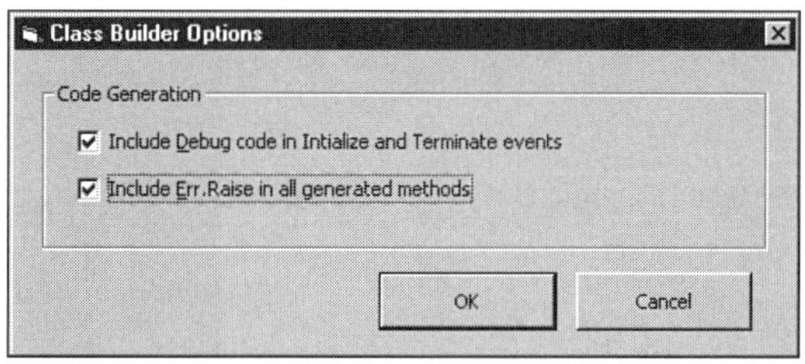

FIGURE 3.13.
The Class Builder Options dialog box.

You can check the first option, "Include Debug code in Initialize and Terminate events," if you want to trace the `Initialize()` and `Terminate()` events. These events are automatically invoked when a class is initialized or terminated, respectively. These events are not always used. The "Include Err.Raise in all generated methods" option will raise an error in an error handler in all the methods you specified earlier.

After you have specified all the properties, methods, events, and options for each class you want to include, choose the File | Update Project menu option to have the Class Builder utility generate the class code for you. Figure 3.14 shows a project with the aforementioned members added.

Listing 3.1 shows the actual code generated from the Class Builder after specifying the `Customers` class members listed earlier. For further explanation of what the code means, refer to the section "Coding Classes," later in this chapter.

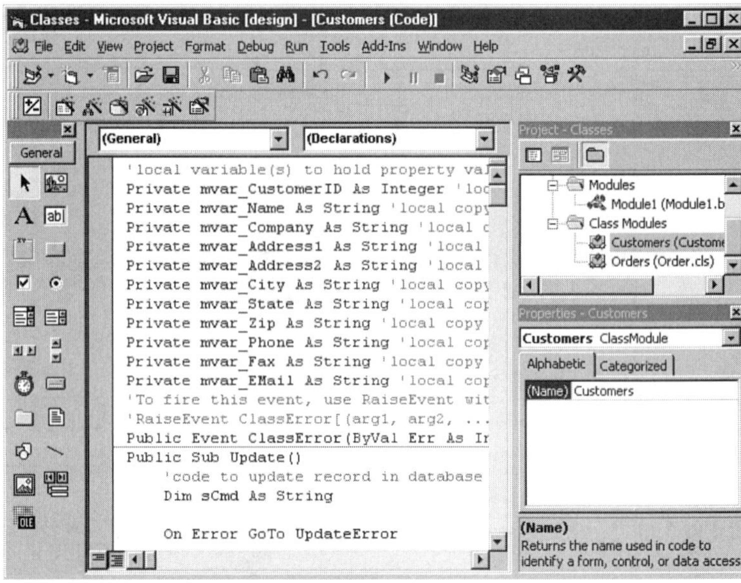

FIGURE 3.14.
The project after the Class Builder-generated code.

Listing 3.1. `Customers` sample class code using the Class Builder.

```
'local variable(s) to hold property value(s)
Private mvar_CustomerID As Integer 'local copy
Private mvar_Name As String 'local copy
Private mvar_Company As String 'local copy
Private mvar_Address1 As String 'local copy
Private mvar_Address2 As String 'local copy
Private mvar_City As String 'local copy
Private mvar_State As String 'local copy
Private mvar_Zip As String 'local copy
Private mvar_Phone As String 'local copy
Private mvar_Fax As String 'local copy
Private mvar_EMail As String 'local copy
'To fire this event, use RaiseEvent with the following syntax:
'RaiseEvent ClassError[(arg1, arg2, ... , argn)]
Public Event ClassError(ByVal Err As Integer)

Public Sub Update()
End Sub

Public Sub Delete()
End Sub

Public Sub Add()
End Sub

Public Property Let EMail(vData As String)
'used when assigning a value to the property, on the left side of an
'assignment.  Syntax: X.EMail = 5
    mvar_EMail = vData
End Property
```

```
Public Property Get EMail() As String
'used when retrieving value of a property, on the right side of an
'assignment.  Syntax: Debug.Print X.EMail
    EMail = mvar_EMail
End Property

Public Property Let Fax(vData As String)
'used when assigning a value to the property, on the left side of an
'assignment.  Syntax: X.Fax = 5
    mvar_Fax = vData
End Property

Public Property Get Fax() As String
'used when retrieving value of a property, on the right side of an
'assignment.  Syntax: Debug.Print X.Fax
    Fax = mvar_Fax
End Property

Public Property Let Phone(vData As String)
'used when assigning a value to the property, on the left side of an
'assignment.  Syntax: X.Phone = 5
    mvar_Phone = vData
End Property

Public Property Get Phone() As String
'used when retrieving value of a property, on the right side of an
'assignment.  Syntax: Debug.Print X.Phone
    Phone = mvar_Phone
End Property

Public Property Let Zip(vData As String)
'used when assigning a value to the property, on the left side of an
'assignment.  Syntax: X.Zip = 5
    mvar_Zip = vData
End Property

Public Property Get Zip() As String
'used when retrieving value of a property, on the right side of an
'assignment.  Syntax: Debug.Print X.Zip
    Zip = mvar_Zip
End Property

Public Property Let State(vData As String)
'used when assigning a value to the property, on the left side of an
'assignment.  Syntax: X.State = 5
    mvar_State = vData
End Property

Public Property Get State() As String
'used when retrieving value of a property, on the right side of an
'assignment.  Syntax: Debug.Print X.State
    State = mvar_State
End Property

Public Property Let City(vData As String)
'used when assigning a value to the property, on the left side of an
'assignment.  Syntax: X.City = 5
```

continues

Listing 3.1. continued

```
    mvar_City = vData
End Property

Public Property Get City() As String
'used when retrieving value of a property, on the right side of an
'assignment.  Syntax: Debug.Print X.City
    City = mvar_City
End Property

Public Property Let Address2(vData As String)
'used when assigning a value to the property, on the left side of an
'assignment.  Syntax: X.Address2 = 5
    mvar_Address2 = vData
End Property

Public Property Get Address2() As String
'used when retrieving value of a property, on the right side of an
'assignment.  Syntax: Debug.Print X.Address2
    Address2 = mvar_Address2
End Property

Public Property Let Address1(vData As String)
'used when assigning a value to the property, on the left side of an
'assignment.  Syntax: X.Address1 = 5
    mvar_Address1 = vData
End Property

Public Property Get Address1() As String
'used when retrieving value of a property, on the right side of an
'assignment.  Syntax: Debug.Print X.Address1
    Address1 = mvar_Address1
End Property

Public Property Let Company(vData As String)
'used when assigning a value to the property, on the left side of an
'assignment.  Syntax: X.Company = 5
    mvar_Company = vData
End Property

Public Property Get Company() As String
'used when retrieving value of a property, on the right side of an
'assignment.  Syntax: Debug.Print X.Company
    Company = mvar_Company
End Property

Public Property Let Name(vData As String)
'used when assigning a value to the property, on the left side of an
'assignment.  Syntax: X.Name = 5
    mvar_Name = vData
End Property

Public Property Get Name() As String
'used when retrieving value of a property, on the right side of an
'assignment.  Syntax: Debug.Print X.Name
    Name = mvar_Name
End Property
```

```
Public Property Let CustomerID(vData As Integer)
'used when assigning a value to the property, on the left side of an
'assignment.  Syntax: X.CustomerID = 5
    mvar_CustomerID = vData
End Property

Public Property Get CustomerID() As Integer
'used when retrieving value of a property, on the right side of an
'assignment.  Syntax: Debug.Print X.CustomerID
    CustomerID = mvar_CustomerID
End Property
```

Add-In

The Add-In option builds a framework for constructing an add-in. Selecting this option will produce standard code for creating an add-in. It must be modified where appropriate. Add-ins are discussed in more detail in Chapter 4, "Add-Ins." There are no options available when you select this type of class module. Visual Basic simply generates the code shown in Listing 3.2. Use it as a reference for determining which Add New Class option you choose.

Listing 3.2. Add-in code generated by Visual Basic.

```
Option Explicit

Implements IDTExtensibility

Public FormDisplayed          As Boolean
Public VBInstance             As VBIDE.VBE
Dim mcbMenuCommandBar         As Office.CommandBarControl
Dim mfrmAddIn                 As New frmAddIn
Public WithEvents MenuHandler As CommandBarEvents  'command bar event handler


Sub Hide()

    On Error Resume Next

    FormDisplayed = False
    mfrmAddIn.Hide

End Sub

Sub Show()

    On Error Resume Next

    If mfrmAddIn Is Nothing Then
        Set mfrmAddIn = New frmAddIn
    End If

    Set mfrmAddIn.VBInstance = VBInstance
    Set mfrmAddIn.Connect = Me
```

continues

Listing 3.2. continued

```
    FormDisplayed = True
    mfrmAddIn.Show

End Sub

'------------------------------------------------------
'this method adds the Add-In to VB
'------------------------------------------------------
Private Sub IDTExtensibility_OnConnection(ByVal VBInst As Object,
➥ByVal ConnectMode As vbext_ConnectMode, ByVal AddInInst As VBIDE.AddIn,
➥ custom() As Variant)

    On Error GoTo error_handler

    'save the vb instance
    Set VBInstance = VBInst

    'this is a good place to set a breakpoint and
    'test various addin objects, properties and methods
    Debug.Print VBInst.FullName

    If ConnectMode = vbext_cm_External Then
        'Used by the wizard toolbar to start this wizard
        Me.Show
    Else
        Set mcbMenuCommandBar = AddToAddInCommandBar("My AddIn")
        'sink the event
        Set Me.MenuHandler = VBInst.Events.CommandBarEvents(mcbMenuCommandBar)
    End If

    If ConnectMode = vbext_cm_AfterStartup Then
       If GetSetting(App.Title, "Settings", "DisplayOnConnect", "0") = "1" Then
           'set this to display the form on connect
           Me.Show
       End If
    End If

    Exit Sub

error_handler:

    MsgBox Err.Description

End Sub

'------------------------------------------------------
'this method removes the Add-In from VB
'------------------------------------------------------
Private Sub IDTExtensibility_OnDisconnection(ByVal RemoveMode As
➥vbext_DisconnectMode, custom() As Variant)

    On Error Resume Next

    'delete the command bar entry
    mcbMenuCommandBar.Delete
```

```
    'shut down the Add-In
    If FormDisplayed Then
        SaveSetting App.Title, "Settings", "DisplayOnConnect", "1"
        FormDisplayed = False
    Else
        SaveSetting App.Title, "Settings", "DisplayOnConnect", "0"
    End If

    Unload mfrmAddIn
    Set mfrmAddIn = Nothing

End Sub

Private Sub IDTExtensibility_OnStartupComplete(custom() As Variant)
    If GetSetting(App.Title, "Settings", "DisplayOnConnect", "0") = "1" Then
        'set this to display the form on connect
        Me.Show
    End If
End Sub

Private Sub IDTExtensibility_OnAddInsUpdate(custom() As Variant)
'
End Sub

'this event fires when the menu is clicked in the IDE
Private Sub MenuHandler_Click(ByVal CommandBarControl As Object,
➥handled As Boolean, CancelDefault As Boolean)
    Me.Show
End Sub

Function AddToAddInCommandBar(sCaption As String) As Office.CommandBarControl
    Dim cbMenuCommandBar As Office.CommandBarControl  'command bar object
    Dim cbMenu As Object

    On Error GoTo AddToAddInCommandBarErr

    'see if we can find the Add-Ins menu
    Set cbMenu = VBInstance.CommandBars("Add-Ins")
    If cbMenu Is Nothing Then
        'not available so we fail
        Exit Function
    End If

    'add it to the command bar
    Set cbMenuCommandBar = cbMenu.Controls.Add(1)
    'set the caption
    cbMenuCommandBar.Caption = sCaption

    Set AddToAddInCommandBar = cbMenuCommandBar

    Exit Function

AddToAddInCommandBarErr:

End Function
```

Coding Classes

Regardless of which of the three options you choose when you add a new class module to your project, you must understand how class modules work and how to code them.

All class modules have a Name property that identifies the name of the class and is referred to in the form of `Project.Class`. This is the project name followed by the class name. In addition, depending on the type of project you create, you will have an Instancing property available. Table 3.2 shows the possible options and when they are available, based on the type of project created. You will notice that the Standard EXE column has all N/A values. This is because although you can use class modules in a standard executable, the class does not have an `Instancing` property.

Table 3.2. Instancing property values with different project types.

Instancing	*Standard EXE*	*ActiveX EXE*	*ActiveX DLL*	*ActiveX Control*	*ActiveX Document DLL*	*ActiveX Document EXE*
`Private`	N/A	Yes	Yes	Yes	Yes	Yes
`PublicNotCreatable`	N/A	Yes	Yes	Yes, Default	Yes	Yes
`SingleUse`	N/A	Yes	No	No	No	Yes
`GlobalSingleUse`	N/A	Yes	No	No	No	Yes
`MultiUse`	N/A	Yes, Default	Yes, Default	No	Yes, Default	Yes, Default
`GlobalMultiUse`	N/A	Yes	No	No	No	Yes

The `Private` setting dictates that no application can create any instances of the class and that only the component you are creating can use these objects.

The `PublicNotCreatable` setting indicates that other applications can use the object, but cannot create more than one instance of the object.

The `SingleUse` setting allows for another application to use the object, but another instance of the component is created, not just another instance of the object.

The `GlobalSingleUse` setting is the same as the `SingleUse` setting with one difference: Other applications view the object as if it were a global function.

The `MultiUse` setting enables other applications to create multiple instances of the object without having to create another instance of the component that calls the object.

Finally, the `GlobalMultiUse` setting is to the `MultiUse` setting as the `GlobalSingleUse` setting is to the `SingleUse` setting. This means that the members of the object can be used as if they were global functions.

The class module also has two events:

- `Initialize()`
- `Terminate()`

The `Initialize()` event is triggered when an instance of the class is created. If you need to initialize any variables or perform some other initializing code, place the code in this event. The `Terminate()` event is triggered when an instance of the class is destroyed. You can place any clean-up code in this event. It is not always necessary to place code in these events.

Adding Property Procedures

You declare properties by inserting property procedures. You can insert a property procedure by selecting the Tools | Add Procedure menu option. This brings up a dialog box that contains the types of procedures you can insert. Figure 3.15 shows how this dialog box looks. Select the Property option and type the name of the property.

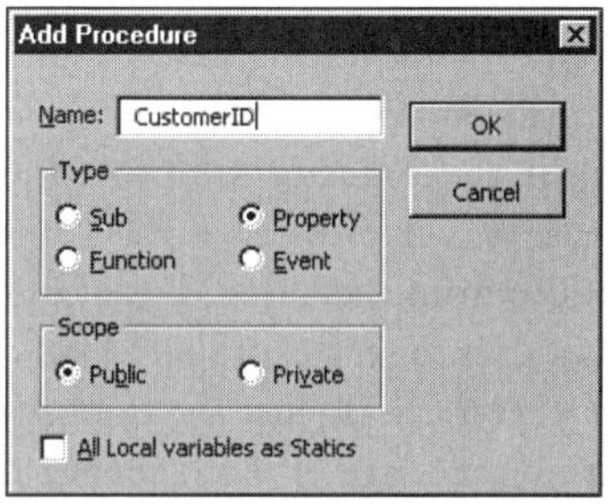

FIGURE 3.15.
The Add Procedure dialog box.

Choose the Public option to make the property available outside the class module. Choose Private to make the property local to the class. Visual Basic will actually create two special types of procedures for use with creating properties. By default, they are called `Property Get` and `Property Let` procedures. There is one other type of property procedure, called `Property Set`. A `Property Get` procedure will be called automatically, like a Visual Basic event, when a property is retrieved in code. For example, if you place the following code in the Debug window for a property declared as `Color`, where `x` is the name of an instance of a class module object, the `Property Get Color()` procedure will automatically be invoked:

```
?x.Color
```

It would then execute any code in that procedure, just as any other Visual Basic procedure. The procedure would be declared like this:

```
Public Property Get Color()
End Sub
```

A `Property Let` procedure, as you might expect, will be invoked when you assign a value to a variable. For example, this code fragment would call the `Property Let Color()` procedure:

```
x.Color = RED
```

The declaration of such a procedure would look like this:

```
Public Property Let Color()
End Sub
```

A `Property Set` procedure is used for assigning an object variable. Suppose you wanted to assign a form inside a property procedure. The following code fragment would automatically call the `Property Set FormName()` procedure:

```
x.FormName = Me
```

The declaration of this type of property looks like this:

```
Public Property Set Color()
End Sub
```

To declare a property as being read-write, you place code in the `Property Get` and `Property Let` procedures. To make a property read-only, you can do one of two things. The first is to place the desired code in the `Property Get` procedure and place a warning message about being read-only in the `Property Let` procedure. The other thing you can do is actually remove the `Property Let` procedure from the Visual Basic code. This will generate a Visual Basic default message when the user tries to set the property. To declare a property as being write-only (such as an action property), you can do just the opposite. You can place code in the `Property Let` procedure and a warning message in the `Property Get` procedure. Otherwise, you can actually remove the `Property Get` procedure from the Visual Basic code.

Likewise, a Friend property is a property that is available only within the project, not the outside world. This means that, for example, Microsoft Excel cannot access the property, but another class within the same Visual Basic project can. Friend properties are written in pairs, like other property procedures with `Get`, `Let`, and `Set`. You would declare a Friend property with this code:

```
Friend Property Get Color()
End Sub
Friend Property Let Color()
End Sub
```

Adding Methods

Adding a method is as simple as declaring a `Public Sub`. In a regular module, a `Public Sub` is a routine that will be available throughout the entire project. In a class module, a `Public Sub` creates a method that is exposed to the outside world. For example, the following code will make a method, called `Add`, available as a member of the class module that contains it:

```
Public Sub Add()
End Sub
```

Likewise, a `Friend Sub` is a subroutine that creates a method, but the method is available only within the project, not the outside world. This means that, for example, Microsoft Excel cannot access the method, but another class within the same Visual Basic project can. You would declare a `Friend` subroutine with this code:

```
Friend Sub Add()
End Sub
```

Adding Events

Before version 5.0, you could not add your own events. Adding an event is different than anything you are probably used to now. You add an event in five steps, as follows:

1. Declare the public event in the `(general)(declarations)` section of the class module. This simply declares the event, it doesn't actually fire it.
2. Within the class module, use the `RaiseEvent` statement to fire the event declared in the previous step. Pass the appropriate number of arguments.
3. In the form that instantiates the class module, you must declare a variable as being of the class module type. You must use the `WithEvents` keyword in the declaration to let Visual Basic know that an event will be fired for this object (class). For example, if you have a class named `Customers`, you can declare something like this:

   ```
   Private WithEvents objCustomers As Customers
   ```
4. In the `form_load` event (or somewhere else if it makes sense) instantiate the class with a line of code similar to this:

   ```
   Set objCustomers = New Customers
   ```
5. Everything you need has been set up except the coding for the actual event itself. You must write a subroutine that executes code as the event is fired. The subroutine name *must* be named with the object variable declared with the `WithEvents` keyword in step 3, followed by an underscore, and finally the name of the event as coded in the class module. This is somewhat of a foreign concept to Visual Basic programmers. For example, the `ClassError` event coded in the `Customers` class and declared in Listing 3.1 with the `objCustomers` variable would have a subroutine coded like this:

   ```
   Private Sub ObjCustomers_ClassError(ByVal Err As Integer)
       MsgBox Str$(Err)
   End Sub
   ```

The object variable `objCustomers` is the name of the object for which the event will be raised. The event follows the object name, such as `_ClassError`. Note that the underscore character between the object name and the event name is necessary.

Putting It All Together

Now it's time to see how it all fits together. The basic concept we are trying to achieve is that the functionality of the system is *encapsulated* into the class modules so that to use the functionality, you do not have to know how the class modules work. Using one of the new classes created earlier (`Customers`), let's see how it all comes together. Consider the code from Listing 3.3, which is the coding for the class module, `Customers`. It is important to understand what is happening.

Listing 3.3. `Customers` class module code.

```
'local variable(s) to hold property value(s)
Private mvar_CustomerID As Integer 'local copy
Private mvar_Name As String 'local copy
Private mvar_Company As String 'local copy
Private mvar_Address1 As String 'local copy
Private mvar_Address2 As String 'local copy
Private mvar_City As String 'local copy
Private mvar_State As String 'local copy
Private mvar_Zip As String 'local copy
Private mvar_Phone As String 'local copy
Private mvar_Fax As String 'local copy
Private mvar_EMail As String 'local copy
'To fire this event, use RaiseEvent with the following syntax:
'RaiseEvent ClassError[(arg1, arg2, ... , argn)]
Public Event ClassError(ByVal Err As Integer)
Public Sub Update()
    'code to update record in database
    Dim sCmd As String

    On Error GoTo UpdateError

    sCmd = "UPDATE Customers "
    sCmd = sCmd & "SET Names = '" & mvar_Name & "',"
    sCmd = sCmd & "Company = '" & mvar_Company & "',"
    sCmd = sCmd & "Address1 = '" & mvar_Address1 & "',"
    sCmd = sCmd & "Address2 = '" & mvar_Address2 & "',"
    sCmd = sCmd & "City = '" & mvar_City & "',"
    sCmd = sCmd & "State = '" & mvar_State & "',"
    sCmd = sCmd & "Zip = '" & mvar_Zip & "',"
    sCmd = sCmd & "Phone = '" & mvar_Phone & "',"
    sCmd = sCmd & "Fax = '" & mvar_Fax & "',"
    sCmd = sCmd & "EMail = '" & mvar_EMail & "' "
    sCmd = sCmd & "WHERE CustomerID = " & mvar_CustomerID
    dbOrders.Execute sCmd
    Exit Sub

UpdateError:
```

```
    RaiseEvent ClassError(Err)
End Sub
Public Sub Delete()
    'code to delete record from database
  Dim sCmd As String
  Dim nRes As Integer

  On Error GoTo DeleteError
  If mvar_CustomerID = 0 Then
      MsgBox "You must enter a customer ID"
        Exit Sub
    End If

    nRes = MsgBox("Confirm Delete", vbOKCancel)
    If nRes = vbOK Then
        sCmd = "DELETE FROM Customers "
        sCmd = sCmd & "WHERE CustomerID = " & mvar_CustomerID & " "
        dbOrders.Execute sCmd
    End If

    Exit Sub
DeleteError:
    RaiseEvent ClassError(Err)

End Sub
Public Sub Add()
    'code to add record to database
    On Error GoTo AddError
    Dim sCmd As String

    sCmd = "INSERT INTO Customers(CustomerID,Name,Company,Address1,
    ➥Address2,City,State,Zip,Phone,Fax,EMail) "
    sCmd = sCmd & "Values (" & mvar_CustomerID & ","
    sCmd = sCmd & "'" & mvar_Name & "',"
    sCmd = sCmd & "'" & mvar_Company & "',"
    sCmd = sCmd & "'" & mvar_Address1 & "',"
    sCmd = sCmd & "'" & mvar_Address2 & "',"
    sCmd = sCmd & "'" & mvar_City & "',"
    sCmd = sCmd & "'" & mvar_State & "',"
    sCmd = sCmd & "'" & mvar_Zip & "',"
    sCmd = sCmd & "'" & mvar_Phone & "',"
    sCmd = sCmd & "'" & mvar_Fax & "',"
    sCmd = sCmd & "'" & mvar_EMail & "')"
    dbOrders.Execute sCmd
    Exit Sub

AddError:
    RaiseEvent ClassError(Err)
End Sub
Public Property Let EMail(vData As String)
'used when assigning a value to the property, on the left side of an
'assignment.  Syntax: X.EMail = 5
    mvar_EMail = vData
End Property
Public Property Get EMail() As String
'used when retrieving value of a property, on the right side of an
'assignment.  Syntax: Debug.Print X.EMail
```

continues

Listing 3.3. continued

```
    EMail = mvar_EMail
End Property
Public Property Let Fax(vData As String)
'used when assigning a value to the property, on the left side of an
'assignment.  Syntax: X.Fax = 5
    mvar_Fax = vData
End Property
Public Property Get Fax() As String
'used when retrieving value of a property, on the right side of an
'assignment.  Syntax: Debug.Print X.Fax
    Fax = mvar_Fax
End Property
Public Property Let Phone(vData As String)
'used when assigning a value to the property, on the left side of an
'assignment.  Syntax: X.Phone = 5
    mvar_Phone = vData
End Property
Public Property Get Phone() As String
'used when retrieving value of a property, on the right side of an
'assignment.  Syntax: Debug.Print X.Phone
    Phone = mvar_Phone
End Property
Public Property Let Zip(vData As String)
'used when assigning a value to the property, on the left side of an
'assignment.  Syntax: X.Zip = 5
    mvar_Zip = vData
End Property
Public Property Get Zip() As String
'used when retrieving value of a property, on the right side of an
'assignment.  Syntax: Debug.Print X.Zip
    Zip = mvar_Zip
End Property
Public Property Let State(vData As String)
'used when assigning a value to the property, on the left side of an
'assignment.  Syntax: X.State = 5
    mvar_State = vData
End Property
Public Property Get State() As String
'used when retrieving value of a property, on the right side of an
'assignment.  Syntax: Debug.Print X.State
    State = mvar_State
End Property
Public Property Let City(vData As String)
'used when assigning a value to the property, on the left side of an
'assignment.  Syntax: X.City = 5
    mvar_City = vData
End Property
Public Property Get City() As String
'used when retrieving value of a property, on the right side of an
'assignment.  Syntax: Debug.Print X.City
    City = mvar_City
End Property
Public Property Let Address2(vData As String)
'used when assigning a value to the property, on the left side of an
'assignment.  Syntax: X.Address2 = 5
    mvar_Address2 = vData
```

```
End Property
Public Property Get Address2() As String
'used when retrieving value of a property, on the right side of an
'assignment.  Syntax: Debug.Print X.Address2
    Address2 = mvar_Address2
End Property
Public Property Let Address1(vData As String)
'used when assigning a value to the property, on the left side of an
'assignment.  Syntax: X.Address1 = 5
    mvar_Address1 = vData
End Property
Public Property Get Address1() As String
'used when retrieving value of a property, on the right side of an
'assignment.  Syntax: Debug.Print X.Address1
    Address1 = mvar_Address1
End Property
Public Property Let Company(vData As String)
'used when assigning a value to the property, on the left side of an
'assignment.  Syntax: X.Company = 5
    mvar_Company = vData
End Property
Public Property Get Company() As String
'used when retrieving value of a property, on the right side of an
'assignment.  Syntax: Debug.Print X.Company
    Company = mvar_Company
End Property
Public Property Let Name(vData As String)
'used when assigning a value to the property, on the left side of an
'assignment.  Syntax: X.Name = 5
    mvar_Name = vData
End Property
Public Property Get Name() As String
'used when retrieving value of a property, on the right side of an
'assignment.  Syntax: Debug.Print X.Name
    Name = mvar_Name
End Property
Public Property Let CustomerID(vData As Integer)
'used when assigning a value to the property, on the left side of an
'assignment.  Syntax: X.CustomerID = 5
    mvar_CustomerID = vData
End Property
Public Property Get CustomerID() As Integer
'used when retrieving value of a property, on the right side of an
'assignment.  Syntax: Debug.Print X.CustomerID
    CustomerID = mvar_CustomerID
End Property
Public Sub Lookup()
    'code to lookup record to database
    Dim sCmd As String
    Dim rsTemp As Recordset

    sCmd = "SELECT * FROM Customers "
    sCmd = sCmd & "WHERE CustomerID = " & mvar_CustomerID & " "
    Set rsTemp = dbOrders.OpenRecordset(sCmd)
    If Not rsTemp.EOF Then
        If Not IsNull(rsTemp.Fields("Name")) Then
            mvar_Name = rsTemp.Fields("Name")
```

continues

Listing 3.3. continued

```
        Else
            mvar_Name = ""
        End If

        If Not IsNull(rsTemp.Fields("Company")) Then
            mvar_Company = rsTemp.Fields("Company")
        Else
            mvar_Company = ""
        End If

        If Not IsNull(rsTemp.Fields("Address1")) Then
            mvar_Address1 = rsTemp.Fields("Address1")
        Else
            mvar_Address1 = ""
        End If

        If Not IsNull(rsTemp.Fields("Address2")) Then
            mvar_Address2 = rsTemp.Fields("Address2")
        Else
            mvar_Address2 = ""
        End If

        If Not IsNull(rsTemp.Fields("City")) Then
            mvar_City = rsTemp.Fields("City")
        Else
            mvar_City = ""
        End If

        If Not IsNull(rsTemp.Fields("State")) Then
            mvar_State = rsTemp.Fields("State")
        Else
            mvar_State = ""
        End If

        If Not IsNull(rsTemp.Fields("Zip")) Then
            mvar_Zip = rsTemp.Fields("Zip")
        Else
            mvar_Zip = ""
        End If

        If Not IsNull(rsTemp.Fields("Phone")) Then
            mvar_Phone = rsTemp.Fields("Phone")
        Else
            mvar_Phone = ""
        End If

        If Not IsNull(rsTemp.Fields("Fax")) Then
            mvar_Fax = rsTemp.Fields("Fax")
        Else
            mvar_Fax = ""
        End If

        If Not IsNull(rsTemp.Fields("EMail")) Then
            mvar_EMail = rsTemp.Fields("EMail")
        Else
            mvar_EMail = ""
```

```
263:        End If
264:    Else
265:        MsgBox "ID does not exist"
266:        mvar_CustomerID = -1
267:    End If
268:
269:End Sub
```

Lines 2–12 declare local copies of variables that equate one-for-one with the properties declared. This is because the property itself is available in the instantiated class that is available in a form or module. The property is not available inside the class; therefore, the value is assigned to a local copy of a variable.

Line 15 declares the `ClassError` event.

Lines 16–39 contain the code for the `Update` method of the `Customers` class. Notice that the code on line 38 raises the `ClassError` event.

Lines 40–62 contain the code for the `Delete` method of the `Customers` class. Notice that the code on line 60 raises the `ClassError` event.

Lines 63–85 contain the code for the `Add` method of the `Customers` class. Notice that the code on line 84 raises the `ClassError` event.

Lines 86–195 declare and code the `Property Let` and `Property Get` procedures for all of the properties of the `Customers` class.

Lines 196–269 contain the code for the `Lookup` method of the `Customers` class.

You can expand this functionality in your own application to include a form for the `Orders` class. You can also take this application one step further and add multiple customers to a collection of customers. Collections are discussed in Chapter 22, "Collections."

Summary

Classes were first introduced in Visual Basic version 4.0. Classes give Visual Basic the possibility to reuse code and create properties, methods, and events with which you can encapsulate code. Encapsulating code is an important concept that enables a developer to create and distribute classes or objects in order to shield other developers and applications from the complexity of the code in the class. The capability to create custom events is new to version 5.0. This is made possible through the use of the `WithEvents` keyword.

This chapter went into great detail in creating classes both manually and with the Class Builder Utility. Use it as a reference for your applications.

4

Add-Ins

An *add-in* is an extension to the Visual Basic design-time environment that enables you to manipulate your project in ways that were not possible before. For example, you can do things like the following:

- Manipulate forms
- Respond to events
- Manipulate projects
- Manipulate source code

Starting with Visual Basic version 4.0, you could write add-ins. However, the number of objects exposed by the Visual Basic IDE was limited. Version 5.0 makes it possible to do many more things by exposing many more objects, properties, methods, and events.

An add-in actually adds one or more menu items to the Visual Basic Integrated Design Environment (IDE) so that the add-in is accessed from this menu option. This chapter teaches you the things you need to know to create an add-in.

CROSS REFERENCE

For more information on writing wizards, refer to Chapter 39, "Creating a Wizard Add-In."

Where to Begin

A good place to begin is to have Visual Basic create the add-in framework for you. You do this by selecting the File | New Project menu option. This brings up the New Project dialog box, which enables you to choose the type of project to create. Choose Addin. Figure 4.1 shows what this dialog box looks like.

Because all add-ins are actually OLE Server (or code component) applications, notice that the type of project is ActiveX EXE. You could also change this to an ActiveX DLL. Also, notice that the Start Mode is set to ActiveX Component instead of Stand Alone.

Note that a reference has automatically been added for you. This reference is for the Visual Basic IDE itself and is listed in Figure 4.2 as the Microsoft Visual Basic 5.0 Extensibility reference. You can view the reference by selecting the Project | References menu option. When this reference is selected, the Extensibility (Visual Basic IDE) objects are made available.

After you have added the reference, the objects, properties, methods, and events are visible in the Object Browser. To invoke this browser, simply press the F2 key. The browser is shown in Figure 4.2.

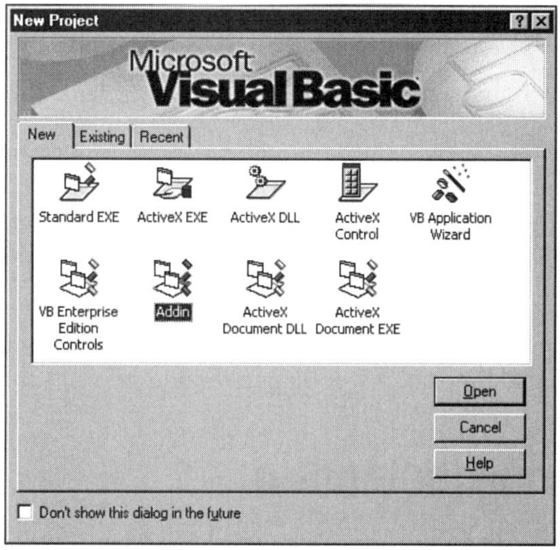

FIGURE 4.1.
Selecting the Addin option to create a framework.

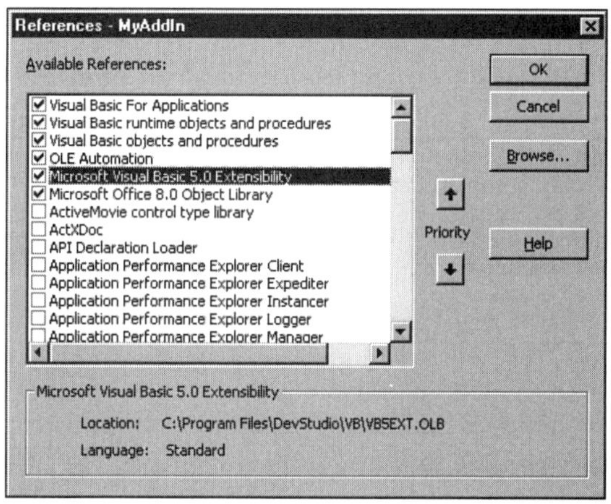

FIGURE 4.2.
The Object Browser showing Extensibility objects.

There really are only two files needed to create the add-in. One is a class module, and the other is a BAS module. The BAS module is needed to create an entry point for the add-in. If there are no visible forms, you specify the start-up form as being `Sub Main()`. It is very likely that even if there is a visible interface, you want to use a `Sub Main()` starting procedure. This allows for a clean entry point into the add-in and also enables you to perform initialization.

The other necessary form is a *class module*. A class is basically one object. Depending on how you construct your subroutines, functions, and variables, this determines which properties, methods, and events are available to the outside world.

CROSS REFERENCE

For more information on Visual Basic classes, refer to Chapter 3, "Classes."

The minimum number of procedures needed in the class module is three: one to initialize the add-in, one to disconnect from the add-in, and one to respond when the Add-In menu option is clicked. If you have more than one menu option, you might (but won't necessarily) have more than one procedure to handle this.

The following sections deal with the topics of initializing (connecting) the add-in, disconnecting from the add-in, and responding to the add-in.

Declaring the Add-In

Because the code on the next few pages shows what is generated by default, the declarations shown in Listing 4.1 are also automatically generated.

Listing 4.1. The `(general)(declarations)` section from the default Create New Add-In Project Wizard.

```
Option Explicit
Implements IDTExtensibility
Public FormDisplayed           As Boolean
Public VBInstance              As VBIDE.VBE
Dim mcbMenuCommandBar          As Office.CommandBarControl
Dim mfrmAddIn                  As New frmAddIn
Public WithEvents MenuHandler As CommandBarEvents 'command bar event handler
```

The first line indicates that every variable must be declared. The next line declares that this module implements the `IDTExtensibility` interface. The following line declares a Boolean flag that indicates whether the form was displayed. Then, a public variable is declared to store the instance of Visual Basic. This is because the instance of Visual Basic passed into the `OnConnection()` event is local to that procedure. You might need it elsewhere, so it must be declared here. Next is a command bar (menu) variable, followed by a new instance of the form, called `frmAddIn`. Finally, and perhaps most importantly, there's a handle to the menu item that will be added later. This menu item is declared `WithEvents` so that you can code for events being fired.

Initializing the Add-In

The class module that you created must have a procedure to initialize or connect to the add-in. This procedure is an event from the VB Extensibility object and must be called `OnConnection()`.

This event is automatically called when Visual Basic attempts to install the add-in. Listing 4.2 shows what the `OnConnection()` procedure looks like when the New Project Wizard creates the add-in framework.

Listing 4.2. The `OnConnection()` event from the default Create New Add-In Project Wizard.

```
Private Sub IDTExtensibility_OnConnection(ByVal VBInst As Object, ByVal
➥ConnectMode As vbext_ConnectMode, ByVal AddInInst As VBIDE.AddIn,
➥custom() As Variant)

    On Error GoTo error_handler

    'save the vb instance
    Set VBInstance = VBInst

    'this is a good place to set a breakpoint and
    'test various addin objects, properties and methods
    Debug.Print VBInst.FullName
    If ConnectMode = vbext_cm_External Then
        'Used by the wizard toolbar to start this wizard
        Me.Show
    Else
        Set mcbMenuCommandBar = AddToAddInCommandBar("My AddIn")
        'sink the event
        Set Me.MenuHandler = VBInst.Events.CommandBarEvents(mcbMenuCommandBar)
    End If

    If ConnectMode = vbext_cm_AfterStartup Then
       If GetSetting(App.Title, "Settings", "DisplayOnConnect", "0") = "1" Then
           'set this to display the form on connect
           Me.Show
       End If
    End If

    Exit Sub

error_handler:

    MsgBox Err.Description

End Sub
```

Notice four parameters being passed into the event. First, Visual Basic itself passes in the `VBInst` object. This variable is a handle to the actual instance of Visual Basic. Because you can actually run more than one instance of Visual Basic, you might need to reference a specific instance handle.

The second argument is the `ConnectMode` object. It is used to determine how the add-in was connected. You do not always use this, but if you need it, the possible settings are as follows:

- `vbext_cm_AfterStartup`—The Initial Open Project dialog box was shown, then the add-in was started.

- `vbext_cm_Startup`—The add-in was started, and then the initial Open Project dialog box was shown.
- `vbext_cm_External`—Another program or component started the add-in.

The third argument is the instance of the add in. Finally, `custom()` is an array that holds user-defined data. Notice that the generated `OnConnection` event contains a call to a function named `AddToAddInCommandBar()`. This function adds the actual menu item to the Visual Basic menu. Listing 4.3 shows this function, which is also generated automatically.

Listing 4.3. The `AddToAddInCommandBar()` event from the default Create New Add-In Project Wizard.

```
Function AddToAddInCommandBar(sCaption As String) As Office.CommandBarControl
    Dim cbMenuCommandBar As Office.CommandBarControl  'command bar object
    Dim cbMenu As Object

    On Error GoTo AddToAddInCommandBarErr

    'see if we can find the Add-Ins menu
    Set cbMenu = VBInstance.CommandBars("Add-Ins")
    If cbMenu Is Nothing Then
        'not available so we fail
        Exit Function
    End If

    'add it to the command bar
    Set cbMenuCommandBar = cbMenu.Controls.Add(1)
    'set the caption
    cbMenuCommandBar.Caption = sCaption

    Set AddToAddInCommandBar = cbMenuCommandBar

    Exit Function

AddToAddInCommandBarErr:
End Function
```

This function passes in one argument: the caption of the menu item. You add this item to the Add-Ins menu option by using the `Add` method of the `VBInstance.CommandBars` object.

Disconnecting the Add-In

The same class module has a procedure that can be used to clean up any variables when the add-in is no longer selected in the Add-In Manager. This procedure is an event from the VB Extensibility object, and must be called `OnDisconnection()`. This event is automatically called when Visual Basic attempts to install the add-in. Listing 4.4 shows what the `OnDisconnection()` procedure looks like when the New Project Wizard creates the add-in framework.

Listing 4.4. The `OnDisconnection()` event from the default Create New Add-In Project Wizard.

```
Private Sub IDTExtensibility_OnDisconnection(ByVal RemoveMode As
➥ vbext_DisconnectMode, custom() As Variant)

    On Error Resume Next

    'delete the command bar entry
    mcbMenuCommandBar.Delete

    'shut down the Add-In
    If FormDisplayed Then
        SaveSetting App.Title, "Settings", "DisplayOnConnect", "1"
        FormDisplayed = False
    Else
        SaveSetting App.Title, "Settings", "DisplayOnConnect", "0"
    End If

    Unload mfrmAddIn
    Set mfrmAddIn = Nothing
End Sub
```

There are two parameters being passed into the event. The first argument is the `RemoveMode` object, which is used to determine how the add-in was disconnected. You do not always use this, but if you need it, the possible settings are as follows:

- `vbext_dm_HostShutdown`—The host application closed the add-in.
- `vbext_dm_UserClosed`—The user closed the add-in.

The second argument, `custom()`, is an array that holds user-defined data.

Handling the Menus

When the menu item is clicked, an event is fired to enable you to respond in some way. This event, the `Click()` event, must be coded. It passes in three arguments. These arguments are not always used but are passed into the event anyway. The first argument is a handle to the menu object `CommandBarControl`. The second, `handled`, is a Boolean value that indicates whether another process or add-in has handled the event already. The third, `CancelDefault`, is another Boolean that indicates whether the code will be executed. If it is not executed, then it has been canceled. This value will be set by another add-in. Listing 4.5 shows the default code generated for the `Click()` event.

Listing 4.5. The `Click()` event from the default Create New Add-In Project Wizard.

```
Private Sub MenuHandler_Click(ByVal CommandBarControl As Object,
➥ handled As Boolean, CancelDefault As Boolean)
    Me.Show
End Sub
```

Additional Events

There are several procedures that the wizard codes by default, but that are not necessary in every add-in. The first procedure is the `OnStartupComplete()` event. It is fired when the startup of the Visual Basic IDE is complete. The event passes in one argument, `custom()`, as an array that holds user-defined data. When this event fires, the code simply shows the instance of the form. Listing 4.6 shows this event.

Listing 4.6. The `OnStartupComplete()` event from the default Create New Add-In Project Wizard.

```
Private Sub IDTExtensibility_OnStartupComplete(custom() As Variant)
    If GetSetting(App.Title, "Settings", "DisplayOnConnect", "0") = "1" Then
        'set this to display the form on connect
        Me.Show
    End If
End Sub
```

The second procedure is used to show the form. This is definitely not a procedure that will be contained in all add-ins. Listing 4.7 shows this procedure, which is coded automatically by the code generator.

Listing 4.7. The `Show()` subroutine from the default Create New Add-In Project Wizard.

```
Sub Show()

    On Error Resume Next

    If mfrmAddIn Is Nothing Then
        Set mfrmAddIn = New frmAddIn
    End If

    Set mfrmAddIn.VBInstance = VBInstance
    Set mfrmAddIn.Connect = Me
    FormDisplayed = True
    mfrmAddIn.Show

End Sub
```

The last procedure is used to hide the form. Again, this is definitely not a procedure that will be contained in all add-ins. Listing 4.8 shows this procedure, which is coded automatically by the code generator.

Listing 4.8. The `Hide()` subroutine from the default Create New Add-In Project Wizard.

```
Sub Hide()

    On Error Resume Next
```

```
    FormDisplayed = False
    mfrmAddIn.Hide

End Sub
```

For more insight into the extensibility features of version 5.0, refer to Table 4.1.

Table 4.1. Extensibility features in Visual Basic 5.0.

Keyword	*Type*	*Description*
`Activate`	Method	Causes the currently selected component to be double-clicked
`ActiveCodePane`	Property	Sets or returns the active `CodePane` object
`ActiveVBProject`	Property	Returns the active project in the Project window
`ActiveWindow`	Property	Returns the active window in the development environment
`Add`	Method	Adds an item to a collection
`AddFromFile`	Method	Adds or opens a project or group
`AddFromGUID`	Method	Adds a reference to the `References` collection using a GUID
`AddFromString`	Method	Adds text to a module
`AddFromTemplate`	Method	Creates a new component from a template
`AddIn`	Object	Returns information about an add-in
`AddIns`	Collection	A collection of `AddIn` objects
`AddToolboxProgID`	Method	Places a component in the toolbox and adds a control reference to the project
`AfterAddFile`	Event	Fires after a component is added to the current Visual Basic project
`AfterChangeFileName`	Event	Fires after a file in the current project has been saved for the first time (or saved with a new name)
`AfterCloseFile`	Event	Fires after a project has been closed
`AfterRemoveFile`	Event	Fires after a file is removed from the active Visual Basic project
`AfterWriteFile`	Event	Fires after a file is written to disk
`BeforeLoadFile`	Event	Fires when a component is added

continues

Table 4.1. continued

Keyword	*Type*	*Description*
`Bindable`	Property	Sets or returns the `Bindable` property associated with a `Member` object
`Browsable`	Property	Sets or returns the `Browsable` attribute associated with a `Member` object
`BuildFileName`	Property	Returns the `MAKE` filename used when the project is built
`BuiltIn`	Property	A Boolean value indicating whether the reference is a default reference that can't be removed
`Caption`	Property	Returns a `String` containing the title of the active window
`Category`	Property	Sets or returns the `Category` attribute associated with a `Member` object
`ClassName`	Property	Class name for an object
`Clear`	Method	Clears an item from a collection
`Click`	Event	Fires when the user clicks a menu
`Close`	Method	Closes the selected window
`CodeLocation`	Property	Returns the line location in the code module where the member is defined
`CodeModule`	Object	Represents a code module
`CodeModule`	Property	Returns an object representing the code behind the component
`CodePane`	Object	Represents a code pane to manipulate the position text in the code pane
`CodePanes`	Collection	A collection of `CodePane` objects
`CodePaneView`	Property	Returns whether the code pane is in Procedure view or Full Module view
`Collection`	Property	Returns the collection that contains the object with which you are working
`CommandBar`	Object	Object that represents buttons or menus
`CommandBarEvents`	Object	Object that triggers an event when a control on the command bar is clicked
`CommandBarEvents`	Property	References the `CommandBarEvents` object
`CommandBars`	Collection	Collection of `CommandBar` objects
`CompatibleOLEServer`	Property	Sets or returns the compatible ActiveX component of this project

Keyword	*Type*	*Description*
`Connect`	Property	Sets or returns the connected state of an add-in
`ContainedControls`	Property	Returns a collection of the controls in the project
`ContainedVBControls`	Collection	Represents a collection of `VBControl` objects
`Container`	Property	Sets or returns the container of a control
`ControlObject`	Property	References an instance of a control's `IDispatch` pointer
`ControlType`	Property	The type of runtime window that a control creates
`Copy`	Method	Copies to the Clipboard
`Count`	Property	The count of the number of items in a collection
`CountOfDeclarationLines`	Property	Returns the number of lines of code in the `Declarations` section of a code module
`CountOfLines`	Property	Returns the number of lines of code in a code module
`CountOfVisibleLines`	Property	Returns the number of lines visible in a code pane
`CreateEventProc`	Method	Creates an event procedure
`Cut`	Method	Cuts to the Clipboard
`DefaultBind`	Property	Sets or returns the `DefaultBind` attribute of a `Member` object
`DeleteLines`	Method	Deletes a single line or a specified range of lines
`Description`	Property	Sets or returns a description of an object
`Designer`	Property	Returns the object that enables you to access the design characteristics of a component
`DesignerWindow`	Property	Returns the `Window` object that represents the component's designer
`DisplayBind`	Property	Sets or returns the `DisplayBind` attribute of a `Member` object
`DisplayModel`	Property	Sets or returns the display model used by the system
`DoGetNewFileName`	Event	Fires when a Save As operation is performed
`Events`	Object	Supplies properties that enable add-ins to connect to all events
`FileControlEvents`	Object	Represents all events supplied by Visual Basic that support file control

continues

Table 4.1. continued

Keyword	*Type*	*Description*
`FileControlEvents`	Property	Returns an event object of type `FileControlEvents`
`FileCount`	Property	Returns the number of files associated with a given component
`FileName`	Property	Returns the full path name of the group project file
`FileNames`	Property	Returns the current paths
`Find`	Method	Searches the project for a specific string
`FullPath`	Property	A string containing the fully qualified path of the referenced type library
`GetSelection`	Method	Returns the selection in a code pane
`GUID`	Property	A string containing the class identifier of an object
`HasOpenDesigner`	Property	A Boolean value indicating whether the `VBComponent` object has an open designer
`Height`	Property	Standard `Height` property
`HelpContextID`	Property	Context ID for a help file
`HelpFile`	Property	Fully qualified help filename
`Hidden`	Property	Sets or returns the `Hidden` attribute of a `Member` object
`IconState`	Property	Sets or returns the source code control status of an icon
`IDTExtensibility`	Object	Contains methods and procedures that Visual Basic calls for add-ins
`IndexedValue`	Property	Sets or returns a value for a member of a property that is an indexed list or an array
`InSelection`	Property	Sets or returns a control's selection state
`InsertFile`	Method	Inserts a file into a project
`InsertLines`	Method	Inserts lines of code at a specified location in a block of code
`IsBroken`	Property	A Boolean value indicating whether the `Reference` object points to a valid reference in the registry
`IsDirty`	Property	A Boolean indicating whether the component was edited since the last time it was saved

Keyword	*Type*	*Description*
`Item`	Method	Returns the indexed member of a collection
`ItemActivated`	Event	Fires when an item is activated
`ItemAdded`	Event	Fires after an item is added to the project
`ItemReloaded`	Event	Fires after a component is reloaded
`ItemRemoved`	Event	Fires after an item is removed from the project
`ItemRenamed`	Method	Fires after an item is renamed in the project
`ItemSelected`	Event	Fires when a component in the project is clicked
`LastUsedPath`	Property	Sets or returns the last path used for the file dialog boxes
`Left`	Property	Standard `Left` property
`LinkedWindowFrame`	Property	Returns the `Window` object representing the frame that contains the window
`LinkedWindows`	Collection	Contains all linked windows in a linked window frame
`MainWindow`	Property	Returns a `Window` object representing the main window of the Visual Basic IDE
`Major`	Property	Sets or returns the major release number of the project
`MakeCompiledFile`	Method	Compiles the current project
`Member`	Object	Represents a mixture of code-based properties and type library-based attributes
`Members`	Collection	A collection of `Member` objects
`Minor`	Property	Sets or returns the minor release number of the project
`Name`	Property	Sets or returns the name used for an object
`NumIndices`	Property	Returns the number of indices on the property returned by the `Property` object
`Object`	Property	Sets or returns the value of an object returned by a property
`OnAddInsUpdate`	Event	Fires automatically when changes to the `VBADDIN.INI` file are saved
`OnConnection`	Event	Fires when an add-in is connected to the Visual Basic IDE

continues

Table 4.1. continued

Keyword	*Type*	*Description*
`OnDisconnection`	Event	Fires when an add-in is disconnected from the Visual Basic IDE
`OnStartupComplete`	Event	Fires when the startup of the Visual Basic IDE is complete
`Parent`	Property	Returns the object or collection that contains a parent object or collection
`ProcBodyLine`	Method	Returns the first line of a procedure
`ProcCountLines`	Method	Returns the number of lines in the specified procedure
`ProcOfLine`	Method	Returns the name of the procedure that the specified line is in
`ProcStartLine`	Method	Returns the line at which the specified procedure begins
`ProgID`	Property	Returns the programmatic ID for the `VBControl` control
`Properties`	Collection	A collection of `Property` objects
`Property`	Object	Represents the properties of an object that are visible in the Properties window
`PropertyPage`	Property	Sets or returns the `PropertyPage` attribute of a `Member` object
`Quit`	Method	Attempts to exit Visual Basic
`ReadOnlyMode`	Property	Sets or returns a value that determines how the Visual Basic IDE interacts with read-only files
`ReadProperty`	Method	Returns a string from the specified user-defined section and key in the project's VBP or component file
`Reference`	Object	Represents a reference to a type library or a project
`References`	Collection	A collection of `Reference` objects
`ReferencesEvents`	Object	Returned by the `ReferencesEvents` property
`ReferencesEvents`	Property	Returns the `ReferencesEvents` object
`Reload`	Method	Reloads the specified component from disk
`Remove`	Method	Removes an item from a collection
`ReplaceLine`	Method	Replaces an existing line of code with a specified line of code

Keyword	*Type*	*Description*
`RequestChange-FileName`	Event	Fires after specifying a new filename for a component or project, and the name change is completed
`RequestEdit`	Property	Sets or returns the `RequestEdit` attribute of a `Member` object
`RequestWriteFile`	Event	Fires before saving any project component with unsaved changes
`SaveAs`	Method	Saves a component or project to a given location, using a new filename
`Saved`	Property	A Boolean value indicating whether the object was edited since the last time it was saved
`Scope`	Property	Returns whether a member is public, private, or friend
`SelectedVBControls`	Collection	Returns a collection of selected controls on a component
`SelectedVBControls-Events`	Property	Returns all events supported by the controls currently selected on a form
`SetFocus`	Method	Sets the focus of a control
`SetSelection`	Method	Sets the selection in the code pane
`Show`	Method	Makes the specified code pane visible
`StandardMethod`	Property	Sets or returns the `StandardMethod` attribute of a `Member` object
`StartMode`	Property	Sets or returns the start mode of the project
`StartupObject`	Property	Sets or returns the startup component for the project
`Static`	Property	Returns whether the referenced variable or method is declared as `Static`
`TemplatePath`	Property	Returns the full path name where Visual Basic stores template files
`Top`	Property	Standard `Top` property
`TopLine`	Property	Sets or returns the line number of the line at the top of the code pane
`Type`	Property	Returns the type of the currently selected member or project

continues

Table 4.1. continued

Keyword	*Type*	*Description*
`UIDefault`	Property	Sets or returns the `UIDefault` attribute of a `Member` object
`Update`	Method	Updates another object
`Value`	Property	Sets or returns a `Variant` specifying the value of the property
`VBComponent`	Object	Represents a component contained in a project
`VBComponents`	Collection	A collection of `VBComponent` objects
`VBComponentsEvents`	Property	Returns an event object of type `VBComponentsEvents`
`VBControl`	Object	Represents a control on a component in a project
`VBControls`	Collection	A collection of `VBControl` objects
`VBControlsEvents`	Object	Represents a source of events in a Visual Basic project
`VBE`	Property	Returns the root of the `VBE` object
`VBForm`	Object	Returns a component in a project
`VBProject`	Object	Represents a project
`VBProjects`	Collection	A collection of `VBProject` objects
`VBProjectsEvents`	Object	Represents a source of events in a Visual Basic project
`VBProjectsEvents`	Property	Returns an event object of type `VBProjectsEvents`
`Version`	Property	Returns the version of Visual Basic
`Visible`	Property	Standard `Visible` property
`Width`	Property	Standard `Width` property
`Window`	Object	Represents a window in the IDE
`Window`	Property	Returns the window in which the code pane is displayed
`Windows`	Collection	A collection of `Window` objects
`WindowState`	Property	Sets or returns a numeric value specifying the visual state of the window
`WriteProperty`	Method	Writes a value to a file
`Zorder`	Method	Places a specified `MDIForm`, `Form`, or control at the front or back of the z-order within its graphical level

The Starting Point of the Add-In

The starting point of the add-in is a procedure that you must create in a global module called `Main()`. This enables you to perform any initialization needed by your add-in. It also enables you to write code to ensure that the add-in can be found by the Add-In Manager. A sample `Main()` procedure looks like this:

```
Dim ErrCode As Long
ErrCode = WritePrivateProfileString("Add-Ins32", "MyAddIn.Connect", "0",
➥ "vbaddin.ini")
```

This is not actually coded by default; it is used simply to act as a starting point for the add-in. It also does one other thing: It makes sure that the Add-In Manager knows about the existence of the add-in because the `VBADDIN.INI` file contains a listing of the available add-ins. Please note that it must also be registered for the add-in to function. You can access the Add-In Manager by selecting the Add-Ins | Add-In Manager menu option.

After making sure that the `Main()` subroutine is coded in a BAS module, you must instruct the add-in to use this subroutine as the startup object in the General tab when you select the Project | Properties menu option.

Testing and Creating the Add-In

To test the add-in, you need to start another instance of Visual Basic. With the first instance of Visual Basic, run the add-in application. You do not need to compile it first.

Then, with the second instance, you can choose the Add-Ins | Add-In Manager menu option. You should see the name of your add-in in the list box. When you select this option, the menus you have defined for your add-in will be shown.

If you want to debug your add-in, you simply set breakpoints and debug it as you would in any other application, but you need to do this in the first instance. The second instance of Visual Basic acts only as a means to invoke and test the add-in.

Installing the Add-In on a User's System

When you create and run an add-in, the add-in will be registered automatically on your system. But what do you do if you want to distribute it to someone else? It must be registered in the system registry, as do all OLE components. You do this by one of the following methods:

- Install the application using the Setup Wizard
- Manually register the add-in

To manually register the add-in, you can use the REGSVR utility; however, you need to create an OLE DLL instead of an EXE file. Here is the format:

```
REGSVR dllname
```

In this case, *dllname* is the name of the DLL you are trying to register.

Summary

Add-ins are very versatile and easy to create. However, in order to be able to build them quickly, you must have some knowledge of how they work. Use this chapter as a reference to create add-ins for your own use, and you will quickly be able to build tools that speed up application development.

5

Testing and Debugging

Testing and debugging is an extremely important part of Visual Basic programming. The first part of this chapter covers general testing concepts. The second part discusses how to debug as well as gives pointers on how track down nasty bugs. It also gives some precautions for avoiding bugs in the first place.

One way to help fix bugs is to use a lot of comments. Comments do not get compiled in with the final project, so there's no reason not to place plenty of comments in your code. Comments allow other developers to understand the code you write.

Make sure to use the `Option Explicit` keywords. The `Option Explicit` keywords are placed in every `(general)(declarations)` section of every form, module, and class module in a project. This ensures that every variable must be declared before it is used and helps to avoid problems with variable spelling errors. If you do not use these keywords, a spelling error will be considered a new variable name.

You can possibly avoid bugs by using naming conventions. Naming conventions identify not only the scope of a variable, but the type of variable used. This can help you verify that bugs don't start because if you don't use conventions, many times a reference is made to a variable that actually had its value changed in a different procedure. You might not be aware of this because it was not immediately apparent what the scope of the variable was. Another example of why you want to use variable naming conventions is so that you understand what the datatype G. the variable is. If you just call a variable `x`, it is not apparent what the datatype is. This can cause problems when you need to convert to other datatypes. Therefore, using these conventions is a good idea.

Naming Standards and Conventions

To ensure ease of maintaining your code, it is advisable to use naming standards in your code. Many large Information Systems (IS) organizations mandate use of their corporate standards. Most of the time the corporate standards are adopted from the standards set forth by Microsoft Consulting Services. The need for standards apply to the following items:

- Variables
- Object names

These items are discussed in the following sections.

> **NOTE**
>
> Please keep in mind that these naming conventions are by no means "law"; they are suggestions and practices. Many IS departments use at least most of these standards.

Variable Naming Conventions

Variable naming conventions not only deal with how you should name your variables, but also indicate the scope of your variables. For example, you should be able to determine the type and scope of any variable simply by glancing at it. Variable naming conventions follow the general syntax

```
[g/m][a]tName
```

where all indicators before the variable name (prefix) are in lowercase:

`[g/m]` is used only if the variable is declared as global (`Public`) or module level (`Private`). Omit this if the variable used is local to a procedure.

`[a]` is used only if the variable is an array. Omit this if the variable is not an array.

t is the datatype of the variable, as follows:

- `n`—Integer
- `c`—Currency
- `d`—Double
- `b`—Boolean
- `y`—Byte
- `l`—Long
- `g`—Single
- `t`—Date
- `o`—Object
- `s`—String
- `v`—Variant
- `u`—User-defined type

`Name` is the name of the variable, which should be germane to the actual usage of the variable.

As an example, suppose you were using a variable that will be used in a local procedure to increment a count in a loop. Following the standards just listed, you would declare the variable like this:

```
Dim nLoopcount As Integer
```

If you wanted to declare a module-level variable in the `(general) (declarations)` section that will be used as a `String` array to store last names retrieved from a database, you would declare the variable like this:

```
Dim masLastname(100) As String
```

If you were to declare a `Public Currency` to hold sales tax, you would declare the variable like this:

```
Public gcSalestax As Currency
```

If you wanted to declare a constant in a BAS module to hold the sales tax rate, you would name the variable in uppercase and declare it like this:

```
Public Const ggRATE = 0.05
```

Notice that in this example the rate is being used as a single datatype, even though it is not explicitly declared as such.

Object Naming Conventions

Object naming conventions are as important to objects (such as forms and controls) as variable naming conventions are to variables. Object naming conventions follow this general syntax, where `o` is the object type, as described in Table 5.1:

```
oName
```

Table 5.1. Proposed object names and abbreviations.

Object Name	*Abbreviation*
3D Check Box	`chk`
3D Command Button	`cmd`
3D Frame	`fra`
3D Group Push Button	`psh`
3D Option Button	`opt`
3D Panel	`pnl`
Animated Button	`ani`
Check Box	`chk`
Combo Box	`cbo`
Command Button	`cmd`
Communications	`com`
Data	`dat`
Databound Combo Box	`dbc`
Databound Grid	`dbg`
Databound List Box	`dbl`
Directory List Box	`dir`

Object Name	*Abbreviation*
Drive List Box	`drv`
File List Box	`fil`
Form	`frm`
Frame	`fra`
Gauge	`gau`
Graph	`gra`
Grid	`grd`
Horizontal Scroll Bar	`hsb`
Image	`img`
Image List	`iml`
Key Status	`key`
Label	`lbl`
Line	`lin`
List Box	`lst`
List View	`lsv`
MAPI	`map`
Masked Edit	`mas`
Menu	`mnu`
Multimedia	`mci`
OLE Container	`ole`
Option Button	`opt`
Outline	`out`
Picture Box	`pic`
Picture Clip	`clp`
Progress Bar	`pro`
Remote Data Control	`rdc`
Rich Text Box	`rtb`
Shape	`shp`
Slider	`sli`
Spin Button	`spn`
SSTab	`tab`
Status Bar	`sta`

continues

Table 5.1. continued

Object Name	*Abbreviation*
Tab Strip	`str`
Text Box	`txt`
Timer	`tmr`
Toolbar	`tbr`
Treeview	`trv`
Vertical Scroll Bar	`vsb`

`Name` is the name of the variable, which should be germane to the actual usage of the variable. As an example, if you had a form used to input employee information, you would name the form `frmEmployee`.

If you need to place a text box on a form that stores the last name, you would name the control `txtLastName`.

One final example is that if you need to place a combo box on a form that lists all possible last names, you would name the control `cboLastName`.

Notice from Table 5.1 that there are some items duplicated, such as 3D Command Button and Command Button. If you want, you could use something like `3cb`, but usually, if a 3D command button is used at all, it is used everywhere throughout the project. This potentially means that there is no need to differentiate between the two different command buttons. Again, these prefixes are only suggestions. There is nothing cast in stone. The most important thing is that you maintain some sort of consistency. It is a good idea for all programming shops to either use this list or come up with some standards of their own.

Testing

Testing can be a very tedious part of the development process. However, it is extremely important. Testing can make the difference between a great software package and terrible one. Because of the nature of some types of applications, testing can seem impossible. This is why you need to develop a test plan. A *test plan* is a way to document how you are going to perform the testing.

Developing a Test Plan

A test plan is usually a documented path through which you will ensure that your application is sound. There is no "standard" test plan. Each company should evaluate the benefit of developing a sound test plan versus the time it takes to develop the plan. Many organizations don't take the time to develop a sound test plan. They figure the longer it takes to develop and implement a test plan, the longer it takes to get the software on the user's desktop.

I have worked for companies that have done everything from developing extensive test plans to developing no test plans at all. Because time is money, some companies feel that they are losing money by developing elaborate test plans and performing adequate testing. However, this attitude will ultimately be the demise of the software package. Users will lose confidence. Therefore, I suggest at least some type of test plan be implemented.

A test plan can be as simple as an Excel spreadsheet or Word document. It can be as complex as a custom application that tracks testing or actually performs the testing. Another option is to use Microsoft Test. It is a useful tool to perform mouse clicks and keystrokes and records results of repetitive tasks, which you would have to do manually by following your spreadsheet or document. The test plan can be broken into different types of testing, if necessary. The types are as follows:

- Unit (Component) testing
- Integration testing
- System-wide testing

Your test plan should outline how you will test the following, if applicable:

- Operating systems
- Different RAM configurations
- Different databases (Access, SQL Server, Oracle, and so on)
- Microsoft Office integration
- Individual "standard" features
- Individual "customized" features
- Different LAN environments (NT Server, Novell, and so on)
- Different printers for reports (laser, color, and so on)
- Different CPU types (386, 486, 586, Alpha, MIPS, and so on)

A very basic test plan could look like this:

Retail Order Taking System Test Plan, Version 1.0

Scope

This application allows access by two types of users. There is an "ADMIN" or administrator-level user and a general-level user. The general-level user is allowed to look up any data throughout the system and enter new customers. The only thing that the administrator-level user can do is override prices.

The system consists of three screens:

- Customer Entry/Review
- Order Entry/Review
- Reports/Invoices

Each of the screens conform to Windows standards.

Testing Plan

Testing shall consist of verifying the following:

- All command buttons on all three forms
- Security differences between general and administrator levels
- Database access for the three types of databases that can be used (Access, SQL Server, and Oracle)

Testing Verification

To verify that all possibilities have been tested, the following tables are used as a checklist. Table 5.2 is a checklist for testing the command buttons. Table 5.3 is for testing the security levels. Table 5.4 is for testing database access.

Table 5.2. Command button functionality checklist.

Screen	*Command Button*	*Tested By/Date*	*Notes*
Customer Entry	New		
	Lookup		
	Save		
	Print		
	Close		
Order Entry	New		
	Lookup		
	Save		
	Print		
	Close		
Reports	Select		
	Print		
	Close		

Table 5.3. Security functionality checklist.

Screen	*Security*	*Tested By/Date*	*Notes*
Customer Entry	General		
	Admin		
Order Entry	General		
	Admin		
Reports	General		
	Admin		

Table 5.4. Database access checklist.

Screen	*Database Type*	*Tested By/Date*	*Notes*
Customer Entry	Access 2.0		
	SQL Server 6.5		
	Oracle 7.1		
Order Entry	Access 2.0		
	SQL Server 6.5		
	Oracle 7.1		
Reports	Access 2.0		
	SQL Server 6.5		
	Oracle 7.1		

If nothing else, even a simple test plan can help show management what you did to help ensure that the system will work the way it was intended. These checklists can be made extremely detailed, if necessary. Again, this depends on the company's policy on testing.

Some companies have the developers themselves do the testing. Others have a quality assurance (QA) department perform the testing. There is also the possibility of both. For more information on detailed project testing, consult the Microsoft Consulting Service (MCS). They have many plans to help companies develop test plans, as well as general project management and design. They can be reached on the World Wide Web at `http://www.microsoft.com/servad/msconsult.htm`.

Debugging

During the testing process, you most definitely will find some bugs. However, sometimes these bugs can be elusive. This section will dispel some of the problems associated with debugging. Start first by learning the environment in which debugging takes place—within the Visual Basic IDE itself.

New to Version 5.0

The Debugging IDE

Version 5.0 enables you to include a debugging toolbar, either floating or docked. Figure 5.1 shows a floating Debug toolbar that contains 12 buttons.

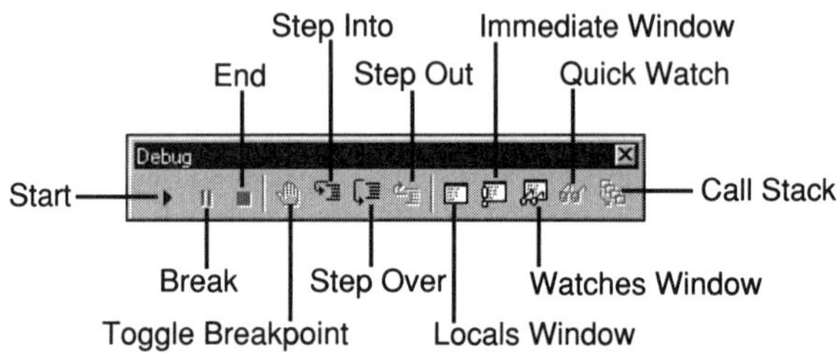

FIGURE 5.1.
A floating Debug toolbar.

As with all Visual Basic 5.0 toolbars, you can add it to the toolbar region or allow it to float. If the toolbar is not showing at all, you can click the right mouse button while the mouse is anywhere over the docked toolbar region to see a list of toolbars. Check the Debug toolbar. Alternatively, you can select the View | Toolbars menu option and choose the Debug toolbar.

The Start, Break, and End buttons are self explanatory. The Toggle Breakpoint option simply toggles a breakpoint on and off. A breakpoint is shown as a red line across the line of code. This indicates that the code will be put in break mode, which enables you to either trace the execution of the code or query the state or values of variables. Figure 5.2 shows a code window with a breakpoint set.

The Step Into button executes the current line of code. However, if the current line is the entry point into a procedure, it will step into that procedure and every other procedure it encounters.

The Step Over button executes each line of code in the current procedure, but steps over any subsequent procedure that is called. Even though the cursor does not stop anywhere within subsequent procedures, they are actually executed.

New to Version 5.0

The Step Out button is a new feature in Visual Basic. It executes all lines remaining in the current procedure and stops executing on the line after the line that called the current procedure.

FIGURE 5.2.
A breakpoint set in code.

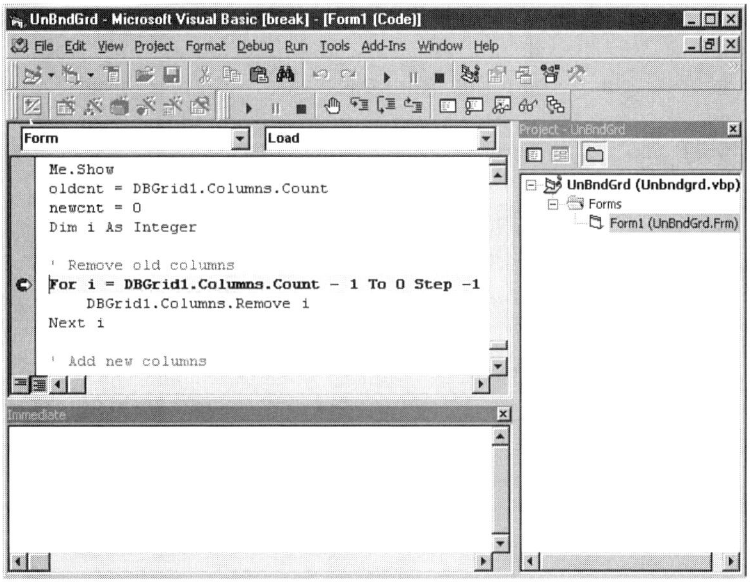

The Locals Window button is another new feature in Visual Basic. It brings up a window of the variables that are local to a procedure. Figure 5.3 shows the Locals window, which is located at the bottom of the figure.

FIGURE 5.3.
The Locals window.

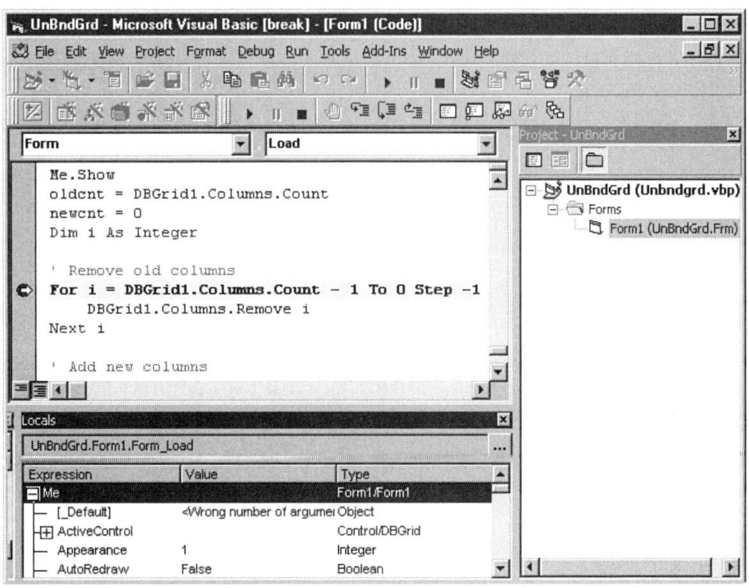

The Immediate Window button is probably the most common debugging tool. It is used to query and set the values of variables and objects and is sometimes referred to as the Debug window. Figure 5.4 shows the Immediate window, which is located at the bottom of the figure.

FIGURE 5.4.
The Immediate window.

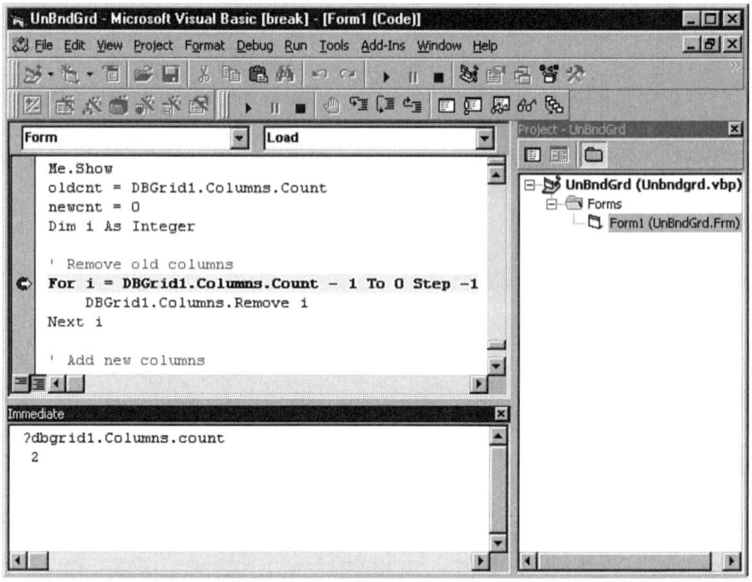

You use the Watches Window button to display any watches you have added. A *watch* is a way to query the value of a variable or many variables at one time. A watch is very useful because you can configure it to automatically break the code when specific conditions exist. This is discussed in the next section, "Design Time/Break Mode Debugging." Figure 5.5 shows the Watches window.

You use the Quick Watch button to determine the value of a single variable within which the cursor is located inside the code. Visual Basic version 5.0 also incorporates a provision for a quick watch when the mouse pointer is located over a variable that is in the context of a running procedure. Figure 5.6 shows the Quick Watch window.

The final toolbar button, the Call Stack button, is used to show all procedures that have been called but have not yet completed. Because Visual Basic is an event-driven language, it is possible to have many calls in the call stack. That's because events can be fired due to external influences, such as a timer event firing, not just by user intervention. Figure 5.7 shows the Call Stack window.

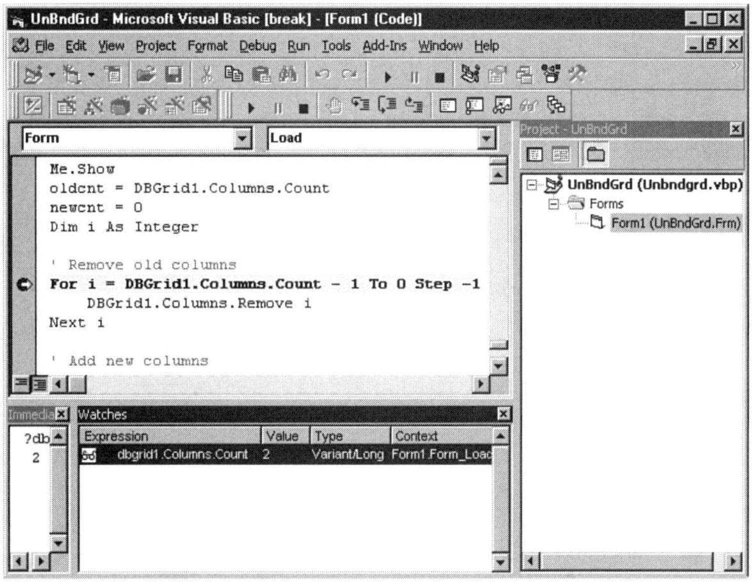

FIGURE 5.5.
The Watches window.

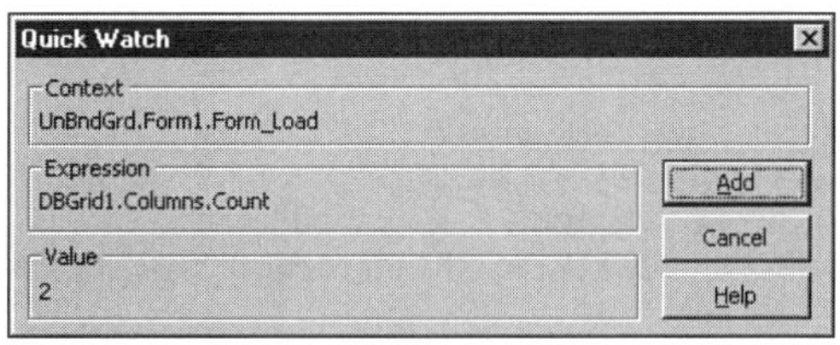

FIGURE 5.6.
The Quick Watch window.

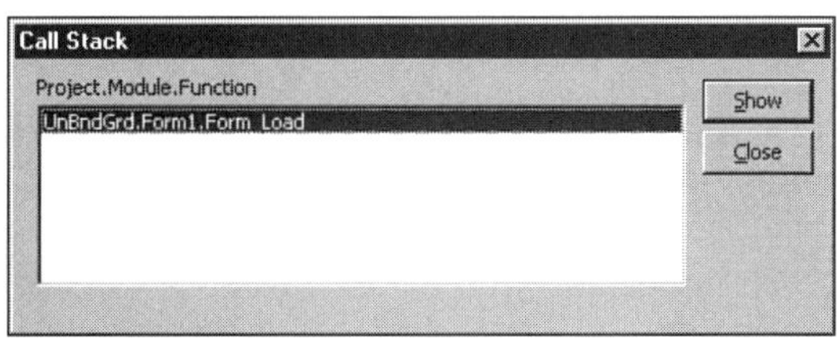

FIGURE 5.7.
The Call Stack window.

Design Time/Break Mode Debugging

Debugging is most commonly done in break mode, although breakpoints and watches can be set up in design time. If you are not sure why a procedure of code is not working as expected, you must set a breakpoint and step through the code. You set the breakpoint above where you believe the problem to be. If you are not sure exactly where the problem is, set the breakpoint on the first possible line. It is not possible to place a breakpoint on any code line that is a comment, a line label, a variable declaration, or a hidden module.

Consider the code from the `StatusUpdate()` event of the multimedia control in the CD player application in Chapter 35, "Developing a CD Player Application." It is a procedure that serves almost as a shell for the `PopulateDisplay()` procedure. Suppose that the display was not being populated correctly. You do not know if it is the `PopulateDisplay()` procedure, the multimedia control, or the processing in the `StatusUpdate()` event. The code looks like this:

```
Private Sub MMControl_StatusUpdate()

    'declare variables
    Dim loopcount%  'loop counting variable
    Dim x%          'most significant byte
    Dim x1%         'next significant byte
    Dim x2%         'least significant byte

    'if there is no disk, then clear all displays
    If MMControl.Mode = mciModeReady Then
        Call ClearAll
        Exit Sub
    End If

    'populate current track time
    x% = ((MMControl.Position) And &HFF00&) \ &H100
    x1% = ((MMControl.Position) And &HFF0000) \ &H10000
    PopulateDisplay PTIME, Format$(x%, "00") + Format$(x1%, "00")
    DoEvents
    DoEvents

    'populate current track
    x% = (MMControl.Position) And 255
    PopulateDisplay PTRACK, Format$(x%, "00")
    'force track property so that correct time is calculated
    MMControl.Track = x%
    DoEvents
    DoEvents

    'populate current track length
    x% = ((MMControl.TrackLength) And 255)
    x1% = ((MMControl.TrackLength) And &HFF00&) \ &H100
    PopulateDisplay PTRACKLENGTH, Format$(x%, "00") + Format$(x1%, "00")
    DoEvents
    DoEvents

    'populate colons
    For loopcount% = 0 To 3
       pictColon(loopcount%).Picture = LoadResPicture(FindCorrectBitmap(COLON),
       ➥ 0)
    Next loopcount%
    DoEvents
    DoEvents

    'populate total number of tracks
    PopulateDisplay PTOTALTRACK, Format$(MMControl.Tracks, "00")
    DoEvents
    DoEvents
```

```
    'populate total length of disk
    x% = (MMControl.Length) And 255
    x1% = ((MMControl.Length) And &HFF00&) \ &H100
    x2% = Int(x% / 60)
    PopulateDisplay PTOTALLENGTH, Format$(x2%, "0") + Format$(x% Mod 60, "00") +
    ➥ Format$(x1%, "00")
    DoEvents
    DoEvents

End Sub
```

Suppose the current track was not being populated. You might start by placing a breakpoint on the line that reads

```
x% = (MMControl.Position) And 255
```

First, you want to make sure that the `MMControl.Position` is actually changing when the track is changed. Run the project and change tracks using the buttons in the multimedia control. If it does not change, there is your problem. If it does change with the new track, make sure you are performing the bitwise operation with the correct number, 255.

CROSS REFERENCE

For more information about multimedia, refer to Chapter 11, "Multimedia."

Because the number 255 is correct in this case, the problem appears to be in the `PopulateDisplay()` procedure, or possibly the arguments that are passed to it. Here is the line of code that calls this routine:

```
PopulateDisplay PTRACK, Format$(x%, "00")
```

Check the value of `PTRACK` by typing `?PTRACK` in the Immediate (Debug) window or by choosing Quick Watch. If this is correct, then check the value of `x%`. This should be the same value returned from the prior line of code, which performed the bitwise operation with the constant `255`. If that is correct, then you need to verify that what is returned from the `Format$()` function is the format expected. In this case, a two-digit number is expected. If everything looks right, then the problem must be in the `PopulateDisplay()` procedure. The procedure looks like this:

```
Private Sub PopulateDisplay(WhichArray As Integer, texttodisplay$)

    'declare variables
    Dim FirstDigit%      'first integer converted from packed integer(LSB)
    Dim SecondDigit%     'second integer converted from packed integer
    Dim ThirdDigit%      'third integer converted from packed integer
    Dim FourthDigit%     'fourth integer converted from packed integer
    Dim FifthDigit%      'fifth integer converted from packed integer
```

```
If WhichArray = PTIME Then
  'CURRENT RUNNING TIME
  FirstDigit% = Val(Mid$(texttodisplay$, 4, 1))
  pictTime(0).Picture = LoadResPicture(FindCorrectBitmap(FirstDigit%), 0)

  SecondDigit% = Val(Mid$(texttodisplay$, 3, 1))
  pictTime(1).Picture = LoadResPicture(FindCorrectBitmap(SecondDigit%), 0)

  ThirdDigit% = Val(Mid$(texttodisplay$, 2, 1))
  pictTime(2).Picture = LoadResPicture(FindCorrectBitmap(ThirdDigit%), 0)

  FourthDigit% = Val(Mid$(texttodisplay$, 1, 1))
  pictTime(3).Picture = LoadResPicture(FindCorrectBitmap(FourthDigit%), 0)
ElseIf WhichArray = PTRACK Then
  'CURRENT TRACK
  FirstDigit% = Val(Mid$(texttodisplay$, 2, 1))
  pictTrack(0).Picture = LoadResPicture(FindCorrectBitmap(FirstDigit%), 0)

  SecondDigit% = Val(Mid$(texttodisplay$, 1, 1))
  pictTrack(1).Picture = LoadResPicture(FindCorrectBitmap(SecondDigit%), 0)
ElseIf WhichArray = PTOTALTRACK Then
    'TOTAL TRACKS
    FirstDigit% = Val(Mid$(texttodisplay$, 2, 1))
    pictTotalTrack(0).Picture = LoadResPicture(FindCorrectBitmap
    ➥(FirstDigit%), 0)

    SecondDigit% = Val(Mid$(texttodisplay$, 1, 1))
    pictTotalTrack(1).Picture = LoadResPicture(FindCorrectBitmap
    ➥(SecondDigit%), 0)
ElseIf WhichArray = PTRACKLENGTH Then
    'TRACK LENGTH
    FirstDigit% = Val(Mid$(texttodisplay$, 4, 1))
    pictLength(0).Picture = LoadResPicture(FindCorrectBitmap
    ➥(FirstDigit%), 0)

    SecondDigit% = Val(Mid$(texttodisplay$, 3, 1))
    pictLength(1).Picture = LoadResPicture(FindCorrectBitmap
    ➥(SecondDigit%), 0)

    ThirdDigit% = Val(Mid$(texttodisplay$, 2, 1))
    pictLength(2).Picture = LoadResPicture(FindCorrectBitmap
    ➥(ThirdDigit%), 0)

    FourthDigit% = Val(Mid$(texttodisplay$, 1, 1))
    pictLength(3).Picture = LoadResPicture(FindCorrectBitmap
    ➥(FourthDigit%), 0)
ElseIf WhichArray = PTOTALLENGTH Then
    'TOTAL LENGTH OF ALL TRACKS
    FirstDigit% = Val(Mid$(texttodisplay$, 5, 1))
    pictTotal(0).Picture = LoadResPicture(FindCorrectBitmap
    ➥(FirstDigit%), 0)

    SecondDigit% = Val(Mid$(texttodisplay$, 4, 1))
    pictTotal(1).Picture = LoadResPicture(FindCorrectBitmap
    ➥(SecondDigit%), 0)

    ThirdDigit% = Val(Mid$(texttodisplay$, 3, 1))
    pictTotal(2).Picture = LoadResPicture(FindCorrectBitmap
    ➥(ThirdDigit%), 0)
```

```
        FourthDigit% = Val(Mid$(texttodisplay$, 2, 1))
        pictTotal(3).Picture = LoadResPicture(FindCorrectBitmap
        ➥(FourthDigit%), 0)

        FifthDigit% = Val(Mid$(texttodisplay$, 1, 1))
        pictTotal(4).Picture = LoadResPicture(FindCorrectBitmap
        ➥(FifthDigit%), 0)
    End If

End Sub
```

As you can see from the code, each branch of code is used to populate a specific area of the display. Therefore, make sure that the correct area of the display is being populated by placing a breakpoint in the branch that contains the line of code which reads

```
ElseIf WhichArray = PTRACK Then
```

If the code does not break in this branch, then the problem is located in the branching logic. Stepping through the code, you need to verify that the actual digits are being correctly calculated by using the `Mid$()` function. If they are, the problem must be within the actual resource file that contains the bitmaps.

Sometimes debugging can be a little more tedious. In the earlier example, there were only two calls, so tracking was very easy. However, some bugs are very elusive because as your application becomes more complex, so does the debugging.

I have seen developers spend much time tracking down a problem as simple as the screen's mouse pointer changing from `vbHourglass` to `vbDefault` before a form is finished loaded. Therefore, on a slow computer, a complicated initialization process can make a user think that the computer is locked up. The reality is that the mouse pointer simply changed too soon. This can be virtually impossible to track by using breakpoints and stepping into the code, which is precisely why watches were invented. You can set a watch on the `Mousepointer` property of the `Screen` object. Set the breakpoint to break when the value changes anywhere in the project, as shown in Figure 5.8.

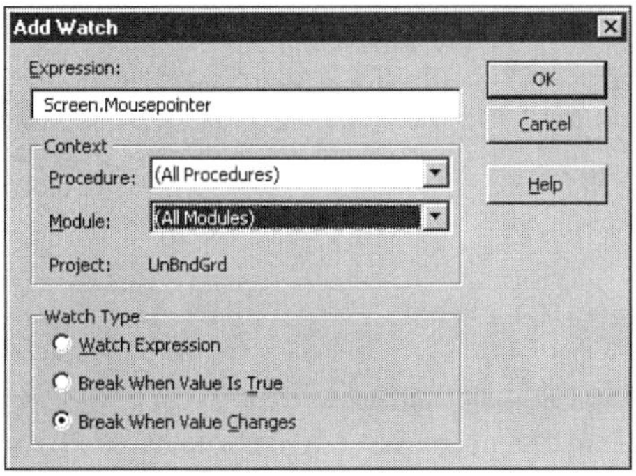

FIGURE 5.8.
Configuring a watch for the screen's `Mousepointer` *property.*

Now, after the watch is set, it will be very easy to see which procedure in a chain of many procedures sets the `Mousepointer` property prematurely.

Runtime Debugging

There is actually no runtime component of Visual Basic that can help you debug; however, you can write something into your code to help in this process. If you have an error handler in your Visual Basic procedures, you can write out a log containing the errors that occur. This can help you identify the what, when, where, and why about errors.

Consider this sample code:

```
Private Sub Form_Load()

   'declare variables
   Const CURR_PROC = "Form_Load"
   Const DEBUG_FILE = "C:\DEBUG.LOG"
   Dim sCmd As String
   Dim wsTemp As Workspace
   Dim rsTemp As Recordset
   Dim dbTemp As Database
   Dim nFile As Integer

   'handle errors
   On Error GoTo LoadError

   'get free file handle
   nFile = FreeFile()

   'open File
   Open DEBUG_FILE For Output As #nFile

   ' Create Workspace object.
   Set wsTemp = DBEngine.CreateWorkspace("", "admin", "")

   'open database
   Set dbTemp = wsTemp.OpenDatabase("C:\Program Files\DevStudio\VB\BIBLIO.MDB")

   'retrieve authors records
   sCmd = "SELECT * FROM Authors"
   Set rsTemp = dbTemp.OpenRecordset(sCmd)

   'close the file
   Close #nFile

   Exit Sub
LoadError:
   'show error on screen
   MsgBox Error$

   'write error to file
   Print #nFile, "Procedure: " & CURR_PROC + " " & Error$

   'run the rest of the procedure
   Resume Next
End Sub
```

Because the error handler is placed at the beginning of the procedure, and the constant CURR_PROC is assigned to be the same as the name of the current procedure, any error will write out a log file. This log file is simply a text file of any error that occurs. This log file could also write out values of any variables. This is a sample log file that is generated if your DAO object reference is to anything other than DAO 3.5. DAO stands for Data Access Objects and is covered in more detail in Chapter 28, "Database Concepts." The log file is as follows:

```
Procedure: Form_Load ActiveX component can't create object
Procedure: Form_Load Object variable or With block variable not set
Procedure: Form_Load Object variable or With block variable not set
```

Summary

Testing and debugging can help you develop quality applications in a shorter period of time. The time it takes to develop an application first depends on how well you have designed the application. Then it depends on how well you put together a test plan. Finally, when bugs do surface, it helps to be able to quickly track or debug them. Visual Basic 5.0 provides many tools to make debugging your applications very easy.

II

The Windows Execution Environment

6

The Registry

The Windows Registry is a centralized database that contains information about your computer's configuration, hardware, and software. The Registry is used by many processes, such as the following:

- Booting
- System initialization
- Logon
- Executing programs

In the Windows environment, the Registry essentially has made it possible to get rid of all of the MS-DOS–based configuration files, such as these:

- `AUTOEXEC.BAT`
- `CONFIG.SYS`
- `SYSTEM.INI`
- `WIN.INI`

These files are still used for DOS windows and the command prompt. The Registry makes it possible for many programs to share information contained in a Registry key. For example, much information about profiles is used with all aspects of Microsoft Exchange, Mail, and other communications programs. This is possible because it is all stored in one place.

You can think of the Registry as a repository for any process that needs to write configuration-type data for later retrieval. Using `.INI` files to store data is no longer recommended. Microsoft is now using the Registry to store initialization and configuration data. However, the API functions to retrieve `.INI` files are still supported in the Windows API and the WIN32 API.

CAUTION

It is not advised that you change any of the Registry values unless you know what you are doing. This could have adverse effects on the system such as cause it to stop responding, or even prevent it from booting into Windows 95 or Windows NT.

Almost all applications read and write from the Registry. If an application doesn't work correctly, I would recommend making sure that the application (and all of its components) are registered correctly. However, this can be a daunting task. It is such a huge database that, unless you know what you're looking for, you can get lost. This chapter attempts to dissect the Registry to help you understand how it works.

There are two programs used to edit the Registry. They are `REGEDIT.EXE` and `REGEDT32.EXE`. These programs are discussed under the Windows 95 and Windows NT sections that follow, but as a quick overview, Windows 95 uses only REGEDIT.EXE. It is a 32-bit application that enables you to dive into the Registry. Windows NT installs both files; however, there is one problem. If you have upgraded your operating systems on your machine, starting with Windows 3.1, the REGEDIT.EXE program is not the same as the one that is installed under Windows 95. It is the same one that is installed with Windows 3.1, believe it or not. Also, to make matters more confusing, the REGEDT32.EXE application for use with Windows NT is not the same 32-bit program as the REGEDIT.EXE 32-bit program shipping with Windows 95. The bottom line is that there are several programs that ship with different versions of Windows, but they all aim to accomplish the same thing. My personal preference is to use the REGEDIT.EXE program in Windows 95.

TIP

You can actually use the REGEDIT.EXE program that ships with Windows 95 under Windows NT. The only difference is that there is one hive, HKEY_DYN_DATA, that is not used in Windows NT, but only in Windows 95. Therefore, don't go into that hive.

Be aware that you cannot set security for Registry keys using REGEDIT.EXE. One other limitation is that you cannot edit any key with a datatype of REG_EXPAND_SZ or REG_MULTI_SZ. If you do, you could render the Registry key useless.

Use caution when you use a different Registry editor than the one shipped with your environment. Only experienced users should do this. Also, the only advantage in using a different Registry editor is the personal preference of the Windows 95 look and feel of the editor.

An example of the importance of the Registry is a problem using an early Visual Basic 5.0 beta. If you were to place a Sheridan custom control on a form, for example, you would receive an error message about not having the appropriate design-time license. It would not enable you to use the control. However, fortunately, there was a fix, and quite a simple one. The license information that is, of course, stored in the Registry, was not registered correctly. These controls come with Visual Basic, but Visual Basic failed to register them properly. Therefore, Microsoft released a registration file to take care of the problem.

As time goes on and more files are deleted from your system, your Registry begins to point to invalid files. This can actually slow down your system as the Registry becomes very large. Therefore, Microsoft created a utility called REGCLN.EXE that will clean your Registry. It cycles through all entries in the Registry and sees whether they point to valid locations on the physical disk drives. If not, they are removed. You can find this file on the Visual Basic 5 CD or download it from the Microsoft Web site at http://www.microsoft.com.

Hives

The Registry is divided into sections, called *hives*. These hives are the highest possible hierarchical level in a registry. These hives are labeled as follows:

- HKEY_CLASSES_ROOT
- HKEY_CURRENT_USER
- HKEY_LOCAL_MACHINE
- HKEY_USERS
- HKEY_CURRENT_CONFIG
- HKEY_DYN_DATA (Windows 95 only)

HKEY_CLASSES_ROOT

HKEY_CLASSES_ROOT is a hive that stores information about classes registered on your machine and specifies how the operating system (Windows 95 or Windows NT) knows how to run a file with a specific file extension. This file extension is associated with a specific class (or executable program).

This is assigned automatically by most setup programs. For example, a BAS file is automatically associated with a Visual Basic program. You can change this association in the File Manager by selecting the File | Associate menu option and typing the program name with which to associate a specific file extension.

You can also use the Explorer by selecting View | Options. This brings up a dialog box with three tabs. Choose the File Types tab. The dialog box, shown in Figure 6.1, contains a list of registered class types on your system. From this list you associate a specific file extension. If you would like to change this association, click the Edit button. To make a new association, click the New Type button.

To understand what you are seeing when you view the HKEY_CLASSES_ROOT hive, refer to Figure 6.2, which shows an expanded view of this hive.

Notice that some of the keys have a plus sign (+) located to the left of the file extension name. This indicates that the subkeys located underneath specify an actual program to run for this file extension. Notice that, for example, a .BAS file contains subkeys Shell | Open | Command. You can think of the logic like this: the value for the COMMAND specifies which SHELL program will be OPENed for this file extension.

Any key that does not have a plus sign located to the left of the file extension name means that the value for this key is registered as a class in the HKEY_LOCAL_MACHINE hive.

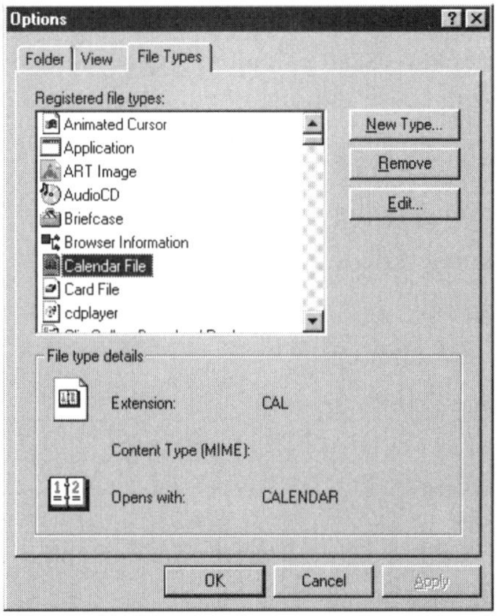

FIGURE 6.1.
The Explorer's Options dialog box.

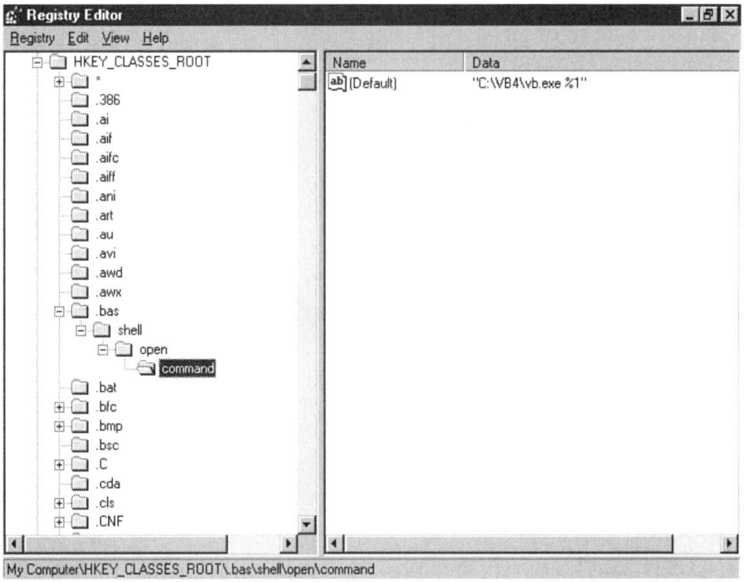

FIGURE 6.2.
An expanded view of the HKEY_CLASSES_ROOT *hive.*

HKEY_CURRENT_USER

HKEY_CURRENT_USER is a hive that stores information about the user currently logged into the computer. The data is also contained in the HKEY_USERS hive (discussed later). This hive is used to quickly access the way a user has opted to configure the system without having to search through the HKEY_USERS hive for the appropriate user. The data for the HKEY_CURRENT_USER hive is copied from the HKEY_USERS hive upon logging on to the computer after booting or choosing Start | Shut Down | Close all programs and log on as a different user.

HKEY_CURRENT_USER stores such information as this:

- Desktop configuration
- Environmental variables
- Software groups
- Network configuration
- Remote access configuration

HKEY_LOCAL_MACHINE

The HKEY_LOCAL_MACHINE hive stores information about all aspects of the local computer. This includes the following:

- Hardware settings
- Software settings
- Application configuration information
- Security settings

HKEY_USERS

The HKEY_USERS hive stores information about all users who are registered on the computer. The information about a specific user, when he or she logs in, is copied to the HKEY_CURRENT_USER hive. Such information includes the following:

- Environmental variables
- Desktop settings (display, screen savers, and so on)
- Software information
- Network connections
- Explorer groups

Each user registered in the Registry is indicated by a unique ID. There is no way to determine which user is assigned which ID. These IDs are constructed in such a way that only these IDs are used for processes. They are actually used as tokens because each one is guaranteed to be unique.

HKEY_CURRENT_CONFIG

The HKEY_CURRENT_CONFIG hive stores system-related information about the current configuration. This configuration is determined upon login. Such information includes the Current Control Set. The Current Control Set is a group of information about the configuration of your computer in its current state, including hardware and software settings.

HKEY_DYN_DATA

The HKEY_DYN_DATA hive stores dynamic information and is available only under Windows 95. The dynamic data makes it easy to determine statistics about a computer without needing to make complex API calls and calculations. The information in the HKEY_DYN_DATA hive includes the following:

- Performance statistics (such as CPU usage)
- Hardware information
- Process/thread information

Registration Files

A *registration file* is a file that can be merged into the Registry. The registration file (with a *.REG file extension) contains information only about a specific program, ActiveX control, or other component. It also can contain information about multiple controls. However, the point is that it is not the entire Registry. Many products come with a *.REG file to enable you to re-register applications in case of problems, without needing to reinstall the application. Consider the SETUP.REG file in the \WINDOWS\SYSTEM directory. The contents look something like this:

```
REGEDIT
(the above line used as a quick check that we are indeed a registration script)

ALL LINES THAT DON'T START WITH 'HKEY_CLASSES_ROOT' ARE COMMENTS.

THIS FILE CONSISTS OF A LIST OF <key> <value> PAIRS. THE key AND value SHOULD
BE SEPERATED BY A " = " mark.

Some of these entries duplicate those found in win.ini, for example, the
file extension associations to executables.  Shell.dll always looks
in the registration database before it looks in win.ini for this
information, so it is efficient to include it here.

ENTRIES FOR NotePad
HKEY_CLASSES_ROOT\.ini = txtfile
HKEY_CLASSES_ROOT\.txt = txtfile
HKEY_CLASSES_ROOT\txtfile = Text File
HKEY_CLASSES_ROOT\txtfile\shell\print\command = notepad.exe /p %1
HKEY_CLASSES_ROOT\txtfile\shell\open\command = notepad.exe %1
```

```
ENTRIES FOR Cardfile
HKEY_CLASSES_ROOT\.crd = crdfile
HKEY_CLASSES_ROOT\crdfile = Card File
HKEY_CLASSES_ROOT\crdfile\shell\print\command = cardfile.exe /p %1
HKEY_CLASSES_ROOT\crdfile\shell\open\command = cardfile.exe %1

ENTRIES FOR Calendar
HKEY_CLASSES_ROOT\.cal = calfile
HKEY_CLASSES_ROOT\calfile = Calendar File
HKEY_CLASSES_ROOT\calfile\shell\print\command = calendar.exe /p %1
HKEY_CLASSES_ROOT\calfile\shell\open\command = calendar.exe %1

ENTRIES FOR Terminal
HKEY_CLASSES_ROOT\.trm = trmfile
HKEY_CLASSES_ROOT\trmfile = Terminal Settings
HKEY_CLASSES_ROOT\trmfile\shell\open\command = terminal.exe %1

ENTRIES FOR Macro Recorder
HKEY_CLASSES_ROOT\.rec = recfile
HKEY_CLASSES_ROOT\recfile = Recorder Macro
HKEY_CLASSES_ROOT\recfile\shell\open\command = recorder.exe %1

ENTRIES FOR Write
HKEY_CLASSES_ROOT\.wri = wrifile
HKEY_CLASSES_ROOT\wrifile = Write Document
HKEY_CLASSES_ROOT\wrifile\shell\print\command = write.exe /p %1
HKEY_CLASSES_ROOT\wrifile\shell\open\command = write.exe %1

ENTRIES FOR Regedit
HKEY_CLASSES_ROOT\.reg = regedit
HKEY_CLASSES_ROOT\regedit = Registration Entries
HKEY_CLASSES_ROOT\regedit\shell\open\command = regedit.exe %1

ENTRIES FOR PBrush SERVER
HKEY_CLASSES_ROOT\.bmp = PBrush
HKEY_CLASSES_ROOT\.msp = PBrush
HKEY_CLASSES_ROOT\*** = PBrush
HKEY_CLASSES_ROOT\PBrush = Paintbrush Picture
HKEY_CLASSES_ROOT\PBrush\shell\print\command = pbrush.exe /p %1
HKEY_CLASSES_ROOT\PBrush\shell\open\command = pbrush.exe %1
HKEY_CLASSES_ROOT\PBrush\protocol\StdFileEditing\verb\0 = Edit
HKEY_CLASSES_ROOT\PBrush\protocol\StdFileEditing\server = pbrush.exe

ENTRIES FOR Packager SERVER
HKEY_CLASSES_ROOT\Package = Package
HKEY_CLASSES_ROOT\Package\protocol\StdFileEditing\verb\0 = &Activate Contents
HKEY_CLASSES_ROOT\Package\protocol\StdFileEditing\verb\1 = &Edit Package
HKEY_CLASSES_ROOT\Package\protocol\StdFileEditing\server = packager.exe


ENTRIES for Sound Recorder
HKEY_CLASSES_ROOT\.wav = SoundRec
HKEY_CLASSES_ROOT\SoundRec = Sound
HKEY_CLASSES_ROOT\SoundRec\shell\open\command = SoundRec.exe %1
HKEY_CLASSES_ROOT\SoundRec\protocol\StdExecute\server = SoundRec.exe
HKEY_CLASSES_ROOT\SoundRec\protocol\StdFileEditing\server = SoundRec.exe
HKEY_CLASSES_ROOT\SoundRec\protocol\StdFileEditing\verb\1 = &Edit
HKEY_CLASSES_ROOT\SoundRec\protocol\StdFileEditing\verb\0 = &Play
```

```
ENTRIES for Media Player
HKEY_CLASSES_ROOT\.mid = MPlayer
HKEY_CLASSES_ROOT\.rmi = MPlayer
HKEY_CLASSES_ROOT\MPlayer = Media Player
HKEY_CLASSES_ROOT\MPlayer\shell\open\command = MPlayer.exe %1

ENTRIES for Word for Windows 2.0
HKEY_CLASSES_ROOT\WordDocument\protocol\StdFileEditing\PackageObjects
```

The preceding is designed to help you understand the contents of a `*.REG` file. The first line of the `*.REG` file must be `REGEDIT`. The rest of the lines are used to enter values into the Registry under the specified hive. Creating a `*.REG` file can be much more convenient than writing a process that calls API functions to set the values in the Registry. This is because all you need to do is write the ASCII text file containing the Registry information and then run the `REGEDIT.EXE` or `REGEDT32.EXE` programs. You can pass the name of the `*.REG` file as an argument, and either of these programs will automatically register the `*.REG` file. Otherwise, you can select the File | Merge option to merge a `*.REG` file.

Most of the time, you'll write or change data only in the `HKEY_CLASSES_ROOT` or the `HKEY_LOCAL_MACHINE` hives because the `HKEY_USERS` hives are automatically maintained as you add, remove, or change information about users. The `HKEY_CURRENT_CONFIG` and `HKEY_CURRENT_USER` hives are copied automatically from the other hives. `HKEY_DYN_DATA` is maintained completely by Windows 95.

In the preceding file printout, notice that there are some lines that do not start with one of the six hive key names. This will cause the `REGEDIT.EXE` or `REGEDT32.EXE` programs to ignore the line, treating it as a comment. All other lines set the `HKEY_CLASSES_ROOT` hive. The subkeys under this hive are used to instruct the operating system, either Windows 95, Windows NT, or even Windows 3.1, which program to associate with a given file extension.

For example, look at the Notepad entries. The first lines set up the keyword `txtfile` with both `*.INI` files and `*.TXT` files. However, the system does not know what `txtfile` means. Therefore, the following three lines define what it means. The next line associates `txtfile` with a string that will be shown in dialog boxes throughout the system as a description. In this case it is `Text File`. The next two lines specify how to print or open the associated file(s). This is done by creating the subkey `\txtfile\shell\print` and assigning the command to `notepad.exe /p %1`. This works only because Notepad understands the `/p` print keyword and accepts a command-line argument, indicated by the `%1`. The `open` command works the same way. It simply doesn't specify the `/p` switch.

The other keys work the same way. This is a very simple example, but it clearly shows how the `*.REG` file works. The alternative is to use API functions to access the Registry. Here are the most commonly used functions:

- `RegCloseKey`
- `RegCreateKey`

- `RegCreateKeyEx`
- `RegEnumKey`
- `RegEnumKeyEx`
- `RegEnumValue`
- `RegOpenKey`
- `RegOpenKeyEx`
- `RegQueryValue`
- `RegSetValue`

These functions, and many others, are covered in detail in Chapter 13, "Using the WIN32 API."

Windows 95

The Registry is actually stored in two separate files, `SYSTEM.DAT` and `USER.DAT`. These files store system- and user-related data, respectively. When the user successfully logs into Windows 95, the `SYSTEM.DAT` and `USER.DAT` files are copied to `SYSTEM.DA0` and `USER.DA0`. These are used as a backup in case there is a problem booting your system, based on changes that might have been made in the Registry in your current session.

The Registry is shown in an Explorer-style tree list view. The hives are described earlier in this chapter. To view these hives, you can use the `REGEDIT.EXE` program, which ships with Windows 95. Figure 6.3 shows what the Windows 95 `REGEDIT.EXE` program looks like.

Windows NT

The Registry is stored in two files. The first is `REG.DAT`, which is used to store `HKEY_CLASSES_ROOT` type information about 16-bit applications only. The other is stored in an unpublished location.

As mentioned earlier, the `REGEDIT.EXE` program installed by Windows NT is one of two versions. The first is a 32-bit application that is installed if you have never had Windows 3.1 installed. The second is a 16-bit application that is installed if you have upgraded at some point from Windows 3.1 to Windows NT. Both have the same filename, but only one is actually installed by Windows NT setup. The difference in the look and feel is totally different. Figure 6.4 shows what the 16-bit Windows NT version looks like and Figure 6.5 shows what the 32-bit `REGEDT32` version looks like.

FIGURE 6.3.
The Registry Editor, Windows 95 REGEDIT.EXE.

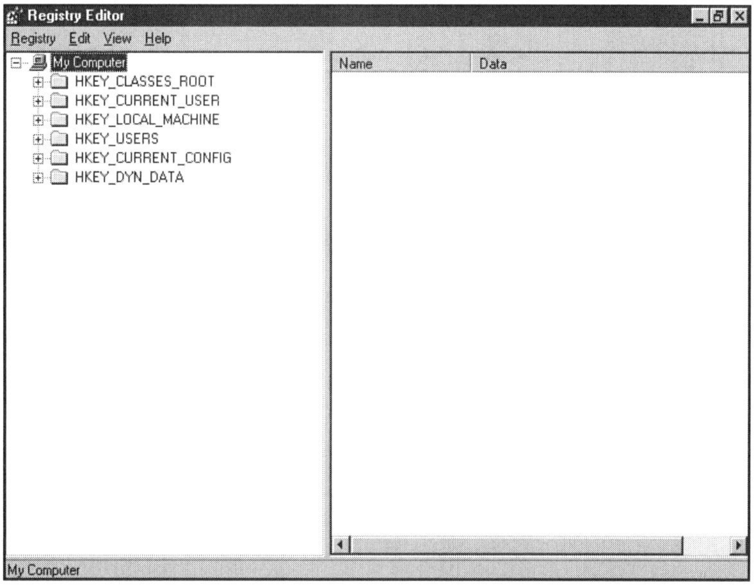

FIGURE 6.4.
The Registry Editor, 16-bit Windows NT REGEDIT.EXE.

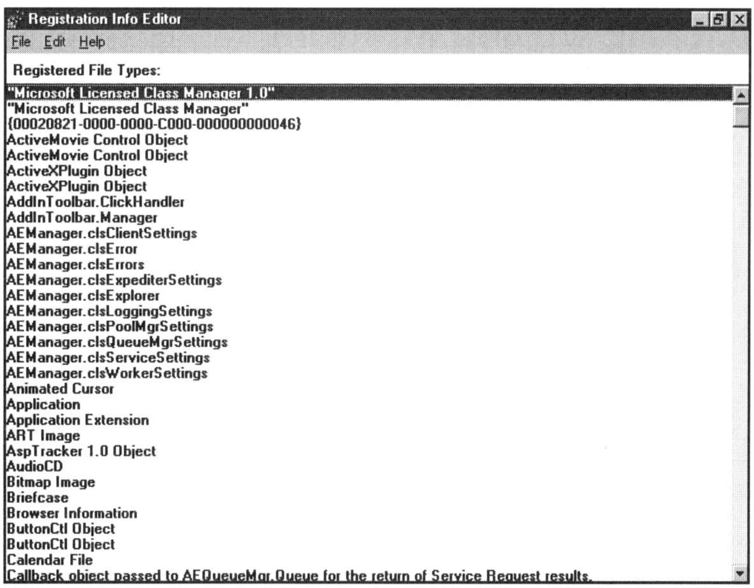

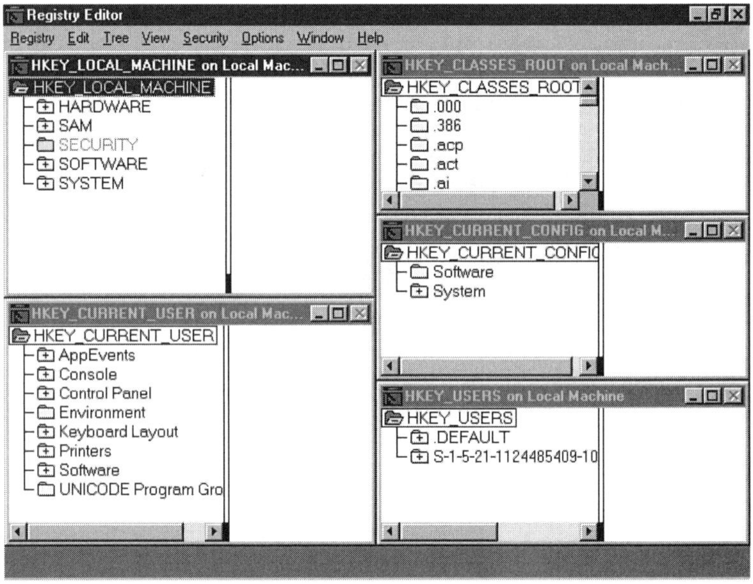

FIGURE 6.5.
The Registry Editor, 32-bit Windows NT `REGEDT32.EXE`.

Backing Up and Restoring Registries

Backing up and restoring registries is really quite simple, and you should do this on a regular basis. You can do so by using the Windows 95 version of the `REGEDIT.EXE` program. Select Registry | Import Registry File or Registry | Export Registry File. Exporting enables you to export the current branch's values or the entire Registry. Figure 6.6 shows what the Export screen looks like.

Note that using the `REGEDT32.EXE` program under Windows NT, you can save only one key at a time by selecting the Registry | Save Key menu option. The key is saved in a file that you specify. Then, to restore the file, choose the Registry | Restore menu option.

If you are using the Windows 3.1 look and feel version of `REGEDIT.EXE`, you can only merge a registration file. This is because this version was only meant to register the classes for file association in the `HKEY_CLASSES_ROOT` hive. To do this, select the File | Merge Registration File menu option.

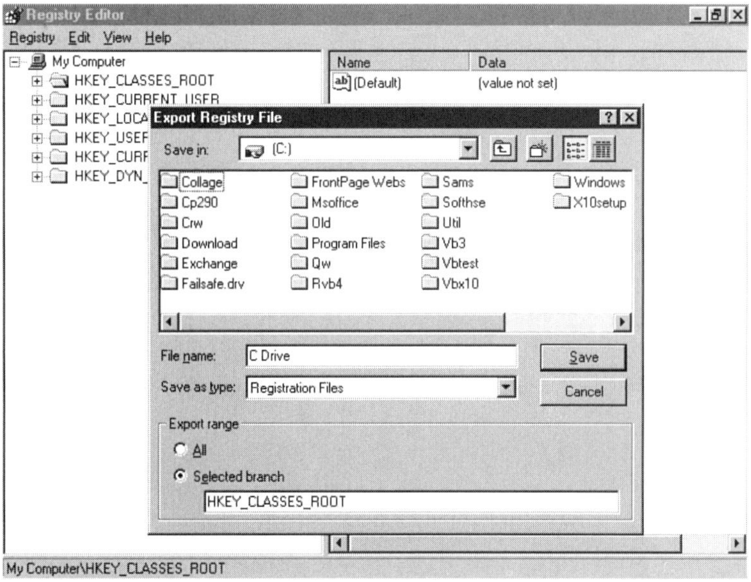

FIGURE 6.6.
The Export Registry File dialog box of the Registry Editor.

Summary

The Registry plays an important part in proper Windows configuration and operation. Many people never edit or look into the Registry because they are afraid of damaging something. Although this is a real possibility, at some point you will need to learn about the Registry. If you understand how it is used, you can quickly diagnose system problems. This chapter gives a good overview of how the Registry works.

7

Working with Files

Working with files is very easy in Visual Basic compared to other programming languages, mainly because you don't have to deal with pointers. Visual Basic takes care of that. There are two major types of files: text files and binary files. Visual Basic enables you to write code using both types.

Text files are files that contain ASCII characters only. There are very few special characters for special purposes. Text files are not divided into a series of records, and you can read them with any text file viewer. A text file is useful, for example, when a vendor needs to convey information to the user, such as in a `READ.ME` or `README.TXT` file. Text files are also called *sequential access files* because the data is accessed sequentially, or one byte after another.

On the other hand, a binary file can contain any character available in the operating system. These characters can include special characters that are not recognizable in the English language. They are merely symbols that represent some other value. Binary files are used for database files, executable files, and many others.

NOTE

The difference in the file types really only determines how the format of a file is interpreted. They all perform the same basic function. However, the different types are designed for the different purposes stated earlier so that maximum performance for a specific purpose can be achieved.

Opening a File

Regardless of which type of file you use, you must open the file before it is written to or read from. The syntax to open a file is

```
Open file [For mode] [Access access] [lock] As [#]filenumber [Len=reclen]
```

where:

`file` is the name of the file to open.

`mode` is the mode in which to open the file. Possible modes are `Append`, `Binary`, `Input`, `Output`, and `Random`.

`access` is the type of access permitted on the file. Possible access modes are `Read`, `Write`, and `Read Write`.

`lock` is the type of access granted to other processes. Possible locks are `Shared`, `Lock Read`, `Lock Write`, and `Lock Read Write`.

`filenumber` is the integer expression of the file number used by Visual Basic. This number is between 1 and 511, inclusive.

reclen is the length of the record in random access files. It is also the number of characters buffered for a sequential access file. Note that this number must be less than or equal to 32,767.

To determine the next available *filenumber*, also called a file handle, use the `FreeFile()` function. This function returns an integer representing the next available file handle.

The `FreeFile()` function can accept one optional argument, either `0` or `1`. If it is `1`, the `FreeFile()` function will return the next available file number in the range of 256 to 511, inclusive. If the argument is `0` or omitted, it will return a number between 1 and 255, inclusive. Note that in Visual Basic version 3.0 and earlier, you could not specify the optional argument.

A *sequential file* (usually a text file) is simply a list of characters stored in a file. It can be opened for `Input`, `Output`, or `Append`. If the file is open for `Input`, this means that you will be reading data from it. If it is opened for `Output`, you will be writing to the file, and an old file will be overwritten. If it is opened for `Append`, you will be writing to the file, but the data will be appended to the end of the file.

A *random access file* is stored in records. These records are made up of a certain number of bytes stored as fields. Each and every record in the file must be exactly the same length. This type of file can be used to store database information.

A *binary file* is a file in which any of the bytes in the file can be read or written to in any location. This type of file is probably the most widely used. Executable files are of this type, as well as device drivers and many other types. The thing to remember about a binary file is that you must know what location in the file to retrieve or store your data. You cannot decipher just by looking at the file where you need to place data or from where you need to retrieve data.

Visual Basic has many standard functions and statements available for use with files. These functions and statements are listed in Table 7.1.

Table 7.1. Standard Visual Basic file functions and statements.

Function/Statement	*Use*	*Pertains To*
`ChDir`	Changes the current directory	Sequential, Random, Binary
`ChDrive`	Changes the current drive	Sequential, Random, Binary
`Close`	Closes all file handles	Sequential, Random, Binary
`Close #`	Closes one file handle	Sequential, Random, Binary
`CurDir/CurDir$`	Returns current path	Sequential, Random, Binary
`Dir`	Returns a variant of the directory matching certain file specifications	Sequential, Random, Binary

continues

Table 7.1. continued

Function/Statement	*Use*	*Pertains To*
`Dir$`	Returns the directory matching certain file specifications	Sequential, Random, Binary
`EOF`	End of file marker	Sequential, Random, Binary
`FileAttr`	Returns the file mode of an open file	Sequential, Random, Binary
`FileCopy`	Copies a file	Sequential, Random, Binary
`FileDateTime`	Retrieves the date and time of a file	Sequential, Random, Binary
`FileLen`	Returns the size of a file in bytes (Long)	Sequential, Random, Binary
`FreeFile`	Returns the next available file handle number	Sequential, Random, Binary
`Get`	Reads data from a file	Random, Binary
`GetAttr`	Returns Integer of file/directory attributes	Sequential, Random, Binary
`Input`	Reads data from a file and returns `Variant`	Sequential, Binary
`Input #`	Reads data from a particular file number	Sequential
`Input$`	Reads data from a file and returns `String`	Sequential, Binary
`Kill`	Deletes a file	Sequential, Random, Binary
`Line Input #`	Reads a line from a particular file number	Sequential
`Loc`	Returns current file position	Random, Binary
`Lock`	Locks a file in a multiuser environment	Sequential, Random, Binary
`LOF`	Returns the size of an open file (bytes)	Sequential, Random, Binary
`MkDir`	Creates a new directory	Sequential, Random, Binary
`Name`	Renames a file or directory	Sequential, Random, Binary
`Open`	Opens a file	Sequential, Random, Binary
`Print #`	Writes data to a file	Sequential
`Put`	Writes data to a file	Random, Binary

Function/Statement	*Use*	*Pertains To*
`Reset`	Closes all open files, writing buffer contents to disk first	Sequential, Random, Binary
`RmDir`	Removes a directory	Sequential, Random, Binary
`Seek`	Returns the current file position	Sequential, Random, Binary
`SetAttr`	Sets attributes of a file or directory	Sequential, Random, Binary
`Type...End Type`	Defines record types	Random
`Unlock`	Unlocks a file in a multiuser environment	Sequential, Random, Binary
`Write #`	Writes data to a particular file number	Sequential

Closing a File

It's a good idea to close the file as soon as you are finished using it to free up valuable resources. Don't wait until the user leaves the application or closes Windows. You can close a file by using the following line, where *`filenumber`* is the number of the open file:

```
Close #filenumber
```

For example, this line closes file number 1:

```
Close #1
```

Working with Text Files

As stated earlier, text files are files that contain only ASCII characters and are often called sequential access files. These files can be opened or created by using the `Open` statement. A sequential access file can be opened for `Input`, `Output`, or `Append`. If the file does not exist, the `Open` statement creates the file. A file opened for `Input` reads text from a file. A file opened for `Output` writes text to a file from the beginning of the file, which effectively erases the file first. A file opened for `Append` appends characters to the end of a file.

Writing Text Files

You write text files by using the Visual Basic sequential file I/O functions. Sequential file I/O means that as each character is written, it is placed at the end of the file. You write a sequential file by using the `Print #` and `Write #` statements.

The Print # Statement

Using Print #, you can write one or more characters at a time. For example, assuming that the file has been opened, you can write one character to file handle number 1 with this line:

```
Print #1, "C"
```

You can also write the contents of a Visual Basic text box by using this line:

```
Print #1, Text1.Text
```

Using the Print # statement, a carriage return and line feed will be placed at the end of the line (Chr$(13) & Chr$(10)). For example, suppose you want to write a text file that contains variable information in a loop. The following is a simple example, but it clearly shows how to write text files:

```
'declare Variables
Dim nFileHandle As Integer       'file handle
Dim nShell As Integer            'shell return variable
Const FILENAME = "C:\TEST.TXT"   'file name
Dim nLoopCount As Integer        'looping variable

'assign file handle
nFileHandle = FreeFile

'open the file
Open FILENAME For Output As #nFileHandle

'process and write out text files
For nLoopCount = 1 To 10
    Print #nFileHandle, "This is Line Number " & Trim$(Str$(nLoopCount))
Next nLoopCount

'close the file
Close #nFileHandle

'view the file with NOTEPAD
nShell = Shell("Notepad " & FILENAME, vbMaximizedFocus)
```

Here's what's happening in the code. First, a file handle is obtained using the FreeFile function. Then, with this handle the Open statement is called to open the text file for output. The following is simply a loop that constructs a string. This string is written out on its own line. Finally, the file handle is closed and the text file is displayed in Notepad as follows:

```
This is Line Number 1
This is Line Number 2
This is Line Number 3
This is Line Number 4
This is Line Number 5
This is Line Number 6
This is Line Number 7
This is Line Number 8
This is Line Number 9
This is Line Number 10
```

To make this more of a practical example, suppose you wanted to write out any errors that occurred in an application. You could create an error log by placing a routine to write out the procedure and error code and string. For example, consider this procedure:

```
Private Sub Command1_Click()

Dim sCmd As String
Dim dbMain As Database
Dim rsTemp As Recordset
Const PROCNAME = "Command1_Click"

On Error GoTo DBError
sCmd = "SELECT Count(*) "
sCmd = sCmd & "FROM Authors "
Set rsTemp = dbMain.OpenRecordset(sCmd)
If Not rsTemp.EOF Then
    If rsTemp.Fields(0) = 0 Then
        MsgBox "There are no authors in the table!"
    End If
End If

DBError:
    Print #gnFileHandle, "Error in " & PROCNAME & ": " & Trim$(Str$(Err)) &
    ➥" " & Error$
    MsgBox Error$
    Exit Sub
    Resume
End Sub
```

This procedure has an error handler that writes out information about the specific error generated to a text file. This is very effective in troubleshooting your application for problems. This example generates an error because the `dbMain` database object is never set. However, if you wanted to use this type of approach in all of your procedures, you would have to copy and reuse this code in all of your procedures, which is not very effective. Therefore, you could actually write a public routine that accesses the `Err` object. You would write something like this:

```
Public Sub HandleError(ByVal PROCNAME As String)
    Print #gnFileHandle, "Error in " & PROCNAME & ": " &
    ➥Trim$(Str$(Err.Number)) & " " & Err.Description
    MsgBox Error$
End Sub
```

Either way, the desired result produces a text file with the errors, such as this:

```
Error in Command1_Click: 91 Object variable or With block variable not set
```

The `Write #` Statement

Using `Write #`, you can write one or more characters at a time as well as one or more fields at a time. For example, if you wanted to write a comma-delimited file for export, the `Write #` statement would be perfectly suited for the task. You simply pass your data arguments, and it automatically formats the output for each field. Suppose, for example, you wanted to generate a text file with two fields. You could use the following format:

```
'process and write out text files
For nLoopCount = 1 To 10
    Write #nFileHandle, "Line Number", nLoopCount
Next nLoopCount
```

You could just as easily do this to export data:

```
sCmd = "SELECT * "
sCmd = sCmd & "FROM Authors "
Set rsTemp = dbMain.OpenRecordset(sCmd)
If Not rsTemp.EOF Then
    rsTemp.MoveFirst
    'write out column names
    Write #nFileHandle, rsTemp.Fields(0).Name, rsTemp.Fields(1).Name,
    ➥rsTemp.Fields(2).Name

    'loop through all records and output data
    Do While Not rsTemp.EOF
       'process and write out text files
       Write #nFileHandle, rsTemp.Fields(0), rsTemp.Fields(1), rsTemp.Fields(2)
       rsTemp.MoveNext
    Loop

End If
```

The `Write #` statement automatically formats the data, as follows:

Field Type	*Formatting*
Text field	Quotes
Numeric field	No formatting
Date field	Universal Date format (inside pound (#) signs)
Null fields	Displays `#NULL#`
Errors	Displays `#ERROR` *`errorcode#`*, where *`errorcode`* is the actual error code at runtime
Boolean field	Displays `#TRUE#` or `#FALSE#`

If you place multiple fields in code, they must be separated by commas. The following formatted output uses the previous code fragment to produce an output. This is just a small fragment of the total output produced.

```
"Au_ID","Author","Year Born"
"1","Jacobs, Russell",#NULL#
"2","Metzger, Philip W.",#NULL#
"3","Boddie, John",#NULL#
"4","Sydow, Dan Parks",#NULL#
"6","Lloyd, John",#NULL#
"8","Thiel, James R.",#NULL#
"10","Ingham, Kenneth",#NULL#
```

```
"12","Wellin, Paul",#NULL#
"13","Kamin, Sam",#NULL#
"14","Gaylord, Richard",#NULL#
"15","Curry, Dave",#NULL#
"17","Gardner, Juanita Mercado",#NULL#
"19","Knuth, Donald E.",#NULL#
"21","Hakim, Jack",#NULL#
"22","Winchell, Jeff",#NULL#
"24","Clark, Claudia",#NULL#
"25","Scott, Jack",#NULL#
"27","Coolbaugh, James",#NULL#
"29","Ladd, Scott Robert",#NULL#
"31","Gabriel, Richard P.",#NULL#
"33","Mitchell, John C.",#NULL#
"35","Smolka, G.",#NULL#
"37","Bowler, Norm",#NULL#
"39","Sundaram, Rangarajan K.",#NULL#
"41","Torkelson, Cary",#NULL#
```

Reading Text Files

Reading text files is also quite simple. You can do it by using the `Input`, `Input #`, or `Line Input #` statements. The `Input` and `Input #` statements are used to read into a variable a certain number of characters for files that have been opened for `Input` or `Binary`. The `Input` statement is a function that returns a specific number of characters into one string variable. For example, the following will read 10 characters into the variable `sTemp` from the file with a file handle `#nFileNum`:

```
sTemp = Input(10, #nFileNum)
```

The `Input #` statement will read one complete line of text from a file and place the values into one or multiple variables. The use of this statement is widely used and shown in the next section, "Searching Through Text Files."

You use the `Line Input #` statement to get one complete line of text. This is used as the counterpart to the `Print #` statement, where a carriage return and line feed are automatically appended.

The `Line Input #` statement can be used like this:

```
Do While Not EOF(nFileHandle)
    Line Input #nFileHandle, TheLine$
    MsgBox TheLine$
Loop
```

This code loops through the entire file and displays each line of text in a message box.

Searching Through Text Files

Searching through a text file to determine how many occurrences of a particular string there are can be very useful. You can use this technique to search through a file for search and replace operations, such as replacing all references of one directory to another directory. To search through a text file for occurrences of a certain string, you must perform the following steps:

1. Open the file.
2. Find the next occurrence of the specified string.
3. Increment the counter to represent the number of occurrences.
4. Continue searching until the end of file is reached.
5. Close the file.

To open the file, use the `Open` statement. To find the number of occurrences of a given string, loop through the open file and count the number of times the `InStr()` Visual Basic function returns a value greater than zero. This indicates that the specified string exists inside the file. The `InStr()` function allows for the possibility to search for case sensitivity. If the argument of 0 is used, the `InStr()` function performs a case-sensitive search. If 1 is used, or if it is omitted, the search is not case-sensitive.

You can use the following code to search for a specific string within a text file. This code returns a message box that contains the number of occurrences of the specified string:

```
Dim nCaseSensitive As Integer
Dim sSearchString As String
Dim nTempPos As Integer
Dim nStringCount As Integer

'set variables
nCaseSensitive = True
sSearchString = "CURRY"

'open the file
Open FILENAME For Input As #nFileHandle

'loop through entire file
Do While Not EOF(nFileHandle)

    'Get a line
    Input #nFileHandle, sLine

    'search for string in the line
    If nCaseSensitive = False Then
        'NOT case sensitive

        'Test to see if the search string exists in this line
        If InStr(1, sLine, Trim$(sSearchString), 1) <> 0 Then

            'initialize nTempPos
            nTempPos = 1

            'the string exists, test for other occurrences in same line
            Do While nTempPos <= Len(sLine)

                If InStr(1, Mid$(sLine, nTempPos, Len(sSearchString)),
                ➥ sSearchString, 1) > 0 Then
```

```
                    nStringCount = nStringCount + 1
                End If
                nTempPos = nTempPos + 1
            Loop
        End If
    Else
        'IS case sensitive

        'Test to see if the search string exists in this line
        If InStr(1, sLine, Trim$(sSearchString), 0) <> 0 Then

            'initialize nTempPos
            nTempPos = 1

            'the string exists, test for other occurrences in same line
            Do While nTempPos <= Len(sLine)
                If InStr(1, Mid$(sLine, nTempPos, Len(sSearchString)),
                ➥ sSearchString, 1) > 0 Then
                    nStringCount = nStringCount + 1
                End If
                nTempPos = nTempPos + 1
            Loop
        End If
    End If

Loop


'display number of occurrences
MsgBox Trim$(Str$(nStringCount))

'close the file
Close #nFileHandle
```

The technique used in this code is really very simple to follow. The code cycles through every line in the text file, one line at a time. As each line is read, the `InStr()` function is used to determine where the next occurrence is. If there is an occurrence, it is counted, and it searches for the next occurrence of the string in the same line. The looping continues until the end of `sLine`. This entire looping process continues until the end of the file is reached.

Your application can incorporate this technique, and even possibly add to it. You can allow a user to define both the search and replace strings to affect a search and replace function. You can use this technique to make a powerful text editor.

Working with Binary Files

Binary files are files that can contain special characters representing some other purpose besides reading text. A binary file is really just a file that contains a series of symbols that do not necessarily mean anything to anyone except the programmer. It is up to the programmer to determine what the scheme is behind how the data is stored.

Binary files can be opened for *random* or *binary* access. A random access file is a file for which any record inside the file can be updated randomly because each record has a certain predefined length. When opening the file, you must use the `Len` argument to tell Visual Basic how long each record is, in bytes. A file opened for `Binary` is similar to a file opened for `Random`, except that each record is not necessarily the same size. This means that, once again, it is up to the programmer to decide how to incorporate some scheme for accessing the file. It could be as simple as using an extra two-byte integer before each record to identify how many bytes are in the following record.

Binary files are probably the most common type of file. Here are just a few examples of binary files:

- Executables
- Drivers
- Fonts
- Help files
- Wave files
- Documents
- DLLs

It is important to note that just because you might not be able to recognize the characters in a file, it doesn't mean that the file has to be a binary file. The term *binary* refers to a mode. However, the general rule is that text files have recognizable characters and binary files do not. For example, this is a fragment of what the binary file, `VB5.EXE`, looks like, as viewed in Notepad:

```
MZ_        ÿÿ  ¸        @                                     _     º ´Í!¸LÍ!
This program cannot be run in DOS mode.$        PE  L 'Ô¬2              à
^       ©       p   @                              _      C_
        ê _     ì ô     ° ôw                        0 ¸' @ë
                                                             .text   _
               '.data   Lz   0  :                 @  À.rsrc   ôw  °  x  T
            @  @.reloc  ¸'  0  "  Ì              @  B_  _  _  _ _ _
_ _ _ _-_ _ _ _ _ _ _ _$ _ _' _ _  _ _  _a
_' __ _C _@ _B _A _? _  _% _& _  _'  _, _ù _y _{ _z _M _e _f
_d _c _ë _x _u _á _õ _ô _Û _ü _/ _. _ú __ _ı _^ _ _ _ _
_ó __ _Õ _È _ _ _H _ _! _ _ _¦ _ _ _ _ _+ _- _ _ _F
_É _ _ _Ä _3 _D _ _Å _! _© _ª _¨ _¤ _" _g _h _0 _" _ï _j
_% _R _û _^ _\ _ü _£ _ _¬ _ _® _* _v _E _ _q _K _s _ _
_ _Ë _ _ _Ü _¿ _ñ _À _ _" _› _õ _ö _ _ _ô _ _: _ó _
_° _ _ _8 _Ñ _> _L _ _Û _p _- __ _ _( _' _ï _í _ _P _"
_) _Œ _& _+ _ _ù _ _   ú "ú 8ú Lú \ú pú ,ú ú ¤ú °ú
ºú Æú àú úú û ,û Hû Xû jû ~û Œû ¯û ¦û ´û Îû äû üû ü *ü <ü
 Pü ü tü „ü _ü ´ü Îü Úü æü òü _ü y y "y 2y <y Ly ^y ty ~y
'y  y °y _y Ìy èy öy _ "_ 6_ H_ R_ `_ j_ z_ †_ __ 2_ Â_ Ò_
 __ ô_ __ ÿ ÿ &ÿ 6ÿ Hÿ Xÿ hÿ vÿ „ÿ "ÿ ¨ÿ ¶ÿ Ìÿ äÿ öÿ
  "  0  B  R  b  r  z  _    ®  À  _  _  ò    4 J `
x ^ _ ¤ ¶ Ì â ô   . L b n ~ _ ¤ ¶ Î
â ô    , < N f v _ ¢ ¬ Â Ò ä
```

```
- , : J V h v ˆ - ¦ 2 Â _ Ü ê _  $ 0 D
V p , '  ® À _ â î ö  * > R f ¦ Œ
¤ ´ Æ Ö è ô _   "  0  B  R ` r  „  _  ¤  2  Â  Ò
 _  ê  ø          & 8 B V n „ _ œ ¬ º Ì à î ü
  0
```

Obviously, this is not understandable. However, the format of the file is predetermined by the developer. This file is understandable to the operating system. You can generate your own specifications for binary files. For example, you can create a binary file called `USER.PWD` that is a binary file with an algorithm for the password, which only you know. This is not terribly secure, but to the average corporate user, it's secure enough.

Writing Binary Files

To write a binary file, you use the `Put #` statement. The `Put #` statement writes one or more characters to a binary file, but it does not append a carriage return and line feed. One advantage of a binary file is that you can read from it or write to it, using different statements, without needing to open the file again. A text file can be opened for input or output, but not both at the same time. Once the file has been opened, every successive `Put #` statement will write characters to the end of the file. The following is the syntax for the `Put #` statement:

```
Put [#]filenumber, [recnumber], varname
```

where:

> *`filenumber`* is the file number assigned when using the `Open` statement.
>
> *`recnumber`* is the record number for a file opened as `Random` or the byte number if it is opened as `Binary`.
>
> *`varname`* is the variable that contains the data to be written.

The *`recnumber`* can be omitted if the file is opened as anything other than `Random` or `Binary`.

For example, consider this code fragment:

```
'assign file handle
    nFileHandle = FreeFile

    'open binary file
    Open "C:\TEST.BIN" For Binary As #nFileHandle

    'write out test string loop
    For nLoopCount = 1 To 10
        Put #nFileHandle, , "Loop Number " & Trim$(Str$(nLoopCount))
    Next nLoopCount

    'close the file
    Close nFileHandle
```

This code looks similar to the other earlier examples, except that the file is opened in a binary mode. Also, the `Put #` statement is used instead of the `Write #` or `Print #` statements, as in the case of a text file. Notice that there are two commas after the file handle number, because the second argument is omitted. This means that the next byte is written directly after the last one. If you wanted to write to a specific position (byte) in the file, you would specify that byte in this position. If the file was opened in Random mode, this number would be the record number to access.

The previous code produces an output which looks like this:

```
Loop Number 1Loop Number 2Loop Number 3Loop Number 4Loop Number 5Loop Number
6Loop Number 7Loop Number 8Loop Number 9Loop Number 10
```

Notice that the text was simply placed one string after the other. Also notice that the text is readable, but it was opened as a binary file because a binary file uses the same Windows character set as a text file. However, as I mentioned earlier, a binary file *usually* contains characters that do not have much readability.

Suppose you wanted to encode this file. You could use a primitive encryption routine to simply take the ASCII value of a character and add a specific number of ASCII characters to it, and return that value instead. Then when you read it, convert it back.

If you write a function to convert the string as described previously, simply change the line that uses the `Put #` statement to something like this:

```
Put #nFileHandle, , ConvertString("Loop Number " & Trim$(Str$(nLoopCount)))
```

Next, write the `ConvertString` function like this:

```
Private Function ConvertString(ByVal sString As String) As String

    Dim nLoopCount As Integer
    Dim sFinal As String

    For nLoopCount = 1 To Len(sString)
        sFinal = sFinal + Chr$(Asc(Mid$(sString, nLoopCount, 1)) + 57)
    Next nLoopCount

    ConvertString = sFinal
End Function
```

This function loops through each character in the string, finds the ASCII value of it, adds 57 to it, and converts it back to a character. Then it concatenates it to the total string that will be returned to the calling procedure. The number 57 is purely arbitrary. It is only used to reach the area of the character set that contains special characters. It could have just as easily been 60, 65, or 70. It does become important, however, when you decode the string. This file now looks like a "typical" binary file. To an untrained eye, the earlier `VB5.EXE` fragment looks like the file contents generated by this new function, as follows:

```
…¨¨©Y‡®¦›_«Yj…¨¨©Y‡®¦›_«Yk…¨¨©Y‡®¦›_«Yl…¨¨©Y‡®¦›_«Ym…¨¨©Y‡®¦›_«Yn…¨¨©Y‡®¦›_«Yo
…¨¨©Y‡®¦›_«Yp…¨¨©Y‡®¦›_«Yq…¨¨©Y‡®¦›_«Yr…¨¨©Y‡®¦›_«Yji
```

Reading Binary Files

You read binary files by using the `Get #` statement. It is essentially the opposite of writing a binary file; however, there are a few differences. The main difference is that you must dimension the string variable into which the `Get #` statement will read data. If you do not, the system will be stuck in an endless loop. Dimensioning a string is assigning a fixed length to a string variable so that it contains a specific number of characters.

The following is the syntax for the `Get #` statement:

```
Get [#]filenumber, [recnumber], varname
```

where:

> *`filenumber`* is the file number assigned when using the `Open` statement.
>
> *`recnumber`* is the record number for a file opened as `Random` or the byte number if it is opened as `Binary`.
>
> *`varname`* is the variable that contains the data to be written.

The *`recnumber`* can be omitted if the file is opened as anything other than `Random` or `Binary`.

The procedure that needs to be written looks like this:

```
'assign file handle
nFileHandle = FreeFile

'open binary file
Open "C:\TEST.BIN" For Binary As #nFileHandle

'declare variables
Dim sRes As String * 1  'stores one character read from file
Dim sFinal As String    'stores final string

'read binary data
sFinal = ""
Do While Not EOF(nFileHandle)
    Get #nFileHandle, , sRes 'ConvertString("Loop Number " &
    ➥Trim$(Str$(nLoopCount)))
    sFinal = sFinal & sRes
Loop

'close the file
Close nFileHandle

'remove last character, which is the EOF marker
sFinal = Left$(sFinal, Len(sFinal) - 1)

'decode the string
sFinal = DecodeString(sFinal)
```

There are two commas after the file handle number in this code because the second argument is omitted, which means that the next byte is read directly after the last one. If you wanted to read starting with a specific position (byte) in the file, you would specify that byte in this position here. If the file was opened in Random mode, this number would be the record number to read.

Notice that before the string is decoded, the right-most character is removed because when the binary file is written to, an End Of File (EOF) marker is placed there. You need to ignore it. It is used by the file control statements only to determine when to stop reading. Otherwise, an `Input past the end of file` error would occur.

The `DecodeString()` function was written to basically reverse what you did in the `ConvertString()` function earlier. The `DecodeString()` function looks like this:

```
Private Function DecodeString(ByVal sString As String) As String

    Dim nLoopCount As Integer
    Dim sFinal As String

    For nLoopCount = 1 To Len(sString)
        sFinal = sFinal + Chr$(Asc(Mid$(sString, nLoopCount, 1)) - 57)
    Next nLoopCount

    DecodeString = sFinal

End Function
```

Notice that it becomes imperative that the arbitrary number chosen earlier (that is, 57) is used here. Using the same number in the decode procedure produces this result:

```
Loop Number 1Loop Number 2Loop Number 3Loop Number 4Loop Number 5Loop Number
6Loop Number 7Loop Number 8Loop Number 9Loop Number 10
```

Using the number 56 produces this result:

```
Mppq!Ovncfs!2Mppq!Ovncfs!3Mppq!Ovncfs!4Mppq!Ovncfs!5Mppq!Ovncfs!6Mppq!Ovncfs!
7Mppq!Ovncfs!8Mppq!Ovncfs!9Mppq!Ovncfs!:Mppq!Ovncfs!21
```

Error Handling with Files

Having some type of error handling in your applications that contain file I/O is important. If no error handling is performed and an error occurs, your application can exit abruptly. This has serious consequences for files because there is data that has not been written, the user loses his changes, and there are one or more file handles that are not closed.

It is important to account for all possible file-handling errors. Table 7.2 lists the possible errors that relate to files.

Table 7.2. Visual Basic file-related errors.

Error Number	*Explanation*
52	Bad filename or number
53	File not found
54	Bad file mode
55	File already open
57	Device I/O error
58	File already exists
59	Bad record length
61	Disk full
62	Input past end of file
63	Bad record number
67	Too many files
68	Device unavailable
70	Permission denied
71	Disk not ready
74	Can't rename with different drive
75	Path/File access error
76	Path not found

CROSS REFERENCE

For more information on testing and debugging, refer to Chapter 5, "Testing and Debugging."

The exception to the rule of error handling is if you are using API functions for INI files. There is no error handling when you are dealing with Windows API functions because the most likely errors to occur are general protection faults. There is no way to "handle" these, only avoid them.

CROSS REFERENCE

For more information on how to avoid errors with Windows API functions, refer to Chapter 13, "Using the WIN32 API."

It is also important to handle errors generated by the Common Dialog control. Error handling can be initiated the same way as discussed in Chapter 2, "Stock Wizards," except you want to change the `CancelError` property of the Common Dialog control to `True`. This will force an error to occur when the user selects Cancel in the Common dialog box. You can then test for this error.

Summary

Most Visual Basic programs work with files in one way or another. Probably the most common type of file to work with is text files. Often, the results of a database query need to be written to a text file so that other programs can read the file. Also, text files are well suited for printing. Therefore, it is important to know how to manipulate files so that the end users of your programs have the most functionality and flexibility.

8

Graphics

Graphics are an important part of Windows applications because they visually enhance the way users interact with the system. There are many techniques demonstrated throughout this chapter that show how to display and manipulate graphics, such as using the `Screen` object, graphic hotspots, and animated icons.

The `Screen` Object

Visual Basic provides a `Screen` object with many properties to easily access and manipulate what the user sees on-screen. The object is accessed just like any other Visual Basic object, such as a `Form` object or a `Control` object. Table 8.1 lists the Visual Basic `Screen` object properties.

Table 8.1. Visual Basic `Screen` object properties.

Property	*Function*
`ActiveControl`	Specifies the control with the focus.
`ActiveForm`	Specifies the form with the focus.
`FontCount`	Number of fonts available for the current display screen.
`Fonts`	Specifies the names of the fonts available for the current display screen. This property is in the form of an array, from `0` to `FontCount - 1`.
`Height`	The height of the screen, always measured in twips.
`MouseIcon`	The icon to be used as the mouse pointer, when the `MousePointer` property is set to 99.
`MousePointer`	The mouse pointer to be used when the mouse is positioned over the screen. If the mouse pointer is over a form that specifies a different mouse, the mouse pointer of that form is used.
`TwipsPerPixelX`	Number of twips for every horizontal pixel. This is a very useful property because the `ScaleMode` doesn't have to be changed to do a calculation.
`TwipsPerPixelY`	Number of twips for every vertical pixel. This is a very useful property because the `ScaleMode` doesn't have to be changed to do a calculation.
`Width`	Width of the screen, always measured in twips.

Centering a Form Automatically

Before Visual Basic version 5.0, you had to center a form in code. Now, there is a property, `StartUpPosition`, which does this automatically for you. You can set it to one of four values, as follows:

- `Manual`—No action occurs
- `CenterOwner`—Centers in the client area
- `CenterScreen`—Centers in the screen
- `WindowsDefault`—Moves to the upper-left part of the screen

Now that the automatic stuff is taken out of the way, you can center the form in code. If you don't handle the placement of the form in code and you have the `StartUpPosition` property set to `0`, the form appears at the coordinates where you left it at design time. The form can appear centered, but if you run your application on a computer with a higher-resolution screen, the forms appear in the upper-left corner of the screen.

For backward compatibility with other versions of Visual Basic, there is a very simple solution to centering the form automatically in a device-independent manner. This means that whatever the resolution, the form appears centered. It can be very useful to have a routine such as the one presented here, `CenterForm()`, that you can call from each form in the `Form_Load()` event. Consider the `CenterForm()` subroutine.

```
Sub CenterForm (F As Form)
    F.Left = (screen.Width - F.Width) / 2
    F.Top = (screen.Height - F.Height) / 2
End Sub
```

The technique is to use the `Screen` object to determine the `Height` and `Width` properties. The form's `Height` and `Width` properties are also used. The routine simply subtracts the form's properties from the screen's properties and divides them by two. If you want to incorporate this from a form's `Form_Load()` event, you call it like this:

```
Private Sub Form_Load()
    CenterForm Me
End Sub
```

You also can use the same technique to center controls, or even offset controls from a certain point on the screen.

The Coordinate System

Visual Basic provides different ways to access the *coordinate system*. The coordinate system allows you to access a specific point for drawing. It is designed to let you, the programmer, choose which unit of measurement is comfortable to you. The different units of measurement ultimately provide the same result, which is to draw graphics at a certain location on a form, picture box, or printer object. Table 8.2 shows the different types of units of measurement possible in the Visual Basic coordinate system.

Table 8.2. Visual Basic coordinate system.

Unit	*Conversion*	`ScaleMode` *Setting*
`Custom`	User-defined scale properties	0
`Twips`	Default unit in Visual Basic (1440 twips per logical inch)	1
`Point`	72 points per logical inch	2
`Pixel`	Base unit of measurement representing the smallest point on a monitor or printer	3
`Character`	120 twips horizontally and 240 twips vertically	4
`Inch`	Physical inch	5
`Millimeter`	Physical millimeter	6
`Centimeter`	Physical centimeter	7

As you can see from looking at Table 8.2, if you normally like working with the smallest possible unit for greater resolution control, you probably want to work with `Pixel`. If you want to work in a more manageable unit, but with less resolution, you probably want to work with `Inch`.

TRIED AND TRUE

Most Windows developers work with `Pixel`.

To change the unit of measurement with which the coordinate system works, use the `ScaleMode` property of the form, picture box, or printer object to set to the desired mode. For example, the following syntax changes the printer coordinate system to respond in inches:

```
Printer.ScaleMode = 5
```

If you want to customize the coordinate system, use the `ScaleHeight`, `ScaleWidth`, `ScaleLeft`, and `ScaleTop` properties of the form, picture box, or printer object. The `ScaleLeft` and `ScaleTop` properties define what the upper-left coordinate will be. The `ScaleHeight` and `ScaleWidth` properties define the relative height and width, respectively, of an object. For example, suppose that you want the upper-left coordinate of the printer to be 100,100 instead of 0,0. Then suppose that you want the height and width of the printable area to be 200 units each. You set up the properties as follows:

```
Printer.ScaleLeft = 100
Printer.ScaleTop = 100
Printer.ScaleHeight = 200
Printer.ScaleWidth = 200
```

NOTE

If you change the `Scale` properties, the `ScaleMode` property is set to `0`, signifying that you are using user-defined coordinates.

The upper-left coordinate of the page will be 100,100. The lower-right coordinate of the page will be 300,300. This is because the `ScaleHeight` and `ScaleWidth` properties specified the height and width, not the absolute coordinate.

Static Graphics

Static graphics are graphics that are not altered at runtime, other than positioning the graphic at a desired location on-screen. For example, a static graphic can be as simple as a line drawn across the screen that is redrawn as the screen is resized.

Graphic Hotspots

A *hotspot* is an area of the screen that, when clicked, produces some desired result. Generally, you don't see the border of the hotspot region. Hotspots are becoming more popular as the information age progresses. Hotspots are incorporated widely in systems that use a touch screen. Many museums use touch screens to convey information interactively. Hotspots can be used in a wide variety of applications, such as maps. The program may be able to present statistics of a certain state when a user touches the area of the screen that represents that state.

You can incorporate hotspots *dynamically*, if necessary. This means that you can allocate or deallocate a hotspot as the program is running. You do not have to predefine all hotspots in advance.

Because there is no hotspot control in Visual Basic, you can use the Image control. The reason you need to use a Visual Basic control instead of drawing a rectangle on-screen is that a hotspot needs to independently recognize a mouse click event. If you draw a rectangle on-screen, the mouse events occur on the form, not on the rectangle.

TRIED AND TRUE

The reason that the Image control is used instead of the Picture Box control is because of its capability to be transparent. The Image control enables the background to show through the image area when a picture is not displayed. The Picture Box control does not have a `Transparent` property, so all you see is a white rectangular box.

The way to allocate the hotspots dynamically (as with most controls in Visual Basic) is to use a control array. You use only one Image control and assign it an index of zero. As the user defines a new hotspot, a new Image control is loaded as part of the control array, increasing its index value by one. The following is a code fragment that shows how a control can be loaded dynamically.

For the next few examples, suppose you had a function called `FindNextHotspotIndex()`. This function's sole purpose is exactly as the name sounds: to find the next control array index for the image controls used as hotspots. The code for this can be found on the CD accompanying this book in the `\HOTSPOT` subdirectory. The function looks like this:

```
Private Function FindNextHotspotIndex() As Integer

    'declare variables
    Dim loopcount%  'loop counting variable
    'handle errors
    On Error GoTo ThisIsTheIndex

    'loop just to test index
    For loopcount% = 0 To HotspotIndex%
        'this is just a dummy condition to find out if the index exists
        If Hotspot(loopcount%).Visible = False Then
        End If
    Next loopcount%
    'if it got to this point, then all indexes are used-allocate one more
    HotspotIndex% = HotspotIndex% + 1
    FindNextHotspotIndex = HotspotIndex%
    Exit Function
ThisIsTheIndex:
    FindNextHotspotIndex = loopcount%
    'avoid errors
    Exit Function
End Function
```

The function simply accesses a property of the control, in this case the `Visible` property, only to test if the control array index exists. If it does not, an error occurs and this index is the one used. Then to call it, use code similar to this:

```
NextAvailHotspot% = FindNextHotspotIndex()
Load Hotspot(NextAvailHotspot%)
```

You probably want to incorporate a routine that automatically moves or resizes the hotspot to the desired location. To do this, you need to know the coordinates of where the hotspot is to be located. It's a good idea to track in a variable where the desired location is. The following is a code fragment taken from the HOTSPOT application on the CD accompanying this book. This application resizes and moves the dynamic hotspot, where `BeginX`, `BeginY`, `EndX`, and `EndY` indicate the desired hotspot region:

```
'Modify Vertically
If EndY > BeginY Then
    Hotspot(NextAvailHotspot%).Height = EndY - BeginY + 10
    Hotspot(NextAvailHotspot%).Top = BeginY
Else
    Hotspot(NextAvailHotspot%).Height = BeginY - EndY + 10
    Hotspot(NextAvailHotspot%).Top = EndY
End If
'Modify Horizontally
If EndX > BeginX Then
    Hotspot(NextAvailHotspot%).Width = EndX - BeginX + 10
    Hotspot(NextAvailHotspot%).Left = BeginX
Else
    Hotspot(NextAvailHotspot%).Width = BeginX - EndX + 10
    Hotspot(NextAvailHotspot%).Left = EndX
End If
```

NOTE

The constant `10` is used to verify that the hotspot completely encompasses the desired area. If this isn't done, the hotspot is on the lines of the rectangle drawn. It is simply a matter of personal preference.

The variables used to track coordinates of the desired location are `BeginX`, `BeginY`, `EndX`, and `EndY`. These variables are assigned after the user draws the area on-screen with the mouse. You don't need to know where the current hotspot is located; you need to know only the index of the hotspot to move. In this case, the hotspot has an index assigned to the variable `NextAvailHotspot%`.

Manipulating Picture Boxes at Runtime

An important part of graphics in Visual Basic is the capability to move picture boxes at runtime. This gives the user a more visually appealing application. For example, suppose that you want to display photographs stored in bitmaps on-screen. If you want to display only one photograph, you probably want to center it on-screen. If you display more than one, you want to manipulate the picture boxes that contain the photographs into some logical pattern so that they are symmetrical within the screen. You can also use the technique of manipulating a picture box at runtime to load and display icons from the disk.

Suppose you want to display up to 54 icons in a single screen by using a single picture box control array. All elements of the control array (other than the one created at design time) are allocated dynamically, which means that as the program needs them, they are loaded and positioned. There is no sense in creating 54 picture boxes and wasting valuable system resources if the user intends to display less than 54 icons! The alternative is to have your application load the picture boxes as it needs them, one per screen.

To manipulate the picture boxes at runtime, you first need to load the next index in the control array. Because element zero is the index created at design time, the next available index is one, and so on. You load a new picture box by using the `Load` command. This loads a new picture box with the next available index number, but it takes on the characteristics as the picture box created at design time.

After the new control is loaded, you can move it anywhere you want on-screen. You'll probably want to automatically determine the location. Suppose you wanted to assign a maximum of six rows of picture boxes, each having nine picture boxes in the row. As a new picture box is created, it is moved to the next position in the row. The next position is determined by the last position, plus a predefined border area. If the last position in a row is filled, the application moves the new picture box to the first position in the next row. The next row is determined by the position of the previous row, plus a predefined border area. These border areas are stored in constants.

NOTE

It's a good idea to use constants so that if you later determine that you need to change the border area, all you have to do is change the value assigned to the constant and not rework your calculations.

There is an application on the CD accompanying this book in the `\ICON` subdirectory that contains the code for loading icons dynamically, up to 54 per screen. The application's main screen is shown in Figure 8.1.

The application defines these constants:

```
Const WIDTHFACTOR = 345      'horizontal space between picture boxes
Const HEIGHTFACTOR = 345     'vertical space between picture boxes
Const BORDERFACTOR = 225     'width of border holding picture boxes
```

The constants are a critical part of making sure the icons line up correctly on the form. Following is a code fragment from the ICON application. It moves the picture boxes so that they line up as six rows and 10 columns of picture boxes:

```
'0 is already loaded at design time
If IconIndex% <> 0 Then
    Load pictIcon(IconIndex%)
    Load pnlLabel(IconIndex%)
End If
pictIcon(IconIndex%).Visible = True
pnlLabel(IconIndex%).Visible = True
'see if this picture box will fit on this line
If IconIndex% <> 0 Then
    If pictIcon(IconIndex%).Width + pictIcon(IconIndex% - 1).Left +
```

```
    ➥pictIcon(IconIndex% - 1).Width +
    ➥WIDTHFACTOR < pnlIconFrame.Width - BORDERFACTOR Then
        'It WILL fit on the line
        'position picture box
        pictIcon(IconIndex%).Left = pictIcon(IconIndex% - 1).Left +
        ➥pictIcon(IconIndex% - 1).Width + WIDTHFACTOR
        pictIcon(IconIndex%).Top = pictIcon(IconIndex% - 1).Top
        'position label box
        pnlLabel(IconIndex%).Left = pictIcon(IconIndex%).Left -
        ➥ ((pnlLabel(IconIndex%).Width - pictIcon(IconIndex%).Width) / 2)
        pnlLabel(IconIndex%).Top = pictIcon(IconIndex%).Top - 225
    Else
        'It Won't fit on the line - use next line
        pictIcon(IconIndex%).Left = pictIcon(0).Left
        pictIcon(IconIndex%).Top = pictIcon(IconIndex% - 1).Top +
        ➥pictIcon(IconIndex% - 1).Height + HEIGHTFACTOR
        'position label box
        pnlLabel(IconIndex%).Left = pictIcon(IconIndex%).Left -
        ➥((pnlLabel(IconIndex%).Width - pictIcon(IconIndex%).Width) / 2)
        pnlLabel(IconIndex%).Top = pictIcon(IconIndex%).Top - 225
    End If
End If
```

The preceding code tests to see whether the previous picture box plus the `WIDTHFACTOR` allow the new picture box to be displayed on the same line without touching the edge. If so, it positions the new picture box in that location. If not, it moves the new picture box to the next line.

It is important not to load index zero. It cannot be loaded or unloaded at runtime because it is the original element in a control array created at design time. That's why the preceding code tests to see whether the index value in question is zero.

FIGURE 8.1.
An icon printing application that can be found on this book's CD.

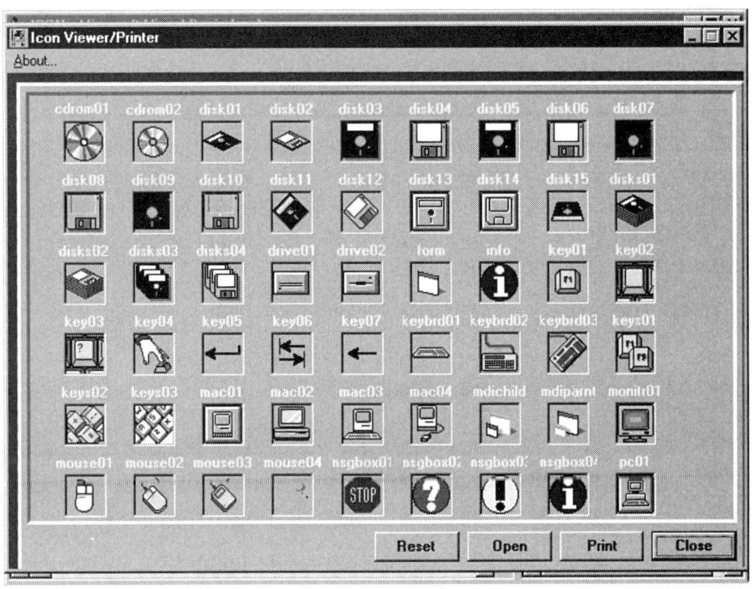

You can use similar tactics in your applications to automatically position picture boxes to suit your needs. The only picture box properties you need to deal with are `Left`, `Top`, `Width`, and `Height`. From these properties, you can test and manipulate the picture boxes in any fashion that suits your application. If your pictures are different sizes, simply adjust the values of the constants declared earlier.

Animated Graphics

Animated graphics are graphics that are altered in some way on a continuous basis at runtime. For example, an animated graphic can be a bitmap floating across the screen, as in the case of a screen saver.

Animated Bounding Box

When you are allocating dynamic hotspots, it is a good idea to visually represent on-screen the desired area of the new hotspot. One method you can use is an *animated bounding box* that visually tells the user that an area of the screen is selected for some purpose. Many desktop publishing programs use this technique.

The animated bounding box, or *rubber band*, is a box that looks like it is moving in a rectangular pattern. The animated bounding box is used by many applications that require the selection of objects. It is used in some programs to represent that a window is selected, or a certain portion of the screen is selected. In Visual Basic, the animated bounding box (from now on referred to as the "rubber band") is used for such a purpose.

There is no simple way to create the rubber band; it is actually an illusion. You create it by using a Timer control and by actually changing the type of *pen* used to draw the rectangle. A pen is how Visual Basic refers to a style of drawing. Pen styles can be solid, inverted, dashed, and so on. You create the illusion by drawing a rectangle using a certain pen, using the Timer control to switch the type of pen used at a precise interval, and redrawing the rectangle using a different pen. This is very similar to the way electronic Christmas lights appear to be moving from one end of the strand to the other. In reality, all that is happening is that every other light is toggling on and off simultaneously. Table 8.3 lists all of the different types of pens available in Visual Basic. They are also called `DrawMode` settings.

Table 8.3. Visual Basic `DrawMode` settings.

Constant	*Mnemonic*	*Description*
1	`BLACKNESS`	Black pen
2	`NOT_MERGE_PEN`	Inverse of setting 15 (`MERGE_PEN`)
3	`MASK_NOT_PEN`	Combination of common colors in background and inverse of the pen

Constant	Mnemonic	Description
4	NOT_COPY_PEN	Inverse of setting 13 (COPY_PEN)
5	MASK_PEN_NOT	Combination of common colors in inverse of display and pen
6	INVERT	Inverse of display color
7	XOR_PEN	Combination of colors in pen and display (but not both)
8	NOT_MASK_PEN	Inverse of setting 9 (MASK_PEN)
9	MASK_PEN	Combination of colors common to both the pen and display
10	NOT_XOR_PEN	Inverse of setting 7 (XOR_PEN)
11	NOP	Turns off drawing
12	MERGE_NOT_PEN	Combination of display color and inverse of pen color
13	COPY_PEN	Default ForeColor
14	MERGE_PEN_NOT	Combination of the pen and inverse of the display
15	MERGE_PEN	Combination of the pen and display colors
16	WHITENESS	White pen

The first step you take in your application is to draw the rectangle using the INVERT pen. Make sure that you declare the INVERSE constant in a module with the value of 6, as listed in Table 8.3. Before you draw the rectangle in the desired location, however, remember the DrawMode setting before you draw the rectangle so you can reset it when you're finished. This is exactly what the application on the CD accompanying this book in the \HOTSPOT subdirectory does. It has a subroutine, called DrawRubberBand(), which illustrates drawing an animated bounding box:

```
Sub DrawRubberBand (ByVal X1, ByVal Y1, ByVal X2, ByVal Y2 As Single)
    'declare variables
    Dim SaveDrawMode%    'holds previous drawing mode
    'save old drawing mode
    SaveDrawMode% = frmMain.DrawMode
    'invert drawing pen
    frmMain.DrawMode = INVERT
    'actually draw line
    Line (X1, Y1)-(X2, Y2), , B
    'revert to saved mode
    frmMain.DrawMode = SaveDrawMode%
End Sub
```

After you draw the rectangle in the INVERT pen, enable a timer so that when the timer() event fires, you can redraw the same rectangle using the SOLID pen.

TRIED AND TRUE

Using a combination of the `SOLID` and `INVERT` pens produces the most visually appealing rubber band. Using other pens can produce adverse effects on-screen.

The action of alternating pens creates the animated look. To draw in `SOLID` pen is as easy as shown previously, but you must substitute for the different pen. How you incorporate this technique is up to you. The point is that you simply alternate between the two pens at a certain frequency, dictated by the Timer control. What happens when the `Timer1_Timer()` event fires is as follows:

```
'save old draw style
SaveDrawStyle% = frmMain.DrawStyle
'force new solid drawstyle
frmMain.DrawStyle = SOLID
'draw a rubber band
DrawRubberBand BeginX, BeginY, EndX, EndY
'return to old drawstyle
frmMain.DrawStyle = SaveDrawStyle%
```

You probably want to start this process of displaying the rubber band at an appropriate time. For example, you might want to start the animation as the rubber band is being drawn or only after it is finished being drawn.

If you want the rubber band to be displayed as it is being drawn, this complicates matters. This is because if you draw a rectangle at one location and a split second later your application needs to redraw another rectangle and erase the previous one to reflect the mouse movement, the transition isn't very smooth. For this reason, the `Form_MouseUp()` event procedure is a good place to put the code.

Animated Icon When Minimized

An animated icon can be useful when an application is minimized. Animated icons are used to represent the fact that some action is taking place in the application, even though it is minimized and "out of sight." This is another way to give the user visual feedback in a graphic way with a touch of flair.

Animated icons are used in many types of applications, such as in a clock, which animates the time while minimized. Other applications can include an animated icon to represent the fact that a process is in progress, or that a CD player application is playing. The CD player scenario is actually used in Chapter 35, "Developing a CD Player Application."

CROSS REFERENCE

Refer to the application in Chapter 35, "Developing a CD Player Application," for more information.

In any of the preceding examples, the animation is performed using the Timer control, just as with most animation in Visual Basic. The Timer control allows for the toggling between predefined icons at a specified interval. You might need to toggle only two icons to create animation, but depending on how much animation is desired, you can toggle more. The animation will appear "smoother" if more icons are used.

To simulate the animation, enable the timer when the form is minimized (`WindowState = 1`) and disable it when it is not minimized (`WindowState = 0` or `3`). Disabling the timer ensures that you do not use too much of the system resources while the application is maximized. You do this because you won't see the icon in this state, anyway. You enable and disable the time in the `Form_Resize()` event procedure. This enables you to query the `Windowstate` property any time the size changes.

The animation occurs when the `timer()` event fires in the Timer control. It toggles the picture property. The following is the code from the `tmrIcon_Timer()` event procedure used in Chapter 35:

```
'toggle icon picture
If frmMain.Icon <> pictIcon(0).Picture Then
    frmMain.Icon = pictIcon(0).Picture
Else
    frmMain.Icon = pictIcon(1).Picture
End If
```

When the `timer()` event occurs from the `tmrIcon` Timer control, it assigns the icon from one of two static picture boxes containing the icons used in the animation. For example, in the application presented in Chapter 35, there are two static picture boxes that contain the icons. If your application uses three icons for the animation, you need to have three picture boxes that are assigned at the appropriate time by the `tmrIcon` Timer control when the `timer()` event occurs.

In the preceding example, the code to toggle between two icons is simple because no matter which icon is displayed, you simply load the other one. You can do this by using only one `If...Then...Else` statement. If you want to toggle among three icons, for example, you can use code such as this:

```
'toggle icon picture
    If frmMain.Icon = pictIcon(0).Picture Then
        frmMain.Icon = pictIcon(1).Picture
    ElseIf frmMain.Icon = pictIcon(1).Picture Then
        frmMain.Icon = pictIcon(2).Picture
    Else
        frmMain.Icon = pictIcon(0).Picture
    End If
```

This code has an `If...Then...Else` statement with a branch for each of the possible icons. If it finds a match, the code loads the icon with the next highest index number. If it finds no match, the code loads the first index. You can use this technique for any number of icons.

3-D Using WIN32 API

The WIN32 API contains a vast array of functions to use for many purposes. Although Chapter 13, "Using the WIN32 API," covers Windows APIs in detail, some graphics functions are significant enough to mention here.

Some controls do not include the capability to appear in a 3-D look. One such control is the Image control, which has no border. However, there is a way to make sure it has the popular 3-D look. This is done through the WIN32 API. There is an application on the CD accompanying this book in the `\3D` subdirectory that is used as the basis for all of the examples presented here. First, take a look at the main screen from this application, as shown in Figure 8.2.

FIGURE 8.2.
The 3D Image application on the CD.

You might think this is no big deal, based on the picture, but what's happening is that the code is calling an API graphics function to draw a box with specific coordinates. The box can have different types of looks, based on the value that's passed to the API function. First, look at the declarations:

```
Option Explicit
'declare type
Type RECT
    Left As Long
    Top As Long
    Right As Long
    Bottom As Long
End Type
'declare constants
Public Const BDR_RAISEDOUTER = &H1
```

```
Public Const BDR_SUNKENOUTER = &H2
Public Const BDR_RAISEDINNER = &H4
Public Const BDR_SUNKENINNER = &H8
Public Const EDGE_RAISED = (BDR_RAISEDOUTER Or BDR_RAISEDINNER)
Public Const EDGE_SUNKEN = (BDR_SUNKENOUTER Or BDR_SUNKENINNER)
Public Const EDGE_ETCHED = (BDR_SUNKENOUTER Or BDR_RAISEDINNER)
Public Const EDGE_BUMP = (BDR_RAISEDOUTER Or BDR_SUNKENINNER)
Public Const BF_LEFT = &H1
Public Const BF_TOP = &H2
Public Const BF_RIGHT = &H4
Public Const BF_BOTTOM = &H8
Public Const BF_TOPLEFT = (BF_TOP Or BF_LEFT)
Public Const BF_TOPRIGHT = (BF_TOP Or BF_RIGHT)
Public Const BF_BOTTOMLEFT = (BF_BOTTOM Or BF_LEFT)
Public Const BF_BOTTOMRIGHT = (BF_BOTTOM Or BF_RIGHT)
Public Const BF_RECT = (BF_LEFT Or BF_TOP Or BF_RIGHT Or BF_BOTTOM)
'declare API function
Public Declare Function DrawEdge Lib "USER32" (ByVal hdc As Long, qrc As RECT,
➥ ByVal edge As Long, ByVal grfFlags As Long) As Boolean
```

The main declaration is the `DrawEdge` function in the USER32 library. It expects four arguments to be passed in, as follows:

- A handle to the device context so it knows where to draw the edge
- A rectangle structure, indicating the specific coordinates to draw
- The type of edge to draw (as noted in the previously listed constants)
- Flags indicating how to draw the edge

Next, look at the code that is executed when the horizontal scroll bar is clicked. It is as follows:

```
Private Sub HScroll1_Change()
    Dim r As RECT
    Dim Mode As Long
    Const FACTOR = 2

    'set scalemode
    Me.ScaleMode = vbPixels

    'set the size and position of the rectangle
    With r
        .Left = Image1.Left - FACTOR + HScroll1.Value
        .Top = Image1.Top - FACTOR + HScroll1.Value
        .Right = Image1.Width + Image1.Left + FACTOR - HScroll1.Value
        .Bottom = Image1.Height + Image1.Top + FACTOR - HScroll1.Value
    End With

    If optOption(0).Value = True Then
        'raised
        Mode = EDGE_RAISED
    ElseIf optOption(1).Value = True Then
        'sunken
        Mode = EDGE_SUNKEN
    ElseIf optOption(2).Value = True Then
        'etched
        Mode = EDGE_ETCHED
    ElseIf optOption(3).Value = True Then
```

```
        'bump
        Mode = EDGE_BUMP
    End If

    'draw
    DrawEdge Me.hdc, r, Mode, BF_RECT
```

This code simply calculates the rectangle to draw in, based on a constant factor of 2 and the position of the horizontal scroll bar. This position can be anything from 1 to 100. The `If...Then...Else` statements test to see which radio button option was chosen so that it knows what type of edge to draw. The way that the effect is achieved in Figure 8.2 is that the horizontal scroll bar was not clicked on the arrow where the `SmallChange` value is 1. It was clicked on the bar where the `LargeChange` value is 10.

Summary

Graphics play an important role in Visual Basic programming. We live in a very visual world where boring applications just won't do. Sometimes an application can be spiced up simply by adding some color. Other times, adding a toolbar with colorful icons can make an application look more interesting. However, for other times, you need animation. This chapter taught you concepts that you can use to add graphics to your own programs.

9

Printing

Printing plays a very important role in Visual Basic. Visual Basic allows for the printing of complex objects by using the `Printer` object and accessing its properties and methods. This chapter delves into not only printing text, but printing graphics as well.

The `Printer` Object

The `Printer` object controls the currently selected printer. The `Printer` object is accessed just as all other Visual Basic objects are accessed, through properties and methods. There can be only one selected (default) printer at a time. Table 9.1 lists the possible `Printer` object properties.

Table 9.1. Possible `Printer` object properties.

Property	*Function*
`ColorMode`	Specifies whether a color printer will print in color or monochrome
`Copies`	Specifies how many copies will be printed
`Count`	The number of printers in the `Printers` collection
`CurrentX`	Specifies the current "X" position using current `ScaleMode`
`CurrentY`	Specifies the current "Y" position using current `ScaleMode`
`DeviceName`	Returns the name of the device that a driver supports
`DrawMode`	Specifies the appearance of the shape or line control
`DrawStyle`	Line style for graphics output
`DrawWidth`	The width of the line
`DriverName`	Returns the name of the device driver for the `Printer` object
`Duplex`	Specifies whether a page is printed on both sides
`FillColor`	Color used to fill shapes
`FillStyle`	Fill style used in filling shapes
`Font`	Font object
`FontBold`	Boolean (Y/N) for selecting a bold font
`FontCount`	Number of fonts available for the currently selected output device
`FontIutalic`	Boolean (Y/N) for selecting an italic font
`FontName`	Name of the currently used font
`Fonts`	The list of every font name available (from 0 to `FontCount` –1)
`FontSize`	The point size of the currently selected font
`FontStrikethru`	Boolean (Y/N) for selecting a strikethrough font
`FontTransparent`	Boolean (Y/N) for selecting a transparent font

Property	Function
FontUnderline	Boolean (Y/N) for selecting an underlined font
ForeColor	The color used in the foreground
hDC	A handle to the device context
Height	The height of the device in twips
Orientation	The orientation of the printer object (Landscape or Portrait)
Page	The current page number
PaperBin	Specifies which paper tray will be used
PaperSize	Specifies the size of paper
Port	Returns the name of the port that will receive the document
PrintQuality	Specifies the print resolution
ScaleHeight	The number of vertical units for an object to measure its height in current ScaleMode
ScaleLeft	The left edge in the current ScaleMode
ScaleMode	Specifies the unit of measurement for coordinates
ScaleTop	The top edge in the current ScaleMode
ScaleWidth	The number of horizontal units for an object to measure its width in current ScaleMode
TrackDefault	Specifies whether the printer will always be the same printer or the Windows default printer
TwipsPerPixelX	Horizontal twips for every pixel
TwipsPerPixelY	Vertical twips for every pixel
Width	The width of the device in twips
Zoom	Specifies the scaling factor of the printed output

In addition to the properties listed here, the Printer object has methods that enable certain actions to occur. Table 9.2 lists the possible Printer object methods.

Table 9.2. Possible Printer object methods.

Method	Function
Circle	Draws a circle, ellipse, or arc
EndDoc	Terminates a document and releases the hDC to the Printer object
KillDoc	Kills the currently printing document from the Print Manager print queue

continues

Table 9.2. continued

Method	*Function*
`Line`	Draws a line in the current `ScaleMode`
`NewPage`	Ends the current page, advances to the next page, and resets the coordinates to the top-left position
`PaintPicture`	Draws the contents of a graphics file
`Print`	Prints a text string on the default printer in the current color and font
`PSet`	Prints a graphics point on the default printer in the current color
`Scale`	Defines a custom coordinate system or resets to `twips`
`ScaleX`	Converts the scale of the X coordinate to the `ScaleMode`'s coordinates
`ScaleY`	Converts the scale of the Y coordinate to the `ScaleMode`'s coordinates
`TextHeight`	The height of text as it prints using font properties in `Scale` coordinates
`TextWidth`	The width of text as it prints using font properties in `Scale` coordinates

Printing Text

Printing text using the `Printer` object is very simple. To print text to a printer, you only have to set the `CurrentX` and `CurrentY` properties (to position the printer "cursor"), use the `Print` method, and call the `EndDoc` method to eject the page. As an example, consider the following code fragment:

```
Printer.CurrentX = 1500
Printer.CurrentY = 750
Printer.Print "Visual Basic 5 Developer's Guide"
Printer.EndDoc
```

The preceding code does not change the `ScaleMode` property. As such, the default unit of measurement, `Twips`, is in effect. This code starts by setting the printer coordinates to 1500,750. It then prints the string `"Visual Basic 5 Developer's Guide"` at these coordinates. Finally, the `EndDoc` method ejects the page. It's that simple.

Because the unit of measurement is `Twips`, the coordinate reference of 1500,750 is a measurement of twips. There are 1440 twips in a logical inch. Therefore, the position of the text is approximately one inch to the right on the X-axis and one-half inch down on the Y-axis. Both of these measurements are from the starting point of 0,0.

NOTE

Most printers have a non-printable border of one-half inch around the perimeter of the page. This means that coordinate 0,0 would not be at the top-left corner of the page, but actually one-half inch to the right on the X-axis and one-half inch down on the Y-axis.

If another `Print` method is used directly after the `Print` method in the previous code listing, the printout will be at the beginning of the next line. This is because there are no symbols specified after the print expression in the code. There are two possible symbols that can affect where the next character is printed. The first, a semicolon (`;`), instructs the printer to print the next character directly after the text just printed. The second, a comma (`,`), instructs the printer to print at the next *print zone*. A print zone is the beginning of a set of 14 columns. What determines the width of a column is the average of the width of all characters in a font, considering the current font size. If you do not append the print expression with a symbol, Visual Basic appends a carriage return. This action positions the "cursor" to the beginning of the next line. If you want to print at a different location, you can put the "cursor" anywhere you desire by using the `CurrentX` and `CurrentY` properties.

Printing Graphics

Printing graphics is different from printing straight text in Visual Basic. Graphics, however, can spruce up the printouts your applications create. For example, you can add a company logo to the top of the page. There are three methods that allow for printing graphics: `Circle`, `Line`, and `PSet`.

The `Circle` Method

The `Circle` method allows for the printing of a circle, ellipse, or arc. It has the following syntax:

```
[object.]Circle[Step](x,y),radius[,[color][,[start][,[end][,aspect]]]]
```

For example, this statement prints a black circle beginning in the middle of a form, 1000, with a radius of 1000 twips, assuming that the `ScaleMode` is set to `Twips`:

```
Me.Circle (Me.Width / 2, Me.Height / 2), 1000    'draw circle
```

The `Line` Method

The `Line` method allows for the printing of a line or rectangle. It has the following syntax:

```
[object.]Line[[Step](x1,y1)]-[Step](x2,y2)[,[color][,B[F]]]
```

TRIED AND TRUE

You cannot use graphics methods in the `Form_Load()` event of a form because Visual Basic will attempt to draw graphics on the `Form` object before it is actually drawn on the screen. It is not drawn until after the `Form_Load()` event is executed. One alternative is to place graphics methods in the `Form_Activate()` event.

You can use the `Line` object to print a line under the header of a page to be printed out. You can do something like this:

```
Printer.Line (0, Printer.TextHeight(Printer.FontSize))-(Printer.ScaleWidth,
➥Printer.TextHeight(Printer.FontSize) + 35), , BF
```

The code uses the `Line` method to print a line across the page, beginning at the left side of the page, just under the text printed at the top of the page. The line extends across the page and down 35 twips, which creates a box. However, you cannot actually see the area inside the box because the top and bottom of the box are so close together that they touch. This, in effect, enables the line to appear thicker. The line can be drawn without using the `BF` option, but then another line of code has to be added to change the `Printer.DrawWidth` property. Instead, you use only one line of code.

You can add a nice touch if you incorporate lines and boxes around headers and other areas of your printed documents. This gives a much more pleasing appearance. By using `ScaleWidth` and `ScaleHeight` properties, you can make this code device-independent, which means that it will work on all printers.

The `PSet` Method

Finally, the `PSet` method allows for the printing of a single point. It has the following syntax:

```
[object.]PSet[Step](x,y)[,color]
```

For example, this statement prints a red point in the middle of a form:

```
Me.PSet (Me.Width / 2, Me.Height / 2), RGB(255, 0, 0)  'draw point
```

Sending Data Directly to the Printer

The concepts presented earlier in the section "The `Printer` Object" send data to the printer via the `Printer` object. Using the `Printer` object is an easy way to efficiently print simple text and graphics. If you want more flexibility in printing, you must send the data directly to the printer. This means that the data is sent directly to the printer port (LPT1, LPT2, and so on), which is controlled by the operating system, and not Visual Basic.

There are two ways to send data directly to the printer. The first method is to write the data exactly as you write data to a text file, using the `Print #` method. The second way also writes to the port, but instead of sending text, a special PCL language is sent. PCL stands for Printer Control Language, which is a special language that uses escape codes to instruct the printer to do specific things.

> **NOTE**
>
> The PCL methods discussed in this chapter work only with printers that support the PCL language, such as the Hewlett Packard LaserJet series II (or compatible) and higher.

To send data directly to the printer, the port must first be opened. You open the port by using the `Open` command. The following code opens the printer for writing:

```
Open "LPT1" For Output As #1
```

All data to be sent to `LPT1` is now referenced by `#1`. You can also open `LPT2` or higher, as long as they are supported on your system. The `#1` listed in the preceding code is known as a *file handle*. You can open multiple file handles, each representing a different printer or even a file.

If you want to open a file with another file handle, simply replace `#1` with the appropriate number. If you don't know what number to use, you can use the Visual Basic `FreeFile()` function. The `FreeFile()` function returns an integer representing the next available file handle. You can use it like this:

```
fHandle% = FreeFile()
Open "LPT1" for output as #fHandle%
```

To write data to the port, use the `PRINT #` command. For example, the following code writes a string directly to the printer port:

```
Print #1, "Visual Basic 5 Developer's Guide"
```

This code fragment clearly shows how you can incorporate the `PRINT #` command to send text directly to the printer port:

```
'initiate error handler
On Error GoTo LoadError

'Open Printer Port
Open "LPT1" For Output As #2
'your code goes here

'close the port
Close #2

'exit
Exit Sub
```

```
LoadError:
Print #2, "Load Error " & Trim$(Str$(Err)) & " - " & Error$
Print #2, Chr$(vbKeyEscape) + "&l0H"
Resume
```

The problem with not using the `Printer` object in Visual Basic is that you have to handle all printing tasks at a lower programming level. Visual Basic's `Printer` object and its methods are not being used to help out in any way. For example, how do you do something like eject a page? You can't use the `Printer.EndDoc` method because as far as the `Printer` object is concerned, the print job never started. In this case, there is a whole range of functions available for using the escape codes mentioned earlier. These escape codes are so named because before every function, an escape character must be sent to alert the printer that the command will follow. Escape codes can be printer-specific, but if a printer conforms to a Hewlett-Packard specification, it should work the same.

Notice the line in the previous code fragment that reads

```
Print #2, Chr$(vbKeyEscape) + "&l0H"
```

It uses this syntax to send an escape code to the printer:

```
Chr$(vbKeyEscape)+command$
```

where *`command$`* is the code of the function and parameters to send to the printer. The purpose of this line is to eject the page. It is done, not through Visual Basic, but by instructing the printer directly to eject the page. The possible escape codes are listed in Table 9.3. The escape character, `Chr$(vbKeyEscape)`, is not shown in Table 9.3 but is necessary to precede each command that will be sent to the printer. The reason it is not shown is for the sake of saving space on every line in the table. Note that anywhere in the table the `#` symbol appears, substitute it for the number pertaining to the code. For example, for `&l#X`, use the code substituting the `#` for the number of copies to print. In this case, to print five copies, send `&l5X`. Also, make sure to use the codes as they are listed because they are case sensitive.

Table 9.3. Common PCL escape codes.

Escape Code	*Function*
`E`	Reset printer
`&l#X`	Number of copies
`&l0H`	Eject page
`&l1H`	Feed from tray
`&l2H`	Manual feed
`&l3H`	Manual envelope feed
`&l1A`	Executive paper size
`&l2A`	Letter paper size

Escape Code	Function
&l3A	Legal paper size
&l26A	A4 paper size
&l80A	Monarch paper size
&l81A	Commercial 10 paper size
&l90A	International DL paper size
&l91A	International C5 paper size
&l#P	Page length number of lines
&l0O	Portrait orientation
&l1O	Landscape orientation
&l#E	Top margin number of lines
&l#E	Text length number of lines
&a#L	Left margin number of lines
&a#M	Right margin number of lines
9	Clear horizontal margins
&l0L	Perforation skip mode disabled
&l1L	Perforation skip mode enabled
&k#H	Horizontal motion index (1⁄20-inch increments)
&l#C	Vertical motion index (1⁄48-inch increments)
&l1D	1 line/inch
&l2D	2 lines/inch
&l3D	3 lines/inch
&l4D	4 lines/inch
&l6D	6 lines/inch
&l8D	8 lines/inch
&l12D	12 lines/inch
&l16D	16 lines/inch
&l24D	24 lines/inch
&l48D	48 lines/inch
&a#R	Cursor positioning—vertical row number
*p#Y	Cursor positioning—number of vertical dots
&a#V	Cursor positioning—number of vertical decipoints
&a#C	Cursor positioning—horizontal row number

continues

Table 9.3. continued

Escape Code	*Function*
`*p#X`	Cursor positioning—number of horizontal dots
`&a#H`	Cursor positioning—number of horizontal decipoints
`=`	Half line feed
`&k0G`	CR=CR, LF=LF, FF=FF
`&k1G`	CR=CR+LF, LF=LF, FF=FF
`&k2G`	CR=CR, LF=CR+LF, FF=CR+FF
`&k3G`	CR=CR+LF, LF=CR+LF, FF=CR+FF
`&f0S`	Cursor push position
`&f1S`	Cursor pop position
`(0A`	HP math symbol set
`(0B`	HP line draw symbol set
`(0D`	ISO 60 Norwegian symbol set
`(1D`	ISO 61 Norwegian symbol set
`(0E`	HP Roman symbol set
`(1E`	ISO 4 UK symbol set
`(0F`	ISO 25 French symbol set
`(1F`	ISO 69 French symbol set
`(0G`	HP German symbol set
`(1G`	ISO 21 German symbol set
`(8G`	HP Greek symbol set
`(0I`	ISO 15 Italian symbol set
`(0K`	ISO 14 JIS ASCII symbol set
`(1K`	HP Katakana symbol set
`(2K`	ISO 57 Chinese symbol set
`(0M`	HP Math 7 symbol set
`(1M`	Technical symbol set
`(8M`	HP Math 8 symbol set
`(0N`	ISO 100 Latin 1 symbol set
`(0O`	OCR A symbol set
`(1O`	OCR B symbol set
`(0S`	ISO 11 Swedish symbol set
`(1S`	HP Spanish symbol set

Escape Code	Function
(2S	ISO 17 Spanish symbol set
(3S	ISO 10 Swedish symbol set
(4S	ISO 16 Portuguese symbol set
(5S	ISO 84 Portuguese symbol set
(6S	ISO 85 Spanish symbol set
(0U	ISO 6 ASCII symbol set
(1U	HP Legal symbol set
(2U	ISO 2 IRV symbol set
(7U	OEM symbol set
(8U	HP Roman 8 symbol set
(10U	PC 8 symbol set
(11U	PC 8 (D/N) symbol set
(15U	HP Pi symbol set
(s1P	Proportional spacing
(s0P	Fixed spacing
(s#H	Primary pitch
(s#V	Primary point size
(s0S	Primary upright style
(s1S	Primary italic style
(s0B	Primary stroke weight medium (0)
(s3B	Primary stroke weight bold (3)
(s0T	Line printer typeface
(s3T	Courier typeface
(s4T	Helvetica typeface
(s5T	Times Roman typeface
(s6T	Letter Gothic typeface
(s8T	Prestige typeface
(s11T	Presentations typeface
(s17T	Optima typeface
(s18T	ITC Garamond typeface
(s19T	Cooper Black typeface
(s20T	Coronet Bold typeface

continues

Table 9.3. continued

Escape Code	*Function*
`(s21T`	Broadway typeface
`(s22T`	Black Condensed typeface
`(s23T`	Century Schoolbook typeface
`(s24T`	University Roman typeface
`(3@`	Primary font default
`)3@`	Secondary font default
`&d0D`	Underline enable fixed
`&d3D`	Underline enable floating
`&d@`	Underline disable
`*c#D`	Font ID#
`*c0F`	Delete all fonts
`*c1F`	Delete all temporary fonts
`*c2F`	Delete last font ID #
`*c4F`	Make font temporary
`*c5F`	Make font permanent
`(#X`	Select primary font with ID #
`)#X`	Select secondary font with ID #
`)s#W[Data]`	Create font header (# of bytes)
`(s#W[Data]`	Download character (# of bytes)
`*c#E`	Character code (ASCII Code # in decimal)
`*t75R`	75 dots/inch printer resolution
`*t100R`	100 dots/inch printer resolution
`*t150R`	150 dots/inch printer resolution
`*t300R`	300 dots/inch printer resolution
`*r0A`	Left graphics margin
`*r1A`	Current cursor position
`*b#W[Data]`	Transfer data (# of rows)
`*rB`	End graphics transfer
`*c#A`	Rectangle horizontal # of dots
`*c#H`	Rectangle horizontal # of decipoints
`*c#B`	Rectangle vertical # of dots
`*c#V`	Rectangle vertical # of decipoints

Escape Code	*Function*
`*c0P`	Fill rectangle area rule
`*c2P`	Fill rectangle area gray scale
`*c3P`	Fill rectangle area HP pattern
`*c2G`	Shape rectangle 2% gray
`*c10G`	Shape rectangle 10% gray
`*c15G`	Shape rectangle 15% gray
`*c30G`	Shape rectangle 30% gray
`*c45G`	Shape rectangle 45% gray
`*c70G`	Shape rectangle 70% gray
`*c90G`	Shape rectangle 90% gray
`*c100G`	Shape rectangle 100% gray
`*c1G`	Pattern 1 horizontal line
`*c2G`	Pattern 2 vertical lines
`*c3G`	Pattern 3 diagonal lines
`*c4G`	Pattern 4 diagonal lines
`*c5G`	Pattern 5 square grid
`*c6G`	Pattern 6 diagonal grid

TIP

You might want to define constants for the values presented in Table 9.3. This would make referencing these codes cleaner and easier.

Sending Graphic Data Directly to the Printer

The previous section covered the basics of sending text data to the printer using the `PRINT #` command. It also showed how to incorporate PCL escape codes. The PCL codes can be taken one step further to print graphics. Because any pixel on the paper can be printed (as long as it is in the printable area), it is just a question of how to actually access those points. It would take forever to use the Visual Basic `PSet` method to write to each individual point.

One very reliable way to do this is to send raster graphics by using the PCL functions available for this. The term *raster graphics* is defined as images that are composed of groups of dots. A raster graphic is sent to the printer as one bit of data for every dot to be printed.

Applications can use PCL raster graphic methods to send bitmaps. The bitmap can be a logo, a font, or some other graphic—the trick is to break the whole bitmap up into small, manageable pieces. Raster graphics can be used for a variety of purposes, such as printing a logo on the top of every page, or only on certain pages. They can also be used to "stamp" graphics across an entire page. This is great for "stamping" the word "Confidential" across a page if it contains certain confidential information. The possibilities are endless because PCL raster graphics enable you to effectively print to any pixel on the printable page.

Creating a Stamp with Raster Graphics

The term *stamp* is used here to represent what a page would look like if someone took a rubber stamp to a piece of paper. This is useful because it ensures that this is done programmatically instead of relying on someone to physically stamp it. One possible way to create the stamp is to treat each character to be "stamped" as its own bitmap that can be stored in a text file. Each line in the text file can represent an individual character to be displayed. On each of the lines, you can determine a scheme for storing the data (what the character looks like) to be sent to the printer.

There are two applications on the CD accompanying this book that are used as a point of discussion. One is a raster graphics editor application, and the other is a raster graphics printer application. The editor is stored in the `\RASTER\EDITOR` subdirectory, while the printing application is stored in the `\RASTER\PRINTER` subdirectory.

The raster graphics editor application enables the user to generate a text file to store data about each character.

This section actually shows you how to perform the stamping on a printout. From this point forward, it is assumed that any text needed to be printed on the page has already been printed using the `PRINT #` command.

Using Table 9.3, you can see the possible PCL escape codes that can be sent to the printer. The codes we are concerned with are the graphics codes.

The first step is to understand how to send the data to the printer. As mentioned earlier, you need to break up the bitmap image into small, manageable pieces that must be represented in bytes. A *byte* is eight bits of data, which means that eight individual pixels on the paper are represented. The eight pixels are physically printable pixels, regardless of whether they are actually printed or left blank.

A raster image printed in the Portrait orientation must be broken up into vertical bytes. A raster image printed in the Landscape orientation must be broken up into horizontal bytes. For example, suppose you have an image that is going to be printed in the Portrait orientation and is 400 pixels wide and 400 pixels high. Because each set of eight pixels is a byte, it is logical to break up the image into 50 bytes, vertically. This means that if you have the image on paper, you can physically draw a vertical line between each set of eight pixels.

After you break up the image into bytes, a decimal value has to be calculated for each byte. If there are 50 bytes in a row to send to the printer, each row has 50 decimals to send to the printer. This is how the printer knows which of the eight bits inside each byte to actually print, and which ones to leave white (unprinted).

The bits are calculated using the standard method of encoding a decimal using the value of 1 for the least significant bit and 128 for the most significant bit. The maximum possible decimal equivalent value for any byte that has all pixels printed is 255. A value of 255 instructs the printer to print eight pixels in a row. If you send 50 decimal values of 255 to the printer, it prints a line 400 pixels wide. If you send 50 decimal values of 255, 400 times (once per row in a 400×400 bitmap), the printer prints a solid square block 400 pixels by 400 pixels.

Now that you understand conceptually how the data is broken up and sent to the printer, consider the case of the raster graphics editor application. Because each character of data is actually its own bitmap, you send the bitmaps to the printer as if they are their own entities, even though the final product looks like one "stamp" of all characters. This particular application uses bitmaps that are 32 pixels by 32 pixels, which means that in the Portrait orientation, 32 rows of four bytes of data are sent to the printer.

To illustrate how these bits and bytes are calculated for a 32 pixel by 32 pixel bitmap, see Figure 9.1, which shows how the bits are calculated for the Portrait orientation. Refer to Figure 9.2 to see how they are calculated in Landscape orientation.

FIGURE 9.1.
How to calculate individual bits in Portrait orientation.

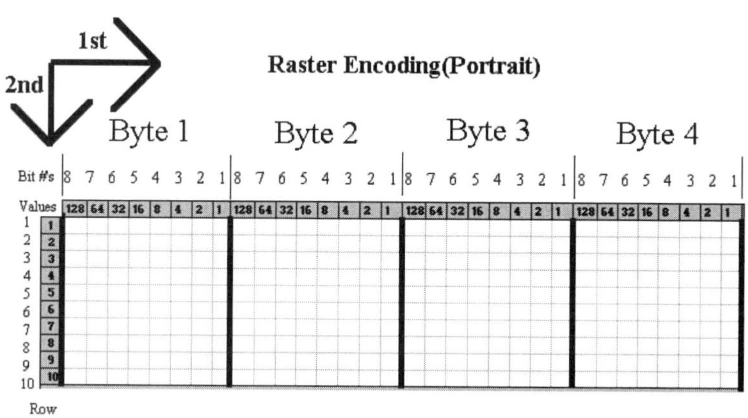

The only difference between Portrait and Landscape is the way in which the individual bits are calculated. Figure 9.1 shows how the bits are calculated for the Portrait orientation, and Figure 9.2 shows how they are calculated in the Landscape orientation.

To calculate the decimal equivalent for Portrait orientation, move from left to right, from the top row to the bottom. Note that the farthest right bit is the least significant bit (value 1), and the farthest left bit is the most significant bit (value 128).

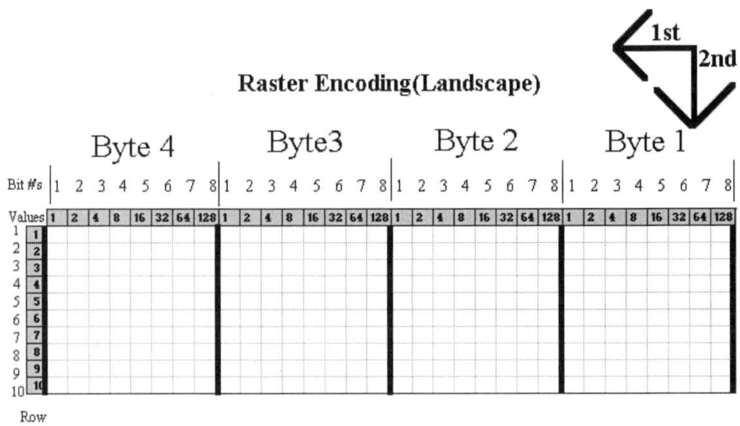

FIGURE 9.2.
How to calculate individual bits in Landscape orientation.

To calculate the decimal equivalent for Landscape orientation, move from right to left, from the top row to the bottom. Note that the leftmost bit is the least significant bit (value 1), and the rightmost bit is the most significant bit (value 128).

To actually start sending the data, the first thing you need to do is to tell the printer what orientation to print in (Portrait or Landscape). You can tell the printer to print in the Portrait orientation by sending the following escape code:

```
Print #1, Chr$(vbKeyEscape) + "&l0O"
```

The next step is to position the printer cursor. Remember, you are not using Visual Basic methods and properties, so you cannot use the `CurrentX` and `CurrentY` properties to position the printer cursor. The cursor can be positioned at any desired location.

Suppose the printer is to start at position 100,100. Again, remember that you are not dealing with Visual Basic properties; you are using the printer's own pixel coordinates, so changing the `ScaleMode` property has no effect on raster graphics. All of the escape codes used in the following examples are listed in Table 9.3. First, instruct the printer to begin printing with the X coordinate at 100 and the Y coordinate at 100:

```
Print #1, Chr$(vbKeyEscape) + "*p100X"
Print #1, Chr$(vbKeyEscape) + "*p100Y"
```

The next thing you need to do is to set the printer resolution. If you want to set it to 75 dots-per-inch, send the following to the printer:

```
Print #1, Chr$(vbKeyEscape) + "*t75R"
```

TRIED AND TRUE

The reason that a resolution of 75 dots-per-inch is used is because it gives a nice size representation on the page. For a 32 pixel by 32 pixel bitmap, at this resolution, the image is approximately one-half inch by one-half inch.

Now that you have told the printer the position and resolution of the graphic, you must tell the printer to be ready to accept the data. Therefore, you must put it into raster graphics mode by sending the following:

```
Print #1, Chr$(vbKeyEscape) + "*r1A"
```

NOTE

After putting the printer in Raster Graphics mode, the printing will begin at the current position as set with the X and Y coordinates earlier. It does not reset to the top-left corner of the page, which is coordinate location 0,0.

Now graphics mode is set, but the printer needs to know how many bytes per line it will receive. Instruct the printer that it will receive four bytes with the following line:

```
Print #1, Chr$(vbKeyEscape) + "*b4W"
```

If you are going to send 50 bytes, send the following:

```
Print #1, Chr$(vbKeyEscape) + "*b50W"
```

The printer needs to know how many bytes to expect to receive so that it can calculate which bits are to be printed correctly. The printer is now ready to accept the actual byte data. To send the byte data, first calculate the decimal equivalent of each byte to be sent, as shown earlier in Figures 9.1 and 9.2. If the printer expects to receive four bytes of data, send the data with the following format, where *decimal* is the decimal you calculate from the individual bits in the byte:

```
Print #1, Chr$(vbKeyEscape) + Chr$(decimal)
```

Here's an example of four bytes being sent to the printer:

```
Print #1, Chr$(vbKeyEscape) + Chr$(255)
Print #1, Chr$(vbKeyEscape) + Chr$(105)
Print #1, Chr$(vbKeyEscape) + Chr$(0)
Print #1, Chr$(vbKeyEscape) + Chr$(255)
```

Because four bytes are expected to be received and four bytes are sent, an entire row is printed. It is your choice to send more data or to end.

If you are to send more data (more rows), you again tell the printer how many bytes of data to expect and then send the data. The printer is still set in the appropriate resolution and still in Raster Graphics mode. Continue to send the data in this fashion. When you have sent all of the data and are ready to finish, you must tell the printer that you are finished with graphics by using the following line:

```
Print #1, Chr$(vbKeyEscape) + "*rB"
```

You can automate the process of calculating the bits and bytes that have to be sent to the printer. As a programmer, you need to keep in mind that whatever scheme you devise to design or display the bitmap, you need to break it up and send it to the printer as described earlier. The raster graphics editor application uses a scheme to enable the user to define the bitmap by using the grid control. The grid is set up in a 32×32 matrix. How the bytes and bits are calculated depends on whether the user wants to print in Portrait or Landscape modes. Therefore, the process is automated by cycling through each and every row and column in the grid control and calculating the decimal equivalents. This is performed in the `CalculateBits()` procedure from the application, as follows:

```
'portrait
If WhichMode$ = "PORTRAIT" Then
    'cycle through for portrait from left to right, top to bottom
    For Row% = 1 To Grid1.Rows - 1
        For Col% = 1 To Grid1.Cols - 1
            Grid1.Row = Row%
            Grid2.Row = Row%
            Grid1.Col = Col%
            'move Grid2's col once for every 8 cols in Grid1
            If Grid1.Col >= 1 And Grid1.Col <= 8 Then
                Grid2.Col = 1
            ElseIf Grid1.Col >= 9 And Grid1.Col <= 16 Then
                Grid2.Col = 2
            ElseIf Grid1.Col >= 17 And Grid1.Col <= 24 Then
                Grid2.Col = 3
            ElseIf Grid1.Col >= 25 And Grid1.Col <= 32 Then
                Grid2.Col = 4
            End If
            'assign Grid2 row
            Grid2.Row = Grid1.Row
            'start at row 0 to check text(to see which bit position this is)
            'each row and col has a header at row 0 and col 0 for which bit
            'position this is
            Grid1.Row = 0
            'build bit representation of which bits are printed
            Select Case (Val(Trim$(Grid1.Text)))
                Case 1:
                    Grid1.Row = Row%
                    If Grid1.Picture = Black.Picture Then
                        Grid2.Text = Val(Trim$(Grid2.Text)) + 1
                    End If
                Case 2:
                    Grid1.Row = Row%
                    If Grid1.Picture = Black.Picture Then
                        Grid2.Text = Val(Trim$(Grid2.Text)) + 2
                    End If
                Case 3:
                    Grid1.Row = Row%
                    If Grid1.Picture = Black.Picture Then
                        Grid2.Text = Val(Trim$(Grid2.Text)) + 4
                    End If
                Case 4:
                    Grid1.Row = Row%
                    If Grid1.Picture = Black.Picture Then
```

```
                    Grid2.Text = Val(Trim$(Grid2.Text)) + 8
                End If
            Case 5:
                Grid1.Row = Row%
                If Grid1.Picture = Black.Picture Then
                    Grid2.Text = Val(Trim$(Grid2.Text)) + 16
                End If
            Case 6:
                Grid1.Row = Row%
                If Grid1.Picture = Black.Picture Then
                    Grid2.Text = Val(Trim$(Grid2.Text)) + 32
                End If
            Case 7:
                Grid1.Row = Row%
                If Grid1.Picture = Black.Picture Then
                    Grid2.Text = Val(Trim$(Grid2.Text)) + 64
                End If
            Case 8:
                Grid1.Row = Row%
                If Grid1.Picture = Black.Picture Then
                    Grid2.Text = Val(Trim$(Grid2.Text)) + 128
                End If
        End Select
    Next Col%
  Next Row%
ElseIf WhichMode$ = "LANDSCAPE" Then
  'cycle through for Landscape bottom to top, left to right
  For Row% = Grid1.Cols - 1 To 1 Step -1
    For Col% = 1 To Grid1.Rows - 1
        Grid1.Col = Row%
        Grid1.Row = Col%
        Select Case (Grid1.Row)
            Case 1 To 8:
                Grid2.Col = 1
            Case 9 To 16:
                Grid2.Col = 2
            Case 17 To 24:
                Grid2.Col = 3
            Case 25 To 32:
                Grid2.Col = 4
        End Select
        'calculate row
        Grid2.Row = (32 - Grid1.Col) + 1
        'start at col 0 to check text(to see which bit position this is)
        'each row and col has a header at row 0 and col 0 for which bit
        'position this is
        Grid1.Col = 0
        'build bit representation of which bits are printed
        Select Case (Val(Trim$(Grid1.Text)))
            Case 1:
                Grid1.Col = Row%
                If Grid1.Picture = Black.Picture Then
                    Grid2.Text = Val(Trim$(Grid2.Text)) + 1
                End If
            Case 2:
                Grid1.Col = Row%
                If Grid1.Picture = Black.Picture Then
```

```
                    Grid2.Text = Val(Trim$(Grid2.Text)) + 2
                End If
            Case 3:
                Grid1.Col = Row%
                If Grid1.Picture = Black.Picture Then
                    Grid2.Text = Val(Trim$(Grid2.Text)) + 4
                End If
            Case 4:
                Grid1.Col = Row%
                If Grid1.Picture = Black.Picture Then
                    Grid2.Text = Val(Trim$(Grid2.Text)) + 8
                End If
            Case 5:
                Grid1.Col = Row%
                If Grid1.Picture = Black.Picture Then
                    Grid2.Text = Val(Trim$(Grid2.Text)) + 16
                End If
            Case 6:
                Grid1.Col = Row%
                If Grid1.Picture = Black.Picture Then
                    Grid2.Text = Val(Trim$(Grid2.Text)) + 32
                End If
            Case 7:
                Grid1.Col = Row%
                If Grid1.Picture = Black.Picture Then
                    Grid2.Text = Val(Trim$(Grid2.Text)) + 64
                End If
            Case 8:
                Grid1.Col = Row%
                If Grid1.Picture = Black.Picture Then
                    Grid2.Text = Val(Trim$(Grid2.Text)) + 128
                End If
        End Select
    Next Col%
  Next Row%
End If
```

Although it is not the only way to calculate the decimal equivalents, the following is the scheme used in the `CalculateBits()` procedure.

There are two branches of code: one for Portrait and one for Landscape. The basic scheme for either mode is to cycle through each row and column (the order of which depends on which orientation is selected) and for each individual cell location to check the bit value of that particular location. Fortunately, with the grid control, each row and column can be labeled in a fixed row. The application simply relies on these labels (row 0 and column 0) to determine what value to use to calculate the decimal equivalents. If the color of the pixel (cell) is black, then it adds the value of this label to the calculated value of the byte.

That is basically what is happening in the code. It looks more complicated than it really is because of the way the code has to cycle through each cell. Refer to Figures 9.1 and 9.2 to see how the cells must be calculated.

Even though this application uses a 32×32 pixel matrix, your application does not have to—it can use any size. You just have to make sure that you manage how you send the data to the printer.

If you want to print multiple bitmaps on the same page, you simply position the cursor to the desired position before printing each bitmap. You can even cycle through bitmaps, automatically incrementing the X or Y coordinates after every bitmap. You can use this method to give a sloping appearance.

Again, as an example, the raster graphics editor application along with the raster graphics printer application uses a routine to print all bitmaps, incrementing the X and Y coordinates automatically. The following code fragment is taken from the `PrintAllText()` routine that calls the `PrintCharacter()` routine once for every bitmap to be printed:

```
'loop through all characters to be printed
For loopcount% = 1 To (Len(PrintText.Text))
    pnlCurChar.Caption = Mid$(PrintText.Text, loopcount%, 1)
    'increment coordinates
    If PortLandMode% = PORTRAIT Then
        XPValue% = XPValue% + Val(HPOffset.Text)
        YPValue% = YPValue% + Val(VPOffset.Text)
    ElseIf PortLandMode% = LANDSCAPE Then
        XLValue% = XLValue% + Val(HLOffset.Text)
        YLValue% = YLValue% + Val(VLOffset.Text)
    End If
    Call PrintCharacter
Next loopcount%()
```

Printing a Picture Box Bitmap Represented On-Screen

There is a way to print the contents of a picture box to the printer. You do this by using the `PaintPicture` method of the `Printer` object. Here's the syntax of the `PaintPicture` method:

```
object.PaintPicture picture, x1, y1, [width1], [height1], [x2], [y2], [width2],
➥ [height2], [opcode]
```

where:

> `x1, y1` is the top-left coordinate of the picture.
>
> `width1` is optional, indicating the width of the picture.
>
> `height1` is optional, indicating the height of the picture.
>
> `x2, y2` are optional, indicating the clipping region of the picture.
>
> `width2` is optional, indicating the width of the clipping region.
>
> `height2` is optional, indicating the height of the clipping region.
>
> `opcode` is optional, indicating special options used when printing the picture, as shown in Table 9.4.

Table 9.4. Constants to be used for *opcode*.

Constant	*Description*
`vbDstInvert`	Inverts the destination bitmap
`vbMergeCopy`	Combines the source bitmap and the pattern
`vbMergePaint`	Combines the inverted source bitmap with the destination bitmap by using the `OR` operator
`vbNotSrcCopy`	Copies the inverted source bitmap to the destination
`vbNotSrcErase`	Inverts the result of combining the destination and source bitmaps by using the `OR` operator
`vbPatCopy`	Copies the pattern to the destination bitmap
`vbPatInvert`	Combines the destination bitmap with the pattern by using the `XOR` operator
`vbPatPaint`	Combines the inverted source bitmap with the pattern by using the `OR` operator
`vbSrcAnd`	Combines the pixels of the destination and source bitmaps by using the `AND` operator
`vbSrcCopy`	Copies the source bitmap to the destination bitmap
`vbSrcErase`	Inverts the destination bitmap and combines the result with the source bitmap by using the `AND` operator
`vbSrcInvert`	Combines the pixels of the destination and source bitmaps by using the `XOR` operator
`vbSrcPaint`	Combines the pixels of the destination and source bitmaps by using the `OR` operator

Based on the syntax listed earlier, you can copy the contents of a Picture box to a printer by simply using these statements:

```
With Printer
    .PaintPicture Picture1.Picture, 100, 100
    .EndDoc
End With
```

Then, you can do some fancier things, such as invert the picture by changing to this line of code:

```
.PaintPicture Picture1.Picture, 100, 100, , , , , , , vbDstInvert
```

Note that you must place commas in the statement for the optional items that you don't fill in.

There is another way to print a picture to the printer. The icon printing application in the `\ICON` subdirectory on the CD accompanying this book uses this other method. The same approach used by this application can be used in your applications. The technique is to actually cycle through each bit in the bitmap, determine its color; and if it isn't white, send it to the printer using standard graphics methods.

The first step is to set the scale mode to pixels. You do this with the following line:

```
WhichIcon.ScaleMode = 3
```

Then, you must cycle through all of the coordinates. The specific order (X then Y, or Y then X) doesn't matter. In this example, the order of the coordinate cycling is first Y, and then X. The X and Y coordinates are assigned based on the screen resolution. This allows for the possibility to print a larger icon than is displayed on-screen.

NOTE

Note that even though this example uses icons, any bitmapped image will work. Even though the picture box is populated with an icon, it really is just a bitmapped image.

CROSS REFERENCE

The `Screen` object is used as the basis of determining the printing resolution. For more information on using the `Screen` object, refer to Chapter 8, "Graphics."

You define the screen resolution by using the `Screen` object. The following code shows how to cycle through each pixel in the picture box and print it if it is not white:

```
'Cycle through y coordinates
For YLoop% = 0 To (WhichIcon.ScaleHeight - 1)
    'assign y coordinate, based on screen resolution
    YAdjust = WhichIcon.Top + (YLoop% * ScrResY)
    'cycle through x coordinates
    For XLoop% = 0 To (WhichIcon.ScaleWidth - 1)
        'assign x coordinate, based on screen resolution
        XAdjust = WhichIcon.Left + OFFSET + (XLoop% * ScrResX)
        'assign particular point to determine color
        XYColor = WhichIcon.Point(XLoop%, YLoop%)
        'for some reason, if the screen repaints(due to moving a window)
        'the color might be -1.
        If XYColor < 0 Then
            XYColor = 7
            m$ = "The window has been moved off the screen." & Chr$(13)
            m$ = m$ + "The icons may not print correctly"
            MsgBox m$
            'center form
            CenterForm Me
```

```
            'force repaint
            Me.Refresh
        End If
        'if color is not white, print point, using screen resolution
        If XYColor <> QBColor(7) Then
            printer.Line (XAdjust, YAdjust)-Step(ScrResX, ScrResY), XYColor, BF
        End If
    Next XLoop%
    DoEvents
Next YLoop%
```

TRIED AND TRUE

If the form is moved off screen or if another window is opened on top of the picture box being printed, `QBColor` will be `-1`. This is an immediate flag that a window has changed. It affects the printout because you are looking at a certain area of the picture box, which will have changed.

Determining Which Printer Fonts Are Present

To determine whether a printer has a certain font, use the `FontCount` and `Fonts` properties for the `Printer` object. The `Fonts` property is actually a Visual Basic *collection*. A collection is a way that Visual Basic keeps track of certain objects or properties.

CROSS REFERENCE

For more information about collections, refer to Chapter 22, "Collections."

The idea is to cycle through all fonts and test for the possibility you are looking for. You might be looking for a certain font or a particular font size. You loop through `0` to `Printer.FontCount - 1` to cover all possibilities in the collection. Because there is no collection for the size of the font, there is a workaround. You can assign the size of the font by using the `FontSize` property of the `Printer` object and then test to see whether it is selected. If it is not, the size is not possible.

As an example, there is a function in the icon printing application, called `FindFont()`. It is used to determine whether the printer has a font with a `FontSize` of six. The following code fragment is from that function:

```
'find out which fonts exist for printer, and use first available in size 6
For loopcount% = 0 To printer.FontCount - 1
    'assign to first available font
    printer.FontName = printer.Fonts(loopcount%)
    'assign to size 6
    printer.FontSize = 6
    'test to see if 6 is still assigned, if so, exit loop
```

```
    If printer.FontSize = 6 Then
        'set variable flag to print text in print routine
        FontFound% = True
        'exit function
        FindFont = True
        Exit Function
    End If
Next loopcount%
```

TRIED AND TRUE

The reason for testing the printer for a font size between 5.5 and 9.5 is because if the printer does not have a font size of exactly 6, it may assign a font size close to 6. It is sufficient to check for the point size + or –.5. It is assumed that if a font size is found in this range, then the setting of the font worked.

In your application, you can use the same technique to display a list of all of the possible fonts for a user's selection. You can then list all font sizes available if a user selects one of those fonts.

The `Printers` Collection

The `Printers` collection enables you to cycle through the printers installed on a user's system. This enables you to print to more than one printer or search for a printer with specific qualities, such as a color printer. You cycle through the printers collection, just like any other collection in Visual Basic. If you wanted to check for a color printer connected to the system, you could do it like this:

```
'declare variables
Dim prt As Printer
Dim nColorFound As Integer

'initialize
nColorFound = False

'check for color printer
For Each prt In Printers
    If prt.ColorMode = vbPRCMColor Then
        nColorFound = True
        Exit For
    End If
Next

If nColorFound = False Then
    MsgBox "There are no color printers!"
End If
```

This code cycles through the collection and checks the `ColorMode` property to see if it is equal to the constant `vbPRCMColor`. If it is equal to the constant, then that specific printer has color capabilities.

Summary

Printing is an important part of Visual Basic programming. In general, Microsoft has made printing extremely simple. The properties and methods you learned in this chapter show how to manipulate the printer object. This chapter also showed you how to do some more complicated printer manipulation by using the PCL codes built into the printer. This enables you to extend the functionality of your programs to manipulate the printer in ways not possible through Visual Basic.

10

Writing Resource Files

Resource files enable you to include in your Visual Basic project resources such as bitmaps, strings, and cursors. The advantage of this is, for example, if you wanted to use many bitmaps in your project, you have one of three choices available:

- You can place hidden picture boxes on your form containing bitmaps and copy them where they need to be on your form at runtime. This is a fast option, but uses many system resources.
- You can load them at runtime using the `LoadPicture` function. This is a very slow option to use and is not recommended.
- You can include a precompiled resource file (as shown in this chapter). This is usually the best option because it is fast and requires little system resources.

Including resource files makes smaller applications because these resources can be loaded at runtime. One of the most popular things to do with a resource file is to localize your application, which means that you can display different language settings depending on where your application is distributed.

In fact, Visual Basic can use the following types of data within a resource file; however, each of the types of data can be a maximum of 64KB:

- Cursor resource
- Bitmap resource
- Icon resource
- Menu resource
- Dialog box
- String resource
- Font directory resource
- Font resource
- Accelerator table
- User-defined resource
- Group cursor
- Group icon

You must create the resource file using a compiler, such as Visual C++ 4.0. The use of this compiler is shown in this chapter, as well as a previous version that many people still use, version 2.0. The compiler will take the resources you've defined and generate a `*.RES` file. You can then add this `*.RES` file to your Visual Basic project.

Visual C++ Version 4.0

Microsoft has made great strides in its C++ compilers. In version 4.0 (and greater), creating a resource file is extremely easy. Suppose you were to create a resource file with three bitmaps, colored red, blue, and green. Then you wanted to load this resource file into Visual Basic and access the bitmaps. Please note that in Visual C++ 4.0, you can only create 32-bit resource files. To create a 16-bit resource file for Visual Basic 4.0, you need to use Visual C++ 2.0.

The example resources shown for Visual C++ 4.0 in this chapter are taken from Chapter 35, "Developing a CD Player Application." Also, the resource file and related files are stored on the CD accompanying this book in the `\CD` subdirectory.

The first thing to do is to start up Visual C++ 4.0. The Integrated Design Environment (IDE) in the Developer Studio looks like Figure 10.1. The Developer Studio is an environment designed by Microsoft to give a common look and feel to all of its visual tools, such as Visual C++, Visual Basic, and Visual FoxPro.

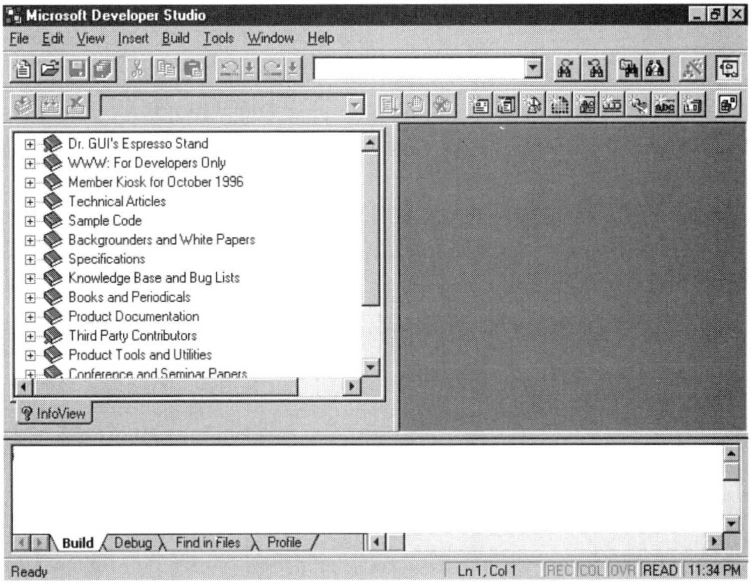

FIGURE 10.1.
The Visual C++ version 4.0 IDE.

Open a new project by selecting File | New. This will bring up the New dialog box, in which you can select the type of file to create. Figure 10.2 shows what this dialog box looks like.

Select the Resource Script option and click OK. Then select Insert | Resource. This will bring up the Insert Resource dialog box shown in Figure 10.3.

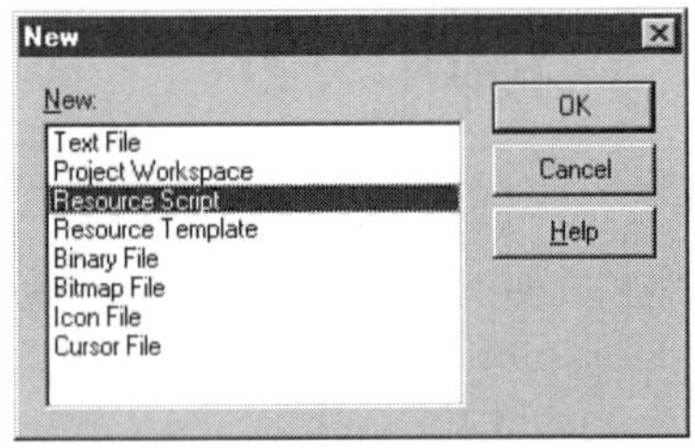

FIGURE 10.2.
The New dialog box.

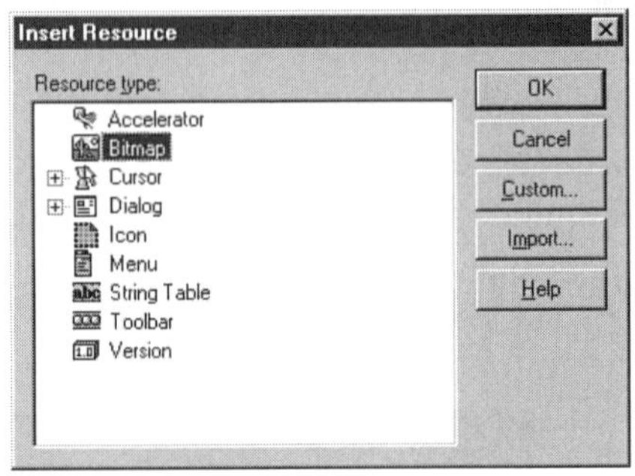

FIGURE 10.3.
The Insert Resource dialog box.

Choose the type of resource to add. Suppose you wanted to create a resource file of bitmaps. Select the Bitmap option and click OK. This will bring up a window to enable you to start drawing your bitmap. Figure 10.4 shows a sample bitmap.

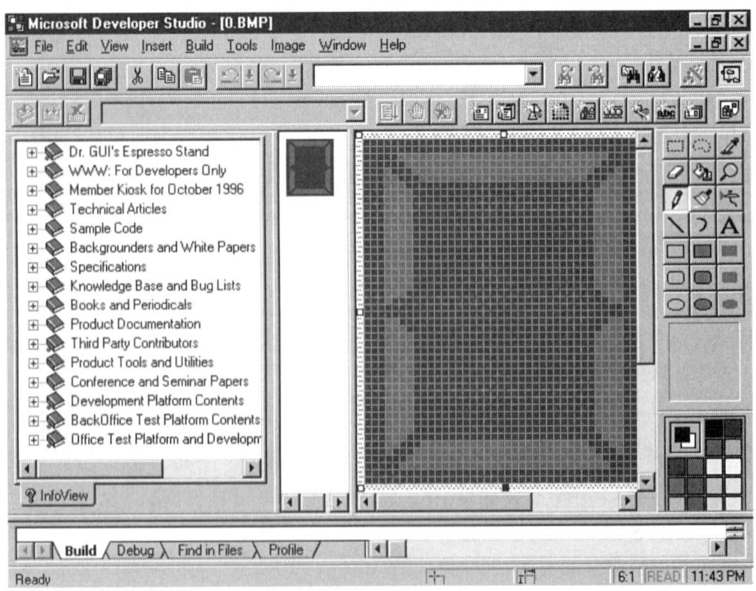

FIGURE 10.4.
The bitmap resource drawn in the resource editor.

After you have drawn your resource, close the editor window. You next need to change the resource ID. This ID is how you will refer to your bitmap in code. You might want to use a scheme so that referring to the resource in code will be easy. For example, if you had bitmaps from 0 to 9, you probably want to name the resources something like 100 to 109. Then, if you apply other colors to the same numeric characters, you could use, for example, 200 to 209.

To rename the default resource ID, select Edit | Properties to bring up the Bitmap Properties dialog box shown in Figure 10.5. Change the name of the resource ID and press Enter.

FIGURE 10.5.
The Resource tab of the Bitmap Properties dialog box.

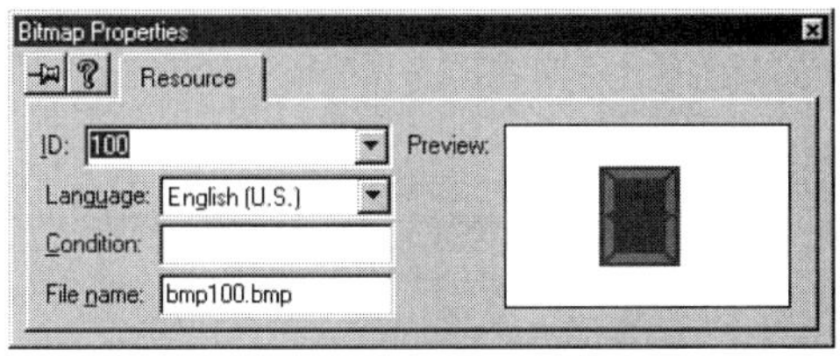

Continue drawing and naming your resources. When you are finished, you will have a screen that looks something like the one in Figure 10.6.

FIGURE 10.6.
The finished resource.

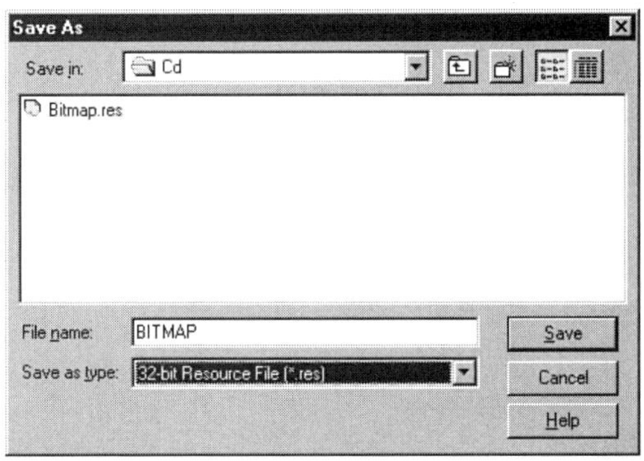

Visual Basic needs a file with a `*.RES` extension. To create this file, simply select File | Save As, and then select the 32-bit Resource File option. This is shown in Figure 10.7.

If you wanted to localize your application, you could also do so with a resource file. To do this, select Insert | Resource and choose String Table. This will enable you to keep a table of strings used for, among other things, error messages. You must, again, come up with some scheme to identify the strings. For example, if you had less than 100 strings, English could be the strings in the 100 series, German in the 200 series, and Spanish in the 300 series. That would enable you to create a string resource like the one shown in Figure 10.8. The resources are shown on the right side of the screen, and each string resource has a corresponding value for the string. These values are how you will refer to the string in code. To change the properties of the string, select Edit | Properties. To add a new string, select Insert | New String.

FIGURE 10.7.
The Save As dialog box.

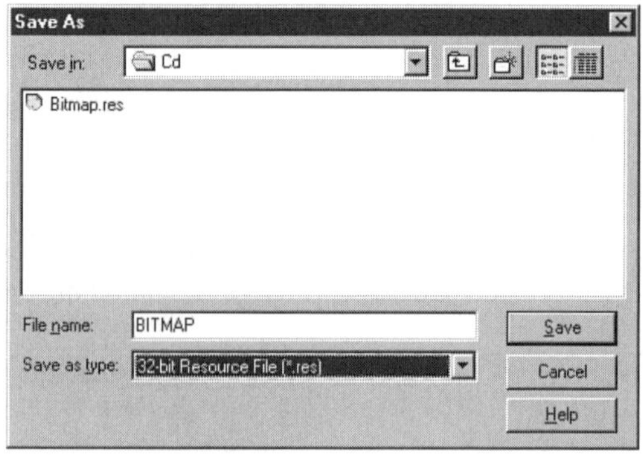

FIGURE 10.8.
Localization string table.

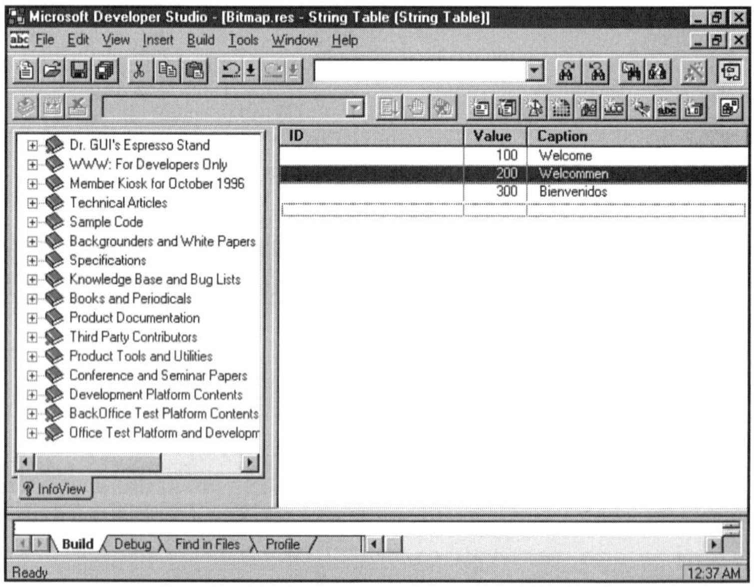

Visual C++ Version 2.0

You will need to use Visual C++ version 2.0 if you need to create a 16-bit resource file for use with Visual Basic 4.0. This section is included in this chapter for backward compatibility and to make the chapter more complete. Creating a resource file in Visual C++ version 2.0 is a bit harder than in version 4.0, but it is still easier than earlier versions. It used to be that you needed many files just to compile the resource file. These files included a `.C` file, an `.RC` resource file, a `.DEF` definition file, and a `.MAK` project file. Version 2.0 almost walks you through the process if you want to create a resource file. However, to create a resource file, you must create a resource DLL. During the process of creating a resource DLL in version 2.0, a resource file (with a `.RES` extension) is automatically generated.

The first step in creating a resource DLL is to create the individual resources. You do this by opening Visual C++ version 2.0 and selecting File | New. Select the Resource Script option. Figure 10.9 shows what Visual C++ looks like after you select these options.

FIGURE 10.9.

A sample resource file with no resources added.

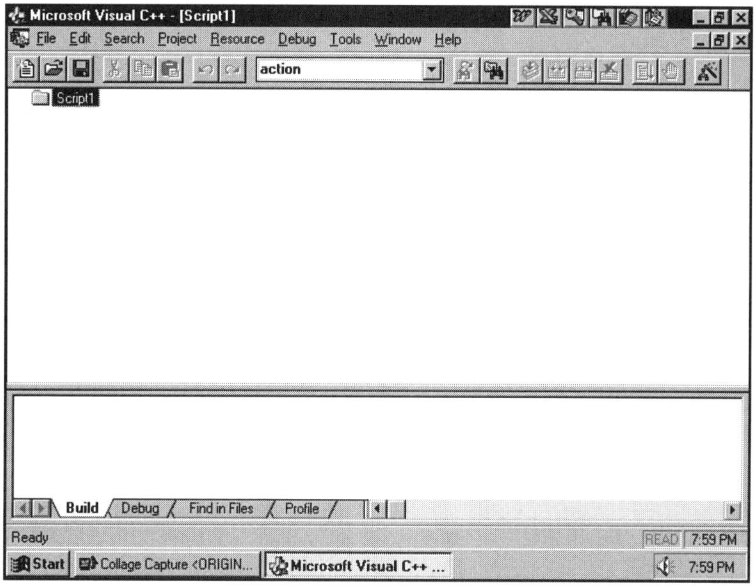

To create a new resource, such as a bitmap, select Resource | New, and pick the type of resource you want to create. If you want to add a bitmap resource, select Bitmap. This invokes an editor that enables you to edit the bitmap.

Use the toolbox to select colors and tools to create the bitmap. After you create the bitmap, you must name it as you call it from Visual Basic. For example, if you create a bitmap of the outside of a house, you might call it `HOUSE_EXTERNAL`. To assign the name of the bitmap, first close the bitmap by either double-clicking the system menu, or by selecting the right mouse button and selecting the Properties option. Of the two system menus in the upper-left corner, it is the lower one. You see a list of the different resources in your resource file. Change the name of the bitmap from whatever the default is to the name that you will refer to from Visual Basic. Note that unless you are using a previous version of Visual Basic, you do not have to place the name of the bitmap in quotes because you will not refer to the bitmap by this name. You will refer to the name specified in the `.H` file generated by Visual C++.

Continue creating bitmaps, icons, cursors, and so on, as described earlier. After you have created all desired resources, save the file by using File | Save. This saves a resource file with an `.RC` file extension. This resource file will be used by the compiler to create the resource DLL.

Figure 10.10 lists what the resource script looks like after resources have been created.

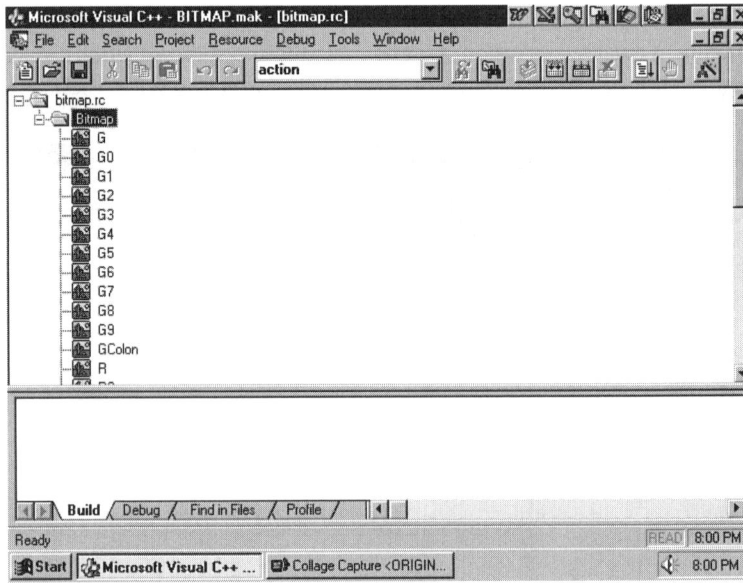

FIGURE 10.10.
A sample resource file with resources added.

Next, you must create a project with which to control how the resource is created. You do this by selecting File | New. From the list of options, select Project. You will be asked "Do you want to close all document windows?". Select Yes. A New Project dialog box will be presented. Figure 10.11 shows what this dialog box looks like.

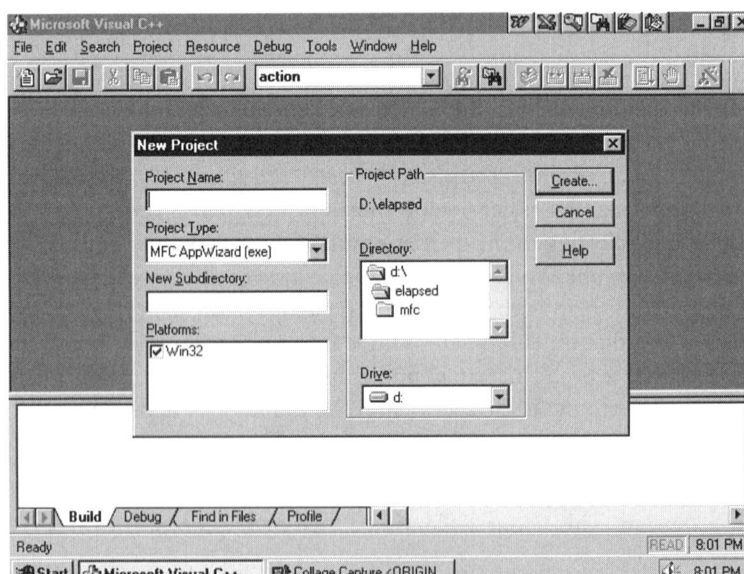

FIGURE 10.11.
The New Project dialog box.

Type the name of your new project. The name can be only eight characters because this will become the base name of the target files as well. Also, select from the pick list the type of project you are trying to create. Select Dynamic-link Library. Also select the target directory for your source files, and click the Create button. This opens another dialog box, labeled Project Files. You need to add the resource file created in the earlier step.

There is only one more step to follow before you are ready to compile the file. Because this is a resource-only DLL, you must select a link option that is not set by default. To do this, select Project | Settings. This will bring up a dialog box that enables you to change many settings for your project. Figure 10.12 shows what this dialog box looks like.

FIGURE 10.12.
The Project Settings dialog box.

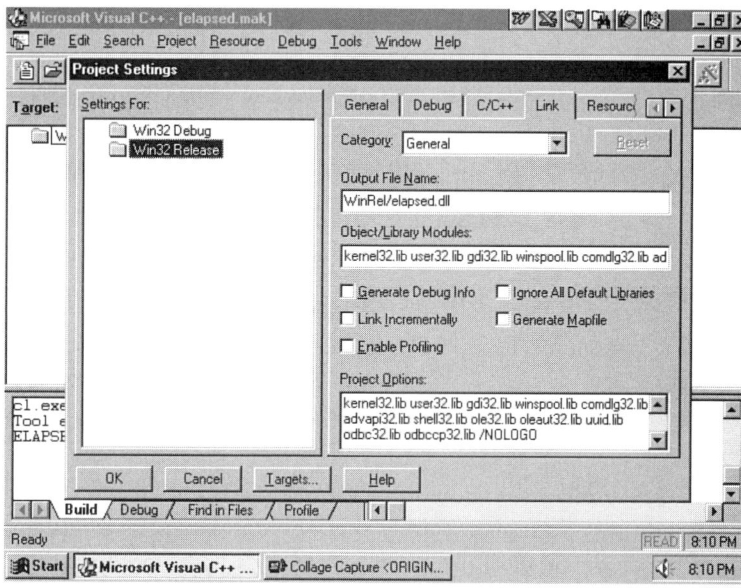

Select the Link tab. For the purposes of this lesson, you will be building a DLL without debug information. Therefore, click the Win32Release option, and then click in the Project Options text box region. Make sure you go to the end of the text box with the cursor. Most likely, the text box lists text beyond the visible region. Type `/NOENTRY` and click OK. Make sure to include the slash. Figure 10.13 shows how the Project Settings dialog box looks after you make these changes.

You are now ready to compile the DLL. Make sure to select the Win32 Release Target option. To start compiling, simply select Project | Rebuild All. When finished, you will have a DLL file that you can use in your Visual Basic projects.

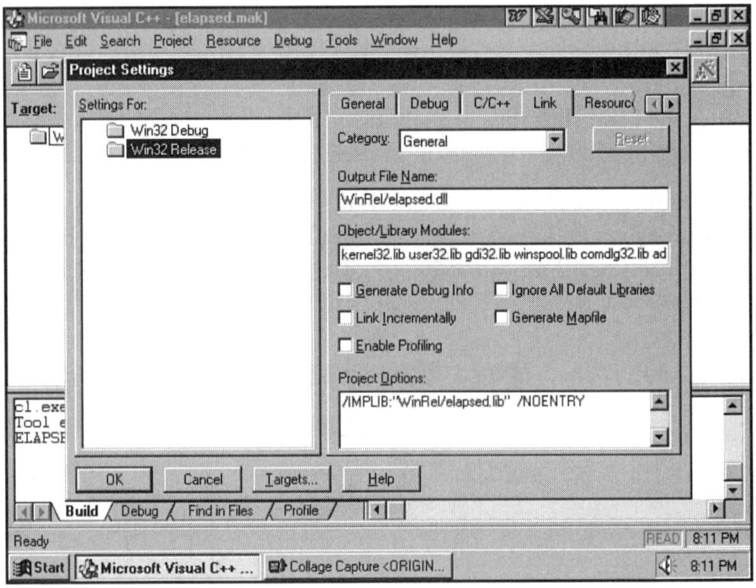

FIGURE 10.13.
The Project Settings dialog box after making changes.

Implementing a Resource File

To include a resource file in your application, select File | Add File, and select the resource file you just created. You can use only one resource file in a Visual Basic project. If you need to include more than one, you must instead create one resource file with all the resources necessary.

After you have added the resource file to the project, you must access these resources individually. To do this, you must identify them by number. If you created the resource file with Visual C++ 4.0, you must use the resource ID that you specified. If you created the resource file with Visual C++ 2.0, you must specify the numbers that are generated automatically when you compile the resource. The numbers are listed in a file with a `.H` extension. These are compiled with the resource file.

TRIED AND TRUE

Even though the `.H` file is generated automatically, you can actually change the resource IDs assigned and recompile. The compiler will only add new resources, not change the IDs of existing resources.

Listing 10.1 shows the resource IDs that were manually changed and recompiled into a resource DLL for Visual C++ version 2.0 only.

Listing 10.1. Manually changed .H file listing for Visual C++ version 2.0.

```
//{{NO_DEPENDENCIES}}
// Microsoft Visual C++ generated include file.
// Used by bitmap.rc
//
#define G0                              100
#define G1                              101
#define G2                              102
#define G3                              103
#define G4                              104
#define G5                              105
#define G6                              106
#define G7                              107
#define G8                              108
#define G9                              109
#define G                               110
#define GColon                          111
#define R0                              200
#define R1                              201
#define R2                              202
#define R3                              203
#define R4                              204
#define R5                              205
#define R6                              206
#define R7                              207
#define R8                              208
#define R9                              209
#define R                               100
#define RColon                          211
#define Y0                              300
#define Y1                              301
#define Y2                              302
#define Y3                              303
#define Y4                              304
#define Y5                              305
#define Y6                              306
#define Y7                              307
#define Y8                              308
#define Y9                              309
#define Y                               310
#define YColon                          311
```

The name just after the `#define` statement is the name of the resource inside the `.RES` file. The number all the way to the right of the line is the resource ID used inside Visual Basic.

The resource file is now ready for use. There are three functions available in Visual Basic to access resource files:

- `LoadResPicture`: Loads a picture resource (bitmap, icon, or cursor)
- `LoadResString`: Loads a string table resource
- `LoadResData`: Loads miscellaneous resource types based on the table listed early in this chapter, such as fonts and accelerator tables

Suppose you wanted to load a picture box on a form with a resource ID of 101. You could do that with this line of code:

```
Picture1.Picture = LoadResPicture(101,0)
```

`LoadResPicture` takes two arguments. The first is the resource ID, and the second is the type of resource, as follows:

- 0—Bitmap
- 1—Icon
- 2—Cursor

You could use the line of code listed previously to possibly change the color based on certain conditions. In this case, you would only need to change the 101 resource to 102 or 103. You could also do this in a variable or loop.

Because the resource file created uses three different colors—green, red, and yellow—each is identified in its own series of numbers. The green bitmaps are in the 100 series, the red bitmaps are in the 200 series, and the yellow bitmaps are in the 300 series. This allows for a mathematical calculation of which resource to use. Each of the bitmaps in each series is the same as the other two series, only the color is different. Therefore, for each color you want, you simply add a factor number to the number represented by each bitmap.

For example, if you wanted to display a green 1, you add the green factor of 100 to the number desired, 1. The result is 101. If you wanted to display a yellow 5, you add the yellow factor of 300 to the number desired, 5. The result is 305. This is what is done in the user-defined function called `FindCorrectBitmap()` in Chapter 35.

Implementing a string table resource is also very easy. You can show the English version of the first string by using the line

```
MsgBox LoadResString(100)
```

It's really that simple. Then, by adding the appropriate factor to the ID, you can display the same message for another language.

Summary

Resource files are a great addition to Visual Basic. They started with version 4.0. Resource files enable you to quickly manipulate images, strings, and other data within your programs. The most common uses for resource files are for localizing applications for use with other countries and for images. Using resource files for images is a very fast and efficient way to use images in your application without needing to load the images from disk. It also frees you from having to distribute the images.

11

Multimedia

Multimedia is becoming more and more of a mainstream technology. It enables the PC to interact with many different types of media. This media can be CD-ROM, audio, video, a combination of these, or even specialized media created by third-party vendors. This technology can greatly enhance an individual's productivity, enjoyment, and knowledge.

Multimedia and Visual Basic

You can access multimedia devices in one of two ways in Visual Basic. The first is through Windows API functions. There are many functions in the Windows API that enable access and control of multimedia devices. The other way is through the Multimedia Control Interface (MCI) control that comes with Visual Basic. This control is really a nice interface to the Windows API functions. You access properties of the control, and the control makes the appropriate Windows API function calls. The MCI control is a very good way to access the API functions, and as such, is the main focus of this chapter.

CROSS REFERENCE

If you want to experiment with the API functions, refer to Chapter 13, "Using the WIN32 API," for more information.

The MCI Control

The Multimedia Control Interface (MCI) control enables you to click on the buttons on the control itself (if it is visible and enabled) or to hide the control and access it only in code, allowing you to design a custom interface.

CROSS REFERENCE

The application in Chapter 35, "Developing a CD Player Application," uses the buttons on the control itself. In this application, you will see the MCI control in action.

About the MCI Control

The MCI control is used as the interface to the Microsoft multimedia functions built into Windows. It has many properties that greatly simplify using multimedia. These properties are listed in Table 11.1.

Table 11.1. MCI control unique properties.

Property	*Datatype*	*Description*
`AutoEnable`	Integer(Boolean)	Automatically enables the appropriate buttons when a CD or file is ready to play
`BackEnabled`	Integer(Boolean)	Enables the appropriate button
`EjectEnabled`	Integer(Boolean)	Enables the appropriate button
`NextEnabled`	Integer(Boolean)	Enables the appropriate button
`PauseEnabled`	Integer(Boolean)	Enables the appropriate button
`PlayEnabled`	Integer(Boolean)	Enables the appropriate button
`PrevEnabled`	Integer(Boolean)	Enables the appropriate button
`RecordEnabled`	Integer(Boolean)	Enables the appropriate button
`StepEnabled`	Integer(Boolean)	Enables the appropriate button
`StopEnabled`	Integer(Boolean)	Enables the appropriate button
`BackVisible`	Integer(Boolean)	Makes the appropriate button visible
`EjectVisible`	Integer(Boolean)	Makes the appropriate button visible
`NextVisible`	Integer(Boolean)	Makes the appropriate button visible
`PauseVisible`	Integer(Boolean)	Makes the appropriate button visible
`PlayVisible`	Integer(Boolean)	Makes the appropriate button visible
`PrevVisible`	Integer(Boolean)	Makes the appropriate button visible
`RecordVisible`	Integer(Boolean)	Makes the appropriate button visible
`StepVisible`	Integer(Boolean)	Makes the appropriate button visible
`StopVisible`	Integer(Boolean)	Makes the appropriate button visible
`CanEject`	Integer(Boolean)	`True` if media type can eject
`CanPlay`	Integer(Boolean)	`True` if media type can play
`CanRecord`	Integer(Boolean)	`True` if media type can record
`CanStep`	Integer(Boolean)	`True` if media type can step one frame at a time
`Command`	String	Specifies which MCI command to execute
`DeviceID`	Integer	ID of the currently open device
`DeviceType`	String	Specifies type of media to play
`Error`	Integer	Last error from MCI control
`ErrorMessage`	String	Message of last error from MCI control
`FileName`	String	Filename to play if media is file based
`Frames`	Long	Number of frames for `STEP` command to skip

continues

Table 11.1. continued

Property	*Datatype*	*Description*
`From`	Long	Specifies starting point of playing sequence
`hWndDisplay`	Integer	Handle of display in Visual Basic for video files
`Length`	Long	Length of media
`Mode`	Long	Mode of open MCI device
`Notify`	Integer(Boolean)	`True` if MCI uses notification services
`NotifyMessage`	String	Message from the `Done` event if `Notify` is `True`
`NotifyValue`	Integer	Value of result from last MCI command
`Orientation`	Integer	0 for horizontal, 1 for vertical
`Position`	Long	Current position of MCI control
`RecordMode`	Integer	0–Insert, 1–Overwrite
`Shareable`	Integer(Boolean)	`True` if another program can share MCI device
`Silent`	Integer(Boolean)	`True` if sound is off
`Start`	Long	Starting position of current media
`TimeFormat`	Long	Time reporting format
`To`	Long	Specifies ending point of playing sequence
`Track`	Long	Track for use with `TrackLength` and `TrackPosition`
`TrackLength`	Long	Length of track in `Track` property
`TrackPosition`	Long	Position of track in `Track` property
`Tracks`	Long	Number of tracks in media
`UpdateInterval`	Integer	Number of milliseconds between `StatusUpdate` events
`UsesWindows`	Integer(Boolean)	`True` if media type uses a window for output
`Wait`	Integer(Boolean)	`True` if MCI completes command before returning control

One nice thing about the control is that it automatically detects when a CD-ROM is in the drive and enables the appropriate buttons, if the `AutoEnable` property is set to `True`. The individual elements of the control (such as play, stop, and so on) are automatically enabled based on additional properties you can set. For example, if you set the `PlayEnabled` property to `False`, then even if the CD-ROM is in the drive, the play button is not enabled. You can even hide buttons that you don't ever want to be enabled. For example, you can hide the Forward and Back buttons if you want. You do this by setting the appropriate `Visible` property to `False`.

For example, if you didn't want the Back button to be visible, you can set the property with the following code, where *control* is the name of your control:

```
control.BackVisible = False
```

Refer to Table 11.1 for a listing of all the properties that are unique to the MCI control. It does not list the properties that are common, such as `Name`, `Height`, and so on.

The key to effectively using the MCI control is to learn how the `StatusUpdate` event works. The `StatusUpdate` event is generated by the control itself. The event is generated at a certain interval that you can set using the `UpdateInterval` property. As you would with the Visual Basic Timer control, you set the interval for the number of milliseconds before the next event is generated. For example, if you want the event to be generated every second, you set the `UpdateInterval` property to `1000`.

You need to understand the `UpdateInterval` property because it is how you receive information from the control to notify the user of certain things. For example, suppose you want to provide a visual feedback to the user about how many seconds have passed since a musical CD has been playing. You update the display on the screen by using the `StatusUpdate` event. If you set the `UpdateInterval` property to `1000`, as long as you put code in the `StatusUpdate` event to find out what the current playing time is, you know that your display will be updated every second.

The application in Chapter 35 uses the `StatusUpdate` event to update the display for the user in the manner described in the previous paragraph.

NOTE

Refer to the application in Chapter 35 to see how the `StatusUpdate` event works.

Using the MCI Control

After you load the MCI control into your project, place it on your form and size it according to your needs. Because the MCI control can access many different types of media, you must tell the control which type to use; you do this by accessing the `DeviceType` property, which accepts a String datatype. The possible device types are listed in Table 11.2.

Table 11.2. Possible values for the `DeviceType` property.

String	*Media Type*
`"AVIVideo"`	Audio Video Interleave (AVI) file
`"CDAudio"`	CD audio from a musical CD

continues

Table 11.2. continued

String	*Media Type*
`"DAT"`	Digital Audio Tape
`"DigitalVideo"`	Digital Video Files
`"MMMovie"`	Multimedia Movie file
`"Other"`	Undefined type
`"Overlay"`	Overlay image
`"Scanner"`	Scanner
`"Sequencer"`	Musical Instrument Digital Interface (MIDI) file
`"VCR"`	Video Cassette Recorder (VCR)
`"VideoDisc"`	Video Disc
`"WaveAudio"`	WAV audio file

In Windows 3.1, these device types had to be listed in the `SYSTEM.INI` file under the `[MCI]` section. In Windows 95 and Windows NT, they are listed in the Registry. They are listed in the `HKEY_LOCAL_MACHINE` hive, under the `System\Current Control Set\Control\Media Resources\mci` keys. All the listings under this key contain device types.

CROSS REFERENCE

For more information about the Registry, refer to Chapter 6, "The Registry."

You must install drivers in the "Multimedia" section of the Control Panel. By default, you will almost certainly have the appropriate drivers installed.

TRIED AND TRUE

It is possible for the MCI control not to become enabled, without any error notification, just because the driver specified has been physically deleted from the disk.

NOTE

It is possible to use a media type not listed in Table 11.2 as long as it points to a valid driver in the Registry. This allows a third-party provider to construct a driver to work with the MCI control.

After you select the `DeviceType`, you must then open the device. Opening the device is necessary; it tells the device to be ready to begin accessing the type of media specified. You do this by using the `OPEN` command, which has the following syntax, where *`control`* is the name of your MCI control:

```
control.Command = "Open"
```

Here are the commands that can be used with the MCI control:

- `Open`
- `Close`
- `Play`
- `Pause`
- `Stop`
- `Back`
- `Step`
- `Prev`
- `Next`
- `Seek`
- `Record`
- `Eject`
- `Sound`
- `Save`

Typically, the `OPEN` command is used in conjunction with other properties. For example, consider these lines of code, using an MCI control with the `Name` property set to `mmControl`:

```
mmControl.Notify = False
mmControl.Wait = True
mmControl.Shareable = False
mmControl.Command = "Open"
```

If the `Notify` property is set to `True`, the control generates the `Done` event after a command is issued. In most applications, the `Notify` property will not be used, so here it is set to `False`. The `Wait` property is used to determine how your program resumes control after accessing the multimedia device. If the `Wait` property is set to `False`, the MCI control will not wait for the specified media to finish playing before returning control. If the `Wait` property is set to `True`, program control will not return to your program until the specified media is finished playing. The `Shareable` property determines whether another program will be allowed to share the MCI device. This property is set to `True` if it is allowed and `False` if it is not. The values of these properties may change in your programs, but it is important to know that if you are going to set these values, they must be set before issuing the `OPEN` command.

The preceding steps are true for all types of media. The next step depends on a specific type of media. It is used to assign the filename. It is dependent because not all media types accept a filename; for example, if you are playing an audio CD, it does not have a filename. If you are playing a WAV audio file, it has a filename. Otherwise, the MCI control will not know which file to play. If you want to set the filename, use the `FileName` property using the following syntax, where *`control`* is the name of your MCI control, and *`fname`* is the string containing the filename to play:

```
control.FileName = fname
```

After you set the filename, if appropriate, you are ready to play. You start playing the desired media type by issuing the `PLAY` command. Use this syntax, where *`control`* is the name of your MCI control:

```
control.Command = "Play"
```

From this point, you can issue any other commands at your leisure, such as `PAUSE` and `STOP`. To issue these commands, use the syntax listed earlier with the `PLAY` command. For a listing of possible commands, refer to Table 11.1.

When you are finished playing the desired media type, you must close the device for the same reason you must close a Visual Basic file after it is opened: to conserve resources. You can close the device by issuing the `CLOSE` command—using the preceding syntax for the `PLAY` command.

Audio CDs

Playing audio CDs is probably one of the most common uses of multimedia; it enables you to work on your PC while you listen to music from your CD-ROM. All CD-ROM drives have the capability to play music, provided you have a working audio card in your PC connected to speakers or stereo. Windows 95 provides a CD player, but the following sections describe how you can write one yourself.

CROSS REFERENCE

For more information about writing the CD player application, refer to Chapter 35.

You can write a program to control the audio CD by using Visual Basic and the MCI control. Writing this program employs the methods described earlier, but there are some additional concerns when writing the user interface for your program. If you are going to allow the user only to play, stop, and skip through the tracks, the MCI control does this automatically by issuing the appropriate commands. Refer to the previous discussion and Table 11.1 for more information about how to do this. However, if you are going to provide any visual feedback to the user (as any good application does), this becomes a little more difficult.

The `StatusUpdate` event is generated at an interval that is set with the `UpdateInterval` property. When this event is generated, you must query the control to find out some information about the position of the CD. For example, you must find out how far along the CD is inside the current track and how much time has elapsed since the beginning of the disc.

NOTE

The *position* of the CD refers to the amount of time that has elapsed. The position is measured with respect to time, not distance; it is not the physical position of the CD. The position reports time not in a HH:MM:SS format, but in a packed integer format. Refer to the section "Decoding a Packed Integer," later in this chapter, for more information.

You can determine the track time of any track, not necessarily the currently playing track. To do this, you specify which track you want information about by using the `Track` property. Then, you can query the `TrackLength` property to find out the length of the track. Query the `TrackPosition` property to determine what position the CD is currently in.

When you use any of the time-related properties of the MCI control, they need to be decoded because they are in a packed integer format. To do this, shift the bits by a predetermined number, based on the precision of the integer you are trying to decode. By doing this, you can determine the current track time, the current track length, and the total length of the disc.

Decoding a Packed Integer

The MCI control uses *packed integers* to return data from the control. A packed integer makes the data smaller for the control to handle, but it's a pain for programmers! You must decode the integer value to separate it into its usable parts, which are stored in terms of bytes. Depending on the format set with the `TimeFormat` property, the value stored in each byte can be different. For example, if the `TimeFormat` property is set to `2`, the value of byte position 1 is minutes, byte position 2 is seconds, byte position 3 is frames, and byte position 4 is unused. If you change the `TimeFormat` property, the values represented in these bytes will be different.

The technique is to apply bitwise operators to separate the individual byte values stored in the packed integer. The best way to show how this is done is to use a code fragment from the `mmControl_StatusUpdate()` event procedure in Chapter 35. It is used to decode and display the integer value coming from the MCI control. Consider the following, which is looking for the minutes and seconds for the current track:

```
x% = ((MMControl.Position) And &HFF00&) \ &H100
x1% = ((MMControl.Position) And &HFF0000) \ &H10000
```

The `TimeFormat` property is set to `10`. Therefore, you need the values in byte positions 2 (minutes) and 3 (seconds). The first line in this code extracts byte position 2. The second extracts position 3.

This syntax might be a little confusing to some programmers. The easiest way to understand it is to take a specific example. Suppose the position property returned the packed integer value 403308801. This will evaluate to one minute and ten seconds. Let's see why. The first line shows that an `AND` operation is performed with the packed integer and `&HFF00&`. The `&HFF00&` part of the expression evaluates to 65280. Therefore, a bitwise operation is performed between the packed integer and 65280. Then the result is divided by `&H100`, which is 256. The result is 1. The second line shows that an `AND` operation is performed with the packed integer and `&HFF0000&`. The `&HFF0000&` part of the expression evaluates to 16711680. Therefore, a bitwise operation is performed between the packed integer and 16711680. Then the result is divided by `&H100`, which is 65536. The result is 10.

If you wanted to decode the first byte, you would simply perform an `AND` operation on the packed integer with the value 256. You'll notice that each hexadecimal value in the equation is a multiple of 256.

Other Media Types

Other media types are perhaps easier to deal with than the `CDAudio` media type because you do not have to update the screen on a real-time basis. If you want to play a WAV audio file, simply play it. You do not necessarily have to update a display with the elapsed time. This is why everything but audio CDs are grouped into this "Other Media Types" category.

Playing Audio Files

Playing audio files does not require any special techniques as does playing CD information. You must specify the media type by using the `DeviceType` property, as described earlier. You select the audio file by using the standard common dialog control. If you want to play a WAV file, the device type is set by using the following code:

```
control.DeviceType = "WaveAudio"
```

If you want to play a MIDI file, you set the device type by using this code:

```
control.DeviceType = "Sequencer"
```

In both cases, *`control`* is the name of the MCI control in your application.

After the device is opened, you can play your file. For more information about opening the device, see the previous section titled "Using the MCI Control."

Playing Video Files

Playing video files is basically the same as playing audio files, with one exception: The video must be played in some window. The easiest way to play video is to use the standard picture box in Visual Basic. The picture box is well adapted to this, mainly because it handles pictures and provides a handle, which is needed by the MCI control. That's how the MCI control knows where to play the video file.

You can obtain the handle by using the following line, where *`pictControl`* is the name of the Visual Basic picture box to use, and *`control`* is the name of the MCI control in your application:

```
control.hWndDisplay = pictControl.hWnd
```

> **NOTE**
>
> You can play the video file on any window that has the capability of playing a video file, as long as you can obtain its handle. You can get the handle of any window by using the Windows API function `FindWindowA()`. Refer to Chapter 13 for more information on API functions.

Automatically Determining Device Type

If you need to account for all types of devices that your application supports, you can do it with a simple `Select Case` statement. This means you can use a common dialog box to select a filename. You then can determine within your programs what `DeviceType` to select based on the extension of the file. For example, if you are trying to play a wave audio file, use the file extension `.WAV`. If you need to select the appropriate `DeviceType` based on a file extension, and your application supports only files with the extension `.WAV`, `.MID`, `.AVI`, or `.MMM`, you can incorporate code like this:

```
Select Case UCase$((Right$(cmDialog.FileName, 3)))
    Case "WAV":
        'set device type
        Control.DeviceType = "WaveAudio"
    Case "MID":
        'set device type
        Control.DeviceType = "Sequencer"
    Case "AVI":
        'set device type
        Control.DeviceType = "AVIVideo"
        'assign handle of window to display video
        Control.hWndDisplay = pictControl.hWnd
    Case "MMM":
        'set device type
        Control.DeviceType = "MMMovie"
        'assign handle of window to display movie
```

```
        Control.hWndDisplay = pictControl.hWnd
    Case Else:
        'construct message for bad file type
        m$ = "Cannot recognize file type!" + Chr$(13)
        m$ = m$ + "It must be (*.WAV),(*.MID),(*.AVI),(*.MMM)"
        MsgBox m$
End Select
```

Here, `cmDialog` is the control name of your common dialog control, and `control` is the name of your MCI control. `pictControl` is the name of the picture box that plays the video file.

MCI Constants

To help you deal with using the MCI control, sometimes it is helpful not to have to look up constants to use with the control. Therefore, Table 11.3 shows the MCI-related constants.

Table 11.3. MCI-related constants.

Constant	*Description*	*Value*
`mciModeNotOpen`	Device not open	524
`mciModeStop`	Device stop	525
`mciModePlay`	Device play	526
`mciModeRecord`	Device record	527
`mciModeSeek`	Device seek	528
`mciModePause`	Device pause	529
`mciModeReady`	Device ready	530
`mciNotifySuccessful`	Command completed successfully	1
`mciNotifySuperseded`	Command superseded by another command	2
`mciAborted`	Command aborted by user	4
`mciFailure`	Command failed	8
`mciOrientHorz`	Buttons arranged horizontally	0
`mciOrientVert`	Buttons arranged vertically	1
`mciRecordInsert`	Insert recording mode	0
`mciRecordOverwrite`	Overwrite recording mode	1
`mciFormatMilliseconds`	Milliseconds format	0
`mciFormatHms`	Hours, minutes, and seconds format	1
`mciFormatMsf`	Minutes, seconds, and frames format	2
`mciFormatFrames`	Frames format	3

Constant	Description	Value
`mciFormatSmpte24`	24-frame SMPTE format	4
`mciFormatSmpte25`	25-frame SMPTE format	5
`mciFormatSmpte30`	30-frame SMPTE format	6
`mciFormatSmpte30Drop`	30-drop-frame SMPTE format	7
`mciFormatBytes`	Bytes format	8
`mciFormatSamples`	Samples format	9
`mciFormatTmsf`	Tracks minutes, seconds, and frames format	10

Summary

Multimedia has been made very easy with the advent of the MCI control. It handles all of the complex functionality of multimedia. This chapter detailed the use of this control, as does the CD Player application shown in Chapter 35.

12

Dynamic Link Libraries

Dynamic Link Libraries (DLLs) play a very important part in Windows development and operation. Using Visual Basic 4.0, you could create OLE servers, but they were compiled into P-Code. P-Code requires that a runtime DLL be distributed with the DLL. If you wanted any other type of DLL, you had to create them in Visual C++ or some other language. In version 5.0, you can create truly compiled DLLs. Because most organizations need to create DLLs, they now can leverage the existing skill set, instead of needing to find C++ programmers.

A DLL is a library linked dynamically, as opposed to statically. A dynamically linked library does not need to exist when you compile the application. Also, it is not included into the application itself, as would be the case in a static library. A dynamically linked library, or DLL, makes it very easy to upgrade functionality without needing to recompile a complete application. It also lets the application be broken into smaller parts. A statically linked library is a library that is compiled into the application itself, thereby making the application larger. It also means that if a change is made in the library, the entire application needs to be recompiled.

DLLs are usually implemented as in-process components. This means that as they load, they are loaded into the same address space as the application that called them. There are two types of DLLs that you can create with Visual Basic: ActiveX DLLs and ActiveX Document DLLs. This chapter focuses on the ActiveX DLL because it is the type that is used most often.

The type of DLL that you can write in Visual Basic is implemented in the form of an ActiveX Code Object (formerly called an OLE Server). This means that you write objects that can expose properties, methods, and events. What you cannot do in Visual Basic is write a function or subroutine and call it as if it were a function or subroutine in a WIN32 API. You must use object variables and instantiate them.

To clarify, suppose you had a function called `CalcTime`. The only thing this function does is calculate the number of minutes between two times. You cannot write the function in Visual Basic and declare it like this:

```
Declare Function CalcTime Lib "XYZ.DLL" (ByVal sTime1 as String,
➥ByVal sTime2 as String) as Double
```

This is what I call an "API style" DLL, and it must be written in C++. This is discussed later in this chapter under the heading "API Style DLLs." You can write the DLL in Visual Basic, but you would have to write it as an object. Writing the DLL as an object is discussed briefly later in this chapter, but for more detailed information about creating objects, refer to Chapter 3, "Classes."

Declaring a Function from a DLL

To use a function from a DLL, you must declare the function so that Visual Basic knows where to find it, what parameters the function expects, and what the function returns. Declaring a function follows the general syntax

```
DECLARE FUNCTION function LIB "dll" [ALIAS "alias name"]([argument list])
➥ AS return type
```

where the following variables are used:

> `function`: The name of the DLL function used inside your Visual Basic code.
>
> `dll`: The name of the DLL file. Note that the name of the DLL is in quotes.
>
> `alias name`: Aliases are used only if the function name referenced inside Visual Basic code is different from the function name the DLL expects. If the alias name is omitted, Visual Basic expects the function name used inside the code to be the same name as the function inside the DLL itself. If you use an alias name, this is where you enter the name the DLL itself expects. Note that the name of the alias is in quotes.
>
> `argument list`: The names of the arguments passed into the function. If there are none, empty set parentheses are needed.
>
> `return type`: The datatype variable returned from the function.

You do not have to actually supply the return type or parameter type if the name of the function includes a Visual Basic datatype declaration character. For example, the following two declarations are equivalent:

```
Declare Function ShowCursor% Lib "User" (ByVal bShow%)
Declare Function ShowCursor Lib "User" (ByVal bShow%) As Integer
```

Likewise, these declarations are equivalent:

```
Declare Function ShowCursor% Lib "User" (ByVal bShow%)
Declare Function ShowCursor% Lib "User" (ByVal bShow As Integer)
```

Note that the percent (`%`) sign indicates that the function will return an integer. This performs the same declaration as if you declared the function as `As Integer`.

Declaring a Subroutine from a DLL

To declare a subroutine from a DLL, you must declare the subroutine so that Visual Basic knows where to find the subroutine and what parameters the subroutine expects. There is no return value from a subroutine. Declaring a subroutine follows the general syntax

```
DECLARE  SUB sub LIB "dll" [ALIAS "alias name"]([argument list])
```

where the following variables are used:

> `sub`: The name of the DLL routine used inside your Visual Basic code.
>
> `dll`: The name of the DLL file. Note that the name of the DLL is in quotes.
>
> `alias name`: Aliases are used only if the subroutine name referenced inside Visual Basic code is different from the subroutine name the DLL expects. If the alias name is

omitted, Visual Basic expects the subroutine name used inside the code to be the same name as the subroutine inside the DLL itself. If you use an alias name, this is where you enter the name the DLL itself expects. Note that the name of the alias is in quotes.

argument list: The name of the arguments passed into the function. If there are none, empty set parentheses are needed.

Passing Arguments

There are some considerations you need to keep in mind when you pass arguments. These considerations are discussed in the next few sections.

Passing By Value or By Reference

Visual Basic, by default, passes all parameters by reference. This means that the values of variables are not passed, but a 32-bit pointer to the variable is. This method is not always desirable. As a matter of fact, you find that most parameters passed into a DLL function or subroutine are passed by value. The only true exceptions are for strings, arrays, and user-defined types. Because variables default to being passed by reference, you must explicitly declare that the value is being passed by value with the keywords `By Val`. The following shows a fictitious declaration by reference:

```
Declare Function LoadCursorByID Lib "User" Alias "LoadCursor" (hInstance%,
➥lpCursorName&) As Integer
```

This is what the declaration looks like as declared by value:

```
Declare Function LoadCursorByID Lib "User" Alias "LoadCursor"
➥ (ByVal hInstance%,ByVal lpCursorName&) As Integer
```

NOTE

Generally, if you forget to declare the parameter type as `ByVal`, you get only a Bad DLL Calling Convention error. You can, however, get a General Protection Fault. The worst case scenario is that Windows locks up entirely. All these problems can be avoided by declaring your API functions correctly.

TRIED AND TRUE

As a general rule, if you are not sure whether to pass the variable by value or by reference, it is safer to pass by value. The worst that can happen is that an unexpected value is passed. If you blindly pass by reference, you can modify a value in memory that has nothing to do with your program. It's not advisable to blindly pass by value rather than by reference. You should first consult the documentation or Help file concerning the DLL you are trying to use.

New to Version 5.0

Passing Strings

Passing strings from Visual Basic to a Visual Basic DLL is generally not a problem. Visual Basic uses a string datatype, called a `BSTR`. This type of string contains a header, which specifies information about the string. Therefore, passing it either by value or by reference will generally not cause a problem. The problem occurs when you pass the string by reference to a DLL procedure not written in Visual Basic.

In this case, the DLL string datatype is called an `LPSTR`. It is a pointer to a null-terminated string. If you pass a string `ByVal` from Visual Basic, it will convert the string into the appropriate type. However, if you pass by reference from Visual Basic to a DLL written in C++, you might have Invalid Page Fault or General Protection Fault problems.

Function Pointers

Function pointers pass the address of a function that you write (a user-defined function) as an argument to a DLL procedure. This is a topic that is foreign to most Visual Basic programmers, but not to C++ programmers, primarily because Visual Basic programmers generally do not deal with pointers. The main advantage in doing this is that many other WIN32 API functions and DLL procedures can be accessed from Visual Basic that were not possible before.

The capability of Visual Basic version 5.0 to support function pointers is made possible through the use of the `AddressOf` keyword. It is used in the parameter, before the function name. It specifies to pass the address of the function (or subroutine) to the DLL procedure.

CROSS REFERENCE

Function pointers are discussed in much more detail in Chapter 13, "Using the WIN32 API."

Modeless Considerations

There is a point that is worth noting about modeless forms: A *modeless* form is a form (used as a dialog box) that enables the focus to be shifted to another form. This is the opposite of a modal form, which forces the user to respond before continuing. An in-process component written by Visual Basic that accesses a modeless component will not work correctly unless it internally communicates with the client's message loop.

Therefore, the communication link between the two processes must support this. At the time of this writing, there are only two Microsoft products that support the modeless form of communication with in-process components created in Visual Basic. They are any application created with Visual Basic 5.0 (including VBA 5.0) or later and Microsoft Office 97 or later.

For an in-process component, or DLL, to determine whether an application supports the display of a modeless form, there is a new property available in version 5.0. This property is called `NonModalAllowed`. It is a Boolean property that, if `True`, can display modeless forms. If it is `False`, it cannot.

Writing DLLs

As mentioned earlier, you can write DLLs in either Visual Basic or Visual C++. However, there is a distinct difference as to when each must be used. You can use Visual Basic only to create objects that must expose properties, methods, and events to achieve some function. You must use Visual C++ if you want to create a DLL that you can declare as an API function. Each is described in the following sections.

Code Components

Code components is the new term for the former OLE Server. These components can be written in Visual Basic and must expose properties, methods, and events. However, you do not necessarily need to expose all three. For example, suppose you wanted to create a DLL that you can write in Visual Basic. The only purpose for the DLL is to expose some functions. Functions are written in OLE Servers as `Public` functions. Therefore, suppose you wanted to use the scenario discussed earlier where the desired function returns the number of minutes elapsed between two supplied times. In a standard Visual Basic function in a BAS module, you would code it like this:

```
Public Function CalcTime(ByVal sTimeStart As String, ByVal sTimeEnd As String)
➥ As Double
   CalcTime = DateDiff("n", sTimeStart, sTimeEnd)
End Function
```

It's a very simple function that uses the `DateDiff` function to return the difference between the two times. However, you must now write this function so it is exposed to the outside world. To do this, you must create an ActiveX DLL project.

The first step is to open a new project. Do this by selecting the File | New Project menu option. This brings up a dialog box that enables you to select the type of project to create. Figure 12.1 shows what this dialog box looks like.

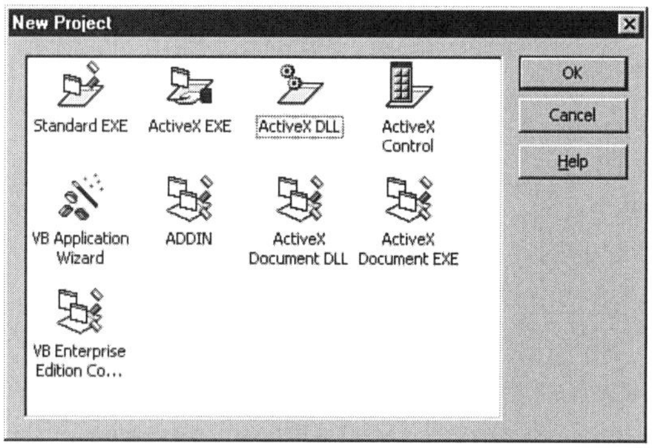

FIGURE 12.1.
Creating a new ActiveX DLL project.

This sets up a template for your ActiveX DLL. Notice that there is one class module created for you. You need to expose the function shown earlier. Therefore, simply place this code in the class module. Next, change the name of the class by clicking on the class module and pressing the F4 key, and then change the name to something such as `TimeFunctions`. In this way, you can create other related functions and place them in the same class module.

CROSS REFERENCE

For more information about creating properties, methods, and events, refer to Chapter 3, "Classes."

Compiling the DLL

Compiling the DLL is as easy as compiling any Visual Basic project. There are a couple of points worth mentioning. They are discussed in the following sections.

Base Addresses

In a 32-bit operating system, in-process components are shared between processes to ensure that resources are conserved. However, this is true only if the component can be loaded at its base address. Therefore, it is recommended that you alter the base addresses of your components.

To alter the base address, choose the Project | Properties menu option, which brings up a dialog box that contains four tabs. Choose the Compile tab. You'll notice a text box at the bottom labeled DLL Base Address, shown in Figure 12.2.

Notice that the default base address is `&H11000000`. If you do not change the base address, you risk your component's using more memory and taking more time to load. You can choose any address between `&H1000000` and `&H80000000`. These values are between 16MB and 2GB, inclusive. The only restriction is that the base address must be a multiple of 64KB.

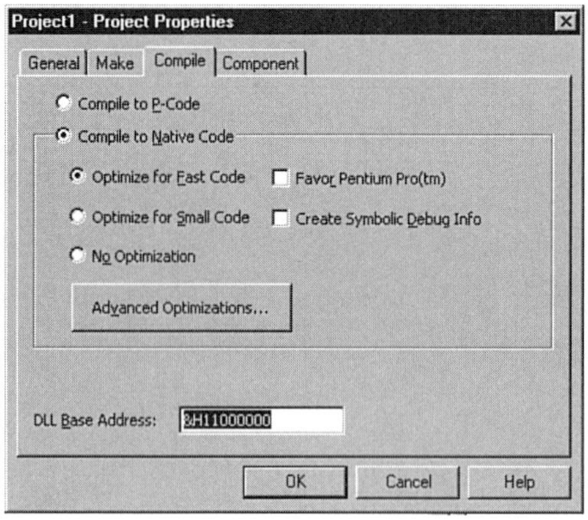

FIGURE 12.2.
Setting the DLL Base Address.

You might be wondering how to choose an address. You couldn't possibly keep track of all the addresses you've used and guarantee that other components don't use any one of those addresses. Therefore, follow Microsoft's lead and generate random numbers. This is actually how class IDs are generated in the Registry.

You can write a Visual Basic program to generate the random address. This program can be a stand-alone executable, or even an OLE Server application. You could also make this part of an add-in so developers can generate this number from a Visual Basic menu. Listing 12.1 shows a function that generates this base address value.

Listing 12.1. Code that generates base addresses at random.

```
Function Generate() As String
    'declare variables
    Dim dVal As Double
    Const STARTVALUE = &H1000000
    Const ENDVALUE = &H80000000
    Const BLOCKSIZE = &H10000

    'start random generator
    Randomize

    'generate random number within range
    dVal = Int((Val(ENDVALUE) - Val(STARTVALUE) + 1) * Rnd + Val(STARTVALUE))

    'test to see if this value is at the 64K boundary
    If dVal Mod Val(BLOCKSIZE) <> 0 Then
        'this is not at the 64K boundary
        dVal = dVal - (dVal Mod Val(BLOCKSIZE))
    End If

    'return hex string
    Generate = "&H" + Trim$(Hex$(dVal))
End Function
```

The code in Listing 12.1 generates a random number within the range of `&H1000000` and `&H80000000`. Then, it tests to see whether the number is at a 64KB boundary. The odds, of course, are that it is not. Therefore, the remainder over the lowest 64KB boundary is subtracted from the value to force it to be at the 64KB boundary.

NOTE

64KB is not the actual value tested. The hexadecimal number, `&H10000`, is actually 65536. Also, if you wanted to know if the hexadecimal number you generate is at the 64KB boundary, just look at the last four digits. They need to be all zeros for the hexadecimal number to be at the 64KB boundary.

Threads

Visual Basic in-process components use a concept called *apartment-model threading*. This provides synchronous access to objects. You can design your DLLs to use either one or multiple threads. However, if you use a single thread, the DLL will be considerably slower. Therefore, you can design your DLL so it uses multiple threads, but there are a couple considerations.

By default, DLLs are single threaded. Therefore, you must take explicit action if you want to make them multithreaded. You do this by first selecting the Project | Properties menu option, which brings up a dialog box that contains four tabs. Select the General tab. Figure 12.3 shows what this dialog box looks like.

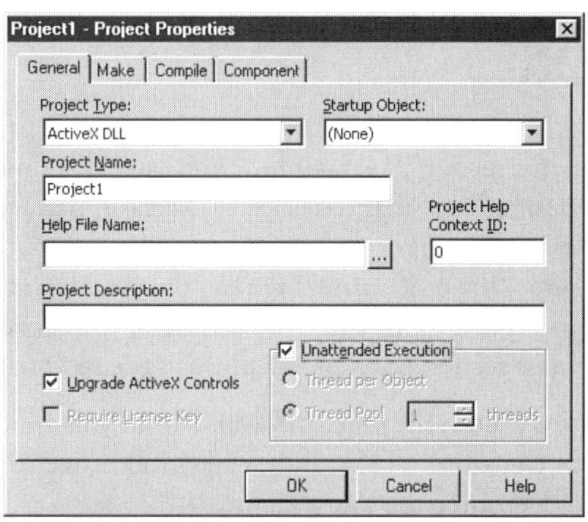

FIGURE 12.3.
Selecting a multithreaded DLL.

Note a check box toward the bottom of the dialog box labeled Unattended Execution. The check box will be enabled only if you have selected a DLL application and there are no forms, controls, user documents, or classes created using ActiveX designers.

Also notice several other options. The first is an option button labeled Thread per Object. Choose this option if each instantiation of an object is to be created on its own thread. Otherwise, the second option, labeled Thread Pool, will instantiate the objects, based on threads available in the pool. The number of threads in the pool is specified in the text box to the right of this option.

The advantage of multithreading your DLLs is that all objects created by the client will be created in the same apartment thread. This is more efficient so that thread boundaries do not have to be crossed. Also, the process call will never be interrupted by another call, which makes it even more efficient.

Testing

To test the OLE Server, you can either run the project and start another instance of Visual Basic to test the new class objects, or actually compile the DLL and then open a new project. For this to work, you must set a reference to the new object. You do this in the Project | References menu option.

Testing the function that you've written takes only two lines of code:

```
Dim objObject As New UserFunctions.TimeFunctions

MsgBox Str$(objObject.CalcTime("10:00am", "2:00pm"))
```

These lines of code simply instantiate the new class, called `TimeFunctions`, in the `UserFunctions` project. Then, the function is called just as any other function would be called, except that the function name must be preceded with the object variable declared just before.

API Style DLLs

Creating an "API Style" DLL requires some knowledge of the C or C++ language. The example listed in this section illustrates how you can call a function in a DLL, written in C, and return the amount of time that has elapsed. This can be very useful because you can time different processes without having to stand over your computer with a stopwatch. You can call this function before the process and then call the function after the process. By subtracting the two times, you can determine the elapsed time of the process. By using the syntax and technique listed in this section, you can adapt this code to your applications.

Begin by creating a DLL file called `TIME.DLL`. In it, you will export one function to simply return the system clock time. This can be called successively. Then, when you subtract the two times, you can determine the elapsed time.

NOTE

The `TIME.DLL` dynamic link library and its associated files are contained on the CD accompanying this book in the `\RESOURCE\TIME` subdirectory.

Creating the Project Framework

To create the framework of the DLL, Visual C++ version 4.0 was used. Open the Developer Studio and select the File | New menu option. Then, choose the Workspace option. You will be presented with a choice of which type of project to open. Figure 12.4 shows what this looks like.

FIGURE 12.4.
The New Project Workspace dialog box.

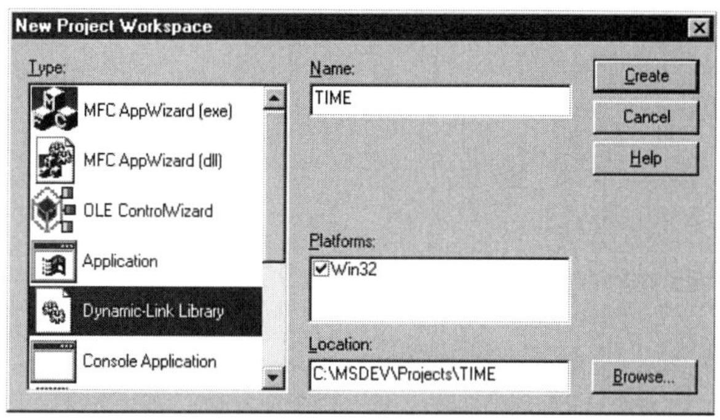

Select the Dynamic-Link Library option and type the name of your DLL, without the DLL extension. You may also select the location of the project's files. In this case, type `TIME` and click the Create command button. This will create a blank project for you.

To create `TIME.DLL`, you must first create a `.CPP` source file. Choose the Insert | Files Into Project menu option, and type `TIME.CPP` to add the new file. Then open the `TIME.CPP` file by double-clicking on the file in the FileView tab. You'll be prompted to create the new file. Simply type the text from the next section.

The `*.CPP` Source File

The `*.CPP` source file contains the code for the actual functions or subroutines that your DLL is to contain. Notice that the function you write is exported with the single declaration:

```
__declspec( dllexport ) double PASCAL FindElapsed(void)
```

The `*.CPP` source code for the `TIME.DLL` file is shown in Listing 12.2.

Listing 12.2. `*.CPP` code to generate an exported function.

```
#include <windows.h>
#include <time.h>
//-----------------------------------------------------------------------------
// Variables
//-----------------------------------------------------------------------------
time_t TimeStruct;
//-----------------------------------------------------------------------------
// Local Prototypes
//-----------------------------------------------------------------------------
__declspec( dllexport ) double PASCAL FindElapsed(void);
//-----------------------------------------------------------------------------
// Actual Function
//-----------------------------------------------------------------------------
__declspec( dllexport ) double PASCAL FindElapsed(void)
{
    return time(&TimeStruct);
}
//-----------------------------------------------------------------------------
// Initialize library. This routine is called when the first client loads
// the DLL.
//-----------------------------------------------------------------------------
BOOL WINAPI DllMain (HANDLE hModule, DWORD fdwReason, LPVOID lpReserved)
{
   switch (fdwReason)
   {
      case DLL_PROCESS_ATTACH:
         /* Code from LibMain inserted here.  Return TRUE to keep the
            DLL loaded or return FALSE to fail loading the DLL.
You may have to modify the code in your original LibMain to
            account for the fact that it may be called more than once.
            You will get one DLL_PROCESS_ATTACH for each process that
            loads the DLL. This is different from LibMain which gets
            called only once when the DLL is loaded. The only time this
            is critical is when you are using shared data sections.
            If you are using shared data sections for statically
            allocated data, you will need to be careful to initialize it
            only once. Check your code carefully.

Certain one-time initializations may now need to be done for
            each process that attaches. You may also not need code from
            your original LibMain because the operating system may now
            be doing it for you.
         */
         break;
case DLL_THREAD_ATTACH:
         /* Called each time a thread is created in a process that has
            already loaded (attached to) this DLL. Does not get called
            for each thread that exists in the process before it loaded
            the DLL.
Do thread-specific initialization here.
         */
         break;
case DLL_THREAD_DETACH:
         /* Same as above, but called when a thread in the process
            exits.
```

```
Do thread-specific cleanup here.
         */
         break;
case DLL_PROCESS_DETACH:
         /* Code from _WEP inserted here.  This code may (like the
            LibMain) not be necessary.  Check to make certain that the
            operating system is not doing it for you.
         */
         break;
   }
/* The return value is only used for DLL_PROCESS_ATTACH; all other
      conditions are ignored.  */
   return TRUE;    // successful DLL_PROCESS_ATTACH
}
```

Notice that in all of the code listed here, there are only a few lines used to actually create the function you will export. This function name is `FindElapsed()`. The code in this function simply returns the time elapsed since midnight. Therefore, this timing process works only within a single day.

The *.DEF Source File

Next, you must create a `*.DEF` source file. Choose the Insert | Files Into Project menu option, and type `TIME.DEF` to add the new file. Then, open the `TIME.DEF` file by double-clicking on the file in the FileView tab. You'll be prompted to create the new file. Simply type in the text from the next section.

The `*.DEF` source file contains the definitions for making the compiled DLL. The `*.DEF` source code for the `TIME.DLL` file is shown in Listing 12.3.

Listing 12.3. The `*.DEF` code to generate an exported function.

```
; TIMEDLL.def : Declares the module parameters for the DLL.
LIBRARY      "TIMEDLL"
DESCRIPTION  'TIMEDLL Windows Dynamic Link Library'
EXPORTS
    ; Explicit exports can go here
    FindElapsed
```

This small amount of code is very necessary. It not only tells the DLL which functions to export, as `FindElapsed()` is shown here, but it will prevent the error message from occurring (see Figure 12.5).

To compile the DLL, simply select the Build | Rebuild All menu option. This will make the 32-bit DLL file.

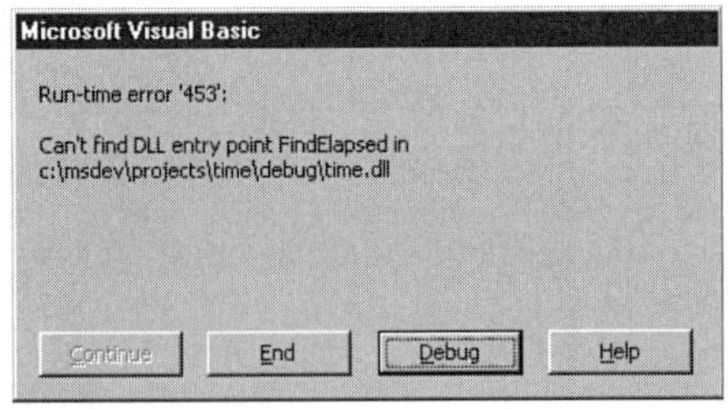

FIGURE 12.5.
The error message that appears if you don't export correctly.

Implementing the DLL in Visual Basic

After you create the DLL, you are ready to use it in your Visual Basic project. The first step in doing this is to declare it as you would an API call. In the case of the `FindElapsed()` function in the `TIME.DLL` file, you declare it like this:

```
Declare Function FindElapsed Lib "time.dll" () As Double
```

You might need to adjust your path to point to the file. This declaration enables you to use the function `FindElapsed()` in your Visual Basic code. You use the same technique presented in this section to write your own functional DLL. This declaration could be used to show the time elapsed since midnight with this line:

```
MsgBox FindElapsed()
```

You could also determine how much time has elapsed from a process by doing something like what is shown in Listing 12.4.

Listing 12.4. Sample Visual Basic code to use a function for elapsed time.

```
Dim dLoopCount As Double
Dim x1
Dim x2

'find first time
x1 = FindElapsed()

'loop for some period of time
For dLoopCount = 1 To 40000
    DoEvents
Next dLoopCount

'find second time
x2 = FindElapsed()

'show difference in seconds
MsgBox Str$(x2 - x1)
```

The code simply calls the DLL function to get the time. Then it runs some process (looping, in this case) and calls the DLL function again. Then the elapsed time is displayed in a message box by subtracting the first time from the second time.

Summary

Creating DLLs in Visual Basic has never been easier. However, these DLLs have their limitations. The DLLs created in Visual Basic are objects that can be called or inserted into an application. Visual Basic does not yet have the capability to create a DLL that can be declared like an API function. This chapter went into detail about creating DLLs both in Visual Basic and in Visual C++ and explains when each language is necessary. You will need to refer to this chapter often as you create DLLs for use with your applications.

13

Using the WIN32 API

The WIN32 API is a set of Application Programming Interfaces (or APIs) that provides the fundamental functionality in the 32-bit Windows operating systems, including Windows 95 and Windows NT. There are 16-bit APIs for Windows 3.1 and Windows for Workgroups, but Visual Basic 5.0 supports only 32-bit operating systems. As such, 16-bit APIs are not covered in this chapter. Because many of the functions in Visual Basic actually make API calls, this chapter does not cover many of those functions. For example, printing is not covered in this chapter because most of the functionality of the `Printer` object is encapsulated as a set of calls to the WIN32 API.

This chapter is designed to give you an overview of how to use WIN32 API functions. It is not intended to be a complete, comprehensive list of all WIN32 API functions. If you want to obtain a comprehensive WIN32 API book, Daniel Appleman's *Visual Basic Programmer's Guide to the Win32 API*, published by Ziff-Davis Press, is an outstanding resource. Every Visual Basic programmer should have this book on his or her desk for reference.

It is important to note that all WIN32 API functions and subroutines are case-sensitive, so pay attention to your typing. Some functions are Windows 95–specific, and even though they are 32-bit API functions, they will not work on the Windows NT platform. Table 13.1 shows these functions.

Table 13.1. Windows 95–specific APIs.

`CheckColorsInGamut`	`GetDeviceGammaRamp`
`CreateColorSpace`	`GetLogColorSpace`
`EnumICMProfiles`	`SetColorSpace`
`GetColorSpace`	`SetICMMode`
`GetICMProfile`	`UpdateICMRegKey`
`LoadImageColorMatcher`	`EnumResLangProc`
`SetDeviceGammaRamp`	`EnumResNameProc`
`SetICMProfile`	`EnumResTypeProc`
`ColorMatchToTarget`	`EnumResourceLanguages`
`DeleteColorSpace`	`EnumResourceNames`
`FreeImageColorMatcher`	

Likewise, some functions are Windows NT–specific, and even though they are 32–bit API functions, they will not work on the Windows 95 platform. There are many more functions unavailable in Windows 95 than there are in Windows NT. Table 13.2 shows these functions.

Table 13.2. Windows NT–specific APIs.

AcceptEx	NetHandleSetInfo
AccessCheck	NetLocalGroupAdd
AccessCheckAndAuditAlarm	NetLocalGroupAddMembers
AddAccessAllowedAce	NetLocalGroupDel
AddAccessDeniedAce	NetLocalGroupDelMembers
AddAce	NetLocalGroupEnum
AddAuditAccessAce	NetLocalGroupGetInfo
AddForm	NetLocalGroupGetMembers
AdjustTokenGroups	NetLocalGroupSetInfo
AdjustTokenPrivileges	NetLocalGroupSetMembers
AllocateAndInitializeSid	NetMessageBufferSend
AllocateLocallyUniqueId	NetMessageNameAdd
AngleArc	NetMessageNameDel
ArcTo	NetMessageNameEnum
AreAllAccessesGranted	NetMessageNameGetInfo
AreAnyAccessesGranted	NetQueryDisplayInformation
BackupEventLog	NetRemoteTOD
BeginUpdateResource	NetReplExportDirAdd
CancelDC	NetReplExportDirDel
ChangeServiceConfig	NetReplExportDirEnum
ClearEventLog	NetReplExportDirGetInfo
CloseDesktop	NetReplExportDirLock
CloseEventLog	NetReplExportDirSetInfo
CloseServiceHandle	NetReplExportDirUnlock
CombineTransform	NetReplGetInfo
ControlService	NetReplImportDirAdd
ConvertThreadToFiber	NetReplImportDirDel
CopySid	NetReplImportDirEnum
CreateWindowStation	NetReplImportDirGetInfo
CreateDesktop	NetReplImportDirLock
CreateFiber	NetReplImportDirUnlock
CreateIoCompletionPort	NetReplSetInfo

continues

Table 13.2. continued

CreatePrivateObjectSecurity	NetScheduleJobAdd
CreateService	NetScheduleJobDel
DdeImpersonateClient	NetScheduleJobEnum
DeleteAce	NetScheduleJobGetInfo
DeleteFiber	NetServerDiskEnum
DeleteForm	NetServerEnum
DeleteService	NetServerGetInfo
DeregisterEventSource	NetServerSetInfo
DestroyPrivateObjectSecurity	NetServerTransportAdd
DuplicateToken	NetServerTransportDel
EndUpdateResource	NetServerTransportEnum
EnumDependentServices	NetSessionDel
EnumDesktopsu	NetSessionEnum
EnumDesktopWindows	NetSessionGetInfo
EnumForms	NetShareAdd
EnumServicesStatus	NetShareCheck
EqualPrefixSid	NetShareDel
EqualSid	NetShareGetInfo
FindClosePrinterChangeNotification	NetShareSetInfo
FindFirstFreeAce	NetStatisticsGet2
FindFirstPrinterChangeNotification	NetUserAdd
FindNextPrinterChangeNotification	NetUserChangePassword
FreeSid	NetUserDel
GetAcceptExSockaddrs	NetUserEnum
GetAce	NetUserGetGroups
GetAclInformation	NetUserGetInfo
GetCurrentFiber	NetUserGetLocalGroups
GetDesktopWindow	NetUserModalsGet
GetFiberData	NetUserModalsSet
GetFileSecurity	NetUserSetGroups
GetForm	NetUserSetInfo
GetKernelObjectSecurity	NetWkstaGetInfo

GetLengthSid
GetNumberOfEventLogRecords
GetOldestEventLogRecord
GetPrivateObjectSecurity
GetProcessWindowStation
GetQueuedCompletionStatus
GetSecurityDescriptorControl
GetSecurityDescriptorDacl
GetSecurityDescriptorGroup
GetSecurityDescriptorOwner
GetSecurityDescriptorSacl
GetServiceDisplayName
GetServiceKeyName
GetSidIdentifierAuthority
GetSidLengthRequired
GetSidSubAuthority
GetSidSubAuthorityCount
GetThreadDesktop
GetTokenInformation
GetUserObjectSecurity
GetWorldTransform
ImpersonateNamedPipeClient
ImpersonateSelf
InitializeAcl
InitializeSecurityDescriptor
InitializeSid
IsValidAcl
IsValidSecurityDescriptor
IsValidSid
LockServiceDatabase
LookupAccountName
LookupAccountSid
LookupPrivilegeDisplayName
NetWkstaSetInfo
NetWkstaTransportAdd
NetWkstaTransportDel
NetWkstaTransportEnum
NetWkstaUserEnum
NetWkstaUserGetInfo
NetWkstaUserSetInfo
NotifyBootConfigStatus
NotifyChangeEventLog
ObjectCloseAuditAlarm
ObjectOpenAuditAlarm
ObjectPrivilegeAuditAlarm
OpenBackupEventLog
OpenDesktop
OpenEventLog
OpenInputDesktop
OpenProcessToken
OpenSCManager
OpenService
OpenThreadToken
PlgBlt
PostQueuedCompletionStatus
PrinterMessageBox
PrivilegeCheck
PrivilegedServiceAuditAlarm
QueryServiceConfig
QueryServiceLockStatus
QueryServiceObjectSecurity
QueryServiceStatus
ReadEventLog
RegisterEventSource
RegisterServiceCtrlHandler
ReportEvent

continues

Table 13.2. continued

LookupPrivilegeName	ResetPrinter
LookupPrivilegeValue	RevertToSelf
MakeAbsoluteSD	ServiceMain
MakeSelfRelativeSD	SetAclInformation
MapGenericMask	SetFileSecurity
MaskBlt	SetForm
ModifyWorldTransform	SetKernelObjectSecurity
MultinetGetConnectionPerformance	SetPrivateObjectSecurity
NetAlertRaise	SetSecurityDescriptorDacl
NetAlertRaiseEx	SetSecurityDescriptorGroup
NetApiBufferAllocate	SetSecurityDescriptorOwner
NetApiBufferFree	SetSecurityDescriptorSacl
NetApiBufferReallocate	SetServiceBits
NetApiBufferSize	SetServiceObjectSecurity
NetFileEnum	SetServiceStatus
NetFileGetInfo	SetThreadDesktop
NetGetAnyDCName	SetThreadToken
NetGetDCName	SetTokenInformation
NetGetDisplayInformationIndex	SetUserObjectSecurity
NetGroupAdd	SetWorldTransform
NetGroupAddUser	StartService
NetGroupDel	StartServiceCtrlDispatcher
NetGroupDelUser	SwitchDesktop
NetGroupEnum	SwitchToFiber
NetGroupGetInfo	TransmitFile
NetGroupGetUsers	UnlockServiceDatabase
NetGroupSetInfo	UpdateResource
NetGroupSetUsers	WaitForPrinterChange
NetHandleGetInfo	

About the WIN32 API

The WIN32 API functions are contained mainly in three Windows DLLs. They are

- USER32.DLL
- KERNEL32.DLL
- GDI32.DLL

There are three basic formats in which an API function can be declared. Each is discussed next.

CROSS REFERENCE

For more information about declaring WIN32 API functions, refer to Chapter 12, "Dynamic Link Libraries."

Some WIN32 API functions enable themselves to be called in all three ways, some in only two ways, and some in only one way. The three ways include the ability to append a character (suffix) to the end of the function or subroutine name. These characters are

- No Character: Standard call from a 16-bit application
- `A`: ANSI single-byte character set
- `W`: Wide Unicode character set

For example, the `GetWindowText()` function is declared with the `A` suffix as

```
Declare Function GetWindowText Lib "user32" Alias "GetWindowTextA"
➥(ByVal hWnd As Long, ByVal lpString As String, ByVal cch As Long) As Long
```

This function expects three arguments and will return a `long` datatype. Notice that the function is declared with an alias, `"GetWindowTextA"`. The alias is the function that actually resides in the WIN32 API. The function call `GetWindowText` is the function call inside Visual Basic. This declaration is the ANSI single-byte character set declaration. This is the one that is most often used.

The 16-bit style declaration looks like this:

```
Declare Function GetWindowText Lib "user32" (ByVal hWnd As Long,
➥ByVal lpString As String, ByVal cch As Long) As Long
```

Notice that there is no alias because the name of the function you will use in Visual Basic is the same name as the actual function in the DLL.

The Unicode declaration would look like this:

```
Declare Function GetWindowText Lib "user32" Alias "GetWindowTextW"
➥(ByVal hWnd As Long, ByVal lpString As String, ByVal cch As Long) As Long
```

Notice the alias `"GetWindowTextW"`. This is the function name inside the DLL itself. In all examples shown, the Visual Basic function call name is `GetWindowText`. This enables you to keep your Visual Basic code constant and to use conditional compile switches to determine which API declaration to use. You could do something like this:

```
'APITYPE can be UNICODE,SINGLE, or WIN16
#Const APITYPE = "UNICODE"
#If APITYPE = "UNICODE" Then
    Declare Function GetWindowText Lib "user32" Alias "GetWindowTextW"
    ➥(ByVal hWnd As Long, ByVal lpString As String,
    ➥ByVal cch As Long) As Long
#ElseIf APITYPE = "SINGLE" Then
    Declare Function GetWindowText Lib "user32" Alias "GetWindowTextA"
    ➥(ByVal hWnd As Long, ByVal lpString As String,
    ➥ByVal cch As Long) As Long
#ElseIf APITYPE = "WIN16" Then
    Declare Function GetWindowText Lib "user32" (ByVal hWnd As Long,
    ➥ByVal lpString As String, ByVal cch As Long) As Long
#End If
```

In the preceding code, you change the `APITYPE` constant before you compile the application. This way, your Visual Basic code never changes because the `GetWindowText` function referenced in code is always the same. Also, Visual Basic knows how to call the API function because it is aliased as appropriate using the compiler switches.

For help with the WIN32 API declarations, Microsoft provides an API text viewer that lists the Visual Basic declarations for all of the exported WIN32 APIs. To use the text viewer, select Start | Programs | Microsoft Visual Basic 5.0 | API Text Viewer. This will bring up a viewer form for viewing and copying one or more API declarations. It also lists constants that can be used in the APIs, as well as type structures. Figure 13.1 shows how the Text API Viewer looks with the WIN32 API loaded.

For faster performance, convert the text to a database instead of having the viewer load the API functions from a text file. You are prompted to do this automatically.

The rest of this chapter is divided into functional areas that show some of the more common features and uses for the WIN32 API.

Registry Functions

Probably the most common use of the WIN32 API functionality is to write to and from the Windows Registry. The Registry is a database used to hold information about the computer, configuration, or software. Using the Registry is the preferred method over storing information in an INI file.

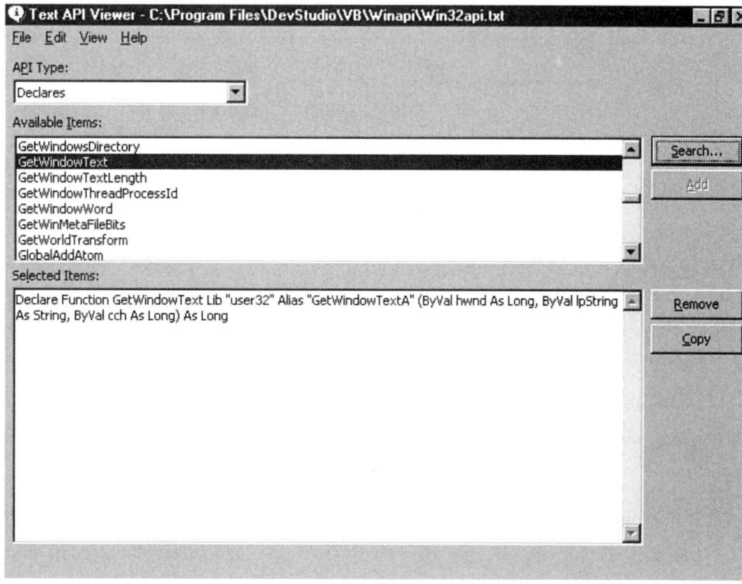

FIGURE 13.1.
The Visual Basic Text API Viewer.

CROSS REFERENCE

For more information about using the Registry, refer to Chapter 6, "The Registry."

There are many WIN32 API functions that help you manipulate the Registry. Table 13.3 lists these functions and their descriptions.

Table 13.3. Registry APIs.

WIN32 API	*Description*
`RegCloseKey`	Closes a Registry key.
`RegConnectRegistry`	Connects to a remote Registry.
`RegCreateKey`	Creates a key.
`RegCreateKeyEx`	Creates a key. This method is recommended.
`RegDeleteKey`	Deletes a key.
`RegDeleteValue`	Deletes a value for an item.
`RegEnumKey`	Enumerates subkeys under a key.
`RegEnumKeyEx`	Enumerates subkeys under a key. This method is recommended.

continues

Table 13.3. continued

WIN32 API	*Description*
`RegEnumValue`	Enumerates values for an item in a key.
`RegFlushKey`	Saves changes to disk immediately.
`RegGetKeySecurity`	Retrieves security attributes for a key.
`RegLoadKey`	Loads Registry information from a file.
`RegOpenKey`	Opens a key.
`RegOpenKeyEx`	Opens a key. This method is recommended.
`RegQueryInfoKey`	Retrieves information about a specified key.
`RegQueryValue`	Retrieves data for an item in a key.
`RegQueryValueEx`	Retrieves data for an item in a key. This method is recommended.
`RegReplaceKey`	Replaces key information with data from disk.
`RegRestoreKey`	Restores key information with data from disk.
`RegSaveKey`	Saves key information to disk.
`RegSetKeySecurity`	Sets security attributes for a key.
`RegSetValue`	Sets the value for an item in a key.
`RegSetValueEx`	Sets the value for an item in a key. This method is recommended.
`RegUnLoadKey`	Unloads information from a key (and subkeys).

For some of these Registry functions to be declared, you must also define user-defined structures, which you can obtain with the text API viewer. They are listed here for the ease of reference. The following are the structures:

```
Type ACL
        AclRevision As Byte
        Sbz1 As Byte
        AclSize As Integer
        AceCount As Integer
        Sbz2 As Integer
End Type

Type SECURITY_ATTRIBUTES
        nLength As Long
        lpSecurityDescriptor As Long
        bInheritHandle As Long
End Type

Type FILETIME
        dwLowDateTime As Long
        dwHighDateTime As Long
End Type
```

```
Type SECURITY_DESCRIPTOR
        Revision As Byte
        Sbz1 As Byte
        Control As Long
        Owner As Long
        Group As Long
        Sacl As ACL
        Dacl As ACL
End Type
```

Also, many WIN32 API Registry functions require the use of constants. These constants can be obtained from the text API viewer, but are presented here for easy reference. The following are the constants:

```
Public Const HKEY_CLASSES_ROOT = &H80000000
Public Const HKEY_CURRENT_CONFIG = &H80000005
Public Const HKEY_CURRENT_USER = &H80000001
Public Const HKEY_DYN_DATA = &H80000006
Public Const HKEY_LOCAL_MACHINE = &H80000002
Public Const HKEY_PERFORMANCE_DATA = &H80000004
Public Const HKEY_USERS = &H80000003
Public Const REG_BINARY = 3
Public Const REG_CREATED_NEW_KEY = &H1
Public Const REG_DWORD = 4
Public Const REG_DWORD_BIG_ENDIAN = 5
Public Const REG_DWORD_LITTLE_ENDIAN = 4
Public Const REG_EXPAND_SZ = 2
Public Const REG_FULL_RESOURCE_DESCRIPTOR = 9
Public Const REG_LINK = 6
Public Const REG_MULTI_SZ = 7
Public Const REG_NONE = 0
Public Const REG_NOTIFY_CHANGE_ATTRIBUTES = &H2
Public Const REG_NOTIFY_CHANGE_LAST_SET = &H4
Public Const REG_NOTIFY_CHANGE_NAME = &H1
Public Const REG_NOTIFY_CHANGE_SECURITY = &H8
Public Const REG_OPENED_EXISTING_KEY = &H2
Public Const REG_OPTION_BACKUP_RESTORE = 4
Public Const REG_OPTION_CREATE_LINK = 2
Public Const REG_OPTION_NON_VOLATILE = 0
Public Const REG_OPTION_RESERVED = 0
Public Const REG_OPTION_VOLATILE = 1
Public Const REG_REFRESH_HIVE = &H2
Public Const REG_RESOURCE_LIST = 8
Public Const REG_RESOURCE_REQUIREMENTS_LIST = 10
Public Const REG_SZ = 1
Public Const REG_WHOLE_HIVE_VOLATILE = &H1
Public Const REG_LEGAL_CHANGE_FILTER = (REG_NOTIFY_CHANGE_NAME Or
➥REG_NOTIFY_CHANGE_ATTRIBUTES Or REG_NOTIFY_CHANGE_LAST_SET Or
➥REG_NOTIFY_CHANGE_SECURITY)
Public Const REG_LEGAL_OPTION = (REG_OPTION_RESERVED Or
➥REG_OPTION_NON_VOLATILE Or REG_OPTION_VOLATILE Or REG_OPTION_CREATE_LINK Or
➥REG_OPTION_BACKUP_RESTORE)
Public Const READ_CONTROL = &H20000
Public Const STANDARD_RIGHTS_ALL = &H1F0000
Public Const STANDARD_RIGHTS_EXECUTE = (READ_CONTROL)
Public Const STANDARD_RIGHTS_READ = (READ_CONTROL)
Public Const STANDARD_RIGHTS_REQUIRED = &HF0000
```

```
Public Const STANDARD_RIGHTS_WRITE = (READ_CONTROL)
Public Const KEY_QUERY_VALUE = &H1
Public Const KEY_CREATE_LINK = &H20
Public Const KEY_CREATE_SUB_KEY = &H4
Public Const KEY_ENUMERATE_SUB_KEYS = &H8
Public Const KEY_EVENT = &H1
Public Const KEY_NOTIFY = &H10
Public Const SYNCHRONIZE = &H100000
Public Const KEY_READ = ((STANDARD_RIGHTS_READ Or KEY_QUERY_VALUE Or
➥KEY_ENUMERATE_SUB_KEYS Or KEY_NOTIFY) And (Not SYNCHRONIZE))
Public Const KEY_SET_VALUE = &H2
Public Const KEY_WRITE = ((STANDARD_RIGHTS_WRITE Or KEY_SET_VALUE Or
➥KEY_CREATE_SUB_KEY) And (Not SYNCHRONIZE))
Public Const KEY_EXECUTE = ((KEY_READ) And (Not SYNCHRONIZE))
Public Const KEY_ALL_ACCESS = ((STANDARD_RIGHTS_ALL Or KEY_QUERY_VALUE Or
➥KEY_SET_VALUE Or KEY_CREATE_SUB_KEY Or KEY_ENUMERATE_SUB_KEYS Or
➥KEY_NOTIFY Or KEY_CREATE_LINK) And (Not SYNCHRONIZE))
Public Const ERROR_SUCCESS = 0
```

You can obtain the actual WIN32 API Registry function declarations from the text API viewer. They are listed here for ease of reference. The Registry functions are declared like this:

```
Declare Function RegCloseKey Lib "advapi32.dll" Alias "RegCloseKey"
(ByVal hKey As Long) As Long
Declare Function RegConnectRegistry Lib "advapi32.dll" Alias
"RegConnectRegistryA" (ByVal lpMachineName As String, ByVal hKey As Long,
phkResult As Long) As Long
Declare Function RegCreateKey Lib "advapi32.dll" Alias "RegCreateKeyA"
(ByVal hKey As Long, ByVal lpSubKey As String, phkResult As Long) As Long
Declare Function RegCreateKeyEx Lib "advapi32.dll" Alias "RegCreateKeyExA"
(ByVal hKey As Long, ByVal lpSubKey As String, ByVal Reserved As Long, ByVal
lpClass As String, ByVal dwOptions As Long, ByVal samDesired As Long,
lpSecurityAttributes As SECURITY_ATTRIBUTES, phkResult As Long, lpdwDisposition
As Long) As Long
Declare Function RegDeleteKey Lib "advapi32.dll" Alias "RegDeleteKeyA"
(ByVal hKey As Long, ByVal lpSubKey As String) As Long
Declare Function RegDeleteValue Lib "advapi32.dll" Alias "RegDeleteValueA"
(ByVal hKey As Long, ByVal lpValueName As String) As Long
Declare Function RegEnumKey Lib "advapi32.dll" Alias "RegEnumKeyA" (ByVal hKey
As Long, ByVal dwIndex As Long, ByVal lpName As String, ByVal cbName As Long)
As Long
Declare Function RegEnumKeyEx Lib "advapi32.dll" Alias "RegEnumKeyExA" (ByVal
hKey As Long, ByVal dwIndex As Long, ByVal lpName As String, lpcbName As Long,
lpReserved As Long, ByVal lpClass As String, lpcbClass As Long,
lpftLastWriteTime As FILETIME) As Long
Declare Function RegEnumValue Lib "advapi32.dll" Alias "RegEnumValueA" (ByVal
hKey As Long, ByVal dwIndex As Long, ByVal lpValueName As String, lpcbValueName
As Long, lpReserved As Long, lpType As Long, lpData As Byte, lpcbData As Long)
As Long
Declare Function RegFlushKey Lib "advapi32.dll" Alias "RegFlushKey"
(ByVal hKey As Long) As Long
Declare Function RegGetKeySecurity Lib "advapi32.dll" Alias "RegGetKeySecurity"
(ByVal hKey As Long, ByVal SecurityInformation As Long, pSecurityDescriptor
As SECURITY_DESCRIPTOR, lpcbSecurityDescriptor As Long) As Long
Declare Function RegLoadKey Lib "advapi32.dll" Alias "RegLoadKeyA" (ByVal hKey
As Long, ByVal lpSubKey As String, ByVal lpFile As String) As Long
```

```
Declare Function RegOpenKey Lib "advapi32.dll" Alias "RegOpenKeyA" (ByVal hKey
As Long, ByVal lpSubKey As String, phkResult As Long) As Long
Declare Function RegOpenKeyEx Lib "advapi32.dll" Alias "RegOpenKeyExA"
(ByVal hKey As Long, ByVal lpSubKey As String, ByVal ulOptions As Long, ByVal
samDesired As Long, phkResult As Long) As Long
Declare Function RegQueryInfoKey Lib "advapi32.dll" Alias "RegQueryInfoKeyA"
(ByVal hKey As Long, ByVal lpClass As String, lpcbClass As Long, lpReserved
As Long, lpcSubKeys As Long, lpcbMaxSubKeyLen As Long, lpcbMaxClassLen As Long,
lpcValues As Long, lpcbMaxValueNameLen As Long, lpcbMaxValueLen As Long,
lpcbSecurityDescriptor As Long, lpftLastWriteTime As FILETIME) As Long
Declare Function RegQueryValue Lib "advapi32.dll" Alias "RegQueryValueA"
(ByVal hKey As Long, ByVal lpSubKey As
String, ByVal lpValue As String, lpcbValue As Long) As Long
Declare Function RegQueryValueEx Lib "advapi32.dll" Alias "RegQueryValueExA"
(ByVal hKey As Long, ByVal lpValueName As String, ByVal lpReserved As Long,
lpType As Long, lpData As Any, lpcbData As Long) As Long
Declare Function RegReplaceKey Lib "advapi32.dll" Alias "RegReplaceKeyA"
(ByVal hKey As Long, ByVal lpSubKey As String, ByVal lpNewFile As String, ByVal
lpOldFile As String) As Long
Declare Function RegRestoreKey Lib "advapi32.dll" Alias "RegRestoreKeyA" (ByVal
hKey As Long, ByVal lpFile As String, ByVal dwFlags As Long) As Long
Declare Function RegSaveKey Lib "advapi32.dll" Alias "RegSaveKeyA" (ByVal hKey
As Long, ByVal lpFile As String, lpSecurityAttributes As SECURITY_ATTRIBUTES)
As Long
Declare Function RegSetKeySecurity Lib "advapi32.dll" Alias "RegSetKeySecurity"
(ByVal hKey As Long, ByVal SecurityInformation As Long, pSecurityDescriptor
As SECURITY_DESCRIPTOR) As Long
Declare Function RegSetValue Lib "advapi32.dll" Alias "RegSetValueA"
(ByVal hKey As Long, ByVal lpSubKey As String, ByVal dwType As Long, ByVal
lpData As String, ByVal cbData As Long) As Long
Declare Function RegSetValueEx Lib "advapi32.dll" Alias "RegSetValueExA" (ByVal
hKey As Long, ByVal lpValueName As String, ByVal Reserved As Long, ByVal dwType
As Long, lpData As Any, ByVal cbData As Long) As Long
Declare Function RegUnLoadKey Lib "advapi32.dll" Alias "RegUnLoadKeyA"
(ByVal hKey As Long, ByVal lpSubKey As String) As Long
```

Manipulating the Registry

Now that the declarations are out of the way, let's begin. The most common things to do with the Registry are create keys, read values, and write values. Therefore, the application on the CD accompanying this book in the `\WIN32\REGISTRY` directory will help you understand how these WIN32 APIs work. This application simply uses the default Visual Basic project name of `Project1` and shows you how to do all three of these functions. Figure 13.2 shows what the application looks like. Please use it as a reference for the following three sections.

Creating a Key

Before you can read or write from a Registry entry, the key must exist. In a 32-bit environment, your code must use the `CreateKeyEx()` function. It will either create a key or open a key if it already exists.

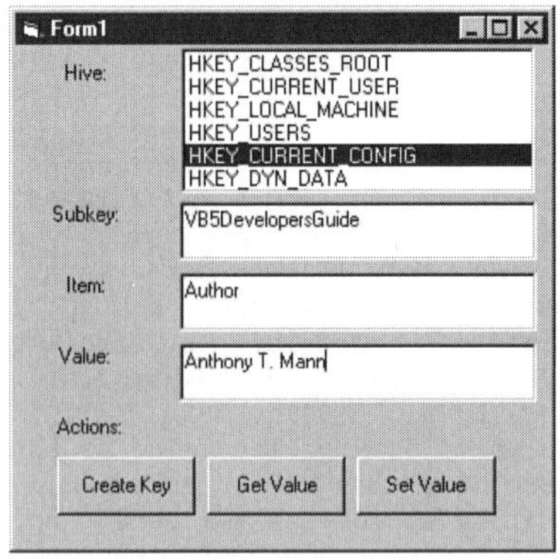

FIGURE 13.2.
The Registry manipulation application.

TRIED AND TRUE

You cannot create a key under the `HKEY_LOCAL_MACHINE` or `HKEY_USERS` hives. If you attempt this, the function will fail because each of these hives is managed totally by Windows.

To create a key, you must supply values as arguments to the WIN32 API function. Listing 13.1 shows how to do this. The code will create a key under the hive listed in the `txtHive` text box. If you want to create multiple successive keys, you can do that in one step by separating the keys with a backspace. For example, instead of creating a key one level down using the following:

```
VB5DevelopersGuide
```

you can create two keys, two levels down, by entering something like this:

```
VB5DevelopersGuide\Details
```

Listing 13.1. Creating a Registry key.

```
Private Sub cmdCreate_Click()

    'for create key
    Dim hKey As Long
    Dim lpSubKey As String
    Dim Reserved As Long
    Dim lpClass As String
    Dim dwOptions As Long
    Dim samDesired As Long
    Dim lpSecurityAttributes As SECURITY_ATTRIBUTES
    Dim phkResult As Long
    Dim lpdwDisposition As Long
    Dim lReturn As Long
```

```
    'other variables
    Dim nLoopCount As Integer

    'assign defaults
    Reserved = 0&
    lpClass = vbNullString
    dwOptions = REG_OPTION_NON_VOLATILE
    samDesired = KEY_ALL_ACCESS

    'find which hive is selected
    For nLoopCount = 0 To lstHive.ListCount - 1
        If lstHive.Selected(nLoopCount) = True Then
            Select Case lstHive.List(nLoopCount)
                Case "HKEY_CLASSES_ROOT"
                    hKey = HKEY_CLASSES_ROOT
                Case "HKEY_CURRENT_USER"
                    hKey = HKEY_CURRENT_USER
                Case "HKEY_LOCAL_MACHINE"
                    hKey = HKEY_LOCAL_MACHINE
                Case "HKEY_USERS"
                    hKey = HKEY_USERS
                Case "HKEY_CURRENT_CONFIG"
                    hKey = HKEY_CURRENT_CONFIG
                Case "HKEY_DYN_DATA"
                    hKey = HKEY_DYN_DATA
            End Select
            Exit For
        End If
    Next nLoopCount

    'assign subkey
    lpSubKey = txtKey.Text

    'create a new key
    lReturn = RegCreateKeyEx(hKey, lpSubKey, Reserved, lpClass, dwOptions,
    ➥samDesired, lpSecurityAttributes, phkResult, lpdwDisposition)
    'display results
    If lReturn <> ERROR_SUCCESS Then
        MsgBox "Error Creating Key"
    Else
        MsgBox "Key Created or Opened"
    End If

    'close key
    lReturn = RegCloseKey(phkResult)
End Sub
```

The code is very easy to follow. First, it declares the variables necessary to manipulate the Registry. Then, defaults are set. The only values that are needed to send through the API function are the hive and the key name. The function will return a handle into the `phkResult` variable and a status into the `lReturn` variable. If the value of this variable is anything except zero, an error occurs. The status is shown in a message box and then the key is simply closed. It is very important to close the key after it is opened.

Writing Data to a Key

After the key exists, you can write data to the key. Data can be written to the `(default)` value, as shown in the Registry, or an item contained within the key. This is very similar to the old way of writing to INI files. The old format used to look like this in a text file:

```
[Key]
Item1=
Item2=
```

Now, these values are recommended to be stored in the Registry. In a 32-bit environment, use the `RegSetValueEx()` function to set a value in the Registry.

To read from an item in a key, you must supply values as arguments to the WIN32 API function. Listing 13.2 shows how to do this. The code will write data to an item listed in the `txtItem` text box, under a key in the hive listed in the `txtHive` text box. This example assumes you will be writing a string value, which is the case most of the time.

Listing 13.2. Writing data to a Registry item.

```
Private Sub cmdSetVal_Click()
    'for query value
    Dim hKey As Long
    Dim lpSubKey As String
    Dim Reserved As Long
    Dim lReturn As Long
    Dim lHandle As Long
    Dim sValue As String
    Dim sItem As String
    Dim lSize As Long
    Dim lpType As Long

    'other variables
    Dim nLoopCount As Integer

    'assign defaults
    Reserved = 0&
    sItem = txtItem.Text
    sValue = txtValue.Text & Chr$(0)
    lSize = Len(sValue)

    'find which hive is selected
    For nLoopCount = 0 To lstHive.ListCount - 1
        If lstHive.Selected(nLoopCount) = True Then
            Select Case lstHive.List(nLoopCount)
                Case "HKEY_CLASSES_ROOT"
                    hKey = HKEY_CLASSES_ROOT
                Case "HKEY_CURRENT_USER"
                    hKey = HKEY_CURRENT_USER
                Case "HKEY_LOCAL_MACHINE"
                    hKey = HKEY_LOCAL_MACHINE
                Case "HKEY_USERS"
                    hKey = HKEY_USERS
```

```
                Case "HKEY_CURRENT_CONFIG"
                    hKey = HKEY_CURRENT_CONFIG
                Case "HKEY_DYN_DATA"
                    hKey = HKEY_DYN_DATA
            End Select
            Exit For
        End If
    Next nLoopCount

    'assign subkey
    lpSubKey = txtKey.Text

    'open key
    lReturn = RegOpenKeyEx(hKey, lpSubKey, Reserved, KEY_ALL_ACCESS, lHandle)

    'Set value
    lReturn = RegSetValueEx(lHandle, sItem, Reserved, lpType,
    ➥ByVal sValue, lSize)

    'display results
    If lReturn <> ERROR_SUCCESS Then
        MsgBox "Error Setting Value"
    Else
        MsgBox "Value Set"
    End If

    'close key
    lReturn = RegCloseKey(lHandle)
End Sub
```

The code is similar to the code in Listing 13.1. First, it declares the variables necessary to manipulate the Registry. Then, defaults are set. The only values that are needed to send through the API function are the handle to the open key in a specific hive, the item to write the data to, and the data itself. Optionally, you can specify the type of data. Before this function is called, the `RegOpenKeyEx()` function is used to return a handle to an existing key. In this example, it will return a value into the `lHandle` variable. The function will return a status into the `lReturn` variable. If the value of this variable is anything except zero, an error occurred. The status is shown in a message box and then the key is simply closed. It is very important to close the key after it is opened.

TRIED AND TRUE

There is something very important you need to consider when you use the `RegSetValueEx()` function. The data in the `RegSetValueEx()` function must be sent `ByVal` if you are sending a string. This way, the string is converted into the type of string which can be used with API functions.

Reading Data From a Key

After the key exists, you can read data from an item in the key. Data can be read from the `(default)` item, as shown in the Registry, or a specific item contained within the key. This is very similar to the old way of writing to INI files. The old format used to look like this in a text file:

```
[Key]
Item1= Value1
Item2= Value2
```

Now, these values are recommended to be stored in the Registry. In a 32-bit environment, use the `RegQueryValueEx()` function, which will return a value from the Registry.

To read from an item in a key, you must supply values as arguments to the WIN32 API function. Listing 13.3 shows how to do this. The code will read data from an item listed in the `txtItem` text box, under a key in the hive listed in the `txtHive` text box. It will place the data in the `txtValue` text box. This example assumes you will be reading a string value, which is the case most of the time.

Listing 13.3. Reading data from a Registry item.

```
Private Sub cmdGetVal_Click()
    'for query value
    Dim hKey As Long
    Dim lpSubKey As String
    Dim Reserved As Long
    Dim lReturn As Long
    Dim lHandle As Long
    Dim sReturn As String
    Dim sItem As String
    Dim lSize As Long
    Dim lpType As Long

    'other variables
    Dim nLoopCount As Integer

    'assign defaults
    Reserved = 0&
    sItem = txtItem.Text
    sReturn = String$(255, Chr$(0))
    lSize = Len(sReturn) + 1

    'find which hive is selected
    For nLoopCount = 0 To lstHive.ListCount - 1
        If lstHive.Selected(nLoopCount) = True Then
            Select Case lstHive.List(nLoopCount)
                Case "HKEY_CLASSES_ROOT"
                    hKey = HKEY_CLASSES_ROOT
                Case "HKEY_CURRENT_USER"
                    hKey = HKEY_CURRENT_USER
                Case "HKEY_LOCAL_MACHINE"
                    hKey = HKEY_LOCAL_MACHINE
```

```
                Case "HKEY_USERS"
                    hKey = HKEY_USERS
                Case "HKEY_CURRENT_CONFIG"
                    hKey = HKEY_CURRENT_CONFIG
                Case "HKEY_DYN_DATA"
                    hKey = HKEY_DYN_DATA
            End Select
            Exit For
        End If
    Next nLoopCount

    'assign subkey
    lpSubKey = txtKey.Text

    'open key
    lReturn = RegOpenKeyEx(hKey, lpSubKey, Reserved, KEY_ALL_ACCESS, lHandle)

    'get value
    lReturn = RegQueryValueEx(lHandle, sItem, Reserved, lpType,
    ➥ByVal sReturn, lSize)

    'display results
    If lReturn <> ERROR_SUCCESS Then
        txtValue.Text = ""
        MsgBox "Error Getting Value"
    Else
        txtValue.Text = Left$(sReturn, lSize - 1)
    End If

    'close key
    lReturn = RegCloseKey(lHandle)
End Sub
```

The code is similar to the code in Listing 13.2. First, it declares the variables necessary to manipulate the Registry. Then, defaults are set. The only values that are needed to send through the API function are the handle to the open key in a specific hive and the item to write the data to. Optionally, you can specify the type of data. Before this function is called, the `RegOpenKeyEx()` function is used to return a handle to an existing key. In this example, it will return a value into the `lHandle` variable and the value into the `sReturn` variable. The function will return a status into the `lReturn` variable. If the value of this variable is anything except zero, an error occurred. The status is shown in a message box and then the key is simply closed. It is very important to close the key after it is opened.

TRIED AND TRUE

There is something very important you need to consider when you use the `RegQueryValueEx()` function. The data in the `RegQueryValueEx()` function must be sent `ByVal` if you are sending a string. This way, the string is converted into the type of string which can be used with API functions.

TRIED AND TRUE

If you attempt to read (query) a value from the `RegQueryValueEx()` function, it must have been opened with the `KEY_QUERY_VALUE` parameter. The example shown in Listing 13.3 was opened with the `KEY_ALL_ACCESS` parameter, which includes the `KEY_QUERY_VALUE` parameter.

New to Version 5.0

Callback Functions

Visual Basic 5.0 now includes an `AddressOf` operator. It is very useful in callback functions, which typically are enumeration functions. These are intended to make successive calls to the function to enumerate (cycle through) a list of items. For example, you can enumerate a list of

- Windows
- Fonts
- Printers
- Resources
- Objects
- Threads
- Many more...

The `AddressOf` operator is used to pass the address of a function, not only a variable. That makes it very useful in some API functions not previously callable from Visual Basic.

This example to follow is contained on the CD accompanying this book in the `\WIN32\ENUM` directory.

You need to know a few things when you use callback functions. The first is that the argument you pass to the `AddressOf` operator needs to be a function. It cannot be a subroutine. The second is that this function used with the `AddressOf` operator needs to exist in a BAS module. It cannot exist in a form or a class module. If it does exist in a form or class module, you will get an "Invalid use of `AddressOf` operator" error message. Third, you need to know what arguments the callback function expects. Daniel Appleman's book, mentioned earlier in the chapter, lists these arguments. If you have his book, these are listed in Appendix A. The only difference in using his custom control and the Visual Basic 5.0 `AddressOf` operator is that you do not use the last parameter, `retval&`.

For the following example, refer to Figure 13.3. It shows what the application looks like. This application simply uses the default Visual Basic project name of `Project1`.

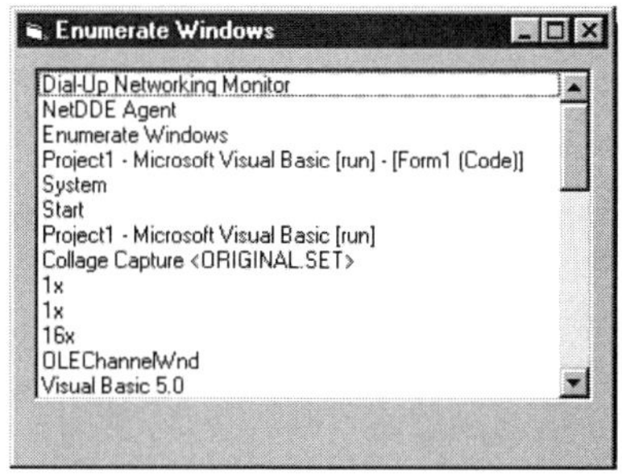

FIGURE 13.3.
The window enumeration application.

To use a callback function, you must create a separate function that will perform the action desired by the callback. The callback function itself automatically will call this function successive times. Listing 13.4 shows a sample function from the application on the CD.

Listing 13.4. Function to perform an action by the callback function.

```
Public Function AddToList(ByVal hwnd As Long, ByVal lParam As Long) As Long
    'declare variables
    Dim sTitle As String
    Dim lLen As Long
    Dim lReturn As Long

    'assign variables
    lLen = GetWindowTextLength(hwnd) + 1
    sTitle = String$(lLen + 1, 0)

    'get the text of the window handle
    lReturn = GetWindowText(hwnd, sTitle, lLen)
    If lReturn > 0 Then
        'add to list box
        Form1.lstWindow.AddItem Left$(sTitle, lReturn)
    End If

    'return value to callback
    AddToList = 1
End Function
```

Notice that this function `AddToList()` has two parameters, `lpfn as Any`, and `lParam as Long`. These parameters are passed by the WIN32 callback function, `EnumWindows()`. The declaration for `EnumWindows()` is

```
Declare Function EnumWindows Lib "user32" (ByVal lpfn As Any,
➥ByVal lParam As Long) As Long
```

Again, the parameters are listed in Daniel Appleman's book described earlier. When you know what the parameters are, you can begin coding your function. At this point, you can assume that the system will call this function, which you are writing.

The `AddToList()` function accepts an `hWnd` parameter, which is a handle to the window produced by the callback function, `EnumWindows()`. The `lParam` parameter is actually a parameter passed by the calling application. It can be anything that you want. It is not used in this case.

After the handle is passed in, there are two WIN32 API functions, `GetWindowTextLength()` and `GetWindowText()`, used to get the text of the window handle passed in. Then, this text is added to the list box on the main form. The following are the declarations for these functions:

```
Declare Function GetWindowText Lib "user32" Alias "GetWindowTextA"
➥(ByVal hwnd As Long, ByVal lpString As String, ByVal cch As Long) As Long
Declare Function GetWindowTextLength Lib "user32" Alias "GetWindowTextLengthA"
➥(ByVal hwnd As Long) As Long
```

Finally, the last line in Listing 13.4 simply returns a value. This value is necessary for the callback because it is a function, but no code actually uses the value.

You can test the `AddToList()` function simply by supplying a valid handle and calling the function directly. When you know it works, you can then use the callback function. Remember, this function is successively called by the callback function. Therefore, it must work before you test the callback function.

To add the callback function used in the application on the CD, Project1, the `EnumWindows()` function is used. It expects an address of a function, and a user-defined parameter to pass to the function. Again, this parameter isn't used in this example. Therefore, the callback function is used with this line of code:

```
lReturn = EnumWindows(AddressOf AddToList, 0&)
```

The `EnumWindows()` API function will return a non-zero value if it succeeds. Notice that this one call to the `EnumWindows()` function produces an entire list of windows. This is because the address of the `AddToList()` function is called automatically by the `EnumWindows()` function.

Summary

The WIN32 API extends the power of Visual Basic by enabling functions to be called that manipulate Windows itself. This is a tremendous tool in being able to write very robust, interactive applications. Visual Basic 5.0 introduces the `AddressOf` operator, which allows the address of a function to be passed to a WIN32 API function so that successive calls can be made to the function, returning successive values as well. This chapter gave a good insight into how Visual Basic uses WIN32 API functions. Use it as an ongoing reference.

14

Integrating with Office 97

Due to the extensible nature of Visual Basic, using and incorporating the features of Office 97, which includes Word, Excel, PowerPoint, and Access, is fairly easy. Each of these products acts as an OLE Server that exports certain properties, methods, and events that are available to the outside world. Visual Basic can take advantage of this functionality. This chapter shows how to build applications using some of the functionality built into Word and Excel.

New Features of Office 97

The are many new features in Office 97. Some of these features are exposed for use in Visual Basic, while others are not. The new features are listed in Table 14.1.

Table 14.1. New features in Office 97.

Product	*Feature*	*Description*
Access	ActiveX Controls	Web controls can be included in Access to provide HTML, FTP, HTTP, and e-mail capabilities.
Access	Customizable Toolbars	Toolbars can be customized to suit your needs.
Access	Database Wizard	Enables you to quickly design over 20 types of databases.
Access	Exposed IDE	Access IDE can be controlled externally because it is an OLE Automation object.
Access	Filter By	Enables you to query based on pieces of information that are known, either by form or by selection.
Access	Import/Export Wizards	Wizards that guide you through the importing or exporting of data.
Access	Improved Form and Report Wizards	Improved design for both the Form Wizard and the Report Wizard.
Access	Internet Replication	Databases can be synchronized or replicated over the Web, using it as a WAN.
Access	Performance Analyzer	Analyzes the performance of your databases and provides suggestions on how it can be improved.
Access	Remove Source Code	Source code can be removed before distribution.

Product	Feature	Description
Access	Simple Query Wizard	Guides you through the design of simple database queries.
Access	Split Database	Gives you the ability to separate one database into multiple databases.
Access	Table Analyzer Wizard	Recommends how relationships should be constructed in tables.
Access	Web Publishing	Publishes your database for Internet/intranet use.
Excel	Asynchronous Queries	Queries can be executed on a separate thread so that the process isn't tied up waiting for the query to finish.
Excel	Charting	Many new features have been added to charting.
Excel	Conditional Formatting	Enables you to format your cells based on certain conditions.
Excel	Custom Cells	You can now create a cell of many smaller cells.
Excel	Distributable Queries	Queries can be distributed to end users.
Excel	Formula Auto-Correct	Automatically corrects the most common typographical formula errors.
Excel	HTML Wizard	Enables you to save a spreadsheet to a specific URL.
Excel	Import From HTML	Imports from an HTML document.
Excel	Language Formulas	Enables you to define formulas not by referencing cell references, but by referencing column titles and names.
Excel	Multi-User Workbooks	Enables multiple users to work on the same workbook at the same time.
Excel	Multiple Undo	Many levels of "Undo" have now been implemented.
Excel	Pivot Table Wizard	Provides an easy way to create pivot tables to display any number of values on one axis against a different number of values on a different axis.
Excel	Range Finder	Automatically highlights cells that make up a formula.

continues

Table 14.1. continued

Product	*Feature*	*Description*
Excel	Visual Printing	Page Break Preview now enables you to view exactly where page breaks will occur.
Office	Administration	Software administration has been greatly improved in all Office products.
Office	Browser Integration	Enables Internet Explorer 3.0 and higher to integrate into all Office document types.
Office	Clean-Up Utility	Gives you the ability to clean up shared components that are not used.
Office	File Format Compatibility	Files can be saved in a previous format for backward compatibility.
Office	Find Fast	Full index searching available for all document types, as well as Web browsing.
Office	FrontPage Integration	Enables FrontPage to view links between Office document types, if they are linked.
Office	Hyperlinks	Internet/intranet hyperlinks can now be included in all Office document types.
Office	IntelliMouse	Support for the new hardware mouse, which provides a scrolling wheel for easy document reading.
Office	More Objects	Many more objects (about 600) are exposed for use with Office 97.
Office	Office Art	A drawing tool that enables you to create 3D graphics.
Office	Office Assistant	3D animated figure designed to give pointers and help you with Office tasks.
Office	Office Binder	Project file that contains many different types of files (such as Excel, Word, PowerPoint, and Access).
Office	Single Toolbar	Now only one toolbar is loaded for all Office products.
Office	SMS support	Systems Management Server support is now integrated into Office.
Office	System Policies	System policies are supported in Office so that they can be used in Windows 95 and Windows NT 4.0.

Product	Feature	Description
Office	VBA Language	Visual Basic for Applications (VBA) is now built into all Office applications.
Office	Viewers	All Office applications can be viewed by distributing viewers, even if they don't have the application itself.
Office	Web Toolbar	Access the Web from all applications.
Outlook	Auto Address	Automatically separates an address into its separate components: Address, City, State, Zip Code.
Outlook	Auto Create	Enables information to be created in one format from another format, saving you the time of cutting and pasting.
Outlook	Auto Name	Automatically separates a name into its separate components: First Name, Last Name, Middle Initial, Suffix, and Salutation.
Outlook	Auto Name Check	Automatically checks names to e-mail recipients.
Outlook	Auto Preview	Displays the first few lines of an e-mail message so that you do not actually have to open it.
Outlook	Auto Voting	Enables you to solicit opinions on a topic from e-mail users before you arrive at a conclusion.
Outlook	E-Mail	Enables you to easily send an e-mail message.
Outlook	Group Scheduling	Enables you to perform group scheduling for meetings.
Outlook	Journal	Personal Information Management system that keeps track of time.
Outlook	Message Flags	Flags a message to remind you that a follow-up action is needed.
Outlook	Message Recall	Recalls a message from a user if it was sent by mistake (as long as the user has not already read it).
Outlook	Outlook	A new feature that integrates many of the common Office tasks, such as writing e-mail, scheduling, contacting, and more.

continues

Table 14.1. continued

Product	*Feature*	*Description*
Outlook	Outlook Forms	Automatic forms for fast data entry and e-mail integration.
Outlook	Task Requests	Enables you to request a task to be completed and tracks the status of the request.
Outlook	Views	Adjusts the Outlook screen for different users.
Outlook	Word Mail	Uses Microsoft Word 97 as the e-mail editor.
PowerPoint	Animated Templates	Attention-grabbing, pre-created templates for animated templates.
PowerPoint	Animation Setting	Text and objects can now be animated in one place.
PowerPoint	Background Spell Checking	The same type of background spell checking in Word is now available in PowerPoint.
PowerPoint	Custom Shows	Enables you to define different shows based on the same presentation.
PowerPoint	Enhanced Auto Content Wizard	Allows for pre-built formatting of specific types of presentations based on simple questions.
PowerPoint	Expand Slide	You can automatically distribute verbose slides on more than one slide.
PowerPoint	Loading Improvements	The loading and saving of files have been greatly improved.
PowerPoint	Slide Finder	You can preview and insert slides based on an existing presentation.
PowerPoint	Summary Slide	You can automatically distribute summary slides based on multiple verbose slides.
Word	Auto Summary	Automatically chooses a summary based on the level of user(s) who need to view the Word document.
Word	Background Grammar Checking	Automatically checks your grammar as you write. You don't need to invoke the option manually.
Word	HTML Pages	You can create Internet/intranet pages without knowing HTML.
Word	Letter Wizard	Helps you in writing letters.

Product	Feature	Description
Word	Table Drawing Tool	Enables you to manually draw tables as you would on a piece of paper.

OLE Automation with Office 97 and Visual Basic

The following sections illustrate the use of Visual Basic with Office 97. For information about the properties, methods, and events exposed by these components, you can use the Object Browser by pressing F2. The Object Browser will not display the reference unless you have explicitly added the reference. You do this by selecting the Project | References menu option. Then you select the appropriate reference, as shown in Table 14.2.

Table 14.2. Reference library files and descriptions.

Product	Office 97 Library	Office 97 Filename
Excel	Excel 8.0 Object Library	`EXCEL8.OLB`
Word	Word 8.0 Object Library	`MSWORD8.OLB`
PowerPoint	PowerPoint 8.0 Object Library	`MSPPT8.OLB`
Access	Access 8.0 Object Library	`MSACC8.OLB`
Office	Office 8.0 Object Library	`MSO97RT.DLL`
Outlook	Outlook 8.0 Object Library	`MSOUTL8.OLB`

Please bear in mind that just because you find an object reference in the type libraries specified in Table 14.2, that does not mean it is exported. For example, the following lines of code will produce an error:

```
Dim objExcel As New Excel.Workbook
MsgBox objExcel.Name
```

Although the declaration in the first line syntactically is correct, Visual Basic does not attempt to instantiate the object until it is referenced. Therefore, the second line fails because the object must be referenced using the `CreateObject` and `GetObject` functions. Therefore, other than to get an idea of how to interface with Office 97, you should consult a book dedicated to showing the methods, properties, and events that are exposed by Visual Basic.

Integrating with Excel

Excel exposes many objects and methods. The first step in integrating with Excel is to assign the reference to the Excel Library, as shown in Table 14.2. Even though this does not help you with every aspect of automation, it does help you find out which objects relate to objects inside Excel before you begin coding.

Suppose you had an array with which you needed to populate data inside Excel. Listing 14.1 shows how you could take code (which generates an array) and populate it inside Excel.

Listing 14.1. Populating data into Excel.

```
Private Sub Command1_Click()

    'declare variables
    Dim objExcel As Object
    Dim objRange As Excel.Range
    Dim nLoopCount1 As Integer
    Dim nLoopCount2 As Integer
    Dim asTempArray(10, 10) As String

    'fill array with values
    For nLoopCount1 = 0 To 10
        For nLoopCount2 = 0 To 10
            asTempArray(nLoopCount1, nLoopCount2) = Chr$(65 + nLoopCount1) &
            ➥Trim$(Str$(nLoopCount2 + 1))
        Next nLoopCount2
    Next nLoopCount1

    'handle errors
    On Error GoTo ExcelError

    'first attempt to get the object if it is running
    Set objExcel = GetObject("Excel.Application")

    If objExcel Is Nothing Then
        Set objExcel = CreateObject("Excel.Application")
    End If

    'add a new workbook
    objExcel.Workbooks.Add

    'set a range for the array to be placed
    Set objRange = objExcel.Range(Cells(1, 1), Cells(UBound(asTempArray, 1)
    ➥+ 1, UBound(asTempArray, 2) + 1))


    'fill the range with the array
    objRange.Value = asTempArray

    'make excel visible
    objExcel.Visible = True

    'exit - all was successful
    Exit Sub

ExcelError:
    If Err <> 432 Then
```

```
        'display error
        MsgBox Error$

        'reclaim memory from object
        Set objExcel = Nothing

        'exit
        Exit Sub
    Else
        'class was not found, attempt to create it
        Resume Next
    End If

End Sub
```

The code in Listing 14.1 uses OLE Automation with Excel to populate Excel with data from an array in Visual Basic. The first step is to create the OLE Automation object. The `GetObject` function is used to find out if the object is already running. If it is, the `GetObject` function obtains a reference to it. If it is not running, an error is generated and trapped. This error is number 432. Therefore, an attempt is made to create the object.

Assuming there are no errors in creating the object, a new workbook is added. This automatically creates three worksheets, and the first one is active by default. Following that, there is an object variable, `objRange`, that has been defined as an Excel range. This is possible because we've included the Excel reference, as shown earlier. The specific range of cells to fill with the data is then assigned to the `objRange` object variable.

The code in Listing 14.1 calculates the range based on the fact that cell 1,1 is the first cell (A1). Then, based on the dimensions of the array, a specific number of cells to the right (X-axis) and down (Y-axis) are calculated based on the fact that the `Ubound` function returns the highest element in the array, which is 10. Therefore, 1 is added to it because it was dimensioned as 10. This means that there are actually 11 elements in the array, ranging from 0 to 10. Adding 1 to the `Ubound` function guarantees that the correct number of cells is calculated. The same is done for the other dimension.

After the range is defined, simply setting the `Value` property of the range to the array will fill the cells. You do not need to pass a specific dimension of the array. Because a reference to the array is actually passed, the range is filled based on how many elements are in the array (or a portion thereof). Finally, Excel is made visible. It is invisible, by default, when the object is being created.

You can enhance this application by saving or printing the spreadsheet. You also can use the code to fill a spreadsheet with the data from a recordset. However, you cannot pass the recordset directly. Instead, you can write a procedure that transforms the recordset into an array (see Listing 14.2).

Listing 14.2. Converting a recordset into an array.

```
Public Sub FillDataArray(asArray(), rsRecord As Recordset)
    'declare variables
    Dim nLoopCount1 As Integer
    Dim nLoopCount2 As Integer

    'handle errors
    On Error GoTo FillError

    'make sure we get correct record count by going to the last record
    rsRecord.MoveLast
    rsRecord.MoveFirst

    'redim the array
    ReDim asArray(rsRecord.RecordCount, rsRecord.Fields.Count)

    'loop through records
    For nLoopCount1 = 0 To rsRecord.RecordCount - 1
            'loop through fields
            For nLoopCount2 = 0 To rsRecord.Fields.Count - 1
               asArray(nLoopCount1, nLoopCount2) = rsRecord.Fields(nLoopCount2)
            Next nLoopCount2

            'move to the next record
            rsRecord.MoveNext
    Next nLoopCount1

    Exit Sub

FillError:
    'display error
    MsgBox Error$
    Exit Sub
End Sub
```

Listing 14.3 shows how this procedure is called.

Listing 14.3. Populating data into Excel from a recordset.

```
Private Sub Command2_Click()
    'declare variables
    Dim objExcel As Object
    Dim objRange As Excel.Range
    Dim dbTemp As Database
    Dim rsTemp As Recordset
    Dim sCmd As String
    Dim asTempArray()


    'handle errors
    On Error GoTo ExcelError
```

```
    'open database
    Set dbTemp = OpenDatabase("BIBLIO.MDB")

    'create SQL statement
    sCmd = "SELECT * FROM Authors"

    'create snapshot from SQL Statement
    Set rsTemp = dbTemp.OpenRecordset(sCmd, dbOpenSnapshot)

    If Not rsTemp.EOF Then
        'force to last then first record to ensure correct count
        rsTemp.MoveLast
        rsTemp.MoveFirst

        'first attempt to get the object if it is running
        Set objExcel = GetObject("Excel.Application")

        If objExcel Is Nothing Then
            Set objExcel = CreateObject("Excel.Application")
        End If

        'add a new workbook
        objExcel.Workbooks.Add

        'set a range for the array to be placed
        Set objRange = objExcel.Range(Cells(1, 1), Cells(rsTemp.RecordCount,
        ➥rsTemp.Fields.Count))

        'fill the range with the array
        Call FillDataArray(asTempArray, rsTemp)

        objRange.Value = asTempArray

        'make excel visible
        objExcel.Visible = True
    End If

    'exit - all was successful
    Exit Sub

ExcelError:
    If Err <> 432 Then
        'display error
        MsgBox Error$

        'reclaim memory from object
        Set objExcel = Nothing

        'exit
        Exit Sub
    Else
        'class was not found, attempt to create it
        Resume Next
    End If

End Sub
```

This code differs from the code in Listing 14.1 in that the database is accessed, a `Recordset` object is generated, and then the `Recordset` object and the temporary array are passed to the `FillDataArray()` procedure.

Integrating with Word

Word also exposes many objects and methods. The drawback to this is that these objects are all exposed through the `Word.Basic` interface, which is a class that must be accessed directly. You cannot, for example, set a reference to a Word object. You must use the `CreateObject` or `GetObject` functions.

One of the most common things to do when integrating with Word is to create a *letter merge process*, which can be a somewhat complex process. A letter merge process takes a predefined template and applies the template to each record in a selected datasource. Word then substitutes fields defined in the template with actual values stored in the database. The result is a merged letter. There are things that need to be set up in Word as well as in specific processes in your code.

Here is the process:

1. Create a header. This tells Word which fields will be available for the merge.
2. Create a template that points to the header.
3. Resolve the data at runtime to create the mail merge based on the template in the previous step and place it in a new document.

You can create a header using Word itself. To do this, open a new document, and then select Tools | Mail Merge. This brings up a dialog box that contains many options to create your Word template. Figure 14.1 shows what this dialog box looks like.

Suppose you wanted to include the following fields on the letter:

- FirstName
- LastName
- Company
- Address
- City
- State
- Zip
- Title
- Salary

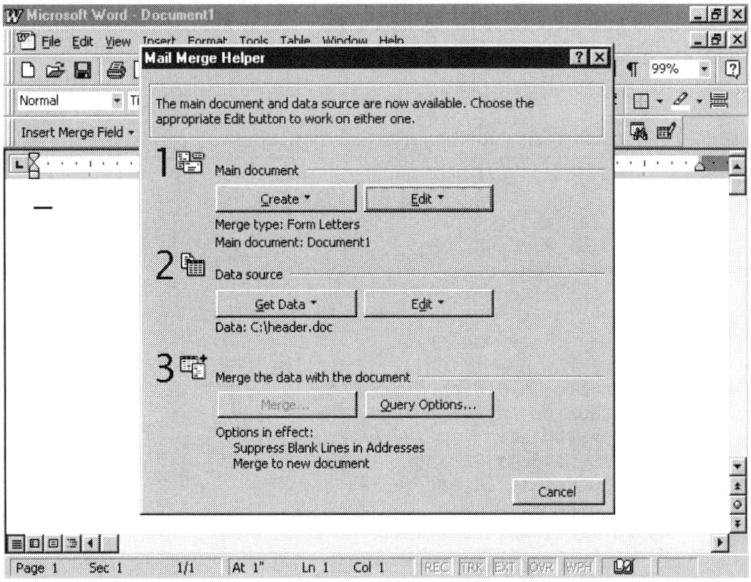

FIGURE 14.1.
The Mail Merge Helper dialog box.

You must select the command buttons in the order presented. First, select the Create | Form Letters menu option. Then click the Main Document button to enable the Get Data command button. Select the Get Data | Header Options menu option. Then select the Create button. This brings up a dialog box in which you can select from the standard fields shown or add your own. Figure 14.2 shows what this dialog box looks like.

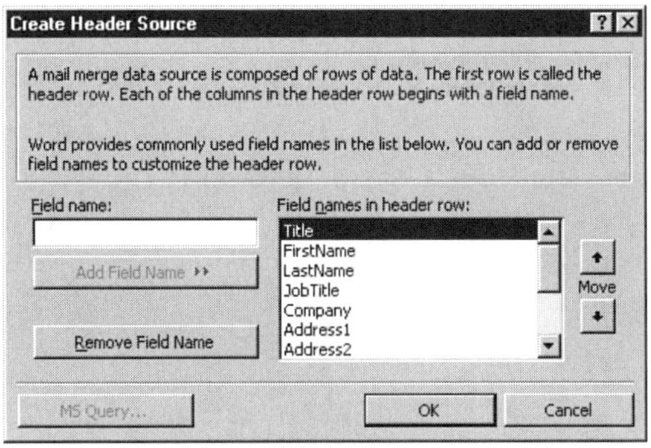

FIGURE 14.2.
The Create Header Source dialog box.

Continue to either select or add the fields so that all of the fields listed earlier are added; then select OK. You are prompted to save the file, which is then used to indicate to your template what fields are available. Now click Close. You will notice a new toolbar button labeled Insert Merge Field. If you click the button, you will see a list of the fields you added. Go ahead and construct your letter, incorporating the merge fields where appropriate. Save the file as your template.

That's all that is necessary in Word. The rest is done in Visual Basic code. Listing 14.4 shows the code needed to create the mail merge.

Listing 14.4. Visual Basic code to perform a mail merge.

```
Private Sub Command1_Click()

    'declare variables
    Dim hHandle1 As Long
    Dim hHandle2 As Long
    Dim lLength As Long
    Dim sTempFile As String
    Dim sTemplateFile As String
    Dim sMergeFile As String
    Dim sDataFile As String
    Dim nFileNum As Integer
    Dim word As Object
    Dim sTempString As String
    Dim nLoopCount As Integer

    'find out if template exists
    On Error GoTo noFile

    'assign template file name
    lLength = 0
    sTempFile = App.Path & "\" & txtTemplate.Text
    lLength = FileLen(sTempFile)
    If lLength = 0 Then
        MsgBox "Template file does not exist!"
        Exit Sub
    Else
        sTemplateFile = sTempFile
    End If

    'assign merge file name
    sMergeFile = App.Path & "\" & txtMerge.Text

    'assign data file name
    sDataFile = App.Path & "\" & "DATA.TXT"

    On Error Resume Next
    'delete merge file
    Kill sMergeFile

    'delete data file
    Kill sDataFile

    On Error GoTo TrapError

    'open data file
    nFileNum = FreeFile
    Open sDataFile For Output As #nFileNum

    'write out first record
    sTempString = "John,Jones,Acme,123 Main Street,New York,NY,11221,
    ➥Marketing Director,52000"
```

```
sTempString = FillQuote(sTempString)
Print #nFileNum, sTempString

'write out second record
sTempString = "Charles,Smith,Acme,456 Elm Way,New York,NY,11222,
➥Sales Director,50000"
sTempString = FillQuote(sTempString)
Print #nFileNum, sTempString

'close the file
Close #nFileNum

'change mouse
Screen.MousePointer = vbHourglass

'change caption
Form1.Caption = "Running Microsoft Word..."

'create word object
Set word = CreateObject("Word.Basic")    'create a WordBasic object

'find word
hHandle1 = FindWindow(0&, "Microsoft Word")

'show word
hHandle2 = ShowWindow(hHandle1, 0)

'change caption
Me.Caption = "Opening Template..."

'open the template
word.fileopen sTemplateFile

'open the data
word.MailMergeOpenDataSource sDataFile

'perform merge
word.mailmergetodoc

'change caption
Me.Caption = "Saving New Document..."

'save merge file
word.filesaveas sMergeFile

'close merge file
word.Fileclose 2

'change caption
Me.Caption = "Opening Merged Document..."

'open merge document
word.fileopen sMergeFile

'show merged document
hHandle2 = ShowWindow(hHandle1, 1)
```

continues

Listing 14.4. continued

```
MergeExit:
    'change caption
    Me.Caption = ""

    'change mouse
    Screen.MousePointer = vbDefault
    Exit Sub

TrapError:
    Select Case Err
        Case 53:    'file not found
            Resume Next
        Case Else:
            MsgBox "Error " & Err & " - " & Error
            DoEvents
            DoEvents
            If Not word Is Nothing Then     'clean up object
                Set word = Nothing
            End If
            Resume MergeExit
    End Select

    Exit Sub
noFile:
    Resume Next

End Sub
```

The code is fairly simple to follow. First, it ensures that the template created in the previous step actually exists. This is imperative for the merge to work. Then a data file is needed. Word will merge the template document along with the data file into a merge document. Therefore, the next section of code makes sure that this data file is deleted (in case a letter was run before this point).

Next, a file handle is opened that enables you to write out several data records. These records could have just as easily come from a database or from some other means. For the sake of example, the code clearly shows the records being written out. Note that for the letter merge to work, you must write out the same number of fields as the number in the header.

To ensure the datatypes are correct, a function called `FillQuote()` is called. This is a user-defined function that makes sure that the final string to be written out contains quotes, as appropriate. Listing 14.5 shows this function.

Listing 14.5. The `FillQuote()` function.

```
Function FillQuote(ByVal sTempString As String) As String
    'this function fills the string with double quotes around each field

    Dim nLoopCount As Integer
    Dim sFinalString As String

    For nLoopCount = 1 To Len(sTempString)
        If Mid$(sTempString, nLoopCount, 1) = "," Then
            sFinalString = sFinalString & Chr$(34) & "," & Chr$(34)
        Else
            sFinalString = sFinalString & Mid$(sTempString, nLoopCount, 1)
        End If
    Next nLoopCount

    sFinalString = Chr$(34) & sFinalString & Chr$(34)
    FillQuote = sFinalString
End Function
```

This function simply ensures that each one of the fields is in double quotes, as noted by `Chr$(34)`.

Now get back to the code in Listing 14.4. The code now creates a reference to the `Word.Basic` object. This line of code actually starts an instance of Word. From here, many methods are executed that are specifically exported by the `Word.Basic` object to manipulate the mail merge functionality. They are well commented above so that you can understand each line of code as it is executed.

This chapter couldn't possibly list every way to interface with Office 97. It was intended to give an overview of some of the ways to interface with the Office 97 components. The two examples presented in this chapter are on the CD accompanying this book in the `\Office\Excel` and `\Office\Word` subdirectories. Also, please refer to the application in Chapter 38, "Data Sharing with Microsoft Office."

Summary

Integrating with Microsoft Office is done through OLE Automation. Office 97 exposes many objects that your Visual Basic programs can access. This chapter showed how you can perform tasks needed most often from both Word and Excel. Use this chapter as a reference when you need to integrate with Office 97.

III

Enterprise-Specific Features

15

Visual SourceSafe

Visual SourceSafe is available in the Enterprise Edition of Visual Basic 5.0 or as a separate product from Microsoft. Visual SourceSafe keeps your source code safely in a proprietary database. This database works very similarly to a library. Users check out source code, make changes, and check it back in. Just as with a library book, once the code is checked out, no one else can check it out. This allows for any number of developers to check out and lock the source code so that changes can be made. After changes have been made, the code can be checked in. After all developers check in the code, an executable (or DLL) can be generated. When you generate an executable or DLL, you can label it as being a specific version.

In addition, the code can be "marked" or "labeled" as a specific version of your program. This enables you to refer to the code for a previous version if it is necessary, or even build an older executable or DLL. This means that you will never lose code again.

One other major advantage of using Visual SourceSafe is that if multiple users do check out a piece of source code, Visual SourceSafe will actually show you the differences when you check it in, so that the changes can be merged together. These differences indicate all of the changes made since the time the code was last checked in.

Installing Visual SourceSafe

You have three options when you install Visual SourceSafe: Server, Custom, and Client (see Figure 15.1). To use Visual SourceSafe, you must deem one computer as a server. This will be the computer used to store all of the source code.

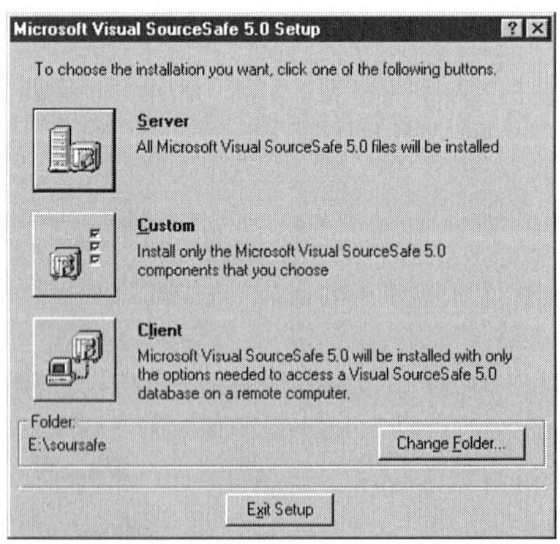

FIGURE 15.1.
Installation options for Visual SourceSafe.

The Server option installs all possible files to the server machine. It installs the Visual SourceSafe database, as well as client programs for the server machine to access the database. In addition, the appropriate files to allow other clients to be set up are added. This means that after you set up the server, you can set up the clients from the server installation. You do not need to insert the CD-ROM again.

The Custom option enables you to choose the type of installation you would like. Choosing this option brings up the Custom dialog box, as shown in Figure 15.2.

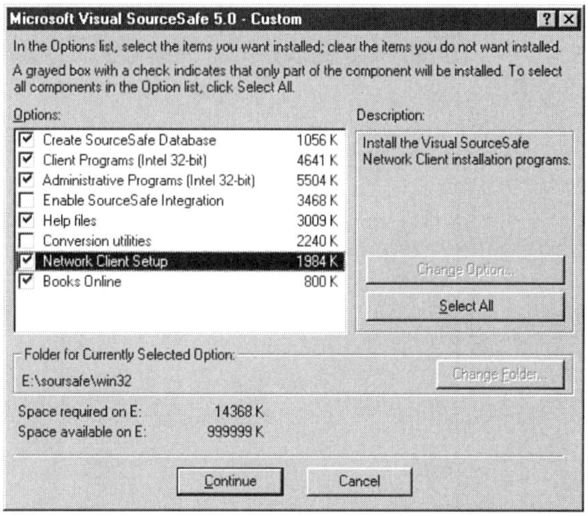

FIGURE 15.2.
Custom installation options.

The following are the choices for the Custom installation:

- Create SourceSafe Database. This option installs the database needed by Visual SourceSafe.
- Client Programs. These programs let you access the database created in the earlier option.
- Administrative Programs. These programs enable you to administer and configure Visual SourceSafe.
- Enable SourceSafe Integration. This registers Visual SourceSafe to be used inside development environments, such as Visual Basic, Visual C++, and Visual FoxPro.
- Help Files.
- Conversion Utilities. These utilities enable you to convert from other version control programs.
- Network Client Setup. This option enables you to install the client programs as part of a network setup.
- Books Online. This option refers to documentation contained on the CD-ROM.

Administering the Server

You administer Visual SourceSafe by selecting Start | Programs | Visual SourceSafe 5.0 Admin. This will bring up the application shown in Figure 15.3.

FIGURE 15.3.
Visual SourceSafe Administrator.

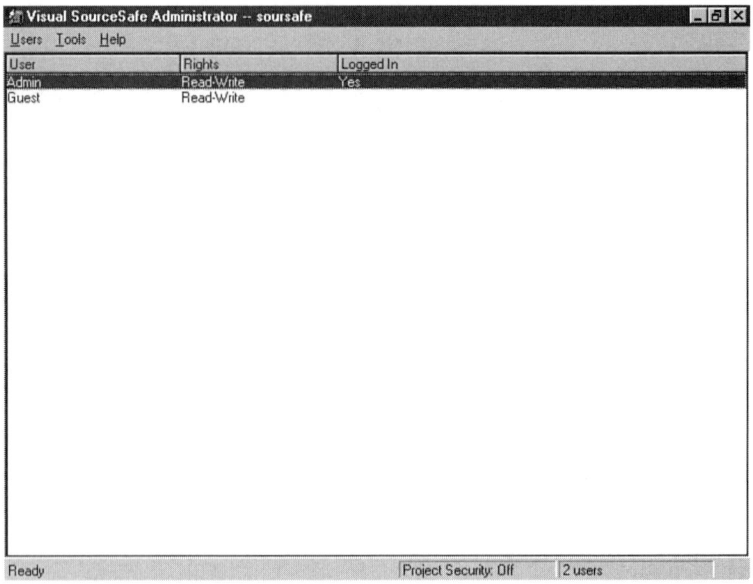

The Administrator will enable you to add new users, change passwords, and add a database. If this is the first time you are using Visual SourceSafe, you must add users who will be accessing the database. Typically, only one database is used in Visual SourceSafe. All of your projects are stored within the database.

To add a new user, select Users | Add User. You will be prompted to add a user's name and password. Passwords are not mandatory. If you leave it blank, there will be no password. It is advisable to have each user's name the same as the network logon ID because the user will not have to enter an ID every time he or she wants to access Visual SourceSafe. The ability to not force the user to type in the logon ID and password is made possible by an option under the Tools | Options menu option. This option is mentioned later in this chapter, in the "Options" section.

You can also delete or edit a user by selecting the appropriate menu option under the Users menu. After you add all appropriate users, the window looks something like Figure 15.4.

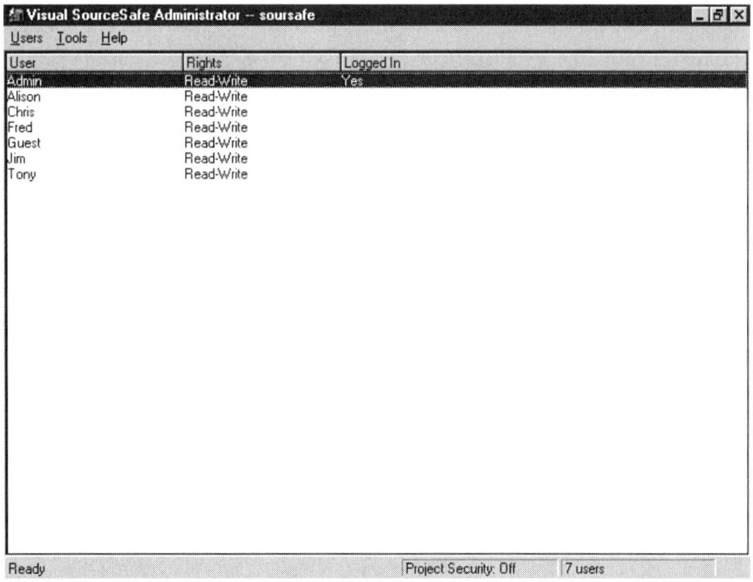

FIGURE 15.4.
Visual SourceSafe after adding users.

Options

There are numerous options that you can configure as the administrator. To select these options, choose Tools | Options. You will see a dialog box showing six different tabs of options. Each is described in the following sections.

General

The General options tab configures general options for Visual SourceSafe as a whole. Figure 15.5 shows this tab.

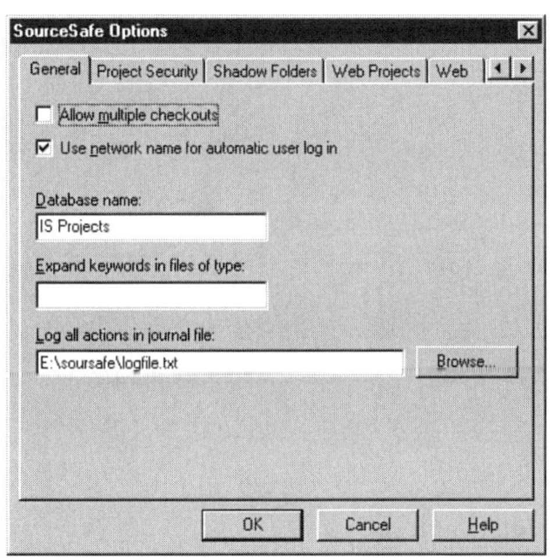

FIGURE 15.5.
The General tab of the Visual SourceSafe Administrator Options.

There are two check boxes in this tab. The first is to allow multiple checkouts. If this option is checked, multiple users can check out the same file. Then, the administrator must merge changes together.

If the second check box—Use network name for automatic user login—is checked, it will pass on to Visual SourceSafe the user ID of the network. This speeds up logging into Visual SourceSafe.

You use the Database name: text box to track the names of your databases. This is especially important when you are using multiple databases because it helps you to track them more efficiently. Remember that you only name a database, you do not give it a filename. Therefore, you do not know where it is stored in Visual SourceSafe.

You use the Expand keywords in files of type: text box to indicate to Visual SourceSafe which keywords need to be expanded. This is a function of Visual SourceSafe in that a Visual SourceSafe keyword will be expanded into a meaningful description or header for the user to understand.

You use the Log all actions in journal file: text box to display the name and path of the journal file that will log all actions.

Project Security

The Project Security options tab enables you to enforce security within your projects. By default, this is turned off. Figure 15.6 shows this tab.

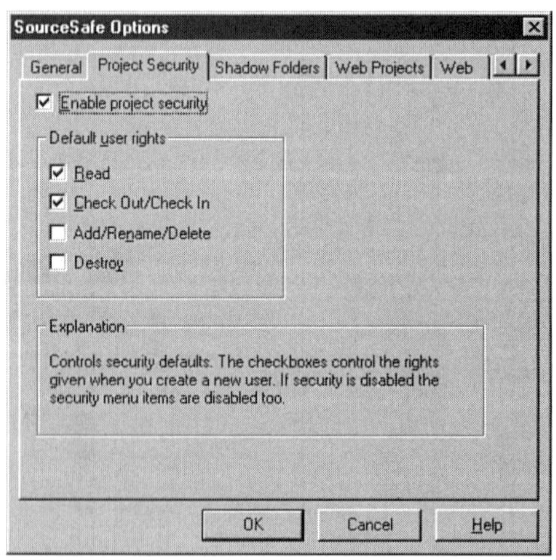

FIGURE 15.6.
The Project Security tab of Visual SourceSafe Administrator Options.

Project Security is turned on when you select the Enable project security check box. Then, you can set the default security for new users. You can choose from the following:

- Read
- Check Out/Check In

- Add/Rename/Delete
- Destroy

It probably is a good idea to give only Read and Check Out/Check In privileges to users by default. Then you can give the other privileges to individual users when they are added.

Shadow Folders

The Shadow Folders options tab enables you to decide whether to shadow a specific project added into Visual SourceSafe. *Shadowing* lets you mirror the current copy of all of the files in the project. Typically, this could be used as a common place to store files to construct a build of your project. This is not necessary in all projects. Figure 15.7 shows this tab.

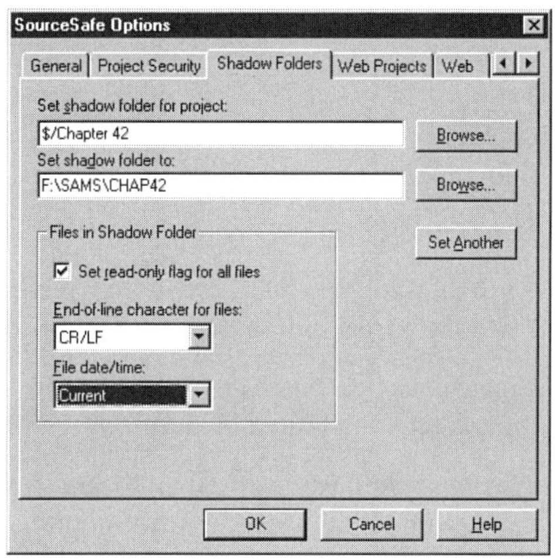

FIGURE 15.7.
The Shadow Folders tab of the Visual SourceSafe Administrator Options.

By default, this option is turned off. If you want to use Shadow Folders, you must select the project to shadow, followed by the folder into which you want to place all of the shadow files. A shadow folder can be a good way to back up your projects.

When those items are selected, you will notice that the frame at the bottom of the dialog box has become enabled. Select Set read-only flag for all files. Also, set the End-of-line character for files: item. Typically, the CR/LF (carriage return/line feed) option is used. Then select the File date/time option.

Web Projects

The Web Projects tab enables you to configure the parameters of a project if it is to be used as a Web-based project. By default, nothing is filled in on this tab. Figure 15.8 shows this tab.

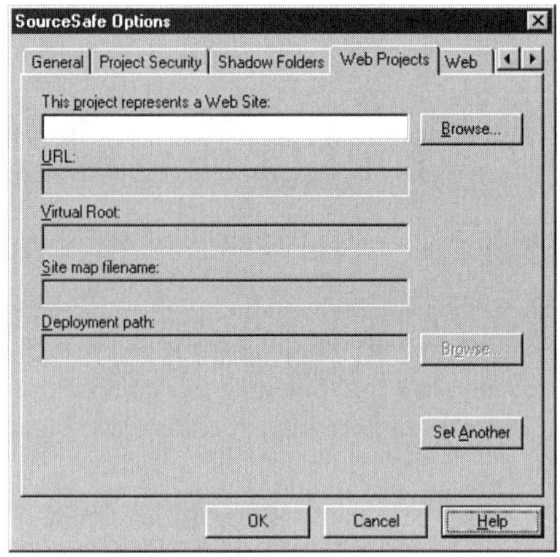

FIGURE 15.8.
The Web Projects tab of the Visual SourceSafe Administrator Options.

There are five text boxes on this tab. Each is used to denote a specific attribute of Web hosting. The first is the This project represents a Web Site: text box. Fill it in to specify the Web project.

Next is the URL: text box. Fill in the Uniform Resource Locator address for the Web project.

Following is the Virtual Root: text box. Not all Web servers support this. Use this option only if you have specified the virtual root in the server software.

You use the Site map filename: text box to specify the site map HTML filename if you plan to support site maps. `SITEMAP.HTM` is used by default.

Finally, the Deployment path: text box is used to specify where you will deploy your project. Typically, this will be an FTP address if this is an Internet project, or even a hard drive location if it is an intranet project.

Use the Set Another command button to be able to set the same parameters for another Web site project.

Web

The Web tab enables you to define the parameters that affect all of your Web projects in Visual SourceSafe. By default, nothing is filled in on this tab (see Figure 15.9).

There are three text boxes that are needed if you plan to deploy from a proxy server. The first is Proxy for deploying over ftp. This is used to specify a proxy server if one is used to deploy over FTP.

Next is the Do not use the proxy for these local servers: text box. Use it to specify local servers that will not use the proxy listed above it. A proxy server enables a user to access the Internet without the need for a modem. It is accessed through a server that acts as a proxy for the client workstations.

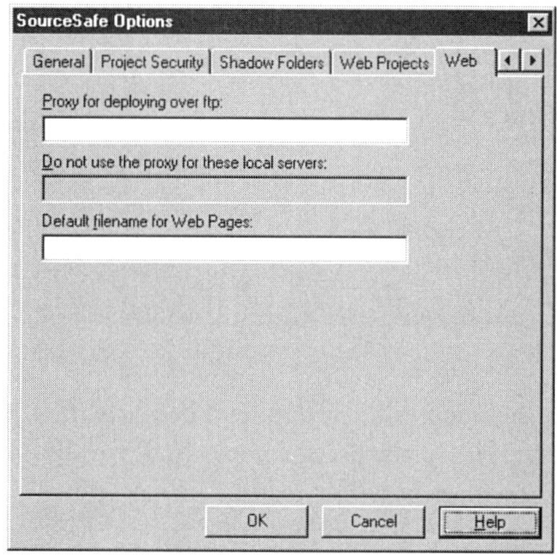

FIGURE 15.9.
The Web tab of the Visual SourceSafe Administrator Options.

Finally, the Default filename for Web Pages: text box is used to specify the default page, such as `INDEX.HTM`, when the user simply types in the URL of the site without a specific page.

File Types

The File Types tab enables you to define the file extensions used for different types of Visual SourceSafe projects. Figure 15.10 shows this tab.

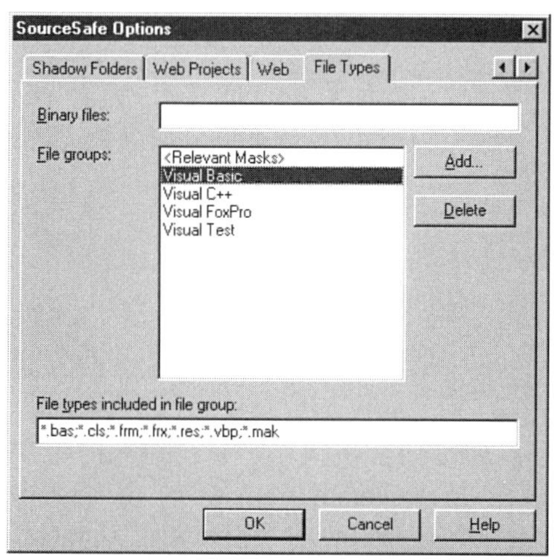

FIGURE 15.10.
The File Types tab in Visual SourceSafe Administrator Options.

The Binary files: text box is used to specify the file extensions of files that will be treated as binary all the time. This will override the Visual SourceSafe automatic detection of the type of file. Each type of file is separated by a comma.

The File groups: list box shows the different project types that can be used in Visual SourceSafe. By default, there are four types shown:

- Visual Basic
- Visual C++
- Visual FoxPro
- Visual Test

To add a new group, select the Add button. Likewise, to remove a group, select the Delete button.

The File types included in file group: text box lists the file extensions that are associated with the highlighted group in the list box above it. Typically, you will not need to change this. You will need to add entries only if you add a new group.

Security

After you enable security in the Options screen, you can manipulate the attributes of security for each user or project. To administer rights per project, select Tools | Rights by Project. This will bring up the Project Rights dialog box shown in Figure 15.11.

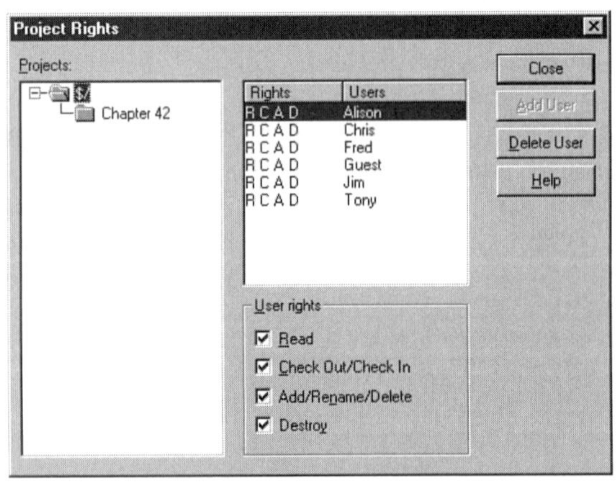

FIGURE 15.11.
Rights by project.

Notice the hierarchy of the projects. The top (root) of Visual SourceSafe is indicated by a `$/` symbol. Under this root symbol is a project called Chapter 42. This is a project that can be assigned its own security or inherit the security from the above (root) structure.

The following are the possible rights shown for each user:

- R—Read
- C—Check Out/Check In

- A—Add
- D—Destroy

To change a right, simply click the appropriate project, select the user, and check or uncheck the appropriate right.

To assign rights by user, first select the appropriate user. Then, select Tools | Rights Assignments For User. This will bring up the dialog box shown in Figure 15.12.

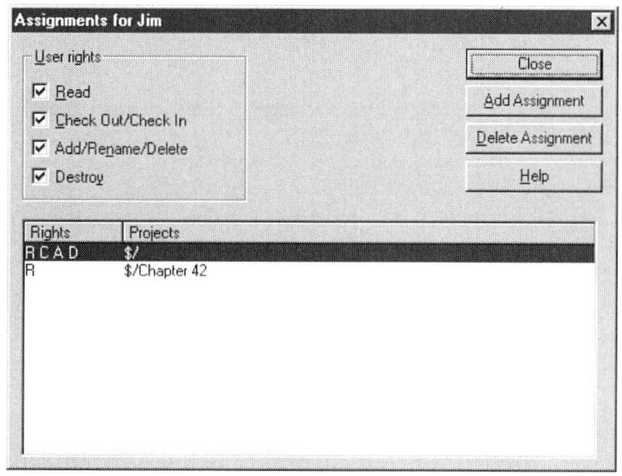

FIGURE 15.12.
Rights by user.

Notice in Figure 15.12 that user Jim has all rights to the root structure, but only Read rights to Chapter 42. You can change this for the chosen user for any project by clicking the appropriate project and then clicking the appropriate right.

Using the Client Utility

To use the client utility, select Start | Programs | Visual SourceSafe 5.0. This will bring up a dialog box that contains a list of all of the projects added into the Visual SourceSafe database. Figure 15.13 shows this dialog box.

The first step is to add the project with which you want to use Visual SourceSafe. To do this, highlight the root with the mouse, and then select File | Create Project. Type the name of the project and any comments you want to add, if appropriate.

After you create the project, you must add files that make up the project. It is important to note that even if the files that made up the project without using Visual SourceSafe are contained in different directories, you must add them all into your Visual SourceSafe project. It does not matter where the files came from—Visual SourceSafe will keep track of them. If you had files in different directories before using Visual SourceSafe because they are shared, Visual SourceSafe can handle that, too. This is discussed later, in the section, "Using Visual SourceSafe Within Visual Basic."

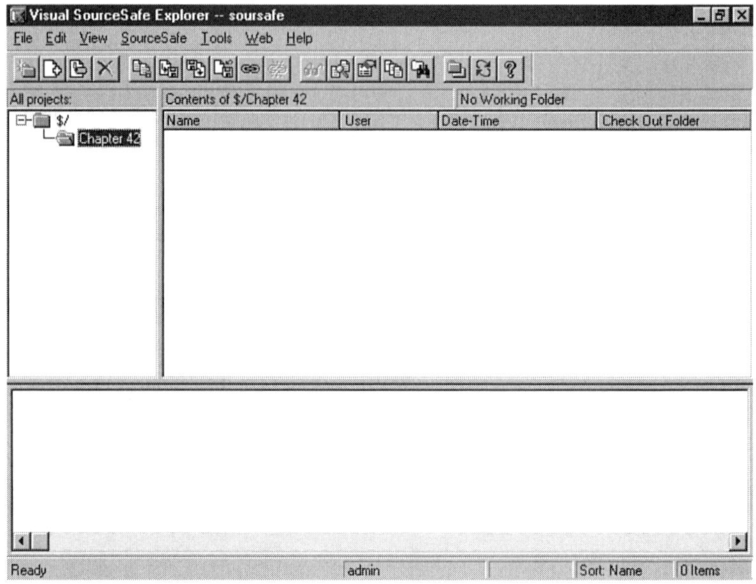

FIGURE 15.13.
The Visual SourceSafe client program.

Adding Files to a Project

To add files to a project, simply select File | Add Files, and then choose the files to add to the project. Suppose you wanted to create a Visual SourceSafe project for tracking the files in the VBMail sample project that comes with Visual Basic. Create the project, and then add the files from the `\Samples\CompTool\VBMail` directory of wherever you installed Visual Basic. Figure 15.14. shows how the dialog box looks while you are adding these files.

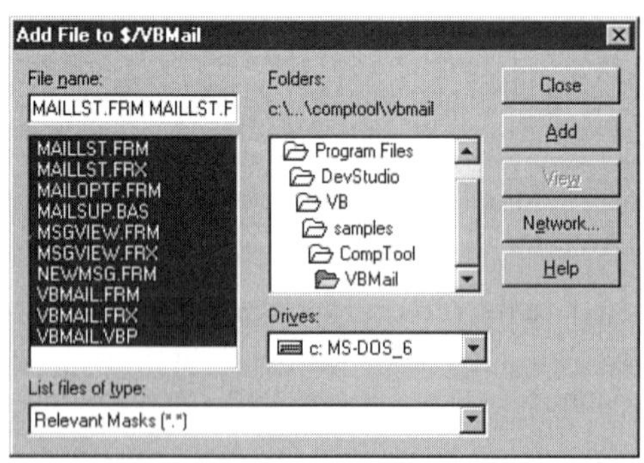

FIGURE 15.14.
Adding files to a project.

You will be prompted to add a comment for each file added into the project. Then, you will be prompted to select a working directory. The concept behind a working directory is that the files in Visual SourceSafe are only for storage. Therefore, a working directory is needed as a place to temporarily store the files you are working on so that Visual Basic has all the files needed for one project stored in one place. Therefore, each user must have one working directory for each project he or she is working on.

If you don't want to accept the working directory proposed, simply click the No button. You can change it later.

After you add all appropriate files, the main Explorer window looks like Figure 15.15.

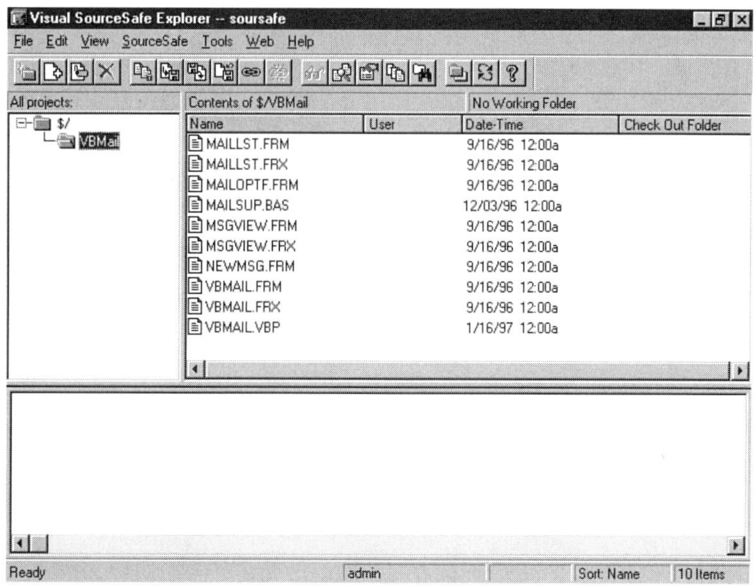

FIGURE 15.15.
Visual SourceSafe Explorer after adding files to a project.

Before you are able to use the files, you must set the working directory. To do this, choose File | Set Working Folder. This will bring up a dialog box for you to select a working folder.

Working with Visual SourceSafe

To work with Visual SourceSafe, you must get the latest version of the checked-in files stored inside Visual SourceSafe itself. You must get all of the files necessary to compile the project. Therefore, simply highlight all of the files listed in the project and choose SourceSafe | Get Latest Version. This will copy all of the latest files into your working folder. Figure 15.16 shows how your Visual SourceSafe Explorer looks after getting the latest project files.

To open the project in Visual Basic, simply open the project in Visual Basic stored in the working folder selected earlier. However, if you do not check out any of the files, you will not be able to save any changes. Therefore, if you plan to change a file, check it out by selecting the appropriate file. Then choose SourceSafe | Check Out. This flags the file in your working directory as read-write and also tells Visual SourceSafe that the file is checked out. Therefore, this will prevent other users from checking it out (unless you have the appropriate option selected in the Tools | Options menu option). Figure 15.17 shows what the Visual SourceSafe Explorer looks like after checking out files. It is very important in Visual Basic to check out all `*.FRM` and `*.FRX` files together. Visual Basic needs both to save a form.

FIGURE 15.16.
Visual SourceSafe Explorer after getting the latest versions.

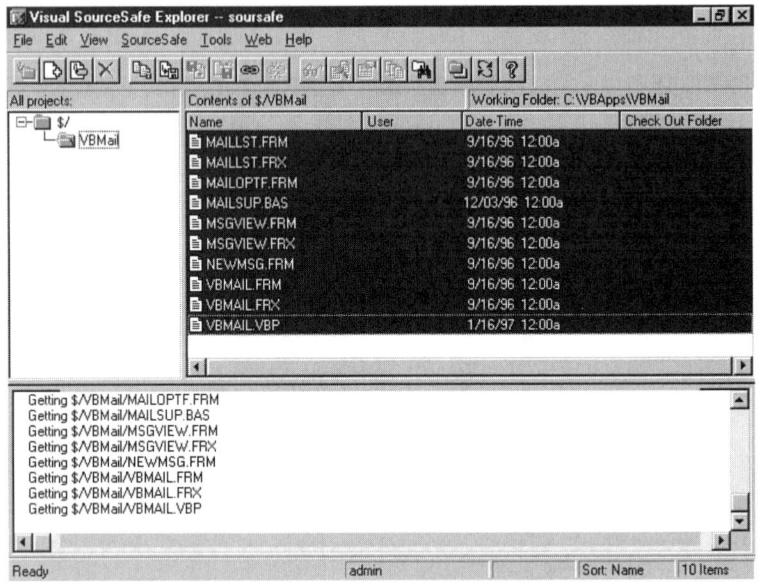

FIGURE 15.17.
Visual SourceSafe Explorer after you check out files.

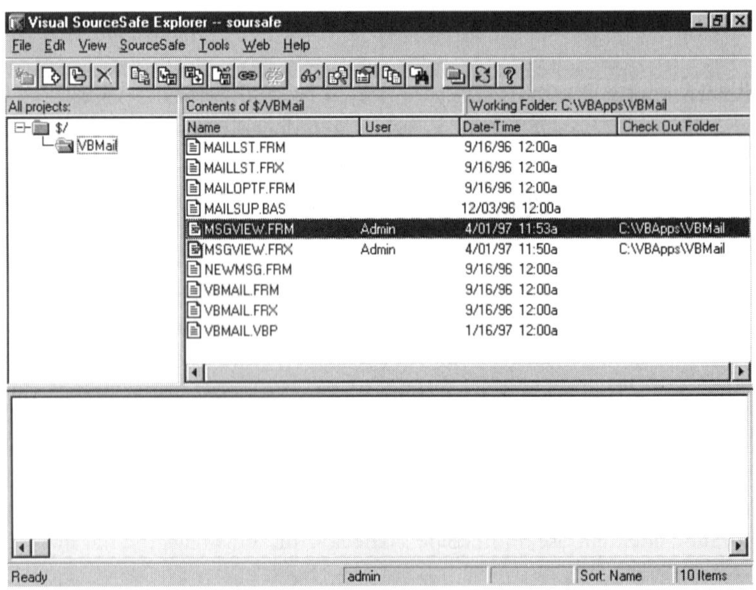

After you make and save changes in Visual Basic, simply check in the files by selecting SourceSafe | Check-In. This will mark the files in your working folder as read-only and also notify Visual SourceSafe itself that the file is checked in.

You can think of Visual SourceSafe as a library. Within this library (the Visual SourceSafe database), there are categories of books (projects). Within these categories are the books themselves (files). These books can be read at home (working folder) only if you check them out. While they are checked out, no one else can read them until you check them back in.

Using Visual SourceSafe Within Visual Basic

Using Visual SourceSafe within Visual Basic is much easier than using the Visual SourceSafe Explorer because it is fully integrated with Visual Basic. To ensure that Visual SourceSafe is set up correctly, set it up from the subdirectory out on the server. This subdirectory, SETUP, will be under the main Visual SourceSafe directory. Set up the client and ensure that the Enable SourceSafe Integration option is checked.

To use Visual SourceSafe within Visual Basic, simply open the project in the working directory. Then, you can access the Visual SourceSafe options by either right-clicking the appropriate form or by using the Tools | SourceSafe menu option within Visual Basic. You will see a list of all possible options. If you use the right-click method, you have the following Visual SourceSafe options:

- Get Latest Version
- Check Out
- Check In
- Undo Check Out

If you use the Tools menu, you have the preceding options plus the following:

- Show History
- Show Differences
- SourceSafe Properties
- Add Files to SourceSafe
- Share Files
- Create Project From SourceSafe
- Run SourceSafe
- Options
- Refresh File Status

You would use the Get Latest Version option because you want to make sure that you are working with the latest versions of all files in your working folder. All files are copied into your working folder. Your working folder is only one subdirectory. You cannot have multiple directories for your working folder.

The Check Out and Check In options are used, of course, to check out and in the files. If the file is checked out, it is read-write. If the file is checked in, it is read-only.

The Undo Checkout option is useful if you checked out the wrong file or files. This does not record the check out in history, as it would be if you simply checked it back in.

Show History shows you the history of a file. The history of the file to date is shown in Figure 15.18.

FIGURE 15.18.
Visual SourceSafe history.

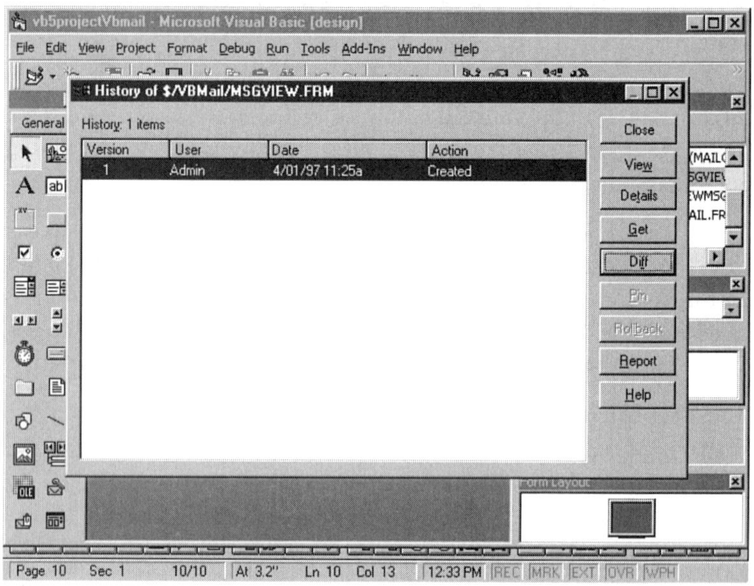

Show Differences is very useful in comparing what is in the working folder with what is in the Visual SourceSafe database. Figure 15.19 shows what the differences look like. Visual SourceSafe will track the differences to not only form controls, but the code as well.

The window on the left is the file shown in the Visual SourceSafe database. The window on the right shows the working folder file.

SourceSafe Properties shows different properties about the file that currently is highlighted. These properties are shown in a screen with four different tabs. Figures 15.20 through 15.23 show these tabs.

FIGURE 15.19.
Visual SourceSafe showing differences.

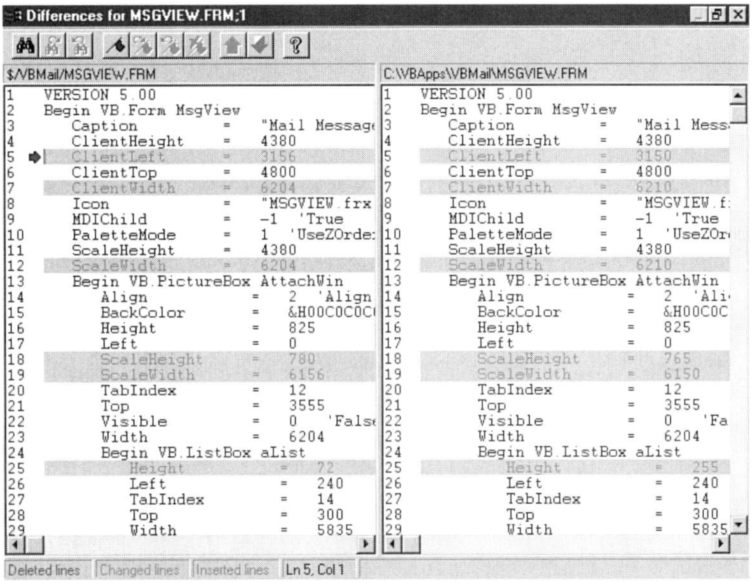

FIGURE 15.20.
The General tab of the Visual SourceSafe properties.

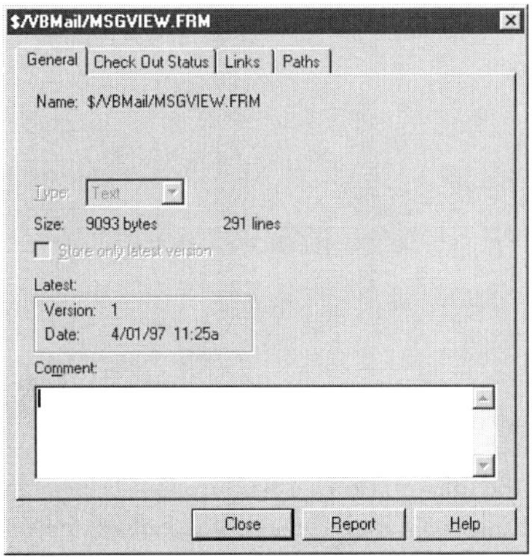

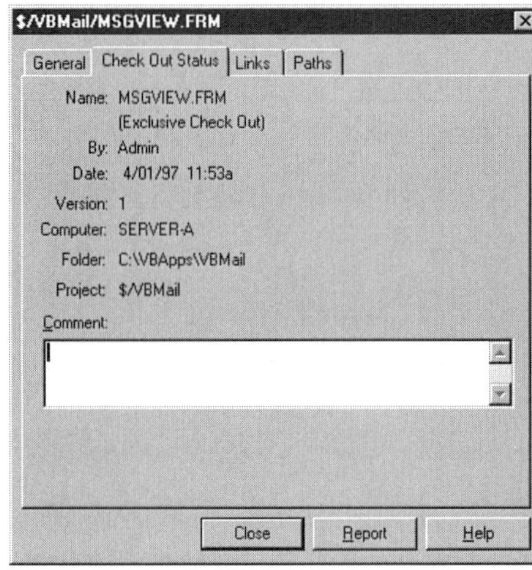

FIGURE 15.21.
The Check Out Status tab of the Visual SourceSafe properties.

FIGURE 15.22.
The Links tab of the Visual SourceSafe properties.

In addition to the information shown on this screen in these four figures, you can print out or store reports about the status of these files. For example, choose the General tab, and then select the Report button. This will bring up a dialog box in which you can choose the destination of the report. Choose the Preview button. This will bring up a report, as shown in Figure 15.24. This can be very useful in troubleshooting and tracking files.

The Add Files To SourceSafe option enables you to add a file from a project into SourceSafe. If all files in a directory have been added, you will receive a message stating that all available files have been added.

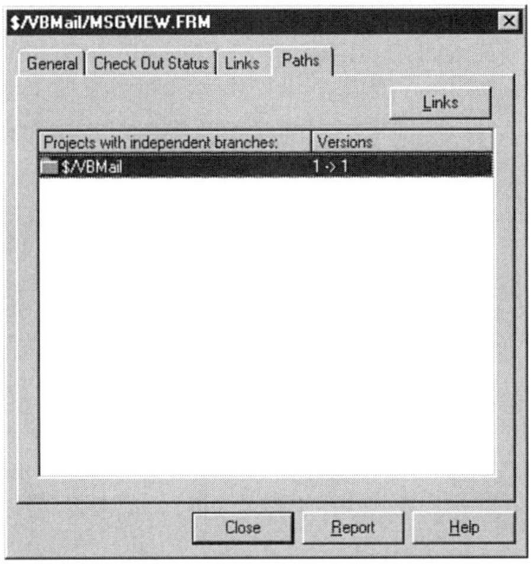

FIGURE 15.23.
The Paths tab of the Visual SourceSafe properties.

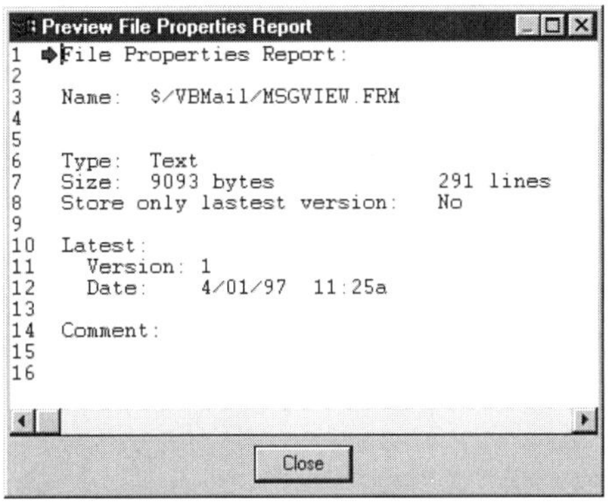

FIGURE 15.24.
Previewing a file properties report in Visual SourceSafe.

The Share Files option is used to share files with another Visual SourceSafe project. This is a very important option. If you choose to share a file, it will store only one copy inside Visual SourceSafe itself. If there are files that contain a lot of routines that you use in all projects, you do not want to store multiple copies of the same file. Therefore, you would store it as a shared file. Then, if you want to view which projects use the shared file, choose the SourceSafe Properties menu option.

The Create Project From SourceSafe menu option creates a local copy of a project added into Visual SourceSafe. This makes it easy to participate in a project that was recently added into Visual SourceSafe.

The Run SourceSafe option simply runs the Visual SourceSafe program. This is exactly the same option as choosing Start | Programs | Visual SourceSafe 5.0.

The Options menu option enables you to configure four different options. These options are configured in the Source Code Control Options dialog box shown in Figure 15.25.

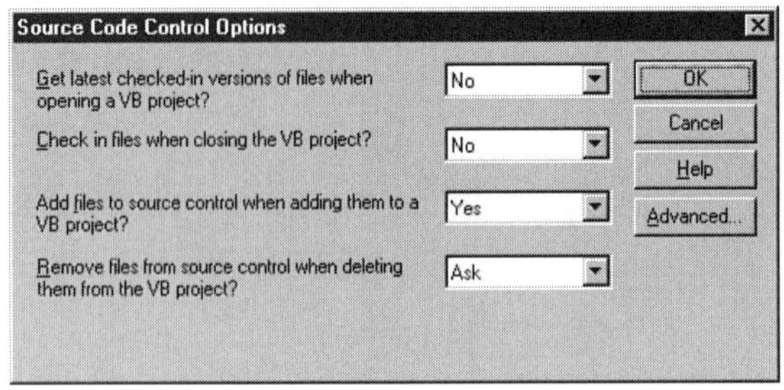

FIGURE 15.25.
The Source Code Control Options dialog box.

Each option has three possibilities, Yes, No, and Ask. The options are

- Get latest checked-in versions of files when opening a VB project?
- Check in files when closing the VB project?
- Add files to source control when adding them to a VB project?
- Remove files from source control when deleting them from the VB project?

Additionally, there is an Advanced button to configure advanced options. The advanced options screen is made up of the following three tabs:

- General
- Local Files
- Integration

The General tab looks like Figure 15.26.

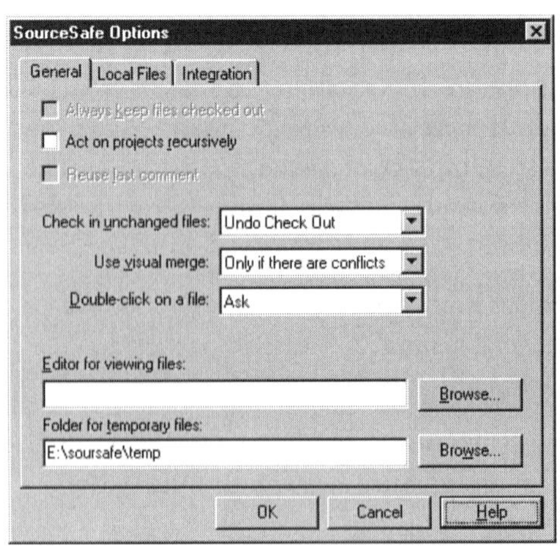

FIGURE 15.26.
The General tab of the Visual SourceSafe advanced options.

The Always keep files checked out option keeps the files checked out into your working folder, even if the files are checked in.

The Act on projects recursively option allows actions that are made to a project affect the entire hierarchy in the project.

The Reuse last comment option simply reuses the last comment for the next command. This makes it very easy to copy comments and reuse them, forcing you to change comments where you need to.

The Check in unchanged files: option automatically checks in files to which you have not made any changes.

The Use visual merge: option allows a visual merge of the files when you are checking in a file.

The Double-click on a file: option affects which command is executed when you double-click on a file.

The Editor for viewing files: text box is used to override the default editor for viewing a file. The default editor is Visual Basic.

The Folder for temporary files: text box is used to indicate which folder will be used to store temporary (work) files. This option is filled in by default.

The Local Files tab of the SourceSafe Option dialog box looks like Figure 15.27.

The Remove local copy after Add or Check In option will delete the copy of the files in your working folder after they are checked in.

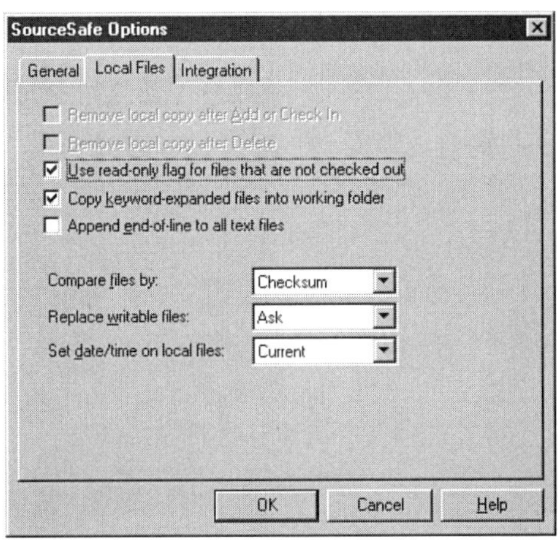

FIGURE 15.27.
The Local Files tab of the Visual SourceSafe advanced options.

The Remove local copy after Delete option will delete the local copy of the files in your working folder after they are deleted.

The Use read-only flag for files that are not checked out option, checked by default, ensures that only checked out files can be overwritten.

The Copy keyword-expanded files into working folder option copies into the working folder a file that might have had a keyword automatically expanded, such as the version number.

The Append end-of-line to all text files option appends a CR/LF character to the end of all text files. This option probably will never be turned off.

The Compare files by: option allows for the comparison of files by a certain method. The default is by CheckSum. Other options include Time and Contents.

Replace writable files: sets the option for what to do for a file that is marked as read-write in your working folder. The possibilities are

- Ask
- Replace
- Skip
- Merge

Set date/time on local files: sets the option for the date and time given to the files in your working folder. These options are

- Current
- Modification
- Check In

The Integration tab of the SourceSafe advanced options looks like Figure 15.28.

FIGURE 15.28.
The Integration tab of the Visual SourceSafe advanced options.

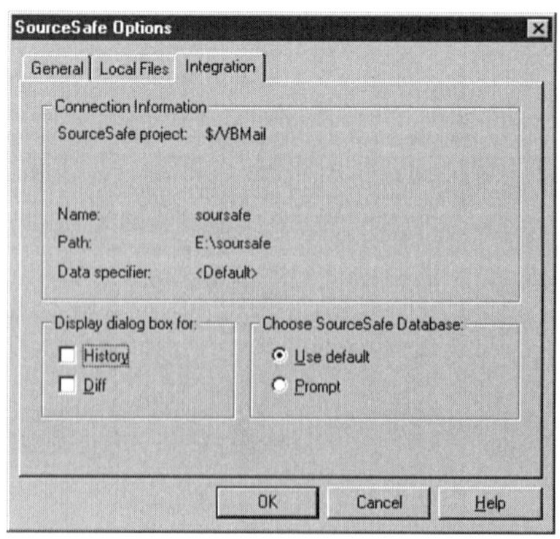

The Display dialog box for: options select whether to display a dialog box for history and differences of files.

The Choose SourceSafe Database: option automatically opens the default database or prompts you for the database to open when Visual SourceSafe is initialized.

The Refresh File Status menu option simply refreshes the status of each file in the project. This includes which files are checked out and who has them checked out.

Labeling a Version

If you are ready to make a build and want to label a version of the project, open the Visual SourceSafe 5.0 application either by selecting Start | Programs | Visual SourceSafe 5.0 or by selecting Tools | SourceSafe | Run SourceSafe within Visual Basic. Then select the project by highlighting it, and choose File | Label. This will bring up a dialog box allowing you to place a label into the box. This flags the project as a specific version label.

Then, to return to a specific version label, simply choose Tools | Show History. You then can select from a specific version of the project.

Summary

Visual SourceSafe is an excellent product to provide source code control. Before version 5.0, this functionality was not supported. There were products on the market, but they were not integrated into Visual Basic. This chapter showed you how to use and administer Visual SourceSafe.

16

Remote Data Objects (RDO)

Remote Data Objects provide for very fast ODBC access to manipulate ODBC databases. The set of Remote Data Objects are referred to as RDO. This acronym will be referenced throughout the rest of this chapter. This concept was introduced first in the 32-bit version of Visual Basic 4.0. However, it is available only in the Enterprise Edition. It has been refined and enhanced to support remote databases better than ever in version 5.0. Because RDO is supported only in the 32-bit version of Visual Basic 4.0 and in Visual Basic 5.0, only the Windows 95 and Windows NT operating systems are supported. Some of the database terms discussed throughout this chapter might be foreign to you, but they are discussed in more detail in Chapter 28, "Database Concepts."

Visual Basic version 5.0, Enterprise Edition only, includes RDO version 2.0. To access any of these objects, you must include a reference to the objects by selecting the Project | References menu option. This will bring up a dialog box. Select the entry Microsoft Remote Data Object 2.0. Figure 16.1 shows what this References dialog box looks like.

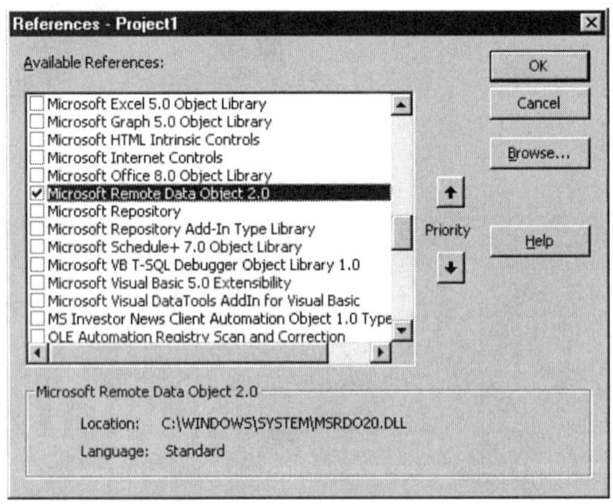

FIGURE 16.1.
The References dialog box, highlighting the RDO 2.0 library.

RDO is to an ODBC data source as Data Access Objects (DAO) is to local data using the JET engine (Access). DAO is another connection method for database access. DAO is provided in all versions of Visual Basic and is much slower than RDO. The main difference is that RDO does not process any queries. It is equivalent to using the `dbPassthrough` option when executing a DAO query.

RDO Hierarchy

To manipulate the RDO objects, consider Table 16.1. It lists the possible objects, about which you learn in detail throughout the rest of this chapter.

Table 16.1. RDO version 2.0 objects.

Object	*Description*
`rdoColumn`	Represents a remote data column.
`rdoColumns`	A collection of `rdoColumn` objects.
`rdoConnection`	Represents an open ODBC connection.
`rdoConnections`	A collection of `rdoConnection` objects.
`rdoEngine`	Top-most level object representing the remote data source.
`rdoEnvironment`	Represents a logical set of connections for a given user.
`rdoEnvironments`	A collection of `rdoEnvironment` objects.
`rdoError`	Represents RDO errors.
`rdoErrors`	A collection of `rdoError` objects.
`rdoParameter`	Represents a parameter for an `rdoPreparedStatement` object.
`rdoParameters`	A collection of `rdoParameter` objects.
`rdoPreparedStatement`	Represents a prepared query definition. This object is obsolete and provided for RDO version 1.0 compatibility only. Use `rdoQuery` instead.
`rdoPreparedStatements`	A collection of `rdoPreparedStatement` objects. This collection is obsolete and provided for RDO version 1.0 compatibility only. Use `rdoQueries` instead.
`rdoQuery`	Represents a defined query.
`rdoQueries`	A collection of `rdoQuery` objects.
`rdoResultset`	Represents the rows of data resulting from a query.
`rdoResultsets`	A collection of `rdoResultSet` objects.
`rdoTable`	Represents the definition of the base table or view of a query.
`rdoTables`	A collection of `rdoTable` objects.

To view all constants and objects available in the RDO library, use the Object Browser by pressing the F2 key, or by selecting the View | Object Browser menu option. Choose the RDO library. Figure 16.2 shows how the RDO library looks in the Object Browser.

Viewing the objects in the Object Browser is very useful for you to understand how the objects relate to each other. Figure 16.3 shows a hierarchical relationship diagram of the top-level RDO 2.0 objects. The properties, methods, and events are listed in Table 16.2.

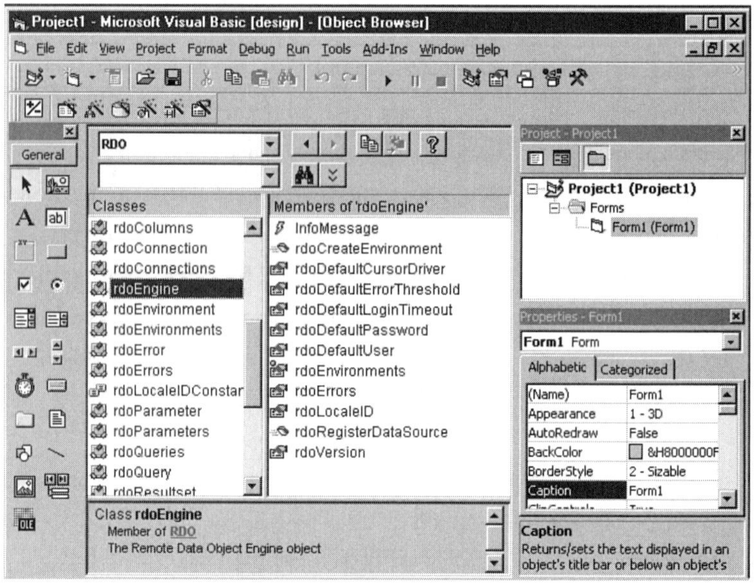

FIGURE 16.2.
The RDO library in the Object Browser.

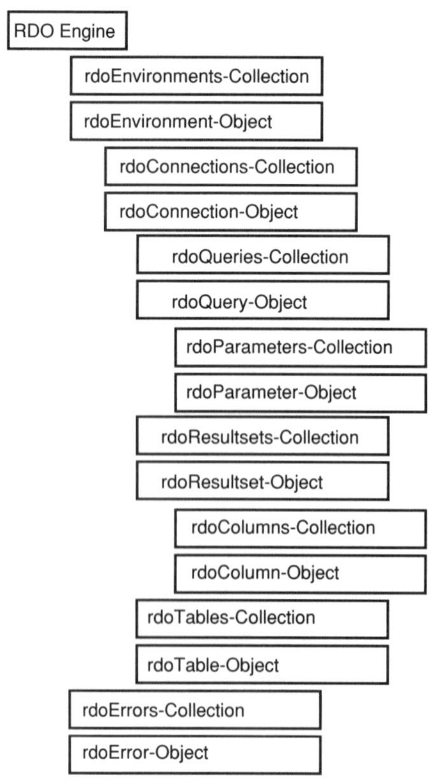

FIGURE 16.3.
A hierarchical RDO 2.0 object diagram.

Table 16.2. RDO 2.0 properties, methods, and events.

Properties	*Methods*	*Events*
	RDO Engine	
rdoDefaultCursorDriver	rdoCreateEnvironment	InfoMessage
rdoDefaultErrorThreshold	rdoRegisterDataSource	
rdoDefaultLoginTimeout		
rdoDefaultPassword		
rdoDefaultUser		
rdoLocaleID		
rdoVersion		
	rdoEnvironments-Collection	
Count	Item	
	Add	
	Remove	
	rdoEnvironment-Object	
CursorDriver	BeginTrans	BeginTrans
hEnv	Close	CommitTrans
LoginTimeout	CommitTrans	RollBackTrans
Name	OpenConnection	
Password	RollbackTrans	
UserName		
	rdoConnections-Collection	
Count	Item	
	Add	
	Remove	
	rdoConnection-Object	
AsyncCheckInterval	BeginTrans	BeforeConnect
Connect	Cancel	Connect
Cursor Driver	Close	Disconnect
hDbc	CommitTrans	QueryComplete
LastQueryResults	CreateQuery	QueryTimeout
LoginTimeout	EstablishConnection	WillExecute
LogMessages	Execute	

continues

Table 16.2. continued

Properties	*Methods*	*Events*
	rdoConnection-Object	
`Name`	`OpenResultset`	
`QueryTimeout`	`RollbackTrans`	
`RowsAffected`		
`StillConnecting`		
`StillExecuting`		
`Transactions`		
`Updatable`		
`Version`		
	rdoQueries-Collection	
`Count`	`Item`	
	rdoQuery-Object	
`ActiveConnection`	`Cancel`	`QueryComplete`
`BindThreshold`	`Close`	`QueryTimeout`
`Connect`	`Execute`	`WillExecute`
`CursorType`	`OpenResultset`	
`ErrorThreshold`		
`hStmt`		
`KeysetSize`		
`LockType`		
`LogMessages`		
`MaxRows`		
`Name`		
`Prepared`		
`QueryTimeout`		
`RowsAffected`		
`RowsetSize`		
`SQL`		
`StillExecuting`		
`Type`		
`Updatable`		

Properties	*Methods*	*Events*
	***rdoParameters*-Collection**	
Count	Item	
	***rdoParameter*-Object**	
Direction	AppendChunk	
Name		
Type		
Value		
	***rdoResultsets*-Collection**	
Count	Item	
	***rdoResultset*-Object**	
AbsolutePosition	AddNew	Associate
ActiveConnection	BatchUpdate	ResultsChanged
BatchCollisionCount	Cancel	Dissociate
BatchCollisionRows	CancelBatch	QueryComplete
BatchingSize	CancelUpdate	RowStatusChanged
BOF	Close	RowCurrencyChange
Bookmark	Delete	WillAssociate
Bookmarkable	Edit	WillDissociate
EditMode	GetRows	WillUpdateRows
hStmt	MoreResults	
LastModified	Move	
LockEdits	MoveFirst	
LockType	MoveLast	
Name	MoveNext	
PercentPosition	MovePrevious	
Restartable	Requery	
RowCount	Update	
Status		
StillExecuting		
Transactions		
Type		

continues

Table 16.2. continued

Properties	*Methods*	*Events*
	rdoResultset-Object	
Updatable		
UpdateCriteria		
UpdateOperation		
	rdoColumns-Collection	
Count	Item	
	Refresh	
	rdoColumn-Object	
AllowZeroLength	AppendChunk	DataChanged
Attributes	GetChunk	WillChangeData
ColumnSize		
BatchConflictValue		
KeyColumn		
Name		
OrdinalPosition		
OriginalValue		
Required		
Size		
SourceColumn		
SourceTable		
Status		
Type		
Updatable		
Value		
	rdoTables-Collection	
Count	Item	
	Refresh	
	rdoTable-Object	
Name	OpenResultset	
RowCount		
Type		
Updatable		

Properties	Methods	Events
	rdoErrors-Collection	
Count	Item	
	Clear	
	rdoError-Object	
Description		
HelpContext		
HelpFile		
Number		
Source		
SQLRetCode		
SQLState		

RDO Properties

There are many properties that enable you to manipulate the RDO objects. Table 16.3 defines these properties as they relate to Figure 16.3 and Table 16.2.

Table 16.3. RDO 2.0 properties.

Property	Definition
AbsolutePosition	Sets or returns the absolute position of the current row in a resultset.
ActiveConnection	Object reference to the current database connection.
AllowZeroLength	Sets or returns whether a text column can allow null values.
AsyncCheckInterval	Sets or returns the number of milliseconds that an asynchronous query waits to check if it is finished.
Attributes	Returns a value indicating miscellaneous attributes of a column in a resultset.
BatchCollisionRows	Returns an array of records that failed the last batch update.
BatchConflictValue	Returns the newer database value than the current value during a batch update conflict.
BatchSize	Sets or returns the number of records in a batch.
BindThreshold	Sets or returns a value specifying the largest column that will automatically be bound through ODBC.

continues

Table 16.3. continued

Property	*Definition*
`BOF`	Returns whether the current row is at the beginning of the resultset.
`Bookmark`	Sets or returns a bookmark to the current row in an `rdoResultset` object.
`Bookmarkable`	Indicates whether an `rdoResultset` object supports bookmarks.
`ChunkRequired`	A Boolean value that indicates whether data must be accessed using the `GetChunk` method.
`Connect`	Sets or returns an ODBC connect string.
`Count`	Returns the number of objects in a collection.
`CursorDriver`	Sets or returns the type of cursor to be created.
`CursorType`	Sets or returns the default type of cursor to use when opening an `rdoResultSet` object.
`Description`	Returns a description of an error.
`Direction`	Sets or returns how a parameter is passed to or from a procedure.
`EditMode`	Returns the state of editing for the current row.
`EOF`	Returns whether the current row is at the end of the resultset.
`hDbc`	Returns an ODBC connection handle.
`HelpContext`	Sets or returns a context ID for a Help file topic.
`HelpFile`	Returns a fully qualified Help file path.
`hEnv`	Returns the ODBC environment handle.
`hStmt`	Returns an ODBC statement handle.
`Item`	Returns a specific item from an RDO collection.
`KeyColumn`	Sets or returns whether this column is part of the primary key.
`KeysetSize`	Sets or returns the number of rows in the keyset buffer.
`LastModified`	Returns the most recently changed (or added) row.
`LastQueryResults`	Returns a reference to the `rdoResultset` object generated by the last query.
`LockEdits`	A Boolean value indicating the type of locking used.
`LockType`	Sets or returns the type of concurrency handling.

Property	*Definition*
`LoginTimeout`	Sets or returns the number of seconds the ODBC driver manager waits before a time-out error.
`LogMessages`	Sets or returns the path of the ODBC trace file to log ODBC messages.
`Maxrows`	Sets or returns the maximum number of rows to be returned from a query.
`Name`	Returns the name of an RDO object.
`Number`	Returns a numeric value of an error.
`OrdinalPosition`	Returns the relative position of an `rdoColumn` object.
`OriginalValue`	Returns the value of a column the way it existed before the last batch.
`Password`	The password used when creating an `rdoEnvironment` object in code.
`PercentPosition`	Sets or returns the location of the current `rdoResultset` row based on a percentage.
`Prepared`	Sets or returns whether the query should be prepared using the `SQLPrepare` or `SQLExecDirect` ODBC API function.
`QueryTimeout`	Sets or returns the number of seconds before an ODBC time-out occurs.
`rdoDefaultCursorDriver`	Returns or sets the cursor library used by the ODBC driver manager.
`rdoDefaultErrorThreshold`	Sets or returns the default value for the `ErrorThreshold` property for `rdoQuery` objects.
`rdoDefaultLoginTimeout`	Sets or returns the default value that indicates how many seconds can elapse before generating an error while connecting to an ODBC data source.
`rdoDefaultPassword`	Sets or returns the default password assigned to any new `rdoEnvironment`.
`rdoDefaultUser`	Sets or returns the default user name assigned to any new `rdoEnvironment`.
`rdoLocalID`	Sets or returns the locale of the RDO library.
`rdoVersion`	Sets or returns version of the RDO library.
`Required`	Sets or returns whether an `rdoColumn` is required.

continues

Table 16.3. continued

Property	*Definition*
`Restartable`	Sets or returns whether an `rdoResultset` object supports the `Requery` method.
`RowCount`	Sets or returns the number of rows in an `rdoResultset` object.
`RowsAffected`	Returns the number of rows affected by an `Execute` method.
`RowsetSize`	Sets or returns the number of rows in an `rdoResultset` cursor.
`Size`	Sets or returns the number of bytes of an `rdoColumn` object.
`Source`	Returns the source of an RDO error.
`SourceColumn`	Returns the name of the original source column name for an `rdoColumn` object.
`SourceTable`	Returns the name of the original source table name for an `rdoColumn` object.
`SQL`	Sets or returns a SQL statement for use in an `rdoQuery` object or `Execute` method.
`SQLRetCode`	Returns the most recent ODBC error.
`SQLState`	Returns the type of error in the `SQLRetCode` property.
`Status`	Sets or returns the status of a row (Modified, Updated, and so on).
`StillConnecting`	A Boolean value that indicates whether a connection is still being attempted.
`StillExecuting`	A Boolean value that indicates whether a query is still executing.
`Transactions`	Indicates whether an object supports transactions.
`Type`	Sets or returns the type or datatype of an object.
`Updatable`	Indicates whether changes can be made to an RDO object.
`UpdateCriteria`	Sets or returns how the `WHERE` clause is constructed in an optimistic batch update operation.
`UpdateOperation`	Sets or returns whether the optimistic batch update should use an `UPDATE` statement or a `DELETE` followed by an `INSERT`.
`UserName`	Sets or returns the user of an `rdoEnvironment` object.
`Value`	Sets or returns the value of an object.
`Version`	Sets or returns the version of an RDO data source.

RDO Methods

RDO objects require methods to be executed to use the objects. Table 16.4 defines these methods as they relate to Figure 16.3 and Table 16.2.

Table 16.4. RDO 2.0 methods.

Method	*Definition*
`Add`	Adds an item to an RDO collection.
`AddNew`	Adds a new row in an `rdoResultset` object.
`AppendChunk`	Appends data from a variant to an `rdoColumn` object.
`BatchUpdate`	Performs an optimistic batch update.
`BeginTrans`	Begins a new transaction.
`Cancel`	Cancels the processing or results of an RDO object.
`CancelBatch`	Cancels all uncommitted changes in the batch mode cursor.
`CancelUpdate`	Cancels any pending updates to an `rdoResultset` object.
`Clear`	Clears all errors in the `rdoErrors` collection.
`Close`	Closes an RDO object.
`ColumnSize`	Returns the size of an `rdoColumn` object.
`CommitTrans`	Commits a transaction.
`CreateQuery`	Creates a new `rdoQuery` object.
`CreatePreparedStatement`	Creates a new `rdoPreparedStatement` object.
`Delete`	Deletes the current row in an `rdoResultset` object.
`Edit`	Allows updates to the data in the current row of an `rdoResultset` object.
`EstablishConnection`	Establishes a connection to an ODBC data source.
`Execute`	Runs an action query.
`GetChunk`	Returns the contents of an `rdoColumn` object with a datatype of `rdTypeLONGVARBINARY` or `rdTypeLONGVARCHAR`.
`GetClipString`	Retrieves multiple rows of an `rdoResultset` into an array.
`GetRows`	Retrieves rows of an `rdoResultset` into an array.
`MoreResults`	Clears pending rows of a resultset. It also returns a Boolean value indicating whether one or more additional resultsets are pending.

continues

Table 16.4. continued

Method	*Definition*
`Move`	Repositions the current row pointer in an `rdoResultset` object.
`MoveFirst`	Moves to the first row in a resultset.
`MoveLast`	Moves to the last row in a resultset.
`MoveNext`	Moves to the next row in a resultset.
`MovePrevious`	Moves to the previous row in a resultset.
`OpenConnection`	Opens a connection to an ODBC data source.
`OpenResultSet`	Creates a new `rdoResultset` object.
`rdoCreateEnvironment`	Creates a new `rdoEnvironment` object.
`Refresh`	Refreshes an RDO object.
`RegisterDataSource`	Registers a new ODBC data source.
`Remove`	Removes an item from an RDO collection.
`Requery`	Updates the data in an `rdoResultset` object.
`Resync`	Fetches the batch conflict values for the current row.
`RollbackTrans`	Rolls a transaction back to the state the database was in before the `BeginTrans` statement.
`Update`	Updates an `rdoResultset` object.

RDO Events

There are a few RDO events that help you respond to conditions when dealing with RDO objects. Table 16.5 defines these events as they relate to Figure 16.3 and Table 16.2.

Table 16.5. RDO 2.0 events.

Event	*Definition*
`Associate`	Fires after a new connection is associated with the object.
`BeforeConnect`	Fires before RDO connects to an ODBC data source.
`BeginTrans`	Fires when the `BeginTrans` method has completed.
`CommitTrans`	Fires when the `CommitTrans` method has completed.
`Connect`	Fires when a connection is established with an ODBC data source.

Event	*Definition*
`DataChanged`	Fires when the value of the column has changed.
`Disconnect`	Fires when a connection has been closed.
`Dissociate`	Fires after a new connection is disassociated with the object.
`InfoMessage`	Fires when informational messages are added to the `rdoErrors` collection.
`QueryComplete`	Fires when an `rdoResultset` returns the first resultset.
`QueryTimeout`	Fires when the query execution time has expired.
`ResultsChanged`	Fires when a new resultset is made available after the `MoreResults` method is executed.
`RollbackTrans`	Fires when the `RollbackTrans` method has completed.
`RowCurrencyChange`	Fires when the resultset has been repositioned.
`RowStatusChanged`	Fires when the data of the current row changes.
`WillAssociate`	Fires before a new connection is associated with the object.
`WillChangeData`	Fires before data is changed in the column.
`WillDissociate`	Fires before the connection is set to nothing.
`WillExecute`	Fires before the execution of a query.
`WillUpdateRows`	Fires before an update to the database occurs.

Using RDO

Now that all objects, properties, methods, and events have been shown hierarchically and defined, it is time to get started using these objects. As stated earlier, using RDO is very much like using DAO. However, there are some differences. These differences and similarities are shown in the next few sections. Because of the nature of RDO, every property, method, and event cannot be shown. The purpose of this discussion is merely to give you enough background to be able to use RDO.

Connecting to a Database

To establish a connection, you must set up a valid ODBC data source. This chapter does not discuss setting up the ODBC data sources. It assumes that this has been already done. The following code fragment shows how to open an RDO connection.

```
'declare variables
Dim rdoCn As rdoConnection
Dim rdoEn As rdoEnvironment

'open environment
Set rdoEn = rdoEnvironments(0)
'open the connection
Set rdoCn = rdoEn.OpenConnection("SQLSERVER")
```

CROSS REFERENCE

For more information about ODBC, refer to Chapter 30, "ODBC."

First, you must declare the connection and environment objects. The environment object with array element zero is the default environment. The `rdoEnvironments(0)` object in RDO is equated to the `Workspaces(0)` object in DAO. You do not "need" to create another workspace in most cases. When the `rdoEnvironments(0)` object is created, the `rdoEngine` parent object created it with the `rdoDefaultUser` and `rdoDefaultPassword` properties.

Because this code did not specify either of these properties, or, if the user name and password was not specified when the connection was opened, the ODBC driver prompts you for the user name and password.

If you want to specify the user name and password, you can assign the default properties as follows:

```
'declare variables
Dim rdoCn As rdoConnection
Dim rdoEn As rdoEnvironment
'assign default properties
rdoEngine.rdoDefaultUser = "sa"
rdoEngine.rdoDefaultPassword = ""

'open Environment
Set rdoEn = rdoEnvironments(0)
'open the connection
Set rdoCn = rdoEn.OpenConnection("SQLSERVER")
```

Likewise, you can assign the user name and password to the `rdoEnvironments(0)` object like this:

```
'declare variables
Dim rdoCn As rdoConnection
Dim rdoEn As rdoEnvironment

'open Environment
Set rdoEn = rdoEnvironments(0)

'assign user name and password
rdoEn.UserName = "sa"
rdoEn.Password = ""
```

```
'open the connection
Set rdoCn = rdoEn.OpenConnection("SQLSERVER")
```

Another way to specify the user name and password is to include a `CONNECT` string in the `OpenConnection` method arguments, like this:

```
'declare variables
Dim rdoCn As rdoConnection
Dim rdoEn As rdoEnvironment

'open Environment
Set rdoEn = rdoEnvironments(0)

'open the connection
Set rdoCn = rdoEn.OpenConnection("SQLSERVER", , , "UID=sa;PWD=")
```

One final way to connect to the database is to use the `EstablishConnection` method of the `rdoConnection` object. You must also specify the `CONNECT` string. Here's how you do it:

```
'declare variables
Dim rdoCn As New rdoConnection
Dim rdoEn As rdoEnvironment

'open Environment
Set rdoEn = rdoEnvironments(0)
'open Connection
With rdoCn
    .Connect = "UID=sa;PWD=;Database=Pubs;DSN=SQLSERVER;"
    .EstablishConnection rdDriverNoPrompt, True
    rdoEn.rdoConnections.Add rdoCn
End With
```

Notice that you can assign the `Connect` property because the previous declaration of the `rdoCn` object was declared as a `New rdoConnection`. This instantiates the `rdoConnection` object. When the connection is established, you must add it to the `rdoConnections` connection with the `Add` method.

Selecting Records

When the connection is established, you can access records by using the `OpenResultSet` method of the `rdoConnection` object. You must assign it to an `rdoResultSet` object. This is very similar to opening a `Recordset` in DAO. Suppose you wanted to select all columns from the Authors table in the PUBS database. You could do it like this:

```
Dim sSQL As String
Dim rdoResult As rdoResultset

'build SQL String
sSQL = "SELECT * FROM Authors"
Set rdoResult = rdoCn.OpenResultset(sSQL)
```

Another way to access records is to use an `rdoQuery` object. This gives you a way to store your queries. You would do that like this:

```
Dim sSQL As String
Dim rdoQuery As New rdoQuery
Dim rdoResult As rdoResultset

'build SQL String
sSQL = "SELECT * FROM Authors"
'assign connection to query object
Set rdoQuery.ActiveConnection = rdoCn
'assign SQL
rdoQuery.SQL = sSQL
'open resultset
Set rdoResult = rdoQuery.OpenResultset(rdOpenForwardOnly, rdConcurReadOnly)
```

One advantage of this type of query is that you can specify more options for the resultset. The options shown here specify that the resultset can scroll only in a forward motion. Also, concurrent users can only read records.

After the resultset is created, you access the columns of data using the `rdoColumns` collection. This is used like the `Fields` collection in DAO. Use it like this:

```
Do While Not rdoResult.EOF
    List1.AddItem rdoResult.rdoColumns(0)
    rdoResult.MoveNext
Loop
```

Likewise, you can access the `rdoColumns` collection by name, as follows:

```
Do While Not rdoResult.EOF
    List1.AddItem rdoResult.rdoColumns("au_id")
    rdoResult.MoveNext
Loop
```

Inserting, Deleting, and Updating Records

After the connection is established, you can begin inserting, deleting, and updating records. Simply build your SQL statement and execute it.

CROSS REFERENCE

For more information about SQL, refer to Chapter 29, "Structured Query Language (SQL)."

You can insert a record like this:

```
'declare new connection
Dim rdoCn As New rdoConnection

'build SQL String
sSQL = "INSERT INTO Authors(au_id,au_lname,au_fname,phone,address,city,state,
➥zip,contract)"
sSQL = sSQL & "VALUES('123-45-6789','Smith','John','303-123-4567',
➥'123 Main Street','Denver',"
sSQL = sSQL & "'CO','80202',1) "
```

```
'Execute SQL
rdoCn.Execute sSQL
```

You can delete a record like this:

```
'declare new connection
Dim rdoCn As New rdoConnection

'build SQL String
sSQL = "DELETE FROM Authors "
sSQL = sSQL & "WHERE au_id ='123-45-6789' "

'Execute SQL
rdoCn.Execute sSQL
```

As you would expect, you would update a record like this:

```
'declare new connection
Dim rdoCn As New rdoConnection

'build SQL String
sSQL = "UPDATE Authors "
sSQL = sSQL & "SET au_lname = 'Jones' "
sSQL = sSQL & "WHERE au_id ='123-45-6789' "

'Execute SQL
rdoCn.Execute sSQL
```

Handling Events

Handling events can be a little difficult to understand if you have never done it before. This is because Visual Basic programmers have been conditioned to code events that already exist. That is, you double-click on a control on a form (or the form itself) and it brings up a code window with the `Click` event. Events in RDO are predefined, but they do not exist in your code unless you code them.

Suppose you wanted to code the `BeforeConnect` event of the `rdoConnection` object. You can look everywhere in your code, but the event code does not exist. You have to write it and declare it.

First, you must declare the event in the `(general)(declarations)` section of a form or module. You would do that like this:

```
'declare object variable to accept events
Private WithEvents rdoCn As rdoConnection
```

This line did a few things. It declared an object variable `rdoCn` as being of type `rdoConnection`. It also defined the scope of the object variable. However, the most important attribute is the `WithEvents` keyword. This instructs Visual Basic to look for the event code as being the name of the object variable, `rdoCn`, followed by an underscore character, then by the name of the event. Refer to the Object Browser for arguments of the event.

Next, for the `BeforeConnect` event, you would write a subroutine like this:

```
Private Sub rdoCn_BeforeConnect(ConnectString As String, Prompt As Variant)
    MsgBox "About to connect!"
End Sub
```

The only way for the coding of these events to work is that you must know the arguments expected by the library. For example, the `BeforeConnect` event has two arguments, `ConnectString` and `Prompt`. You would need to know the arguments in advance. They can be obtained from the vendor who wrote the library that fires the events.

After you indicate to Visual Basic that a procedure is to be called when an event is fired with the `WithEvents` keyword, the procedure is executed, just as any other event would be executed. You place your code in that event. The preceding example simply shows a message box when the event fires.

Asynchronous Queries

Asynchronous queries are very important. They give you, the developer, the possibility of sending a query to the server and not having to tie up the client computer while the results are calculated. The system can be freed up to do other tasks. Then, when the query is finished, you can process the results.

To begin an asynchronous query, you need to use the `rdAsyncEnable` option in either the `OpenResultSet` or `Execute` methods. This will instruct RDO to return control back to the Visual Basic program immediately. Because the query isn't finished yet, you cannot access the `rdoResultSet` object. To determine when you can use the `rdoResultSet` object (that is, when it is finished being populated), you must test for either the `StillExecuting` property to be set to `False` or the `QueryComplete` event to be executed. This indicates that the query is finished. You can do that like this: Declare the following lines in the `(general)(declarations)` section:

```
Option Explicit
Private WithEvents rdoCn As rdoConnection
Private rdoResult As rdoResultset
```

The second line declares an `rdoConnection` as responding to events. The third line declares an `rdoResultset` object.

Then, you can manipulate the RDO objects, like this:

```
'declare variables
Dim rdoEn As rdoEnvironment
Dim sConnect As String
Dim sSQL
Dim rdoQuery As New rdoQuery

'build connect string
sConnect = "UID=sa;PWD=;Database=Pubs;DSN=SQLSERVER;"

'assign environment
Set rdoEn = rdoEnvironments(0)
```

```
'open the connection
Set rdoCn = rdoEn.OpenConnection("SQLSERVER", , , sConnect)

'build SQL String
sSQL = "SELECT * FROM Authors"

'assign connection to query object
Set rdoQuery.ActiveConnection = rdoCn

'assign SQL
rdoQuery.SQL = sSQL

'open resultset
Set rdoResult = rdoQuery.OpenResultset(rdOpenForwardOnly, rdConcurReadOnly,
➥rdAsyncEnable)
```

Notice the `rdAsyncEnable` option in the `OpenResultset` method. It indicates that control should be released back to the Visual Basic program. When the resultset is finished being built, you want to populate a list box with the results. Therefore, you must code the `QueryComplete` event, as follows:

```
Private Sub rdoCn_QueryComplete(ByVal Query As rdoQuery, ByVal ErrorOccured
➥ As Boolean)
    Do While Not rdoResult.EOF
        List1.AddItem rdoResult.rdoColumns("au_id")
        rdoResult.MoveNext
    Loop
End Sub
```

This event occurs only when the query is finished. Therefore, the List1 list box is populated with the results of the resultset, but only using the `au_id` column. In this case, you don't care if an error occurred or not. If an error does occur, the resultset won't be built. If you did care about errors, you could test the `ErrorOccured` flag passed into the event.

Summary

RDO 2.0, included in the Enterprise Edition of Visual Basic 5.0, is a great way to connect to remote databases. It has been vastly improved over RDO 1.0, which shipped with Visual Basic 4.0, to provide very quick access to your data. This chapter provided insight into using RDO in your applications.

17

T-SQL Debugger

Microsoft has included a new feature in the Enterprise Edition of Visual Basic 5.0 called the Transact-SQL Debugger (or T-SQL Debugger for short). It is not compatible with any other version of Visual Basic. Before the T-SQL Debugger existed, debugging stored procedures on SQL Server was very difficult. You had to raise errors under certain circumstances in order to know what was going on within the stored procedure. In other words, you had to devise a custom method of debugging stored procedures. The T-SQL Debugger changes all of that.

CROSS REFERENCE

For more information about stored procedures and SQL Server, refer to Chapter 33, "SQL Server 6.5 Features."

Installation

To install the T-SQL Debugger, you need to know a few things. First, there is a client-side setup and a server-side setup. The client-side setup is installed automatically when you choose the Typical installation option. If you choose the Custom installation option, you must select the SQL Debugging option under Enterprise Features.

The server-side setup is a little more complicated. The first thing to do is to make sure that you install the Service Pack 2 for Windows NT 4.0. This is located on the Visual Basic 5.0 CD-ROM in the `\TOOLS\NT40.SP2` subdirectory. Reboot when prompted.

You must have SQL Server version 6.5 or greater installed. Next, make sure that Service Pack 2 is installed. The Service Pack 2 is located on the Visual Basic 5.0 CD-ROM in the `\TOOLS\TSQL\SQL65.SP2` subdirectory. Reboot when prompted.

NOTE

Make sure that no errors occur when you install the SQL Server 6.5 Service Pack 2. This is important because installing Service Pack 2 alters the database by issuing scripts that are necessary for you to continue. If any errors occur, your database will not be updated. Also, make sure that you reboot each time you are prompted. If you don't, this could affect the overall installation process.

The final server-side component to set up is the actual T-SQL debugger. This is done by running the `SDI_NT4.EXE` program located on the Visual Basic 5.0 CD-ROM in the `\TOOLS\TSQL\SRVSETUP` subdirectory.

Even though you are set up to debug your stored procedures, you should consider a few points before continuing:

- Make sure that the MSSQLServer service is *not* set up to log on as a system account. Make sure that it is set to log on as a local account, as shown in Figure 17.1.

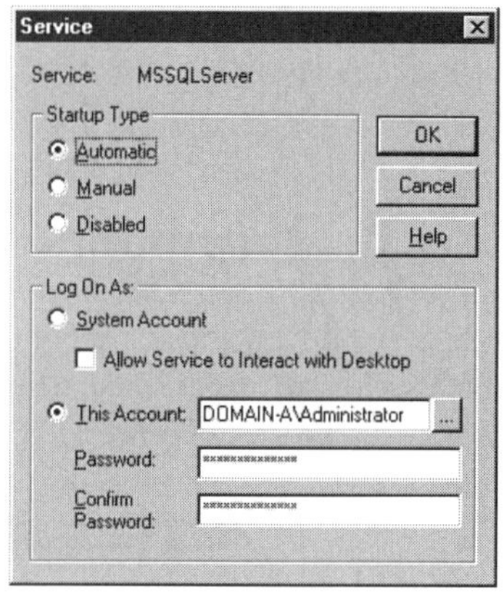

FIGURE 17.1.
MSSQLServer service startup parameters.

- If you are using TCP/IP as a protocol, make sure the machines communicate with each other by going to the command prompt on the server and typing `PING`, followed by the name of the computer you are trying to connect with. For example, Figure 17.2 shows the results of the `PING` command with a computer with the name `NOTEBOOK`.

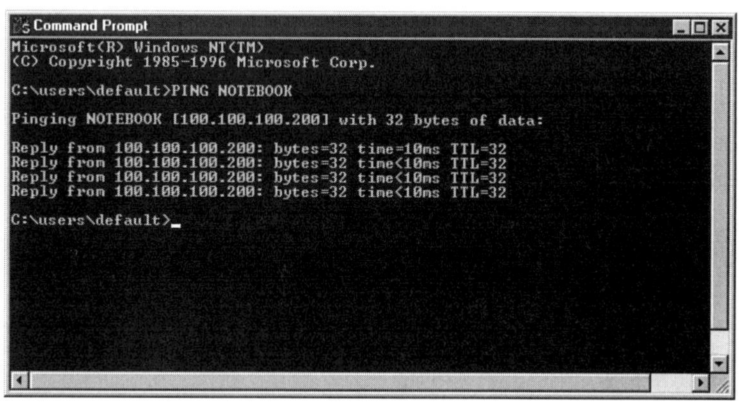

FIGURE 17.2.
Using the `PING` *command.*

- Make sure that you have Remote Data Objects 2.0 or later installed on the client computer.
- Make sure that the RPC Services (Remote Procedure Call and Remote Procedure Locator) are running on the NT Server.

If you have problems, and the system instructs you to look in the client and server logs, the system does not tell you where the logs are located. The server log is actually the Windows NT `Application` event log. The client log, `AUTMGR32.LOG`, is on the client machine in the `\WINDOWS\SYSTEM` subdirectory. Note that this is a cumulative log with the most recent entries at the bottom.

One final note about problems. If everything looks fine and you can't figure out why stored procedures are not debugging, it is best to first reboot the client machine. If that doesn't work, try rebooting the server.

Using the T-SQL Debugger

The T-SQL Debugger is an add-in, and therefore must be selected for use. To do this, select Add-Ins | Add-In Manager Visual Basic. Make sure that there is a check mark next to the VB T-SQL Debugger option, as shown in Figure 17.3.

FIGURE 17.3.
Selecting the T-SQL Debugger for use.

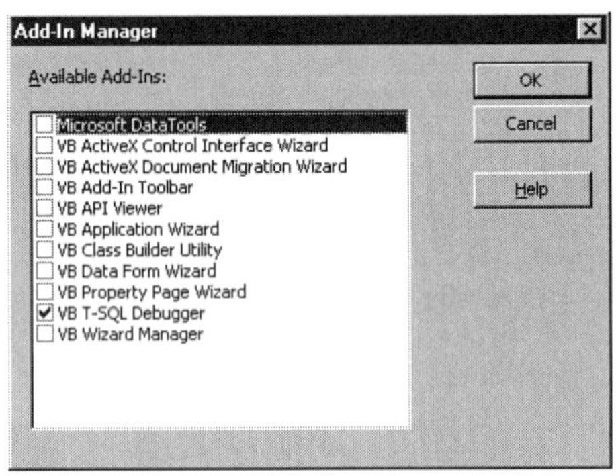

After you have selected it, you'll notice the Automation Manager running. The Automation Manager runs because it is necessary to coordinate Remote Procedure Calls (RPC) with the server. Next, select Add-I | T-SQL Debugger. This will start the debugger.

> **NOTE**
>
> You might notice that the T-SQL Debugger is actually off the screen. This is apparently a problem with the resolution of the add-in that Microsoft didn't take into account. Simply move it to the center of the screen for use.

Creating the Query

When you invoke the T-SQL Debugger, you will notice a screen with three tabs. You must fill in the first tab, Settings, before you are able to continue. The Settings tab is used to establish an ODBC connection with SQL Server. The following fields are required:

- DSN
- SQL Server
- UID
- Password (if there is one)

To begin, select a Data Source Name (DSN). This is a 32-bit Data Source registered with ODBC. If you do not have one on your machine, you can create one by clicking the Register DSN command button. This simply invokes a dialog box to configure a 32-bit DSN.

Next, select or enter the name of the server where SQL Server is installed. For example, you might name your server `SERVER-A`. After you successfully log on, this server will be conveniently added to the drop-down list for future use.

Enter the database. If you leave this blank, the default database (usually Master) will be used. For example, type `pubs`.

UID is the user ID registered with SQL Server. Type a valid user ID, such as `sa`. This is the default administrator logon. Also, type the password if one exists.

Although they are not necessary to change in order for you to continue, the following RDO (Remote Data Objects) options are available:

- Lock Type. This specifies the type of RDO locking that will occur. The possible values are `rdConcurReadOnly`, `rdConcurValues`, `rdConcurLock`, `rdConcurRowver`, and `rdConcurBatch`.
- Result Set. This specifies the type of RDO resultset that will be returned. The possible values are `rdOpenKeyset`, `rdOpenForwardOnly`, `rdOpenStatic`, and `rdOpenDynamic`.
- Options. This specifies miscellaneous options for how the query will be executed. The possible values are `rdNone` and `rdExecDirect`.

Figure 17.4 shows how the Settings tab looks when configured properly.

After the required fields are filled in, you'll notice that the Stored Procedure and Batch Query tabs are enabled. Click the Stored Procedure tab. Clicking this tab will establish an RDO connection with the server. You'll see a list of stored procedures contained within the database (pubs) you selected in the earlier example. You'll see these possible stored procedures:

- `byroyalty`
- `reptq1`

- `reptq2`
- `reptq3`

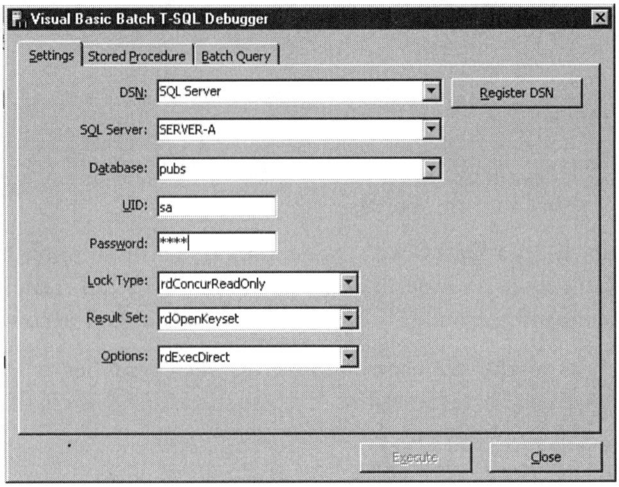

FIGURE 17.4.
The Settings tab of the T-SQL Debugger.

Select the desired stored procedure to run. For example, choose the `byroyalty` stored procedure. Figure 17.5 shows what the Stored Procedure tab now looks like.

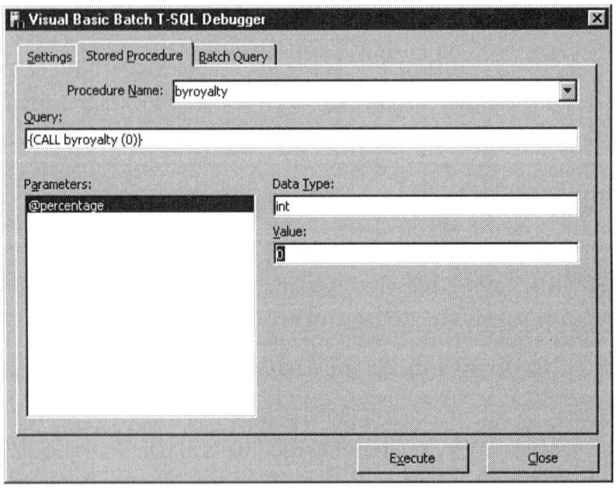

FIGURE 17.5.
The Stored Procedure tab of the T-SQL Debugger.

You'll notice that at the bottom of the screen, the Execute button becomes enabled. This is because the T-SQL Debugger is ready to debug the stored procedure.

Alternatively, you can traverse the list of parameters shown on the left and set values for them in the Value text box. This enables you to try different values to debug the stored procedures. However, as you will see shortly, you can actually change the value in the debugger, just as you would in the Visual Basic debugger. As you change the values, you'll notice the Query text box change to reflect the new values. This is the actual query that will be sent to the server.

NOTE

Although you can actually change the value in the Query text box, it is not recommended because the Value text box does not reflect a change in this case.

If you want to execute the query at this time, refer to the section titled, "Executing the Query," later in this chapter.

You use the Batch Query tab to place text that will be used in a batch query. A *batch query* is a series of SQL statements that are transmitted to the server, one after another, in a group. Figure 17.6 shows a sample batch query. Each item in the batch must be separated by the keyword `GO`.

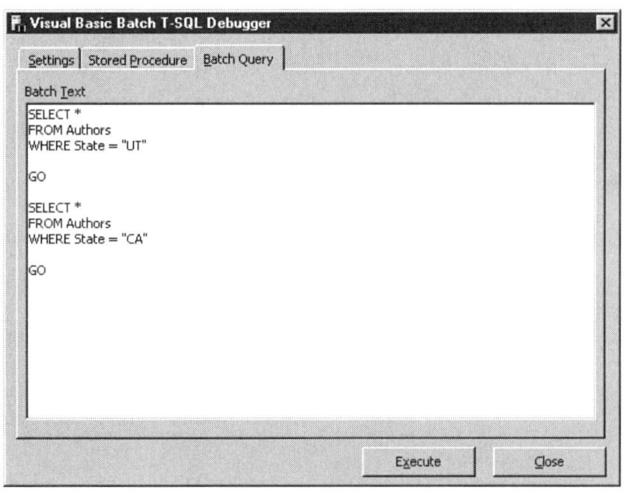

FIGURE 17.6.
The Batch Query tab of the T-SQL Debugger.

Executing the Query

To execute the query, simply click the Execute button. This will establish another connection with the server and place the query in the debugger window. Figure 17.7 shows this window with the `byroyalty` stored procedure.

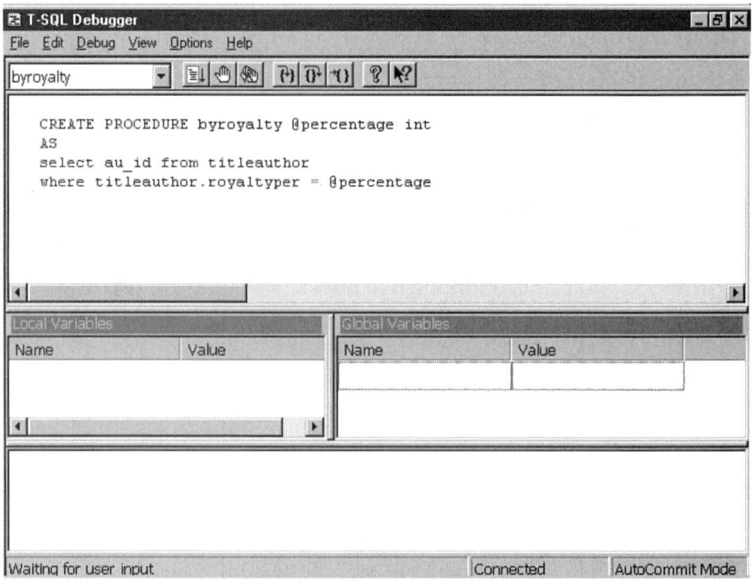

FIGURE 17.7.
The T-SQL Debugger with a stored procedure to execute.

You'll notice the debugger window has four sections in it. The first, which is unlabeled, contains the actual stored procedure text. The second, labeled Local Variables, lists the local variables in the stored procedure. The third, labeled Global Variables, lists variables that are global within SQL Server 6.5. The fourth, also unlabeled, is the results window. To execute the query, click the Go toolbar button, press the F5 key, or select Debug | Go.

If you receive the message shown in Figure 17.8, refer to the steps listed earlier in the "Installation" section or refer to the online help.

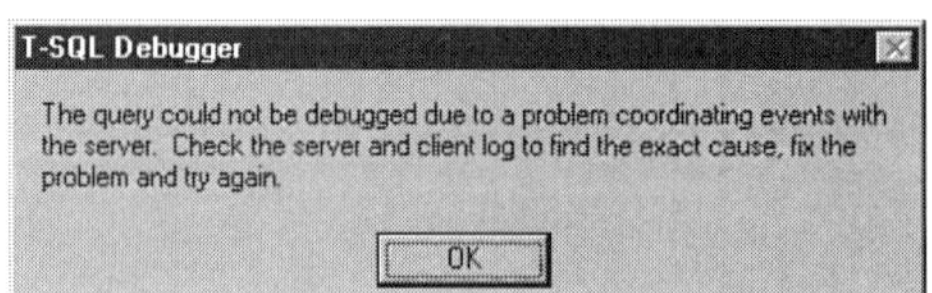

FIGURE 17.8.
A T-SQL Debugger server error.

If you do not receive an error, you'll notice that the stored procedure is executed. This is shown in Figure 17.9.

After you have executed a query, you'll notice the GO toolbar button becomes disabled. To enable it, either select Debug | Restart or press Shift+F5. Now you can execute the query as before.

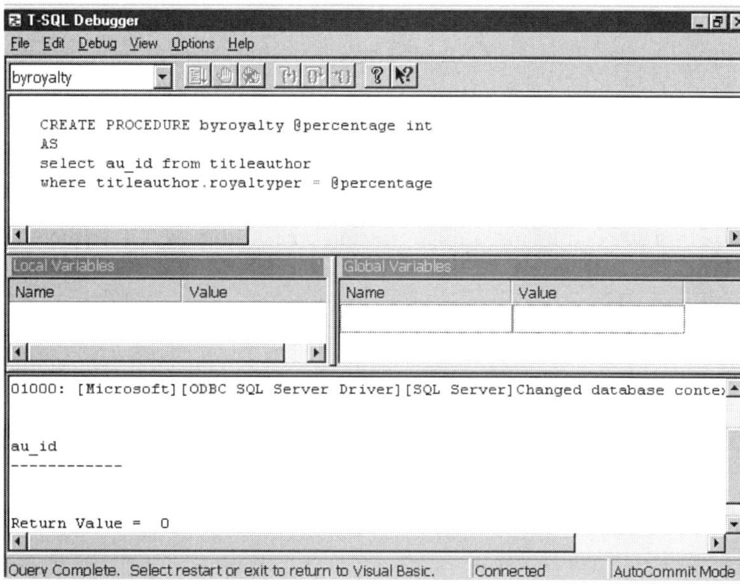

FIGURE 17.9.
The T-SQL Debugger after a stored procedure has been executed.

Debugging Queries

Debugging a query in T-SQL is very similar to the way you debug a query in Visual Basic. You can set breakpoints by clicking a line of text in the query and then selecting the Set/Remove Breakpoint toolbar button, pressing the F9 key, or selecting Edit | Set Breakpoint. You'll notice a red dot in the margin of the line that contains the breakpoint.

After you set a breakpoint, you can step through the code as you would in Visual Basic. You have the following options:

- Step Into
- Step Over
- Run To Cursor

You activate the Step Into option by clicking the Step Into toolbar button, pressing the F8 key, or selecting Debug | Step. The Step Into option executes every line of code. If the code calls a label or another procedure, it will step through each line in that code as well.

You activate the Step Over option by clicking the Step Over toolbar button. There is no hotkey or menu option for this function. The Step Over option executes each line in the current procedure, but not every line of code of a called procedure. The code will be executed, but not every line will be shown.

The Run To Cursor option is achieved by clicking the Run To Cursor toolbar button or selecting Debug | Run To Cursor. There is no hotkey for this function. The Run To Cursor option enables you to determine which line of code will be executed next. You use this function by placing the cursor on the line you want to execute. Just select the function, and all lines of code between where the cursor was and where the cursor currently is will be skipped. This can be very helpful when you are debugging.

While you are debugging code (by setting breakpoints), you can query or set the values of variables. This lets you test different scenarios without having to rerun your query externally. In Figure 17.10 the code is stopped at a breakpoint, showing the values of all local variables.

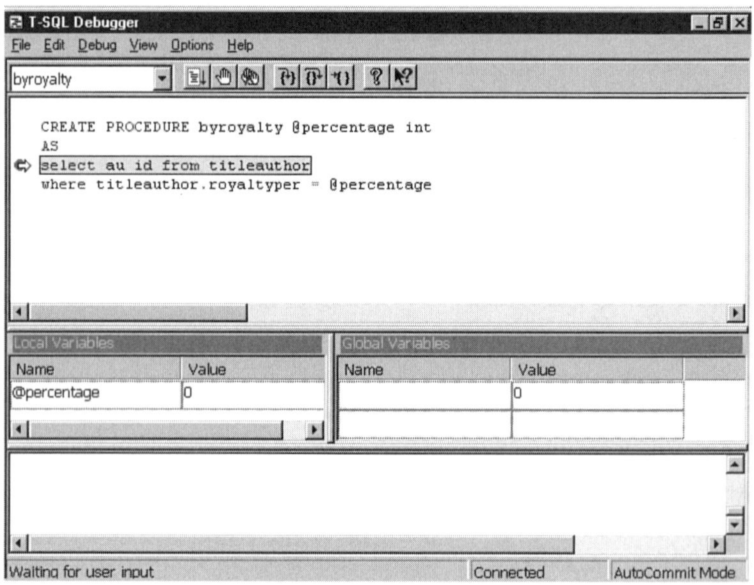

FIGURE 17.10.
The T-SQL Debugger stopped at a breakpoint.

Notice that the value of the `@percentage` variable is `0`. This is shown in the Local Variables section. Another nice way to tell the value of your variables is to place the cursor over the variable: you'll see the value in a tooltip.

To change the value, simply click the Value text box in the Local Variables section and manually change the value. After you have changed it, press Enter. You'll notice by placing the cursor over the variable that it is changed immediately. You can then step through the rest of the procedure and view the results. Change the percentage to 25 to view the results as shown in Figure 17.11. There are two author IDs that are returned at 25 percent.

You use the Global Variables section to query or set the values of global variables. These global variables are stored within SQL Server and are available to all stored procedures and queries. Again, only while debugging can you query or set the value of these options. For example, stop a query at a breakpoint and type the global variable `@@OPTIONS`. This variable is used to store different options within SQL Server. All global variables begin with `@@`. Press Enter and you'll see the value of the global variable. This might not be included in the stored procedure. Figure 17.12 shows what this section looks like.

FIGURE 17.11.
The T-SQL Debugger after a variable value has been changed.

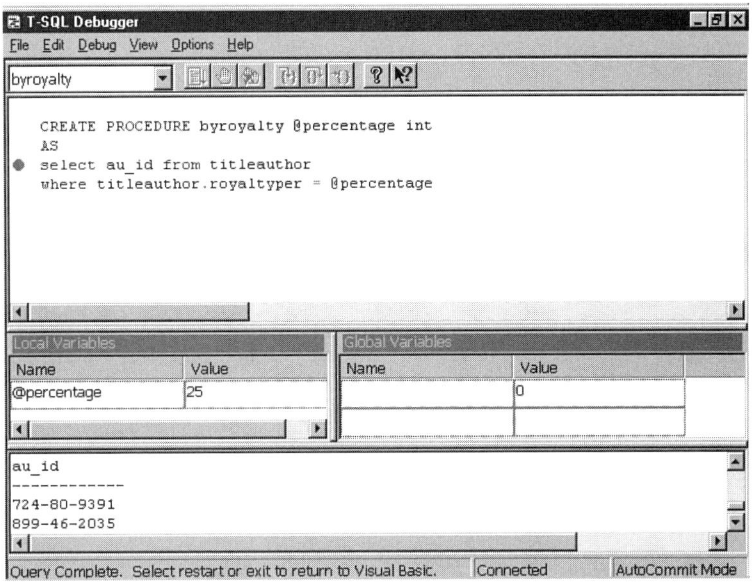

FIGURE 17.12.
The T-SQL Debugger after a global variable has been entered.

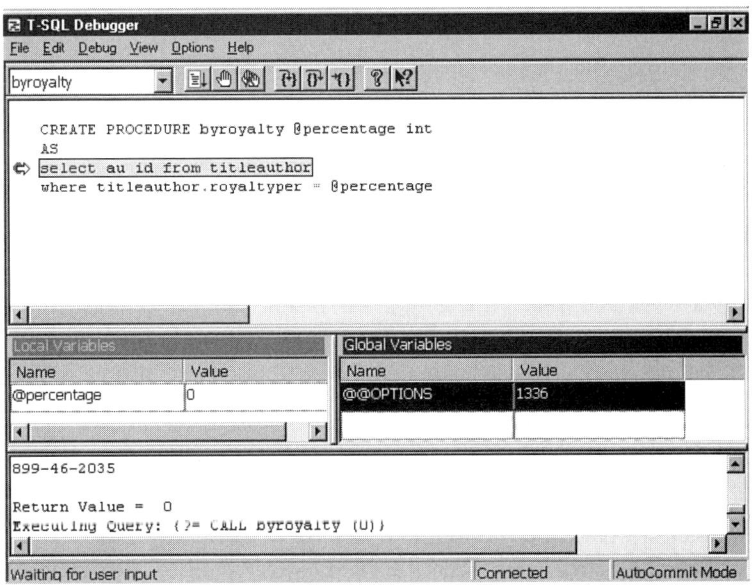

T-SQL Debugger Options

There are two options you can set while using the debugger. One is to view the call stack. If one stored procedure calls another, you'll have more than one query in the call stack. To view this stack, select View | Call Stack. Figure 17.13 shows this window.

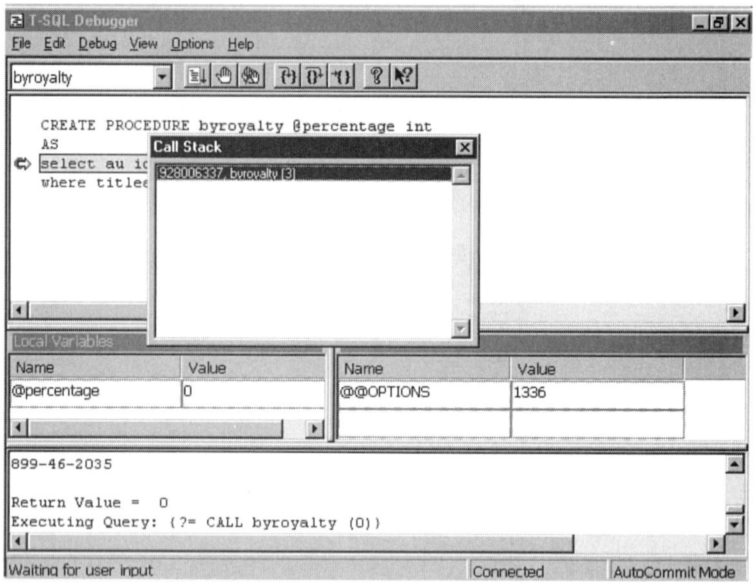

FIGURE 17.13.
The T-SQL Debugger call stack.

The other option is the mode that the debugger is in. There are two choices:

- Auto Commit
- Auto Rollback

You can toggle between these two modes by choosing Options | Safe (Auto Rollback) Mode. If there is a check mark next to this item, then the debugger is in Auto Rollback mode. If there isn't a check mark, then the debugger is in Auto Commit mode. Auto Rollback means that a query will automatically be rolled back if it is not committed in code. Auto Commit mode means that every complete transaction is automatically committed when it is executed.

You can also add a watch to a global variable, just as you can add a watch in Visual Basic. To add a watch, select Edit | Add Watch. This places the watch in the Global Variables section. To remove the watch, simply click the watch and press Delete.

Another nice feature is the ability to view the contents of a temporary table. To view the contents, simply select View | Temp Table Dump. You'll be prompted to type the name of the temporary table. You can then view the results of the table.

You can toggle the Output Window on and off by selecting View | Output Window. If there is a check mark next to the option, the Output Window will be shown.

In addition to these stated options, you can choose your own colors for items in the debug window by selecting Options | Colors. Here's a list of the possible items that can have colors assigned:

- Comment
- Constant
- Datatype
- Function
- Identifier
- Keyword
- Number
- Operator
- String
- Execution Indicator

You can also choose the font for the text in the debugger by selecting Options | Font.

NOTE

You can also debug a stored procedure from within Visual Basic in break mode. You do this via the `UserConnection` object. You can right-click the object and you'll see an option labeled Debug Stored Procedure. This will begin the debugging session listed throughout this chapter.

Summary

Microsoft's introduction of the T-SQL Debugger into the Enterprise Edition of Visual Basic 5.0 is a tremendous improvement. Until now, debugging stored procedures was difficult, if not impossible. You had to devise your own schemes for returning values and error codes from stored procedures. This was cumbersome because the stored procedures had to be recompiled after these schemes were put in place.

The T-SQL Debugger makes it very easy to debug stored procedures. It enables you to step through your stored procedures, as well as query and set the value of variables. Using the T-SQL Debugger saves countless hours of tedious work. This chapter showed you how to use the T-SQL Debugger.

18

Microsoft Transaction Server

The Microsoft Transaction Server (MTS), previously code-named Viper, is designed to make developing and deploying distributed applications, such as Internet and intranet applications, easier. It is useful for deploying 3-tier (or *n*-tier) applications comprising collections of ActiveX objects. MTS is included with the Enterprise Edition of Visual Basic 5.0.

CROSS REFERENCE

For more information about ActiveX, refer to Chapter 19, "Components and Objects," and Chapter 20, "ActiveX Controls."

There are many complexities with developing and deploying distributed applications. Developers must consider some of the following:

- Develop the front end (1st tier)
- Develop the back end (last tier)
- Develop business objects (third tier or n-tier)
- Manage process pools and thread pools for multiple client requests
- Manage locking, concurrency, and database connections

MTS greatly helps with the deployment tasks. This chapter shows the basics of using MTS. It cannot outline every scenario or situation and show how MTS will satisfy your requirements; instead, it is designed to give you an informative overview.

The MTS Architecture

The MTS architecture is made up of the following components:

- MTS components
- MTS executive
- Server processes
- Resource managers
- Resource dispensers
- Distributed Transaction Coordinator (DTC)

MTS components actually are ActiveX components that can be created in Visual Basic 5.0. The components are the core of what a Visual Basic developer should be creating.

MTS executive is the core of MTS. It handles all of the runtime services provided by MTS itself.

Server processes enable you to configure where the MTS process will run. It can be run on any of the following:

- NT Server
- SQL Server
- Internet Information Server
- Exchange Server
- Client computer

Resource managers ensure that data is durable. This means that all transactions are either committed or rolled back, which in turn ensures that MTS data always maintains integrity.

Resource dispensers manage data that is "non-durable." This type of data includes ODBC connections and shared properties. Non-durable describes data that is not related to the actual transaction, such as the reduction of inventory when an item is shipped. There are two parts to the resource dispenser. The first is an ODBC resource dispenser, which handles all of the connections via ODBC and makes sure that these connections are efficient. The second is the shared property manager. A *shared property* is a property that is shared throughout the entire application, across the entire process. Internet applications typically need this type of property.

The Distributed Transaction Coordinator (DTC) is a service that handles a two-phase commit process. The main function of the DTC is to ensure that all resource managers which are involved in a transaction will actually commit or roll back the transaction, as if they were acting as a whole. It's either all or nothing, meaning all parts of the transaction are committed, or no parts are committed. This is a major advance for developers because the DTC ensures the transaction is rolled back even if the network or workstation crashes. The DTC manages the transactions so that if the transaction cannot be completed for any reason, it is rolled back.

Testing MTS

When you install MTS, two sample applications are also installed. They are

- Bank Client: Application that shows how to use a transactional database.
- Hockey: Game application that shows how to use non-transactional components.

Let's test the Bank Client. Testing with a sample application is a good idea before you use MTS for your applications. If you simply run the Bank Client by selecting Programs | Microsoft Transaction Server | Samples | Bank Client, do not change any of the default values. The application looks like Figure 18.1.

Simply click Submit. You will receive the error shown in Figure 18.2 because MTS attempts to create an instance of an ActiveX component that does not yet exist. MTS is attempting to create an object (ActiveX component) called `Bank.MoveMoney`.

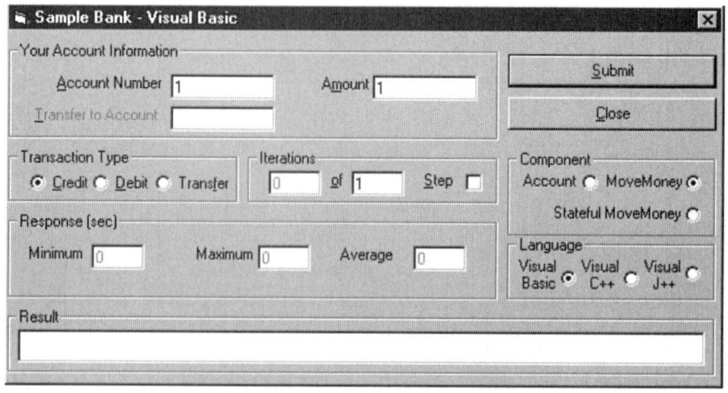

FIGURE 18.1.
A sample Bank Client application.

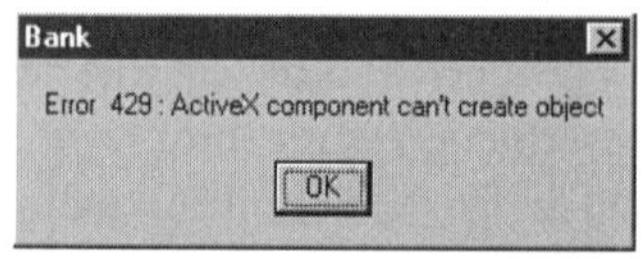

FIGURE 18.2.
The ActiveX error that occurs when the component doesn't exist.

To create the component, start the MTS Explorer by selecting Start | Programs | Microsoft Transaction Server | Transaction Server Explorer. Figure 18.3 shows the MTS Explorer.

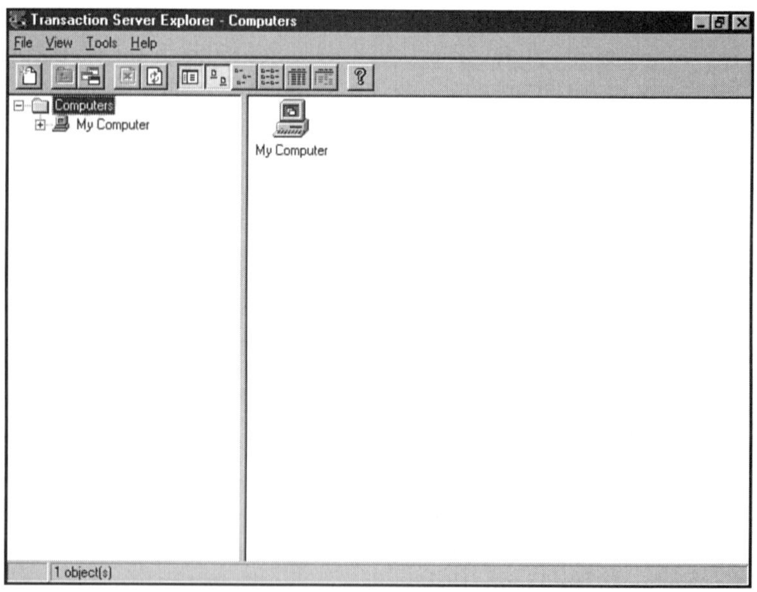

FIGURE 18.3.
The MTS Explorer.

Double-click the My Computer icon, and then double-click the Packages Installed icon. Select File | New. This will bring up the Package Wizard, which is shown in Figure 18.4.

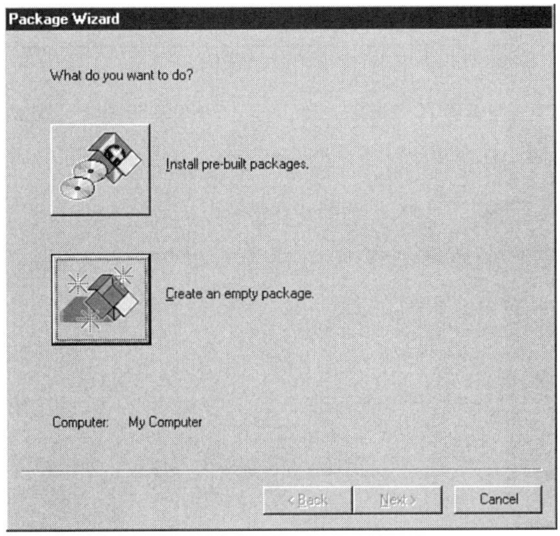

FIGURE 18.4.
The Package Wizard.

Click the Install pre-built packages button. You will see no packages installed. Select the Add button to add a package that comes with the Bank Client sample application. Select the `Sample Bank.PAK` file in the `\MTX\SAMPLES\PACKAGES` folder to add the package, as shown in the Select Package Files dialog box shown in Figure 18.5.

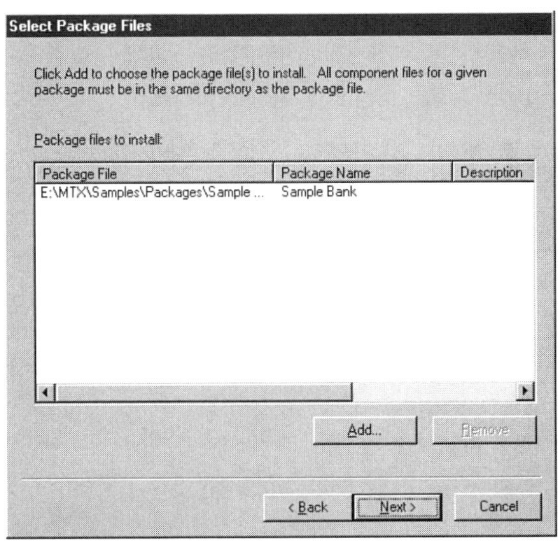

FIGURE 18.5.
Adding a new package.

A `*.PAK` file is a text file that contains the definition of a package. Listing 18.1 shows the `Sample Bank.PAK` file.

Listing 18.1. The `Sample Bank.PAK` file.

```
[{04CF0B76-1989-11D0-B917-0080C7394688} - I1]
Roles=0
InterfaceID={04CF0B72-1989-11D0-B917-0080C7394688}
Description=
AuthLevel=4
ProxyStubDLL=
[{6AAD5F0A-69AD-11D0-B15C-00AA00BA3258} - C1]
Roles=0
Clsid={04CF0B76-1989-11D0-B917-0080C7394688}
Description=
ProgID=Bank.Account.VC
Transaction=Required
RunInASP=Y
RemoteServer=
InProc=N
Local=Y
Remote=N
Internet=N
Security=Y
AuthLevel=4
System=N
CompDLL=vcacct.dll
TypeLib=vcacct.dll
Interfaces=1
[{04CF0B7B-1989-11D0-B917-0080C7394688} - I1]
Roles=0
InterfaceID={04CF0B77-1989-11D0-B917-0080C7394688}
Description=
AuthLevel=4
ProxyStubDLL=
[{6AAD5F0A-69AD-11D0-B15C-00AA00BA3258} - C2]
Roles=0
Clsid={04CF0B7B-1989-11D0-B917-0080C7394688}
Description=
ProgID=Bank.MoveMoney.VC
Transaction=Required
RunInASP=Y
RemoteServer=
InProc=N
Local=Y
Remote=N
Internet=N
Security=Y
AuthLevel=4
System=N
CompDLL=vcacct.dll
TypeLib=vcacct.dll
Interfaces=1
[{4B29E576-69B3-11D0-B15C-00AA00BA3258} - I1]
Roles=0
InterfaceID={4B29E575-69B3-11D0-B15C-00AA00BA3258}
Description=
AuthLevel=4
ProxyStubDLL=
[{6AAD5F0A-69AD-11D0-B15C-00AA00BA3258} - C3]
Roles=0
Clsid={4B29E576-69B3-11D0-B15C-00AA00BA3258}
```

```
Description=
ProgID=Bank.Account
Transaction=Required
RunInASP=Y
RemoteServer=
InProc=N
Local=Y
Remote=N
Internet=N
Security=Y
AuthLevel=4
System=N
CompDLL=Vbacct.dll
TypeLib=Vbacct.dll
Interfaces=1
[{4B29E578-69B3-11D0-B15C-00AA00BA3258} - I1]
Roles=0
InterfaceID={4B29E577-69B3-11D0-B15C-00AA00BA3258}
Description=
AuthLevel=4
ProxyStubDLL=
[{6AAD5F0A-69AD-11D0-B15C-00AA00BA3258} - C4]
Roles=0
Clsid={4B29E578-69B3-11D0-B15C-00AA00BA3258}
Description=
ProgID=Bank.MoveMoney
Transaction=Required
RunInASP=Y
RemoteServer=
InProc=N
Local=Y
Remote=N
Internet=N
Security=Y
AuthLevel=4
System=N
CompDLL=Vbacct.dll
TypeLib=Vbacct.dll
Interfaces=1
[{4B29E57A-69B3-11D0-B15C-00AA00BA3258} - I1]
Roles=0
InterfaceID={4B29E579-69B3-11D0-B15C-00AA00BA3258}
Description=
AuthLevel=4
ProxyStubDLL=
[{6AAD5F0A-69AD-11D0-B15C-00AA00BA3258} - C5]
Roles=0
Clsid={4B29E57A-69B3-11D0-B15C-00AA00BA3258}
Description=
ProgID=Bank.GetReceipt
Transaction=Not supported
RunInASP=Y
RemoteServer=
InProc=N
Local=Y
Remote=N
Internet=N
```

continues

Listing 18.1. continued

```
Security=Y
AuthLevel=4
System=N
CompDLL=Vbacct.dll
TypeLib=Vbacct.dll
Interfaces=1
[{4B29E57C-69B3-11D0-B15C-00AA00BA3258} - I1]
Roles=0
InterfaceID={4B29E57B-69B3-11D0-B15C-00AA00BA3258}
Description=
AuthLevel=4
ProxyStubDLL=
[{6AAD5F0A-69AD-11D0-B15C-00AA00BA3258} - C6]
Roles=0
Clsid={4B29E57C-69B3-11D0-B15C-00AA00BA3258}
Description=
ProgID=Bank.CreateTable
Transaction=Requires new
RunInASP=Y
RemoteServer=
InProc=N
Local=Y
Remote=N
Internet=N
Security=Y
AuthLevel=4
System=N
CompDLL=Vbacct.dll
TypeLib=Vbacct.dll
Interfaces=1
[{4B29E57E-69B3-11D0-B15C-00AA00BA3258} - I1]
Roles=0
InterfaceID={4B29E57D-69B3-11D0-B15C-00AA00BA3258}
Description=
AuthLevel=4
ProxyStubDLL=
[{6AAD5F0A-69AD-11D0-B15C-00AA00BA3258} - C7]
Roles=0
Clsid={4B29E57E-69B3-11D0-B15C-00AA00BA3258}
Description=
ProgID=Bank.UpdateReceipt
Transaction=Requires new
RunInASP=Y
RemoteServer=
InProc=N
Local=Y
Remote=N
Internet=N
Security=Y
AuthLevel=4
System=N
CompDLL=Vbacct.dll
TypeLib=Vbacct.dll
Interfaces=1
[{A2CDA060-2D38-11D0-B94B-0080C7394688} - I1]
Roles=0
```

```
InterfaceID={04CF0B72-1989-11D0-B917-0080C7394688}
Description=
AuthLevel=4
ProxyStubDLL=
[{6AAD5F0A-69AD-11D0-B15C-00AA00BA3258} - C8]
Roles=0
Clsid={A2CDA060-2D38-11D0-B94B-0080C7394688}
Description=
ProgID=Bank.Account.VJ
Transaction=Required
RunInASP=Y
RemoteServer=
InProc=N
Local=Y
Remote=N
Internet=N
Security=Y
AuthLevel=4
System=N
CompDLL=VJAcct.DLL
TypeLib=VJAcct.DLL
Interfaces=1
[{E0EF8090-2D39-11D0-B94B-0080C7394688} - I1]
Roles=0
InterfaceID={04CF0B77-1989-11D0-B917-0080C7394688}
Description=
AuthLevel=4
ProxyStubDLL=
[{6AAD5F0A-69AD-11D0-B15C-00AA00BA3258} - C9]
Roles=0
Clsid={E0EF8090-2D39-11D0-B94B-0080C7394688}
Description=
ProgID=Bank.MoveMoney.VJ
Transaction=Required
RunInASP=Y
RemoteServer=
InProc=N
Local=Y
Remote=N
Internet=N
Security=Y
AuthLevel=4
System=N
CompDLL=VJAcct.DLL
TypeLib=VJAcct.DLL
Interfaces=1
[{6AAD5F0A-69AD-11D0-B15C-00AA00BA3258} - R1]
RoleID={6AAD5F20-69AD-11D0-B15C-00AA00BA3258}
Description=
Name=Managers
[{6AAD5F0A-69AD-11D0-B15C-00AA00BA3258}]
Name=Sample Bank
Description=
System=N
Latency=3
Shutdown=N
Security=N
```

continues

Listing 18.1. continued

```
AuthLevel=4
Components=9
Roles=1
[Packages]
Package1={6AAD5F0A-69AD-11D0-B15C-00AA00BA3258}
Packages=1
Version=1.0
```

Notice that the `*.PAK` file contains the class IDs of the DLLs that make up the components in the package. Select Next from the Select Package Files dialog box to show the next step, the Set Package Identity dialog box. This step enables you to select whether to have the package run under a specific user's account or under the currently logged on user account. Figure 18.6 shows this step.

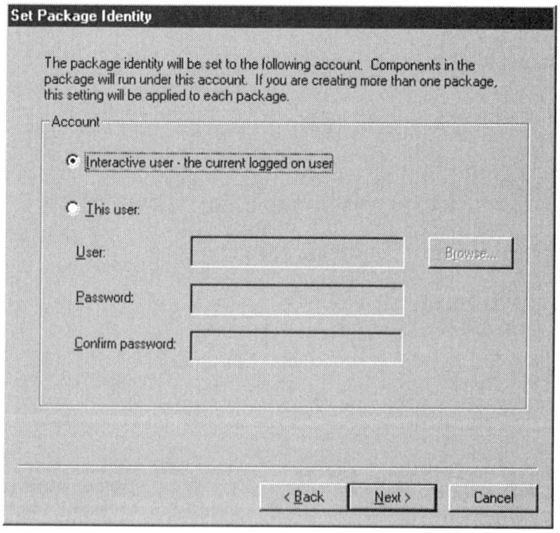

FIGURE 18.6.
Choosing the account under which the package runs.

If you choose a specific user, enter the user's name and password, and click Next to confirm in which directory the package will be created. By default, it will be created in the `\PACKAGES` directory of wherever you installed MTS. This is shown in Figure 18.7.

Click Finish to create the package. Figure 18.8 shows the package after it is created.

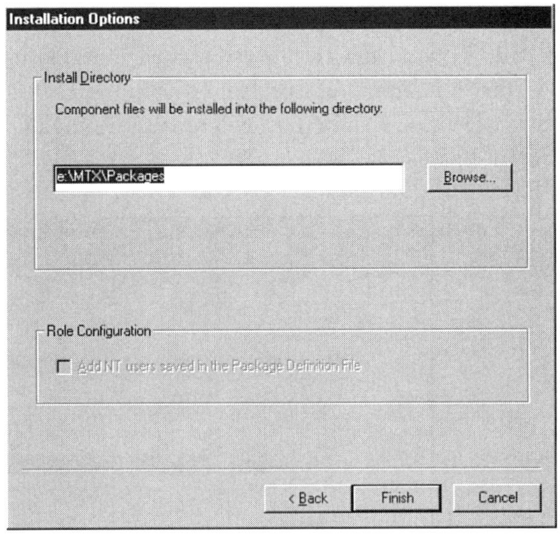

FIGURE 18.7.
Choosing a directory for the package.

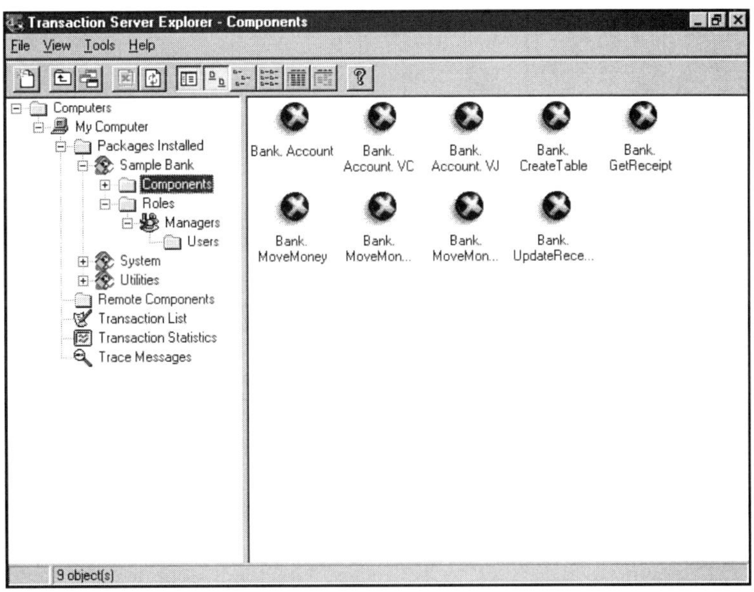

FIGURE 18.8.
The MTS package after you create it.

Next, you must start the DTC service, if it is not already running. If you do not start the DTC service, you will receive an automation error when you run the sample application. To start the service, select the My Computer icon from within the Transaction Server Explorer, and then choose Tools | MS DTC | Start. This will start the MSDTC service in the Control Panel, as shown in Figure 18.9.

FIGURE 18.9.
The MSDTC service in the Control Panel.

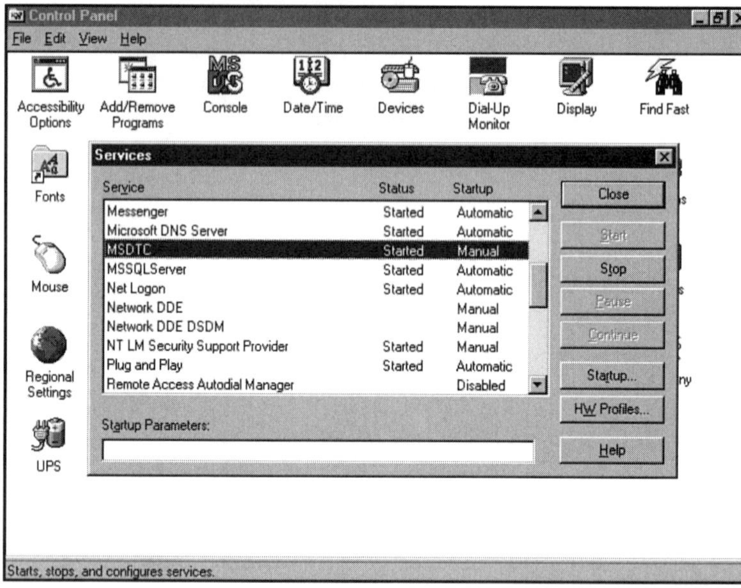

The next step is to set up the ODBC data source used in the Bank Client application. Select Start | Settings | Control Panel to bring up the Control Panel. Then, select the 32-bit ODBC data source icon. Click Add to add a new SQL Server data source. Figure 18.10 shows the parameters you need to add to the data source. Click OK to add the data source.

Now run the sample Bank Client application, which will now actually run. This will bring up the main screen. Simply click the Submit button with all of the default parameters. This will run the application, create an account, and return the balance for the account. This is shown in Figure 18.11.

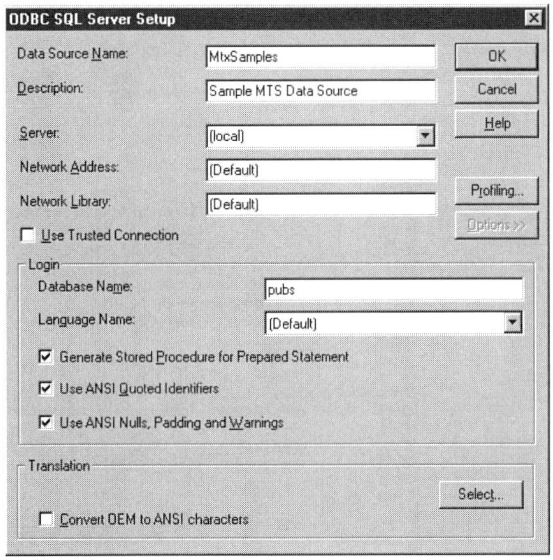

FIGURE 18.10.
Parameters for the ODBC data source.

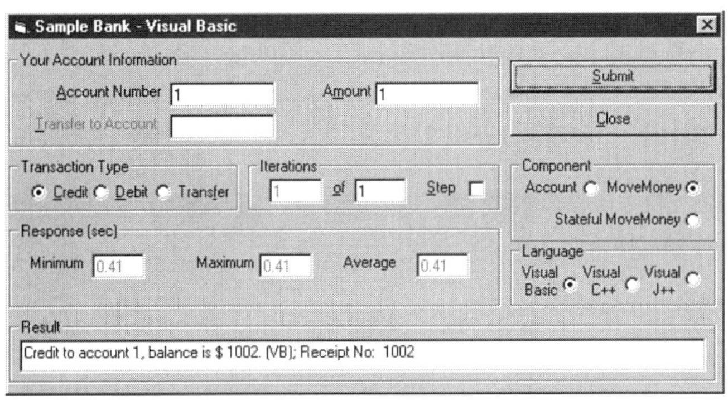

FIGURE 18.11.
The working Bank Client application.

The Bank Client application source code is distributed with the EXE as well. Open the `Bank.VBP` project in Visual Basic 5.0. It is located in the `\Samples\Bank.VB` folder of wherever you installed MTS. The objects that are called and instantiated depend on which of the options you choose in the application. If you choose all of the defaults, the `Bank.MoveMoney` object is called. Figure 18.12 shows the Visual Basic code that performs these actions. The code for this example is installed when you set up MTS. It is a Visual Basic project called `BANK.VBP`. It is stored in the `\Samples\Bank.VB` subdirectory of wherever you installed MTS.

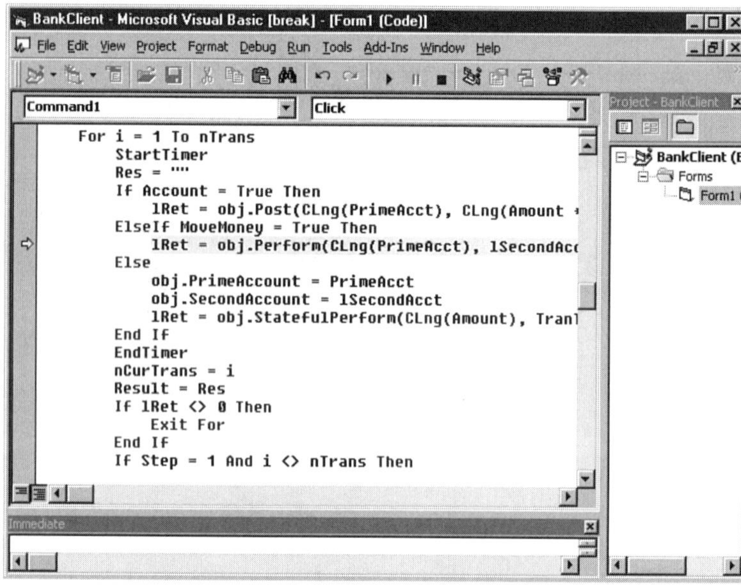

FIGURE 18.12.
The code of the Visual Basic Bank Client application.

Notice that the line shown in Figure 18.12 where the breakpoint is set is calling the `Perform` method of the `Bank.MoveMoney` object. You can view this and every other method by traversing the tree within the MTS Explorer. This is shown in Figure 18.13.

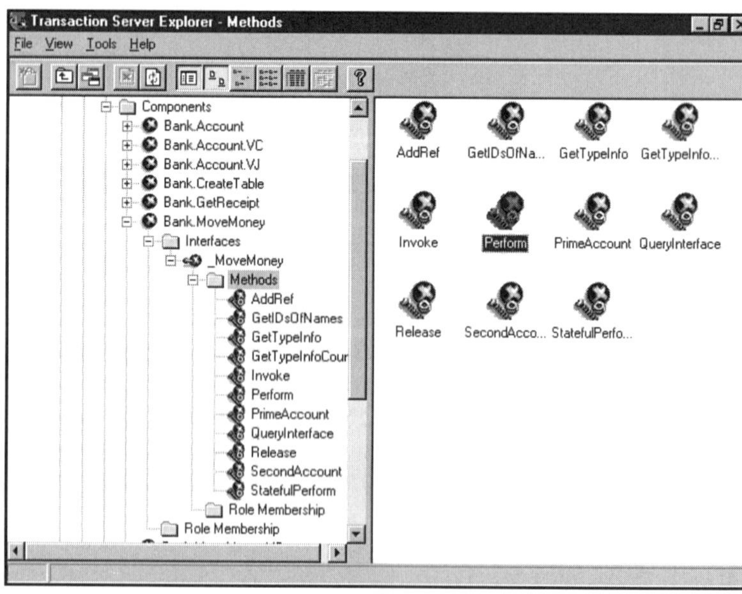

FIGURE 18.13.
Methods and properties for the `Bank.MoveMoney` *object.*

One of the nice features of MTS is that you can view how many objects are instantiated. If you place a breakpoint in the application after the `CreateObject` function, you will notice the object created in the MTS Explorer. To view these objects, click the Components folder, and then select View | Status. This will show in the right pane how many objects are instantiated by a client program. If the number is greater than one, the icon to the left of the class name will actually rotate. This is shown in Figure 18.14.

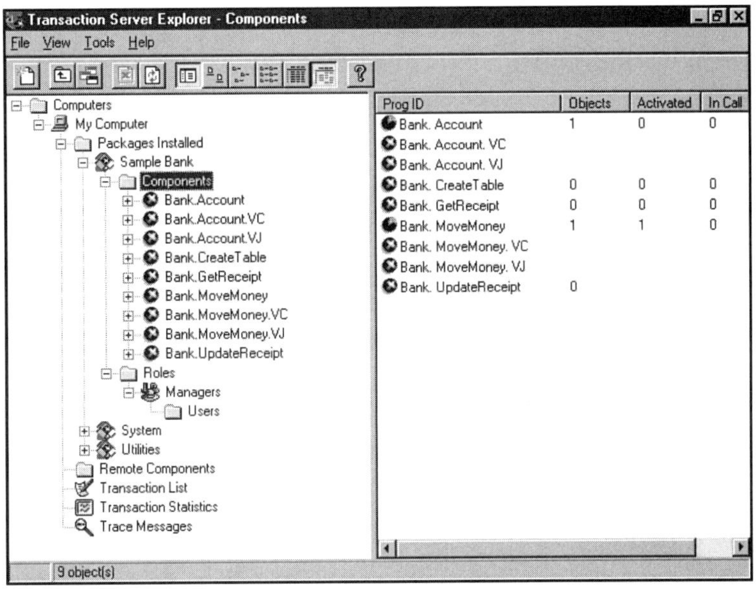

FIGURE 18.14.
Component status showing counts of objects, number of objects activated, and number of objects in call.

Adding Components

To add a component, choose the `Components` folder. Then, select File | New. This will bring up the Component Wizard, as shown in Figure 18.15.

You have two choices in the wizard:

- Install new component(s)
- Import component(s) that are already registered

The Install new component(s) option enables you to install components that are contained within `*.DLL` or `*.TLB` files. You use the Import component(s) that are already registered option to install components that are listed in the Registry. This is shown in Figure 18.16.

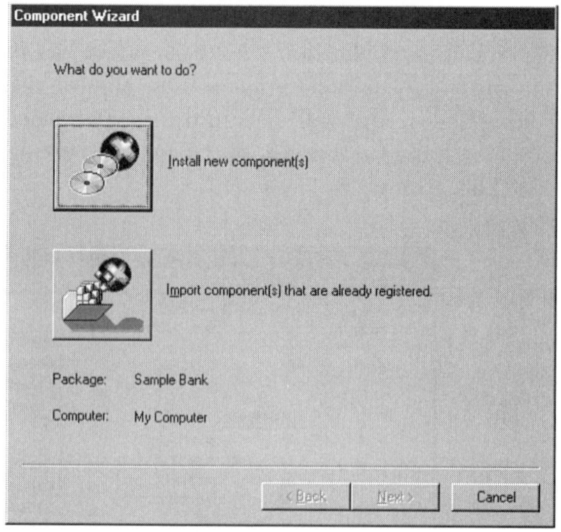

FIGURE 18.15.
The Component Wizard.

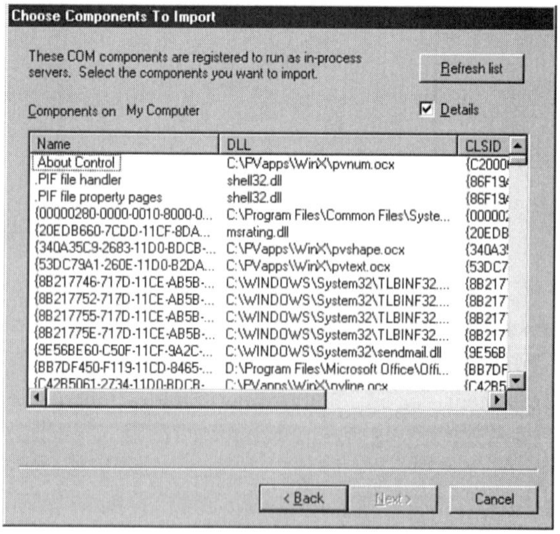

FIGURE 18.16.
The Registry listing of objects.

You can select one or more objects by pressing the Ctrl or Shift keys while using the mouse.

Configuring Properties for an Object

To configure properties for an object, select the desired object under the `Components` folder. It will be located under the Packages Installed folder. Then select File | Properties, or right-click the object itself. This will bring up a Component Properties dialog box that contains the following four tabs:

- General
- Transaction
- Activation
- Security

You use the General tab, shown in Figure 18.17, to show the details of the object and to enable you to store a description for the object.

FIGURE 18.17.
Component properties, General tab.

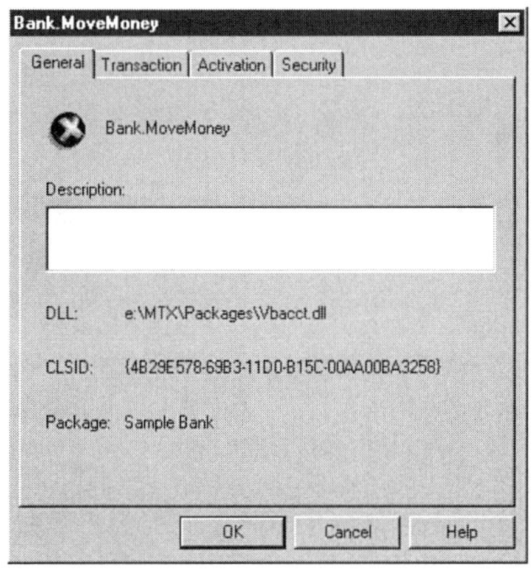

The Transaction tab, shown in Figure 18.18, enables you to select the type of transaction supported by this object. There are four options:

- Requires a transaction
- Requires a new transaction
- Supports transactions
- Does not support transactions

The Activation tab, shown in Figure 18.19, enables you to select how to run a component. The first check box enables you to specify that the object runs in the transaction server environment. This means that it runs under MTS.

The next three options enable you to choose where the component will be created. The following are the choices:

- In the creator's (client) process
- In a server process on this (NT Server) computer
- In a remote server process on the computer

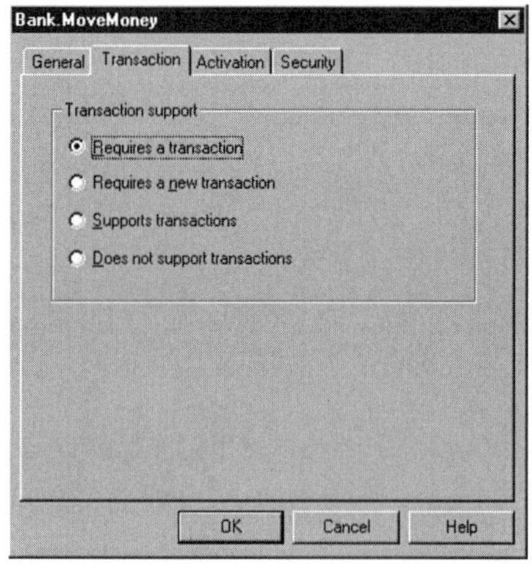

FIGURE 18.18.
Component properties, Transaction tab.

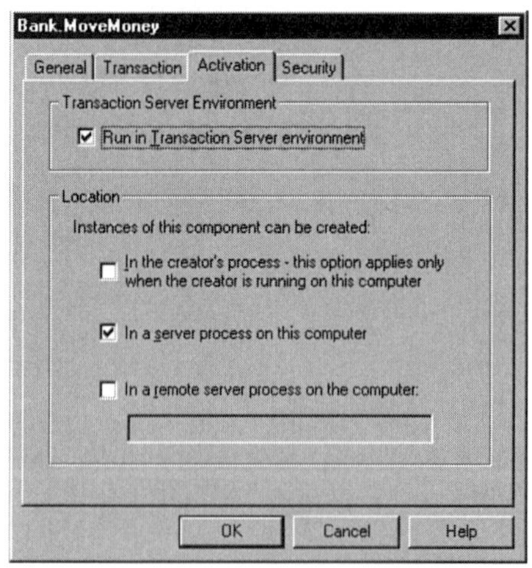

FIGURE 18.19.
Component properties, Activation tab.

The Security tab, shown in Figure 18.20, has only one check box, called Enable authorization checking. If it is checked, security is enabled.

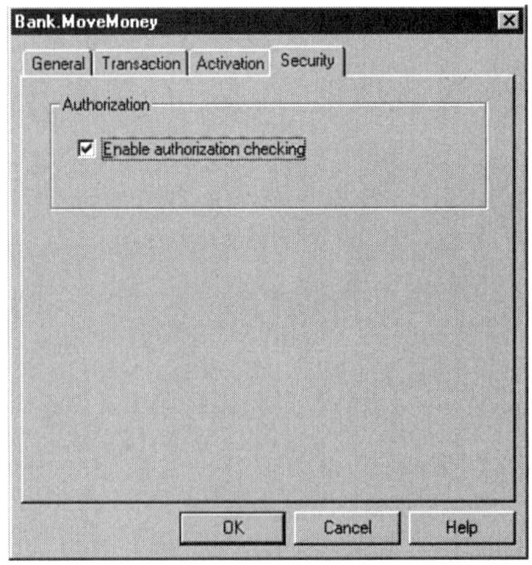

FIGURE 18.20.
Component properties, Security tab.

Summary

This chapter showed how to use Microsoft Transaction Server, or MTS, to deploy and monitor distributed applications. It is a very useful tool that frees the developer from the daunting task of deploying distributed applications and enables him or her to focus on developing. This chapter showed you how to use MTS with a sample application, but your applications will work exactly the same way.

IV

Controls and Containers

19

Components and Objects

Components are based on a reusable, open architecture and can be thought of as "plug-and-play" pieces of software. Components have long been a part of Visual Basic. You have known them in the past as VBXs in versions 1.0, 2.0, and 3.0. Then, version 4.0 introduced OCXs. These were new kinds of components based on OLE, which is, in itself, an open architecture. However, this was not enough. Microsoft decided to develop a very open architecture and base it on most of its products, including Office 97 and Internet Explorer. This new standard is called ActiveX.

ActiveX is based on a standard called the Component Object Model (COM). This model is used by all ActiveX components and by Visual Basic itself.

CROSS REFERENCE

For more information about creating ActiveX controls, refer to Chapter 20, "ActiveX Controls."

Component Object Model

The Component Object Model (COM) is an architecture based on OLE that forms high-level software services. These software services form the basis for how processes and components interact with each other. Here are a few different things that are defined and addressed by COM:

- How to uniquely identify components
- How to determine the interface available to a component
- How to have a component delete itself when it is no longer needed
- How to call other components in a standard format

Component Categories

Component categories are ways of classifying a component to be used for a specific purpose. This purpose essentially identifies its functionality. As do most things, this requires a Registry entry to let applications and other components know about the functionality of the component. Each component is uniquely identified by a Globally Unique Identifier (GUID). The GUID is generated when the control is installed. This way, every component has a guaranteed unique identifier.

A good example of when this categorization is useful is to tell another control or environment that this control does not support being bound to a database. Another example is to determine whether a control is Internet aware.

To have a control support many environments is a good idea. After all, the idea behind a component is for it to be platform- as well as operating system-independent, if possible. If the component cannot be supported in a specific environment, that is really where the component categories come in. These categories prevent the component from being used in an environment that does not let it function correctly (or at all).

A category does not have to be globally accepted. For example, the Internet component category is globally accepted. On the other hand, you can have a category that is unique to your organization; however, implementing it is a different story.

For older components that do not use a component category, Microsoft has set up a specific category called CATID_ControlV1. This is solely to support older controls that do not support categories, but only control keywords.

ActiveX

ActiveX is a new technology that is based on OLE and COM (described earlier). Active replaces the VBX and OLE Control architectures. It is everything that these technologies were, plus it has many new features. ActiveX is much more than components. It is a whole new standard for many Microsoft products. Here are some terms that circle around the ActiveX technology:

- Active Platform: Active Platform is a term that describes a set of services used in Internet/intranet situations. This means that either the server or the client utilizes ActiveX technologies.
- Active Desktop: Active Desktop is a term that describes the use of ActiveX technology on the client. This includes scripting, components, and dynamic HTML on the desktop.
- Active Server: Active Desktop is a term that describes the use of ActiveX. In contrast, Active Server refers to scripting, components, and dynamic HTML on the server. Dynamic HTML is a function of Internet Information Server version 3.0, which incorporates a technology known as Denali.

CROSS REFERENCE

For more information about Denali, refer to Chapter 24, "Special Considerations."

- ActiveX controls: ActiveX controls (or ActiveX components) are components that utilize the ActiveX technology and can be developed in Visual Basic 5.0.
- Active Documents: Active Documents are documents (such as Excel spreadsheets, Word documents, and PowerPoint presentations) that can be viewed in a browser.

Objects

Objects are ActiveX components that expose properties, methods, and events to ActiveX clients. You can create ActiveX clients using Visual Basic as well as ActiveX Server Objects. These objects encapsulate key business functions and make these functions available through well-defined properties and methods to the outside world.

Created objects can act as the middle layer in a three-tiered client/server application. Sometimes this middle layer is called a *business object server*.

CROSS REFERENCE

For more information about the three-tiered architecture, refer to Chapter 32, "Visual Basic's Role in Client/Server Computing."

Business Object Servers

Business object servers is a term which specifies that you have written an OLE Automation Server application that encapsulates certain business rules or functions. One reason for creating a business object server is when you want to sell most of your source code, but you don't want to release proprietary algorithms and procedures. Creating an OLE Automation Server application enables you to "break out" part of your code into another logical piece. These servers can be installed on a local machine or a remote server. Your Visual Basic applications can call the methods and procedures exposed by these business object servers. Examples of business object servers can be as simple as creating a server application that performs tasks that you use in your everyday Visual Basic code, such as centering a form. It can be as complex as a Visual Basic application issuing instructions to the business object server to notify when a network connection or database connection is lost. Visual Basic enables you to create these OLE Automation Servers, which means that you can write your own applications with Visual Basic that expose methods and properties to the outside world.

There are two types of OLE Automation Servers: in-process and out-of-process. The in-process server is a DLL file created in Visual Basic that runs in the same thread process space as the programs that use them. An out-of-process server is a stand-alone executable file created in Visual Basic that runs in its own address space. It actually invokes another thread process.

Creating OLE Automation Servers involves inserting a class module. This class module will define a class name that can be viewed in the system Registry or by using the code shown in Listing 19.1, later in this chapter.

When inserting a class module, Visual Basic automatically creates two events: `Initialize()` and `Terminate()`. You do not have to place code in these events to create an OLE Automation

Server. Note that you cannot create your own custom events with an OLE Automation Server application.

To create an OLE Automation Server application, first open a new ActiveX project by selecting File | New Project. Next, select the ActiveX DLL option. This will automatically add a class module to your project. Change the `Name` property to the name you want to call the class. While you have the Properties dialog box open, make sure that the `Instancing` property is set to `MultiUse`. This will enable the class module to be seen outside the application. Setting the `Instancing` property to `MultiUse` enables the calling application to create multiple instances of your object.

Defining Custom Methods

To create a custom method for a particular object, you declare a subroutine or function inside a class module. The code in the subroutine or function can be written to do exactly what you want done when the method is activated. The only difference is that because this is in a class module, you define the subroutine or method as being `Public`, which instructs Visual Basic to expose the method to the outside world. For example, suppose you want to encapsulate the functionality of the code to enumerate all OLE classes on a client system. This is done in Listing 19.1. Instead of populating a list box with all of the class names, the OLE Automation Server application returns a string containing all of the class names on a particular machine, separated by the pipe symbol (¦). This method will be called `CreateClasses`. You must first insert a `Public` function by selecting Tools | Add Procedure and then typing `CreateClasses` and selecting the `Function` option button. Be sure that the `Public` option is clicked. After the empty function is created, insert the code shown in Listing 19.1.

Listing 19.1. The function listing for creating an OLE Automation Server custom method.

```
Public Function CreateClasses() As String
    'declare variables
    Dim lResults As Long        'result status after opening key
    Dim sSubKey As String       'sub key containing class ID
    Dim sSubKey1 As String      'sub key containing key under class ID
    Dim lResult As Long         'result status after getting class ID's
    Dim lResult1 As Long        'result status after getting sub keys
    Dim nPos As Integer         'position of null terminator
    Dim lSubKey As Long         'loops through Class ID Indexes
    Dim lSubKey1 As Long        'loops through sub key indexes
    Dim sKeyResult As String    'result string containing class ID
    Dim sKeyResult1 As String   'result string containing sub key
    Dim lHandle As Long         'handle of class ID key
    Dim lHandle1 As Long        'handle of sub key ID
    Dim sValue As String        'result string containing class name
    Dim sString As String       'holds string of classes

    'open CLASS ID(CLSID) key
    lResults = RegOpenKey(HKEY_CLASSES_ROOT, "CLSID", lHandle)
    lSubKey = 0
    'loop through all class ID's
```

continues

Listing 19.1. continued

```
    Do Until lResult <> 0
        sSubKey = Space$(1028)
        lResult = RegEnumKey(lHandle, lSubKey, sSubKey, 1028)
        nPos = InStr(sSubKey, Chr$(0))
        If nPos > 0 Then
            sKeyResult = Left$(sSubKey, nPos - 1)
            'get handle for this item
            lResults = RegOpenKey(lHandle, sKeyResult, lHandle1)
            lSubKey1 = 0
            lResult1 = 0
            'loop through all subsequent sub-keys
            Do Until lResult1 <> 0
                sSubKey1 = Space$(1028)
                lResult1 = RegEnumKey(lHandle1, lSubKey1, sSubKey1, 1028)
                nPos = InStr(sSubKey1, Chr$(0))
                If nPos > 0 Then
                    sKeyResult1 = Left$(sSubKey1, nPos - 1)
                    'if the key is "PROGID" then this is the value we need
                    If UCase$(sKeyResult1) = "PROGID" Then
                        'get value
                        sValue = Space$(1028)
                        lResults = RegQueryValue(lHandle1, sKeyResult1, sValue,
                        ➥1028)
                        nPos = InStr(sValue, Chr$(0))
                        If nPos > 0 Then
                            'add to string
                            sString = sString + Left$(sValue, nPos - 1) + "¦"
                        End If
                    End If
                End If
                lSubKey1 = lSubKey1 + 1
            Loop
        End If
        lSubKey = lSubKey + 1
    Loop

    'remove trailing pipe
    If Right$(sString, 1) = "¦" Then
        sString = Left$(sString, Len(sString) - 1)
    End If

    'return string
    CreateClasses = sString
End Function
```

This is the only code needed to expose a custom method from your OLE Automation Server application. However, it is not quite ready to run. A BAS module is needed because any in-process OLE Automation Server application needs to have a `Sub Main()` procedure as the starting point. It does not necessarily need any code, but it must exist. Therefore, create this procedure in a BAS module. Also, the BAS module is necessary to declare any API functions or `Public` variables. Note that any public variables declared will appear to the outside world as properties (see the section titled "Defining Custom Properties," later in this chapter). For this example of an OLE Automation Server, you need to declare the three API functions and one constant in a BAS module. They are declared with this code:

```
Declare Function RegOpenKey Lib "advapi32.dll" Alias "RegOpenKeyA"
➥(ByVal hKey As Long, ByVal lpSubKey As String, phkResult As Long) As Long
Declare Function RegEnumKey Lib "advapi32.dll" Alias "RegEnumKeyA"
➥(ByVal hKey As Long, ByVal dwIndex As Long, ByVal lpName As String, ByVal
➥cbName As Long) As Long
Declare Function RegQueryValue Lib "advapi32.dll" Alias
➥"RegQueryValueA" (ByVal hKey As Long, ByVal lpSubKey As String,
➥ByVal lpValue As String, lpcbValue As Long) As Long
Public Const HKEY_CLASSES_ROOT = &H80000000
```

CROSS REFERENCE

For more information about the WIN32 API, refer to Chapter 13, "Using the WIN32 API."

The final step is to assign how the server will look in the Registry editor, as well as in the References Visual Basic dialog box. You do this by selecting Project | Properties and then the General tab. Whatever you enter in the Project Description text box is shown under the Visual Basic References menu. If you were to search the Registry, you would see an entry in the format *ProjectName.ProjectDescription*.

Suppose you named your class (by using the property sheet for the class module) `ClassIDApp`. To use your new class module, you need to create another Visual Basic application and write only three lines of code in the `Form_Load()` event, as shown in Listing 19.2.

Listing 19.2. Implementing the new class.

```
Dim objNew as ClassIDApp
Dim sTemp as String
sTemp = objNew.CreateClasses
```

Of course, you need to parse the `sTemp` string, looking for the pipe symbols. Then you can do whatever you want with the individual items, such as populate a list box. For more information about testing and implementing the new class, see the "Testing the OLE Automation Server" section later in this chapter.

Defining Custom Properties

To create a custom property, you must declare variables as being `Public` in the `(general)` `(declarations)` section of the class module. This instructs Visual Basic to make these properties available outside your application.

As an example of how to declare custom properties, suppose you wanted to create a property that returns the number of classes in the example in Listing 19.1. You would declare a `Public` integer in the class module like this:

```
'declare RegistrationInfo Class Properties
Public NumClasses As Integer
```

If you need to declare variables used only to hold and calculate values in your class procedures, but you don't want to expose them to the outside world, you would declare them as being `Private`.

To assign a value to a property, you simply assign the variable as you would any other variable. For example, to increment the count of the number of classes found in the example earlier and make the count available, you need only to increment the value of `NumClasses` (see Listing 19.3).

Listing 19.3. Code fragment showing how to assign the `Public` variable `NumClasses`.

```
If nPos > 0 Then
    'add to string
    sString = sString + Left$(sValue, nPos - 1) + "¦"
    NumClasses = NumClasses + 1
End If
```

Then, to access the count, you would simply access the `NumClasses` property of the object you created, just as you would any other Visual Basic property. If you created a new class named `objNew`, you could return the number of classes by tying this in the Debug window:

```
?objNew.NumClasses
```

There is one problem with using this approach. The property is read-write, which means that you could assign a value to the property that does not actually indicate the number of classes returned from the OLE Automation Server. Therefore, another approach is to create a property procedure.

Property Procedures

Visual Basic 4.0 introduced a new type of procedure called a *property procedure.* A property procedure is very useful if you need to take some type of action when an exposed property is accessed or set. For example, the `NumClasses` property (defined earlier) needs to be read-only. Therefore, you need to add a property procedure.

There are three types of property procedures:

- `Property Let` sets a value of a property procedure.
- `Property Get` gets a value of a property procedure.
- `Property Set` sets an object reference in a property procedure.

Each one of these is used in certain circumstances. It is important to know that blank procedure templates are created for each of the `Let`, `Get`, and `Set` property procedures, even if you do not use them. For example, if you wanted to declare a property called `NumClasses`, you could either declare a `Public` variable `NumClasses` in the `(general) (declarations)` section (as done earlier) or declare a property procedure. The advantage of declaring a property procedure is that you can make the property read-only or write-only. To make a property read-only, you place code only in the `Property Get` procedure and not in the `Property Let` or `Property Set` procedures. Conversely, if you wanted to make a property write-only, you place code in the `Property Let` procedure only and none in the `Property Get` and `Property Set` procedures. If you need a property to be read-write, you set either `Property Let` and `Property Get` *or* `Property Set` and `Property Get`. With all this in mind, suppose you wanted to create the read-only property, as described in the earlier scenario. You would write code like this:

```
Public Property Get NumClasses()
    NumClasses = TempNumClasses
End Property
```

This example assumes that you have declared an integer, `TempNumClasses`, in the `(general) (declaration)` section as being `Private`. It is used as a temporary working variable. It also assumes that you have entered code in the `CreateClasses()` routine to increment the `Private` integer `TempNumClasses`. To create the property procedure, you can either type the code in the code window or select Tools | Add Procedure. This presents you with a dialog box to select the type of procedure. Figure 19.1 shows what this dialog box looks like.

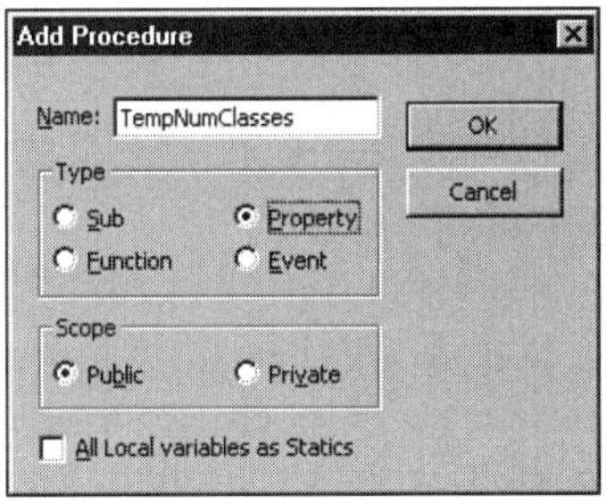

FIGURE 19.1.
The Add Procedure dialog box.

Select the Public and Property options. Also, type the name of the desired property, such as `NumClasses`, and click OK. All `Let`, `Get`, and `Set` property procedures will be created for you.

Version Issues

The potential for compatibility problems exists when you create an OLE Automation Server application, distribute it to customers, and then change the code and redistribute it. It is for this reason that Visual Basic enables you to choose from three different types of versioning compatibility:

- No compatibility
- Project compatibility
- Binary compatibility

No compatibility is obvious. It does not check for OLE Automation Server compatibility. You use project compatibility to make sure that your entire project is compatible with a project that you specify. You use binary compatibility to maintain a project that has been compiled using the component. In either the Project or Binary options, you specify the project with which to compare compatibility. Figure 19.2 shows what the Component tab looks like.

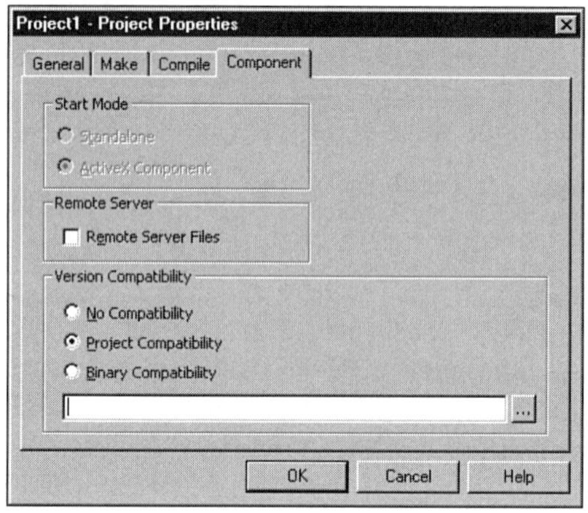

FIGURE 19.2.
The Project Properties, Component tab.

If you have specified a filename, Visual Basic will warn you of potential conflicts when you create another executable.

Testing the OLE Automation Server

You do not need to compile the OLE Automation Server into an executable or DLL to be able to test it. However, you do need to do a few things. You must enter the application description by selecting Project | Properties. This is the description that appears when you register the OLE Automation Server application. You must also select the OLE Server option button.

> **TRIED AND TRUE**
>
> Try not to enter a long name. If you do, you will not be able to see the entire name when you enable the OLE Automation Server.

After selecting these options, you must run the application with a full compile. You do this by using the Ctrl+F5 key combination or by selecting Run | Start With Full Compile.

After the application is running, you must start another instance of Visual Basic and create code to use the object, such as in Listing 19.1. Before you run the application, you must select the appropriate reference to the OLE Automation Server you just created with the first instance of Visual Basic. You do this by selecting Project | References. This option presents a dialog box of all the objects that are available on your system, including the OLE Automation Server application that is running. Figure 19.3 shows what this dialog box looks like, with the new OLE Automation Server application class.

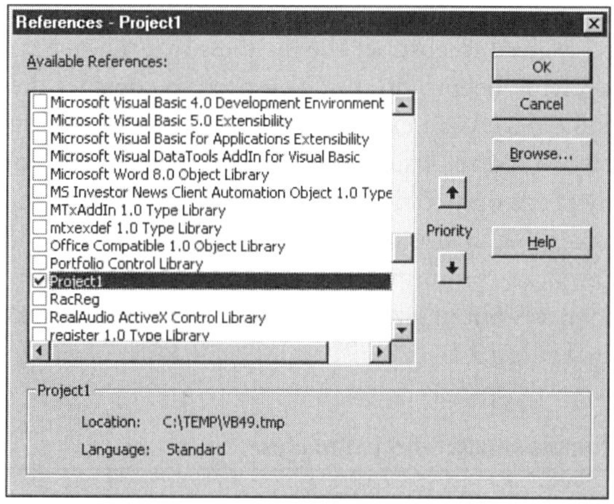

FIGURE 19.3.
The References dialog box with the OLE Automation Server application class.

You must check the reference of the name of your OLE Automation Server application. If you do not check the reference, the application will not know how to create the object class. At this point, you can run the application and see if it works. You can set breakpoints and debug the first instance of Visual Basic as you would any other application.

After you know the OLE Automation Server application works the way you expect, you can create the OLE DLL file by using File | Make DLL. This actually registers the OLE Automation Server on your system at the same time. The registration of an OLE Automation Server application is performed automatically when you distribute your OLE Automation Server by using the SETUP toolkit. If, for some reason, you need to manually register the OLE Automation Server DLL, you can use the `REGSVR32.EXE` program included with Visual Basic. To use the `REGSVR32.EXE` program, you need to supply a command-line argument, which is the name of the DLL to register. Note that it must be a 32-bit DLL to use this program. For a 16-bit DLL, use the `REGSVR` program. In either case, you would use the program like this, where *`DLL`* is the name of your DLL:

```
REGSVR32 DLL
```

Creating a Client/Server Middle Tier

The middle tier in a client/server application is used to contain business rules. You enforce these rules by making the first tier (the User Interface layer) talk directly to the middle-tier object. The third tier (Database Abstraction layer) accepts calls from the middle tier.

CROSS REFERENCE

For more information about the three-tiered architecture, refer to Chapter 32, "Visual Basic's Role in Client/Server Computing."

Suppose you wanted to abstract the business rules and encapsulate them into an object. You first have to decide how to do this. You need to consider the reason for putting functionality into the middle tier. As an example, take the PUBS database, which comes with SQL Server. Suppose you wanted to abstract the operations necessary for the Authors table. The middle tier probably needs only to delete, look up, and add records. It needs properties related to the columns in the table. It also needs events to communicate with the first tier. There needs to be at least one event to communicate the status of the operation. You need to think of this, not in terms of a database, but in terms of objects. The possible `AUTHOR` object could have the attributes contained in Table 19.1.

Table 19.1. Sample `AUTHOR` object attributes.

Properties	*Methods*	*Events*
`AuthorID`	`Add`	`Operation()`
`LastName`	`Delete`	
`FirstName`	`Lookup`	
`Phone`		
`Address`		
`City`		
`State`		
`Zip`		

Coding the Middle Tier

Visual Basic 5.0 has greatly simplified the creation of middle tiers through the use of the Class Utility Wizard. The first step is to create a new ActiveX DLL project by selecting File | New Project and then choosing the ActiveX DLL option. This creates a new project.

Then, to use the wizard, you must make sure it is selected for use. Do this by selecting Add-Ins | Add-In Manager and then selecting VB Class Builder Utility, as shown in Figure 19.4.

To run the Class Builder, select Add-Ins | Class Builder Utility. Figure 19.5 shows the Class Builder Utility.

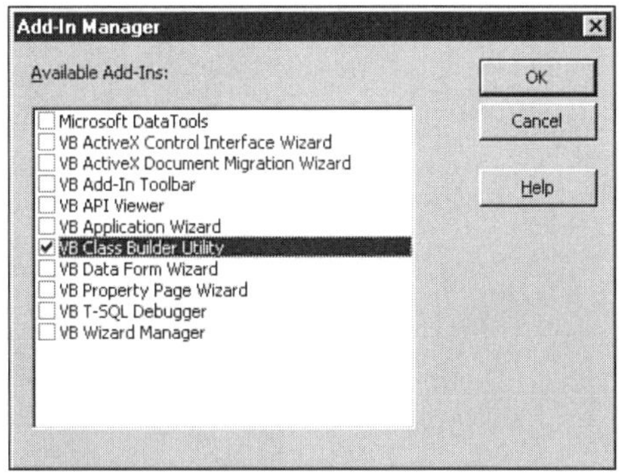

FIGURE 19.4.
Selecting the Class Builder Utility.

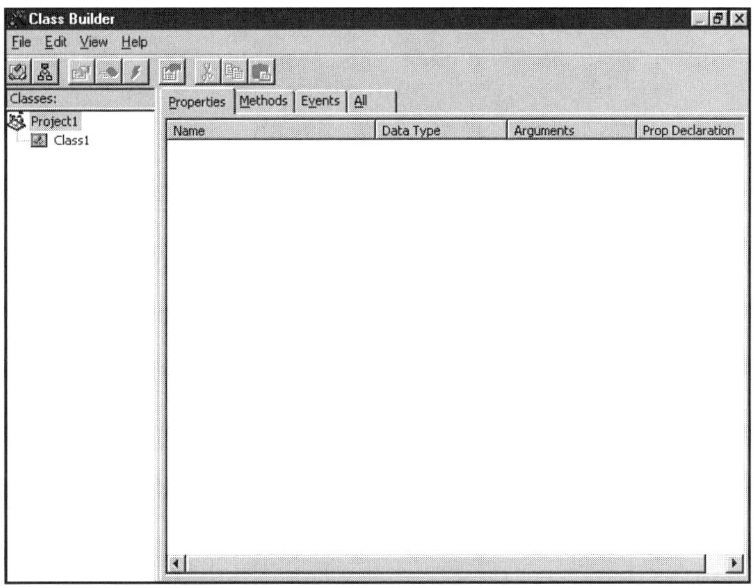

FIGURE 19.5.
The empty Class Builder Utility.

Highlight the class to which you want to add the members. Then, click the Add Properties toolbar icon. This brings up a dialog box like the one shown in Figure 19.6.

Add properties according to Table 19.1. You want to make sure that these are `Public` properties, because they are going to be exposed outside the application. Continue until all properties are added.

Then, add the methods described in Table 19.1. Do this by clicking the Add Methods toolbar icon. This brings up a dialog box like the one shown in Figure 19.7.

There are no arguments with these methods. The system will know which author to add, delete, or look up based on the properties set.

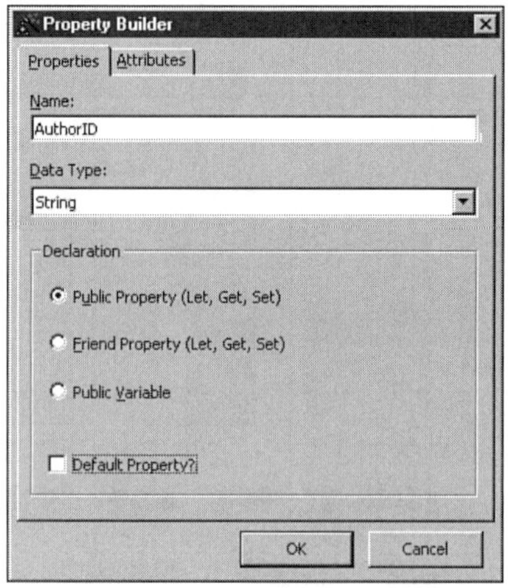

FIGURE 19.6.
Adding a property.

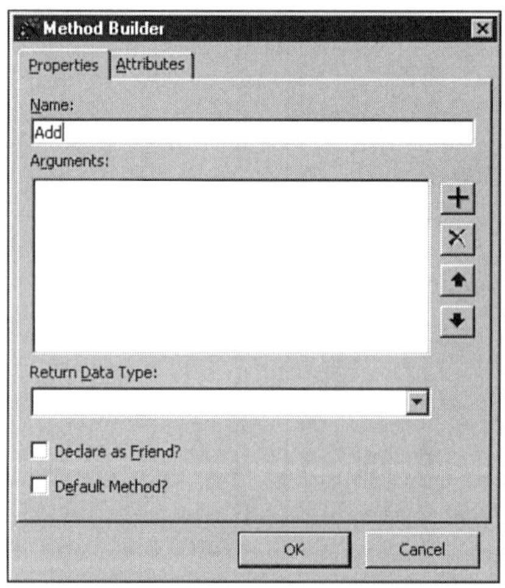

FIGURE 19.7.
Adding a method.

Continue with the other two methods. Then, add the one event by clicking the Add Events toolbar icon. This brings up a dialog box like the one shown in Figure 19.8.

For this event, you do need an argument because you need to know what type of operation happened. Therefore, put in a `Status` variable as an integer. Do this by clicking the + icon, which brings up the Add Arguments dialog box. Type `Status` and select Integer, as shown in Figure 19.9. Make sure to click the ByVal option.

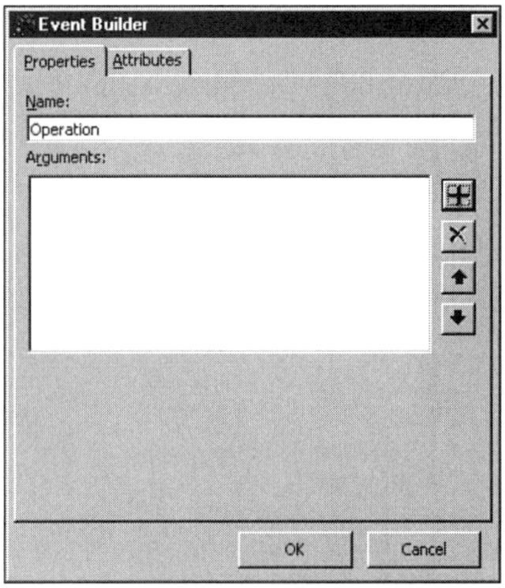

FIGURE 19.8.
Adding an event.

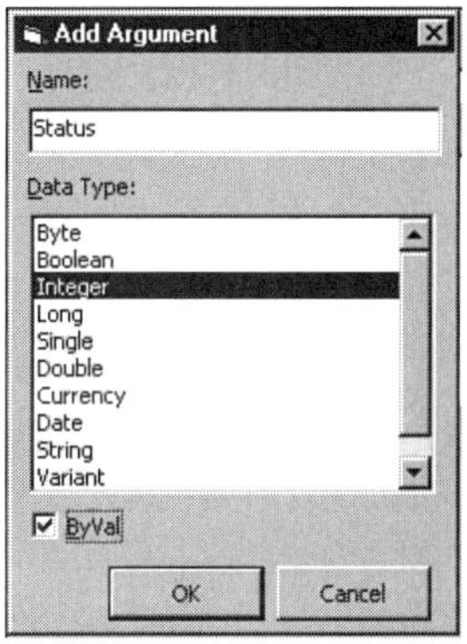

FIGURE 19.9.
Adding an argument to an event.

When you are finished, the Class Builder appears as shown in Figure 19.10.

Select File | Update Project. Now your project is updated with the class information, and you are ready to code.

Because the code shown here uses Remote Data Objects, make sure that there is a reference to Remote Data Objects by selecting Project | References and selecting the Microsoft Remote Data Object 2.0 option, as shown in Figure 19.11.

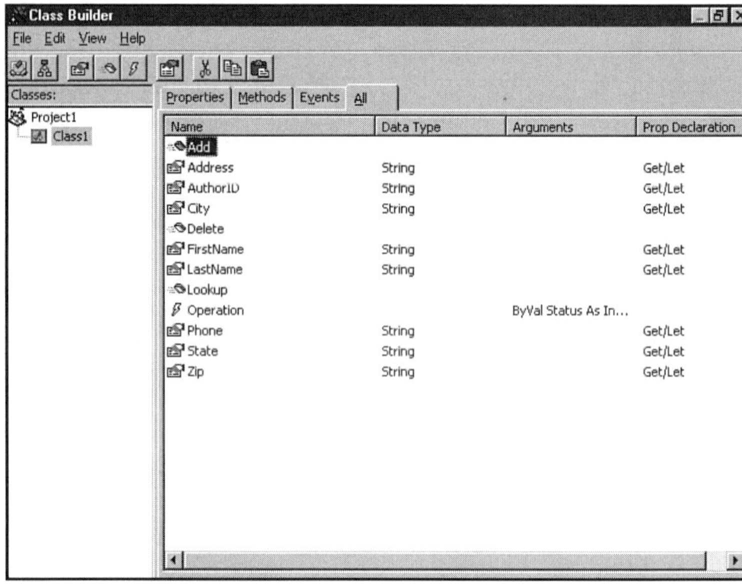

FIGURE 19.10.
The completed Class Builder.

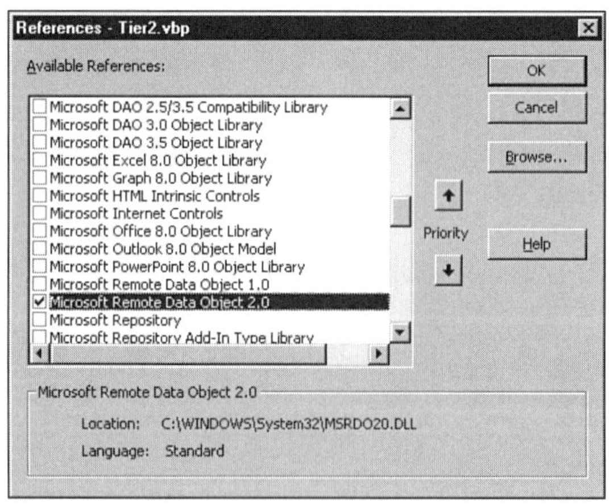

FIGURE 19.11.
Selecting the RDO 2.0 reference.

Much of the code is built for you when you use the Class Builder. The properties are already coded, as are the events. The only thing left to do is code the events and raise the events in the Tier 1 code.

The object of this exercise is for you to be able to fill data in the properties of the object, execute some methods, and get data. The Tier 1 application has no idea how or from where the data comes. This is precisely what the middle tier is supposed to do. The code for this tier is available on the CD-ROM accompanying this book in the TIER2 subdirectory.

The first concept is that the connection to the server should be opened when the object is instantiated (`Initialize()` event), and the connection should be closed when the object is closed (`Terminate()` event). This example uses Remote Data Objects.

CROSS REFERENCE

For more information about RDO, refer to Chapter 16, "Remote Data Objects (RDO)."

The code in the `Initialize()` event of the class module looks like this:

```
Private Sub Class_Initialize()

    'Connect to SQL Server

    Set rdoEn = rdoEnvironments(0)
    With rdoCn
        .Connect = "UID=sa;PWD=;Database=Pubs;DSN=LocalServer;"
        .EstablishConnection rdDriverNoPrompt, True
        rdoEn.rdoConnections.Add rdoCn
    End With

End Sub
```

CROSS REFERENCE

For more information about ODBC, refer to Chapter 30, "ODBC."

It simply establishes the connection. The code to close the connection in the `Terminate()` event looks like this:

```
Private Sub Class_Terminate()
    'close the active connection
    rdoCn.Close

End Sub
```

This works within the class module because the variables are declared in the `(general)(declarations)` section, like this:

```
Private rdoCn As New rdo.rdoConnection
Private rdoEn As rdo.rdoEnvironment
```

The code that handles the properties is generated automatically by the Class Builder. This includes everything from the declarations, which look like this:

```
Option Explicit
'SQL Server variables
Private rdoCn As New rdo.rdoConnection
Private rdoEn As rdo.rdoEnvironment
```

```
'local variable(s) to hold property value(s)
Private mvarAuthorID As String 'local copy
Private mvarLastName As String 'local copy
Private mvarFirstName As String 'local copy
Private mvarPhone As String 'local copy
Private mvarAddress As String 'local copy
Private mvarCity As String 'local copy
Private mvarState As String 'local copy
Private mvarZip As String 'local copy
'To fire this event, use RaiseEvent with the following syntax:
'RaiseEvent Operation[(arg1, arg2, ... , argn)]
Public Event Operation(ByVal Status As Integer)
```

to the code inside the property procedures themselves:

```
Public Property Let Zip(ByVal vData As String)
'used when assigning a value to the property, on the left side of an
'assignment.  Syntax: X.Zip = 5
    mvarZip = vData
End Property
Public Property Get Zip() As String
'used when retrieving value of a property, on the right side of an
'assignment.  Syntax: Debug.Print X.Zip
    Zip = mvarZip
End Property
Public Property Let State(ByVal vData As String)
'used when assigning a value to the property, on the left side of an
'assignment.  Syntax: X.State = 5
    mvarState = vData
End Property
Public Property Get State() As String
'used when retrieving value of a property, on the right side of an
'assignment.  Syntax: Debug.Print X.State
    State = mvarState
End Property
Public Property Let City(ByVal vData As String)
'used when assigning a value to the property, on the left side of an
'assignment.  Syntax: X.City = 5
    mvarCity = vData
End Property
Public Property Get City() As String
'used when retrieving value of a property, on the right side of an
'assignment.  Syntax: Debug.Print X.City
    City = mvarCity
End Property
Public Property Let Address(ByVal vData As String)
'used when assigning a value to the property, on the left side of an
'assignment.  Syntax: X.Address = 5
    mvarAddress = vData
End Property
Public Property Get Address() As String
'used when retrieving value of a property, on the right side of an
'assignment.  Syntax: Debug.Print X.Address
    Address = mvarAddress
End Property
Public Property Let Phone(ByVal vData As String)
'used when assigning a value to the property, on the left side of an
'assignment.  Syntax: X.Phone = 5
    mvarPhone = vData
```

```
End Property
Public Property Get Phone() As String
'used when retrieving value of a property, on the right side of an
'assignment.  Syntax: Debug.Print X.Phone
    Phone = mvarPhone
End Property
Public Property Let FirstName(ByVal vData As String)
'used when assigning a value to the property, on the left side of an
'assignment.  Syntax: X.FirstName = 5
    mvarFirstName = vData
End Property
Public Property Get FirstName() As String
'used when retrieving value of a property, on the right side of an
'assignment.  Syntax: Debug.Print X.FirstName
    FirstName = mvarFirstName
End Property
Public Property Let LastName(ByVal vData As String)
'used when assigning a value to the property, on the left side of an
'assignment.  Syntax: X.LastName = 5
    mvarLastName = vData
End Property
Public Property Get LastName() As String
'used when retrieving value of a property, on the right side of an
'assignment.  Syntax: Debug.Print X.LastName
    LastName = mvarLastName
End Property
Public Property Let AuthorID(ByVal vData As String)
'used when assigning a value to the property, on the left side of an
'assignment.  Syntax: X.AuthorID = 5
    mvarAuthorID = vData
End Property
Public Property Get AuthorID() As String
'used when retrieving value of a property, on the right side of an
'assignment.  Syntax: Debug.Print X.AuthorID
    AuthorID = mvarAuthorID
End Property
```

The majority of the code is inside the methods. A blank shell for the methods is generated by the Class Builder. After the three methods are coded, Tier 2 is finished.

Start with the `Lookup` method. It's a good place to start because there is data already in the server. This lets you test to find out even if you can set and get data from each property. The code for the `Lookup` method looks like this:

```
Public Sub Lookup()
    'declare variables
    Dim sCmd As String
    Dim rdoRs As rdoResultset

    'clear errors
    rdo.rdoEngine.rdoErrors.Clear

    'construct SQL statement
    sCmd = "SELECT * FROM Authors "
    sCmd = sCmd & "WHERE au_id = '" & AuthorID & "' "
    Set rdoRs = rdoCn.OpenResultset(sCmd)
    'respond
```

```
    If rdo.rdoEngine.rdoErrors.Count > 0 Then
        'there was an error
        RaiseEvent Operation(-1)
    ElseIf rdoCn.rdoResultsets(0).EOF = True Then
        'no results
        RaiseEvent Operation(-2)
    Else
        'all was OK

        'First, Clear all except ID
        LastName = ""
        FirstName = ""
        Phone = ""
        Address = ""
        City = ""
        State = ""
        Zip = ""

        'populate with results
        LastName = rdoCn.rdoResultsets(0).rdoColumns("au_lname").Value
        FirstName = rdoCn.rdoResultsets(0).rdoColumns("au_fname").Value
        Phone = rdoCn.rdoResultsets(0).rdoColumns("phone").Value
        Address = rdoCn.rdoResultsets(0).rdoColumns("address").Value
        City = rdoCn.rdoResultsets(0).rdoColumns("city").Value
        State = rdoCn.rdoResultsets(0).rdoColumns("state").Value
        Zip = rdoCn.rdoResultsets(0).rdoColumns("zip").Value

        'raise the event that everything is ok
        RaiseEvent Operation(0)
    End If

End Sub
```

This code is quite simple to follow. An SQL statement is built using the value of the `AuthorID` property. It is sent to the server and a resultset is built. Before doing this, the `rdoErrors` object is cleared. This means that if there are any errors during the operation, you know that what is contained in the object is current. There are three different statuses that can be produced:

- 1—An error occurred.
- 2—There were no records returned.
- 0—The operation was successful.

If the operation was successful, the values coming from the database are populated into the property values. This makes it very easy to get data from the database from other applications.

The next method to code is the `Add` method because you don't want to test the `Delete` method yet on data you currently need. Therefore, if the `Add` is done first, you can add erroneous data for the purpose of deleting it afterward. The code for the `Add` method looks like this:

```
Public Sub Add()
    'declare variables
    Dim sCmd As String

    'clear errors
    rdo.rdoEngine.rdoErrors.Clear
```

```
    'construct SQL statement
    sCmd = "INSERT INTO Authors(au_id,au_lname,au_fname,phone,address,city,
    ➥state,zip,contract) "
    sCmd = sCmd & "VALUES ('" & AuthorID & "','"
    sCmd = sCmd & LastName & "','"
    sCmd = sCmd & FirstName & "','"
    sCmd = sCmd & Phone & "','"
    sCmd = sCmd & Address & "','"
    sCmd = sCmd & City & "','"
    sCmd = sCmd & State & "','"
    sCmd = sCmd & Zip & "',"
    sCmd = sCmd & "0)"
    rdoCn.Execute (sCmd)

    'respond
    If rdo.rdoEngine.rdoErrors.Count > 0 Then
        'there was an error
        RaiseEvent Operation(-1)
    Else
        'all was OK

        'raise the event that everything is ok
        RaiseEvent Operation(0)
    End If
End Sub
```

This code, too, is easy to follow. It builds an `INSERT` SQL statement, based on the values retrieved from the properties. There is only one major difference between this method and the `Lookup` and `Delete` methods. This method adds data into an additional column, for which there is no property. This column is the "contract" column. It requires a non-null value. Therefore, a value must be supplied. However, the value is not important in this example. That's why you see the following line right above the `Execute` line. It sends the value of `0` to that column:

```
sCmd = sCmd & "0)"
```

The final method is the `Delete` method, which works basically the same as the others. It builds an SQL statement and deletes the record. It then clears the values of all of the properties because they are no longer valid. The code looks like this:

```
Public Sub Delete()
    'declare variables
    Dim sCmd As String

    'clear errors
    rdo.rdoEngine.rdoErrors.Clear

    'construct SQL statement
    sCmd = "DELETE FROM Authors "
    sCmd = sCmd & "WHERE au_id = '" & AuthorID & "' "
    rdoCn.Execute (sCmd)
    'respond
    If rdo.rdoEngine.rdoErrors.Count > 0 Then
        'there was an error
        RaiseEvent Operation(-1)
    Else
        'all was OK
```

```
        'Clear all
        AuthorID = ""
        LastName = ""
        FirstName = ""
        Phone = ""
        Address = ""
        City = ""
        State = ""
        Zip = ""

        'raise the event that everything is ok
        RaiseEvent Operation(0)
    End If
End Sub
```

Testing the Middle Tier

To test the middle tier that was created in the previous section, you must first run the application. There is no visual interface, so you will not see much. You then start another instance of Visual Basic. Open a new project by selecting File | New Project. A standard EXE will be fine for testing. Choose the reference of the application in Project | References. You will see the reference listed as Tier2, as shown in Figure 19.12.

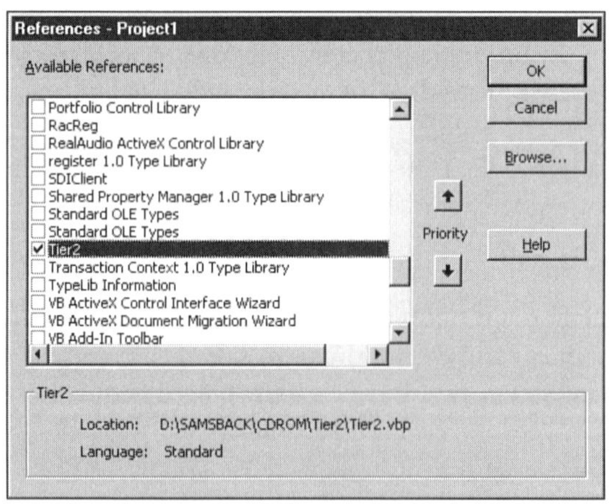

FIGURE 19.12.
Selecting the Tier2 reference.

When the reference is set, you can begin coding. The `(general)(declarations)` section must contain at least two lines, as follows:

```
Option Explicit
Private WithEvents objAuthor As Author
```

The `WithEvents` keyword indicates that an event will be fired for this object, declared as `objAuthor` from the class module `Author`. Then, you must instantiate the object with the `New` keyword in the `Form_Load()` event. Here's how it's done:

```
Private Sub Form_Load()
    'declare variables
    Dim sMsg As String
    'instantiate object
    Set objAuthor = New Author

    'specify an ID
    objAuthor.AuthorID = "238-95-7766"

    'Lookup
    objAuthor.Lookup

    'construct messagebox
    sMsg = "Last Name:" & objAuthor.LastName & Chr$(13)
    sMsg = sMsg & "First Name:" & objAuthor.FirstName & Chr$(13)
    sMsg = sMsg & "Phone:" & objAuthor.Phone & Chr$(13)
    sMsg = sMsg & "Address:" & objAuthor.Address & Chr$(13)
    sMsg = sMsg & "City:" & objAuthor.City & Chr$(13)
    sMsg = sMsg & "State:" & objAuthor.State & Chr$(13)
    sMsg = sMsg & "Zip:" & objAuthor.Zip

    'display message
    MsgBox sMsg

End Sub
```

After the object is instantiated, the properties and methods can be accessed, just like any other object. The code here sets the `AuthorID` property and then looks it up. The values are displayed in a message box. If there are any errors, this routine will catch them:

```
Private Sub objAuthor_Operation(ByVal nStatus As Integer)
    'handle event
    If nStatus <> 0 Then
        MsgBox Str$(nStatus)
    End If
End Sub
```

Notice the function name. It's the name of the object, followed by an underscore character, followed by the name of the event raised in Tier 2. It passes in the argument expected, as outlined in the Class Builder Utility, earlier. This routine simply displays a message box if there was an error during any operation. That's all there is to it.

The preceding code is not the most elegant code, but it definitely gives you an idea of the types of things you can do with multitier architecture. It also gives you a good background on how to create these tiers with Visual Basic.

Summary

Components and objects are very easy to create in Visual Basic 5.0. One of the most important ways to use these objects is for creating and using the middle tier in a three- or more-tiered client/server application. The middle tier is often referred to as a business object server because it encapsulates key business rules into one server object.

Visual Basic enables you to create objects which have properties, methods, and events that you define. These properties, methods, and events are called members of the object or class. This chapter outlined how to create and use components and objects. Use this chapter to build your knowledge and skills so that you can incorporate components and objects into your own applications. Also, make sure to read Chapter 20, "ActiveX Controls."

20

ActiveX Controls

ActiveX controls are software components that can be used in a variety of applications and environments. ActiveX controls are based on the Components Object Model (COM), which is an open architecture. An open architecture allows for different vendors to create reusable components. Before ActiveX controls, Microsoft released a different kind of open architecture, called a Visual Basic Extension (VBX). Then came the OLE Control Extension (OCX), which was based on OLE. However, this architecture was not open enough. It is important to note that because the VBX was based on a 16-bit architecture, it is not compatible with Visual Basic 5.

The open standard of ActiveX controls was designed to enable the components developed using this standard to be widely used. The full Microsoft Office suite uses ActiveX controls, as does all of the tools in the Visual Tools suite, and, maybe most importantly, so does the Internet Explorer.

ActiveX used on the Internet enables vendors to create and package small components that can contain optimized packages of functionality without the end user even knowing how to program. Visual Basic developers have been familiar with this type of convenience since version 1.0 (about six years ago). It is now so widespread that learning how to create your own ActiveX controls gives you a big advantage over those who cannot.

The ActiveX components that you create can be

- Sold to developers
- Used to enhance your corporate Web presence
- Used to enhance and encapsulate a total application

The rest of this chapter is dedicated to helping you develop ActiveX controls. The example that is built throughout this chapter is located in the `ActiveX` directory on the CD-ROM accompanying this book. ActiveX controls can be created in all versions of Visual Basic 5.0, including the Control Creation Edition (CCE), which is included on the CD-ROM that accompanies this book.

Developing the ActiveX Control User Interface

You can use Visual Basic to develop ActiveX controls. Prior to version 5.0, you had to develop OCXs and VBXs in C or C++, which was a tedious task. Visual Basic programmers had to learn C++, which is quite a bit different than Visual Basic. Microsoft has taken great steps to make the functionality available in Visual Basic.

An ActiveX control really encapsulates the functionality of both code or forms. Therefore, your ActiveX control can have no visual interface, if you want.

Creating the ActiveX Project

To begin creating an ActiveX control (or component), you must tell Visual Basic that this is the type of project you are creating. Do this by selecting File | New Project, and then choose the ActiveX Control icon, as shown in Figure 20.1.

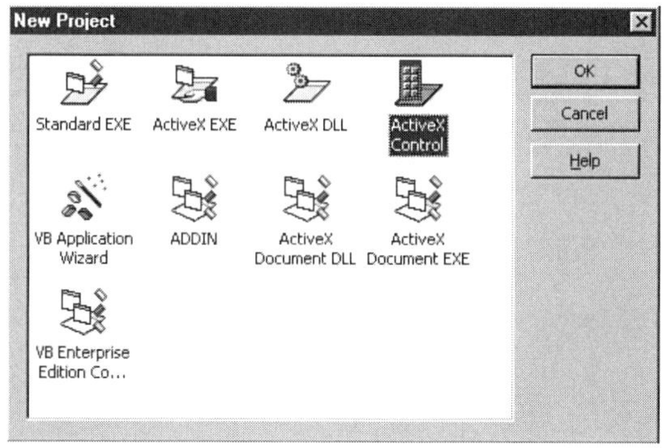

FIGURE 20.1.
Creating a new ActiveX control project.

After you create the project, the screen at first glance will look just like any other new project. However, you'll notice in the Project window that a user control has been created. Figure 20.2 shows what the newly created project looks like. The form-like design window is where you create your ActiveX control (if it has a visual interface). The code pane is where you place code related to the visual interface. This is what controls the functionality behind the visual interface. Notice one more thing: the new icon in the bottom-right part of the toolbox. This is a placeholder for an icon representing your new ActiveX control. It is disabled because your ActiveX control's visible interface must be closed for you to be able to use it. You'll learn about that later.

ActiveX controls (called *user controls* in Visual Basic) have specific properties, methods, and events that manipulate behavior. To see these properties, methods, and events and their descriptions, see the Visual Basic Help file.

At this point, you can start to create your ActiveX control. You can place other controls on it and manipulate code, just as if it were a regular form.

NOTE

If you place third-party controls on the form, you will need to distribute them as you would any project containing these controls. Furthermore, in order to use the control at design time, the end user also needs to possess a license for the control, just as you did.

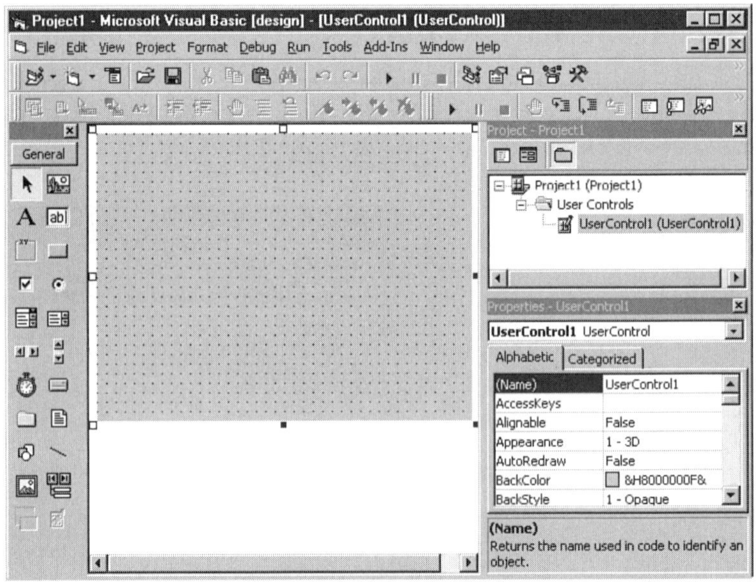

FIGURE 20.2.
The newly created ActiveX control project.

Suppose you wanted to create a common dialog box to use for files. You could place these three intrinsic controls on the form:

- Drive List
- Directory List
- File List

The entire form presented represents your ActiveX control. This control should be renamed to something more appropriate. In this case, `FileControl`. To rename the control, click the outer border or surface of the control in the visual window and change the `Name` property in the property window, as shown in Figure 20.3.

That's all that is necessary to create a very elementary control. Because no code is behind it yet, nothing will happen to the control, but you're probably anxious to test it.

Testing the ActiveX Control

To test the ActiveX control, you need to open another project inside the same window. Select File | Add Project. This will, again, bring up a dialog box of what type of project to add. This is not critical. You can select any of the EXE or DLL type projects to create a group of projects. The first project is your ActiveX control project and the second is your test project. To avoid confusion, rename your test project from the default name to something meaningful, such as `TestActiveX`.

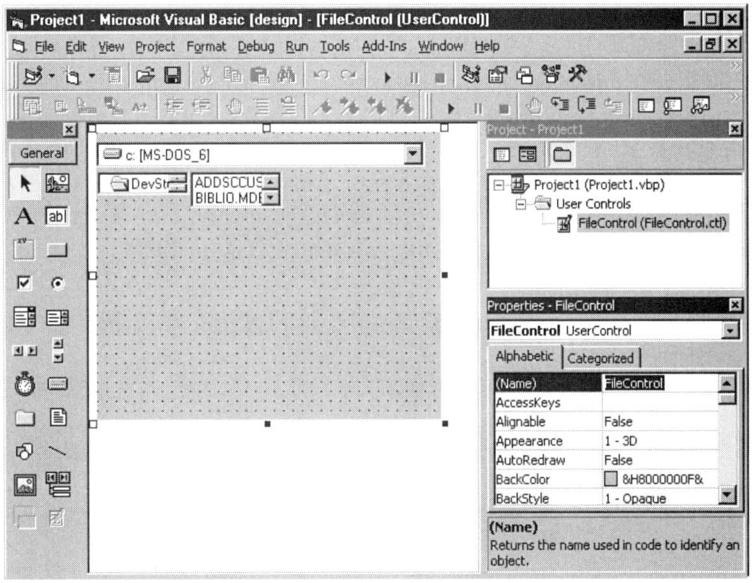

FIGURE 20.3.
The ActiveX control after placing intrinsic controls on it.

Double-click the ActiveX control in the Project window to bring up the visual interface for the ActiveX control. Now, close this window. As soon as you do, you'll see the icon placeholder for your control become enabled, which means that it is ready to test. Double-click the form in the TestActiveX project. Then, drag and drop the new ActiveX control in the Control Panel onto your form, as you would any other control. Figure 20.4 shows how this looks.

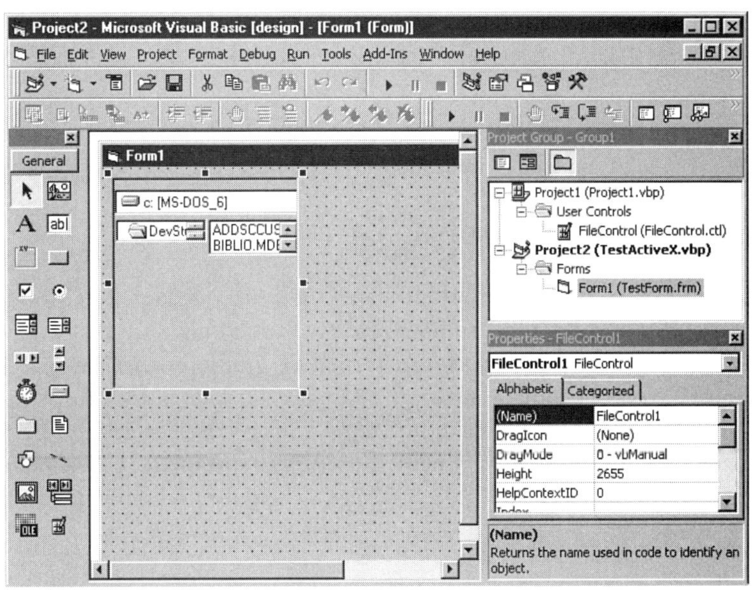

FIGURE 20.4.
Testing your new control.

Notice that you do not even have to run the project for this to be tested. The control reacts immediately. This is true also if there is code behind the control, as you will see later. Even though the control is placed on a form, you can still edit the control. Simply open the ActiveX control project window and perform any necessary changes. However, you'll notice one thing. As stated earlier, you need to close the ActiveX control's visual window in order to test the control and to make it available to your other projects in the group. Because you already have placed the control on your test project's form, if you do not close the ActiveX control, you'll see hash marks within the control, as shown in Figure 20.5.

FIGURE 20.5.
The test project showing hash marks.

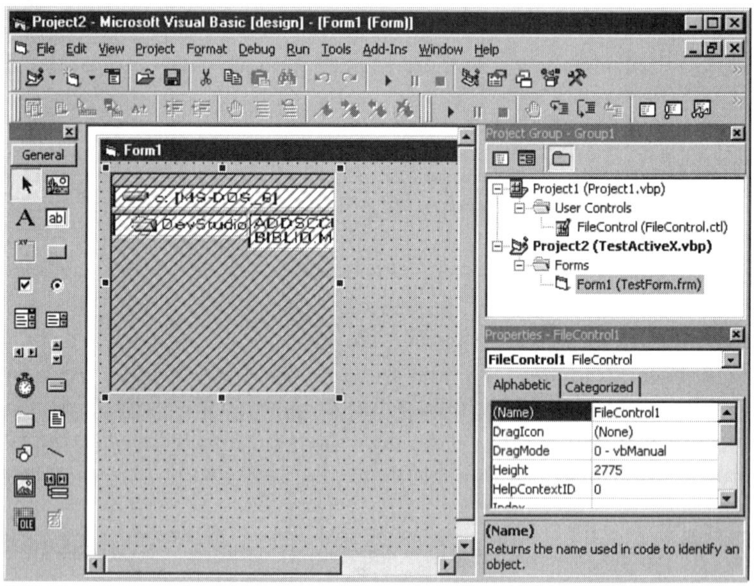

Now that you know the basic concepts of developing and testing a control, you are able to refine your design and make it more user friendly. The possibilities are limitless.

Refining the ActiveX Control

Now that you understand how to create a basic ActiveX control, it's time to refine its functionality and make it useful. You have placed controls on a form that will act like a file common dialog box. Placing the controls on a form does nothing unless there is code behind them. There are two pieces of code necessary. The first is the code needed to perform all of the internal operations, such as changing the directory (folder) display when the drive changes. The second is the code needed to expose desired properties and methods to the outside world. Then, if necessary, you can create a property page to help the user develop faster.

The first step in this example is to make sure that when the drive changes, so does the directory (folder) control. You can do this with the following code:

```
Private Sub Drive1_Change()
    On Error Resume Next
    Dir1.Path = Drive1.Drive
End Sub
```

Then, when the directory changes, so does the file contents for that control. This can be done with this simple code:

```
Private Sub Dir1_Change()
    On Error Resume Next
    File1.Path = Dir1.Path
End Sub
```

One nice feature to add would be the capability to automatically resize the controls on the form whenever the control is resized. This is a very common feature. It is done, as you would expect, in the `Resize()` event, as follows:

```
Private Sub UserControl_Resize()
    'resize controls
    Const FACTOR = 100

    'resize drive control
    Drive1.Left = FACTOR
    Drive1.Width = UserControl.Width - (FACTOR * 2)

    'resize directory control
    Dir1.Left = FACTOR
    Dir1.Width = ((UserControl.Width - FACTOR) * 0.5) - FACTOR
    Dir1.Height = UserControl.Height - FACTOR - Dir1.Top

    'resize file control
    File1.Left = Dir1.Width + (FACTOR * 2)
    File1.Width = ((UserControl.Width - FACTOR) * 0.5) - FACTOR
    File1.Height = UserControl.Height - FACTOR - File1.Top

End Sub
```

The `FACTOR` constant is used solely to act as a spacer so that the controls are not placed at the left, right, top, and bottom edges of the control. Also, the multiplication factor, 0.5, is used so that the File List control and Directory List control are spaced evenly across the form. Figures 20.6 and 20.7 show the code in action. Each figure shows the control being sized differently.

Notice in both cases, the project was not run. Only the ActiveX control window was closed. This makes for very rapid application development.

Changing the Icon in the Toolbox

Changing the icon in the toolbox is as simple as setting a property—you must set the `ToolboxBitmap` property. It can be set to a maximum of 16×15 pixels. If you use a larger bitmap or icon, it will be scaled down automatically. You can use a program such as Microsoft Paint to construct your icons. Figure 20.8 shows the icon in Microsoft Paint, and Figure 20.9 shows the icon in the toolbox.

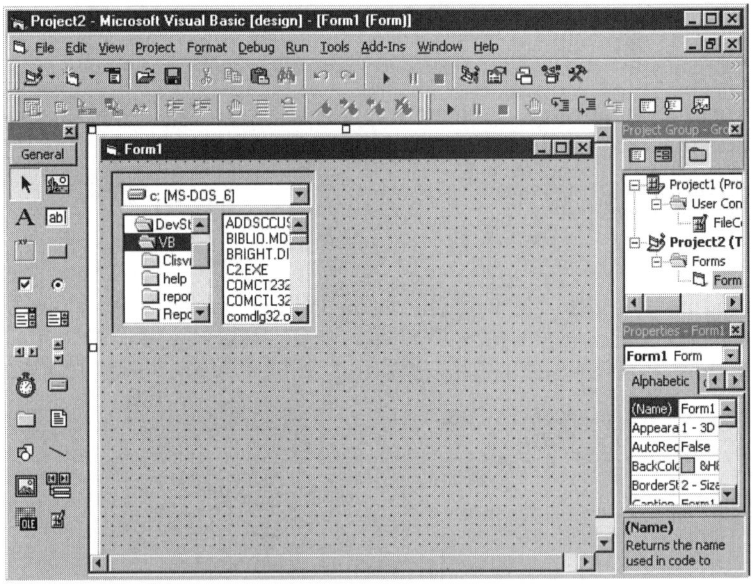

FIGURE 20.6.
The ActiveX control using the resize code in one position.

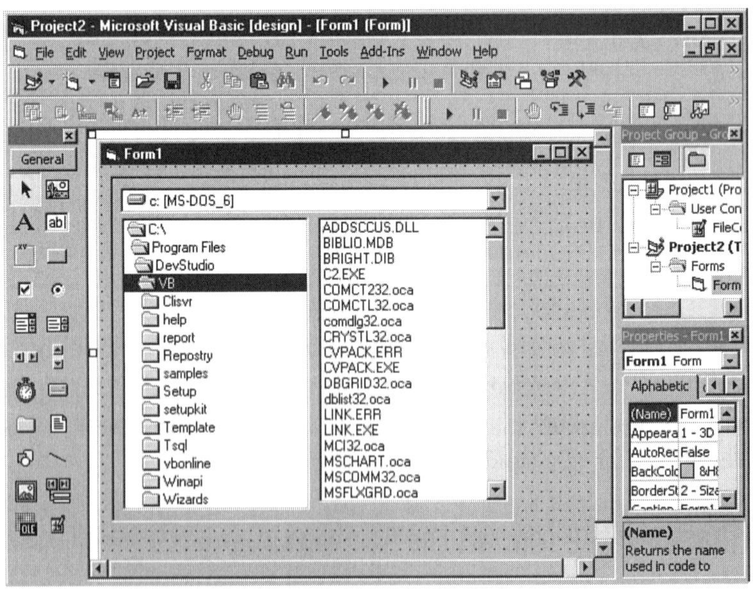

FIGURE 20.7.
The ActiveX control using the resize code in a different position.

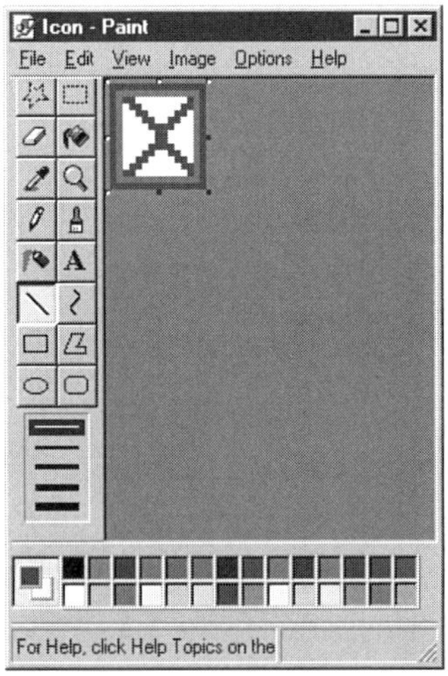

FIGURE 20.8.
Designing an icon in Microsoft Paint.

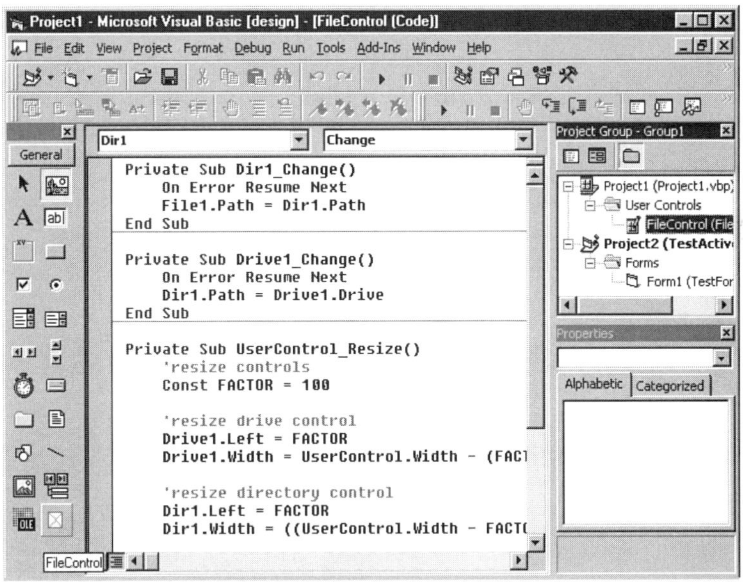

FIGURE 20.9.
The icon shown in the new ActiveX toolbox.

Multiple ActiveX Controls in One File

If you want to include more than one ActiveX control in your distributed OCX file, you can do so by selecting Project | Add User Control. This enables you to create a new control or simply select an existing one.

Continue doing this until all controls are visible under the project in the Project window. When you distribute your ActiveX file, all controls are also distributed and show up in the toolbar.

Developing the ActiveX Control Public Interface

The public interface is defined by the properties, methods, and events exposed by the object, called members. To define members, Microsoft has included a nice tool called the ActiveX Control Interface Wizard. This tool is an add-in available only when selected. To make sure it is selected, choose Add-Ins | Add-In Manager, which brings up the dialog box shown in Figure 20.10. Click the VB ActiveX Control Interface Wizard option and click OK. This makes the wizard available for use.

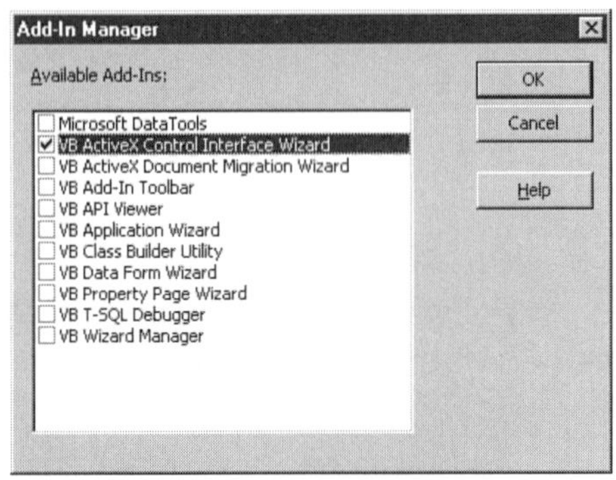

FIGURE 20.10.
Selecting the ActiveX Control Interface Wizard.

To use the wizard, choose Add-Ins | ActiveX Control Interface Wizard. This wizard will guide you through a series of steps to create your public interface. Figure 20.11 shows the opening screen of the wizard.

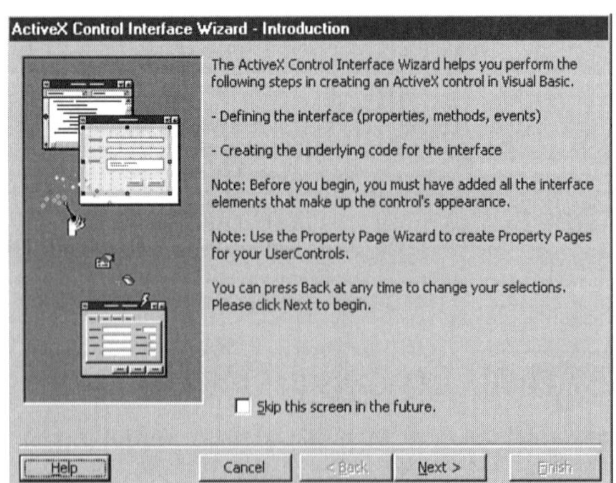

FIGURE 20.11.
The opening screen for the ActiveX Control Interface Wizard.

The first step is to choose the standard properties, methods, and events that are supported by the control. What determines this is the properties, methods, and events that are available to each individual standard or third-party control. If the members are supported by the underlying control, it will be supported in the new user ActiveX control.

For this example, choose the following:

- `BorderStyle` property
- `Change()` event
- `Enabled` property
- `Refresh` method

These selected members are shown in Figure 20.12.

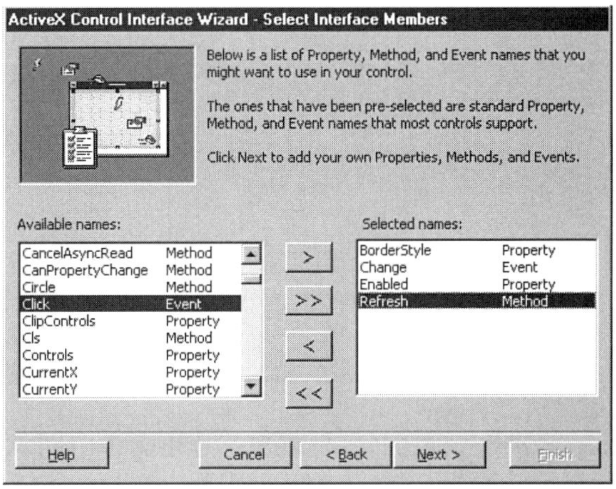

FIGURE 20.12.
Selecting standard properties, methods, and events with the Control Interface Wizard.

The next step is to create your own custom properties, methods, and events. Suppose you want to allow access to any or all of the three controls contained in your ActiveX control. You could create the following properties:

- `DriveEnabled`
- `DirEnabled`
- `FileEnabled`

These properties will be available to your ActiveX control. The code behind them will manipulate the standard properties and methods available to the underlying controls that make up the new ActiveX control.

You would specify these properties successively by clicking the New button. This brings up the Add Custom Member dialog box in Figure 20.13. Type the name of the property and choose Property.

Continue until all properties are added (see Figure 20.14).

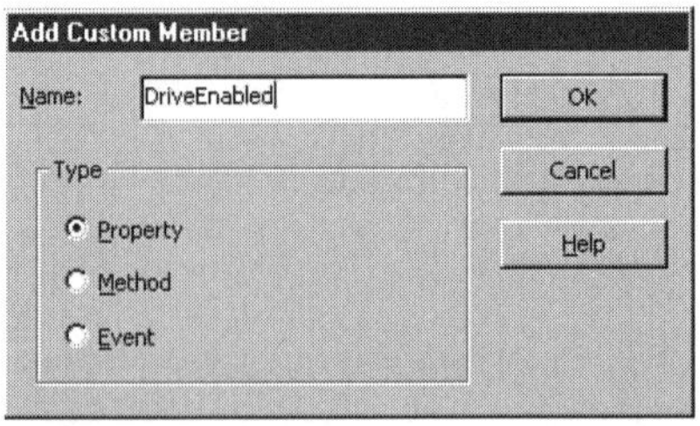

FIGURE 20.13.
Creating a new custom property.

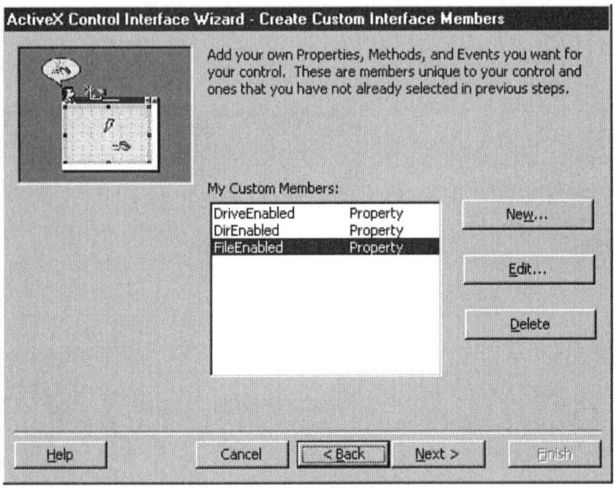

FIGURE 20.14.
The Create Custom Interface Members dialog box with properties created.

The next step is to map each of the custom members defined to members available to the control. For example, the `Change()` event needs to be mapped to the `PathChange()` event of the `File1` control because it will always change when any of the three controls change. The `DriveEnabled` property needs to be mapped to the `Enabled` property of the `Drive1` control. Table 20.1 lists the mappings of the new control, and Figure 20.15 shows the mappings performed in the wizard.

Table 20.1. Mappings for the new ActiveX control.

ActiveX Member	*Maps to Control*	*Maps to Property, Method, or Event*
`BorderStyle`	`User Control`	`BorderStyle`
`Change()`	`File1`	`PathChange()`
`DirEnabled`	`Dir1`	`Enabled`
`DriveEnabled`	`Drive1`	`Enabled`
`Enabled`	`User Control`	`Enabled`
`FileEnabled`	`File1`	`Enabled`
`Refresh`	`User Control`	`Refresh`

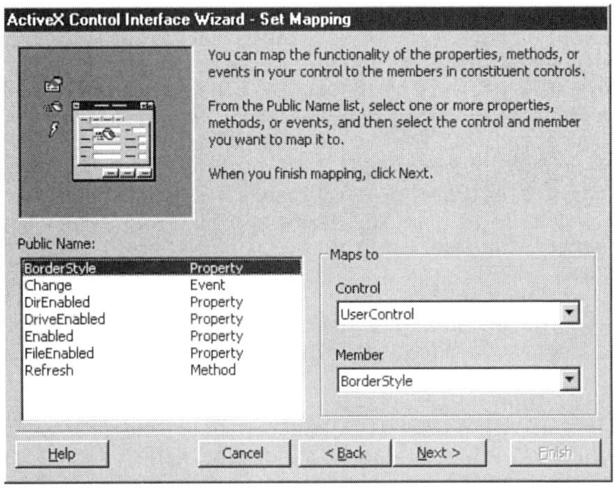

FIGURE 20.15.
The new interface members mappings.

The final screen enables you to view a summary report if you want, and to finish creating the public interface. Figure 20.16 shows this screen.

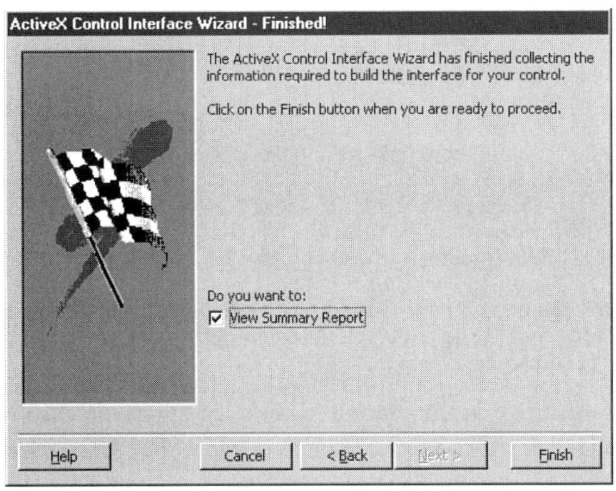

FIGURE 20.16.
The final step of the Control Interface Wizard.

When you click Finish, the summary screen will be presented, if you have checked the Summary check box. The summary looks like this:

```
Below is a To Do list of items required to complete the testing and debugging
of your UserControl.
A) Create a test program for your UserControl
There are two ways to set up a test program for your UserControl, depending on
whether you inserted the control in a Standard EXE, or created an ActiveX
Control project for it.
If you created an ActiveX Control project, the following steps will set up a
test program:
```

```
1)  Save your UserControl.
2)  Close your UserControl's designer, to put the control in run mode.
3)  If you haven't already created a test project, add a Standard EXE project
by selecting Add Project from the File menu.
4)  In the Toolbox, double-click your UserControl's icon to place an instance
of your UserControl on Form1, in the Standard EXE project.  You can move and
resize the control as needed.
5)  Save the project group. In later development and test sessions, you can
open both projects at once by opening the project group.
If you inserted the UserControl in an existing Standard EXE project, follow
these steps:
1)  Save your UserControl.
2)  Close your UserControl's designer, to put the control in run mode.
3)  In the Project window, double-click Form1 in the Standard EXE project, to
open its designer.
4)  In the Toolbox, double-click your UserControl's icon to place an instance
of your UserControl on Form1.  You can move and resize the control as needed.
B) Test your control's behavior at design time, and at run time.
1)  Select the control you placed on Form1 in the test project, and press F4
to open the Properties window. Verify that you can see and change the
properties you added to your control.
2)  Close Form1 and reopen it, and verify that the property values for your
control were correctly saved and retrieved.
3)  Double-click the control you placed on Form1, and verify that the
appropriate events appear in the right- hand (Procedure) drop down of the code
window.
4)  Add test code to the event procedures for your control.
5)  Add other controls, and put code in their event procedures to test the
run-time behavior of your control's properties and methods.
6)  Press F5 to run the test project, and test your control's run-time behavior.
You can modify your control by running the Wizard again, and selecting
your UserControl.
Use the Property Page Wizard to create Property Pages for your UserControls.
For more information on creating and testing ActiveX Controls, please read
Chapter 4, "Creating an ActiveX Control," and
Chapter 9, "Building ActiveX Controls."
Chapter 6, "General Principles of Component Design," and Chapter 7, "Debugging,
Testing, and Deploying ActiveX Components," contain additional information
➥you may find useful.
```

The chapters shown in the preceding code are the chapters from the documentation included on the Visual Basic CD-ROM. When you close the summary screen, your interface is created. You won't have an obvious visual clue that it has been created, but you'll know when you test it. To test it, you must try every property, event, and method available to your new control.

If you bring up the property window, you'll see the new controls, as shown in Figure 20.17.

You also must code your events, as you would with any event. For example, you could try the `Change()` event like this:

```
Private Sub FileControl1_Change()
    MsgBox "Path Changed"
End Sub
```

You could try the method like this:

```
FileControl1.Refresh
```

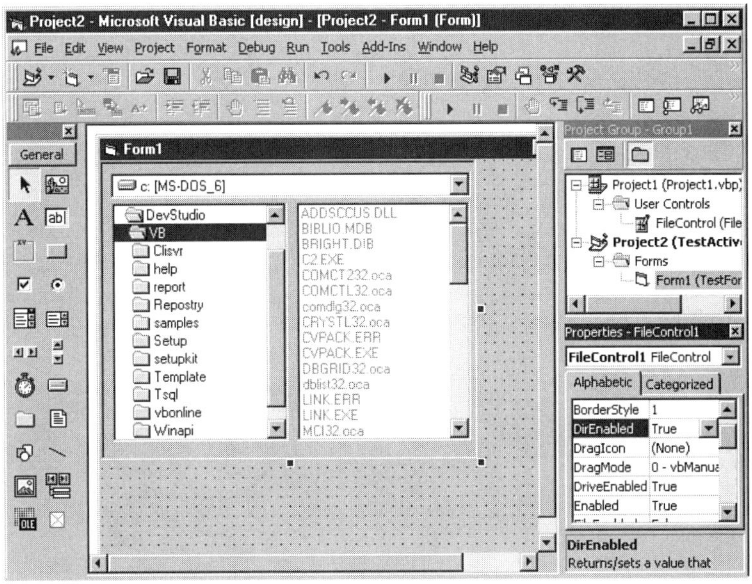

FIGURE 20.17.
The ActiveX control after you have used the Control Interface Wizard.

That's all there is to it. Don't forget to save your project.

Adding Property Pages

Property pages are a way to group like functionality together. If you want to add one or more property pages to your ActiveX control, you must do so by using the Property Page Wizard add-in. You must select this add-in for use by selecting Add-Ins | Add-In Manager. This brings up a dialog box showing the registered add-ins. Select the VB Property Page Wizard option, as shown in Figure 20.18.

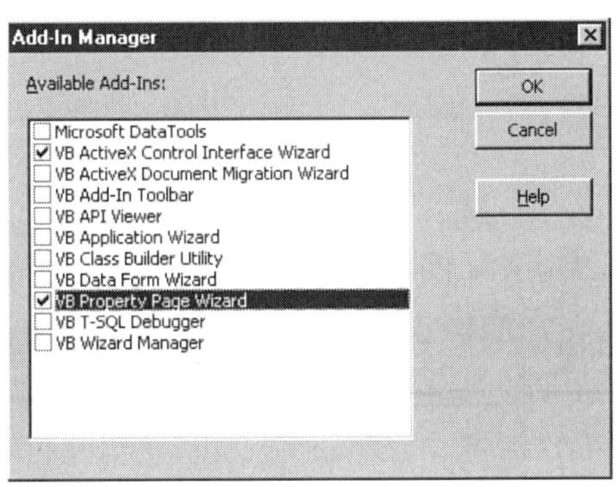

FIGURE 20.18.
Selecting the Property Page Wizard.

Next, select Add-Ins | Property Page Wizard. This brings up a Property Page Wizard for you to select options in a series of successive steps. The opening screen simply serves as an entry point into the wizard. Figure 20.19 shows this screen.

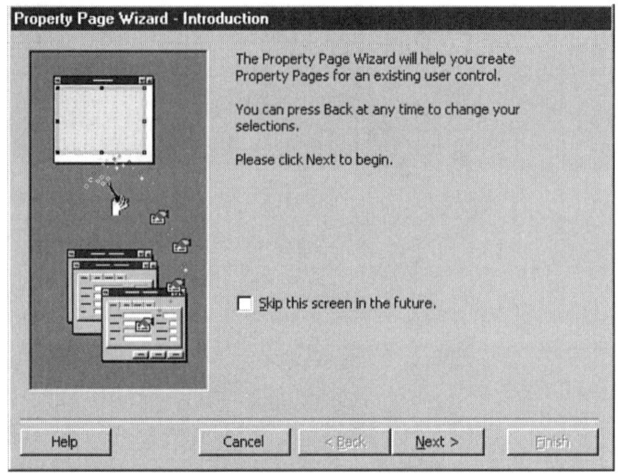

FIGURE 20.19.
The Property Page Wizard opening screen.

Click Next. This now enables you to add the pages you want. For example, consider the example earlier that had these five properties:

- `BorderStyle`
- `DirEnabled`
- `DriveEnabled`
- `Enabled`
- `FileEnabled`

The `BorderStyle` and `Enabled` properties affect the control as a unit, whereas the `DirEnabled`, `DriveEnabled`, and `FileEnabled` properties affect only a specific portion of the control. Therefore, it might make sense to group them like this:

- Components
- Control

Click the Add button in the wizard to add the two categories for the property pages mentioned here. Figure 20.20 shows what this screen should look like after doing this.

The next step is to add the properties to their respective pages. You do this by dragging and dropping or double-clicking the property. Figure 20.21 shows the pages after assigning properties.

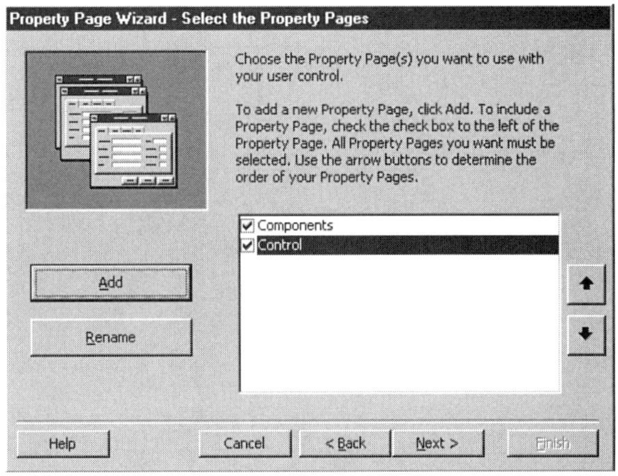

FIGURE 20.20.
The Property Page Wizard after you have defined the pages.

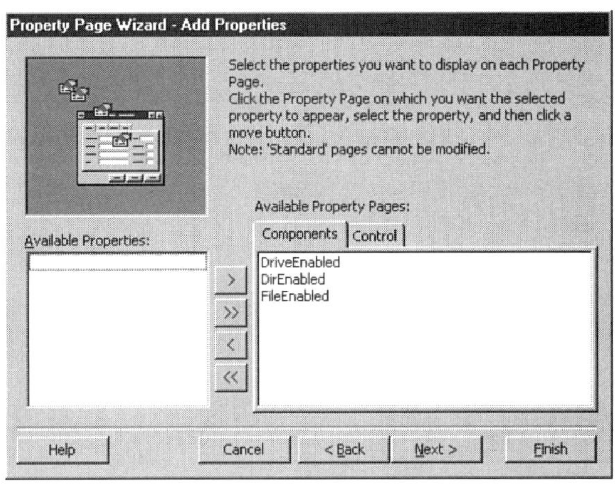

FIGURE 20.21.
The Property Page Wizard after you have assigned properties to the pages.

The next option simply enables you to choose a summary report and complete the process. Figure 20.22 shows this final step.

After you create the property page, you can use it in your controls. It appears as a custom property. Double-click this property and you will see your property page, as shown in Figure 20.23.

Distributing the ActiveX Control

To distribute the ActiveX control, you first need to make the OCX file. You do this by selecting File | Make Project1.OCX. Before you do this, you might want to change the name of your project to something like CustomFile. The ActiveX control will now be registered on your system.

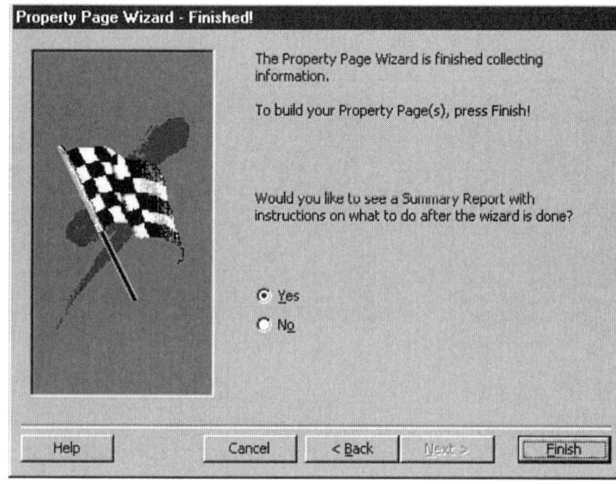

FIGURE 20.22.
The property page final step.

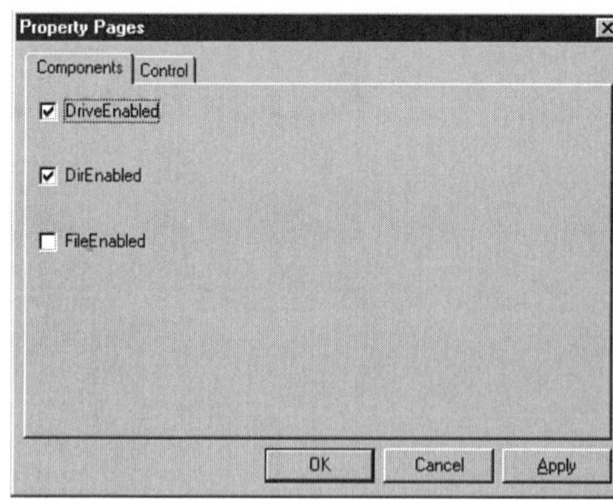

FIGURE 20.23.
The property page in use.

To distribute it to other users, you need to use the Setup Wizard that comes with Visual Basic.

CROSS REFERENCE

For more information about using the Setup Wizard, refer to Chapter 2, "Stock Wizards."

Summary

The ability to create ActiveX controls within Visual Basic 5.0 is a tremendous enhancement. Never before could you create an insertable component within Visual Basic. You always had to create the component in C or C++. ActiveX components can be used in your desktop applications or on the Web.

This chapter showed you how to design and create ActiveX controls. You can build on this knowledge to create ActiveX controls for your own applications.

21

OLE and OLE Automation

Object linking and embedding (OLE) is a powerful process that enables applications to communicate with each other reliably. However, there is a difference between OLE and OLE Automation. They are both based on OLE principles. There are four basic types of OLE:

- Linking
- Embedding
- OLE Automation
- ActiveX controls

The first type of OLE is *linking*, which means that an object in the container document is only linked to the server document. This is very similar to Dynamic Data Exchange (DDE) except that it's much more reliable. DDE is a technology used in the past to communicate between two processes. The server document is the document that contains the object to be linked in the container document. Linking conserves memory because there is no copy of the linked object in the container application. The drawback is that it is not portable. In other words, if you have a Word document with a linked spreadsheet, you cannot copy the document to a disk, load it on another machine, and have the spreadsheet visible. If an object is linked, the container document increases in size only by the amount of overhead necessary to link the document. It does not contain the object itself.

On the other hand, *embedding* actually makes a copy of the object and embeds it into the container document. This is the second type of OLE. It has more overhead, but it provides for faster updates and more portability. This means that if you have a Word document with a linked spreadsheet, you can copy the document to a disk, load it on another machine, and have the spreadsheet visible and active.

The third type of OLE is *OLE Automation*, which makes it possible to access another application's objects programmatically. For example, from Visual Basic you can access Microsoft Excel's `Print` method programmatically. OLE Automation greatly increases the power and productivity of the Visual Basic programming language. OLE Automation opens up the door to a world of possibilities. It enables you to take advantage of reusing code so that you do not have to reinvent the wheel every time you need to perform some function.

An application that makes the objects it contains available to other applications is said to "expose its objects." An application that exposes its objects is referred to as a server application, an OLE Automation server, an OLE Server application, a public object, an exposed object, or most recently, an ActiveX code component. Any OLE Server application must be registered with the Registry. This enables your Visual Basic application to be able to find the server application that is exposing its objects. Each OLE Server must be registered. Remote OLE Servers must be administered by the Remote Automation Connection Manager (discussed in the section, "Remote Automation Connection Manager") or an OLE client will not be able to find the component.

NOTE

Not every server application exposes objects. This means that just because a server application is registered in the Registry, it does not have to expose objects. Also, if it does expose objects, it does not necessarily mean that every object inside the application is exposed.

If you have ever written a DLL, you can apply this analogy. Even though your DLL has many functions and subroutines in it, only the ones you explicitly export are available to the "outside world." This is because as the author of the DLL, you have chosen, for some reason, that only those functions or subroutines will be available to other applications. The OLE Server application works the same way.

The fourth type of OLE is *ActiveX controls*. These controls are based on the OLE architecture and the Component Object Model (COM). ActiveX controls are covered in more detail in Chapter 20, "ActiveX Controls."

OLE Container Control

The OLE Container control is an ActiveX control that comes with all versions of Visual Basic. It is used to place an instance of different types of ActiveX objects on a Visual Basic form. For example, you can place an instance of an actual Excel spreadsheet on your form. Most types of these objects support *in-place activation* (a term that describes the fact that if you double-click on the object itself, an instance of the host application will be invoked that enables you to edit the object). The OLE Container control is shown in Figure 21.1 in the Visual Basic toolbox.

FIGURE 21.1.
The OLE Container control.

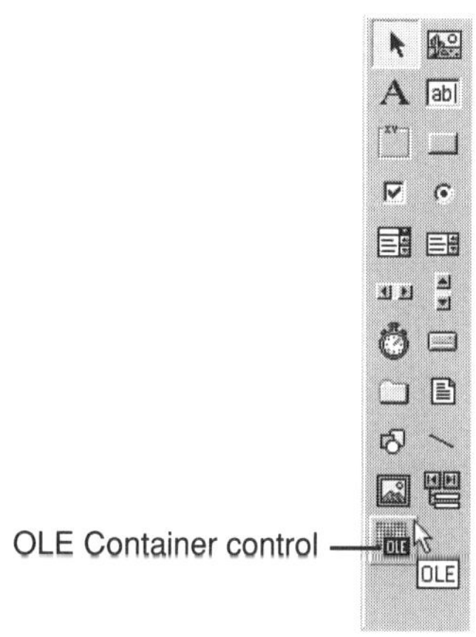

When you place the container on the form, you will be presented with a list of choices of registered OLE types that you can use. Figure 21.2 shows a sample of registered OLE types that can be inserted. After it is assigned, this reference will be set in the `Class` property. Likewise, you do not have to select the class now; you can do so in code. This way you can verify that the class exists on the client's computer before making the reference.

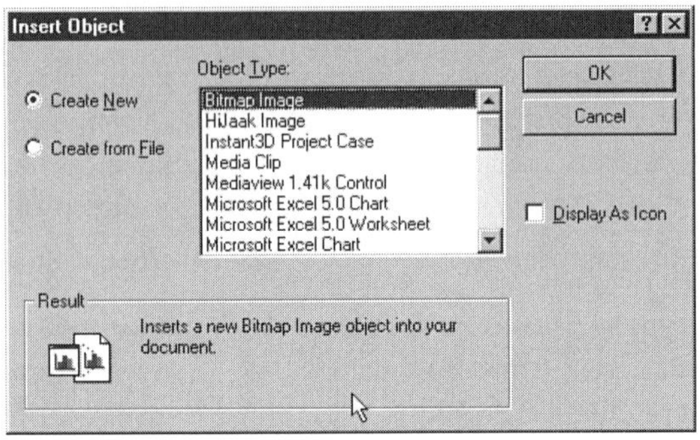

FIGURE 21.2.
The OLE Container control showing registered OLE types.

Along with the class property, there are many other properties that enable you to manipulate the OLE Container control to suit your needs. Table 21.1 shows these properties.

Table 21.1. OLE Container control properties.

Property	*Description*
`Action`	Causes some action to occur as follows: 0—Creates an embedded object. 1—Creates a linked object from the contents of a file. 4—Copies the object to the Clipboard. 5—Copies data from the system Clipboard to an OLE Container control. 6—Retrieves the OLE data from the application that supplied the object and displays that data as a picture. 7—Opens an object. 9—Closes an object. 10—Deletes an object. 11—Saves an object to a data file. 12—Loads an object from a data file. 14—Displays the Insert Object dialog box. 15—Displays the Paste Special dialog box.

Property	Description
	17—Updates the list of verbs an object supports.
	18—Saves an object to the earlier OLE 1.0 format.
`Appearance`	Standard VB property.
`AppIsRunning`	Boolean property to set or return whether the application that created the object is actually running.
`AutoActivate`	Boolean property to set or return whether in-place activation is enabled.
`AutoVerbMenu`	Boolean property to set or return whether an object's verbs (methods) are available with a right mouse click.
`BackColor`	Standard VB property.
`BackStyle`	0—Transparent.
	1—Opaque (default).
`BorderStyle`	Standard VB property.
`Class`	Specifies the type of class with which to create the object.
`Container`	Standard VB property.
`Data`	Sets or returns a Long handle to the object that contains data in specified format.
`DataChanged`	Boolean flag that specifies whether data has been changed for the object.
`DataField`	Standard VB property.
`DataText`	Sets or returns a string for an object.
`DisplayType`	0—Displays the object's contents (default).
	1—Displays object icon.
`DragIcon`	Standard VB property.
`DragMode`	Standard VB property.
`Enabled`	Standard VB property.
`FileNumber`	Visual Basic file number to use when saving or retrieving data from a file.
`ForeColor`	Standard VB property.
`Format`	Sets or returns the format for data when communicating with an object.
`Height`	Standard VB property.
`HelpContextID`	Standard VB property.

continues

Table 21.1. continued

Property	*Description*
`HostName`	Sets or returns a user-readable name for the object's application. This property is not always set by the host application.
`hWnd`	Standard VB property.
`Index`	Standard VB property.
`Left`	Standard VB property.
`lpOleObject`	Returns the address of the OLE object. This is useful in API calls.
`MiscFlags`	Sets or returns miscellaneous flags for OLE objects. Possible values are `vbOLEMiscFlagMemStorage` (stores the object in memory) or `VbOLEMiscFlagDisableInPlace` (overrides in-place activation, if it is supported).
`MouseIcon`	Standard VB property.
`MousePointer`	Standard VB property.
`Name`	Standard VB property.
`Object`	Returns a handle to an object used in an automation task.
`ObjectAcceptFormats`	String array containing the list of formats an object can accept for use in the `Format` property.
`ObjectAcceptFormatsCount`	Returns the number of formats an object can accept. This is helpful for cycling through an enumeration of formats.
`ObjectGetFormats`	String array containing the list of formats an object can produce for use in the `Format` property.
`ObjectGetFormatsCount`	Returns the number of formats an object can produce. This is helpful for cycling through an enumeration of formats.
`ObjectVerbFlags`	An array that returns the state of a given menu item, as follows: `vbOLEFlagChecked`—Menu item is checked. `vbOLEFlagDisabled`—Menu item is disabled and not grayed. `vbOLEFlagEnabled`—Menu item is enabled. `vbOLEFlagGrayed`—Menu item is disabled and grayed. `vbOLEFlagSeparator`—Menu item is a separator bar.
`ObjectVerbs`	Array that returns a specific menu verb for an object.
`ObjectVerbsCount`	Returns the number of verbs an object supports.
`OLEDropAllowed`	Boolean that returns whether the object supports OLE drop operations.

Property	*Description*
`OLEType`	Returns the type of OLE used in the container, as follows: `vbOLELinked`—Linked object. `vbOLEEmbedded`—Embedded object. `vbOLENone`—No object in the container.
`OLETypeAllowed`	Sets or returns the type of OLE an object can use, as follows: `vbOLELinked`—Linked object. `vbOLEEmbedded`—Embedded object. `vbOLEEither`—Either linked or embedded objects.
`Parent`	Standard VB property.
`PasteOK`	Boolean that indicates whether the Clipboard contents can be pasted into the OLE Container.
`Picture`	Standard VB property.
`SizeMode`	Sets or returns how an image is displayed and sized, as follows: `vbOLESizeClip`—The object is displayed in actual size, up to the area of the OLE container borders. `vbOLESizeStretch`—The object is stretched to fill up the area of the OLE Container borders, but doesn't maintain proportions. `vbOLESizeAutoSize`—The OLE Container control is automatically resized to display the entire object. `vbOLESizeZoom`—The object is stretched to fill up the area of the OLE Container borders (as much as possible), but doesn't maintain proportions.
`SourceDoc`	Sets or returns the filename to use for the object. For example, this is a Word document or Excel spreadsheet.
`SourceItem`	Item to be linked (not embedded) within the source document. For example, this could be a single cell in a spreadsheet.
`TabIndex`	Standard VB property.
`TabStop`	Standard VB property.
`Tag`	Standard VB property.
`Top`	Standard VB property.

continues

Table 21.1. continued

Property	*Description*
`UpdateOptions`	Specifies how a linked object is updated as follows: `vbOLEAutomatic`—Updated automatically when changed. `vbOLEFrozen`—Updated only when object in source application is saved. `vbOLEManual`—Manually updated with the `Update` method.
`Verb`	Integer specifying which item in the `ObjectVerbs` collection to issue when setting the `Action` property.
`Visible`	Standard VB property.
`WhatsThisHelpID`	Standard VB property.
`Width`	Standard VB property.

Taking Advantage of OLE Automation in Visual Basic

As stated earlier, OLE Automation is a powerful feature of Visual Basic that enables your application to use objects and methods exposed by other applications. For example, you could use Microsoft Word's spell checker, thesaurus, or grammar checker. You could incorporate the very powerful calculation features of Excel. You could even write your own OLE Server applications (see the section, "Business Object Servers," later in this chapter). OLE Automation gives much more flexibility over the OLE Container control discussed in the previous section.

To determine which objects are exposed for certain applications and registered, you can use the Tools | References menu option. This opens a dialog box for all of the OLE Automation libraries that are registered with the system. These libraries usually have an `*.OLB` or `*.TLB` extension for applications and an `*.OLA` or `*.TLB` extension for OLE controls. You might find a `*.DLL` extension in some cases. Figure 21.3 shows the References dialog box. Keep in mind that your References dialog box might look different, depending on which libraries have been registered with the Registry.

If you check an item in the References dialog box, the exposed objects will then be visible through the Object Browser. You invoke the Object Browser either by pressing the F2 key, or by selecting the View | Object Browser menu option. Suppose you have Microsoft Excel loaded (and registered) on your system; you checked Microsoft Excel 5.0 Object Library in the References dialog box. When you invoke the Object Browser and select this library, it will look like Figure 21.4.

This might lead you to believe that every possible OLE Automation application that exposes its objects is listed in the References dialog box. However, this is not true. As with everything, there are exceptions. Not every application has a type library (`*.OCA`, `*.OCB`, or `*.TLB`) that is used by the References dialog box. The most commonly used application that does not show up in the References dialog box is Microsoft Word 6.0. Eventually, most or all products that expose objects will have a type library to make it easier for you to use its exposed objects. For now, however, it's a little more difficult. There is a way for you to determine which OLE objects are on your system, but there's a drawback to using this method. It lists all OLE object classes, not only the ones that support OLE Automation. For example, this method will list `AVIFile` as a class. This is a valid class name, but it does not support OLE Automation.

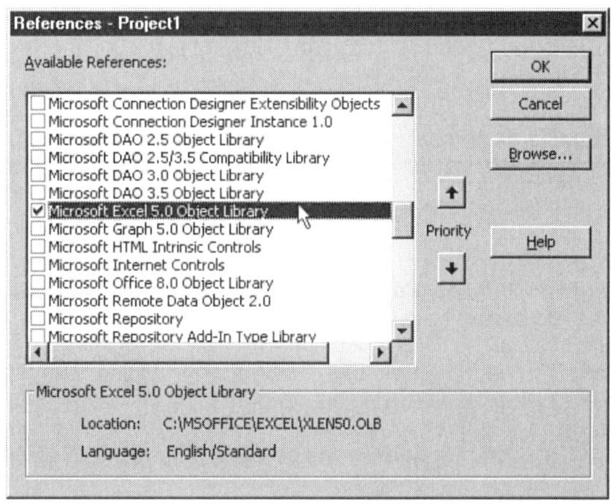

FIGURE 21.3.
The References dialog box.

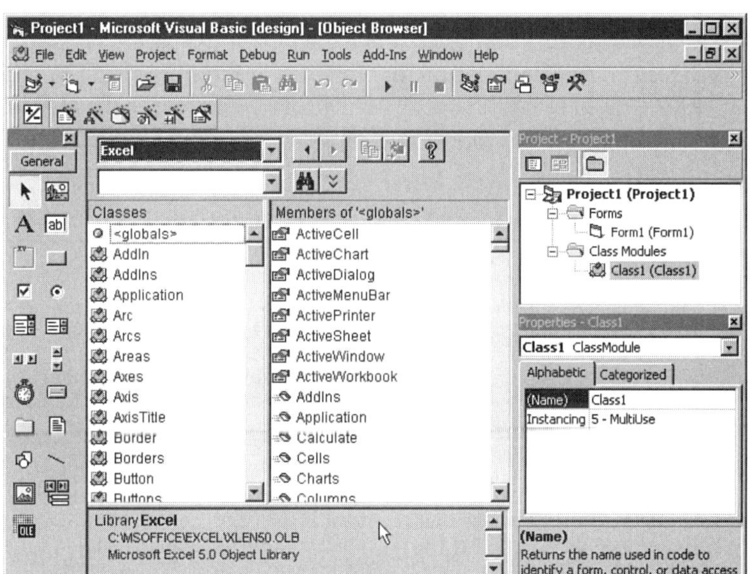

FIGURE 21.4.
The Excel library loaded into the Object Browser.

To determine all OLE classes on your system, you need to use 32-bit API functions. You must declare three API functions and one constant. The three API functions allow the opening and querying of Registry key values. The constant identifies the Registry hive you will be accessing. In this case, it is the `HKEY_CLASSES_ROOT` hive.

CROSS REFERENCE

For more information about the Registry, refer to Chapter 6, "The Registry." For more information about using the WIN32 API, refer to Chapter 13, "Using the WIN32 API."

First, place the code declarations from Listing 21.1 in a `*.BAS` module.

Listing 21.1. Constants and declarations needed for class listing.

```
'registry constant
Global Const HKEY_CLASSES_ROOT = &H80000000

' Registry API prototypes
Declare Function RegEnumKey Lib "advapi32" Alias "RegEnumKeyA" (ByVal hKey As
➥Long, ByVal dwIndex As Long, ByVal lpName As String,
➥ByVal cbName As Long) As Long
Declare Function RegOpenKey Lib "advapi32" Alias "RegOpenKeyA" (ByVal hKey As
➥Long, ByVal lpSubKey As String, phkResult As Long) As Long
Declare Function RegQueryValue Lib "advapi32" Alias "RegQueryValueA" (ByVal
➥hKey As Long, ByVal lpSubKey As String, ByVal lpValue As String,
➥lpcbValue As Long) As Long
```

Next, write a routine that places the names of all the classes on your system into a list box. First, create a form and insert a list box on it. Next, from the `Form_Load()` event, reference a procedure, called `CreateClasses()`. The final step is to write the `CreateClasses()` subroutine. The code listing for it is shown in Listing 21.2.

Listing 21.2. A subroutine to obtain a list of available classes.

```
Public Sub CreateClasses()

    'declare variables
    Dim lResults As Long           'result status after opening key
    Dim sSubKey As String          'sub key containing class ID
    Dim sSubKey1 As String         'sub key containing key under class ID
    Dim lResult As Long            'result status after getting class ID's
    Dim lResult1 As Long           'result status after getting sub keys
    Dim nPos As Integer            'position of null terminator
    Dim lSubKey As Long            'loops through Class ID Indexes
    Dim lSubKey1 As Long           'loops through sub key indexes
    Dim sKeyResult As String       'result string containing class ID
    Dim sKeyResult1 As String      'result string containing sub key
    Dim lHandle As Long            'handle of class ID key
    Dim lHandle1 As Long           'handle of sub key ID
```

```
    Dim sValue As String        'result string containing class name

    'open CLASS ID(CLSID) key
    lResults = RegOpenKey(HKEY_CLASSES_ROOT, "CLSID", lHandle)

    lSubKey = 0
    'loop through all class ID's
    Do Until lResult <> 0
        sSubKey = Space$(1028)
        lResult = RegEnumKey(lHandle, lSubKey, sSubKey, 1028)
        nPos = InStr(sSubKey, Chr$(0))
        If nPos > 0 Then
            sKeyResult = Left$(sSubKey, nPos - 1)

            'get handle for this item
            lResults = RegOpenKey(lHandle, sKeyResult, lHandle1)

            lSubKey1 = 0
            lResult1 = 0

            'loop through all subsequent sub-keys
            Do Until lResult1 <> 0
                sSubKey1 = Space$(1028)
                lResult1 = RegEnumKey(lHandle1, lSubKey1, sSubKey1, 1028)
                nPos = InStr(sSubKey1, Chr$(0))
                If nPos > 0 Then
                    sKeyResult1 = Left$(sSubKey1, nPos - 1)

                    'if the key is "PROGID" then this is the value we need
                    If UCase$(sKeyResult1) = "PROGID" Then
                        'get value
                        sValue = Space$(1028)
                        lResults = RegQueryValue(lHandle1, sKeyResult1,
                        ➥sValue, 1028)
                        nPos = InStr(sValue, Chr$(0))
                        If nPos > 0 Then
                            lstObject.AddItem Left$(sValue, nPos - 1)
                        End If
                    End If
                End If
                lSubKey1 = lSubKey1 + 1
            Loop
        End If
        lSubKey = lSubKey + 1
    Loop

End Sub
```

Basically, how the code works is that every Registry subkey is opened under the `CLSID` key. `CLSID` is short for *class identification.* If it, in turn, has a subkey called `PROGID`, then the value of this subkey is used.

To implement OLE Automation in your programs, you must declare an object variable. This is the interface means by which Visual Basic communicates with OLE Automation objects. After you have created the object variable, reference that object variable. It, in turn, points to the specific OLE Automation object.

To create an object variable in Visual Basic, you need to use the `CreateObject()` function and assign it to a variable declared as being of type `Object`. For example, the following declares an object variable named `objExcel` as being of type `Object`:

```
Dim objExcel as Object
```

You then need to create the type of object you want to use with OLE Automation and assign it to your object variable. Suppose you wanted to create a Microsoft Excel object. You would do so with this line of code:

```
objExcel = CreateObject("Excel.Application.5")
```

The way you would know the class name for the creation of the Excel object is from the previous discussion. You would use the code in Listing 21.2 to determine the class name of the object to open, or you could consult the documentation for the OLE Server application. Microsoft Press has some excellent books for developers, such as the *Excel Developer's Kit* and the *Word Developer's Kit.* These books list the objects exposed by the respective applications. Also, an excellent reference is the Developer's Network Library, also available from Microsoft.

Suppose you wanted to use Microsoft Word to check the spelling of the text in a text box. The next few sections show you how to use OLE Automation to perform functions in Microsoft Word. However, a more detailed discussion is in Chapter 14, "Integrating with Office 97." This eliminates the need to buy a third-party library to check spelling. Again, you need to declare an object variable and assign it to the Microsoft Word object called `Word.Basic`. You would open the object like this:

```
Set objWord = CreateObject("Word.Basic")
```

The `CreateObject` function creates a new object, regardless of whether an object exists already or not. To create a Word object if Microsoft Word is running, use the `GetObject` function. You open the object like this:

```
Set objWord = GetObject("Word.Basic")
```

You might wonder how to ensure in your code that only one object is created. Typically, you issue a `GetObject` function. If it fails, you issue a `CreateObject` function. You would do that like this:

```
Dim objWord As Object

On Error Resume Next
Set objWord = GetObject(, "Word.Basic")
If objWord Is Nothing Then
    Set objWord = CreateObject("Word.Basic")
    If objWord Is Nothing Then
        MsgBox "Object did not get created!"
    End If
End If
```

Now that the object is created, you can actually call any methods, properties, functions, and subroutines that have been exposed. Suppose you had text in a text box for which you want to check the spelling. Because the objective is only to "borrow" the functionality of the spell checker, in code you have to actually insert all of the text in the text box into Word, spell check the text, close Word, and return focus to the text box. If you had a text box, named `txtText1`, you could invoke the spell checker as shown in Listing 21.3.

Listing 21.3. Invoking Microsoft Word's spell checker.

```
'handle errors
On Error GoTo OLEError

'assign objWord to word.basic class
Set objWord = CreateObject("Word.Basic")

'initialize flag
Selected% = False

'start new file
objWord.FileNew

'clear selection
objWord.editclear

If txtText1.SelText <> "" Then
    'flag selected
    Selected% = True

    'insert only selected text
    objWord.INSERT txtText1.SelText
Else
    'insert all text from VB Text box
    objWord.INSERT txtText1.TEXT
End If

'position to beginning
objWord.startofdocument

'position to end, selecting all in between
objWord.endofdocument (1)

'invoke spell checker
objWord.Toolsspelling

'position to beginning
objWord.startofdocument

'position to end, selecting all in between
objWord.endofdocument (1)

'cut selection to clipboard
objWord.editcut

If Selected% = False Then
    'nothing was selected, replace whole text
    txtText1.TEXT = Clipboard.GetText(1)
Else
    'text was selected, replace only selected text
    LeftText$ = Left$(txtText1.TEXT, txtText1.SelStart)
```

continues

Listing 21.3. continued

```
    RightText$ = Right$(txtText1.TEXT, Len(txtText1.text) -
    ➥ (txtText1.SelStart + txtText1.SelLength))
    txtText1.TEXT = LeftText$ + Clipboard.GetText(1) + RightText$
End If

'close the file
objWord.FileClose (2)

'Make sure text box has focus
txtText1.SetFocus

'exit
Exit Sub

OLEError:

'Make sure text box has focus
txtText1.SetFocus

'show error
MsgBox Error$

'resume
Resume Next
```

Here is the theory behind what the code is doing: First, a Word object is created and activated. Using `Word.Basic` will create a Word object, regardless of the version of Word installed on your system. It will create either a version 6.0, 7.0, or 8.0 object. Then, one of two things happens. If there is no text selected in the Visual Basic text box, all of the text from the text box is inserted into the object document. Otherwise, if there is text selected in the Visual Basic text box, only the selected text is inserted into the object document. This ensures that only the desired text is spell checked. The standard Microsoft Word dialog box appears if there is an incorrectly spelled word, using the `ToolsSpelling` Word function. Other related functions are shown in Table 21.2. Then, all of the text in the text box is selected and copied to the Clipboard. From the Clipboard, the text is placed back into the Visual Basic text box. That's all there is to it.

Table 21.2. Microsoft Word functions used in spell checking.

Keyword	*Description*
`StartOfDocument`	Positions the insertion point at the beginning of the document
`EndOfDocument`	Positions the insertion point at the end of the document (but selects everything in between)
`EditClear`	Deletes the selected text
`Insert`	Inserts text at the insertion point
`ToolsSpelling`	Invokes the spell checker
`EditCut`	Removes the selected text and places it in the Clipboard

OLE Automation really is very simple, considering all of the functionality you get from it. You can incorporate this into your applications, but the basic code and functions accessed do not change.

Business Object Servers

Business object servers is a term which specifies that you have written an OLE Automation Server application that encapsulates certain business rules or functions. In a three-tiered client/server application, this is sometimes referred to as the *middle tier*.

CROSS REFERENCE

For more information about three-tiered client/server applications, refer to Chapter 32, "Visual Basic's Role in Client/Server Computing."

Another reason for creating a business object server is if you want to sell most of your source code, but not release proprietary algorithms and procedures. Creating an OLE Server application enables you to "break out" part of your code into another logical piece. These servers can be installed on a local machine or a remote server. Your Visual Basic applications can call the methods and procedures exposed by these business object servers. Examples of using business object servers can be as simple as creating a server application that performs tasks that you use in your everyday Visual Basic code, such as centering a form. It can be as complex as a Visual Basic application issuing instructions to the business object server to notify you when a network connection or database connection is lost.

Visual Basic enables you to create these OLE Automation servers inside Visual Basic itself. This means that you can write your own applications with Visual Basic that expose methods and properties to the outside world. Please note that you must have either the Professional or Enterprise edition to create OLE Automation servers.

There are two types of OLE Automation servers: in-process and out-of-process. The in-process server is a DLL file created in Visual Basic that runs in the same process space as the programs that use them. An out-of-process server is a stand-alone executable file created in Visual Basic that runs in its own address space. It actually invokes another process. Generally, an in-process server will run faster than an out-of-process server because less overhead is required and process boundaries do not have to be crossed.

Creating OLE Automation servers involves inserting at least one class module. This class module defines a class name that can be viewed in the system Registry or by using the code in Listing 21.2.

CROSS REFERENCE

For more information about class modules, refer to Chapter 3, "Classes."

When inserting a class module, Visual Basic automatically creates two events: `Initialize()` and `Terminate()`. You do not have to place code in these events to create an OLE Server. Note that before version 5.0, you could not create your own custom events with an OLE Server application.

To create an OLE Server application, first insert a class module by selecting the Insert | Class Module menu option. This inserts a class module. Change the name property to the name you want to call the class. Next, you must change the `Instancing` property.

CROSS REFERENCE

For more information about the `Instancing` property, refer to Table 3.2 in Chapter 3. This table shows all of the possible combinations for the `Instancing` property for all the different project types.

Chapter 3 also describes how to define custom properties, methods, and events for the OLE Server applications.

There are few design considerations when you are creating an ActiveX code component (OLE Server) for use on the local desktop versus distributing the object on a remote server. This is because Microsoft designed distributed COM this way. The only difference is how you deploy the objects. There are several major advantages to creating distributed ActiveX components, however.

The first is that you can have the component access your remote database. This makes it possible to have only one entry point and only one place to access your database. This increases security. It also makes your code easier to maintain. The other reason is that the majority of the resource-intensive tasks can be completed on the server, not on the client's machine.

Version Issues

There is the potential for compatibility problems when you create an OLE Server application, distribute it to customers, and then change the code and redistribute it.

It is for this reason that Visual Basic enables you to enter the name of the executable file when you select the Component tab under the Project | Properties menu option. Figure 21.5 shows what this tab looks like.

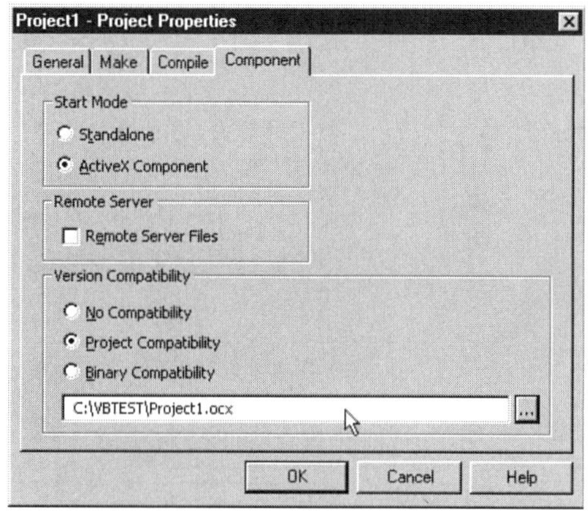

FIGURE 21.5.
The Component tab.

The text box entry field enables you to enter the name of a file with which compatibility will be tested. If you enter a filename here, Visual Basic will warn you of potential conflicts when you compile the project.

Testing the OLE Server

You do not need to compile the OLE Server into an executable or DLL to be able to test it. You do need to do a couple of things first, however.

In the dialog box shown in Figure 21.5, you must enter the application description. This is the description that will appear when you register the OLE Server application. You must also select the ActiveX Component option button.

TRIED AND TRUE

Try not to enter a long name. If you do, you will not be able to see the entire name when you enable the OLE Server.

After selecting these options, you must run the application with a full compile. You do this by selecting Ctrl+F5 or by selecting the Run | Start With Full Compile menu option.

When the application is running, you must start another instance of Visual Basic and create code to use the object. Before you run the application, you must select the appropriate reference to the OLE Server you just created with the first instance of Visual Basic. You do this by selecting the Project | References menu option. This option presents a dialog box of all the objects available on your system, including the OLE Server application that is running. Figure 21.6 shows this dialog box, with the new OLE Server application class, listed as `Project1`.

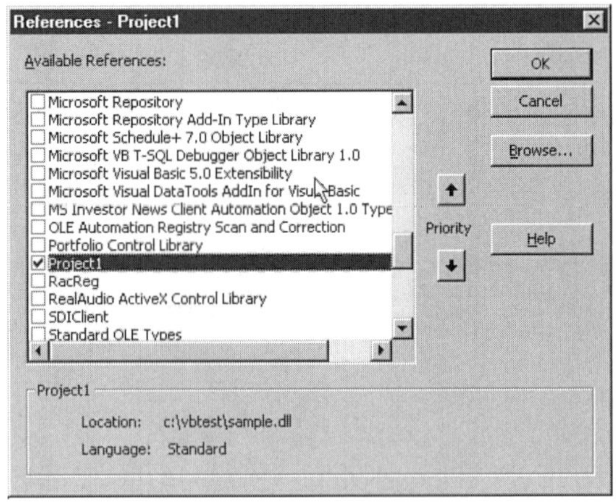

FIGURE 21.6.
The References dialog box with the OLE Server application class.

You must check the reference of the name of your OLE Server application. If you do not check the reference, the application will not know how to create the object class. At this point, you can run the application to see whether it works. You can set breakpoints and debug the first instance of Visual Basic as you would any other application.

When you know the OLE Server application works the way you expect, you can compile the application. This will actually register the OLE Server on your system at the same time. The registration of an OLE Server application is performed automatically when you distribute your OLE Server by using the SETUP toolkit. If, for some reason, you need to manually register the OLE Server DLL, you can use the `REGSVR32.EXE` program for 32-bit applications. Both programs are included in the `\CLISVR` subdirectory of wherever you installed Visual Basic.

Remote OLE Automation

An OLE client application cannot actually create an object that was created as an in-process OLE Server application if the OLE Server application is on a remote computer. For example, if the OLE Server application is on a file server in another building, an OLE client application you are writing at your workstation cannot create the OLE Automation object. There is a way around this, however. The Enterprise edition only of Visual Basic enables you to administer and register remote OLE Servers.

This is possible because the Remote Automation Manager utility is an out-of-process OLE Server application, which then can run an in-process OLE Server application (your OLE Automation Server application) because it is then on the same machine. It is just as if the instructions executed from the client computer are relayed to the Remote Automation Manager. It then administers calls to your OLE Automation server.

Remote Automation works on a principle called *distributed COM.* Distributed COM is an extension of the Component Object Model (COM) that enables modules (ActiveX components) that are capable of making remote procedure calls to access objects that reside remotely. "Remote" objects do not necessarily exist on the local machine, but rather on a server.

It would be incomplete for you to build a component solution (that is, an OLE Automation server) without the ability to deploy those servers on remote computers. Therefore, Microsoft has provided three tools in the Enterprise edition to deploy Remote Automation Servers:

- Client Registration utility
- Remote Automation Connection Manager (Enterprise edition only)
- Pool Manager

Each of the tools are discussed in the following sections. However, this discussion is not intended to replace either the online or printed documentation covering each of these tools. It is intended as a brief overview only.

Client Registration Utility

The Client Registration utility is provided to enable an OLE Automation server application for remote execution. It is run on the client machine and comes in two versions: one for 16-bit applications and one for 32-bit applications. Each is basically used as a command-line utility for other programs, such as setup programs.

The Remote Automation Connection Manager is a good alternative solution to managing the registration in a Windows environment. However, if you wanted to use the command-line utility, it is called `CLIREG32.EXE`.

First, you must specify a `*.VBR` file (the Visual Basic Registration file). It is created when you create the OLE Server application's `*.EXE` or `*.DLL` file. This file is automatically created only if you select the Remote Server Support Files check box under the Options command button. There are many command-line options available to this utility. Figure 21.7 shows a dialog box of these options.

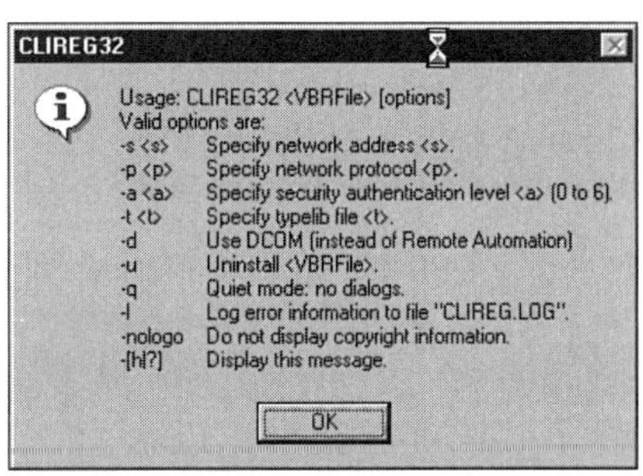

FIGURE 21.7.
Command-line options available to Client Registration Utility.

Remote Automation Connection Manager

The Remote Automation Connection Manager (RACM) is an alternative means of registering OLE Automation servers. It is available only in the Enterprise edition. It provides a nice visual interface so that you do not have to remember path names of your OLE Servers, as you do using the Client Registration utility.

To run the RACM utility, simply double-click the Program Manager group item installed by Visual Basic, or run the `RACMGR32.EXE` file. This file is located in the `\CLISVR` subdirectory of wherever you installed Visual Basic, Enterprise edition. Figure 21.8 show what the RACM looks like after you run it.

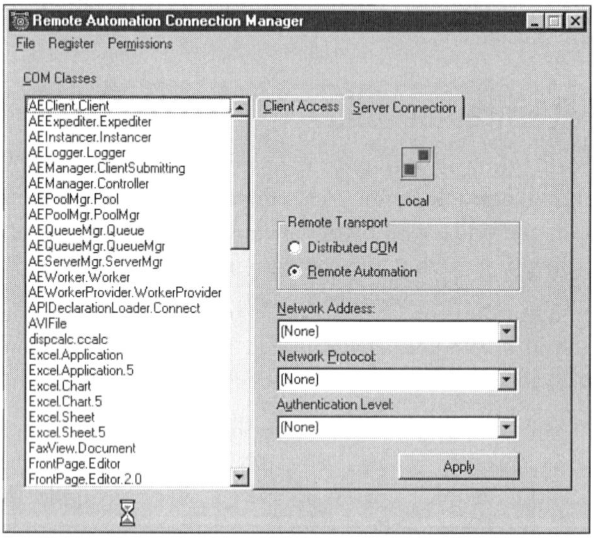

FIGURE 21.8.
The Remote Automation Connection Manager (RACM).

RACM displays a list of all the classes registered in the Registry on your machine. This is very similar to the results of the routine listed in Listing 21.2. The nice thing about this utility is that you can change access information for more than one class at a time. There are two tabs: Client Access and Server Connection. These two tabs enable you to configure how the OLE Automation Server will be accessed from both the client and the server (as demonstrated later).

The Server Connection tab enables you to test and debug any remote automation server on a local machine. You also can configure the component(s) for remote use. Surprisingly, the component can even be running. To configure the Server Connection tab, you must specify these five things:

- Type of Connection—The type of connection can either be "local" or "remote." Figure 21.8 shows a local connection. This can be toggled by either selecting the appropriate option when you click the right mouse button or selecting the Register | Remote menu option or the Register | Local menu option.

- Network Address—Enter the name of your network machine where the OLE Server application is installed.
- Network Protocol—Enter the type of network protocol you are using to connect to the OLE Server application.
- Authentication Level—Specifies the level of data integrity to be guaranteed between server and client. This value cannot be set to `(none)`.
- Remote Transport—The type of transport can be either Distributed COM or Remote Automation.

The Client Access tab enables you to control the security features of the OLE Automation server. There are four options that apply to all classes, not only the ones selected. These are system-wide security features. Here are the possible options:

- Disallow All Remote Creates—Makes it impossible for any remote access clients to create and use objects.
- Allow Remote Creates by Key—Enables you to select which classes a remote access client can create. In this case, you need to check the Remote Activation check box for each class that can be created.
- Allow Remote Creates by ACL—Enables you to select which users or groups a remote access client can create. In this case, you need to select the individuals or groups that can create instances of a class. This can be configured separately by class.
- Allow All Remote Creates—Enables any object to be created by a remote access client.
- Allow Remote Activation—This check box simply enables an OLE Server to be remotely activated, if checked. By default, it is not checked.

Pool Manager

The Pool Manager is not installed in the Program Manager group upon Visual Basic installation. Instead, it is actually a sample application. Therefore, you must have chosen to install sample applications to use it. This application is probably one of the most useful samples. It allows for the capability to automatically load OLE Server applications. Because the application itself must load the OLE Server (if it is not already loaded), it is an advantage to have the Pool Manager load the OLE Server. This makes response time faster for client applications.

It's important to realize that if a client makes a call to a Remote Automation server, the server must be loaded (or created) if it is not already running. Therefore, depending on the size of the OLE Server, it can take a relatively long period of time just to load. This can be only a few extra seconds, but that could make a big difference. The Pool Manager makes sure that it maintains a pool of objects that have already been created, thereby speeding up response time from the clients.

You can run the Pool Manager simply by opening the PMGR-SVR project in the `\SAMPLES\ENTPRIS\POOLMGR` subdirectory under your Visual Basic directory. The Pool Manager sample can be customized to fit your needs. Figure 21.9 shows what this Pool Manager sample looks like.

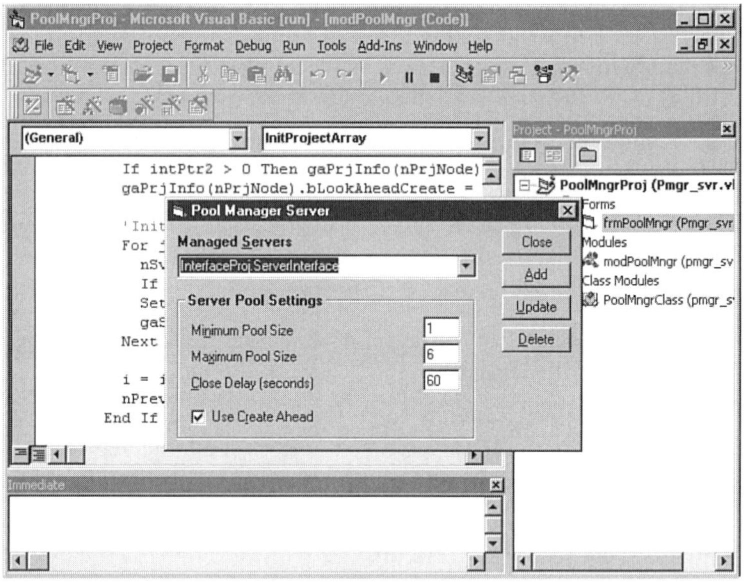

FIGURE 21.9.
The Pool Manager.

Please note that there is no Help file available for this utility; however, there is some information available from the "Visual Basic Books Online" menu option.

Summary

Creating an OLE Server has never been easier. OLE Servers play a big part in distributed computing. This chapter showed not only how to create these OLE Servers, but how to implement and distribute them using the administrative tools. Building upon this knowledge, you can create your own OLE Servers to perform unlimited functionality.

22

Collections

Collections play an important role in Visual Basic. They have existed in Visual Basic since version 1.0. A *collection* is a way of grouping similar objects (classes). The advantage of this is that you can loop through a collection in code to test for a specific property value or perform some action to all or some of the items in the collection. Without collections, which are allocated dynamically, you would need to know in advance how many items in a particular group of like objects exist. This is similar to the way arrays are treated. It is important to note that some collections are zero-based, and others are one-based. Microsoft is heading toward using the one-based collections for new features, and zero-based collections for backward compatibility. A zero-based collection or array starts with the index zero (0) and continues up to the count of the number of items in the collection or array, minus one (1). A one-based collection or array starts with the index one (1) and continues up to the count of the number of items in the collection or array.

For example, the `Fields` collection of a DAO object is zero-based, whereas any collection you create using the `Collection` class is one-based.

Using Collections

A collection enables you to access its members by using properties and methods. As stated earlier, collections have existed in Visual Basic from the beginning. You could not, however, create your own collections, but now you can. This topic is discussed in the section titled "Creating Collections," later in this chapter.

The following is a list of some of the collections in Visual Basic:

- Forms
- Controls
- RDO Objects
- DAO Objects
- Errors

To access and manipulate a collection, you must use the properties and methods associated with the collection. These are shown in Table 22.1.

Table 22.1. Collection-related properties and methods.

Keyword	*Type*	*Description*
`Add`	Method	Adds an item to a collection
`Append`	Method	Appends an item to a collection
`Count`	Property	Returns the number of items in a collection
`Item`	Property	Identifies a specific item in a collection

Keyword	*Type*	*Description*
`Parent`	Property	Returns an object representing the parent object of the collection
`Refresh`	Method	Refreshes the data in a collection
`Remove`	Method	Removes an item from a collection

As an example, suppose you issued a statement to a database, and you retrieve records into a `Recordset` object. The `Recordset` object is responsible for creating the child objects and collections, such as the `Fields` collection. Consider this code fragment, which clearly shows how you can build a `Recordset` object and cycle through every item in the collection (in this case, the `Fields` collection). This code looks for any null value in any of the fields. If it finds one, it displays a message and exits.

```
'declare variables
Dim dbTemp As Database
Dim rsTemp As Recordset
Dim sCmd As String
Dim nLoopCount As Integer

'open database
Set dbTemp = Workspaces(0).OpenDatabase("BIBLIO.MDB")

'build SQL String
sCmd = "SELECT * FROM Authors"

'open recordset
Set rsTemp = dbTemp.OpenRecordset(sCmd, dbOpenSnapshot)

'test for EOF
If Not rsTemp.EOF Then
    'all is OK
    For nLoopCount = 0 To rsTemp.Fields.Count - 1
        'test for null values
        If IsNull(rsTemp.Fields(nLoopCount)) Then
            'display message and exit
            MsgBox "There are Null Values"
            Exit For
        End If
    Next nLoopCount
End If
```

The nice thing about a collection is that you do not need to know how many items exist. In the previous code, you simply loop from `0` to the `Count - 1`. The reason you need to subtract one is that if there are 10 items, the indexes will be from 0 to 9.

You can loop through other collections in much the same way. For example, you can loop through the `Forms` collection, which is maintained by Visual Basic itself. Suppose you had three forms named `frmA`, `frmB`, and `frmC`. You can test to see whether a specific form, `frmB`, is visible with the following code:

```
'loop through forms collection
For nLoopCount = 0 To Forms.Count - 1
    'test for specific form
    If Forms(nLoopCount) Is frmB Then
        'test the visible property
        If frmB.Visible = True Then
            MsgBox "The form is visible!"
        End If
    End If
Next nLoopCount
```

Creating Collections

Now that you've reviewed how to access collections, it's time to create one. You create a collection by using the `Collection` object. The `Collection` object is a built-in Visual Basic class that is used to simply house "collections" of data. The data can be anything—it can even be a collection of collections.

There are pros and cons to using either collections or arrays. A collection is always stored in a `Variant` data type. Because the `Variant` data type carries with it a lot of overhead, you might want to consider using arrays instead. Arrays are much more efficient, but they can be more cumbersome to use. They are also very limited in their usage. This is the main advantage of using a collection. Its usage is virtually limitless.

To create the most simple collections, you declare a collection variable, like this:

```
Dim colForms As New Collection
```

Notice the `New` keyword. It is used to instantiate a new `Collection` class. Now you can use the methods and properties of the `Collection` class that are shown in Table 22.1. For example, you can add to a collection using the `Add` method, like this:

```
colForms.Add frmEmployee
```

The `Add` method can accept up to four arguments. Here's the syntax for the `Add` method:

```
object.Add item[, key][, before][, after]
```

where:

> *`object`* is the collection that will have the item added to it.
>
> *`item`* is the item to add to the collection.
>
> *`key`* is a key that will be referenced by a string (that is, if you plan to reference by strings instead of indexes).
>
> *`before`* is a relative position before which the item is inserted in the collection. This cannot be used if the *`after`* argument is specified.
>
> *`after`* is a relative position after which the item is inserted in the collection. This cannot be used if the *`before`* argument is specified.

As you would expect, you can remove an item from a collection by using the `Remove` method. Here's an example:

```
colForms.Remove 2
```

This will remove the second item from a collection. Also, if you know the name of the item you need to remove, you can do so like this:

```
colForms.Remove "frmEmployee"
```

To reference a specific item in a collection, you would use the `Item` property. If you are familiar with DAO, this really works just like accessing the `Fields` property of a DAO object. You reference an item like this:

```
Set frmCurrent = colForms.Item(1)
```

If the item you are referencing is a string, you can also pass the string to the `Item` property, like this:

```
sCurrent = colForms.Item("CurrentForm")
```

Enumerating Through a Collection

A collection, again, is a means to store miscellaneous data items. These are items that can be stored in a Variant data type. As these items are added to or removed from a collection, the unique index assigned to each item in the collection changes. This is a great feature of collections that does not happen in arrays. Suppose you have an array dimensioned like this:

```
Dim TempArray(10) As Integer
```

This indicates that the highest index available in the array is 10. This actually gives you 11 elements, 0 through 10. You can fill all 11 elements with this code:

```
Dim TempArray(10) As Integer
Dim nLoopcount As Integer

For nLoopcount = 0 To 10
    TempArray(nLoopcount) = nLoopcount
Next nLoopcount
```

You can test the number of elements in the array with the `UBound` function, like this:

```
x = UBound(TempArray)
```

This returns the highest element in the array. If you wanted to remove the fifth element of the array, you must redimension it with the `ReDim` statement. However, you'll need to write code to reorder the data so that the sixth data item becomes the new fifth item, and so on. This is *way* too much work. After all this work is done, you can then enumerate through a collection without needing to skip item number 5. Instead, use a collection, where you can dynamically add and remove items at will. This forces the indexes to be sequential, allowing you to enumerate through the collection.

Enumerating is a process in which you cycle through each element in a collection (or an array). You can enumerate through a collection in one of two ways. The first is through the use of a looping variable. Here's an example:

```
Dim nLoopCount As Integer

For nLoopCount = 1 To colProcs.Count
    'display count
    MsgBox colProcs.Item(nLoopCount)
Next nLoopCount
```

The major problem with looping through a collection using a `For...Next` loop is that you must know whether the collection or array is zero- or one-based. This example will work because the collection is one-based. However, if it were an array, it would not work because an array is zero-based and the first item (element zero) would be skipped. Also, you would get a `Subscript out of range` error when it reached the last item because this item would not exist in a zero-based array. However, there is a better way: using the `For Each...Next` statements. Here's an example:

```
'declare variable
Dim nLoopCount As Variant

For Each nLoopCount In colProcs
    'display count
    MsgBox colProcs.Item(nLoopCount)
Next nLoopCount
```

Your control variable in a `For Each...Next` loop must be either an object or a Variant. Even though this code is using the loop as an integer, it cannot be declared as such. It must be declared as a Variant.

Creating a Call Stack

Visual Basic has a call stack that keeps internally a list of calls to subroutines and functions. As you enter a new procedure, it gets added to a stack. As you leave a procedure, it is removed from a stack. This is a very useful feature, but it works only in design mode. Suppose you needed to find out at runtime how many procedures are in the stack. You can use collections to track this. Listing 22.1 contains sample code that shows you how.

Listing 22.1. Building and testing a call stack.

```
Dim colProcs As New Collection
Private Sub Form_Load()
    'assign sub name
    Const SUBNAME = "Form_Load"

    'add subroutine
    colProcs.Add SUBNAME, SUBNAME
    'call other sub
    Call Sub1
```

```
    'display count
    MsgBox Str$(colProcs.Count)

    'remove sub name
    colProcs.Remove SUBNAME
End Sub
Private Sub Sub1()
    'assign sub name
    Const SUBNAME = "Sub1"

    'add subroutine
    colProcs.Add SUBNAME, SUBNAME
    'call other sub
    Call Sub2

    'display count
    MsgBox Str$(colProcs.Count)
    'remove sub name
    colProcs.Remove SUBNAME
End Sub
Private Sub Sub2()
    'assign sub name
    Const SUBNAME = "Sub2"

    'add subroutine
    colProcs.Add SUBNAME, SUBNAME
    'call other sub
    Call Sub3

    'display count
    MsgBox Str$(colProcs.Count)

    'remove sub name
    colProcs.Remove SUBNAME
End Sub
Private Sub Sub3()
    'assign sub name
    Const SUBNAME = "Sub3"

    'add subroutine
    colProcs.Add SUBNAME, SUBNAME

    'display count
    MsgBox Str$(colProcs.Count)

    'remove sub name
    colProcs.Remove SUBNAME
End Sub
```

In this code, three subroutines are called successively from the `Form_Load` event. As you enter a procedure, the procedure name is added to a collection. Notice that it is added with the following line:

```
colProcs.Add SUBNAME, SUBNAME
```

The reason for this is that the first `SUBNAME` is the string expression signifying the procedure to add to the collection. The second `SUBNAME` is used as a unique key so that you can then remove the procedure name by using a string reference (instead of having to remove it by numeric index). This is a very simple example, but if you wanted to implement this project-wide, you could come up with a scheme to define the `SUBNAME`. It might be a combination of module, form, or class name, appended with the procedure name.

Using the Collection Builder Utility

The Collection Builder is a utility contained in the Class Builder utility. Collection Builder is an add-in that helps you to build collections. For it to be invoked, you must make sure that the add-in is selected in the Add-In Manager. Do this by selecting Add-Ins | Add-In Manager. Figure 22.1 shows the Add-In Manager. Select the VB Class Builder Utility check box.

FIGURE 22.1.
The Add-In Manager with the VB Class Builder Utility selected.

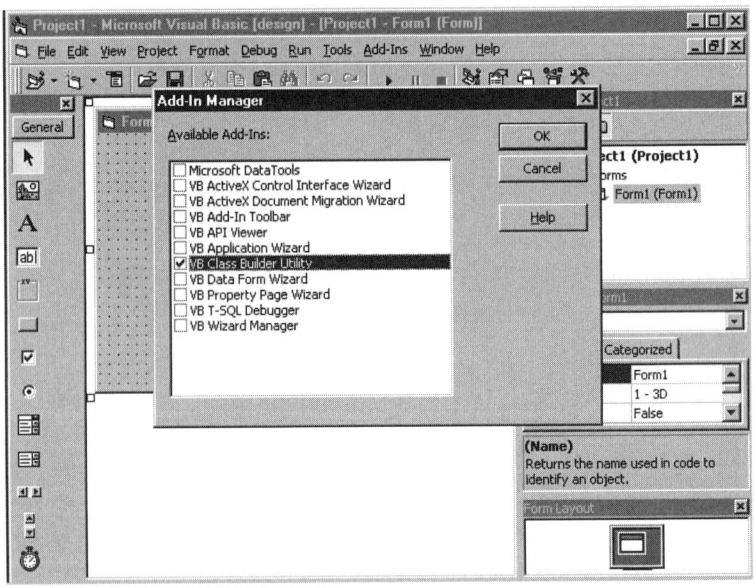

After you select the add-in, invoke it by selecting Add-Ins | Class Builder Utility. Next, select File | New | Collection or click the Add New Collection toolbar button to begin creating a new collection. Figure 22.2 shows what the Collection Builder utility looks like.

You must enter or select three pieces of information under the Properties tab. The first is simply the name of the collection you are creating. By default, the name is `Collection1`.

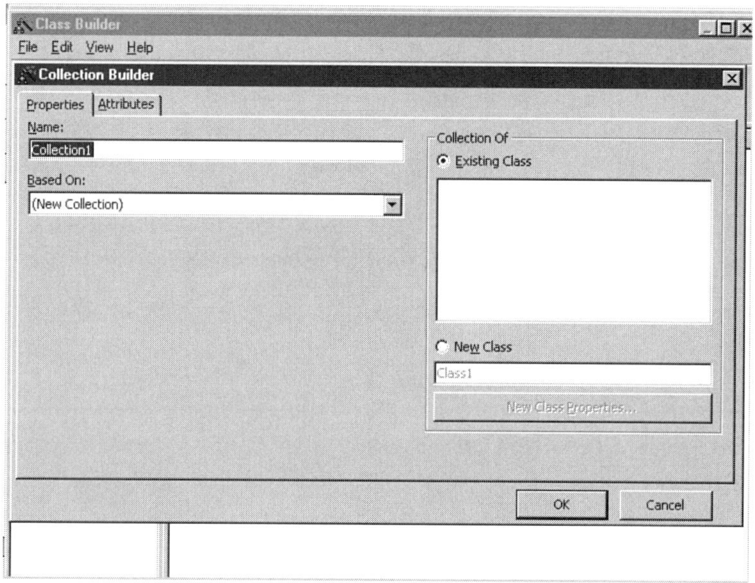

FIGURE 22.2.
Adding a new collection.

The second is to define the basis of the new collection. If it is based on a new collection, the default (New Collection) will be sufficient. Otherwise, select from the proposed list of existing collections.

The third is to define what type of collection this is. If it is a collection of existing class objects, click the Existing Class radio button and choose from the listed classes. Otherwise, click the New Class radio button and enter a name. You can define the properties of the new class by clicking the New Class Properties button.

Figure 22.3 shows the results of choosing a new collection, named `colStack`, and basing it on a new class, named `clsStack`.

The `colStack` collection can then be implemented the same as the one in Listing 22.1. However, using the Collection Builder utility makes it easier to add custom properties, methods, and events.

NOTE

For more information about using the Class Builder utility, refer to Chapter 3, "Classes."

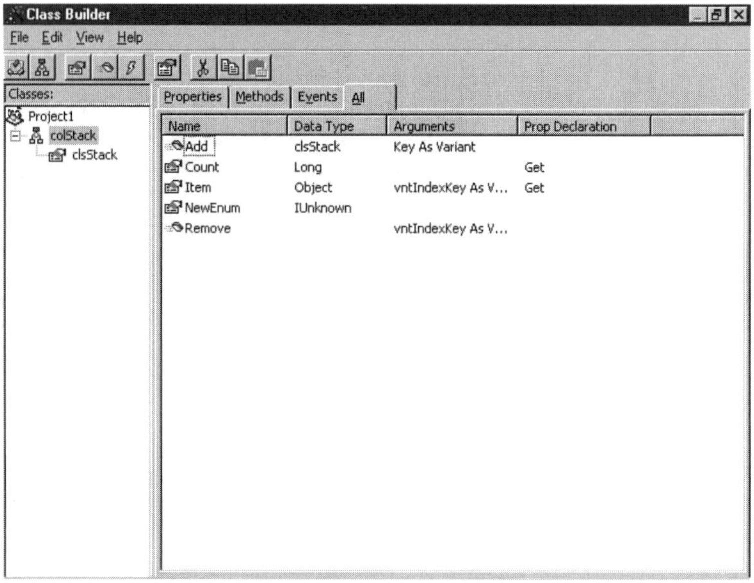

FIGURE 22.3.
The new collection.

Summary

Collections can be tremendously useful in Visual Basic. They enable you to add, remove, or reference items that share similar characteristics. A collection provides a means for the storage of those items without having to know in advance how many items will be added, removed, or referenced. Collections are built dynamically. Use caution when using collections, however, because they can use more overhead than conventional arrays.

V

Communications, Internet, and Intranet Building

23

The Internet

The Internet has become quite popular. As such, the public demands more and more from it. Therefore, like anything, the more features you add, the more complex it becomes. This chapter will help you understand some of those confusing Internet terms. This chapter also discusses the Internet from a Microsoft point of view. Some of the tools and terminology might be different for other Internet-related vendors.

Although the Internet has been popular for only the last few years, it actually has been around for more than 25 years. It was designed, maintained, and built by the U.S. government and was primarily used by universities and research facilities.

The Internet has grown into what it is today fairly rapidly. In the late 1980s the Internet had grown to allow for only text to be transmitted. Even at this primitive stage, the need to determine standards existed. Therefore, the protocol was determined to be TCP/IP, which stands for Transmission Control Protocol/Internet Protocol. TCP/IP allows packets of information to be grouped in such a way that each packet contains data, as well as the source and destination of the packet. Along with the need to develop a protocol, more standards were necessary. First, there was the need for some addressing technique, and the Uniform Resource Locator (URL) was developed. A URL provides a way for an Internet browser to be able to access an Internet Web site in a consistent way. A browser enables you to explore or "surf" the World Wide Web. There is a subtle difference between the Internet and the World Wide Web. The World Wide Web is a subset of the Internet, which also includes e-mail, file transfer, and other technologies, such as video conferencing.

As these specifications were refined, different Web browsers hit the market. There are three main Web browsers:

- Mosaic
- Netscape
- Microsoft Internet Explorer (MSIE)

Mosaic was the first browser. Then came Netscape, which rapidly became the predominant browser. Microsoft was late to market with its browser, but it was an instant hit, and today, Microsoft Internet Explorer is rapidly gaining market share.

Accessing a page on the Web is possible because Internet Service Providers (ISPs) have access to the backbone of the Internet and agree to host your Web site for a fee. Typically for around $50–$60 per month, an ISP will store on a server all of the files that encompass your Web site, which starts with a home page. From this page, you can have the users link to other pages on your Web site, all of which will be stored or "hosted" by the ISP.

Microsoft Internet Technologies

Many key technologies make the Internet work. The technologies discussed in this chapter are promoted and developed primarily by Microsoft. This ensures that they stay on top of the Internet industry.

ActiveX

ActiveX is an extensible technology that actually enhanced and replaced the OCX. The OLE Control eXtension, or OCX, was the first OLE-enabled component, introduced in Visual Basic 4.0. ActiveX controls are reusable components that enable you to take advantage of functionality without having to spend a lot of hours writing code. You can take advantage of someone else's knowledge and time simply by using the ActiveX control in your Web site. You can use Visual Basic to create your own ActiveX controls.

NOTE

For more information about ActiveX controls, read Chapter 20, "ActiveX Controls."

You can develop ActiveX controls in Visual Basic and deploy them onto your Internet site. You can allow them to be automatically downloaded when needed by the Web clients. ActiveX allows for your Web content to be very dynamic because the control can allow for animation or even manipulation of the HTML code itself.

ActiveX controls do not use a lot of overhead, as their predecessors (OCXs) did because they are used only when they are needed. This can actually free up quite a lot of resources, depending on the control. The next few sections discuss terminology centered around the ActiveX technology.

DCOM

DCOM (or Distributed Component Object Model) is a key technology related to ActiveX. It is a protocol that defines how ActiveX will work in a distributed environment. In this case, the Internet is acting like a huge Wide Area Network (WAN). The need for DCOM came when it was determined that these components needed to communicate with each other in a secure, reliable, and efficient manner. Although DCOM is not required for an ActiveX control to function, without DCOM, the ActiveX control will be loaded across the Internet.

DCOM works with all types of ActiveX-related components, including ActiveX controls, VBScript, JScript, and Java applets.

Active Documents

An Active Document is a document that can be viewed (along with other Internet content) as you would view it in a word processor, such as Word. This means that if you were to view a Word document across the Web, your browser would show all of the menus and toolbars you would expect to see if you opened Word itself. This gives great flexibility in Web content. You must use MSIE 3.0 or later to view Active Documents.

This technology actually was based on OLE documents, with which you could have a container in Visual Basic to act as a host for the document. The document then would be opened in Word, but Word would be displayed in the container area.

Quite often, you'll search the Web for information on a specific topic. In the past, you either had to view the document in Web page form or download the Word document for viewing and printing offline. Now with Active Documents, you can actually view the document in your browser directly, without the intermediate steps. This is advantageous to the Web page developer as well because an existing document will not have to be converted into an HTML page for viewing in a browser. Ultimately, this means less time spent in creating your Web pages.

Active Documents also refer to spreadsheets, not just Word documents. Very often, you need to communicate data to a client using a spreadsheet. This, too, is incorporated into Active Documents.

Active Scripting

Active Scripting is an important part of the ActiveX technology. Scripting can be done in any scripting language, such as VBScript or JScript. VBScript allows your Web page to react in a Visual Basic–like way. This is the most popular way for Visual Basic developers to create meaningful Web pages. For example, how does the Web page know what to do when you click a command button? It knows because of a script that was written to react to the button being clicked.

VBScript is a subset of the Visual Basic (VB) and Visual Basic for Applications (VBA) languages. It contains the same syntax, functions, and features, except that it will not enable you to directly manipulate anything on the client's computer. For example, you cannot write to and from files or access a client's security.

VBScript also enables you to trap and respond to any event generated by an ActiveX control. Therefore, if you actually want to respond to a Windows message, you must implement a process called *subclassing* to intercept Windows messages. Desaware actually makes one such control. You can visit the Desaware site at `http://www.desaware.com`.

Active Server

Active Server is a term that indicates that ActiveX scripts can actually run on the server, instead of the client (browser). However, in order for you to take advantage of Active Server, you must be running Internet Information Server (IIS) version 2.0 or greater. This allows for a very dynamic Web site.

The key to this dynamic content is Active Server Pages (ASP). Active Server Pages are secure because they are part of IIS. An Active Server Page can send content to the MSIE browser dynamically, based on certain conditions that exist on the server. For example, suppose the user wanted to request all of the sales data for a specific company. The Active Server Page could actually create the HTML document, based on that data, and send the HTML to the browser dynamically. The server is doing all of the work, which is much faster and more extensible than the browser doing the work on the client side.

Another advantage of an Active Server Page is that you can detect which browser a client is using and generate the HTML code based on which features that client supports.

NOTE

For more information about determining types of browsers and other special features, refer to Chapter 24, "Special Considerations."

Active Server Pages also can integrate with any ODBC database, such as SQL Server, Oracle, Sybase, and Access.

Internet Explorer

The Internet Explorer from Microsoft, at the time of this publication, is the second most widely used browser. The most widely used browser is Netscape. However, Microsoft is gaining market share very rapidly. Microsoft is continually enhancing the browser to enable you to do more and more things. In the future, you will be using this browser for many things other than Web browsing because of its extensible capabilities and fantastic-looking pages. If you plan to use Internet Explorer to view and manipulate ActiveX controls, you will need version 3.0 or greater, which you can download from the Microsoft Web site at `http://www.microsoft.com/IE`.

VBScript

VBScript is a scripting language that is a subset of the Visual Basic language. You can use it to write interpreted code for use in any Web browser that supports it, such as Internet Explorer 3.0 and higher. This code can be very useful in responding to events generated by the browser and user actions. The scope of scripting is beyond this book.

Script Debugger

At the end of 1996, Microsoft released a product called Script Debugger for Internet Explorer. Script Debugger enables you to debug HTML pages containing VBScript or JScript by extending MSIE version 3.01 or greater.

Script Debugger is used very much like the debugger in Visual Basic. It includes the following features:

- Breakpoints
- Call stack
- The capability to step through code
- Syntax coloring
- Immediate pane for testing and assigning variables
- A road map showing related Web pages

At the time of this writing, the Script Debugger was available as a free download at the Microsoft Web site. The address is `http://www.microsoft.com/intdev/scriptie/scriptie.htm`. You invoke the Script Debugger by selecting the View | Source menu option from MSIE. This brings up a window showing an MDI application, which serves as the debugger. The first window is a road map of your Web site (if available). For example, Figure 23.1 shows the Microsoft Web site (`http://www.microsoft.com`) in the debugger.

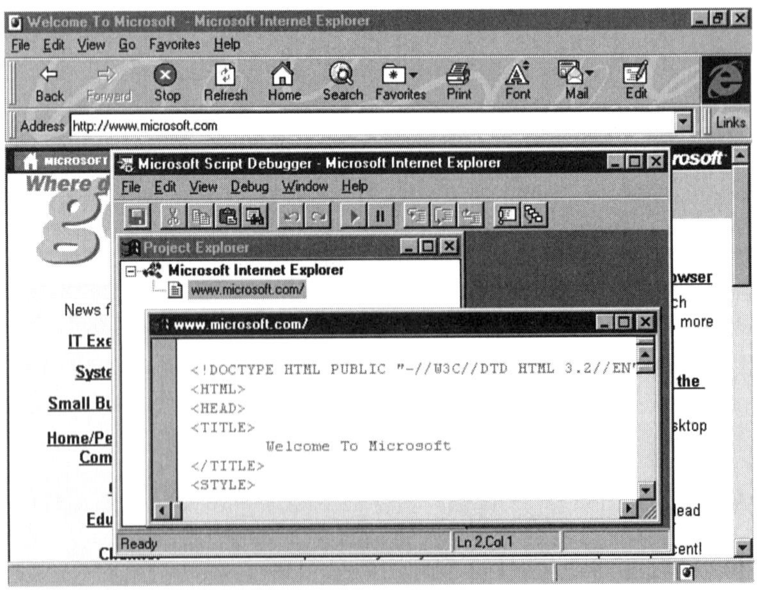

FIGURE 23.1.
The Microsoft Web site shown in the Script Debugger.

To test the debugger, you can insert breakpoints just as you would in Visual Basic, by pressing the F9 key. To test this, Microsoft provides a special Web page at `http://www.microsoft.com/intdev/scriptie/blend.htm`. Figure 23.2 shows what this page looks like.

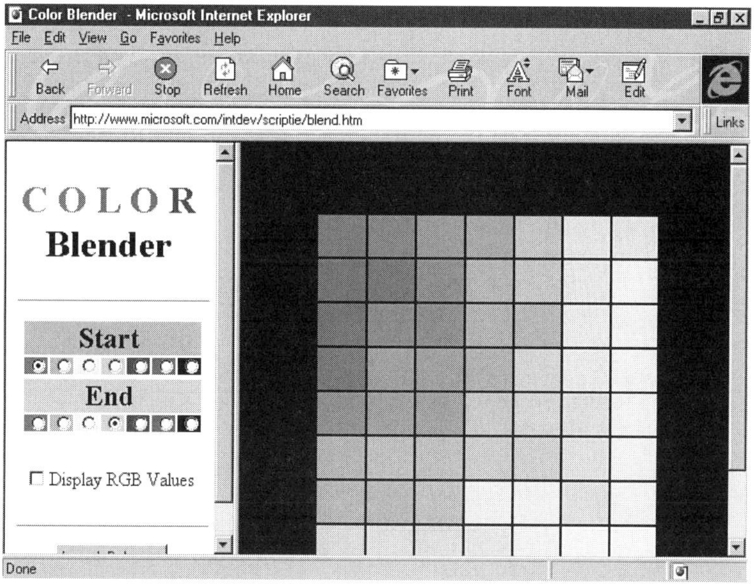

FIGURE 23.2.
The Script Debugger test page.

Again, to invoke the Script Debugger, select the View | Source menu option. Figure 23.3 shows what the debugger looks like on the test page. Notice that there is a road map available for two different Web pages, as well as the breakpoint set by pressing the F9 key.

If you look at the HTML source code for the page, you can see that you would debug it the same way you would debug a Visual Basic application. Listing 23.1 shows the HTML source code for the `blend.htm` Web page.

Listing 23.1. The HTML source code for `blend.htm`.

```
<html>

<title>  Color Blender </title>

<script>

    //******************************************************************//
    //                                                                  //
    //  Based on code from the hIdaho ColorCenter at:                   //
    //          http://www.hidaho.com/colorcenter/ccpad.html            //
    //******************************************************************//
```

continues

Listing 23.1. continued

```
function initArray() {

// Initialize a new array

  this.length = initArray.arguments.length
  for (var i = 0; i < this.length; i++)
    this[i+1] = initArray.arguments[i]
}

var hexChars = "0123456789ABCDEF";

// Convert a decimal to hex string
function Dec2Hex (Dec) {
  var a = Dec % 16;
  var b = (Dec - a)/16;
  hex = "" + hexChars.charAt(b) + hexChars.charAt(a);
  return hex;
}

// Create a blending of the colors
function blendColors(doc, begin, end, stepsArg) {
  var steps = stepsArg -1 ;

  var redA     = begin.charAt(0) + begin.charAt(1),
      red_valA = parseInt(redA,'16'),
      redB     = end.charAt(0) + end.charAt(1),
      red_valB = parseInt(redB,'16'),
      red_int  = ((red_valB - red_valA) / steps) * -1,
      grnA     = begin.charAt(2) + begin.charAt(3),
      grn_valA = parseInt(grnA,'16'),
      grnB     = end.charAt(2) + end.charAt(3),
      grn_valB = parseInt(grnB,'16'),
      grn_int  = ((grn_valB - grn_valA) / steps) * -1,
      bluA     = begin.charAt(4) + begin.charAt(5),
      blu_valA = parseInt(bluA,'16'),
      bluB     = end.charAt(4) + end.charAt(5),
      blu_valB = parseInt(bluB,'16'),
      blu_int  = ((blu_valB - blu_valA) / steps) * -1;

  var step = 2,
      red = red_valA,
      grn = grn_valA,
      blu = blu_valA;

  doc.AddColor(begin);

  while ( steps >= step ) {
    red -= red_int;
    red_round = Math.round(red);
    red_hex = Dec2Hex(red);

    grn -= grn_int;
    grn_round = Math.round(grn);
    grn_hex = Dec2Hex(grn);
```

```
    blu -= blu_int;
    blu_round = Math.round(blu);
    blu_hex = Dec2Hex(blu);

    doc.AddColor(red_hex + grn_hex + blu_hex);

    step++;
  }
  doc.AddColor(end);
}

</script>

<frameset cols="200,*">
    <frame src="picker.htm" name="Color Picker">
    <frame src="table.htm" name="Color Table">
</frameset>


</html>
```

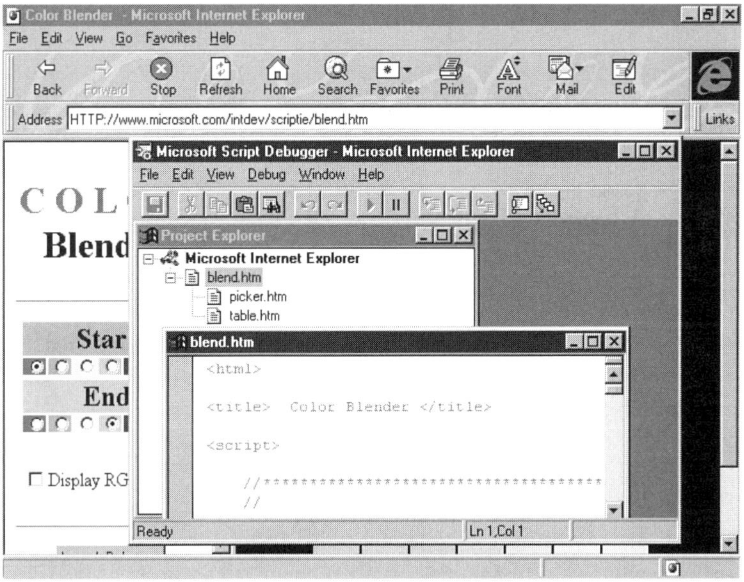

FIGURE 23.3.
The Script Debugger test page inside Script Debugger.

In the same page, you can invoke the Immediate pane by pressing the Ctrl+G key combination or by selecting the Immediate pane toolbar option. Figure 23.4 shows the Immediate pane in the Script Debugger.

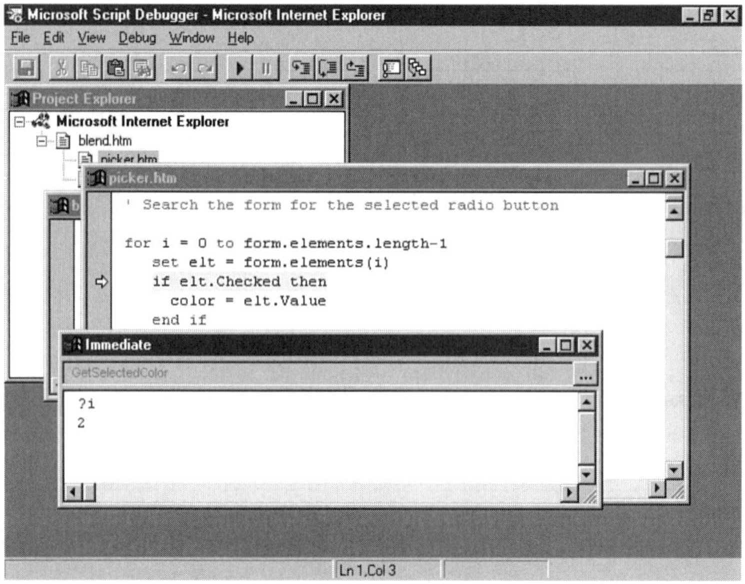

FIGURE 23.4.
The Script Debugger's Immediate pane.

As you can see, the Script Debugger is very much like the Visual Basic debugger. It enables you to quickly and easily debug script files inside your HTML documents.

Internet Information Server

Internet Information Server (IIS) is a Web server that is tightly integrated with Windows NT. A Web server usually is a dedicated, high-powered computer that handles all of the requests coming from Web browsers. IIS can be used by ISPs to deliver Internet service or by a corporation to deliver intranet service. IIS can be used to support HTTP version 1.0, as well as FTP and Gopher services.

IIS is easy to install, manage, and configure, and because of the tight integration with Windows NT Server, IIS is fast, secure, and easy to set up, run, and administer.

IIS includes a built-in search engine, called Index Server. It also includes many management tools to enable administrators to easily manage IIS. Also, HTML wizards are provided.

IIS 3.0 includes full support for VBScript, Visual Basic, JavaScript, and Java components. IIS 3.0 also supports Just In Time compiling (JIT).

Normandy

Normandy is the code name for a new set of Internet servers available from Microsoft that help customers conduct business on the Internet. Normandy is built on the IIS concept (discussed earlier), so it delivers a robust, scaleable Internet solution. Normandy is actually a family of related products, incorporating nine servers and services (see Table 23.1). Each of these items plays an important role in the complete picture of serving a robust Internet system.

Table 23.1. The Normandy family of product servers.

Product	*Description*
Internet News Server	Used to meet high-traffic loads for newsgroups and information.
Internet Chat Server	Allows for real-time voice communications among many conversations through the Internet.
Internet White Pages and Locator Server	Acts the same as the telephone White Pages, enabling you to easily find users of a system, based on how the administrator sets it up.
Information Retrieval System	A search engine that provides full-text searches across one or multiple Web sites.
Content Replication System	A replication engine that replicates any type of content on one or more servers, which can be used to divert traffic to another server or simply as a backup.
Personalization System	Delivers personalized content from your Web server. For example, the Investment Manager at the Microsoft Web site `http://investor.msn.com` stores the personalized portfolios of each user.
Internet Mail Server	Used to send and receive Internet mail for either the SMTP or POP3 protocols. It is robust enough to be scaled into handling millions of users.
Membership System	Used to provide customer subscription–based access. It also generates a billing event for an external billing engine. Used as a centralized authentication system for your customers.
Merchant Server	Enables users to "shop" your Internet site. It provides the capability for clients to select from specific items for purchase.

Web Page Development

You can create Web pages in several ways. However, the underlying language used to define your pages is HTML, which stands for HyperText Markup Language.

NOTE

For more information about HTML, refer to Chapter 25, "HTML Primer."

You can create these HTML pages by writing the HTML yourself, or you can use a code generator, such as Microsoft FrontPage or Visual InterDev. You can use these products to create a page visually, and then they can generate the HTML code for you.

After the HTML code is generated, you must send it to the server so that other Web browsers can access the HTML. You do this by using a protocol called FTP, which stands for File Transfer Protocol. FTP is a protocol that defines how files will be transmitted over the Internet.

FrontPage 97

FrontPage 97 is a visual Web page development and deployment tool that enables you to drag and drop controls onto a Web page, much like Visual Basic. In turn, it actually develops the HTML code for you. FrontPage is a Rapid Development Tool (RAD) for building professional-quality Internet or intranet sites.

FrontPage has more than 30 built-in templates, which you can use to build one page or entire Web sites, based on a specific look. You can also insert links, called *hyperlinks*, to other sites or pages within your own site.

FrontPage comes with two separate pieces. The first is the Explorer, which is a road map of your entire Web site. You can use it to easily see which pages link to other pages in your site. The second piece is the Editor, which you can use to create individual pages by dragging and dropping ActiveX controls from the toolbar onto the "form."

FrontPage fully supports VBScript, ActiveX controls, and applets. Therefore, Internet Explorer fully supports FrontPage. This makes for a richer experience for the user. At approximately $150, it is well worth the money to rapidly develop your site. It is so easy to use that you can have a site up and running within a day.

E-Mail

Although electronic mail (or *e-mail*) is transmitted over the Internet, it is different than the Web. You can have an ISP host your Web site without allowing you to send or receive e-mail. Therefore, there is another charge for you to be able to send and receive e-mail. This charge is probably between $10 and $30 per month.

If your ISP is using IIS, then the e-mail that is supported is either SMTP or POP3 protocols. MSIE supports both, and so does a Microsoft Exchange client.

Terminology

Because the Internet has grown at such a rapid pace, the terminology for different aspects of the Internet can be confusing. Table 23.2 describes the Internet-related terms.

Table 23.2. Internet terminology.

Term	*Description*
FTP	File Transfer Protocol. Used to transfer files from the Internet to a client (or vice versa).
Telnet	Alternative protocol used to log on to remote computers.
Gopher	A menu-driven system for accessing text information.
HTTP	HyperText Transfer Protocol. Used to transmit HTML documents.
HTML	HyperText Markup Language. This is the standard language that is used to generate the visual interface shown in Web browsers.
TCP/IP	Transmission Control Protocol/Internet Protocol. The protocol of the Internet.
VBScript	Visual Basic scripting language for HTML documents.
ActiveX	Extensible controls based on OLE and DCOM for use in your Web pages.
JavaScript	Scripting language based on Java instead of Visual Basic.
Applet	A small, self-contained application used in Web pages.
CGI	Common Gateway Interface. Used to enable a client to interact with a server.
DNS	Domain Name System. Because the Internet works on a protocol, called TCP/IP, DNS resolves a user-friendly description to the TCP/IP address needed by the Internet.
ISAPI	Internet Server API.
ISP	Internet Service Provider.
Internet	External global network.
Intranet	An internal network.
POP3	Post Office Protocol, version 3.0.
IIS	Internet Information Server.
SMTP	Simple Mail Transfer Protocol.
JIT	Just In Time compiling. Used to achieve greater processing speeds.
Usenet	Bulletin Board network for special-interest topics and groups carried over the Internet.

continues

Table 23.2. continued

Term	*Description*
Packets	Groups of data to be transmitted over the Internet.
URL	Uniform Resource Locator. This is a unique identifier for a Web page or site.

Summary

The Internet is a very important technology that has become very popular over the last several years. Microsoft is committed to this technology. With the advent of ActiveX, you can create and incorporate components into your Web pages and view them across the Internet.

Visual Basic 5.0 can create these ActiveX components, which can include special functionality or even other components. This is a tremendous new feature of Visual Basic 5.0 and is discussed further in Chapter 20, "ActiveX Controls."

24

Special Considerations

Special considerations in this chapter refers to special considerations given to your Internet and intranet applications to make them dynamic and exciting. Much of this functionality takes place on the server. Server-side functionality can provide benefits such as determining what functionality your browser supports, counting how many visitors you have to your site, showing tips of the day, and others.

Server-side functionality is made possible by a technology code named Denali, which was the code name for an ActiveX scripting technology on the server. This was also referred to as Dynamic HTML. These scripts can be written in VBScript, JScript, or any other scripting language because the pages are interpreted by the scripting engine. This makes it possible for the server to construct the HTML page dynamically, based on certain conditions, and send it to the local browser. The browser only knows to display the HTML. It does not care where it came from.

Denali will run on the following Web servers:

- Microsoft Internet Information Server (IIS) version 2.0 and higher
- Peer Web Services (PWS), which ships with Windows NT Workstation 4.0
- Peer Web Services (PWS), which ships with Windows 95

PWS is sometimes known as a personal Web server. In either case, Denali runs as an Internet Server Application Programming Interface (ISAPI) application. It contains three different technologies that make it function:

- Scripting—Allows for dynamic content.
- Components—Insertable objects.
- State Management—Manages connections and objects.

Making Denali Work

As mentioned earlier in the chapter, Denali works with a scripting engine on the server to produce dynamic HTML pages. The script must include a directive to Denali. This directive is a pair of delimiters that looks like this:

```
<% %>
```

This means that Denali will process everything between these tags. Everything outside of these tags will be passed through Denali to be resolved by your browser.

CROSS REFERENCE

For more information about HTML tags, refer to Chapter 25, "HTML Primer."

All Denali scripts are stored as Active Server Pages, which have an extension of `*.ASP`. This extension has a special meaning for the server. For Denali to function, you must install Active Server Pages on the server. At the time of this writing, Denali was only supported on Internet Information Server version 3.0 and the Personal Web Server. These scripts are placed (and linked) to any directory specified by the virtual root. You specified the virtual root directory when you installed the Web server. To verify the virtual root in IIS, select Start | Programs | Microsoft Internet Server | Internet Service Manager. This will bring up the dialog box shown in Figure 24.1.

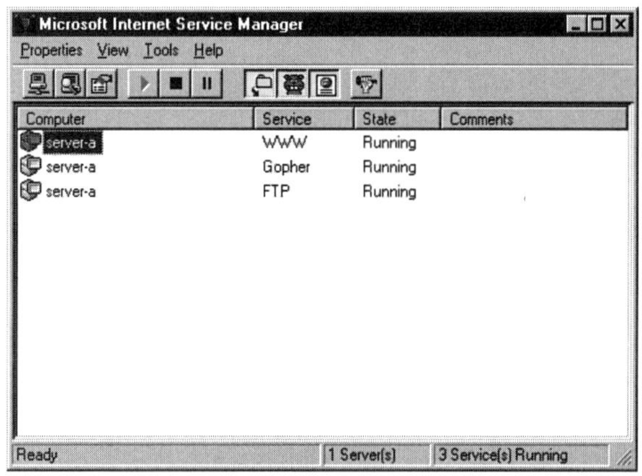

FIGURE 24.1.
The IIS Service Manager.

Double-click the WWW service. This will bring up the WWW Service Properties dialog box. Next, select the Directories tab. This will list all of the virtual directories for your server. Notice the highlighted line in Figure 24.2, which was created for this example. It will be used as a basis for the following discussion. To run an Active Server Page named `TEST.ASP` in the browser, you would type the following:

```
http://server-a/asp/test.asp
```

Substitute *`server-a`* for the name of your server and *`asp`* for the name of your virtual root directory. A virtual root is an actual directory structure that is mapped to an alias. It is this alias which is referred to in your Web browser.

To create the virtual directory, click Add. This will bring up the Directory Properties dialog box shown in Figure 24.3.

The Directory text box is the actual directory on your server. The Virtual Directory Alias text box is the directory for the server where the user will map to the actual directory. One final important note is that you must check the Execute check box. This will allow the Active Server Page to function correctly.

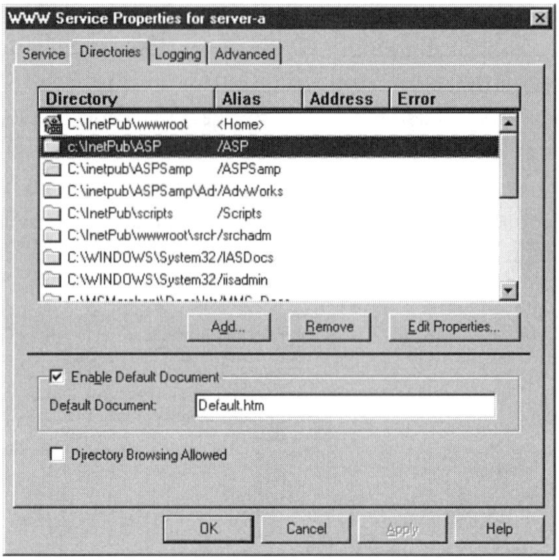

FIGURE 24.2.
The IIS Service Manager, viewing alias directories.

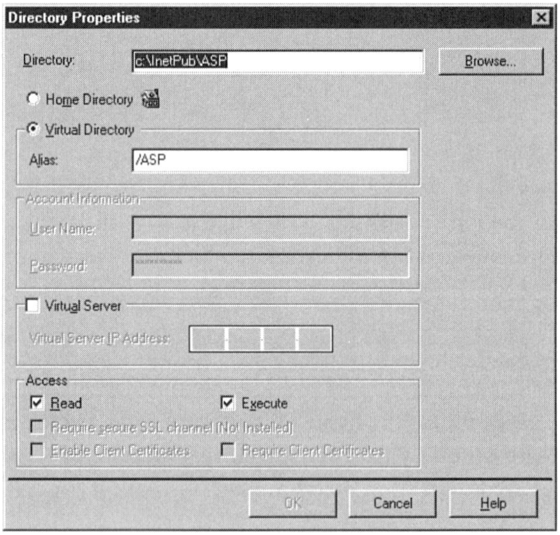

FIGURE 24.3.
Adding a virtual root in IIS Service Manager.

ASP Coding

Coding for an Active Server Page (ASP) can be either easy or difficult. This is similar to a Visual Basic application. You can write one line of code or write a complete Client/Server application.

Let's take a simple ASP. The objective is to display six lines of text, increasing the font on each line, and labeling each line. This is shown in Figure 24.4.

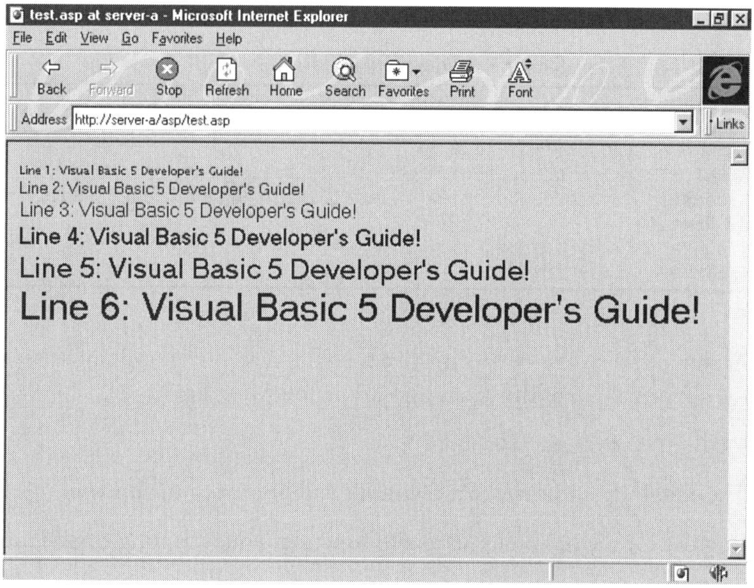

FIGURE 24.4.
Simple ASP showing six lines of text, increasing in font size on each line.

The static HTML to develop this page looks like the code in Listing 24.1.

Listing 24.1. HTML used to display Figure 24.4.

```
<HTML>
<BODY>

<FONT SIZE=1>
Line 1: Visual Basic 5 Developer's Guide!<BR>

<FONT SIZE=2>
Line 2: Visual Basic 5 Developer's Guide!<BR>

<FONT SIZE=3>
Line 3: Visual Basic 5 Developer's Guide!<BR>

<FONT SIZE=4>
Line 4: Visual Basic 5 Developer's Guide!<BR>

<FONT SIZE=5>
Line 5: Visual Basic 5 Developer's Guide!<BR>

<FONT SIZE=6>
Line 6: Visual Basic 5 Developer's Guide!<BR>

</BODY>
</HTML>
```

This code is very tedious, and it is not dynamic at all. It simply displays the text. Would you be surprised to know that this HTML page was actually created from an Active Server Page? It's true. The Active Server script looks like Listing 24.2.

Listing 24.2. Active Server Page dynamic HTML.

```
<HTML>
<BODY>
<% For nLoopCount = 1 To 6 %>
<FONT SIZE=<% = nLoopCount %>>
Line <% = CStr(nLoopCount)%>: Visual Basic 5 Developer's Guide!<BR>
<% Next %>
</BODY>
</HTML>
```

As stated earlier, the `<% %>` directive specifies that a script will interpret the command. Notice the abnormal use of the equal sign in the following line:

```
<FONT SIZE=<% = nLoopCount %>>
```

The equal sign indicates that the result will be sent to the browser.

In order for the preceding scripts to function, your scripting engine must know two things:

- The scripting language
- Whether to run the script on the server or client

Denali will know this based on special tag keywords, called `<SCRIPT> </SCRIPT>`. It accepts arguments, as follows:

```
<SCRIPT LANGUAGE=VBScript RUNAT=Server>
```

However, this line of code does not need to be explicitly stated. The defaults will be listed in a file called `GLOBAL.ASA` on the IIS server. The file contains all of the default values.

Denali Objects

There are several objects intrinsically built into Denali. They include the following:

- `Request`—Represents the request of information from the server.
- `Response`—Represents the response from the request for information from the server.
- `Server`—Represents an instance of the Web server.
- `Application`—Represents a running browser application.
- `Session`—Represents an instance of a running browser window.

The `Request` Object

The `Request` object has five methods:

- `Write`—Sends information directly to a browser.
- `Redirect` —Redirects a user to a different URL.
- `ContentType` —Controls the type of content you send.
- `Cookies` —Sets cookie values.
- `Buffer` —Buffers information.

The `Request` object has five collections:

- `QueryString`—The values of variables in the HTTP query string.
- `Form`—The values of form elements in the HTTP request.
- `Cookies`—The values of cookies sent in the HTTP request.
- `ClientCertificate`—The values of fields stored in the client certificate that is sent in the HTTP request.
- `ServerVariables`—The values of predetermined server environment variables.

The `Response` Object

The `Response` object has eight methods:

- `AddHeader`—Sets the HTML header name to a value.
- `AppendToLog`—Adds a string to the end of the Web server log.
- `BinaryWrite`—Writes the given information to the current HTTP output.
- `Clear`—Erases any buffered HTML output.
- `End`—Stops processing the `.ASP` file and returns the current result.
- `Flush`—Sends buffered output immediately to the browser.
- `Redirect`—Redirects to a different URL.
- `Write`—Writes a variable to the current HTTP output as a string.

The `Response` object has five properties:

- `Buffer`—Indicates whether page output is buffered.
- `ContentType`—Specifies the HTTP content type for the response.
- `Expires`—Specifies the length of time before a page cached on a browser expires.
- `ExpiresAbsolute`—Specifies the date and time on which a page cached on a browser expires.
- `Status`—The value of the status line returned by the server.

The `Response` object has one collection:

- `Cookies`—Specifies cookie values.

The `Server` Object

The `Server` object has four methods:

- `CreateObject`—Creates an instance of a server component.
- `HTMLEncode`—Applies HTML encoding to the specified string.
- `MapPath`—Maps the specified virtual path—either the absolute path on the current server or the path relative to the current page—into a physical path.
- `URLEncode`—Applies URL encoding rules, including escape characters, to the string.

The `Server` object has one property:

- `ScriptTimeout`—The amount of time that a script can run before it times out.

The `Application` Object

The `Application` object has two methods:

- `Lock`—Prevents other clients from modifying `Application` object properties.
- `Unlock`—Enables other clients to modify `Application` object properties.

The `Application` object has two events:

- `Application_OnEnd()`—Fires when all instances of the browser are closed.
- `Application_OnStart()`—Fires when the browser starts.

The `Session` Object

The `Session` object has one method:

- `Abandon`—Destroys a `Session` object.

The `Session` object has two properties:

- `SessionID`—Returns the identifier for a session for this user.
- `Timeout`—The timeout period for the session state for this application.

In addition, there are a few base components that provide additional functionality:

- `AdRotator`—Used to rotate between different advertisements.
- `BrowserType`—Determines browser capabilities.

- `NextLink`—Useful for tracking links for the Forward and Back buttons on the browser.
- `TextStream`—Used to control file I/O.
- `ADO`—Used for connecting to active databases.

To use these components (those that are not themselves objects), you must instantiate the component with the `MSWC` class. For example, you must instantiate the `BrowserType` component like this:

```
Set BrowserType = Server.CreateObject("MSWC.BrowserType")
```

The `AdRotator` Component

The `AdRotator` component has one method:

- `GetAdvertisement`—Gets the specifications for the next scheduled advertisement from a data file.

The `AdRotator` component has three properties:

- `Border`—Specifies the size of the border around the advertisement.
- `Clickable`—Specifies whether the advertisement is a hyperlink to a URL.
- `TargetFrame`—Specifies the name of the frame in which to display the advertisement.

The `BrowserType` Component

The `BrowserType` component, also called the Browser Capabilities component, does not have any properties per se. The properties available depend on the entries listed in a file called `BROWSCAP.INI`. This file usually exists in the `\WINDOWS\SYSTEM32\INETSRV\ASP\CMPNTS` subdirectory on the server where IIS was installed. The following are the default properties:

- `ActiveXControls`—Specifies whether the browser supports ActiveX controls.
- `Backgroundsounds`—Specifies whether the browser supports background sounds.
- `beta`—Specifies whether the browser is beta software.
- `browser`—Specifies the name of the browser.
- `cookies`—Specifies whether the browser supports cookies.
- `frames`—Specifies whether the browser supports frames.
- `javascript`—Specifies whether the browser supports JScript.
- `platform`—Specifies the platform on which the browser runs.
- `tables`—Specifies whether the browser supports tables.
- `vbscript`—Specifies whether the browser supports VBScript.
- `version`—Specifies the version number of the browser.

The `NextLink` Component

The `NextLink` component, which is also called the Content Linking component, has eight methods:

- `GetListCount`—Counts the number of items linked in the content linking List file.
- `GetNextURL`—Gets the URL of the next page listed in the Content Linking List file.
- `GetPreviousDescription`—Gets the description line of the previous page listed in the Content Linking List file.
- `GetListIndex`—Returns the index of the current page in the Content Linking List file.
- `GetNthDescription`—Gets the description of the Nth page listed in the Content Linking List file.
- `GetPreviousURL`—Gets the URL of the previous pages listed in the Content Linking List file.
- `GetNextDescription`—Gets the description of the next page listed in the Content Linking List file.
- `GetNthURL`—Gets the URL of the Nth page listed in the Content Linking List file.

The `TextStream` Object

The `TextStream` object has nine methods:

- `Close`—Closes a file.
- `Read`—Reads a specific number of characters in a file.
- `ReadAll`—Reads all lines in a file.
- `ReadLine`—Reads one line of a file.
- `Skip`—Skips a specific number of characters in a file.
- `SkipLine`—Skips one line in a file.
- `Write`—Writes a specific number of characters to a file.
- `WriteLine`—Writes one line in a file.
- `WriteBlankLines`—Writes a specific number of blank lines to a file.

The `TextStream` object has four properties:

- `AtEndOfLine`—Indicates whether the file pointer is at the end of a line.
- `AtEndOfStream`—Indicates whether the file pointer is at the end of the file.
- `Column`—Indicates the column number within a line where the file pointer is located.
- `Line`—Indicates the line number within a file where the file pointer is located.

The Active Data Object

The Active Data Object (ADO) has quite a complex object model, similar to that of Remote Data Objects (RDO). For more information about this model, refer to the diagrams and text in the Active Server Pages HTML online documents.

Determining Browser-Specific Features

Determining browser-specific features is quite easy with the `BrowserType` component. It reads the `BROWSCAP.INI` file on the server to determine the specific capabilities of a browser. Figure 24.5 shows the results of the ASP code described in Listing 24.3.

FIGURE 24.5.
Browser-specific features.

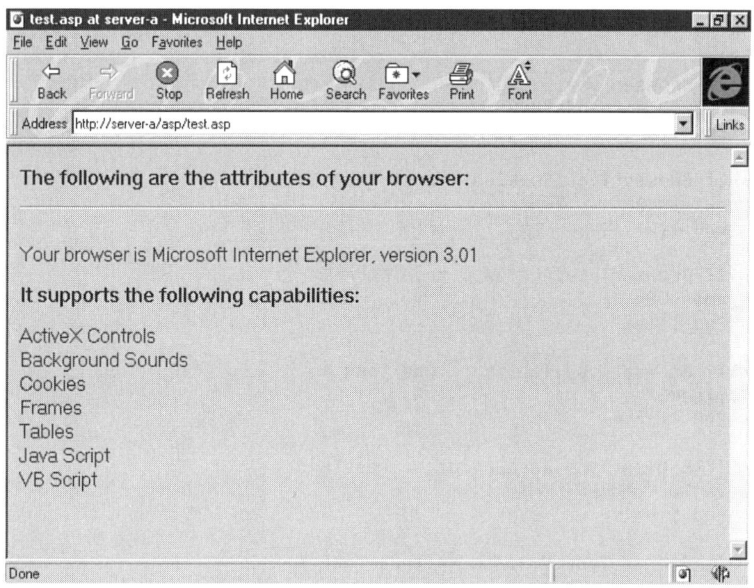

Listing 24.3 shows the ASP code used to generate the dynamic HTML shown in Figure 24.5.

Listing 24.3. Browser-specific code.

```
<HTML>
<BODY>
<% Set BrowserType = Server.CreateObject("MSWC.BrowserType")  %>

<% 'Display Header %>
<B>The following are the attributes of your browser: </B><HR><BR>
```

continues

Listing 24.3. continued

```
<% 'Find Out Browser Type %>
<% If BrowserType.Browser = "IE" Then %>
Your browser is Microsoft Internet Explorer, version <% = BrowserType.
➥Version %><BR><BR>
<% Else %>
Your browser is NOT Microsoft Internet Explorer<BR>
<% End If %>

<% 'Display Header %>
<B>It supports the following capabilities: </B><BR><BR>

<% 'Find Out Capabilities %>

<%If BrowserType.ActiveXControls = true Then %>
ActiveX Controls<BR>
<%End If%>

<%If BrowserType.BackgroundSounds = true Then %>
Background Sounds<BR>
<%End If%>

<%If BrowserType.Cookies = true Then %>
Cookies<BR>
<%End If%>

<%If BrowserType.Frames = true Then %>
Frames<BR>
<%End If%>

<%If BrowserType.Tables = true Then %>
Tables<BR>
<%End If%>

<%If BrowserType.JavaScript = true Then %>
Java Script<BR>
<%End If%>

<%If BrowserType.VBScript = true Then %>
VB Script<BR>
<%End If%>

</BODY>
</HTML>
```

The code first creates an `MSWC.BrowserType` object. This is actually the object that does all of the work. The code simply accesses each of the properties and displays an HTML line indicating the supported feature. Notice that all of the VBScript lines are contained within the `<% %>` directives. Not all of the HTML lines are displayed within these directives.

Displaying the Number of Visits

There is no magic being performed to display the number of times a person visits a Web page. Many developers are confused by this. The theory is quite simple. IIS contains a file called `GLOBAL.ASA`, which is placed in the sample `AdvWorks` directory. It contains default values and procedures to be used upon initializing the `Session` and `Application` objects. These objects are initialized automatically when the browser runs a specific Web page. The file was modified and copied to the default directory where the ASP file in Listing 24.3 exists. Listing 24.4 shows this modified file.

Listing 24.4. Modified `GLOBAL.ASA` file contents.

```
<SCRIPT LANGUAGE=VBScript RUNAT=Server>
SUB Application_OnStart
' This script executes when the first user comes to the site.
' Open file and read the number of visitors so far
VisitorCountFilename = Server.MapPath  + "\visitors.txt"
Set FileObject = Server.CreateObject("Scripting.FileSystemObject")
Set Out= FileObject.OpenTextFile (VisitorCountFilename, 1, FALSE, FALSE)
' Initialize soft visitor counter here
Application("visitors") = Out.ReadLine
' Store physical file name of file containing the visitor count
Application("VisitorCountFilename") = VisitorCountFilename
END SUB
</SCRIPT>

<SCRIPT LANGUAGE=VBScript RUNAT=Server>
SUB Application_OnEnd
' This script executes when the server shuts down or when global.asa changes.
' Overwrites the existing visitors.txt file
Set FileObject = Server.CreateObject("Scripting.FileSystemObject")
Set Out= FileObject.CreateTextFile (Application("VisitorCountFilename"), TRUE,
➥ FALSE)
Out.WriteLine(application("visitors"))
END SUB
</SCRIPT>

<SCRIPT LANGUAGE=VBScript RUNAT=Server>
SUB Session_OnStart

' Increase the visitor counter
Application.lock
Application("visitors")= application("visitors") + 1
t_visitors = application("visitors")
Application.unlock
Session("VisitorID") = t_visitors

' Periodically, save to file
If t_visitors MOD 15 = 0 Then
SET FileObject = Server.CreateObject("Scripting.FileSystemObject")
```

continues

Listing 24.4. continued

```
Set Out= FileObject.CreateTextFile (Application("VisitorCountFilename"), TRUE,
➥ FALSE)
Application.lock
Out.WriteLine(t_visitors)
Application.unlock
End If
END SUB
</SCRIPT>
```

The basic theory is that these four events are fired automatically:

- `Application_OnStart`
- `Application_OnEnd`
- `Session_OnStart`
- `Session_OnEnd`

These events are used to retrieve data from a file called `VISITORS.TXT`. The value is read and stored in a `Visitors` variable, and the number is incremented and written out when the application ends. This means that all instances of the browser must be closed before the value of the variable is written out. This way, if you have multiple windows open or if you hit Refresh multiple times, the counter won't be incremented.

The majority of this code is based on the `FileSystemObject` object. Refer to the HTML online help shipped with IIS for further information about this object.

Your dynamic HTML can simply display the counter with this line of code:

```
You are visitor number: <% = Application("visitors") %><BR>
```

All initialization has already been performed by the `GLOBAL.ASA` file.

Displaying Tips of the Day

Displaying tips of the day is very similar to displaying the number of visitors in that it uses a file that stores the tips. The tips are picked from the list at random. This example assumes that you have a file called `TIPS.TXT` in the same directory as the ASP file. Listing 24.5 shows the contents of this file.

Listing 24.5. The `TIPS.TXT` file.

```
Don't drink and drive!
Don't talk to strangers!
Be kind to others!
It's good to be the king!
Share this book with your friends!
```

Obviously, you could add more tips. The code used to traverse this file at random is shown in Listing 24.6.

Listing 24.6. Code to randomly choose a tip.

```
<HTML>
<BODY>
Tip of the Day:<HR>

<%
CONST UPPER = 5
CONST LOWER = 1
TipFile =  Server.MapPath("tips.txt" )
Set FileObject = Server.CreateObject("Scripting.FileSystemObject")
Set File = FileObject.OpenTextFile (TipFile, 1, FALSE, FALSE)

Randomize
Rand = Int((UPPER - LOWER + 1) * Rnd + LOWER)
For nLoopCount = 1 to Rand
Application("Tip") = File.ReadLine
Next
%>

<% = Application("Tip") %><BR>
</BODY>
</HTML>
```

The code opens a file object of the `TIPS.TXT` file and sets it to the `File` variable. Then a random number is generated between 1 and the number of tips in the `TIPS.TXT` file, as shown by the constant `UPPER`. The code then loops from 1 to the random number chosen and reads a line from the `File` file handle. After the line is read, it is displayed in the browser. This is shown in Figure 24.6.

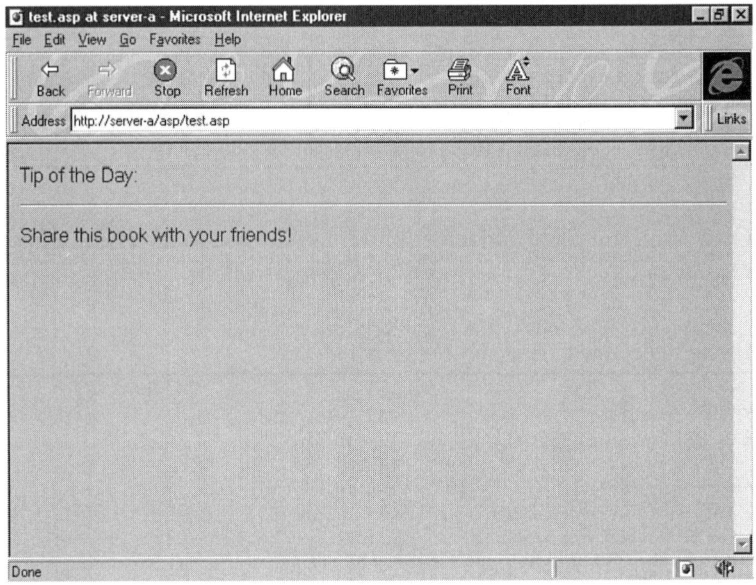

FIGURE 24.6.
Displaying the tip of the day.

Summary

With the advent of Denali, scripting on the HTML server makes creating dynamic Web pages possible. A dynamic Web page is a page of HTML code that is generated at the time of the request for the page by the browser. Therefore, it can react to special considerations that are coded in your scripts, known as Active Server Pages (ASPs). This chapter shows you how to create ASPs and to take into account special considerations, such as tips of the day, the number of visitors to your Web site, and features supported by a specific Web browser. Use these examples to make your own Web pages more dynamic and exciting.

25

HTML Primer

HTML stands for HyperText Markup Language—the language of the Internet. It is this language that tells a Web browser, such as Microsoft Internet Explorer, how to display information in the browser. It specifies things such as the following:

- Text to display on the screen
- Font names
- Font sizes
- Location of pictures to display
- Justification

HTML is based on a series of codes, called tags, which mean special things to the interpreter. HTML is an interpreted language, like Visual Basic.

HTML is a text file that can be edited in any text editor, such as Notepad or even Microsoft Word. There are even programs that generate the HTML for you (FrontPage, for example). The purpose of this chapter is to teach you the basics of HTML so that you can read, alter, and understand the language of the Internet.

An HTML page usually has one of two file extensions. One is `*.HTM` and the other is `*.HTML`. For example, if you have a welcome screen, this might be called `WELCOME.HTM` or `WELCOME.HTML`.

It is important to note that this chapter is designed to present only a primer to the HTML language, so that the codes and tags are not foreign to you when you read the other Internet chapters. However, this chapter cannot possibly cover every HTML feature. There are many great Sams books that cover this topic in its entirety. An excellent book on HTML is Laura Lemay's *Teach Yourself Web Publishing with HTML 3.2 in 14 Days, Professional Reference Edition.*

HTML as a Language

HTML is a very powerful interpreted language used by all Internet browsers. Some browsers enable you to view, or even change, the HTML of a document. Before beginning, look at Microsoft Internet Explorer version 3.0. This browser, from now on, is referred to as MSIE. It is shown in Figure 25.1.

The browser shows a sample page from the Macmillan Computer Publishing Web site. The address is `http://www.mcp.com`. To further enhance the lessons in this chapter, a listing of the HTML source code from the very same page is shown in Listing 25.1. This was obtained by clicking the View | Source menu option in MSIE.

FIGURE 25.1.
Microsoft Internet Explorer version 3.0.

Listing 25.1. MCP Web site HTML source text.

```
<html>
<head><title>Macmillan Publishing USA</title>
</head>
<SCRIPT LANGUAGE="JavaScript">
<!-- Beginning of JavaScript Applet -------------------
function scrollit_r2l(seed)
{
var m1  = "Order online or call 1-800-716-0044 -- ";
var m2  = "Today's special -- The AICPA's Uniform CPA Exam, 1997 Edition,
➥regularly $55.00, today only $41.25";
var msg=m1+m2;
var out = " ";
var c   = 1;
if (seed > 100) {
seed--;
var cmd="scrollit_r2l(" + seed + ")";
timerTwo=window.setTimeout(cmd,100);
}
else if (seed <= 100 && seed > 0) {
for (c=0 ; c < seed ; c++) {
out+=" ";
}
out+=msg;
seed--;
var cmd="scrollit_r2l(" + seed + ")";
    window.status=out;
timerTwo=window.setTimeout(cmd,100);
}
```

continues

Listing 25.1. continued

```
else if (seed <= 0) {
if (-seed < msg.length) {
out+=msg.substring(-seed,msg.length);
seed--;
var cmd="scrollit_r2l(" + seed + ")";
window.status=out;
timerTwo=window.setTimeout(cmd,100);
}
else {
window.status=" ";
timerTwo=window.setTimeout("scrollit_r2l(100)",75);
}
}
}
// -- End of JavaScript code -------------- -->
</SCRIPT>
<body bgcolor="#ffffff" text="#000000" link="#990000" vlink="#000000"
➥alink="#ffffff" background="/general/pix/macpub_pix/yelbar.gif"
onLoad="timerONE=window.setTimeout('scrollit_r2l(100)',500);">
<table border="0" cellspacing="0" cellpadding="0" width="620">
<tr>
<!--BEGIN LEFT BAR COLUMN-->
<td align="left" valign="top" width="120" rowspan="2">
<center>
<a href="/index.html">
<img src="/general/pix/macpub_pix/isl_yel.gif" border="0" width="81"
➥height="74"></a>
</center>
<p>
<font size="3"><b>
<!--DATE-->
<img src="/general/pix/days/sun_y.gif">
January 12, 1997
<!--/DATE-->
<P></b></font>
<!--FEATURED BOOK-->
<a href="/general/featured/macpub.html"><img src="/bookstore/default/covers/8/
➥611918c.gif" alt="Book Of The Day"></a>
<!--/FEATURED BOOK-->
<img src="/general/pix/macpub_pix/feabk_trans.gif" alt="25% Off Today's
Featured Book!" width="114" height="39">
<p>
<!--BEGIN TOPICS-->
<img src="/general/pix/macpub_pix/topics_mpu.gif" alt="Topics" width="115"
➥height="30"><br>
<font size="2">
<a href="macpub/busin_mpu.html">
Business & Finance</a><BR>
<a href="/mcp">
Computing</a><BR>
<a href="macpub/edu_mpu.html">
Education & Training</a><BR>
<a href="macpub/fic_mpu.html">
Fiction & Nonfiction</a><BR>
<a href="macpub/gen_mpu.html">
General Interest</a><BR>
<a href="macpub/health_mpu.html">
```

```
Health, Sports & Fitness</a><BR>
<a href="macpub/life_mpu.html">
Lifestyle</a><BR>
<a href="/mgr/howell">
Pets</a><BR>
<a href="macpub/travel_mpu.html">
Travel & Entertainment</a>
<BR><BR><BR>
<!--BEGIN PUBLISHERS-->
<img src="/general/pix/macpub_pix/publish_mpu.gif" alt="Publishers"
➥width="115" height="30"><br>
<a href="/mcp">
MACMILLAN COMPUTER PUBLISHING</a><br>
<a href="/hayden/adobe/">
Adobe Press</a><BR>
<a href="/brady/">
BradyGAMES</a><BR>
<a href="/hayden/">
Hayden Books</a><BR>
<a href="/lycos">Lycos Press</a><br>
<a href="/newriders/">
New Riders</a><BR>
<a href="/que/">
Que</a><BR>
<a href="/queet/">
Que Education & Training</a><BR>
<a href="/sams/">
Sams Publishing</a><BR>
<a href="/waite/">
Waite Group Press</a><BR>
<a href="/zdpress/">
Ziff-Davis Press</a>
<BR><BR><BR>
<a href="/macdigital">
MACMILLAN DIGITAL</a><br>
<a href="/ssi">
SSI Distribution Services</a>
<BR><BR><BR>
<A href="/mgr">
MACMILLAN GENERAL REFERENCE</A><br>
<a href="/mgr/idiot">
Alpha Books</a><BR>
<a href="/mgr/arco">
ARCO</a><BR>
<a href="/mgr/arco/cassell.html">
Cassell's Foreign Language Dictionaries</a><BR>
<a href="/mgr/arco/harrap.html">
Harrap's Dictionaries</a><BR>
<a href="/mgr/howell">
Howell House Books</a><BR>
<a href="/mgr/lasser">
J.K. Lasser</a><BR>
<a href="/mgr/macmillan">
Macmillan Books</a><BR>
<a href="/mgr/cooking">
Macmillan Cooking
<a href="/mgr/gardening">
Macmillan Gardening</a><BR>
```

continues

Listing 25.1. continued

```
<a href="/mgr/travel">
Macmillan Travel</a><BR>
<a href="/mgr/websters">
Webster's New World</a>
<BR><BR><BR>
<a href="/mlr">
MACMILLAN LIBRARY REFERENCE</a><br>
<a href="/mlr/gkhall">
G.K. Hall & Co.</a><BR>
<a href="/mlr/macref">
Macmillan Reference</a><BR>
<a href="/mlr/schirmer">
Schirmer Books</a><BR>
<a href="/mlr/scribner">
Charles Scribner's Sons Reference</a><BR>
<a href="/mlr/thorndike/">
Thorndike Press</a><BR>
<a href="/mlr/twayne">
Twayne Publishers</a>
</font>
</td>
<!--BLANK SKINNY COLUMN-->
<td width="25" valign="top" rowspan="2">
<BR>
</td>
<td align="left" colspan="3" valign="top" width="475">
<!--INSERT BANNER AD ROTATER-->
<center>
<A HREF="/que/bookshelf/"><IMG alt="Que's Digital Bookshelf" WIDTH=460
HEIGHT=55 border="1" SRC="/ad_banners/ad_digit.gif"></A>
<img src="/general/pix/macpub_pix/head3_anim.gif" alt="Macmillan Publishing
➥USA" width="442" height="82">
<BR>
<a href="/bookstore/do-searches.html">
<img src="/general/pix/macpub_pix/click.gif" alt="Click to search for books"
➥width="230" height="28" border=0"></a>
<BR>
<font size="2">
<a href="/mcp/search/">Search</a> ¦
<a href="/bookstore/do-bookstore.html">Bookstore</a> ¦
<a href="/nrp/wwwyp/index.html">Yellow Pages</a>  ¦
<a href="/general/whats_new/">What's New</a>  ¦
<a href="/general/news17/">Newsletter</a>  ¦
<a href="/softlib/software.html">Software Library</a> ¦
<a href="/refdesk/index.html">Links</a> ¦
<a href="/survey/index.html">Win a T-Shirt</a> ¦
<a href="/general/support/index.html">Talk to Us</a>  ¦
<a href="/online/vendors">Advertisers</a>  ¦
<a href="/macpub/site_map.html">Site Map</a> ¦
<a href="/index.html">SuperLibrary Home</a>
</font>
</center>
<BR>
<font size="3">
Welcome to Macmillan Publishing USA, home of the world's largest computer book
publisher, the reference division of Simon & Schuster and the publishing
operation of Viacom Inc. Examples of Macmillan's most popular brands include
```

```
Betty Crocker,
Frommer's, Weight Watcher's, Que, Sams, Burpee, Lasser, Arco, and Webster's
New World. Here's where you'll find the right tools, topics and references
➥for all of your needs. Enjoy!
</font>
<p>
<p>
<b>Our Newest Releases</b><br>
<center>
<APPLET codebase="/mgr" code="NavigatorTicker11.class" width="475" height="28">
<PARAM name="count" value="20">
<PARAM name="msg0" value=" Late Night ActiveX -- \\http://
➥www.superlibrary.com/cgi-bin/bag?isbn=1-56276-448-9&last=/bookstore">
<PARAM name="msg1" value=" LightWave Power Guide -- \\http://
➥www.superlibrary.com/cgi-bin/bag?isbn=1-56205-633-6&last=/bookstore">
<PARAM name="msg2" value=" Kids Do the Web -- \\http://www.superlibrary.com/
➥cgi-bin/bag?isbn=1-56830-315-7&last=/bookstore">
<PARAM name="msg3" value=" Inside JavaScript -- \\http://www.superlibrary.com/
➥cgi-bin/bag?isbn=1-56205-593-3&last=/bookstore">
<PARAM name="msg4" value=" The Official Gamelan Java Directory --
➥\\http://www.superlibrary.com/cgi-bin/bag?
➥isbn=1-56276-449-7&last=/bookstore">
<PARAM name="msg5" value=" Laura Lemay's Web Workshop: Microsoft FrontPage --
➥\\http://www.superlibrary.com/cgi-bin/bag?
➥isbn=1-57521-149-1&last=/bookstore">
<PARAM name="msg6" value=" Deconstructing Web Graphics  -- \\http:
➥//www.superlibrary.com/cgi-bin/bag?isbn=1-56205-641-7&last=/bookstore">
<PARAM name="msg7" value=" Most Popular Web Sites -- \\http://www.
➥superlibrary.com/cgi-bin/bag?isbn=0-7897-0792-6&last=/bookstore">
<PARAM name="msg8" value=" Internet Games Directory  -- \\http://www.
➥superlibrary.com/cgi-bin/bag?isbn=0-7897-1055-2&last=/bookstore">
<PARAM name="msg9" value=" Microsoft Certified Professional Visual Basic 4.0
➥Exam Guide -- \\http://www.superlibrary.com/cgi-bin/bag?
➥isbn=0-7897-0864-7&last=/bookstore">
<PARAM name="msg10" value=" Killing Time -- \\http://www.superlibrary.com/
➥cgi-bin/bag?isbn=0-02-861340-6&last=/bookstore">
<PARAM name="msg11" value="  The Baseball Encyclopedia and CD-ROM -- \\http://
➥www.superlibrary.com/cgi-bin/bag?isbn=0-02-861435-6&last=/bookstore">
<PARAM name="msg12" value=" Betty Crocker's New Cookbook -- \\http://www.
➥superlibrary.com/cgi-bin/bag?isbn=0-02-860395-8&last=/bookstore">
<PARAM name="msg13" value=" Frommer's Europe from $50 a Day '97 -- \\http:
➥//www.superlibrary.com/cgi-bin/bag?isbn=0-02-860635-3&last=/bookstore">
<PARAM name="msg14" value=" J.K. Lasser's your Income Tax 1997 -- \\http:
➥//www.superlibrary.com/cgi-bin/bag?isbn=0-02-861381-3&last=/bookstore">
<PARAM name="msg15" value=" The Complete Idiot's Guide to Writing The Perfect
➥Resume  -- \\http://www.superlibrary.com/cgi-bin/bag?
➥isbn=0-02-861093-8&last=/bookstore">
<PARAM name="msg16" value=" The Complete Idiot's Guide to Etiquette -- \\http:
➥//www.superlibrary.com/cgi-bin/bag?isbn=0-02-861094-6&last=/bookstore">
<PARAM name="msg17" value=" Webster's New World Dictionary and Thesaurus --
➥\\http://www.superlibrary.com/cgi-bin/bag?
➥isbn=0-02-861318-X&last=/bookstore">
<PARAM name="msg18" value=" The Complete Dog Book -- \\http://www.
➥superlibrary.com/cgi-bin/bag?isbn=0-87605-464-5&last=/bookstore">
<PARAM name="msg19" value=" LSAT Supercourse with Tests on Disk  -- \\http:
➥//www.superlibrary.com/cgi-bin/bag?isbn=0-02-861311-2&last=/bookstore">
<PARAM name="speed" value="7">
<PARAM name="txtco" value="0,0,0">
```

continues

Listing 25.1. continued

```
<PARAM name="bgco" value="255,255,255">
<PARAM name="linkco" value="180,25,21"></APPLET>
</center>
</td>
</tr>
<tr>
<!--BEGIN WIDE MIDDLE COLUMN-->
<td width="340" valign="top" align="left">
<BR><BR>
<B>Browse our books by subject:</B><br>
<FORM method = "POST" action = "/cgi-bin/find-books.cgi"  >
<select NAME="search_term">
<option selected>American Studies
<option>Authors
<option>Business
<option>CD-ROM Software
<option>Computers
<option>Cooking
<option>Dictionaries
<option>Education
<option>Fiction
<option>Filmmakers
<option>Finance
<option>Fine Arts
<option>Gardening
<option>Health and Self Improvement
<option>History
<option>Humor
<option>Literary Themes and Genres
<option>Literature
<option>Masterwork Studies
<option>Music
<option>Personal Finance
<option>Pets
<option>Piano
<option>Professional
<option>Reference
<option>Religion and Philosophy
<option>Science
<option>Social
<option>Sports
<option>Test Preparation
<option>Theatre/Film/Dance
<option>Travel
<option>Vocal/Choral
</select>
<input type="hidden" name="by_some" value="by_subject">
<input type="hidden" name="and_or" value="as_and">
<input type="hidden" name="home_page" value="">
<input type=submit value="Go to">
</form>
<p>
<BR>
<!--BEGIN FEATURES-->
<!-- nov-15: -->
<!-- nov-11:CIG to Perfect Resume -->
<img src="/general/pix/mgr_pix/610938c.gif" align="left" border="1"
```

```
hspace="5" width="95" height="125">
<a href="/cgi-bin/bag?isbn=0-02-861093-8&last=/bookstore">
<B><font size="+1">The Complete Idiot's Guide to Writing the Perfect Resume
➥</font></b></a><p>
<font size="3">
<B>
By Susan Ireland</b>
<P>
This step-by-step guide features resume templates for various industries, networ
king strategies, and resume writing tips. Click on the topics below to see
examples of "resume tips" excerpted from the book:
<ul>
<LI><A href="/mgr/business/tip1.html">TIP 1:</a> Your Resume is About Your
➥ Future, Not Your
Past
<LI><a href="/mgr/business/tip2.html">TIP 2:</a> Dates... How Far Back to Go
➥on Your Resume
<LI><a href="/mgr/business/tip3.html">TIP 3:</a> Resume Scanning: Who's
➥Reading Your
Resume?
</ul>
<a href="http://www.superlibrary.com/cgi-bin/placeorder?express=0-02-861093-8">
<font size="2">[ORDER NOW]</font></a>
<br clear="all"><hr><!-- nov-19: -->
<!-- nov-14:SuperSeek -->
<a href="/superseek"><img src="/general/pix/features/superseek.gif" border="0">
➥<b><font size="+1">Super search using SuperSeek</font></b></a>
<p>
Can't find what you're looking for? Use the Internet's "card catalog".
     Using our metasearch SuperSeek you can
     search the Information SuperLibrary Bookstore, USENET
     internet news archives and the Internet's most popular search
     engines, including Deja News, Excite, Inktomi, New Riders
     World Wide Web Yellow Pages, Lycos, the Magellan,
     Yahoo, and Infoseek.
<!--END FEATURES-->
<hr>
<BR>
<BR>
<BR>
<center>
<table>
<tr>
<td>
<A HREF="http://rs.internic.net/scout/report">
<IMG SRC="/general/pix/scoutsel.gif" border="0" ALT="Scout
Report Selection" valign="top"></A></td><td>
<a href="http://bx.com"><img alt= "bx.com" border=0 src="/general/pix/
➥macpub_pix/bxaward.gif"></a>
</td>
</tr>
</table></CENTER>
<P>
<P>
<P>
<center>
<font size="2">
<i>
```

continues

Listing 25.1. continued

```
<BR><BR><BR>
<center>
<font size="2">
<i>For comments or technical support for our books and software,
select <A HREF = "/general/support/index.html"  >Talk to Us</A>.
<br>
&#169; 1997, Macmillan Publishing USA, a
Simon &amp; Schuster Company.
</i>
</font>
</center>
</i>
</font>
</center>
</td>
<!--BEGIN VERTICAL RULE COLUMN-->
<td width="15" valign="top" align="center">
<P>
<BR>
<img src="/general/pix/macpub_pix/yelbox.gif" height="900" width="1">
</td>
<!--BEGIN RIGHT NARROW COLUMN-->
<td width="120" align="left" VALIGN="TOP">
<!--VERTICAL SPACER-->
<BR><BR>
<img src="/general/pix/macpub_pix/update_mpu.gif" alt="Updates" width="100"
➥ height="30">
<a href="/general/whats_new/">
<B>
What's New</a></b><BR>
Keep up with our latest online features.
<p>
<a href="/cgi-bin/find-books.cgi?category=New+Releases">
<B>
New Releases</a></b><BR>
The latest releases from Macmillan, available now in our <a href="/bookstore
➥/do-bookstore.html">online bookstore</a>.
<P>
<a href="/general/news17/">
<B>
The Information SuperLibrary&#153; Newsletter</a></b><br>
Features, contests, columns,computing and entertainment from Macmillan
➥Publishing.
<P>
<a href="/nrp/wwwyp/index.html">
<B>
New Riders Official WWW Yellow Pages</a></b><br>
The premiere business directory for the Net.
<P>

<a href="/sales_prog/sales.htm">
<B>
Sales Programs</a></b><br>
Opportunities for retailers, resellers, government, education, and corporate
➥customers.
<P>
<a href="/refdesk/reqform.html">
<B>
```

```
Mailing Lists</a></b><BR>
Get updates on the newest books from Macmillan.
<P>
<a href="/superseek/index.cgi">
<B>
SuperSeek</a></b><BR>
A meta-search for the Internet's most popular search engines.
<P>
<a href="/authors/events/">
<B>
Author Events</a></b><BR>
Online conferences and book signings by Macmillan's authors.
<P>
<a href="/general/jobs">
<B>
Job Openings at Macmillan</a></b><BR>
We're looking for a few good people.
</td>
</tr>
</table>
</body>
</html>
```

Tags are most often used in pairs. These tags, which specify certain features that the HTML engine understands, begin with a less-than (<) sign and end with a greater-than (>) sign. Also, the closing tag, which specifies the bottom of the set of instructions that encompasses the tag, is indicated by the forward slash (/). Notice that there is a set of tags that encompasses the entire area of the source code, sometimes referred to as a script. The script begins with the line

```
<html>
```

and ends with the line

```
</html>
```

This specifies which language engine to use. Theoretically, you can use any interpretive language. Everything in the middle of this is the HTML script used to build the page. Notice that the tags are used in pairs. Everywhere throughout this chapter, it is to be understood that a tag is used in pairs, unless explicitly denoted otherwise.

Testing HTML

You can test HTML in MSIE itself. You do not need to be connected to the Internet. You can simply specify the HTML file. Suppose you had a file called `WELCOME.HTM`. You could open it in MSIE by typing the address field

```
file://c:\welcome.htm
```

or just simply

```
c:\welcome.htm
```

This enables the HTML engine to process this page only. The HTML source code used for this test is shown in Listing 25.2.

Listing 25.2. HTML source code used in this example.

```
<html>
<head><title>Welcome to my web page</title>
<body>
This is my web page!
</body>
</head>
</html>
```

Figure 25.2 shows how to test the HTML in MSIE, using the HTML source code from Listing 25.2.

FIGURE 25.2.
Testing your HTML.

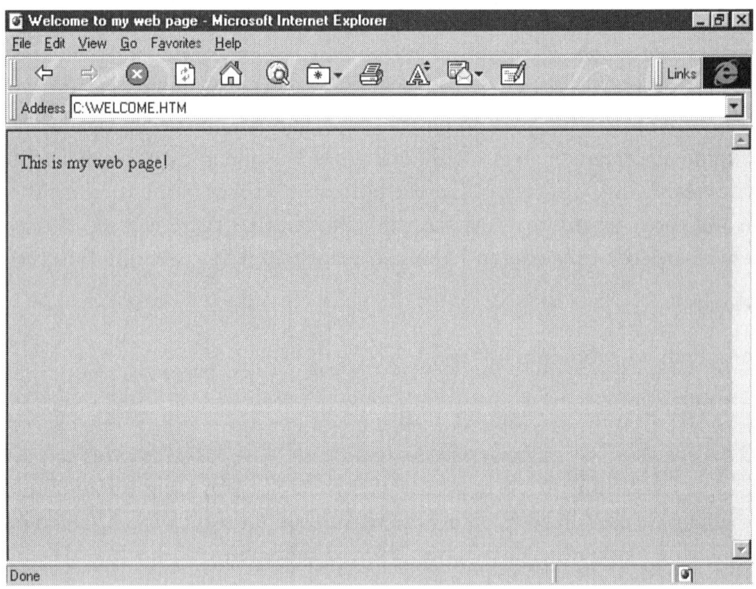

Notice the title specified is in the title bar of MSIE. The body of the page is displayed between the body tags.

HTML Syntax

The following sections describe how to use the most common features of HTML.

Headings

Headings are specified by <Hx> tags, where *x* is the number of the tag, between 1 and 6. This indicates the font size and amount of bold used in the heading text. 1 is the biggest and uses the most bold text, and 6 is the smallest and uses the least bold. The source code for this example is shown in Listing 25.3.

Listing 25.3. HTML headings.

```
<html>
<head><title>Welcome to my web page</title>
<body>
<H1>This is my web page, Heading 1!</H1>
<H2>This is my web page, Heading 2!</H2>
<H3>This is my web page, Heading 3!</H3>
<H4>This is my web page, Heading 4!</H4>
<H5>This is my web page, Heading 5!</H5>
<H6>This is my web page, Heading 6!</H6>
</body>
</head>
```

Figure 25.3 shows the difference between the various types of headings, using the HTML source from Listing 25.3.

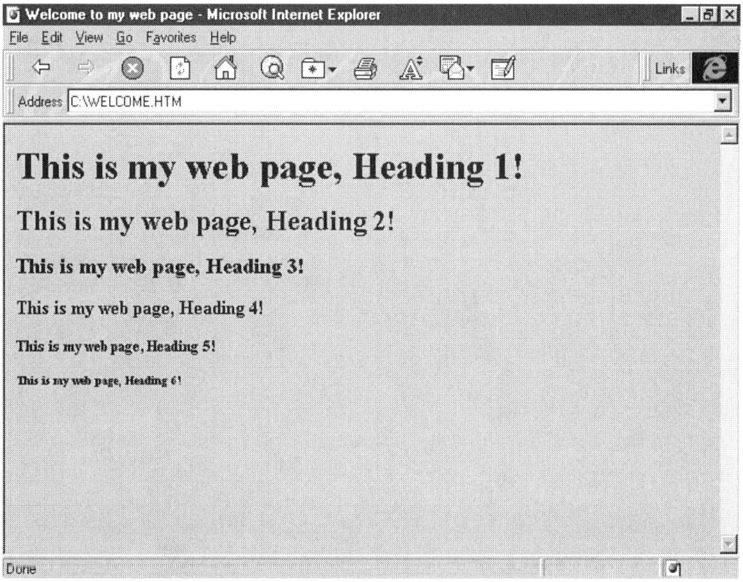

FIGURE 25.3.
Different headings.

Paragraphs

Paragraphs are specified by <P> tags and mark the beginning and ending of a paragraph. The source code used to show paragraph tags is shown in Listing 25.4.

Listing 25.4. HTML paragraph tags.

```
<html>
<head><title>Welcome to my web page</title>
<body>
<H1>This is my web page, Heading 1!</H1>
<P>
It is really cool the way that the HTML is so easy to use in the browser.
</P>
<P>
It is also really cool that it can be edited in a text editor, such as notepad.
</P>
</body>
</head>
```

There is no limit to the number of <P> tags you use; however, they must be terminated with a </P> tag. Figure 25.4 shows the results of using the HTML source from Listing 25.4. Notice that there is no extra carriage return/line feed after the first paragraph. It was placed in the browser automatically.

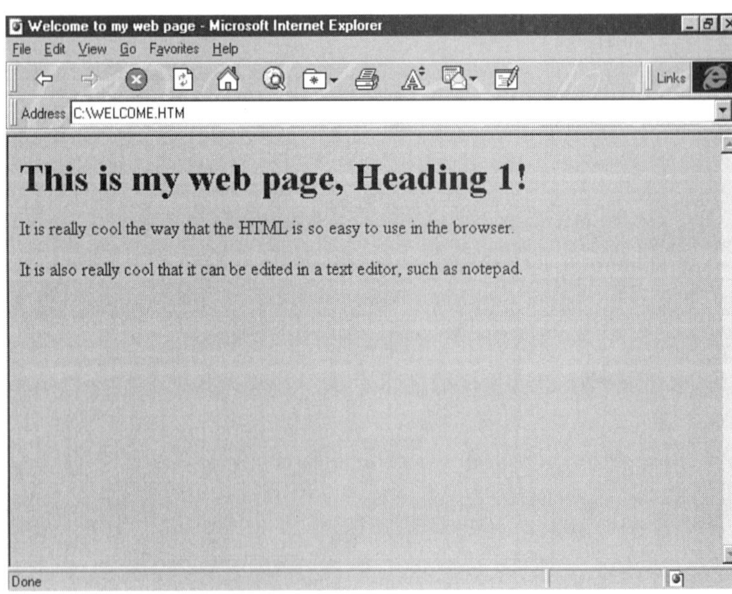

FIGURE 25.4.
Paragraphs.

Emphasis

You can emphasize text placed in your HTML document in several ways. For example, you can use any of the following pairs of tags:

- `<B></B>` for bold typeface.
- `<I></I>` for italic typeface.
- `<EM></EM>` for emphasized typeface. (This may differ on other browsers.)
- `<STRONG></STRONG>` for stronger text (bold). (This may differ on other browsers.)

The source code used to illustrate emphasis is shown in Listing 25.5.

Listing 25.5. HTML emphasis tags.

```
<html>
<head><title>Welcome to my web page</title>
<body>
<H1>This is my web page, Heading 1!</H1>
<P>
It is really <B>cool</B> the way that the <I>HTML</I> is so easy to use in the
➥ browser.
</P>
<P>
It is also <EM>really</EM> cool that it can be edited in a text editor,
➥<STRONG>such as notepad</STRONG>.
</P>
</body>
</head>
```

Figure 25.5 shows the results of using the HTML source from Listing 25.5. It shows all of the tags discussed. You should use the `<EM>` or `<STRONG>` tags if you do not know the browser's capabilities because if the browser doesn't have the capability to display bold, for example, the `<STRONG>` tag will at least offer some type of display to offset the text. The `<BOLD>` tag, if it is not supported, is ignored.

Lists

You can organize the text placed in your HTML document into lists in several ways. For example, you can use any of the following pairs of tags:

- `<OL></OL>` specifies a numbered (ordered) list.
- `<UL></UL>` specifies a bulleted (unordered) list.
- `<LI>` identifies an item in the list. (This is not used in pairs.)

The source code used to illustrate lists is shown in Listing 25.6.

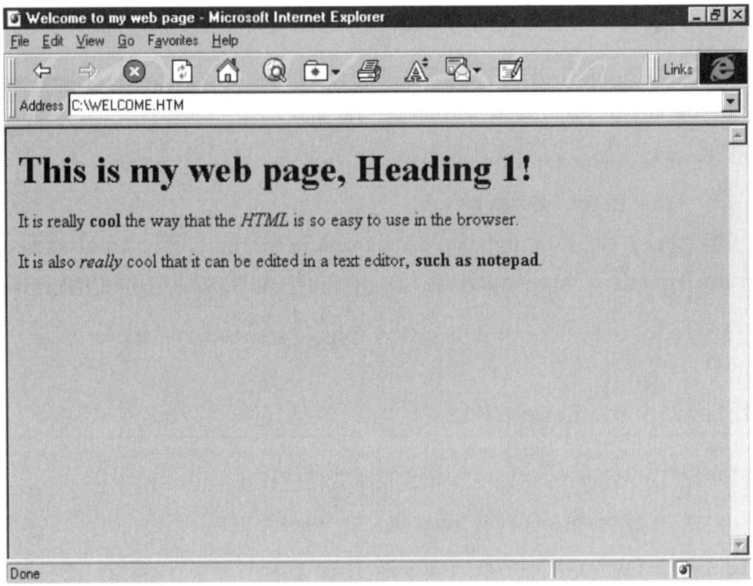

FIGURE 25.5.
Emphasis.

Listing 25.6. HTML lists.

```
<html>
<head><title>Welcome to my web page</title>
<body>
<H1>This is my web page, Heading 1!</H1>
<P>
It is really <B>cool</B> the way that the <I>HTML</I> is so easy to use in the
➥ browser.
</P>
<P>
It is also <EM>really</EM> cool that it can be edited in a text editor,
➥<STRONG>such as notepad</STRONG>.
</P>
<P>
The browser supports lists, like this:
<UL>
<LI>Specifying an unordered list #1
<LI>Specifying an unordered list #2
<LI>Specifying an unordered list #3
</UL>
<OL>
<LI>Specifying an ordered list #1
<LI>Specifying an ordered list #2
<LI>Specifying an ordered list #3
</OL>
</P>
</body>
</head>
```

Figure 25.6 shows the result of using the HTML source code from Listing 25.6. It shows all of the tags discussed.

FIGURE 25.6.
Lists.

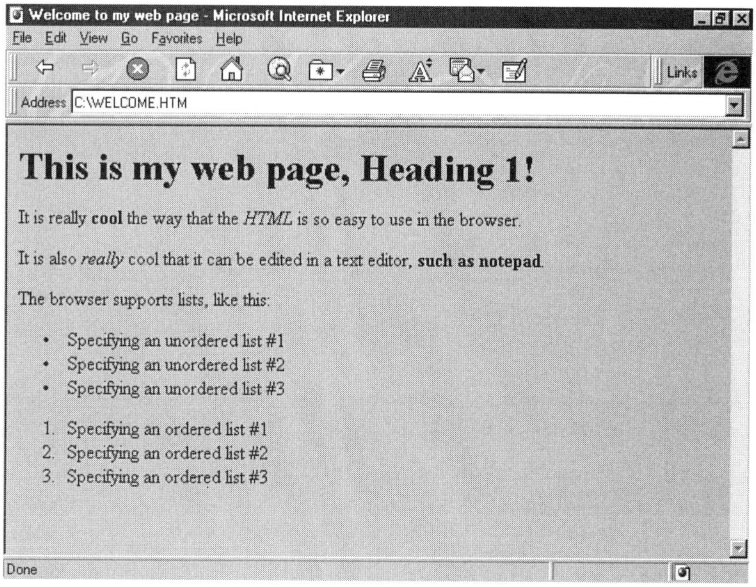

Aligning Text

You can automatically align the text placed in your HTML document. Aligning text consists of using an HTML attribute, not a tag, which means that the attribute is specified with the tag. You can use any of the following attributes:

- `ALIGN=CENTER` centers the text within the tag.
- `ALIGN=RIGHT` right-justifies the text within the tag.

Note that there is no left justification because the text is always left justified, unless specified otherwise. Suppose you wanted to center the heading but make one of the paragraphs right justified. This is shown in Listing 25.7.

Listing 25.7. Aligning text.

```
<html>
<head><title>Welcome to my web page</title>
<body>
<H1 ALIGN=CENTER>This is my web page, Heading 1!</H1>
<P>
It is really <B>cool</B> the way that the <I>HTML</I> is so easy to use in the
➥ browser.
</P>
```

continues

Listing 25.7. continued

```
<P ALIGN=RIGHT>
It is also <EM>really</EM> cool that it can be edited in a text editor,
➥<STRONG>such as notepad</STRONG>.
</P>
<P>
The browser supports lists, like this:
<UL>
<LI>Specifying an unordered list #1
<LI>Specifying an unordered list #2
<LI>Specifying an unordered list #3
</UL>
<OL>
<LI>Specifying an ordered list #1
<LI>Specifying an ordered list #2
<LI>Specifying an ordered list #3
</OL>
</P>
</body>
</head>
```

Figure 25.7 shows the result of using the HTML source code from Listing 25.7. Notice the left and right justification.

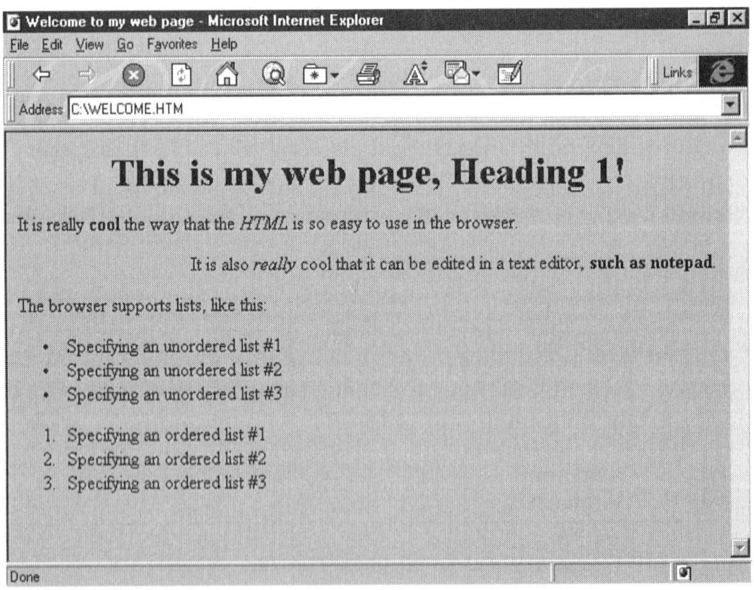

FIGURE 25.7.
Aligning text.

Backgrounds

You can add a background to your HTML document; the background can be a color or an image. To add a background, you use an HTML attribute, not a tag, which means that the attribute is specified with the tag. These specific attributes are specified in the `<body>` tag. You can use any of the following attributes:

- `BGCOLOR=#`*`rrggbb`* indicates a specific color using the red, green, and blue hexadecimal equivalents.
- `BACKGROUND=`*`image`* (where *`image`* is a specific image to be used).

If you want to specify a background color, it might be helpful for you to consult the Visual Basic constants for colors. For example, the constant `vbYellow` has a value of `0xFFFF`. You simply leave out the `0x` in the hexadecimal value. You can also specify a background image. Notice in the following listing that the `TARGET.GIF` file is specified as being a `file:` protocol. This means that it gets the image from disk, instead of another Web page or some other place. This particular image is taken from FrontPage. Each is shown in Listing 25.8. You can also change the colors of your text by specifying the RGB values of the text in your other tags. For example, if you want to change the color of a paragraph, you can specify these attributes in the `<P>` tag. This shows how to change the colors; however, links are discussed later. These attributes are as follows:

- `TEXT=#`*`rrggbb`* indicates a specific color for the body text using the red, green, and blue hexadecimal equivalents.
- `LINK=#`*`rrggbb`* indicates a specific color of a link using the red, green, and blue hexadecimal equivalents.
- `ALINK=#`*`rrggbb`* indicates a specific color of an active link using the red, green, and blue hexadecimal equivalents.
- `VLINK=#`*`rrggbb`* indicates a specific color of a visited link using the red, green, and blue hexadecimal equivalents.

Listing 25.8. HTML backgrounds.

```
<html>
<head><title>Welcome to my web page</title>
<body BGCOLOR=FFFF BACKGROUND=file:\TARGET.GIF>
<H1 ALIGN=CENTER>This is my web page, Heading 1!</H1>
<P>
It is really <B>cool</B> the way that the <I>HTML</I> is so easy to use in the
➥ browser.
</P>
<P ALIGN=RIGHT>
It is also <EM>really</EM> cool that it can be edited in a text editor,
➥ <STRONG>such as notepad</STRONG>.
</P>
<P>
```

continues

Listing 25.8. continued

```
The browser supports lists, like this:
<UL>
<LI>Specifying an unordered list #1
<LI>Specifying an unordered list #2
<LI>Specifying an unordered list #3
</UL>
<OL>
<LI>Specifying an ordered list #1
<LI>Specifying an ordered list #2
<LI>Specifying an ordered list #3
</OL>
</P>
</body>
</head>
```

Figure 25.8 shows the results of using the HTML source code from Listing 25.8. It shows how to include backgrounds. Note that in the `<body>` tag, a background color as well as an image is specified. Because the image is specified last, it takes precedence. It is left in for the purpose of the example.

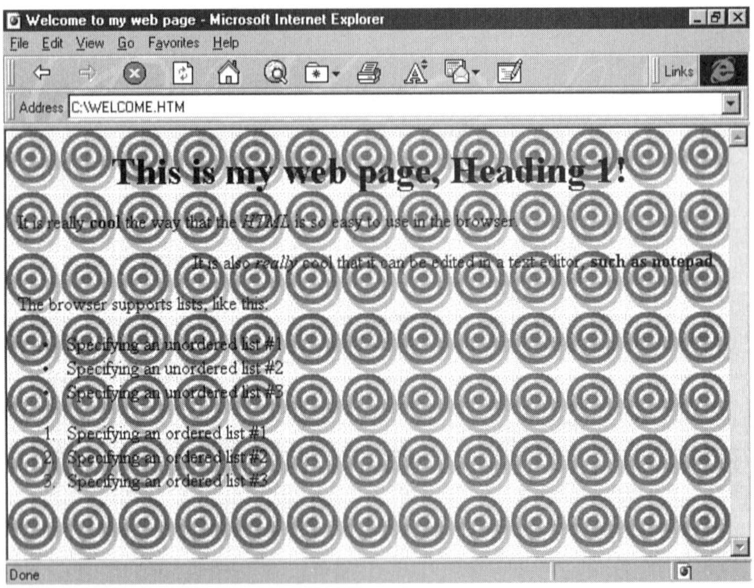

FIGURE 25.8.
HTML backgrounds.

Images

Images are one of the most popular types of data to display on a Web page. It is just as easy to display an image as it is to do anything else in HTML. Adding an image consists of adding an `<IMG>` tag. This tag is not used in pairs. You can then specify attributes of the `<IMG>` tag. For example, you can use any of the following attributes:

- `SRC=`*`image`* where *`image`* specifies the actual image to use.
- `ALT=`*`text`* where *`text`* is the text that should be displayed in the image box while the image is not present.
- `BORDER=`*`n`* where *`n`* is the number of pixels to use in the border.

You can specify any or all of the attributes wherever you want to place the `<IMG>` tag. Each attribute is shown in Listing 25.9.

Listing 25.9. HTML images.

```
<html>
<head><title>Welcome to my web page</title>
<body>
<H1 ALIGN=CENTER>This is my web page, Heading 1!</H1>
<P>
<IMG SRC=file:\Target.gif ALT=Target1 BORDER=5>
It is really <B>cool</B> the way that the <I>HTML</I> is so easy to use in the
➥ browser.
</P>
<P>
<IMG SRC=file:\Target.gif ALT=Target2 BORDER=5>
It is also <EM>really</EM> cool that it can be edited in a text editor,
➥<STRONG>such as notepad</STRONG>.
</P>
<P>
The browser supports lists, like this:
<UL>
<LI>Specifying an unordered list #1
<LI>Specifying an unordered list #2
<LI>Specifying an unordered list #3
</UL>
<OL>
<LI>Specifying an ordered list #1
<LI>Specifying an ordered list #2
<LI>Specifying an ordered list #3
</OL>
</P>
</body>
</head>
```

Figure 25.9 shows the result of using the HTML source code from Listing 25.9. It shows how to include images as well as how to place an image before the text in a paragraph.

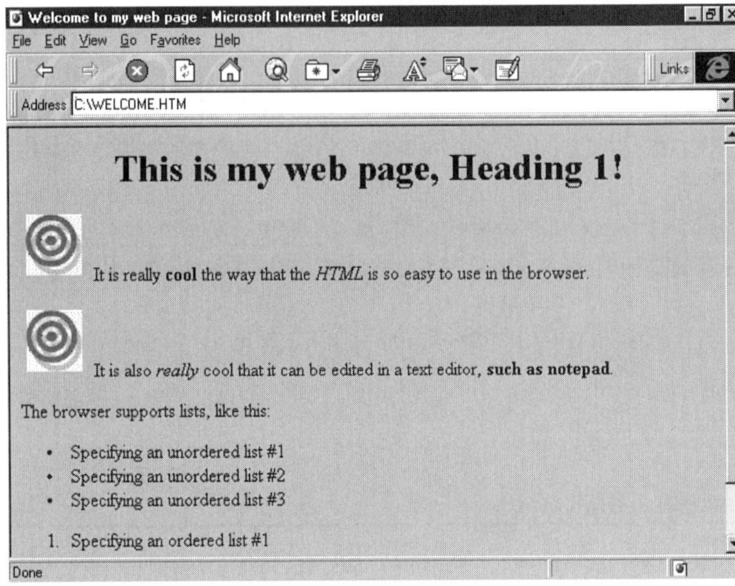

FIGURE 25.9.
HTML images.

Anchors and Links

Very few Web pages do not include some type of link, either to another page, internally to its own Web site, or to some other Web site. A link contains two main parts. One is called an anchor, which is a pair of tags, marked by `<A>` and `</A>`. An anchor is to a Web page what a line label is to Visual Basic: it's a way to label a specific part in your HTML documents. The other part is called the attributes. You can specify these attributes of the `<A>` tag using either of the following:

- `HREF=`*`reference`* where *`reference`* is the Internet uniform resource locator (URL) or reference within the same page.
- `NAME=`*`label`* where *`label`* is the name of an internal anchor so that users don't have to scroll down a long document.

You can specify either of these attributes wherever you want to place the `<A>` tag. Both are shown in Listing 25.10. This code illustrates the use of these attributes by specifying an anchor in the text at the bottom of the page and a link to that text at the top of the page.

Listing 25.10. HTML links.

```
<html>
<head><title>Welcome to my web page</title>
<body>
<H1 ALIGN=CENTER>This is my web page, Heading 1!</H1>
<P>
<A HREF=#List3>
```

```
Link to Ordered List #3
</A>
</P>
<P>
<IMG SRC=file:\Target.gif ALT=Target1 BORDER=5>
It is really <B>cool</B> the way that the <I>HTML</I> is so easy to use in the
➥ browser.
</P>
<P>
<IMG SRC=file:\Target.gif ALT=Target2 BORDER=5>
It is also <EM>really</EM> cool that it can be edited in a text editor,
➥<STRONG>such as notepad</STRONG>.
</P>
<P>
The browser supports lists, like this:
<UL>
<LI>Specifying an unordered list #1
<LI>Specifying an unordered list #2
<LI>Specifying an unordered list #3
</UL>
<OL>
<LI>Specifying an ordered list #1
<LI>Specifying an ordered list #2
<A NAME=List3>
<LI>Specifying an ordered list #3
</A>
</OL>
</P>
</body>
</head>
```

It is important to note that MSIE anchors are case sensitive. Therefore, `#LIST3` is not the same as `#List3`. Also, if you do not include the pound (#) sign, this feature will not work. It is used to specify an internal link to an anchor. Figure 25.10 shows the result of using the HTML source from Listing 25.10. It shows how to include images as well as how to place an image before the text in a paragraph.

Visual Effects

There are many visual effects you can include in your Web page, such as breaks and lines. You can use any of the following tags:

- `<BR>` for a line break, similar to carriage return/line feed. This is not used in pairs.
- `<HR>` places a horizontal line on the page.

Furthermore, the `<HR>` tag can have attributes specified that will control the behavior of the tag. You can use any of the following attributes:

- `SIZE=n` where *n* specifies the thickness of the line. 2 is the default.
- `WIDTH=n` where *n* is either the number of pixels or the percentage of the document width that the line should be in width. The document width is the default.

- ALIGN=*placement* where *placement* is either LEFT, CENTER, or RIGHT. CENTER is the default.

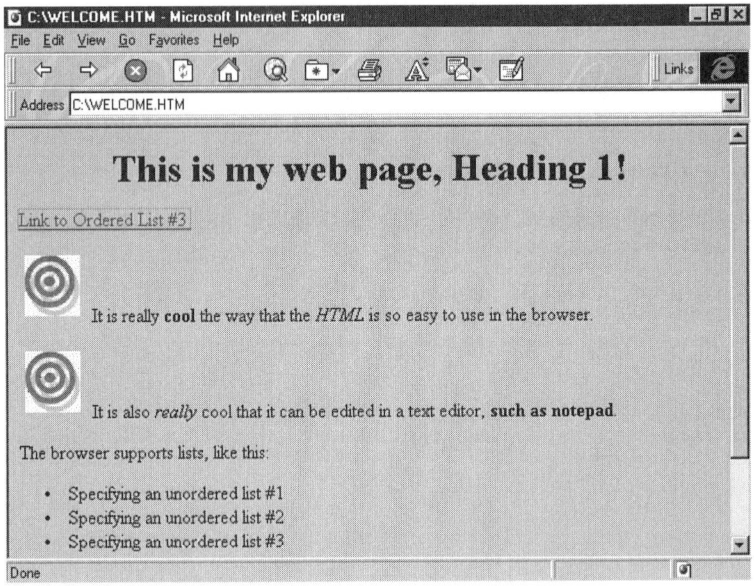

FIGURE 25.10.
HTML links.

Using the <BR> tag will force a carriage return in the text. This can be very important because, if you do not use them, the text is automatically wrapped within the client area of the browser. Therefore, it can break differently based on its font, resolution, window position, and other factors.

You can specify any or all of the attributes wherever you want to place the <HR> tag. Each is shown in Listing 25.11. This code illustrates the use of both line breaks (carriage returns) and horizontal lines.

Listing 25.11. Visual effects.

```
<html>
<head><title>Welcome to my web page</title>
<body>
<H1 ALIGN=CENTER>This is my web page, Heading 1!</H1>
<P>
<A HREF=#List3>
Link to Ordered List #3
</A>
</P>
<P>
<IMG SRC=file:\Target.gif ALT=Target1 BORDER=5>
It is really <B>cool</B> the way that<BR>the <I>HTML</I> is so easy to use in
➥ the browser.
</P>
```

```
<HR SIZE=3 WIDTH=75%>
<P>
<IMG SRC=file:\Target.gif ALT=Target2 BORDER=5>
It is also <EM>really</EM> cool that it can be edited in a text editor,
➥<STRONG>such as notepad</STRONG>.
</P>
<P>
The browser supports lists, like this:
<UL>
<LI>Specifying an unordered list #1
<LI>Specifying an unordered list #2
<LI>Specifying an unordered list #3
</UL>
<OL>
<LI>Specifying an ordered list #1
<LI>Specifying an ordered list #2
<A NAME=List3>
<LI>Specifying an ordered list #3
</A>
</OL>
</P>
</body>
</head>
```

Figure 25.11 shows the result of using the HTML source code from Listing 25.11. It shows a forced line break (<BR>)and a horizontal line with a size of 3 and the width as 75 percent of the document width.

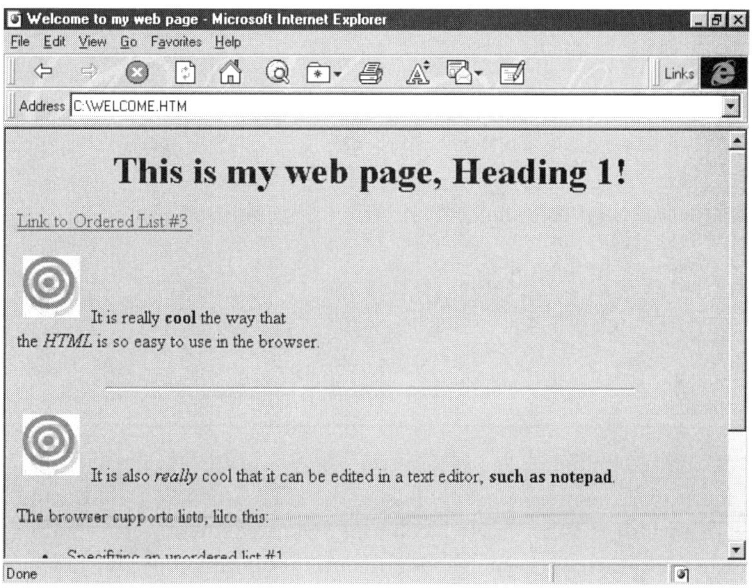

FIGURE 25.11.
HTML links.

Tables

Tables play an important part in HTML. Text alone is nice, but today, many things need to be displayed in a table format, such as price lists. You can use the following tags with tables:

- <TABLE></TABLE> indicates a table.
- <TR></TR> specifies a complete row in a table.
- <TD></TD> specifies where a column is broken within a row.

Suppose you wanted to create a table showing three product items and their prices. This is shown in Listing 25.12.

Listing 25.12. Creating tables.

```
It is really <B>cool</B> the way that<BR>the <I>HTML</I> is so easy to use in
➥ the browser.
</P>
<HR SIZE=3 WIDTH=75%>
<P>
<IMG SRC=file:\Target.gif ALT=Target2 BORDER=5>
It is also <EM>really</EM> cool that it can be edited in a text editor,
➥<STRONG>such as notepad</STRONG>.
</P>
<TABLE BORDER=1>
<TR><TD>P001</TD><TD ALIGN=RIGHT>$5000.00</TD></TR>
<TR><TD>P002</TD><TD ALIGN=RIGHT>$2500.00<TD></TR>
<TR><TD>Z001</TD><TD ALIGN=RIGHT>$20.95<TD></TR>
</TABLE>
<P>
The browser supports lists, like this:
<UL>
<LI>Specifying an unordered list #1
<LI>Specifying an unordered list #2
<LI>Specifying an unordered list #3
</UL>
<OL>
<LI>Specifying an ordered list #1
<LI>Specifying an ordered list #2
<A NAME=List3>
<LI>Specifying an ordered list #3
</A>
</OL>
</P>
</body>
</head>
```

Figure 25.12 shows the result of using the HTML source from Listing 25.12. It builds a table with a width of 1 that has two columns and three rows. You can combine attributes discussed earlier in this chapter (such as alignment, for example).

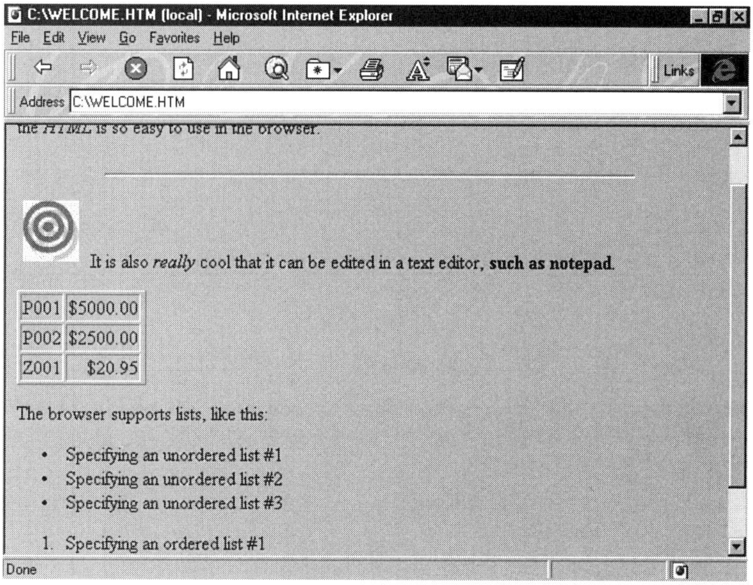

FIGURE 25.12.
Creating HTML tables.

Forms

Forms are used widely to solicit input from users in order to perform some action. The following pages are used to show the development of a form that can be used to send data to a database.

Creating Forms

An HTML form is very similar to a form in Visual Basic, except that you cannot drag and drop controls onto the form. A form must be denoted as such in your code with the `<FORM></FORM>` tags. This indicates where the form starts and stops. You must create the controls in your HTML scripts. There is one specific tag that you can use to create forms: the `<INPUT>` tag. (Note that it is not used in pairs.) Use the `<INPUT>` tag to specify a form object. The way that it knows what type of object to create, such as a text box or a command button, is by an attribute called `TYPE`. The different attributes available are as follows:

- `SIZE=`*`n`* where *`n`* specifies the number of characters.
- `MAXLENGTH=`*`n`* where *`n`* is the number of characters to allow in the field.
- `CHECKED` indicates whether this item is selected by default for a check box or radio button.
- `NAME=`*`val`* where *`val`* is the name of the field.
- `PROMPT=`*`pmt`* where *`pmt`* is the message to appear before a text field.

- `TYPE=t` where *t* is the type of input field. *t* can be `text`, `password`, `check box`, `radio`, `submit`, `reset`, and `hidden`.
- `VALUE=v` where *v* is the value of a button or a label for the type submit or reset.

The code in Listing 25.13 creates a form for submitting a request for information on a specific product. It utilizes many of the techniques outlined earlier, such as using tables and headings.

Listing 25.13. Creating forms with a table.

```
<html>
<head><title>Welcome to my web page</title>
<body>
<H1 ALIGN=CENTER>This is my web page, Heading 1!</H1>
<P>
If you would like information about a specific product, please fill out the
➥form below and click "Submit"
<FORM>
<TABLE BORDER=1>
<TR><TD><INPUT TYPE="CHECKBOX" NAME="chk1"></TD><TD>P001</TD><TD ALIGN=RIGHT>
➥$5000.00</TD></TR>
<TR><TD><INPUT TYPE="CHECKBOX" NAME="chk2"></TD><TD>P002</TD><TD ALIGN=RIGHT>
➥$2500.00<TD></TR>
<TR><TD><INPUT TYPE="CHECKBOX" NAME="chk3"></TD><TD>Z001</TD><TD ALIGN=RIGHT>
➥$20.95<TD></TR>
</TABLE>
<BR>
Name:<BR><INPUT TYPE="TEXT" NAME="text1" SIZE=50><BR>
Address:<BR><INPUT TYPE="TEXT" NAME="text2" SIZE=50><BR>
City:<BR><INPUT TYPE="TEXT" NAME="text3" SIZE=25>
State:  <INPUT TYPE="TEXT" NAME="text4" SIZE=2>
Zip:  <INPUT TYPE="TEXT" NAME="text5" SIZE=10><BR>
<INPUT TYPE="SUBMIT" NAME="Submit">
<INPUT TYPE="RESET" NAME="Reset">
</FORM>
</P>
</body>
</head>
```

Figure 25.13 shows the results of using the HTML source from Listing 25.13. It builds a form that enables you to select products from a table and input a name and address.

Additional Form Functionality

Many times you need to select from a list of possible values in a list box or a drop-down list box. Both of these are produced from a `<SELECT></SELECT>` tag. This tag has different attributes available, which are as follows:

- `SIZE=n` where *n* specifies the number of items.
- `MULTIPLE` indicates whether the select list can have multiple items selected.
- `NAME=val` where *val* is the name of the field.

- `<OPTION>` is a tag inside the `<SELECT>` tag that specifies different options and is used to encapsulate parameters for those options.
- `SELECTED` indicates whether this item is selected by default.
- `VALUE=v` where *v* is the value of a field.

FIGURE 25.13.
Creating HTML forms with tables.

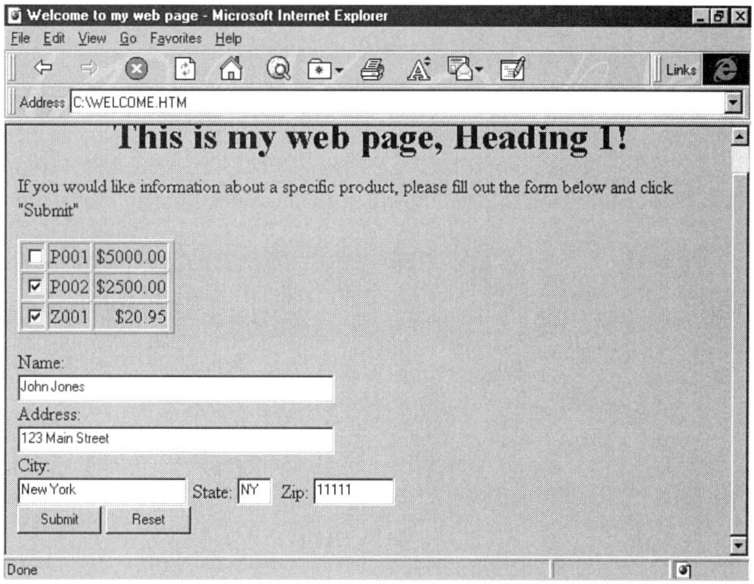

An alternative to listing items in a table is to place them in a selection list. A selection list is simply a list of items, one on each line. You can use the tags and attributes listed here to provide a selection list. Therefore, the code in Listing 25.14 creates a form for submitting a request for information on a specific product, but uses a selection list instead of a table.

Listing 25.14. Creating forms with a selection list.

```
<html>
<head><title>Welcome to my web page</title>
<body>
<H1 ALIGN=CENTER>This is my web page, Heading 1!</H1>
<P>
If you would like information about a specific product, please fill out the
➥form below and click "Submit"
<FORM>
<SELECT>
<OPTION VALUE=1>P001
<OPTION VALUE=2>P002
<OPTION VALUE=3>Z001
</SELECT>
<BR>
Name:<BR><INPUT TYPE="TEXT" NAME="text1" SIZE=50><BR>
```

continues

Listing 25.14. continued

```
Address:<BR><INPUT TYPE="TEXT" NAME="text2" SIZE=50><BR>
City:<BR><INPUT TYPE="TEXT" NAME="text3" SIZE=25>
State:  <INPUT TYPE="TEXT" NAME="text4" SIZE=2>
Zip:  <INPUT TYPE="TEXT" NAME="text5" SIZE=10><BR>
<INPUT TYPE="SUBMIT" NAME="Submit">
<INPUT TYPE="RESET" NAME="Reset">
</FORM>
</P>
</body>
</head>
```

Figure 25.14 shows the result of using the HTML source code from Listing 25.14. It builds a form that enables you to select products from a selection list and to input a name and address.

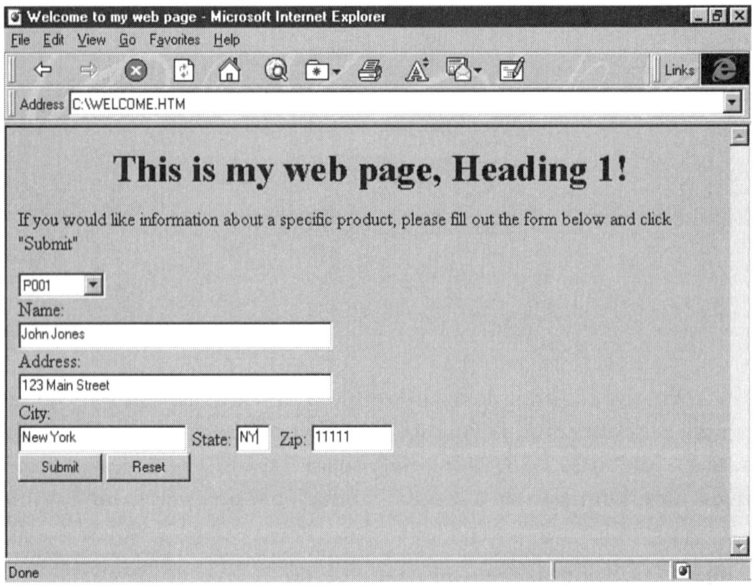

FIGURE 25.14.
Creating HTML forms with selection lists.

Summary

HTML is a very important part of the Internet because all browsers support it. You can create very attractive Web pages by using HTML. Therefore, it is very important to become familiar with HTML. This chapter gives a good overview of how HTML works.

Your Web pages can be enhanced greatly with the use of VBScript, which is a subset of the Visual Basic language for making interactive Web pages. VBScript is outside the scope of this book, but Sams Publishing has many good books on this subject.

One final note is that it is important to keep in mind that HTML is a very small part of the total Internet picture. Also, the Internet is rapidly changing, as is the HTML language itself. Because the Internet is such a hot topic, as a developer, it is very important to keep current.

26

MAPI and Microsoft Exchange

MAPI stands for *Messaging Application Programming Interface.* It is the basis for Microsoft Exchange and other MAPI-compliant systems. A MAPI-compliant system is a messaging system that complies with all of the specifications laid out by Microsoft to use the Messaging API. Messaging services are typically used in an office environment to enable PC users to send messages and files to each other electronically. To be able to do this, there must be some type of messaging server in place, such as Microsoft Exchange. The messaging server does the routing and holds the addresses for each of the users.

The front end can be any number of systems. Microsoft Exchange, for example, comes with a front end to enable a user to send and receive messages and files via the mail server. However, Microsoft Exchange as a front end can be limited because it is not programmable. With Visual Basic, you can include the MAPI control in your project and create a customized front end for the MAPI-compliant back-end server. This chapter shows you how to do this. The MAPI control comes only with the Professional and Enterprise Editions of Visual Basic.

MAPI Support Within Visual Basic

Although Windows includes an API that contains functions to access messaging services, called MAPI, there are two ActiveX controls included with Visual Basic, which makes accessing MAPI easier. They are

- MAPI Session
- MAPI Message

CROSS REFERENCE

For more information about using the MAPI Session and MAPI Message controls, refer to Chapter 36, "Developing a MAPI/Microsoft Exchange Application."

You use the MAPI Session control to establish a connection to a MAPI-compliant messaging system, such as Microsoft Exchange. You use the MAPI Message control to handle all aspects of messaging, such as sending and receiving e-mail and attachments. Creating the MAPI session consists of logging onto the MAPI-compliant system and returning a handle to that session. A *session* is the connection made by logging onto the MAPI-compliant system. The MAPI Message control is used to send and receive messages as well as all message-related functions.

CAUTION

If there is no MAPI-compliant system present on the PC and if you attempt to load or run an application that contains the MAPI controls, you receive an error because the controls themselves look for the MAPI components. If the components are not present, you cannot load or run the application. In Windows 95 and Windows NT, you must configure mail by setting up Microsoft Exchange.

NOTE

Earlier versions of Visual Basic used an `Action` property to invoke a MAPI function. Visual Basic 5.0 uses one method for each of the corresponding values to which the `Action` property can be assigned. Please note that for backward compatibility, Visual Basic 5.0 still supports the `Action` property. Table 26.1 shows which of the new methods correspond to the earlier `Action` properties, to help with backward compatibility.

Table 26.1. Corresponding `Action` properties to methods.

Action Property Setting	*Corresponding Method*
MESSAGE_FETCH	Fetch
MESSAGE_SENDDLG	Send
MESSAGE_SEND	Send
MESSAGE_SAVEMSG	Save
MESSAGE_COPY	Copy
MESSAGE_COMPOSE	Compose
MESSAGE_REPLY	Reply
MESSAGE_REPLYALL	ReplyAll
MESSAGE_FORWARD	Forward
MESSAGE_DELETE	Delete
MESSAGE_SHOWADBOOK	Show
MESSAGE_SHOWDETAILS	Show
MESSAGE_RESOLVENAME	ResolveName
RECIPIENT_DELETE	Delete
ATTACHMENT_DELETE	Delete
mapSignOn	SignOn
mapSignOff	SignOff

There are two types of MAPI functions: *simple* and *extended*. The simple MAPI functions are a set of functions that can handle most of the everyday messaging tasks and are a subset of the extended MAPI functions. Extended MAPI functions are available in Windows, provide extended capabilities, but are not included with the MAPI custom controls. The MAPI custom controls use simple MAPI functions only. You access these functions by specifying values for properties in the custom controls. Table 26.2 lists the simple MAPI functions and message types found in the Messaging API.

Table 26.2. Simple MAPI functions and message types.

Function	*Used For*
`MAPILogon()`	Begins a MAPI session.
`MAPIFindNext()`	Returns the ID of the next message of a specified type.
`MAPIReadMail()`	Reads a mail message.
`MAPISaveMail()`	Saves a mail message.
`MAPIDeleteMail()`	Deletes a mail message.
`MAPISendMail()`	Sends a mail message. Allows more flexibility than `MAPISendDocuments`.
`MAPISendDocuments()`	Sends a mail message using a dialog box.
`MAPIAddress()`	The address of the mail message.
`MAPIResolveName()`	Resolves incomplete name references.
`MAPIDetails()`	Dialog box showing message details.
`MAPILogoff()`	Ends a MAPI session.
`MapiFile()`	Message type containing file attachment information.
`MapiMessage()`	Message type containing message information.
`MapiRecip()`	Contains recipient information.

These MAPI functions are handled by the Visual Basic ActiveX controls. Table 26.3 lists the MAPI Session control's unique properties. Table 26.4 lists the MAPI Message control's unique properties.

Table 26.3. The MAPI Session control's unique properties.

Property	*Datatype*	*Used For*
`Action`	Integer	1-Logon, 2-Logoff (for backward compatibility)
`DownloadMail`	Boolean	Download messages upon logon if `True`
`LogonUI`	Boolean	Logon dialog box is displayed if `True`

Property	Datatype	Used For
NewSession	Boolean	Specifies a new session if True
Password	String	Password used to log on
SessionID	Long	Session handle
UserName	String	User name used to log on

Table 26.4. The MAPI Message control's unique properties.

Property	Datatype	Used For
Action	Integer	Specifies an action to take (for backward compatibility)
AddressCaption	String	Caption on address book window
AddressEditFieldCount	Integer	Specifies which controls to place on the address book
AddressLabel	String	Specifies the appearance of the "To" edit control in the address book
AddressModifiable	Boolean	True if the address book can be modified
AddressResolveUI	Boolean	True if address book is to resolve misspelled or incomplete names
AttachmentCount	Long	Number of attachments for the particular message index
AttachmentIndex	Long	The currently indexed attachment
AttachmentName	String	Name of the currently indexed attachment
AttachmentPathName	String	Full path of the currently indexed attachment
AttachmentPosition	Long	Position of the currently indexed attachment within body of message
AttachmentType	Integer	Specifies the type of attachment
FetchMsgType	String	Type of message to fetch
FetchSorted	Boolean	True if messages are to be sorted
FetchUnreadOnly	Boolean	True if only to fetch unread messages
MsgConversationID	String	Specifies message set identifier
MsgCount	Long	The number of messages
MsgDateReceived	String	Date that the currently indexed message is received

continues

Table 26.4. continued

Property	*Datatype*	*Used For*
`MsgID`	String	String identifier of the currently indexed message
`MsgIndex`	Long	Index of the currently indexed message
`MsgNoteText`	String	Specifies the text body of the message
`MsgOrigAddress`	String	Mail address of the message originator
`MsgOrigDisplayName`	String	Originator's name of the currently indexed message
`MsgRead`	Boolean	`True` if currently indexed message has been read
`MsgReceiptRequested`	Boolean	`True` if return receipt is requested
`MsgSent`	Boolean	`True` if currently indexed message has been sent
`MsgSubject`	String	Specifies the message subject for the currently indexed message
`MsgType`	String	Specifies the type of message
`RecipAddress`	String	Address of the currently indexed recipient
`RecipCount`	Long	Total number of recipients in the currently indexed message
`RecipDisplayName`	String	Name of the currently indexed recipients
`RecipIndex`	Long	Index for use with recipients
`RecipType`	Integer	Specifies the type of the currently indexed recipient
`SessionID`	Long	Session ID from MAPI Session control

In addition to the properties mentioned earlier for both controls, there are also a few methods used to manipulate the controls. Table 26.5 lists the methods available for the MAPI Session control, and Table 26.6 lists the methods available for the MAPI Message control.

Table 26.5. MAPI Session control methods.

Method	*Used To*
`SignOff`	Log out of the MAPI-compliant system
`SignOn`	Log on to the MAPI-compliant system

Table 26.6. MAPI Message control methods.

Method	*Used To*
`Compose`	Compose a new message
`Copy`	Copy the currently indexed message to the compose buffer
`Delete`	Delete a message, recipient, or attachment
`Fetch`	Fetch messages from the server
`Forward`	Forward messages to another recipient
`Reply`	Reply to the currently indexed message
`ReplyAll`	Reply to all message recipients
`ResolveName`	Resolve (look up) a recipient name in the address book
`Save`	Save a message or attachment to disk
`Send`	Send a message in the compose buffer to the MAPI-compliant server
`Show`	Either show details of the message sender or invoke the address book, based on an argument passed to the method

Logging Onto and Out of a MAPI-Compliant System

If you intend to write your own MAPI-compliant front end, your user must log on to the system. Logging on registers the user as a valid user to the back-end server. To log on to a MAPI-compliant system, use the MAPI Session control, which is very easy to use. You log on either by using the `SignOn` method, by setting the `Action` property to `1`, or by using the Visual Basic constant `mapSignOn`. You also can request that the system search for your messages, if there are any, when you log on. To do this, set the `DownloadMail` property to `True` before you log on.

For example, consider this code for logging on:

```
If menu_LogonMsg.Checked = True Then
    MAPISession1.DownloadMail = True
Else
    MAPISession1.DownloadMail = False
End If
'handle errors
On Error GoTo LogonError
'logon
If MAPISession1.SessionID = 0 Then
    MAPISession1.SignOn
End If
'assign mapi session id
MAPIMessages1.SessionID = MAPISession1.SessionID
```

The code in your application won't vary much, because these properties must be set to the values indicated in the preceding code to perform the desired logon function. The only real difference is the control names of the MAPI Session and MAPI Message controls. After a session is started, it is important that the `SessionID` of the MAPI Session control has a handle to it. This handle is an integer value that the MAPI Message control needs. Therefore, you must assign the value after logging on to or out of a MAPI-compliant system. You assign a value by using the last line shown in the preceding code.

When you want to close the application, you must log off to conserve system resources on the server and clear the user's ID number. To log off the MAPI-compliant system, use the `SignOff` method, or simply set the `Action` property of the MAPI Session control to `2`, or by using the Visual Basic constant `mapSignOff`. You log out of the mail system by using the following line of code:

```
MAPISession1.SignOff
```

If you do not assign the `SessionID` of the MAPI Session control to the `SessionID` of the MAPI Message control, you can't perform any messaging functions.

Invoking the MAPI Address Book

A MAPI-compliant application has an address book located on the MAPI-compliant server. The address book allows the user to search for recipients to send messages and files to. You invoke the MAPI address book by using the Message control and setting the `Show` method, or by assigning a value to the `Action` property. The address book would have been created by a system administrator and will appear automatically. It is assumed that you have logged in to the MAPI-compliant system, as stated in the previous section.

You invoke the address book by using the `Show` method and passing an argument of `False`, like this:

```
MAPIMessages1.Show False
```

Before you invoke the address book, you can specify the appearance and characteristics the address book will have. For example, you can specify that you want to choose a recipient to receive a carbon copy of the message you send to someone else. This line usually appears in a document as `CC:` followed by the name of the individual.

To specify how the address book will appear, you can set the `AddressEditFieldCount` property. The possible options are listed in Table 26.7.

Table 26.7. `AddressEditFieldCount` property options.

Value	*Description*
`0`	No editing controls. Only browsing is allowed.
`1`	Only the `To:` edit box is presented.
`2`	The `To:` and `CC:` edit boxes are presented.

Value	Description
3	The `To:`, `CC:`, and `BCC:` edit boxes are presented.
4	All possible edit boxes supported by the mail system are presented.

You also must set the `MsgIndex` property to `-1` before opening the address book. This ensures that the names selected in the address book are put into the recipient-related properties for the MAPI Message control. For example, consider the following code to invoke the address book. Your application will not be much different. By design, the code must be used in this way:

```
'enable the To: box to be shown on address book
MAPIMessages1.AddressEditFieldCount = 1
'set index to -1 to enable saving of names chosen(automatically)
MAPIMessages1.MsgIndex = -1
'invoke address book
MAPIMessages1.Show
```

After the address book is closed, you need to retrieve the addresses you have selected and return them to the MAPI application. You do this by looping through all of the recipients chosen and processing the names in any way your application is designed to. For example, if you simply want to populate a list box with all of the names chosen from the address book, you can use the following code fragment:

```
'clear list box
lstTo.Clear
'loop through all recipients and populate
For loopcount% = 0 To MAPIMessages1.RecipCount - 1
    'assign index
    MAPIMessages1.RecipIndex = loopcount%
    'add to name
    lstTo.AddItem MAPIMessages1.RecipDisplayName
Next loopcount%
```

Sending a Message

To send a message through a MAPI-compliant system by using the MAPI custom controls, you must first log on, construct the message, address it, and then send it. The preceding sections described how to log on and address the message. Constructing the message is an extremely simple task; it is really just one text string that is sent. You can hard code this string into your application, or you can use a text box, allowing the user to construct a dynamic message.

There are many possibilities for sending a message. For example, you can construct a form in which the user fills in the blanks and sends a formatted text message to recipients. You also can have Microsoft Exchange send and receive forms for the users to fill out.

To send a message, you must first set the `MsgIndex` property of the MAPI Message control to `-1`, which enables the control to compose a message. Then you must tell the control that you want to begin composing the message by, once again, using the `Compose` method or by setting the `Action` property. Setting the `Action` property to `6` starts this action. You also can declare a constant; `MESSAGE_COMPOSE` for the value of `6`.

After the composition of the message has begun, you can specify the subject of the message by using the `MsgSubject` property. You assign the string you send as the message by using the `MsgNoteText` property. After all the strings have been assigned, you actually send the message by invoking the `Send` method or by setting the `Action` property to `3`. You can also declare a constant, `MESSAGE_SEND`, for the value of `3`. You use the `Send` method like this:

```
MAPIMessages1.Send
```

You can build a string to send a message like this:

```
'set msgindex to enable compose buffer
MAPIMessages1.MsgIndex = -1
'clear compose buffer
MAPIMessages1.Compose
'assign recipients
Call BuildToList
'allow mail system to resolve bad names
MAPIMessages1.AddressResolveUI = True
'assign subject
MAPIMessages1.MsgSubject = txtSubject.Text
'build message
msg$ = frmRemark.txtGreeting.Text + Chr$(13)
msg$ = msg$ + "APPLICATION:" + Chr$(9) + txtApplication.Text +
➥Chr$(13) + Chr$(13)
msg$ = msg$ + "VERSION:" + Chr$(9) + txtVersion.Text + Chr$(13) + Chr$(13)
If lstChanges.ListCount > 0 Then
    msg$ = msg$ + "CHANGES:" + Chr$(9)
End If
'build list of changes
For loopcount% = 0 To lstChanges.ListCount - 1
    If lstChanges.List(loopcount%) <> "" Then
        msg$ = msg$ + lstChanges.List(loopcount%) + Chr$(13)
        'if this is not the last item in the list, add 2 tabs to line up
        If loopcount% < lstChanges.ListCount - 1 Then
            msg$ = msg$ + Chr$(9) + Chr$(9)
        End If
    End If
Next loopcount%
'add new line before closing remark
msg$ = msg$ + Chr$(13)
'add closing string to message
msg$ = msg$ + frmRemark.txtClosing.Text
'send actual text
MAPIMessages1.MsgNoteText = msg$
'change cursor
screen.MousePointer = vbHourglass
'actually send message
MAPIMessages1.Send
'change cursor
screen.MousePointer = vbDefault
'show message
MsgBox "Message Sent!"
```

The preceding code is used to construct a message and place it in the `msg$` variable. Then, this message variable is sent through the mail system. Understanding every line of code is not important; you just need to understand the concept.

Manually Receiving a Message

To manually receive a message with the MAPI custom controls, you use the `Fetch` method or use the `Action` property for the MAPI Message control. Set the `Action` property to `1`. You also can declare a constant, `MESSAGE_FETCH`, for the value of `1`. If you want to retrieve only unread messages, you can set the `FetchUnreadOnly` property to `True`. If there are any messages after you invoke the `Fetch` method or set the `Action` property, the `MsgCount` property contains a nonzero value. You can cycle through the messages using the `MsgCount` property and build a list of subjects by using the `MsgSubject` property.

For each possible message waiting, there is a `MsgIndex` property associated with it. For example, if there are two messages, there are indexes `0` and `1`, respectively, associated with them. This enables you to access the individual messages. This is very similar to how you access a control array in Visual Basic.

Consider using the following code to retrieve messages:

```
'set to fetch all messages
MAPIMessages1.FetchUnreadOnly = False
If MAPISession1.SessionID <> 0 Then
    'fetch messages
    MAPIMessages1.Fetch
    If MAPIMessages1.MsgCount > 0 Then
        'there are messages waiting-show inbox form
        frmInbox.Show
        DoEvents
        'display number of messages
        frmInbox.pnlNumMsg.Caption = MAPIMessages1.MsgCount
        'clear list box
        frmInbox.lstMessage.Clear
        'populate messages
        For loopcount% = 0 To MAPIMessages1.MsgCount - 1
            'change index
            MAPIMessages1.MsgIndex = loopcount%
            'get subject
            frmInbox.lstMessage.AddItem MAPIMessages1.MsgSubject
        Next loopcount%
    End If
End If
```

The preceding code requests the messages for the particular logon ID. If there are messages waiting, they are shown in a form called frmInbox. To determine if there are messages waiting, use the `MsgCount` property. If this property is greater than `0`, there are messages waiting.

The code then cycles through a list of all available messages and populates a list of the subject content. The code accesses individual messages by using the `MsgIndex` property, and it accesses the individual subjects by using the `MsgSubject` property.

Finding Attachments for a Message

A message not only contains the text part of the message, but can also contain *attachments*. Attachments are files attached to the messages. For example, if you want to send a Microsoft Word document to a recipient as an attachment and explain what the document is used for, you can do this in the same message.

For each possible message waiting, there is a `MsgIndex` property associated with it. For example, if there are two messages, there are indexes `0` and `1`, respectively, associated with them. This lets you access the individual messages. This is very similar to the way in which you access a control array in Visual Basic. However, for each individual `MsgIndex`, there can be one or more attachments. These attachments are accessed through the `AttachmentIndex` property. If you want to determine how many attachments there are, you can access the `AttachmentCount` property.

In your application, you can build a list of attachments for each message. You could have a user click on a specific message, and then build a list of attachments for the user. The following code determines whether there are attachments:

```
'find all attachments and build string
For loopcount% = 0 To frmmain.MapiMessages1.AttachmentCount - 1
    'assign index
    frmmain.MapiMessages1.AttachmentIndex = loopcount%
    'assign name to string
    Attach$ = Attach$ + frmmain.MapiMessages1.AttachmentName
    'append semi-colon if not last item
    If loopcount% < frmmain.MapiMessages1.AttachmentCount - 1 Then
        Attach$ = Attach$ + ";"
    End If
Next loopcount%
```

You use the same technique for attachments as for messages. In other words, just as you can loop through the total number of messages and index them individually, there is a total number of attachments, each of which can be indexed individually. You use the `AttachmentCount` property to obtain the total number of attachments. You find the individual index of any one attachment by using the `AttachmentIndex` property. To find out the attachment filename of the indexed attachment, use the `AttachmentName` property. Your application must use the same theory to build a list of attachments as presented here, although the specific methods can vary.

Deleting a Message or Attachment

The MAPI controls enable you to delete messages or attachments. To delete a message, invoke the `Delete` method or use the `Action` property to delete the currently indexed message. Setting this property to `10` deletes the message. You can also declare a constant, `MESSAGE_DELETE`, for the value of `10`. The MAPI-compliant system gives you no warning. You must check to make sure the user wants to continue with this action.

The `Delete` method can accept one argument, an argument that tells the system what to delete. Table 26.8 shows the possible arguments.

Table 26.8. `Delete` method arguments.

Constant	*Value*	*Description*
`mapMessageDelete`	`0`	Deletes all components of the currently indexed message
`mapRecipientDelete`	`1`	Deletes the currently indexed recipient
`mapAttachmentDelete`	`2`	Deletes the currently indexed attachment

The following code fragment deletes the currently indexed message and ensures that the item is deleted from the list box in which it is listed:

```
'do delete
frmmain.MapiMessages1.Delete
'remove item from lstMessage
lstMessage.RemoveItem lstMessage.listindex
```

You can use the same technique to delete attachments. The only difference is that you set the `Action` property to `15`. You also can declare a constant, `ATTACHMENT_DELETE`, for the value of `15`.

You can delete an attachment with the following line of code:

```
MapiMessages1.Action = ATTACHMENT_DELETE
```

You can even take this one step further and delete all attachments at one time, which is what the application in Chapter 35, "Developing a CD Player Application," does. It does this with the following code:

```
'loop through all attachments and delete
For loopcount% = 0 To frmmain.MapiMessages1.AttachmentCount - 1
    'do delete
    frmmain.MapiMessages1.Action = ATTACHMENT_DELETE
Next loopcount%
```

Polling for New Messages

Chances are that you want to be automatically notified when a new message comes in. You do this by setting a *polling frequency*. A polling frequency is a way for your program to check at certain intervals whether there are messages. Polling can't be done continuously because that eats up system resources. Therefore, you probably want to set a polling frequency somewhere in the range of five to ten minutes, which means that the application checks for new messages every five to ten minutes. If any new messages have been received in that time, you must notify the user in some way. You can put up a message box or even change the icon used if the application is minimized.

Polling presents a unique problem for Visual Basic because you must use a timer control to schedule the polling. The problem is that the timer control can have its `Interval` property set only to a maximum value of `65535`, which is just over one minute. What if you want to poll every five minutes? There is a solution. You use an integer variable in Visual Basic to count the number of minutes that have passed. For example, set the Timer's `Interval` property to `60000`.

This generates the `Timer` event once a minute. In the `Timer` event code, keep adding one to the counter variable you are using. When this counter variable gets to the polling interval you want, manually check for messages, as described in the earlier section, "Manually Receiving a Message." Your code in the `Timer` event might look like this:

```
CurrentInterval& = CurrentInterval& + 1
```

Consider, as an example, this polling code:

```
'check to see if polling time has elapsed
If CurrentInterval& = DesiredInterval& Then
    If MAPISession1.SessionID <> 0 Then
        'fetch only new messages
        MAPIMessages1.FetchUnreadOnly = True
        'fetch messages
        MAPIMessages1.Fetch
        'test for new messages - this insures that the message will only be
        ➥displayed
        'once, and not once each polling period!
        If MAPIMessages1.MsgCount > 0 And MAPIMessages1.MsgCount >
        ➥NewMessages% Then
        If frmMain.WindowState = 1 Then
                'form is minimized then assign In icon
                frmMain.Icon = pictMailIn.Picture
            Else
                'advise about new message
                MsgBox "You have new message(s)!"
            End If
            'increment number of new messages
            NewMessages% = NewMessages% + 1
        End If
        'set back to fetch all messages
        MAPIMessages1.FetchUnreadOnly = False
    End If
    'reset current interval&
    CurrentInterval& = 0
End If
```

If the desired interval equals the current interval, the system only checks for new messages by setting the `FetchUnreadOnly` property to `True`. After the new messages are received, the property is set back to `False`. If there are new messages, the user is notified by either a message box or by changing the icon, depending on the state of the window.

Summary

The messaging API (MAPI) is a very convenient way to send and receive messages and files through a MAPI-compliant mail system from your Visual Basic applications. Visual Basic includes two ActiveX controls to make it very easy to access MAPI functions. These two controls are called MAPI Session and MAPI Message.

You can use the techniques shown in this chapter and the application in Chapter 36, "Developing a MAPI/Microsoft Exchange Application," to build your own MAPI applications.

27

TAPI

Telephony Application Programming Interface (TAPI) is a set of telephony functions encapsulated in an API. It allows for device independence in communication between your computer and a telephone line. Device independence is a term that refers to the fact that your application does not care what type of device it is communicating with. From the application's point of view, the code is the same for all types of devices. This API supports many different aspects of telephone communications, such as

- Call waiting
- Voice mail
- Conferencing
- Automatic dialing
- Access to news data and information services
- Caller ID

TAPI 2.0 is tightly integrated into the Windows NT 4.0 operating system as a 32-bit preemptive multitasking and mutlithreaded API. At the time of this writing, TAPI version 2.0 was not available in Windows 95, but version 1.4 was, which is a 16-bit version. Therefore, this chapter discusses the 16-bit TAPI version.

CROSS REFERENCE

For further information about TAPI, refer to Chapter 37, "Developing a TAPI Application."

The Background of Telephony

Telephony has really improved over the years. The regular phone line with which we communicate on a regular basis is called the Plain Old Telephone System (POTS). From that, Integrated Services Digital Network (ISDN) emerged, which is a protocol that is becoming more popular. It allows for much faster communication (almost four times faster) and allows data transmission at the same time as voice communication.

Next, the switched 56KB protocol was invented along with the T1. Each require special equipment, but provide very fast communication—T1 actually is the backbone of the Internet. TAPI can handle each of these types of communication. The nice thing about TAPI is that you do not need to change your TAPI code to make it compatible with different communication mediums.

Using TAPI

Using TAPI can be quite difficult from Visual Basic. Therefore, it is best to use TAPI with an ActiveX control that encapsulates the functionality of many of the TAPI functions. However, some TAPI functions are quite easy to use. For example, you use the `tapiRequestMakeCall` API function to dial a call. This is shown in the application in Chapter 37.

To make a call, you must have installed a TAPI provider, such as the Economical Service Provider (ESP). This provider is available from the Microsoft FTP site. The address is `FTP.MICROSOFT.COM`. It is in the `\Developr\TAPI` directory. To view the TAPI providers on your system, select Programs | Control Panel, and then select the Telephony applet, shown in Figure 27.1. A TAPI provider becomes available to the Telephony application when the `*.TSP` file is in the `\WINDOWS\SYSTEM` directory. It also needs any supporting files. For example, for the ESP provider, there is an `ESP.TSP` file and an `ESPEXE.EXE` file. Each must be placed in the `\WINDOWS\SYSTEM` directory.

FIGURE 27.1.
The Telephony applet.

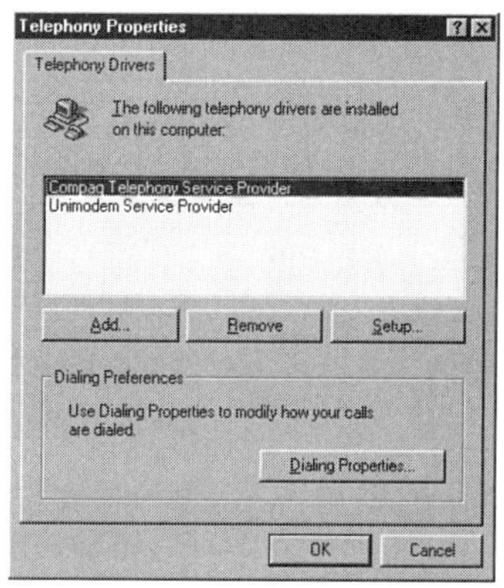

After you have installed a telephony provider, you can test telephony with one of the two different applications, `TB13.EXE` and `TB14.EXE`. The `TB` stands for Telephony Browser.

Each of these applications essentially works in the same way. The only difference is that the `TB13.EXE` application works with TAPI version 1.3 (16-bit), and `TB14.EXE` works with TAPI version 1.4 (32-bit). If you are using Windows 95 or Windows NT, use `TB14.EXE`. If you are using the ESP TAPI service provider, it works with both `TB13.EXE` and `TB14.EXE`. This chapter focuses on the `TB14.EXE` application, which is shown in Figure 27.2.

In the figure, notice on the left side a list of 117 functions available in TAPI 1.4. Understanding how to use this application takes some time and practice. To make it a little easier, Microsoft designed the toolbar to basically guide you from left to right. The available functions are shown in Table 27.1.

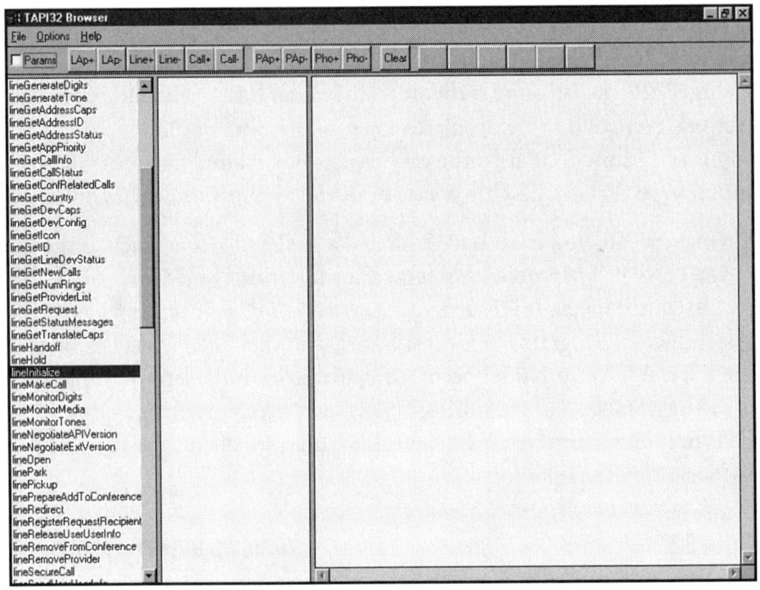

FIGURE 27.2.
The `TB14.EXE` *application.*

Table 27.1. TAPI 1.4 functions available in the TAPI browser.

`lineAccept`	`lineSendUserUserInfo`
`lineAddProvider`	`lineSetAppPriority`
`lineAddToConference`	`lineSetAppSpecific`
`lineAnswer`	`lineSetCallParams`
`lineBlindTransfer`	`lineSetCallPrivilege`
`lineClose`	`lineSetCurrentLocation`
`lineCompleteCall`	`lineSetDevConfig`
`lineCompleteTransfer`	`lineSetMediaMode`
`lineConfigDialog`	`lineSetNumRings`
`lineConfigDialogEdit`	`lineSetStatusMessages`
`lineConfigProvider`	`lineSetTerminal`
`lineDeallocateCall`	`lineSetToList`
`lineDevSpecific`	`lineSetupConference`
`lineDevSpecificFeature`	`lineSetupTransfer`
`lineDial`	`lineShutdown`
`lineDrop`	`lineSwapHold`
`lineForward`	`lineTranslateAddress`
`lineGatherDigits`	`lineTranslateDialog`

```
lineGenerateTone              lineUncompleteCall
lineGetAddressCaps            lineUnhold
lineGetAddressID              lineUnpark
lineGetAddressStatus          phoneClose
lineGetAppPriority            phoneConfigDialog
lineGetCallInfo               phoneDevSpecific
lineGetCallStatus             phoneGetButtonInfo
lineGetConfRelatedCalls       phoneGetData
lineGetCountry                phoneGetDevCaps
lineGetDevCaps                phoneGetDisplay
lineGetDevConfig              phoneGetGain
lineGetIcon                   phoneGetHookSwitch
lineGetID                     phoneGetIcon
lineGetLineDevStatus          phoneGetID
lineGetNewCalls               phoneGetLamp
lineGetNumRings               phoneGetLamp
lineGetProviderList           phoneGetRing
lineGetRequest                phoneGetStatus
lineGetStatusMessages         phoneGetStatusMessages
lineGetTranslateCaps          phoneGetVolume
lineHandoff                   phoneInitialize
lineHold                      phoneOpen
lineInitialize                phoneNegotiateAPIVersion
lineMakeCall                  phoneNegotiateExtVersion
lineMonitorDigits             phoneSetButtonInfo
lineMonitorMedia              phoneSetData
lineMonitorTones              phoneSetDisplay
lineNegotiateAPIVersion       phoneSetGain
lineNegotiateExtVersion       phoneSetHookSwitch
lineOpen                      phoneSetLamp
linePark                      phoneSetRing
linePickup                    phoneSetStatusMessages
linePrepareAddToConference    phoneSetVolume
lineRedirect                  phoneShutdown
```

continues

Table 27.1. continued

`lineRegisterRequestRecipient`	`tapiGetLocationInfo`
`lineReleaseUserUserInfo`	`tapiRequestDrop`
`lineRemoveFromConference`	`tapiRequestMakeCall`
`lineRemoveProvider`	`tapiRequestMediaCall`
`lineSecureCall`	`Open all lines`
`lineSendUserUserInfo`	`Open all phones`
`lineSetAppPriority`	`Close handle`
`lineSecureCall`	`Dump buffer contents`

As you can see from the table, there are only a few categories of functions:

- `line` functions
- `phone` functions
- `tapi` functions
- Other functions

The `line` functions affect mostly the telephone line as a whole. The `phone` functions affect the actual telephone device. The `tapi` functions deal with TAPI and the service providers. The other functions are simply for use within your application.

To begin using the TAPI browser, first you must initialize the line with the `lineInitialize` TAPI function either by double-clicking the function to the left or selecting the LAp+ toolbar button. This will initialize the line. Figure 27.3 shows the results of doing this. It returned successfully and the number of line devices available from the provider is 3.

If you intend to dial out, the next step is to open a line. You can do this by double-clicking the `lineOpen` function or by selecting the Line+ toolbar button. Then, you can make a call with the `lineMakeCall` function. Also, you can click the Call+ toolbar button. Figure 27.4 shows the results of doing this.

Notice that you never told TAPI what number to dial. This and almost all other parameters are set by first clicking the Params check box in the upper-left corner of the application. Now double-click the `lineMakeCall` function. Double-clicking this function will bring up a dialog box, as shown in Figure 27.5.

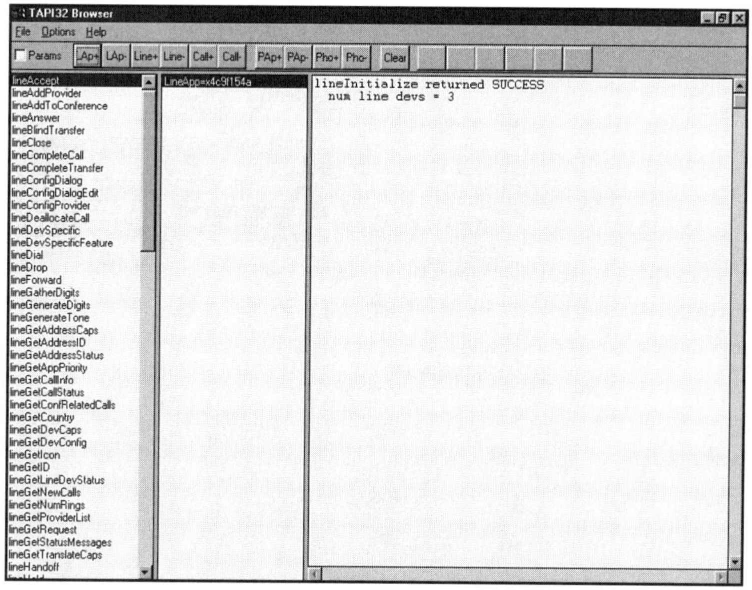

FIGURE 27.3.
The results of the `lineInitialize` *function.*

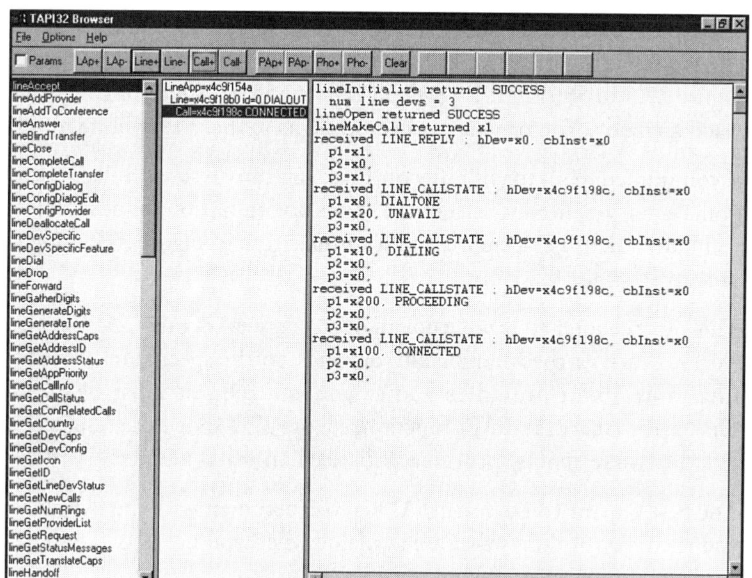

FIGURE 27.4.
The results of the `lineMakeCall` *function.*

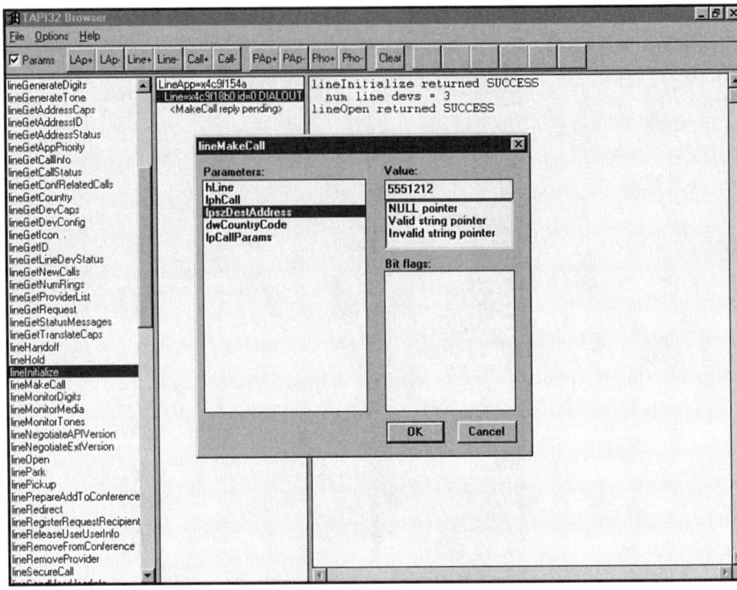

FIGURE 27.5.
The parameters for the `lineMakeCall` *function.*

Each of the parameters can have one or more values, depending on the data type. This parameter is a string where you simply specify the number to dial. The number has been changed in Figure 27.5 to 5551212. By default, it is 55555, which is, of course, not sufficient enough to reach anybody. You need at least seven digits to dial a telephone number.

If you wanted to set the number of rings, you can do so with the `lineSetNumRings` TAPI function. Again, you need to select the Params option button to specify the number of rings, unless you know what the default is and want to accept it. Figure 27.6 shows the parameters for the `lineSetNumRings` function.

This short chapter gives you enough of an overview of how TAPI works and how the API itself works. Much of the functionality depends on the specific telephony provider you use. One final note about providers is that you can request a list of providers by selecting the `lineGetProviderList` TAPI function. Figure 27.7 shows the results of this function. It clearly lists the two telephony providers registered on my computer.

The best way for you to learn TAPI is to experiment with the sample application. It will teach you the types of things that are available when you use TAPI, even if many of them are not available through Visual Basic yet.

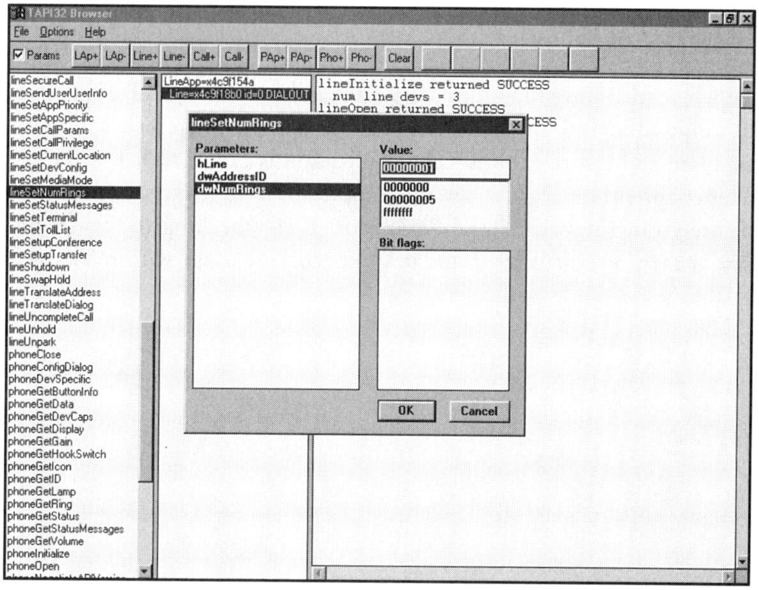

FIGURE 27.6.
The parameters for the `lineSetNumRings` *function.*

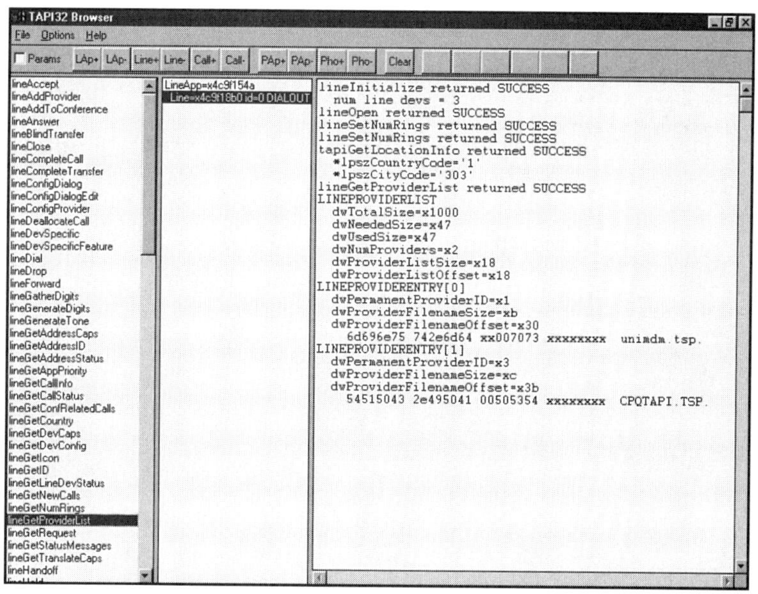

FIGURE 27.7.
Parameters for the `lineGetProviderList` *function.*

Summary

Very few telephony functions are available through Visual Basic applications. Telephony can be quite difficult to understand and troubleshoot. Therefore, Microsoft provides two tools to simulate and test telephony. The application is called `TB14.EXE` for testing 32-bit telephony. This chapter shows how to use these applications to make sure your system functions correctly before you write your Visual Basic code. Keep checking the SoftHouse Web site at `http://www.vbasic.com` for current updates to telephony usage within Visual Basic.

VI

Databases

28

Database Concepts

There are many important concepts circling around databases. Now more than ever, many technologies are used when discussing and planning databases. This chapter discusses many of these terms in an effort to clarify their meaning.

Design Considerations

Designing a database has greatly been enhanced with Access 97, which includes wizards to create databases. The following is a list of the database wizards included with Access 97:

- Address Book
- Asset Tracking
- Book Collection
- Contact Management
- Donations
- Event Management
- Expenses
- Household Inventory
- Inventory Control
- Ledger
- Membership
- Music Collection
- Order Entry
- Picture Library
- Recipes
- Resource Scheduling
- Service Call Management
- Students and Classes
- Time and Billing
- Video Collection
- Wine List
- Workout

CROSS REFERENCE

For more information about using these wizards, refer to Chapter 31, "Database Applications with Access 97."

These wizards simplify the database creation process by enabling you to answer questions about how you will use the database. The wizards then create a normalized data structure based on the results of those questions.

Normalizing the Database

Normalizing a database means that the database is separated into multiple related tables. This ensures that data is not duplicated. Typically, you do this to avoid storing redundant data. Many times this means storing data into many "lookup" tables.

Normalization often makes the size of the database smaller, as well as often improves performance. This is the case only when indexes are placed correctly on tables. If you do not place indexes on columns, or place them on the wrong columns, normalizing the data actually will slow it down. If the indexes are correct, many times there will be few indexes per table. Therefore, `INSERT`, `UPDATE`, and `DELETE` SQL statements have increased performance.

The downside of normalization is that queries can become dramatically more complex. Therefore, a good rule of thumb is to normalize the database so that no more than four joins exist between tables.

If you have a database that already exists in an unnormalized fashion, you might not be able to redesign the entire database. However, you might consider the implications of normalizing only some of the tables. This can still be of great benefit.

For an example of data that is not normalized, refer to Table 28.1.

Table 28.1. Unnormalized data.

Customer ID	*Last Name*	*First Name*	*SaleDate*	*Item*	*Description*	*Price*	*Qty.*
101	Smith	John	12/01/94	X105	Widget	59.95	1
101	Smith	John	12/15/94	X105	Widget	59.95	12
102	Jones	Fred	12/01/94	X126	Widget Accessory	19.95	1

It is easy to query the data in this table, but the storage size would grow to be huge. The last names and descriptions are repeated, as are the prices. Supposing the table is called ORDERS, a query to ask for all orders for customer 101 would be

```
SELECT *
FROM ORDERS
WHERE CustomerID = 101
```

Now consider normalizing the data. The table needs to be broken into three separate tables. You need one table to store customer information, one to store product information, and one to store order information. The first step would be to make the customers table. Table 28.2 shows this table, called CUSTOMERS.

Table 28.2. The normalized CUSTOMERS table.

CustomerID	*LastName*	*FirstName*
101	Smith	John
102	Jones	Fred

Then, break out the products part of the unnormalized table and call it PRODUCTS, as shown in Table 28.3.

Table 28.3. The normalized PRODUCTS table.

Item	*Description*	*Price*
X105	Widget	59.95
X126	Widget Accessory	19.95

Finally, the unnormalized ORDERS table, shown in Table 28.1, is reorganized as shown in Table 28.4.

Table 28.4. The normalized ORDERS table.

CustomerID	*SaleDate*	*Item*	*Qty.*
101	12/01/94	X105	1
101	12/15/94	X105	12
102	12/01/94	X126	1

Now that the data is normalized into three tables, querying the data becomes more difficult because it must join across three tables. The query now looks like this:

```
SELECT O.CustomerID, C.LastName, C.FirstName, O.SaleDate, O.Item,
➥P.Description, P.Price, O.Qty
FROM ORDERS O, CUSTOMERS C, PRODUCTS P
WHERE C.CustomerID = O.CustomerID
AND P.Item = O.Item
AND C.CustomerID = 101
```

CROSS REFERENCE

For more information about SQL, refer to Chapter 29, "Structured Query Language (SQL)."

Now that you understand the concept of normalizing the database (or tables), it is important to understand that indexing the columns incorrectly actually will slow the database down.

Indexes

Indexes are extremely important in a database. They are used by the database optimizer to access the data quickly. Depending on the type of database you are using, different types of indexes will be available. Very often, you will decide to place an index on a column or series of columns in a table, based on how the table is accessed. Also, you might want to place one index on each set of columns accessed. For example, suppose you accessed the ORDERS table by using the following conditions:

- `CustomerID`
- `SaleDate`
- `CustomerID, SaleDate`

The types of indexes you create depend on the database you are using. The first column, CustomerID, is the primary key of the CUSTOMERS table, which means that each customer ID is unique. There will be no duplicate values in the table. Therefore, most likely, a clustered index (SQL Server) or a No Duplicate index (Access) will be placed on this column.

Then, a nonclustered index (SQL Server) or duplicate index (Access) will be placed not only on the SaleDate column, but on the combination of CustomerID and SaleDate. All of these types of indexes are discussed in the next two sections.

SQL Server

SQL Server has two types of indexes available:

- Clustered
- Nonclustered

A *clustered index* stores the physical order of rows in the same order as the indexed order of rows. This can greatly increase the access speed. Only one clustered index is allowed in a single table. `UPDATE` and `DELETE` SQL operations are often accelerated by clustered indexes, because these operations require much reading. Typically, you would not have a table without a clustered index, especially if the table is normalized.

Do not use a clustered index on a column that will be used when you are inserting a lot of data into a table, such as an identity (counter) column. Because data is stored in a physical order, performance can be degraded if you do this. While one row is being inserted into the last data page, it locks the data page. Then all other rows to be inserted must wait until the lock is free.

A *nonclustered index* stores data in a logical order of a table. The physical order in which the data lies (clustered index) is not the same as the indexed order. Instead, a nonclustered index points to where the data is. You can have as many as 249 nonclustered indexes per table.

Access 97

Access 97 (as well as prior versions) has two types of indexes available:

- Yes (duplicates OK)
- Yes (no duplicates)

Not allowing duplicates is very similar to having a clustered index. Selecting an index that allows duplicates is similar to using a nonclustered index. For more information about clustered and nonclustered indexes, see the previous section.

Relationships

Indexes are like relationships. A relationship defines how one table associates with another. The possible relationships are

- One-to-one
- One-to-many
- Many-to-many

The concept of relationships seems to be quite simple, but when it comes to actually defining them for a database, it can become difficult. Therefore, the next few sections define how to use and define relationships.

One-to-One Relationships

A one-to-one relationship identifies a relationship in which a field in one table can have (or relate to) only one value in the related table. Consider tables A and B in Tables 28.5 and 28.6. They relate to each other by the CustomerID column in a one-to-one relationship.

Table 28.5. One-to-one relationship, table A.

CustomerID (Primary Key)	*LastName*	*FirstName*
101	Smith	John
102	Jones	Fred

Table 28.6. One-to-one relationship, table B.

CustomerID (Primary Key)	*CreditTerms*
101	Net 30
102	Cash

One CustomerID in table A can have, at most, one CustomerID in table B. Likewise, one CustomerID in table B can have, at most, one CustomerID in table A.

One-to-Many Relationships

A one-to-many relationship probably is the most common type of relationship. It identifies a relationship in which a field in one table can have (or relate to) many values in the related table. Consider tables A and B in Tables 28.7 and 28.8. They relate to each other by the CustomerID column in a one-to-many relationship.

Table 28.7. One-to-many relationship, table A.

CustomerID (Primary Key)	*LastName*	*FirstName*
101	Smith	John
102	Jones	Fred

Table 28.8. One-to-many relationship, table B.

CustomerID	*SaleDate*	*Item*	*Qty.*
101	12/01/94	X105	1
101	12/15/94	X105	12
102	12/01/94	X126	1

One CustomerID in table A can have many CustomerIDs in table B. Likewise, many CustomerIDs in Table B can have, at most, one CustomerID in table A.

Many-to-Many Relationships

A many-to-many relationship identifies a relationship in which a field in one table can have (or relate to) many values in the related table, as well as the reverse being true. The field in the related table can have many values in the first table. Consider tables A and B in Tables 28.9 and 28.10. They relate to each other by the Item column in a many-to-many relationship.

Table 28.9. Many-to-many relationship, table A.

CustomerID	*SaleDate*	*Item*	*Qty.*
101	12/01/94	X105	1
101	12/15/94	X105	12
102	12/01/94	X126	1

Table 28.10. Many-to-many relationship, table B.

Item	*Category*
X105	Electronics
X105	Audio
X105	Video
X126	Clothing
X126	Shirts

Many items in table A can relate to many items in table B. Likewise, many items in table B can relate to many items in table A.

Connecting to Databases

You can connect to your databases in three ways. You can connect via open database connectivity (ODBC), native connections, or DB libraries. ODBC is a database-independent standard by which you can connect to virtually any database. Native connections really refers to Microsoft Access and DAO, which is described later in this chapter in the section "DAO." DB libraries are libraries that provide functionality to a specific type of database on a specific network. Usually this is more difficult to use than ODBC, but it is faster.

CROSS REFERENCE

For more information about ODBC, refer to Chapter 30, "ODBC."

DAO

DAO is used to communicate with Microsoft Access and other ODBC data sources through the JET engine. This engine is the driving technology behind Microsoft Access databases. A developer can take advantage of the objects exposed by DAO to directly manipulate the data source through the JET engine. Usually, DAO is used with Microsoft Access databases. There are four versions of DAO in use today:

- 2.0: DAO 2.0 is a 16-bit implementation for programmatic access to database objects. It was first included with Microsoft Access 2.0 in April 1994.
- 2.5: DAO 2.5 is a 32-bit implementation of the JET engine. It was included later in 1994 with the Access 2.0 service pack. The major enhancement of this version was that more datatypes were available, as well as full VBA support.
- 3.0: DAO 3.0 is also a 32-bit implementation of the JET engine. It was made available late in 1995. It was intended for use in the Windows 95 and Windows NT operating systems. The major enhancement in this version was to resolve record conflict locking problems.
- 3.5: DAO 3.5 handles all of the processing for Access 97 and Visual Basic 5.0. It was available early in 1997. DAO 3.5 now includes services that support data definition (DDL), multiusers, workgroup security, referential integrity, and replication. One of the most significant improvements is a mode called ODBCDirect. It enables you to access ODBC data sources directly, thereby bypassing the JET engine. This lets you take advantage of the remote data source's processing capabilities.

ODBCDirect provides an alternative to workspaces when you only need to execute queries or stored procedures against a back-end server, such as Microsoft SQL Server, Oracle, or Sybase. This also is useful when your client application needs to perform batch updates or asynchronous query execution.

DAO exposes many objects, properties, methods, and events to help you manipulate database objects. Table 28.11 lists objects for DAO 3.5.

Table 28.11. DAO 3.5 objects.

Property	*Description of Use*
`Connection`	Represents an object containing information about current connections
`Connections`	Collection of `Connection` objects
`Container`	Represents an object holding information about objects grouped into a container
`Containers`	Collection of container objects
`Database`	Object pointing to a physical database
`Databases`	Collection of database objects
`DBEngine`	Object representing the JET database engine
`Document`	Object representing information about an instance of a database, table, query, or relationship object

continues

Table 28.11. continued

Property	*Description of Use*
`Documents`	Collection of `Document` objects
`Error`	Object representing details about DAO errors
`Errors`	Collection of `Error` objects
`Field`	Object pointing to a physical field in a table
`Fields`	A collection of all of the fields in a table
`Group`	Represents a group of user accounts with like permissions
`Groups`	Collection of `Group` objects
`Index`	Object pointing to a particular index in a table
`Indexes`	Collection of all the indexes in a table
`Parameter`	Represents a `QueryDef` parameter
`Parameters`	Collection of `Parameter` objects
`Property`	Represents properties of a `DAO` object
`Properties`	Collection of `Property` objects
`QueryDef`	Definition of a query stored in a database
`QueryDefs`	Collection of `QueryDef` objects
`Recordset`	Object representing records in a base table
`Recordsets`	Collection of `Recordset` objects
`Relation`	Object representing the relationship between fields in tables or queries
`Relations`	Collection of `Relation` objects
`Table`	Object pointing to a physical table
`TableDef`	Object pointing to the structure of a table
`TableDefs`	Collection of `TableDef` objects
`User`	Object representing a user account
`Users`	Collection of `User` objects
`Workspace`	Defines a session for a user
`Workspaces`	Collection of `Workspace` objects

To use DAO, you must declare the object variables. You must also make sure that you assign references to the DAO libraries that contain the DAO objects and functions. To assign a reference, select Tools | References. There are four library references you must consider assigning:

- Microsoft DAO 3.0 Object Library
- Microsoft DAO 3.5 Object Library

- Microsoft DAO 2.5/3.0 Compatibility Library
- Microsoft DAO 2.5/3.5 Compatibility Library

You can assign a reference to only one of the preceding four libraries in one project. If you attempt to assign more than one reference, you will receive the following error:

```
Name conflicts with existing module, project, or object library.
```

There are two basic syntaxes for opening a database. One is

```
Set database = OpenDatabase(databasename[,exclusive[,read-only[,source]]])
```

where:

> `databasename` is the name of the database you are trying to open.
>
> `exclusive` is a Boolean flag for exclusive use of the database.
>
> `read-only` is a Boolean flag to mark the database as read-only.
>
> `source` is the ODBC connect string, if applicable.

A more preferable syntax is to use the `Workspaces` collection as follows:

```
Set database = Workspaces(0).OpenDatabase(databasename[,exclusive[,read-only
➥[,source]]])
```

where all objects are the same as listed in the preceding syntax except that the `Workspaces(0)` object is used. This specifies the first workspace element in the `Workspaces` collection (refer to Table 28.11).

Using workspaces is recommended for multiuser databases. This allows the database engine to differentiate between the different users.

There are two basic syntaxes each for creating dynaset-type, snapshot-type, and table-type recordsets. A *dynaset* is a recordset that allows the underlying tables to be updated. On the other hand, a *snapshot* is basically a "snapshot" or picture of the data and does not allow the underlying tables to be updated. They are essentially read-only. A *table* is, of course, an updatable view of a table. The syntax for creating any of the recordsets mentioned in this paragraph is

```
Set recordset = database.OpenRecordset(source[,type[,options]])
```

where:

> `database` is the name of the database opened with the `OpenDatabase` method.
>
> `type` is the type of recordset to open, either `dbOpenDynaset`, `dbOpenSnapshot`, or `dbOpenTable`. These constant values are declared in the library to which you had set a reference earlier.
>
> `options` sets specific options of the database, such as read-only, forward-only, and many others.

The other syntax is to actually omit the source argument inside the `OpenRecordset` method and use it as an object of the database name. In other words, you can follow this syntax:

```
Set recordset = database.source.OpenRecordset([type[,options]])
```

In the preceding syntax, if you omit *`type`*, then the `OpenRecordset` method will automatically create a table-type `Recordset` object.

A `QueryDef` is very useful for storing predetermined queries with the Microsoft JET database. You could say that a `QueryDef` object is to Access as a stored procedure is to SQL Server.

The syntax for creating a `QueryDef` object is as follows:

```
Set querydef = database.CreateQueryDef(name[,sqltext])
```

If you are no longer using a recordset, it is a good idea to close the recordset using the `Close` method. It is not needed in every situation. For example, if the recordset is local to a procedure, it will automatically be closed when the procedure is exited.

Bound Controls

A *bound control* is a control that you will assign to one or more columns (fields) of data in a database. Assigning the control to data allows for that data to be populated automatically without code. All you have to do is set a few properties. You do not need to write any code. They are called bound controls because they are bound to a data control.

Basically, you assign the data control to get the records you want. You can assign it to the results of an SQL statement, or even to an entire table. Then you *bind* a bound control to the data control mentioned previously. Therefore, there are a minimum of two controls needed when you use a bound control.

CROSS REFERENCE

For more information about SQL, refer to Chapter 29, “Structured Query Language (SQL).”

Suppose you have an Access table named SUPPLIER and want to have a `DBListbox` present all of the possible names of the suppliers. You do not want to show any other data in the list box. You can do this by placing a data control on a form. You would then need to set the following properties:

- `Connect`
- `DatabaseName`
- `RecordSource`

The `Connect` property tells the data control what type of database you will be connected to. By default, Access is selected for you. The `DatabaseName` property is used to select the database corresponding to the `Connect` property. For this example, it will be set to `ORDER.MDB`. The `RecordSource` property will be used to select a table inside the database. For this example, it will be set to `INVENTORY`. This is the minimum required to set up the data control. However, you still need to set up the DBListBox control.

Place a DBListBox on your form. It is very simple to bind this to the data control. You need to set only two properties on the DBListBox control to list the possible supplier names from the data control:

- `RowSource`
- `ListField`

The `RowSource` property will be the name of the data control in the previous step. By default, this name will be `Data1`. This choice will be available in the drop-down list for the `RowSource` property. Select this row source. The `RowSource` property specifies the data source that will provide the DBListBox with data. Next is the `ListField` property, which tells the DBListBox which field (or column) to list from the `RowSource` property. The drop-down list for this property will show all available columns. Remember that the choices you see here were set up when you selected values for the properties in the data control earlier. Select the "supplier" option, and notice that the `BoundColumn` property will automatically be filled with the value `"supplier"`.

Now when you run your application, the DBListBox presents a list of all of the possible values in the `ORDER.MDB` database's SUPPLIER table. If you want to have a field updated automatically in a table, you would need to manipulate the `DataSource` and `DataField` properties.

The DBComboBox works very similarly to how a DBListBox works. The DBGrid is different. Suppose you wanted to have a "full-table" view of the SUPPLIER table in the `ORDER.MDB` file used earlier. You would simply set up the data control as you would for use with any other bound control. Then after placing the DBGrid control on your form, you would at least set the `DataSource` property to the name of the data control. You can click the Custom tab on the DBGrid control to set up extended options, such as limiting the ability to add new records and updating or deleting existing records.

RDO and RDC

Remote Data Objects (RDO) is a set of 32-bit objects used similarly to DAO, except that it is used to connect to remote (ODBC) databases. Remote Data Control (RDC) is a control used to bind controls to an ODBC remote database.

CROSS REFERENCE

For more information about RDO and RDC, refer to Chapter 16, "Remote Data Objects (RDO)."

DB Libraries

VBSQL is a database library (or DB Library) ActiveX custom control available from Microsoft. This tool is a great way to connect to SQL Server without having to use ODBC. Therefore, it is very fast. It also provides many functions that are tailored to SQL Server and are not available through ODBC.

This custom control is part of the DB-Library for Visual Basic that is incorporated into the Microsoft SQL Server Programmer's Toolkit. You can purchase this toolkit from Microsoft directly, and it is available on the Developer Network CDs.

You use the control in two ways. First, because all ActiveX controls are actually DLLs, the functions that are exported inside them can be declared and used directly in Visual Basic. Second, you use it as you would use any other custom control in that it generates custom events. You can use these to respond to certain actions that occur in your application, such as error handling.

Using the VBSQL ActiveX Control

To use the VBSQL ActiveX control, follow these steps during the programming process:

- Handle errors
- Initialize the DB-Library (VBSQL)
- Open an SQL Server connection
- Send any required Transact-SQL statements to the server
- Process results
- Close the SQL Server connection

This section cannot possibly cover how to use all of the functions in the VBSQL ActiveX control. It also is not intended to provide enough information so that you do not need to purchase the DB-Library for Visual Basic. It does, however, provide enough information about connections, command execution, processing results, and closing the connection.

You can handle errors in two ways. It is a good idea to at least invoke a standard error handler, as you would for any type of routine or event procedure. Also, it is a good idea to respond to errors generated by the VBSQL ActiveX control itself. When a DB-Library related error occurs, the VBSQL ActiveX control generates an `Error()` event. It passes in the error number, error string, and severity of the error, as well as some other parameters.

You initialize and close the library, as well as execute Transact-SQL statements, by accessing functions in the VBSQL itself. You declare these functions as you would declare any other DLL functions. Table 28.12 lists the possible functions in the VBSQL control.

CROSS REFERENCE

For more information about declaring and calling DLLs (and APIs) from your Visual Basic application, refer to Chapter 13, "Using the WIN32 API."

Table 28.12. Functions available in VBSQL.

Function	*Description*
`SqlAData$`	Returns data in a `COMPUTE` clause.
`SqlADLen&`	Returns the length of data in a `COMPUTE` clause.
`SqlAltColId%`	Returns the ID of the column specified in the `COMPUTE` clause.
`SqlAltLen%`	Returns the maximum length of the data in a COMPUTE column.
`SqlAltOp%`	Returns the type of aggregate function in a COMPUTE column.
`SqlAltType%`	Returns the datatype of a COMPUTE column.
`SqlAltUType&`	Returns the user-defined datatype of a COMPUTE column.
`SqlBCPColfmt%`	Specifies the operating system (OS) format for columns for BCP (bulk copy) operations.
`SqlBCPColumnFormat%`	Specifies the input format for BCP operations.
`SqlBCPColumns%`	Specifies the number of columns in the OS file for BCP operations.
`SqlBCPControl%`	Changes default settings for BCP operations.
`SqlBCPExec%`	Executes a BCP procedure.
`SqlBCPInit%`	Initializes a BCP procedure.
`SqlBCPSetL%`	Enables/disables BCP procedures.
`SqlByList$`	Returns the bylist of a COMPUTE row. A bylist is a list of columns specified with the `BY` clause.
`SqlCancel%`	Cancels the execution of a statement and clears the results buffer.
`SqlCanQuery%`	Cancels pending rows in the results buffer.
`SqlChange$`	Determines whether a command has changed the current database.
`SqlClose`	Closes a single connection.
`SqlClrBuf`	Clears rows from the row buffer.
`SqlClrOpt%`	Clears SQL Server options.

continues

Table 28.12. continued

Function	*Description*
`SqlCmd%`	Adds Transact-SQL to the transact (send) buffer.
`SqlCmdRow%`	Indicates whether a current statement can return rows.
`SqlColBrowse%`	Indicates whether a column can be updated using VBSQL browse functions.
`SqlColInfo%`	Returns information about a column.
`SqlColLen%`	Returns the maximum length of data in a column.
`SqlColName$`	Returns the name of the column in a resultset.
`SqlColSource$`	Returns the source column name for a resultset.
`SqlColType%`	Returns the datatype of a result column.
`SqlColUType&`	Returns the user-defined datatype of a result column.
`SqlCount&`	Returns the number of rows affected by a Transact-SQL statement.
`SqlCurCmd%`	Returns the number of the current statement in the command buffer.
`SqlCurRow&`	Returns the number of the current row in the row buffer.
`SqlCursor%`	Performs a cursor action on a particular row.
`SqlCursorClose`	Closes an open cursor.
`SqlCursorColInfo%`	Returns information about a column in a cursor.
`SqlCursorData$`	Returns data of a specified row and column in a cursor.
`SqlCursorFetch%`	Fetches a block of rows of data from a client or transparent server cursor.
`SqlCursorFetchEx%`	Fetches a block of rows from an explicit server cursor.
`SqlCursorInfo%`	Returns row and column information for a cursor.
`SqlCursorInfoEx%`	Returns detailed information about a cursor.
`SqlCursorOpen%`	Opens a cursor.
`SqlData$`	Returns the string of data in a specified column.
`SqlDataReady%`	Indicates whether SQL Server has finished processing a command.
`SqlDateCrack%`	Converts SQL date formats.
`SqlDatLen&`	Returns the length of data in a given column.
`SqlDead%`	Tests to see whether a connection is still active.
`SqlExec%`	Sends a Transact-SQL statement to the command buffer.
`SqlExit`	Closes all open connections.
`SqlFirstRow&`	Returns the number for the first row in the row buffer.

Function	Description
`SqlFreeBuf`	Clears command buffer.
`SqlFreeLogin`	Frees memory allocated to a login ID.
`SqlGetAltColInfo%`	Returns information about an aggregate column in a resultset.
`SqlGetChar$`	Returns a character in the command buffer.
`SqlGetColumnInfo%`	Returns column information about the current resultset.
`SqlGetMaxProcs%`	Determines the maximum number of simultaneous open connections.
`SqlGetOff%`	Determines whether the command buffer is empty.
`SqlGetPacket%`	Returns the tabular data packet size.
`SqlGetRow%`	Sets a specific row in the row buffer.
`SqlGetTime%`	Sets the response timeout from SQL Server.
`SqlHasRetStat%`	Determines whether a stored procedure has a return status.
`SqlInit$`	Initializes VBSQL.
`SqlIsAvail%`	Determines whether a connection is available.
`SqlIsCount%`	Determines whether the count returned is real or accurate.
`SqlIsOpt%`	Determines the status of SQL Server options.
`SqlLastRow&`	Returns the number of the last row in the row buffer.
`SqlLogin%`	Allocates a login.
`SqlMoreCmds%`	Determines whether more statements are in the command buffer.
`SqlMoreText%`	Sends all or part of an image or text datatype to SQL Server.
`SqlName$`	Returns the name of the current database.
`SqlNextRow%`	Reads data from the next data row.
`SqlNumAlts%`	Returns the number of columns in a `COMPUTE` clause.
`SqlNumCols%`	Returns the number of columns in the current resultset.
`SqlNumCompute%`	Returns the number of `COMPUTE` clauses.
`SqlNumOrders%`	Returns the number of `ORDER BY` clauses.
`SqlNumRets%`	Returns the number of return values from a stored procedure.
`SqlOk%`	Verifies that a batch command is OK or correct.
`SqlOpen%`	Opens an SQL Server connection.
`SqlOpenConnection%`	Opens a login record and establishes a server connection.
`SqlOrderCol%`	Returns a specified column in the `ORDER BY` clause.
`SqlProcInfo%`	Returns information about SQL Server connection.

continues

Table 28.12. continued

Function	*Description*
`SqlPrType$`	Converts the SQL Server token value to a string.
`SqlQual$`	Returns the `WHERE` clause from the current row in the row buffer.
`SqlResults%`	Sets up the next statement in the command buffer for processing.
`SqlRetData$`	Returns the stored procedure return value.
`SqlRetLen&`	Returns the length of a return parameter from a stored procedure.
`SqlRetName$`	Returns the name of the parameter returned from a stored procedure.
`SqlRetStatus&`	Returns the return status from a stored procedure.
`SqlRetType%`	Returns the datatype of a stored procedure return parameter.
`SqlRows%`	Determines whether the current SQL statement returns rows.
`SqlRowType%`	Determines whether the current row is a regular row or a COMPUTE row.
`SqlRpcExec%`	Executes a stored procedure.
`SqlRpcInit%`	Initializes a stored procedure.
`SqlRpcParam%`	Adds a parameter to a stored procedure.
`SqlRpcSend%`	Sends a stored procedure to SQL Server.
`SqlSend%`	Sends the contents of the command buffer to SQL Server, but does not wait for a response.
`SqlSendCmd%`	Sends the contents of the command buffer.
`SqlServerEnum%`	Lists the names of available SQL Servers.
`SqlSetAvail`	Marks a connection available for general use.
`SqlSetLApp%`	Sets the login application name.
`SqlSetLHost%`	Sets the login workstation name.
`SqlSetLNatLang%`	Sets the login language used.
`SqlSetLoginTime%`	Sets the login timeout to connect to SQL Server.
`SqlSetLPacket%`	Sets the tabular data packet size for login.
`SqlSetLPwd%`	Sets the login password.
`SqlSetLSecure%`	Flags the login as being secure.
`SqlSetLUser%`	Sets the login user name.
`SqlSetLVersion%`	Sets the version of SQL Server being used, 6.0 or 4.2.

Function	*Description*
`SqlSetMaxProcs%`	Sets the maximum number of open connections to SQL Server.
`SqlSetOpt%`	Sets SQL Server-VBSQL options.
`SqlSetTime%`	Sets timeout for results and command processing.
`SqlStrCpy%`	Copies a portion of the command buffer to a string.
`SqlStrLen%`	Returns the length of the command buffer.
`SqlTabBrowse%`	Determines whether a table can be updated by browse functions.
`SqlTabCount%`	Returns the number of tables in a `SELECT` statement.
`SqlTabName$`	Returns the name of a specified table.
`SqlTabSource$`	Returns the name and number of a derived table.
`SqlTextUpdate1Row%`	Updates one row of results in a text or image datatype column.
`SqlTextUpdateManyRows&`	Updates all rows of results in a text or image datatype column, starting with the current row.
`SqlTsNewLen%`	Returns the length of a timestamp column after a browse-mode update.
`SqlTsNewVal$`	Provides information about a timestamp column after a browse-mode update.
`SqlTsNewVal&`	Returns an identifier of a timestamp column after a browse-mode update.
`SqlTsPut%`	Puts a new value into a timestamp column.
`SqlTsUpdate%`	Updates a value in a timestamp column.
`SqlTxPtr$`	Returns an identifier for a text or image datatype in the current row.
`SqlTxTimeStamp$`	Returns a timestamp value for a text or image datatype in the current row.
`SqlTxTsNewVal$`	Provides information about a timestamp column for a text or image datatype in the current row.
`SqlTxTsPut%`	Puts a new timestamp value for a text or image datatype in the current row.
`SqlUpdateText%`	Updates existing text or image data.
`SqlUse%`	Sets current database.
`SqlWinExit`	Exits and unregisters the VBSQL library from the application.
`SqlWriteText%`	Sends a text or image datatype value to SQL Server.

Using the functions listed in Table 28.12, you can establish a connection, execute Transact-SQL statements, and close connections. You also can perform many detailed administrative tasks.

Before you can execute any Transact-SQL statements, you must first initialize the library. You do this with the `SqlInit$()` function. This function registers your application with VBSQL so that no other applications using the library will clash with yours. `SqlInit$()` will return a string message of the status of the initialization. If the string is empty, then there was a problem during initialization. You can initialize the library like this:

```
msg$ = SqlInit$()
If msg$ = "" Then
    MsgBox "Could not initialize library!"
    End
EndIf
```

If the string was not empty, the library is initialized. Then you must use the `SqlOpenConnection%()` function to log in to SQL Server. You use the following syntax to do this:

```
Conn% = SqlOpenConnection (Server, LoginID, Password, Workstation, Application)
```

Supplying the appropriate parameters in the preceding line of code will open a connection to the specified server using the specified login, password, and workstation. `SqlOpenConnection` uses the application name, if supplied, to identify your application from others in SQL Server. `Conn%` in the preceding line of code will then be used by the other functions listed in Table 28.12. The connection is now established.

NOTE

Note that the `SqlOpenConnection%()` function actually replaces two functions used in conjunction. They are `SqlLogin%()` and `SqlOpen%()`.

To execute a Transact-SQL statement, you use two basic functions: `SqlCmd%()` and `SqlExec%()`. First, you specify two parameters to the `SqlCmd%()` function. The first is the connection number returned from `SqlOpenConnection%()` in the preceding line of code. The next is the string representing the command to send to the server. The syntax is as follows:

```
res% = SqlCmd(conn%, Cmd$)
```

If `res%` is not equal to the constant `SUCCEED` (which is declared as the value `1`), then an error occurred. Otherwise, the string, `Cmd$`, is placed into the internal command buffer, waiting to be sent. To send the command to SQL Server, use the `SqlExec%()` function. It accepts only one argument, which is the connection returned from `SqlOpenConnection%()`. It has this syntax:

```
res% = SqlExec%(conn%)
```

Once again, if `res%` is not equal to `SUCCEED`, then there was an error. Otherwise, the command succeeded and the results buffer will be filled with any results coming back from SQL Server. Note that not all commands will return results. In this case, the result buffer will be empty. You can test to see whether there were results returned by using the `SqlResults%()` function. This function accepts one parameter, which is the connection returned by `SqlOpenConnection%()` in the preceding line of code. It returns the status of whether there are results, and follows this syntax:

```
res% = SqlResults%(conn%)
```

If `res%` is not equal to `SUCCEED`, an error occurred, which means that there are no results. If `res%` is equal to `SUCCEED`, then there were results returned by SQL Server. You can manipulate the results buffer by using the `SqlNextRow%()` and `SqlData$()` functions. The `SqlNextRow%()` function enables you to access the next row of data in the resultset returned by SQL Server. `SqlData$()` enables you to read the data in the row allocated by `SqlNextRow%()`. The two work hand-in-hand. You would generally loop through all rows of data and process it in some way. To loop through the rows of data, you could use this code:

```
Do Until SqlNextRow(conn%) = NOMOREROWS
    'Process data here
Loop
```

Here, `NOMOREROWS` is declared as the constant value `-2`. During the loop, you can process the results in any way you see fit. For example, you might want to fill a grid with the data. Another possibility is to write the data to a file. To access the actual data value returned, use the `SqlData$()` function, which accepts two arguments. The first is, of course, the connection returned by `SqlOpenConnection%()`. The second is the column of the data you want to access in the resultset. It returns a string representing the value returned for a particular column in the current row. For example, suppose you wanted to execute this SQL statement:

```
SELECT CustomerID, ZipCode
FROM Customer
ORDER BY CustomerID
```

You explicitly asked for two columns of data to be returned. Therefore, you know which columns to ask for. What if you didn't know how many columns would be returned, such as in the following SQL statement:

```
SELECT *
FROM Customer
ORDER BY CustomerID
```

In this case, you have no idea how many columns will be returned.

CROSS REFERENCE

For more information about SQL, refer to Chapter 29, "Structured Query Language (SQL)."

To determine how many columns are in the resultset, you can use the `SqlNumCols%()` function. This function accepts one argument, the connection returned by `SqlOpenConnection%()`, and returns an integer representing the number of columns in the resultset. It uses this syntax:

```
res% = SqlNumCols%(conn%)
```

Therefore, you can loop through all available columns until there are no more rows.

After you are finished using the connection opened by `SqlOpenConnection%()`, you must close the connection. This is similar to closing a file handle in Visual Basic after it is opened. To close a connection, you use either the `SqlClose%()` or the `SqlExit` subroutine. `SqlClose%()` accepts only one parameter, which is the connection returned by `SqlOpenConnection%()`. `SqlExit` does not accept any parameters. Neither subroutine returns any value. The difference between the two is that `SqlClose%()` closes a specific connection number, and `SqlExit` closes all open connections to SQL Server. `SqlClose%()` uses this syntax:

```
Call SqlClose%(conn%)
```

`SqlExit` uses this syntax:

```
Call SqlExit
```

You must do one final thing. You must unregister the library from your application by using the `SqlWinExit` subroutine. It does not accept any arguments and does not return any values. It is generally the last VBSQL function called before terminating the application, and it uses this syntax:

```
Call SqlWinExit
```

Multiuser Considerations

Most databases must handle multiple users connecting to the database at the same time. This creates some problems, however. The problems exist with concurrency. *Concurrency* is a term that indicates how concurrent (multiple) users handle data at the same time. This is done in a couple of ways.

The first way is with standard record locking. There are two types of record locking, *pessimistic* and *optimistic*.

Pessimistic locking is a term used to describe the fact that a recordset is locked as soon as the `Edit` method is invoked. This is the default method for JET workspaces. This method is safer than optimistic locking, but can tie up the database for longer periods of time because while the recordset is in the `Edit` mode, the records in the recordset are locked. This forces all pending transactions to wait until the records are updated.

Optimistic locking is just the opposite of pessimistic locking. The records are not locked when you perform the `Edit` method, but when you use the `Update` method instead. Therefore, as a developer, you must account for the fact that one user, User A, can be looking at data on the screen. Then another user, User B, executes an `Update` method. If the same data is changed on User A's screen and an `Update` method is executed, effectively the data for User B is lost.

Summary

Many concepts center around using databases. With each of these concepts comes terminology and acronyms, such as DAO, RDO, SQL, tables, indexes, and many others. In this chapter, you learned each of these terms along with syntax and usage to help you use these technologies in your own programs. In addition to the database topics discussed in this chapter, please read the other database chapters.

29

Structured Query Language (SQL)

Structured Query Language (SQL) has quickly become the standard relational database language. SQL gives you a way to impose standards when you use a relational database. There still are some relational databases that do not support SQL, but the vast majority of them do. Here's a list of some of the relational databases that support SQL:

- SQL Server
- Access
- Sybase
- Oracle
- Informix
- SQLBase
- Ingres

NOTE

It is very important to note that this chapter covers some of the basics of the SQL language—that is, the American National Standards Institute (ANSI) SQL language. It is not database specific, which means that certain database engines can have a slightly different syntax. This also means that some of the code presented might not work correctly for a given database engine. You must consult the documentation for your specific database engine to be sure.

This SQL standard can be used in either a client/server environment or in a stand-alone environment. Either way, SQL is the language used to query the *database engine.* A database engine is the heart of the database; it is how the database vendor decides the database operates and functions, how data is stored, how syntax is used, and how processing occurs.

You can actually use SQL to do more than construct queries. Using SQL implies that you are querying the database to get data returned from it. In fact, there is much more to it than this. You use SQL to insert new data, update existing data, and even control the parameters of the database engine.

SQL can be sent to a database engine by many means. The database engine comes with some sort of interactive tool for sending SQL statements to get some result. This is sometimes referred to as Interactive Structured Query Language (ISQL).

This chapter deals with SQL as a whole. The subject of SQL can be, and has been, the subject of entire books. This one chapter cannot cover every aspect of SQL, but it does cover the basics. It also does not get into specific database engines. There are certain things common in all SQL databases. These basic commonalties are the subject of the rest of this chapter. However, for the purpose of providing examples, the following sample data is used. The data is broken up into four tables, shown in Tables 29.1 through 29.4.

Table 29.1. The INVENTORY table.

Product ID	*Description*	*Supplier ID*	*Quantity*
MS001	Visual Basic	M001	45
MS002	Word For Windows	M001	100
MS003	Excel	M001	10
SO001	OCX-10 Home Automation/VB Interface	S002	145

Table 29.2. The SALES table.

Product ID	*Staff ID*	*Date Sold*	*Quantity Sold*
MS001	D001	8/26/96	5
SO001	M001	8/26/96	5

Table 29.3. The STAFF table.

Staff ID	*Last Name*	*First Name*
D001	Duck	Donald
M001	Mann	Anthony
M002	Mouse	Mickey

Table 29.4. The SUPPLIER table.

Supplier ID	*Supplier*
B001	Borland
I001	Intuit
M001	Microsoft
S001	Sams Publishing
S002	SoftHouse

The tables are shown to give you an idea of the structure of a database and how the fields relate to each other. Designing databases is not the topic of this chapter; however, it is important to see how the data relates so that the examples presented later make sense.

Using Tables 29.1 through 29.4, you can see that the INVENTORY table contains a list of all the items a company can stock. The table also contains a field for the quantity in stock and the product ID used to identify when a sale is made in the SALES table. Listing the description of the product every time a sale occurs is inefficient. There is also a supplier ID field that identifies the company that supplies the product from the SUPPLIER table.

The SALES table relates to the tables discussed in the preceding paragraph, but the SALES table also has a field for the staff ID (the person selling the item). The name of the person selling the item is looked up in the STAFF table, based on the staff ID.

That is how the four tables relate to each other. Each of the tables contains very simple data. However, if the database is designed correctly, it makes no difference how much data is in the tables.

Retrieving Data

By far, the most common SQL statement is the `SELECT` statement. This statement is used to retrieve rows of data from a table as well as for many other purposes (which are presented in the rest of this chapter). To use this statement, you must either know the names of the columns in the table you are trying to receive, or you can use an asterisk to specify all columns. The statement has the following general syntax:

```
SELECT [ALL¦DISTINCT] [TOP xx [PERCENT]] select_list
FROM table_names
[WHERE {search_criteria¦join_criteria}
[{AND¦OR search_criteria}]]
[GROUP BY [ALL]aggregate_free_expression [,aggregate_free_expression...]]
[HAVING search_conditions]
[ORDER BY {field_list} [ASC¦DESC]]
```

where:

> `ALL` specifies that every row is returned, including duplicates. (This is the default and need not be used.)
>
> `DISTINCT` specifies that only non-duplicate rows are to be returned.
>
> `TOP` specifies that you would like only the top *xx* number of records returned. You may also specify the `PERCENT` keyword after the number *xx*. This returns only the top *xx* percentage of the total records to be returned. See the section "Limiting the Selection" for more information.
>
> *`select_list`* is the list of column names in the tables to return, separated by commas.
>
> *`table_names`* is the list of tables that return data.
>
> *`search_criteria`* is the list of column names in the tables to return.
>
> *`join_criteria`* is the list of column names in one table that joins to other column names in a different table.

`aggregate_free_expression` is an expression that does not include an aggregate. Refer to Table 29.6 for a list of aggregate functions that cannot be included in this expression.

`field_list` is a list of the columns the data is sorted on.

`ASC` specifies that the sort order is ascending. (This is the default and need not be used.)

`DESC` specifies that the sort order is descending.

If you are not intimately familiar with SQL, the preceding information can seem pretty confusing. Let me simplify it by providing examples from the sample tables used in Tables 29.1 through 29.4.

Selecting Records

NOTE

The keywords throughout this chapter, such as `SELECT`, `FROM`, and so on, are not case sensitive. They are listed here in uppercase to set them apart from the regular text, but you can type them in lowercase.

To use the `SELECT` statement you must know what you want to select and from what. This means that you need to know the column names and the table names you are trying to select. If you do not know the column names, you must use an asterisk. This selects all columns in the tables. For example, if you want to select all values from the Supplier column in the SUPPLIER table, you use this statement:

```
SELECT Supplier
FROM SUPPLIER
```

Or you could use this:

```
SELECT *
FROM SUPPLIER
```

NOTE

Even though the keywords are not case sensitive, some databases have case sensitive column names and table names. For this example, the table names have been designed in uppercase, while the column names have been designed in lowercase. Columns are sometimes referred to as *fields* and column names as *field names.* They are synonymous.

NOTE

Even though an SQL statement can consist of many lines of text, it is actually one statement. To help you understand this concept, as a general rule, a statement will consist of all lines of SQL text between two `SELECT` keywords.

Also, even though these SQL text lines are shown on separate lines, they actually can be put on one line. They are generally constructed on multiple lines because they are easier to read. The SQL standard calls for the database engine (whichever one is used) to ignore the carriage return between SQL keywords in the statement.

The preceding SQL statement produces a complete list of the suppliers in the `SUPPLIER` table, but the order returned is the order in which they are entered into the table. If you want to sort the list alphabetically, you can use this statement:

```
SELECT Supplier
FROM SUPPLIER
ORDER BY Supplier
```

The `ORDER BY` keyword (sometimes referred to as the `ORDER BY` *clause*) needs a column name to know which column to sort on. This ensures that the data is ordered by the Supplier column. By default, the data is ordered in ascending order. To sort in descending order, use this statement:

```
SELECT Supplier
FROM SUPPLIER
ORDER BY Supplier DESC
```

If you want to select multiple columns, use the following statement:

```
SELECT Supplier,Supplier_ID
FROM SUPPLIER
ORDER BY Supplier
```

This statement selects the `Supplier` column first, followed by the `Supplier_ID` column. All values in the table are returned because you did not limit the search. Two columns are selected in the preceding statement (which, coincidentally, is the total number of columns in the SUPPLIER table). However, if you have a table with 100 columns and you want to select all of the columns, you don't have to type in the names of all 100 columns. You can select all columns in a table with a statement like this:

```
SELECT *
FROM SUPPLIER
ORDER BY Supplier
```

The asterisk indicates that all columns are selected from the SUPPLIER table. The table is still sorted by the `Supplier` column in ascending order.

Limiting the Selection

You do not have to return all data from a table; you can limit the number of rows returned by using the `WHERE` keyword. Suppose that you want to find out what the supplier ID is for SoftHouse. You want to limit the number of rows in the SUPPLIER table to all rows in which the supplier is equal to `"SoftHouse"`. You can do this with the following code:

```
SELECT *
FROM SUPPLIER
WHERE Supplier = "SoftHouse"
ORDER BY Supplier
```

The data returned is only the data that matches the `WHERE` keyword (also referred to as the `WHERE` clause). If there is no supplier named SoftHouse, then no rows are returned.

NOTE

The string literal in the `WHERE` clause is case sensitive. Therefore, `"SoftHouse"` is not the same as `"SOFTHOUSE"`.

It is also important to note that some implementations of SQL require the use of single quotes (apostrophes) instead of double quotes.

The `ORDER BY` clause is not necessary in the preceding statement, but it doesn't hurt it either. This is because, by design, each supplier appears in the SUPPLIER table only once. Because you are looking for only one supplier, the order is irrelevant. However, if you are looking for more than one supplier, it does become relevant. For example, suppose that you are looking for `"SoftHouse"` or `"Microsoft"`. Use this SQL statement:

```
SELECT *
FROM SUPPLIER
WHERE Supplier = "SoftHouse" OR Supplier = "Microsoft"
ORDER BY Supplier
```

In this case, two rows are returned: first the `"Microsoft"` row and then the `"SoftHouse"` row. This is because of the `ORDER BY` clause.

Another way to write the preceding statement is to use the `IN` keyword. The `IN` keyword enables you to list a range of values to test for. The values are separated by a comma. The preceding statement is rewritten as this:

```
SELECT *
FROM SUPPLIER
WHERE Supplier IN ("SoftHouse","Microsoft")
ORDER BY Supplier
```

Using the `IN` keyword can generally save a lot of typing because the column name does not have to be repeated. Table 29.5 lists additional keywords that can be used in the `WHERE` clause.

Table 29.5. Keywords that can be used in a `WHERE` clause.

Keywords	*Purpose*
`IN`	Tests for values in a range
`NOT IN`	Tests for values not in a range
`LIKE`	Tests for values that are like a value
`NOT LIKE`	Tests for values that are not like a value
`IS NULL`	Tests for values that are null
`IS NOT NULL`	Tests for values that are not null
`AND`	Tests for multiple conditions
`OR`	Tests for either of two conditions
`BETWEEN`	Tests for values between a set of values
`NOT BETWEEN`	Tests for values not between a set of values
`EXISTS`	Tests for values that exist
`NOT EXISTS`	Tests for values that do not exist
`ANY`	Tests for any values
`ALL`	Tests for all values

A very common necessity is to return values that, for example, start with a certain letter, such as "S." You can do this by using the `LIKE` keyword.

If you want to return all rows from the SUPPLIER table for a supplier starting with an "S," use this statement:

```
SELECT *
FROM SUPPLIER
WHERE Supplier LIKE "S%"
ORDER BY Supplier
```

This statement returns rows containing the suppliers `"SAMS Publishing"` and `"SoftHouse"`. The following is the syntax for using the `LIKE` keyword, where you might have a percent sign either before the *`constant`*, after the *`constant`*, or both:

```
LIKE "[%]constant[%]"
```

The *`constant`* is the value for which you are testing. The percent signs are wildcard symbols, just like asterisks in DOS. If you are looking for any supplier that has an "S" in its name, use this statement:

```
SELECT *
FROM SUPPLIER
WHERE Supplier LIKE "%S%"
ORDER BY Supplier
```

NOTE

Microsoft Access uses an asterisk (*) wildcard symbol in place of the percent sign (%) when accessed through DAO. The percent sign applies to SQL Server and other client/server databases, as well as Access via ODBC. The rest of the syntax is the same. Also, the expression placed between wildcard symbols is case sensitive.

NOTE

You must use at least one percent sign in a `LIKE` clause. If you don't, no rows are returned.

Because the `SELECT` keyword is used to return values, you can even go so far as to return a value that is not part of the database. This is referred to as a *calculated column*. For example, you can return a percentage of the quantity in the INVENTORY table. Instead of the following SQL statement, which returns the quantity that is actually in the database

```
SELECT Quantity
FROM INVENTORY
```

you can use this SQL statement to return 10 percent of the quantities:

```
SELECT Quantity * .10
FROM INVENTORY
```

This works only for a numeric datatype. You cannot do this if `Quantity` is a string.

Another way to limit the number of records returned is to use the `TOP` keyword. For example, suppose you wanted to test an SQL statement to determine whether you have used the correct syntax. However, you do not want to return potentially millions of rows of data for a test. You can use the optional `TOP` keyword to limit the number of rows.

The `TOP` keyword without the following `PERCENT` keyword returns only the first *xx* number of records of the total recordset. For example, the following will return only the first 10 records from the Supplier table:

```
SELECT TOP 10 *
FROM SUPPLIER
ORDER BY Supplier
```

If there were 250 records in the table, only the first 10 would be returned. Likewise, this example will return the first 10 percent of the total records from the Supplier table:

```
SELECT TOP 10 PERCENT *
FROM SUPPLIER
ORDER BY Supplier
```

Again, if there were 250 records in the table, only the first 25 would be returned.

Joins

A *join* is a way to return data from two tables. The key to doing this is that you must "join" or "*link*" the columns of data between the two tables so the database engine knows how to look it up. You create the join in the `WHERE` clause. If you want to select all items in the INVENTORY table but also with the company that supplied each item, you have to do a join between the INVENTORY table and the SUPPLIER table. This is because there is a column (Supplier_ID) that is common to both tables, and this column is what the join is based on. This is also called a *common key*, which is a "key" field that is used as a join. For the SUPPLIER table, it is the primary key, which means that this is the column used to access a row in the table. It is not the primary key in the INVENTORY table because it is not used to access a row in this table. The Product_ID column is the primary key in that table. Again, how to determine primary keys and database design is not the purpose of this chapter.

To perform the join mentioned here, use this code:

```
SELECT Supplier, Description, Quantity
FROM SUPPLIER s, INVENTORY i
WHERE i.Supplier_ID = s.Supplier_ID
ORDER BY Supplier
```

This statement selects the Supplier, Description, and Quantity columns from the SUPPLIER and INVENTORY tables. For every occurrence of a supplier ID in the INVENTORY table, the supplier is looked up using the same Supplier_ID column, and the values are assigned to be equal.

The individual letters `s` and `i` you see in the preceding code are *aliases*. You use these to identify a column in a table that has the same name in another table you are trying to access. If you do not specify this alias, you receive an error telling you that the column name is ambiguous. This alias gives the database engine a way to decipher which column you are referring to. The alias name goes after the table names in the `FROM` clause. The alias name can be any unique value (treated as a string without quotes) as long as it is not the name of a table you are trying to access.

After the alias is established in the `FROM` clause, you can reference it by using this format, where *`alias`* is the name of the alias defined and *`column`* is the name of the column in the table that is aliased:

```
alias.column
```

For example, consider the `WHERE` clause in the previous statement:

```
WHERE i.Supplier_ID = s.Supplier_ID
```

It follows the syntax of *`alias.column`* on each side of the `=` sign. After the alias is established, you can use it in any of the SQL clauses that are part of that same statement.

If you are trying to select (return) columns in different tables, you must also reference the alias to avoid any ambiguity. Even if you are not selecting columns with the same name, you may still use the alias. For example, the following is not incorrect:

```
SELECT s.Supplier, i.Description, i.Quantity
FROM SUPPLIER s, INVENTORY i
WHERE i.Supplier_ID = s.Supplier_ID
ORDER BY s.Supplier
```

It performs the same function. However, it does introduce a possible element of error. At least one field in the `ORDER BY` clause needs to be in the `SELECT` clause. If you change the last line to the following, you receive an error because the Supplier column does not exist in the INVENTORY table:

```
ORDER BY i.Supplier
```

You can create even more complex joins. Suppose that you want to select the supplier, product description, and quantity, but return only the rows in the INVENTORY table where the supplier is `"Microsoft"`. You have to do a join again to the SUPPLIER table because the only reference to supplier in the INVENTORY table is an ID, Supplier_ID, which is used as a lookup key in the SUPPLIER table. You can do the join with this statement:

```
SELECT s.Supplier, i.Description, i.Quantity
FROM SUPPLIER s, INVENTORY i
WHERE i.Supplier_ID = s.Supplier_ID
AND s.Supplier = "Microsoft"
ORDER BY s.Supplier
```

Again, the `ORDER BY` clause is not absolutely necessary because there can be only one row in the SUPPLIER table with the name `"Microsoft"`.

You can use the techniques and topics discussed here to join many multiple tables in your application. However, remember that the more joins you do, the longer it takes the database engine to come back with the results.

Aggregates

An *aggregate* is a mathematical SQL function. Table 29.6 lists the types of SQL aggregates that are available.

Table 29.6. SQL aggregates.

Aggregate	*Purpose*
`COUNT()`	Counts the number of rows returned
`SUM()`	Sums the number of rows returned
`AVG()`	Averages the number of rows returned
`MAX()`	Finds the maximum value in the rows returned
`MIN()`	Finds the minimum value in the rows returned

In each of the aggregates listed, an expression (typically a column name) is expected in the parentheses. However, the expression can be any valid SQL expression.

If you want to find out how many rows are returned from this statement:

```
SELECT s.Supplier, i.Description, i.Quantity
FROM SUPPLIER s, INVENTORY i
WHERE i.Supplier_ID = s.Supplier_ID
ORDER BY s.Supplier
```

you can use this statement instead:

```
SELECT COUNT(*), s.Supplier, i.Description, i.Quantity
FROM SUPPLIER s, INVENTORY i
WHERE i.Supplier_ID = s.Supplier_ID
ORDER BY s.Supplier
```

This statement returns four columns, the count of the number of rows returned, the supplier, the description, and the quantity. The joins in the statement were discussed earlier in the "Joins" section.

When using an aggregate function, you can use a `GROUP BY` clause to tell the database engine how to do the calculation. For example, if you want to sum the number of items stocked for each supplier, you must use a `GROUP BY` clause. If you don't, how does the database engine know how to return the sum? Refer to Table 29.1 to follow this example. Would the database engine sum the quantities for each Product_ID, Description, Supplier_ID, or a combination of the three? That's where the `GROUP BY` clause comes in. In this scenario, you can perform the necessary function by using this statement:

```
SELECT SUM(Quantity)
FROM SUPPLIER s, INVENTORY i
WHERE i.Supplier_ID = s.Supplier_ID
GROUP BY s.Supplier
ORDER BY s.Supplier
```

This means that for every new supplier, the Quantity is summed. If the `GROUP BY` clause is omitted, only one row is returned, and it is the sum of all quantities.

Inserting Data

Without inserting data, there would never be the need to perform any `UPDATE`, `DELETE`, or `SELECT` statements. Inserting rows (or records) into a table requires an `INSERT` statement. The syntax of the `INSERT` statement is

```
INSERT [INTO] table[(column_list)]
VALUES{(insert_values)}¦sql_select_statement
```

where:

> *`table`* is the name of the table to insert into.
>
> *`column_list`* is a listing of columns that have data inserted, separated by commas.

insert_values is the list of values to be inserted into the columns in *column_list*. There must be the same number of values in the *insert_values* list as in the *column_list* list.

sql_select_statement is an alternative way to insert values into a table. You can select values of another table to be inserted. In this case, you do not use the `VALUES` keyword. You must make sure that the number of columns you are returning in your SQL statement is the same number as in the *column_list* list.

NOTE

Microsoft Access requires the `INTO` keyword, SQL Server does not.

To use the `INSERT` statement to insert a new supplier into the SUPPLIER table, you can use this statement:

```
INSERT SUPPLIER(Supplier_ID,Supplier)
VALUES ("C001","Crystal Services")
```

The row is simply inserted into the table. Here are some considerations, however:

- Does the primary key field already exist?
- Are you concerned about case sensitivity?
- Are you inserting values using the correct datatype?

These questions are very important. Except for the case sensitivity question, the questions presented here can result in errors if they are not addressed properly.

For example, the following will result in error:

```
INSERT SUPPLIER(Supplier_ID,Supplier)
VALUES (1,"Crystal Services")
```

The Supplier_ID column does not expect a numeric datatype; it expects a string datatype. If you are not going to include any characters, you must construct the SQL statement this way:

```
INSERT SUPPLIER(Supplier_ID,Supplier)
VALUES ("1","Crystal Services")
```

Instead of inserting into a table by hard coding the values, you can also insert by selecting the values from another table. Suppose that you have a table, MASTER, which also has Supplier_ID and Supplier columns from which you are going to select values. You can insert all items from the MASTER table like this:

```
INSERT SUPPLIER(Supplier_ID,Supplier)
SELECT Supplier_ID,Supplier
FROM MASTER
```

On the other hand, if you only wanted to insert based on a certain value from the MASTER table, you could construct your SQL `SELECT` statement based on any valid SQL rule. You could do this:

```
INSERT SUPPLIER(Supplier_ID,Supplier)
SELECT Supplier_ID,Supplier
FROM MASTER
WHERE Supplier="Crystal Services"
```

As presented in the "Retrieving Data" section earlier in the chapter, the `WHERE` clause limits the number of rows returned.

Deleting Data

Deleting rows (or records) from a table requires a `DELETE` statement. The syntax of the `DELETE` statement is

```
DELETE FROM table
[WHERE search_conditions]
```

where:

> *`table`* is the name of the table to delete from.
>
> *`search_conditions`* are any valid SQL expressions to limit the number of rows deleted.

The `DELETE` statement deletes an entire row or rows in the database. You cannot delete only one column.

You can use the `DELETE` statement to delete all rows in the SUPPLIER table by using this statement:

```
DELETE FROM SUPPLIER
```

> **CAUTION**
>
> There is no confirmation when you use the `DELETE` statement. If the statement is executed, the rows are deleted. It's that simple. Be very careful when you use the `DELETE` statement.

If you want to delete the rows only where the supplier is a certain value, you do it like this:

```
DELETE FROM SUPPLIER
WHERE Supplier = "Borland"
```

This statement deletes all values in the SUPPLIER table where the Supplier is `"Borland"`.

> **NOTE**
>
> You must be careful when you delete (or update) a row in a table in case a value relates to a value in a different table. If it does, it is possible to "orphan" a row of data in the other table. This means that the value related to data in the table from which you deleted now has no way to be referenced. This means that the row in this second table is just taking up space.
>
> There are ways around this that are not within the scope of this chapter, as stated earlier. When you design the database, you can place a trigger on the column so that this doesn't happen inadvertently.

Updating Data

Updating rows (or records) in a table requires an `UPDATE` statement. The syntax of the `UPDATE` statement is

```
UPDATE table
SET assignment_list
[WHERE search_conditions]
```

where:

> *`table`* is the name of the table to insert into.
>
> *`assignment_list`* is a listing of all updates that will take place.
>
> *`search_conditions`* are any valid SQL expressions to limit the number of rows updated.

If you want to update the Supplier_ID column of the SUPPLIER table, you can use the `UPDATE` statement:

```
UPDATE SUPPLIER
SET Supplier_ID="XXX"
```

All rows in the Supplier_ID column are updated to `"XXX"`. To prevent this from happening, you need to limit the search by using a `WHERE` clause with any valid SQL expression. You can limit the updating as described earlier to only where the Supplier is equal to `"Borland"`. You do this as follows:

```
UPDATE SUPPLIER
SET Supplier_ID="XXX"
WHERE Supplier = "Borland"
```

CAUTION

There is no confirmation when you use the UPDATE statement. If the statement is executed, the rows are updated. It's that simple. Be very careful when you use the UPDATE statement.

On the other hand, if you only want to update based on a certain value from the another table, you can use any valid SQL SELECT statement in place of *assignment_list* in the syntax presented earlier. Suppose that you have a table, MASTER, that also has Supplier_ID and Supplier columns out of which you are going to select values. You can insert an item from the MASTER table to update a record in the SUPPLIER table like this:

```
UPDATE SUPPLIER
SET Supplier_ID = (SELECT Supplier_ID
FROM MASTER
WHERE Supplier = "SoftHouse")
WHERE Supplier = "SoftHouse"
```

The last two lines of the preceding statement look like they are repeated. In actuality, they are not. Notice the parentheses around the statement between the second and fourth lines. This is actually a query within a query. The inner query selects from the MASTER table the supplier ID where the supplier is "SoftHouse".

The outer query, which is the UPDATE statement, updates the Supplier_ID column to the value returned from the inner query, but limits the rows for which this applies to where the supplier is equal to "SoftHouse". If the last line is not present, all rows in the Supplier_ID column are updated.

The query within a query concept (called *nested queries*) opens up more possibilities for you when you use the SQL language. As you develop more advanced applications that retrieve data, you'll find that understanding SQL is vital.

Transactions

A *transaction* is a very important part of proper database design. A transaction provides a way to wrap a series of critical SQL statements together as a group. This way, if something fails, the database can revert to the state it was in before the statements were issued. The following three statements handle transactions:

- BEGINTRANS marks the beginning of a transaction.
- COMMITTRANS marks the end of a transaction.
- ROLLBACK rolls the transaction back to the state the database was in before the BEGINTRANS was issued.

You indicate the beginning of the group of statements with the BEGINTRANS keyword. If there are no errors, the transaction is ended with the COMMITTRANS keyword. This commits all statements that are executed since the BEGINTRANS was issued. However, if there is an error, it must be handled in an error handler. The error handler must tell the database not to issue any of the statements executed since the BEGINTRANS was issued. This is done with the ROLLBACK keyword.

The reason that the database is able to do this is because internally it stores the data in a transaction log. The transaction log stores the data in the state that it was at the time the BEGINTRANS was issued. If it needs to be rolled back, the system can do that because there is a snapshot of the data as it was.

A good example of when you might use transactions is in an order entry/accounting application. In one transaction, with one order, you want to do the following things:

- Let the shipping department know about the items to be shipped
- Update the customer's record
- Decrease inventory

All of these items need to be handled at once. If any of them fail, then all need to fail. For example, if the SQL statement to decrease the inventory fails and you don't force the customer's record and the shipping department transactions to fail, there is no integrity between the sets of data. The customer's record would say that an item was ordered. The shipping department would ship the item. However, the inventory would not decrease. As this situation continues, the inventory database would show a large number of items, but these items wouldn't actually exist because the shipping department keeps receiving orders to ship them out. This code fragment illustrates this concept:

```
'Handle Error
On Error Goto SaveError
'Begin the transaction
BeginTrans
'Instruct the shipping department to ship the item
sCmd = "INSERT INTO Shipping(Cust_ID, Stock_Num, Qty) "
sCmd = sCmd + "VALUES (101, '119945A', 2) "
'issue statement
dbMain.Workspaces(0).Execute sCmd

'Update the customer's record
sCmd = "INSERT INTO Order(Cust_ID, Stock_Num, Qty, Price, Date) "
sCmd = sCmd + "VALUES (101, '19945A', 2, 19.95, '12/15/96') "
'issue statement
dbMain.Workspaces(0).Execute sCmd

'Update inventory
sCmd = "UPDATE Inventory "
sCmd = sCmd + "SET On_Hand = On_Hand - 2 "
sCmd = sCmd + "WHERE Stock_Num = '19945A' "
'issue statement
dbMain.Workspaces(0).Execute sCmd
```

```
'there were no errors, commit
CommitTrans
Exit Sub

'error handler
SaveError:
    MsgBox Error$
    Rollback
    Exit Sub
```

Data Definition Statements

You can use data definition statements to create or alter the database structure itself. You can use them to do the following:

- Create tables
- Add columns to tables
- Add indexes on tables
- Delete tables and indexes

These statements are issued from Visual Basic just as any other statement would be issued—by using the `EXECUTE` method of the database object.

Creating Tables

To create a table, you use the `CREATE TABLE` keywords. These keywords use the syntax

```
CREATE TABLE table (field1 type [(size)] [index1] [, field2 type [(size)]
➥[index2] [, ...]]
[, multifieldindex [, ...]])
```

where:

> *`table`* is the name of the table to be created.
>
> *`field1, field2...`* are the names of fields to be created in the new table. (At least one field must be created at this time.)
>
> *`type`* is the datatype of the new field.
>
> *`size`* is the field size in characters for a text field.
>
> *`index1, index2...`* specify a `CONSTRAINT` clause defining a single-field index.
>
> *`multifieldindex`* specifies a `CONSTRAINT` clause defining a multiple-field index.

Suppose you wanted to create a table named Orders. This table would have five columns, Cust_ID, Stock_Num, Qty, Price, and OrderDate. Also, there would be a primary key index on the Cust_ID column:

```
CREATE TABLE Orders (Cust_ID Double CONSTRAINT PKey PRIMARY KEY, Stock_Num
➥TEXT(10), Qty Integer, Price CURRENCY, OrderDate DATE)
```

If you want to make Cust_ID, Stock_Num, and OrderDate the primary key, you would do so like this:

```
CREATE TABLE Orders (Cust_ID Double, Stock_Num TEXT(10), Qty Integer,
➥Price CURRENCY, OrderDate DATE, CONSTRAINT PKey PRIMARY KEY(Cust_ID,
➥Stock_Num, OrderDate))
```

Adding or Deleting Columns and Indexes

To alter a table, use the `ALTER TABLE` keywords with the following syntax:

```
ALTER TABLE table {ADD {[COLUMN] field type[(size)] [CONSTRAINT index] I
CONSTRAINT multifieldindex} ¦
DROP {[COLUMN] field I CONSTRAINT indexname} }
```

where:

> *table* is the name of the table to be altered.
>
> *field* is the name of the field to be added to or deleted from the table.
>
> *type* is the datatype of the field.
>
> *size* is the field size in characters for text fields.
>
> *index* is the index for the field.
>
> *multifieldindex* is the definition of a multiple-field index to be added to the table.
>
> *indexname* is the name of the multiple-field index to be removed.

Suppose you wanted to add a Ship_Date column to the previous example. You could do that like this:

```
ALTER TABLE Orders
ADD COLUMN Ship_Date DATE
```

If you wanted to then delete a column, you could do that like this:

```
ALTER TABLE Orders
DROP COLUMN Ship_Date
```

You can use this same general syntax to add or delete indexes. The only difference is that you must follow the rules for the `CONSTRAINT` clause, which follows one of two basic syntaxes. The first is for a single field index, which follows the basic syntax

```
CONSTRAINT name {PRIMARY KEY ¦ UNIQUE ¦
REFERENCES foreigntable [(foreignfield)]}
```

where:

> *name* is the name of the index to be created.
>
> *forcigntablc* is the name of the foreign table containing the field or fields specified by *foreignfield1*, *foreignfield2*, and so on.
>
> *foreignfield1, foreignfield2...* are the names of the fields in *foreigntable* specified by *ref1* and *ref2*. This field can be omitted if the referenced field is the primary key of *foreigntable*.

The second is for a multiple field index, which follows this basic syntax:

```
CONSTRAINT name
{PRIMARY KEY (primary1[, primary2 [, ...]]) ¦
UNIQUE (unique1[, unique2 [, ...]]) ¦
FOREIGN KEY (ref1[, ref2 [, ...]]) REFERENCES foreigntable [(foreignfield1
➥[, foreignfield2 [, ...]])]}
```

where:

> `name` is the name of the index to be created.
>
> `primary1, primary2...` are the names of the fields to be designated as the primary key.
>
> `unique1, unique2...` are the names of the fields to be designated as a unique key.
>
> `ref1, ref2...` are the names of foreign key fields that refer to fields in another table.
>
> `foreigntable` is the name of the foreign table containing the field or fields specified by `foreignfield1`, `foreignfield2`, and so on.
>
> `foreignfield1, foreignfield2...` are the names of the fields in `foreigntable` specified by `ref1` and `ref2`. This field can be omitted if the referenced field is the primary key of `foreigntable`.

Deleting Tables and Indexes

Deleting tables or indexes requires a very simple SQL statement. It is done by using the `DROP` keyword. Of course, you know the name of the table to delete, but it can be difficult to know the name of an index. If you created it, you would know the naming conventions you've used. For example, a primary key index could be called Pkey. However, if you've used some other tool to create the tables and indexes, you might not know the name. One thing you could do is cycle through the `Indexes` collection to determine all index names.

CROSS REFERENCE

For more information about collections, refer to Chapter 22, "Collections."

The `DROP` keyword is used with the general syntax

```
DROP {TABLE table ¦ INDEX index ON table}
```

where:

> `table` is the name of the table to delete or the name of the index to delete that resides in a table.
>
> `index` is the name of the index to delete.

If you wanted to delete the table Orders, you would do so like this:

```
DROP TABLE Orders
```

TRIED AND TRUE

You will receive no confirmation prompt before the table or index is deleted. Issuing the statement will perform the action.

NOTE

Client/server databases, such as SQL Server, also enable you to `DROP` databases, provided that you have the appropriate permissions to do so.

Summary

SQL is a very important topic because it has become the standard language of most databases. SQL varies slightly between different databases, but the core components discussed in this chapter are common to most databases, except where noted. This chapter gives a good insight into SQL and how it is used. Please use this chapter as an ongoing reference for your database projects.

30

ODBC

ODBC stands for Open Database Connectivity. ODBC provides an application-independent way to connect to a multitude of databases. Provided that you obtain the correct driver, ODBC enables you to connect to any database. This chapter describes ODBC and some of the tools you can use to manipulate and test ODBC drivers and connections.

Regardless of the database to which you connect, called the Database Management System (DBMS), the database needs to process SQL statements. This is done in five steps, as follows:

1. The SQL statement is parsed so that the DBMS knows about specific clauses, such as `SELECT`, `FROM`, and `WHERE`.
2. The SQL statement is validated for accuracy in table and column names.
3. A query plan is generated to determine how the SQL statement will be executed.
4. The DBMS determines how to optimize the query by using indexes, if appropriate. Relatively speaking, this process can take the longest amount of time of all the processes because there are potentially thousands of ways to optimize a query. However, it is worth the overhead of determining how to optimize the query, as opposed to running the query without using an index.
5. The SQL statement is executed.

CROSS REFERENCE

For more information about using SQL, refer to Chapter 29, "Structured Query Language (SQL)."

ODBC enables you to call and issue three different types of SQL statements:

- Embedded SQL
- SQL modules
- Call-level interface

Embedded SQL is the type of SQL statement that is placed in code. You build it using different variables, objects, and control statements in your Visual Basic code.

An *SQL module* is a group of procedures called from Visual Basic. Each of these procedures contains a single SQL statement for processing. Parameters are passed to and from the procedure to enable data to flow in and out of the procedure.

A *call-level interface*, or CLI, is a specification developed to make ODBC an open, extensible environment.

The Background of ODBC

Many years ago, a company typically used one type of database. As databases became more flexible and companies needed to link enterprise-wide data, there was the need for one code base to access multiple databases. Therefore, ODBC was invented. It enabled developers to write one application that could access multiple types of databases. The only thing that needed to change was the ODBC driver.

ODBC has been greatly enhanced over the years. In the beginning it was very slow, but it has been refined so that it makes calls directly to the ODBC API, which is an application programming interface that provides direct access to ODBC drivers. ODBC has become the standard for connecting to remote databases.

ODBC SDK

The Microsoft ODBC Software Development Kit (SDK) is used to develop ODBC drivers in C++. Although this is not the topic of this chapter, it is worth noting some of the great tools that come with the SDK. The examples in this chapter are shown with the ODBC SDK version 3.0.

One of the tools is the 32-bit ODBC Administrator, sometimes referred to as the ODBC Data Source Administrator. There are six main tabs shown in the Administrator:

- User DSN
- System DSN
- File DSN
- ODBC Drivers
- Trace
- About

The User DSN tab enables you to configure an ODBC data source for use by one user only. Figure 30.1 shows what the User DSN tab looks like.

If you want to add a new data source, simply click the Add button. This invokes a dialog box to create a new data source. Figure 30.2 shows this dialog box.

If you want to edit a data source, click the Configure button. A dialog box that you are probably already familiar with, the SQL Server Setup dialog box, is invoked. This dialog box is very similar to the one that assigns an ODBC driver to a data source included since ODBC was created. Figure 30.3 shows this dialog box.

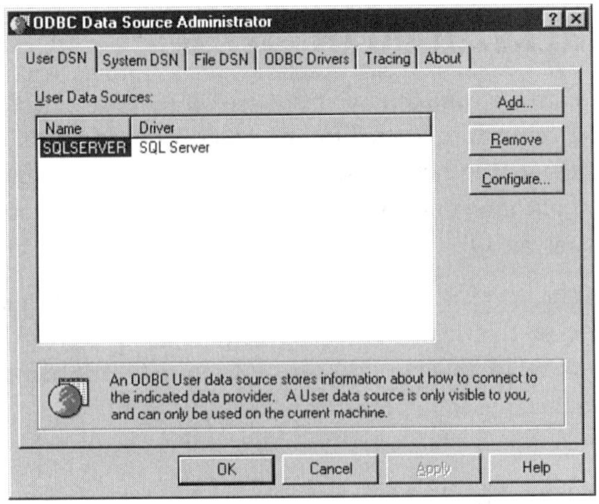

FIGURE 30.1.
The User DSN tab of the ODBC Administrator.

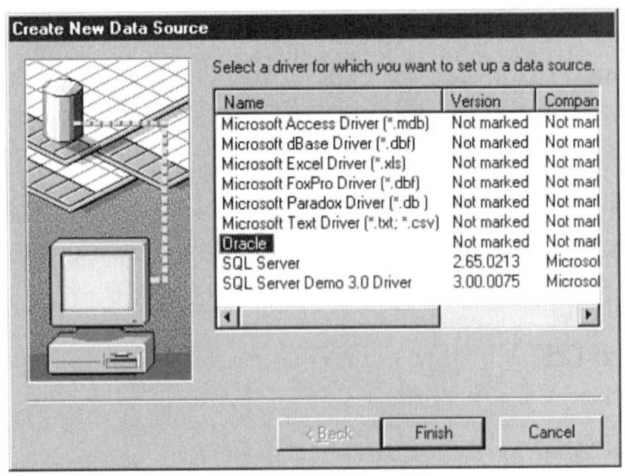

FIGURE 30.2.
The Create New Data Source dialog box of the ODBC Administrator.

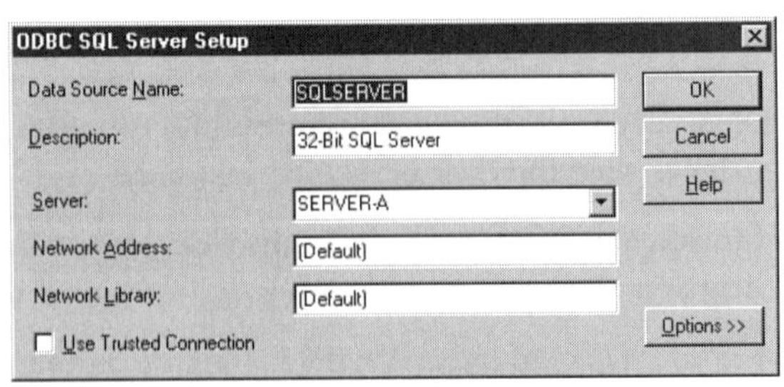

FIGURE 30.3.
The ODBC SQL Server Setup dialog box of the ODBC Administrator.

The next tab is the System DSN tab. You use it to set up data sources that will be used by multiple users on one computer. Again, if you need to add a new data source, select the Add button. Most Windows NT–based Web servers require that the data source be added as a system DSN. Figure 30.4 shows the System DSN tab.

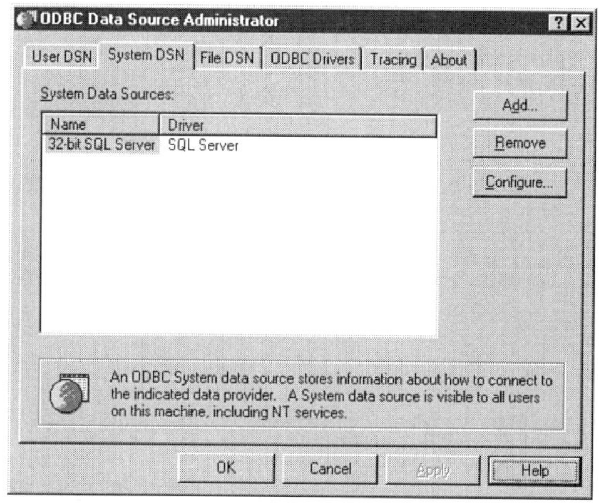

FIGURE 30.4.
The System DSN tab of the ODBC Administrator.

The next tab is the File DSN tab, which is used to set up a file-based data source, such as an Access database. Figure 30.5 shows this tab. If you want to add a new data source, select the Add button. This enables you to select an ODBC driver (see Figure 30.6).

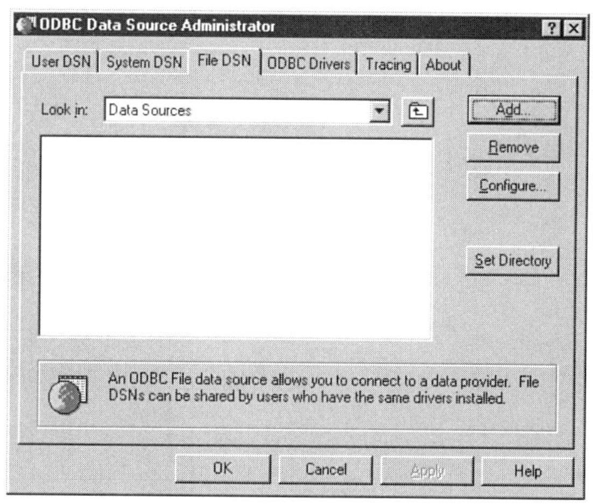

FIGURE 30.5.
The File DSN tab of the ODBC Administrator.

Click the Next button to assign the name of the data source. This enables you to assign a data source name to the file-based data source (see Figure 30.7).

Click the Next button. This brings up a review dialog box of the actions you have chosen in the previous steps. Figure 30.8 shows what the dialog box looks like.

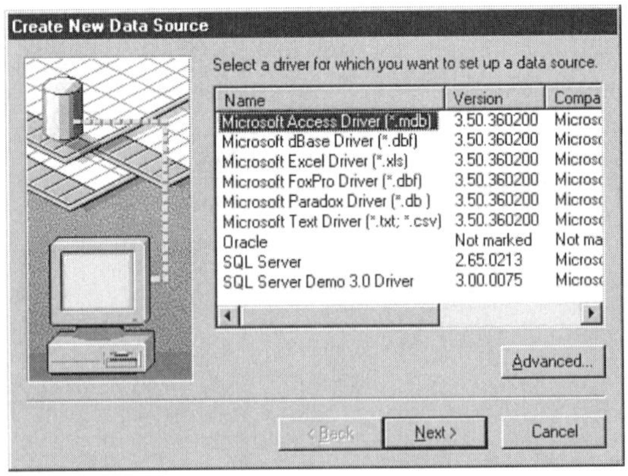

FIGURE 30.6.
Creating a new data source with the ODBC Administrator.

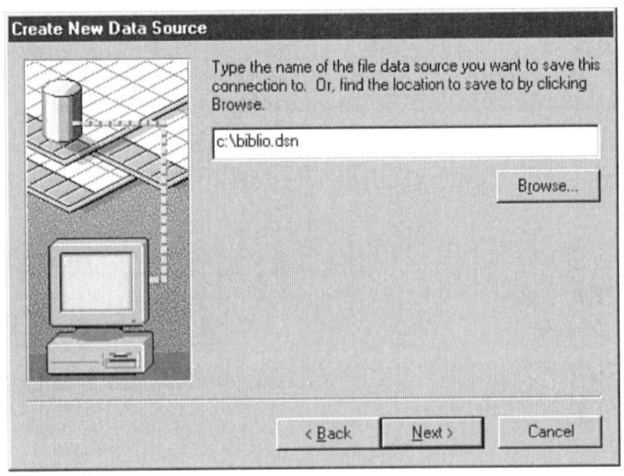

FIGURE 30.7.
Selecting a data source name in the Create New Data Source dialog box of the ODBC Administrator.

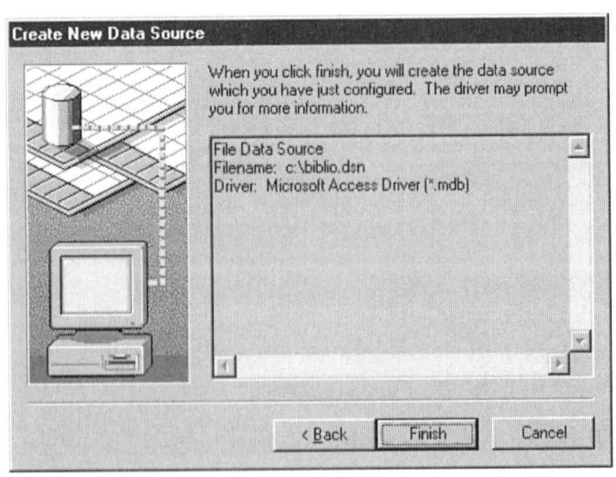

FIGURE 30.8.
Reviewing DSN settings in the Create New Data Source dialog box of the ODBC Administrator.

Click the Finish button. This brings up a dialog box for you to select the actual database name to connect to the file data source name. Figure 30.9 shows what this dialog box looks like.

FIGURE 30.9.
The ODBC Microsoft Access 97 Setup dialog box of the ODBC Administrator.

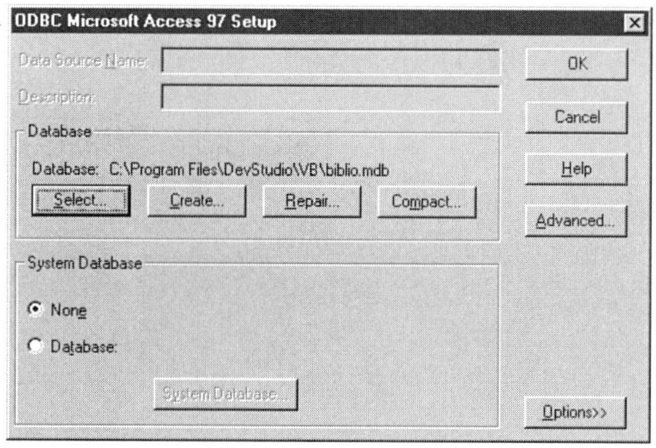

Click the Select button to select the database through a common dialog box.

The next tab, ODBC Drivers, simply lists the ODBC drivers installed on your system. Figure 30.10 shows the ODBC Drivers tab.

FIGURE 30.10.
The ODBC Drivers tab of the ODBC Administrator.

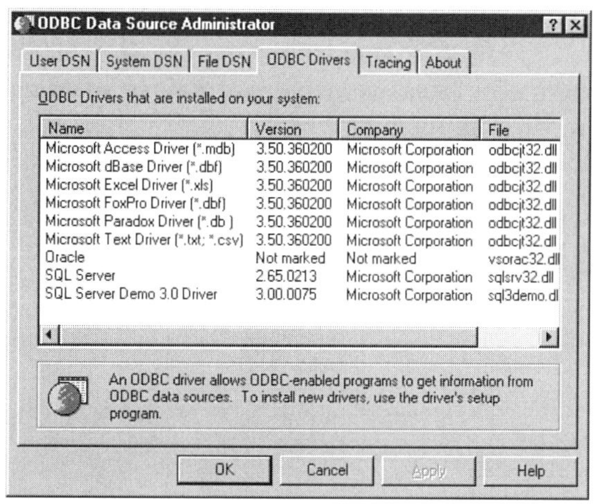

The Tracing tab enables you to trace the ODBC calls made by ODBC drivers. You have three options:

- Don't trace
- All the time
- One-time only

The Don't trace option, of course, turns off ODBC tracing. The All the time option specifies that ODBC tracing will always occur. The One-time only option allows ODBC tracing only once. If you opt for ODBC tracing, the calls made through the ODBC driver will be logged to a filename that you specify in the Log file Path text box. By default, this path is `\SQL.LOG` in the current drive. Figure 30.11 shows the Tracing tab.

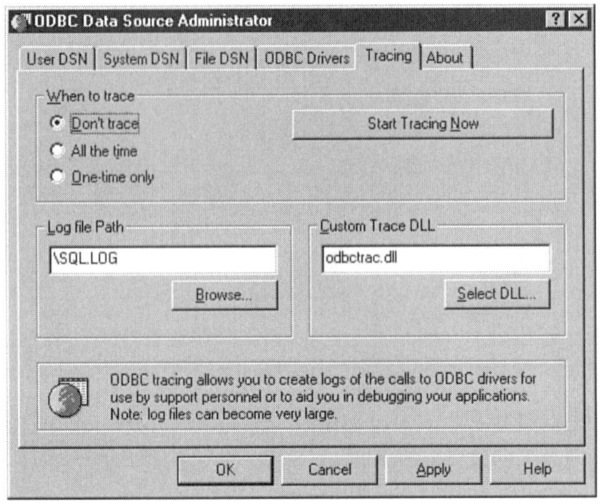

FIGURE 30.11.
The Tracing tab of the ODBC Administrator.

Tracing can help you debug your applications, or even to understand more about making ODBC API calls. Listing 30.1 shows a sample trace file after you simply log on. Unless you are actually going to use this log, you probably want to turn it off because, as you can see from Listing 30.1, the log can become quite large.

Listing 30.1. Sample ODBC trace.

```
ADMNDEMO        fff1098d:fffe07bd     ENTER SQLAllocHandle
        SQLSMALLINT                   1 <SQL_HANDLE_ENV>
        SQLHANDLE           0x00000000
        SQLHANDLE *         0x0040fa74

ADMNDEMO        fff1098d:fffe07bd     ENTER SQLSetEnvAttr
        SQLHENV             0x006615a0
        SQLINTEGER                  200 <SQL_ATTR_ODBC_VERSION>
        SQLPOINTER                  3
        SQLINTEGER                    -6

ADMNDEMO        fff1098d:fffe07bd     EXIT  SQLSetEnvAttr  with return code 0
➥(SQL_SUCCESS)
        SQLHENV             0x006615a0
        SQLINTEGER                  200 <SQL_ATTR_ODBC_VERSION>
        SQLPOINTER                  3
        SQLINTEGER                    -6

ADMNDEMO        fff1098d:fffe07bd     ENTER SQLAllocHandle
        SQLSMALLINT                   2 <SQL_HANDLE_DBC>
        SQLHANDLE           0x006615a0
        SQLHANDLE *         0x00520024
```

```
ADMNDEMO        fff1098d:fffe07bd    EXIT  SQLAllocHandle  with return code 0
➥(SQL_SUCCESS)
        SQLSMALLINT                    2 <SQL_HANDLE_DBC>
        SQLHANDLE             0x006615a0
        SQLHANDLE *           0x00520024 ( 0x006606a0)

ADMNDEMO        fff1098d:fffe07bd    ENTER SQLDriverConnectW
        HDBC                  0x006606a0
        HWND                  0x00000444
        WCHAR *               0x00000000
        SWORD                          0
        WCHAR *               0x00660750
        SWORD                        512
        SWORD *               0x0064fc36
        UWORD                          1 <SQL_DRIVER_COMPLETE>

ADMNDEMO        fff1098d:fffe07bd    EXIT  SQLDriverConnectW  with return code
➥1 (SQL_SUCCESS_WITH_INFO)
        HDBC                  0x006606a0
        HWND                  0x00000444
        WCHAR *               0x00000000
        SWORD                          0
        WCHAR *               0x00660750 [      122] "DSN=32-bit SQL Server;
        ➥UID=sa;PWD=;WSID=NOTEBOOK;DATABASE=pubs"
        SWORD                        512
        SWORD *               0x0064fc36 (122)
        UWORD                          1 <SQL_DRIVER_COMPLETE>

ADMNDEMO        fff1098d:fffe07bd    ENTER SQLGetInfo
        HDBC                  0x006606a0
        UWORD                         47 <SQL_USER_NAME>
        PTR                   0x00520052
        SWORD                         30
        SWORD *               0x0064fc38

ADMNDEMO        fff1098d:fffe07bd    ENTER SQLGetInfoW
        HDBC                  0x006606a0
        UWORD                         47 <SQL_USER_NAME>
        PTR                   0x0066152c
        SWORD                         60
        SWORD *               0x0064fc38

ADMNDEMO        fff1098d:fffe07bd    EXIT  SQLGetInfoW  with return code 0
➥(SQL_SUCCESS)
        HDBC                  0x006606a0
        UWORD                         47 <SQL_USER_NAME>
        PTR                   0x0066152c [        6] "dbo"
        SWORD                         60
        SWORD *               0x0064fc38 (6)

ADMNDEMO        fff1098d:fffe07bd    EXIT  SQLGetInfo  with return code 0
➥(SQL_SUCCESS)
        HDBC                  0x006606a0
        UWORD                         47 <SQL_USER_NAME>
        PTR                   0x00520052 [        3] "dbo"
        SWORD                         30
        SWORD *               0x0064fc38 (3)
```

continues

Listing 30.1. continued

```
ADMNDEMO        fff1098d:fffe07bd    ENTER SQLGetInfo
        HDBC                0x006606a0
        UWORD                        2 <SQL_DATA_SOURCE_NAME>
        PTR                 0x00520070
        SWORD                       30
        SWORD *             0x00000000

ADMNDEMO        fff1098d:fffe07bd    ENTER SQLGetInfoW
        HDBC                0x006606a0
        UWORD                        2 <SQL_DATA_SOURCE_NAME>
        PTR                 0x006613c8
        SWORD                       60
        SWORD *             0x0064fc02

ADMNDEMO        fff1098d:fffe07bd    EXIT  SQLGetInfoW  with return code 0
➥(SQL_SUCCESS)
        HDBC                0x006606a0
        UWORD                        2 <SQL_DATA_SOURCE_NAME>
        PTR                 0x006613c8 [       34] "32-bit SQL Server"
        SWORD                       60
        SWORD *             0x0064fc02 (34)

ADMNDEMO        fff1098d:fffe07bd    EXIT  SQLGetInfo  with return code 0
➥(SQL_SUCCESS)
        HDBC                0x006606a0
        UWORD                        2 <SQL_DATA_SOURCE_NAME>
        PTR                 0x00520070
        SWORD                       30
        SWORD *             0x00000000

ADMNDEMO        fff1098d:fffe07bd    ENTER SQLAllocHandle
        SQLSMALLINT                  3 <SQL_HANDLE_STMT>
        SQLHANDLE           0x006606a0
        SQLHANDLE *         0x00520028

ADMNDEMO        fff1098d:fffe07bd    EXIT  SQLAllocHandle  with return code 0
➥(SQL_SUCCESS)
        SQLSMALLINT                  3 <SQL_HANDLE_STMT>
        SQLHANDLE           0x006606a0
        SQLHANDLE *         0x00520028 ( 0x006609d4)

ADMNDEMO        fff1098d:fffe07bd    ENTER SQLGetFunctions
        HDBC                0x006606a0
        UWORD                       54
        UWORD *             0x0064fc3a

ADMNDEMO        fff1098d:fffe07bd    EXIT  SQLGetFunctions  with return code 0
➥(SQL_SUCCESS)
        HDBC                0x006606a0
        UWORD                       54
        UWORD *             0x0064fc3a (1)

ADMNDEMO        fff1098d:fffe07bd    ENTER SQLGetFunctions
        HDBC                0x006606a0
        UWORD                       40
        UWORD *             0x0064fc3a
```

```
ADMNDEMO        fff1098d:fffe07bd    EXIT  SQLGetFunctions  with return code 0
➥(SQL_SUCCESS)
        HDBC                0x006606a0
        UWORD                       40
        UWORD *             0x0064fc3a (1)

ADMNDEMO        fff1098d:fffe07bd    ENTER SQLGetFunctions
        HDBC                0x006606a0
        UWORD                       53
        UWORD *             0x0064fc3a

ADMNDEMO        fff1098d:fffe07bd    EXIT  SQLGetFunctions  with return code 0
➥(SQL_SUCCESS)
        HDBC                0x006606a0
        UWORD                       53
        UWORD *             0x0064fc3a (1)

ADMNDEMO        fff1098d:fffe07bd    ENTER SQLGetFunctions
        HDBC                0x006606a0
        UWORD                       65
        UWORD *             0x0064fc3a

ADMNDEMO        fff1098d:fffe07bd    EXIT  SQLGetFunctions  with return code 0
➥(SQL_SUCCESS)
        HDBC                0x006606a0
        UWORD                       65
        UWORD *             0x0064fc3a (1)

ADMNDEMO        fff1098d:fffe07bd    ENTER SQLGetFunctions
        HDBC                0x006606a0
        UWORD                       60
        UWORD *             0x0064fc3a

ADMNDEMO        fff1098d:fffe07bd    EXIT  SQLGetFunctions  with return code 0
➥(SQL_SUCCESS)
        HDBC                0x006606a0
        UWORD                       60
        UWORD *             0x0064fc3a (1)

ADMNDEMO        fff1098d:fffe07bd    ENTER SQLGetFunctions
        HDBC                0x006606a0
        UWORD                       70
        UWORD *             0x0064fc3a

ADMNDEMO        fff1098d:fffe07bd    EXIT  SQLGetFunctions  with return code 0
➥(SQL_SUCCESS)
        HDBC                0x006606a0
        UWORD                       70
        UWORD *             0x0064fc3a (1)

ADMNDEMO        fff1098d:fffe07bd    ENTER SQLGetFunctions
        HDBC                0x006606a0
        UWORD                       56
        UWORD *             0x0064fc3a
```

continues

Listing 30.1. continued

```
ADMNDEMO        fff1098d:fffe07bd    EXIT  SQLGetFunctions  with return code 0
➥(SQL_SUCCESS)
        HDBC                0x006606a0
        UWORD                       56
        UWORD *             0x0064fc3a (1)

ADMNDEMO        fff1098d:fffe07bd    ENTER SQLGetFunctions
        HDBC                0x006606a0
        UWORD                       52
        UWORD *             0x0064fc3a

ADMNDEMO        fff1098d:fffe07bd    EXIT  SQLGetFunctions  with return code 0
➥(SQL_SUCCESS)
        HDBC                0x006606a0
        UWORD                       52
        UWORD *             0x0064fc3a (1)

ADMNDEMO        fff1098d:fffe07bd    ENTER SQLGetFunctions
        HDBC                0x006606a0
        UWORD                       67
        UWORD *             0x0064fc3a

ADMNDEMO        fff1098d:fffe07bd    EXIT  SQLGetFunctions  with return code 0
➥(SQL_SUCCESS)
        HDBC                0x006606a0
        UWORD                       67
        UWORD *             0x0064fc3a (1)

ADMNDEMO        fff1098d:fffe07bd    ENTER SQLGetFunctions
        HDBC                0x006606a0
        UWORD                       66
        UWORD *             0x0064fc3a

ADMNDEMO        fff1098d:fffe07bd    EXIT  SQLGetFunctions  with return code 0
➥(SQL_SUCCESS)
        HDBC                0x006606a0
        UWORD                       66
        UWORD *             0x0064fc3a (1)
```

The final tab, About, is used to show data about each of the core ODBC components selected. Figure 30.12 shows this tab.

ODBC API

The ODBC Application Programming Interface (API) is the core of ODBC functionality. Each ODBC driver uses these functions to communicate with ODBC. It has been argued that using the API is much faster than using the ODBC driver. The drivers are usually optimized so that they make the calls to the ODBC API very efficiently.

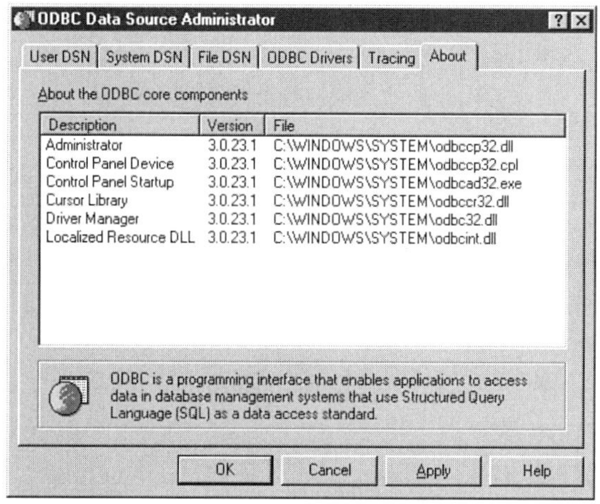

FIGURE 30.12.
The About tab of the ODBC Administrator.

Visual Basic and ODBC

Visual Basic utilizes ODBC through the use of the `OpenDatabase` method, which will return a reference to a `Database` object. Most developers have used this method to open an Access database. Using the `OpenDatabase` method through ODBC is not that much different than using it with Access.

First, consider the syntax of the `OpenDatabase` method. It is as follows:

```
Set database = Workspace.OpenDatabase( databasename[, options[,
➥read-only [, source]]])
```

where:

`Workspace` is the name of the optional database workspace to be used. If omitted, the default workspace is used.

`databasename` is the name of the Access `*.MDB` file or the name of your database in an ODBC data source.

`options` specifies whether the database is opened exclusively for Access databases. For ODBC data sources, `options` specifies how the ODBC driver will prompt if all of the information necessary to connect to the database is not supplied. Possible options for ODBC data sources are

- `dbDriverNoPrompt`: Will not prompt if any connect data is missing. If not enough information is supplied, a runtime error will occur.
- `dbDriverPrompt`: Will prompt for connect data, regardless of whether it is supplied.

- `dbDriverComplete`: Will prompt for any missing connect data. This is the default setting.
- `dbDriverCompleteRequired`: Will prompt if any data required to connect to an ODBC data source is missing, but will not prompt if the data is not required for the connection.

`read-only` is a Boolean flag indicating whether the database should be opened for read-only or read-write operations.

`source` is the ODBC connect string source. The connect string has parameters that are required specific to a data source. However, most data sources accept these parameters:

- `DSN`: The name of the data source, as registered with the ODBC driver manager.
- `UID`: The user ID used to log onto the ODBC database.
- `PWD`: The password used to log onto the ODBC database.
- `DRIVER`: Specifies a specific ODBC driver to use.
- `DATABASE`: Indicates the database to use once connected to the data source.
- `SERVER`: The name of the remote server that contains the database.
- `WSID`: The workstation identifier.
- `APP`: The name of the application requesting the ODBC data source.

Next, suppose you wanted to open the pubs database, installed automatically with SQL Server. You could create a string of all of the connect parameters necessary by the ODBC driver. Then use the `OpenDatabase` method to connect to the ODBC data source. This is shown in the following example:

```
Dim dbPubs As Database
Dim sConnect As String
sConnect = "ODBC;DATABASE=pubs;UID=sa;PWD=;DSN=SQLServer"
Set dbPubs = Workspaces(0).OpenDatabase("SQLServer", dbDriverNoPrompt,
➥True, sConnect)
```

After you connect to the ODBC data source, issuing commands and retrieving data is virtually the same as it would be from Access. The preceding example assumes that an ODBC driver is named SQLServer. To set up an ODBC data source, select the ODBC setup program in the Windows Control Panel.

ODBC API Sample Applications

A few sample applications come with the ODBC API SDK. Here's a list of them:

- Cursor Sample
- ODBC Test
- Query Sample
- Table Administrator Sample

These applications are very useful in helping you to test or debug your ODBC API functions as well as new ODBC data sources you have set up.

Cursor Sample

Cursor Sample is an application that is used to test cursors. This program demonstrates the use of the block cursor, scrolling, positioned update, and delete capabilities of the ODBC Cursor Library. Figure 30.13 shows this application.

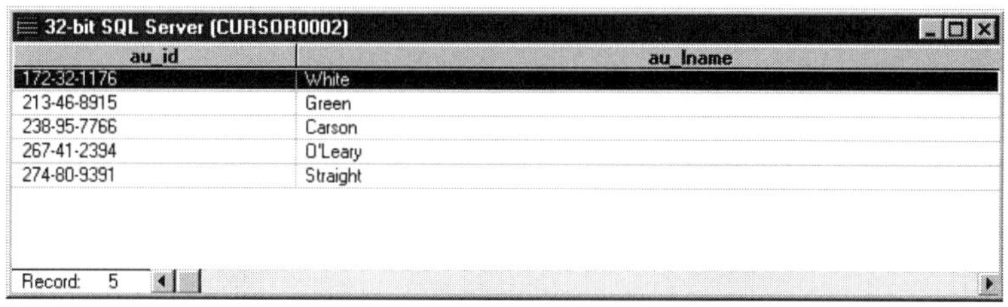

FIGURE 30.13.
The Cursor Sample application.

ODBC Test

The ODBC Test application helps you to test ODBC drivers. It enables you to test ODBC functions in three different categories:

- ODBC functions
- Environmental (Function) tools
- Automated tests

Figure 30.14 shows this application.

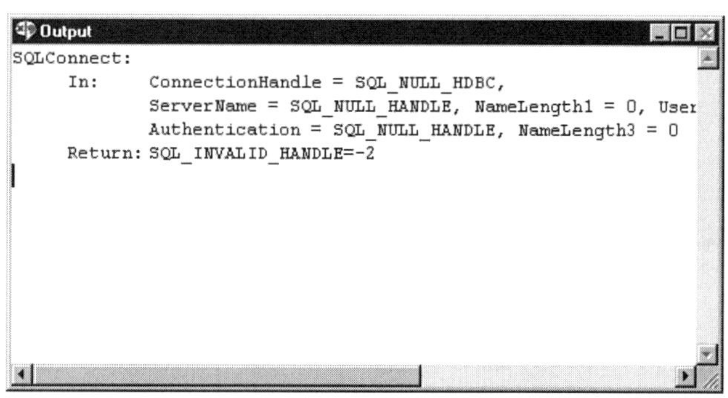

FIGURE 30.14.
The ODBC Test application.

Query Sample

Query Sample is an application that demonstrates how you can open multiple, simultaneous ODBC connections. Figure 30.15 shows this application.

FIGURE 30.15.
The Query Sample application.

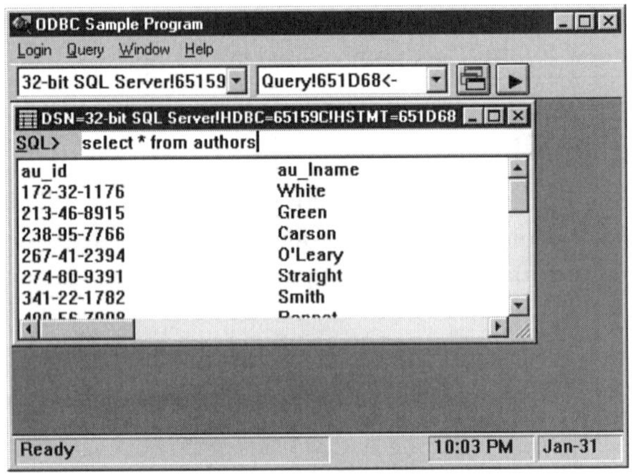

Table Administrator Sample

The Table Administrator Sample (or Admin Demo) demonstrates the use of ODBC to issue SQL statements and return results. Figure 30.16 shows this application.

FIGURE 30.16.
The Table Administrator Sample application.

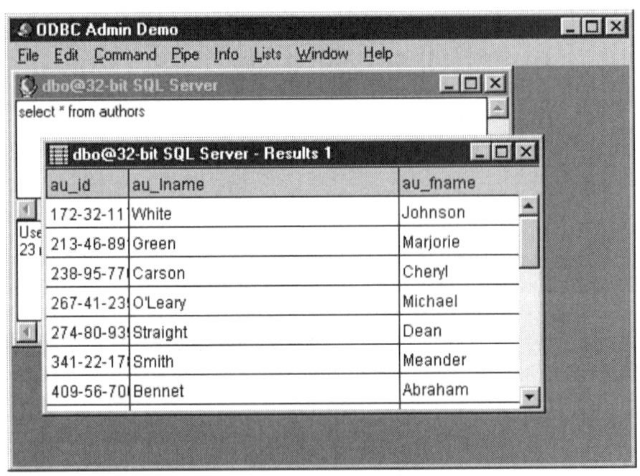

Summary

ODBC is an important technology used as a standard means to manipulate databases. ODBC drivers are provided by the database vendor so that a developer can be shielded from the complexities of knowing how to send SQL statements to different types of databases. This chapter explained how ODBC is used to connect to databases, as well as some of the tools contained in the ODBC SDK. It also showed how to create ODBC data sources using the ODBC drivers from database vendors. Use this chapter to help you develop your ODBC database applications.

31

Database Applications with Access 97

Microsoft Access has come a long way since version 1.0. As expected, Access 97 makes it extremely easy to design and create databases. Throughout the rest of this chapter, Access 97 is described in detail.

Creating a New Database in Access 97

Creating a new database within Access 97 is a snap. Simply select the File | New Database menu option, which brings up a dialog box like the one shown in Figure 31.1. Select the Databases tab.

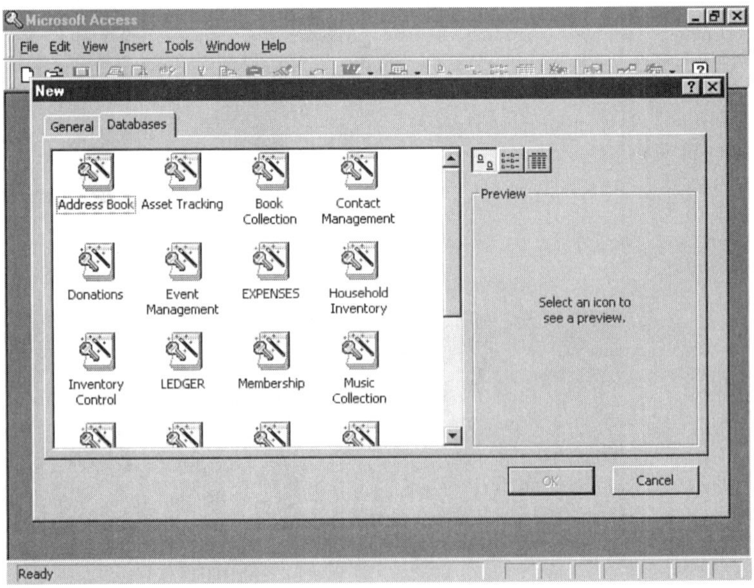

FIGURE 31.1.
The New database dialog box.

This dialog box enables you to select from many different types of databases. A wizard will be presented for each option to ask questions about the type of database you are creating.

Select the Time and Billing option. This brings up the dialog box in Figure 31.2 to let you save the newly created database.

This specific wizard presents you with a series of successive questions. The answers to these questions help the wizard determine how to set up the database. The first step is to show a summary of the types of questions that will be asked. Figure 31.3 shows this dialog box.

The next step is to select the fields in each of the 11 different categories of information to collect. This step is shown in Figure 31.4.

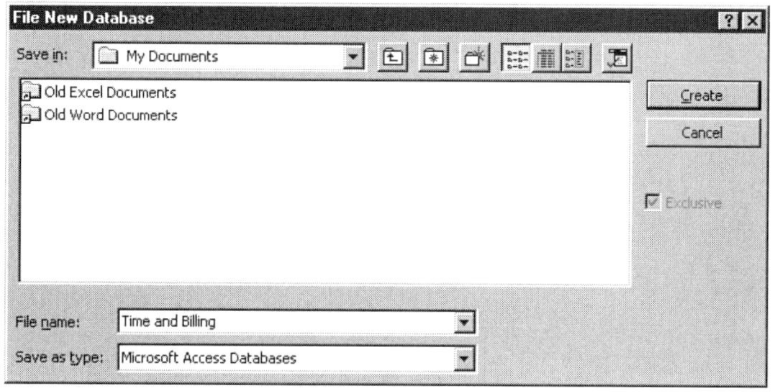

FIGURE 31.2.
The File New Database dialog box.

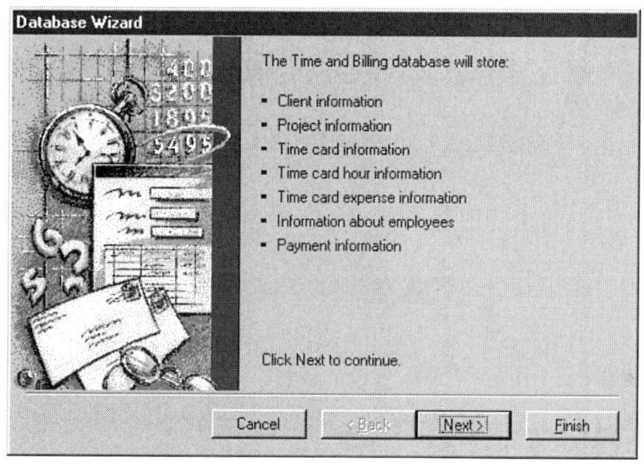

FIGURE 31.3.
The introduction screen of the Database Wizard.

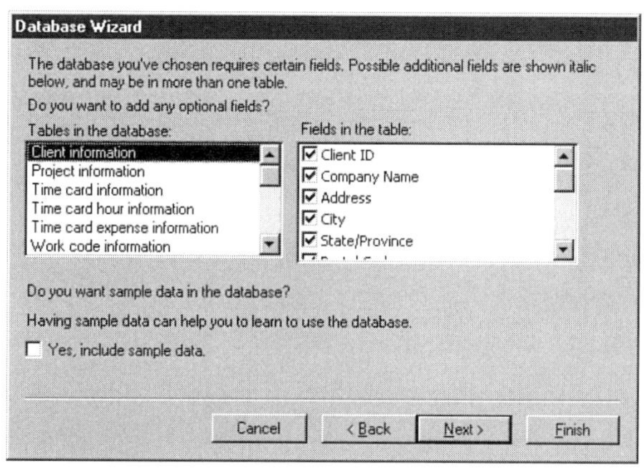

FIGURE 31.4.
Selecting tables and fields in the Database Wizard.

Furthermore, you have the option in this step to include sample data. After you have clicked each of the categories on the left and selected the appropriate fields on the right, you are ready to move to the next step.

Step 3 enables you to pick the style to be shown in your database. If you do not plan to use Access 97 for the front end of your application, this doesn't matter so much. You are using the wizard only to create the database structure. Figure 31.5 shows step 3.

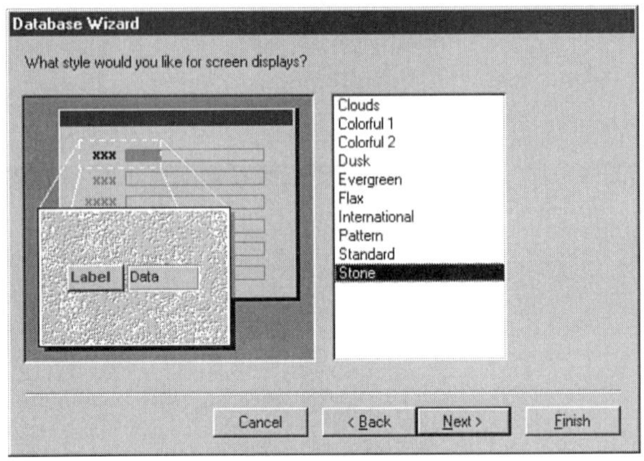

FIGURE 31.5.
Selecting a style for the screens in the Database Wizard.

You can choose from 10 different styles:

- Clouds
- Colorful 1
- Colorful 2
- Dusk
- Evergreen
- Flax
- International
- Pattern
- Standard
- Stone

Select the Stone style. The next step is to choose a style for printed reports. Figure 31.6 shows the dialog box for choosing the style.

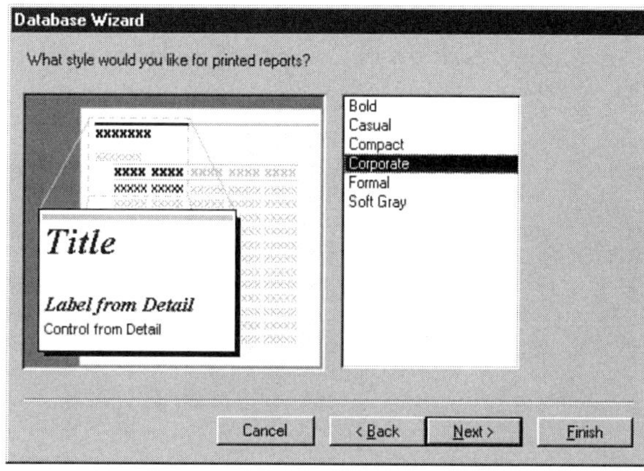

FIGURE 31.6.
Selecting a style for reports.

You can choose from six different styles:

- Bold
- Casual
- Compact
- Corporate
- Formal
- Soft Gray

Select the Corporate style. The next step enables you to pick a title for the database on your reports, as well as choose a picture to place on the reports. Figure 31.7 shows this step.

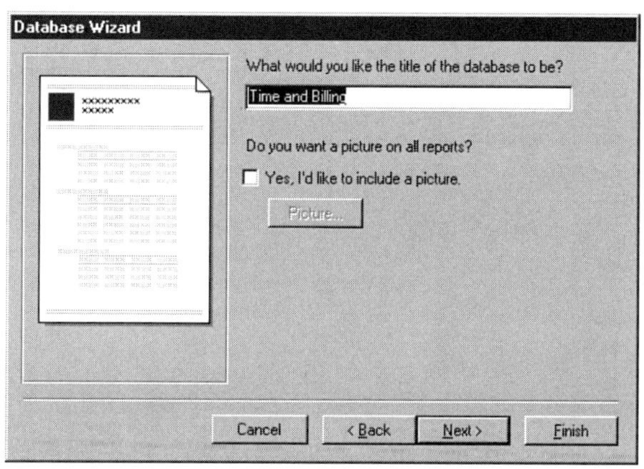

FIGURE 31.7.
Selecting the title of the database in the Database Wizard.

Enter Time and Billing into the text box. The final step enables you to create the database. When you are ready, choose the Finish button, and your database will be created. This is shown in Figure 31.8.

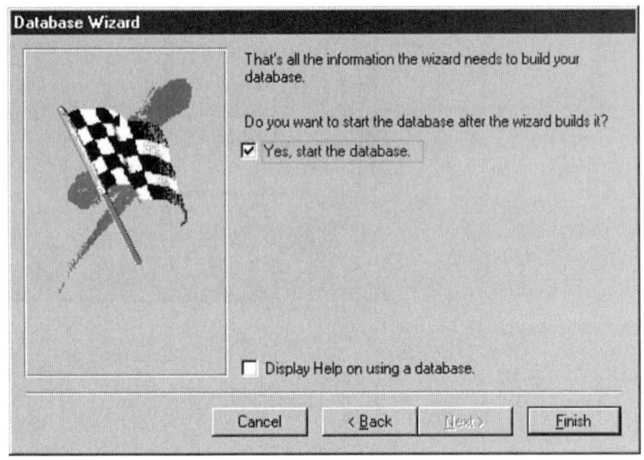

FIGURE 31.8.
The final step of the Database Wizard.

After the database is created, you will not be able to use it until you enter your company information (if you've chosen to use this category in step 2). You will be presented with an Access 97 form to enter your company information in the style you have chosen. Figure 31.9 shows the My Company Information form.

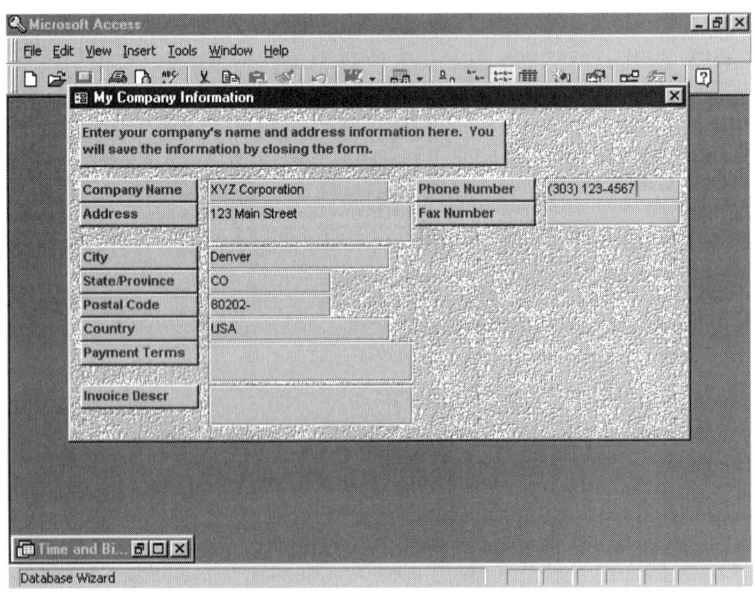

FIGURE 31.9.
The My Company Information form.

Now the database is completely created. The wizard has completed all tables, reports, code, and queries. However, it is likely that you wanted only the table structure to be created, not all the forms, reports, and queries. Figure 31.10 shows what the application looks like in Access 97 when you first open the newly created database.

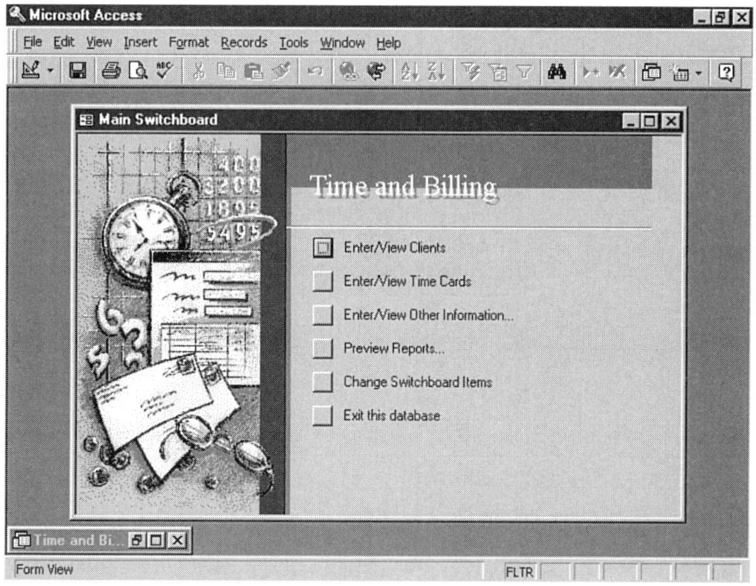

FIGURE 31.10.
The new application created by the wizard.

When the wizard creates the database, indexes and relationships are also created. You can view the relationships by choosing the Tools | Relationships menu option, which brings up the screen shown in Figure 31.11.

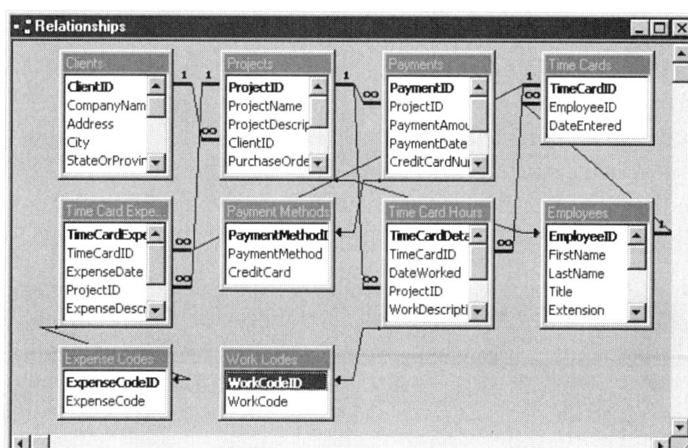

FIGURE 31.11.
Relationships created by the Database Wizard.

Access 97 and Visual Basic

With a database that has been created in Access 97, you can take advantage of many of the same features available in Access 95 or Access 2.0. For example, you can open the database in the Visual Data Manager. To do this, choose the Add-Ins | Visual Data Manager menu option in Visual Basic 5.0. Next, choose the File | Open Database | Microsoft Access menu option. Choose the Time and Billing database created in the earlier steps. This enables you to view and alter the structure or data of the database. Figure 31.12 shows the Time and Billing database in the Visual Data Manager.

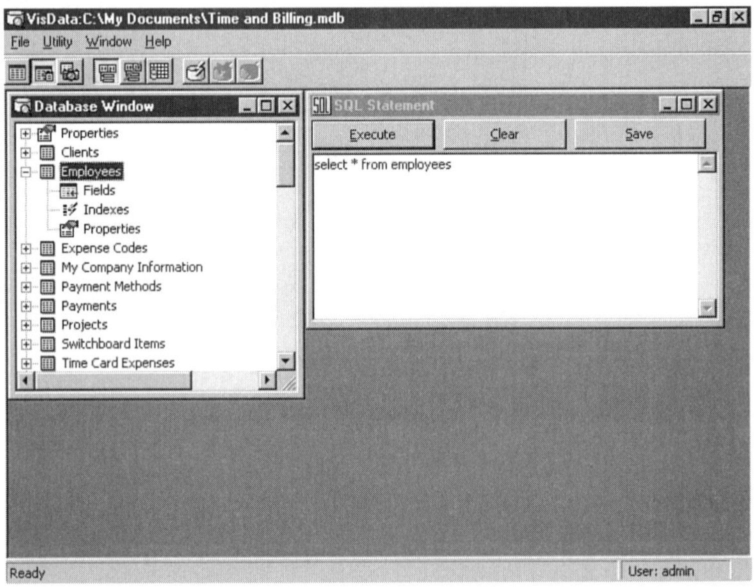

FIGURE 31.12.
The Visual Data Manager showing the Time and Billing database.

One other possibility is to use the Data Form Wizard in Visual Basic. The Data Form Wizard creates a form that looks like a data-bound form in Access 97, but in Visual Basic 5.0. The Data Form Wizard is an add-in that can save you a lot of time. For the add-in to be available, you must make sure that it is available. To do this, select Add-Ins | Add-In Manager Visual Basic. You will see the VB Data Form Wizard menu option. Make sure that this is checked to make it available in the Add-Ins menu. Figure 31.13 shows the Add-In Manager.

Now, the Data Form Wizard is available from the Add-Ins menu option. Choose Add-Ins | Data Form Wizard. This brings up a wizard that asks you to answer a series of questions.

CROSS REFERENCE

For more information about using wizards, refer to Chapter 2, "Stock Wizards."

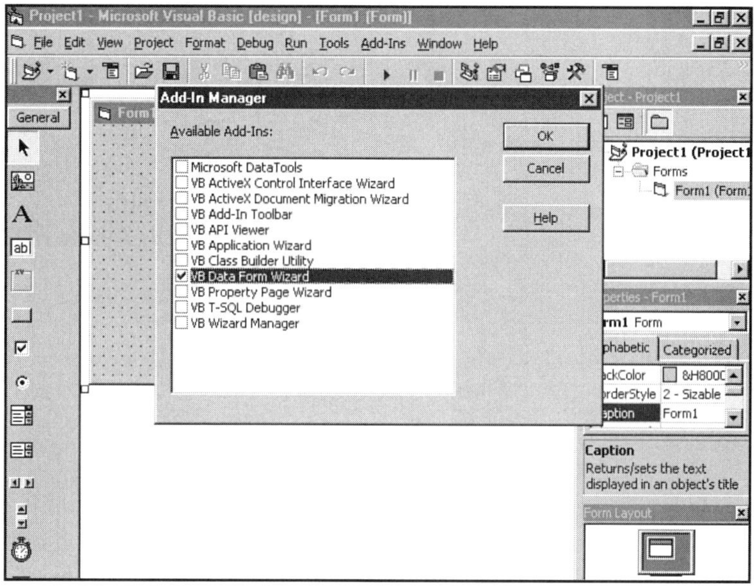

FIGURE 31.13.
The Visual Basic Add-In Manager.

The first step simply presents you with a summary of the results of the wizard. Figure 31.14 shows this opening screen.

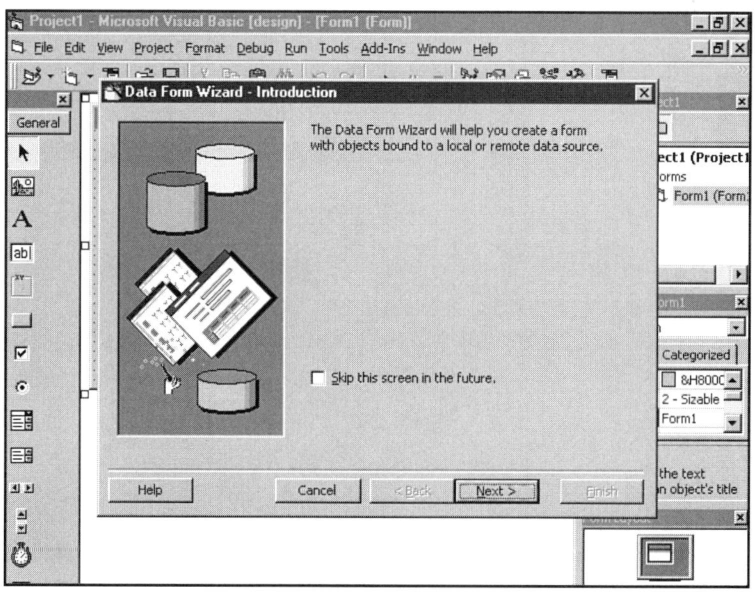

FIGURE 31.14.
The Introduction step of the Data Form Wizard.

The next step, Database Type, shown in Figure 31.15, enables you to choose the type of database. Choose Access.

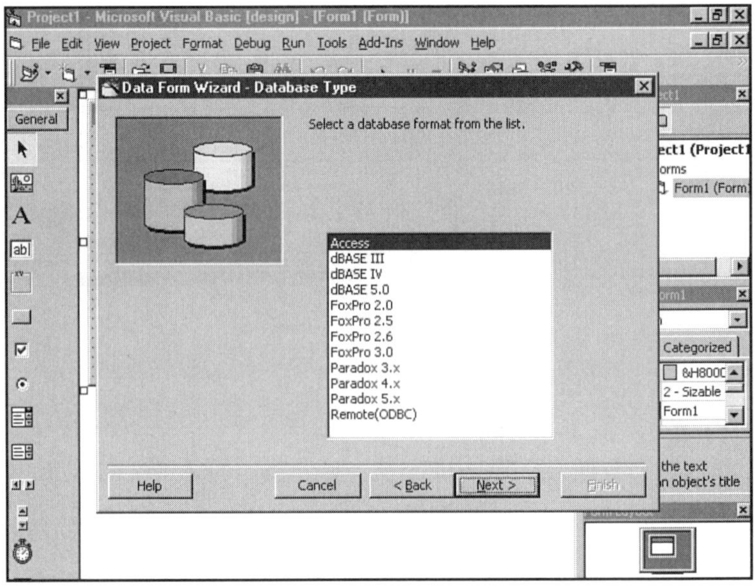

FIGURE 31.15.
The Database Type step of the Data Form Wizard.

In step 3, the Database screen, you select the name of the data source to use (see Figure 31.16). You can choose to show sources from tables or queries. In this case, uncheck the Queries option because you know that the Database Wizard (described earlier) created queries for use with reports, but you do not need them at this point.

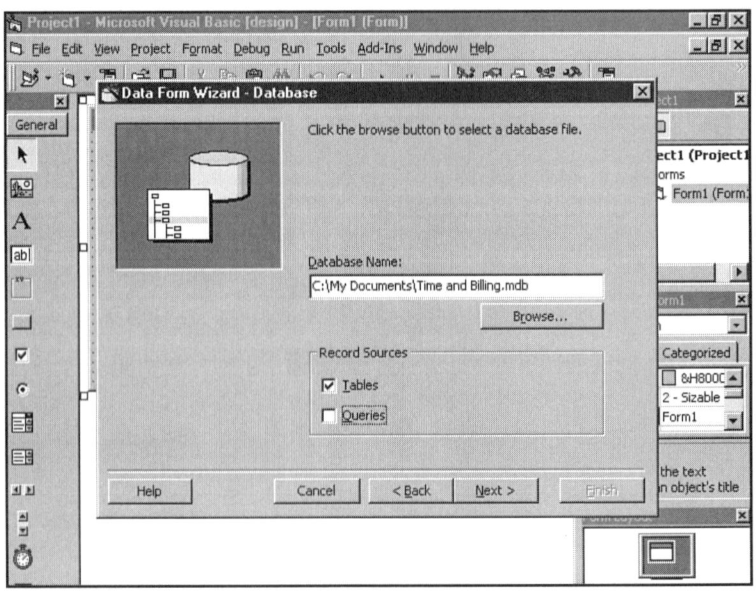

FIGURE 31.16.
The Database step of the Data Form Wizard.

In step 4, the Form screen, you select the type of form to create. There are three choices:

- Single record
- Grid (Datasheet)
- Master/Detail

The Single record option displays all selected fields, one record at a time. The Grid (Datasheet) option displays all records in a grid format. The Master/Detail option enables you to show a one-to-many relationship between two tables. The "many" part of the relationship is being shown in the grid. These options are shown in Figure 31.17. For this example, choose the Single record option.

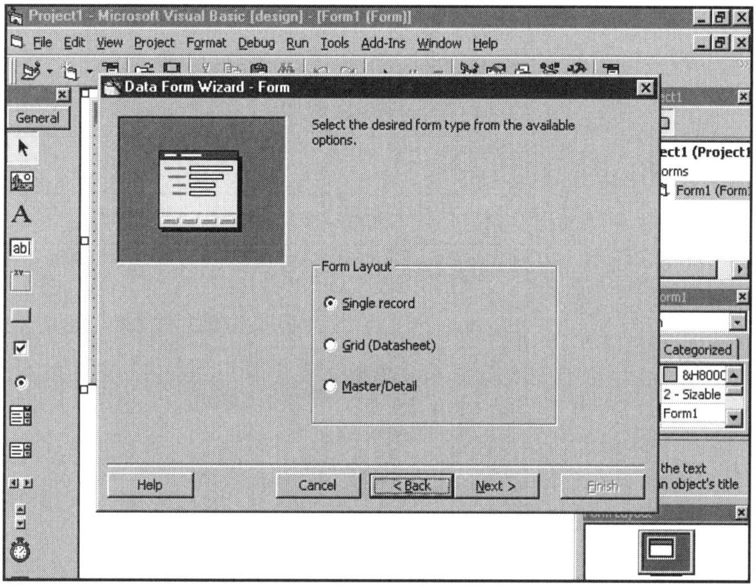

FIGURE 31.17.
The Form step of the Data Form Wizard.

In the next step, the Record Source screen, you choose the record source from which to build the form. Figure 31.18 shows this step. Choose the Employees table and select all the fields.

Next, you must choose which buttons will be placed on the form. Figure 31.19 shows what step 6, the Control Selection screen, looks like.

The final step, Finished!, enables you to choose a name for the form. The default is the name of the table with an "frm" prefix. In this case, frmEmployees is the default. Figure 31.20 shows this final step. Choose the Finish button to create the form.

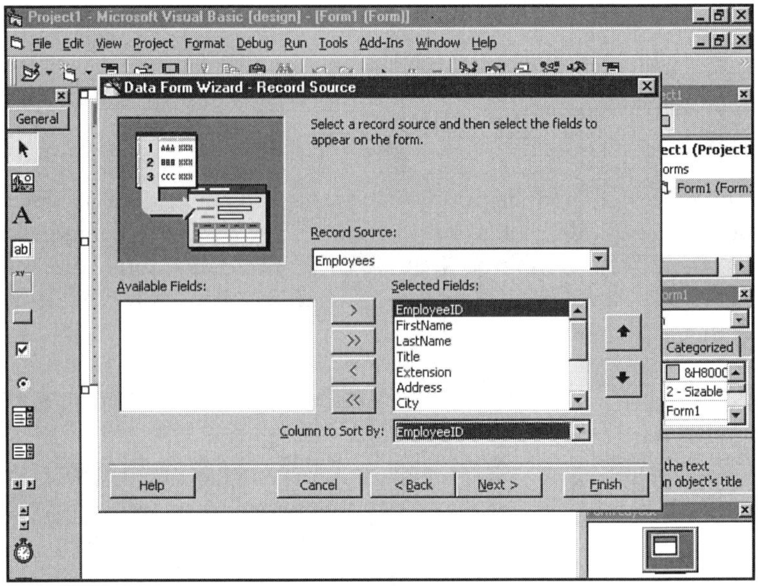

FIGURE 31.18.
The Record Source step of the Data Form Wizard.

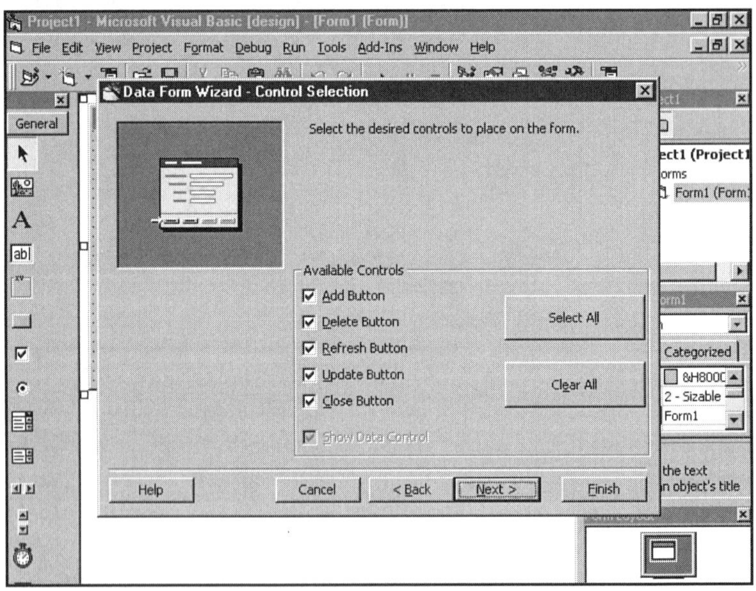

FIGURE 31.19.
The Control Selection step of the Data Form Wizard.

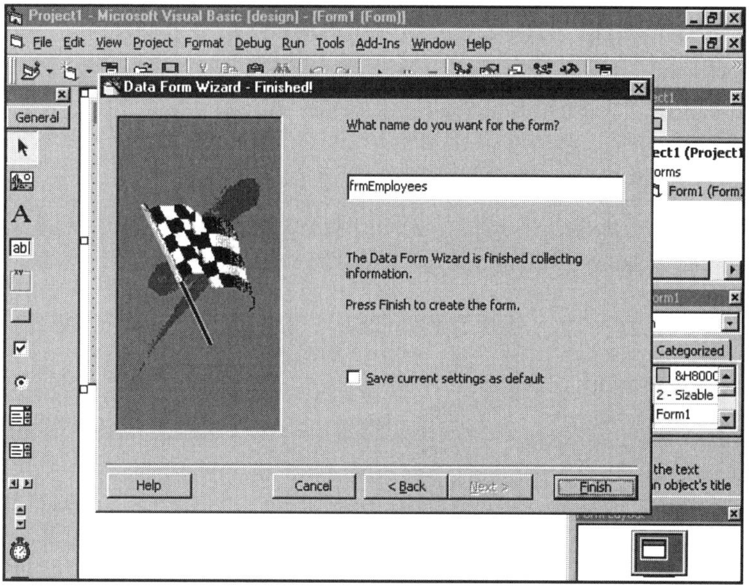

FIGURE 31.20.
The Finished! step of the Data Form Wizard.

Now the form is finished (see Figure 31.21). This was very simple—all you had to do was answer a few questions. Not one line of code was written. You can run your project, of course, by pressing the F5 key.

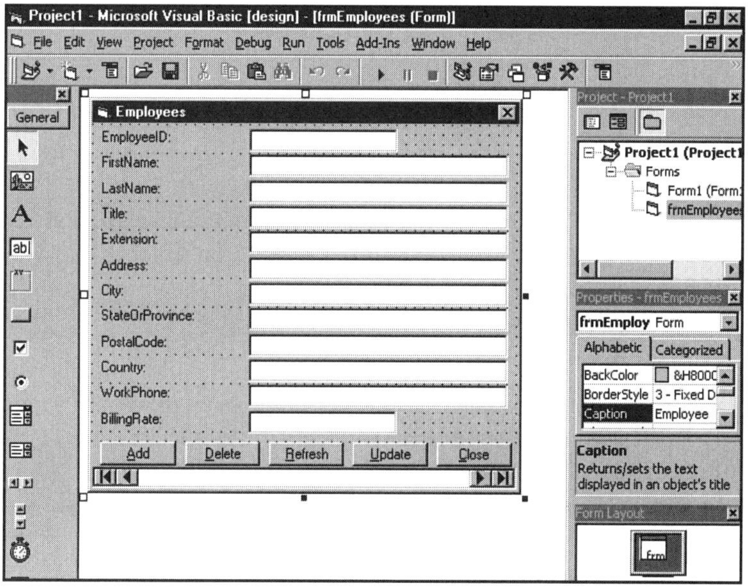

FIGURE 31.21.
The completed form.

Automation with Access 97 from Visual Basic

This chapter cannot adequately show everything that you can do with Access from Visual Basic. Instead, it teaches you the basics so that you can learn from the concepts. This enables you to take the ball and run with it.

As with all automation, you must select a reference to the objects. In this case, you must select the Project | References menu option. Then select the option labeled Microsoft Access 8.0 Object Library. Figure 31.22 shows this reference selected.

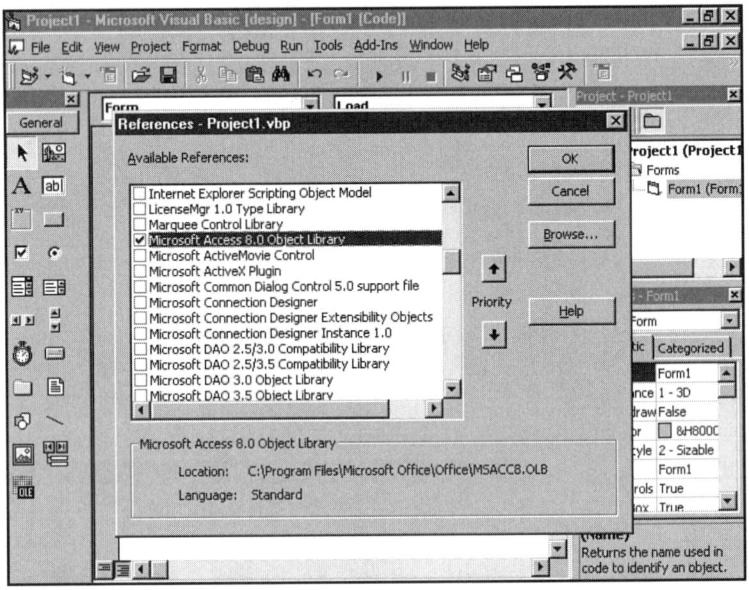

FIGURE 31.22.
The Microsoft Access 8.0 Object Library reference selected.

After you have selected the reference, the easiest way to determine which objects are available is to press the F2 key to view the Object Browser and then select Access in the Library drop-down list. Figure 31.23 shows what the Object Browser looks like with this library selected.

Running an Access Report from Visual Basic

To run a report generated in Access 97 from Visual Basic, you must instantiate an object reference to Access 97. Listing 31.1 shows the code to run the report. This code is available on the CD-ROM accompanying this book in the `\Office\Access` subdirectory.

Listing 31.1. Code to run an Access report from Visual Basic.

```
Private Sub Form_Load()
    'handle errors
    On Error GoTo LoadError

    'change the mouse
    Screen.MousePointer = vbHourglass
```

```
    'create new object variable
    Dim objAccess As New access.Application

    'open database
    objAccess.OpenCurrentDatabase ("TIME AND BILLING.MDB")

    'maximize access
    objAccess.DoCmd.Maximize

    'run report in print preview mode
    objAccess.DoCmd.OpenReport "Client Listing", acViewPreview

    'restore report
    objAccess.DoCmd.Restore

    'maximize report
    objAccess.DoCmd.Maximize
    'change the mouse
    Screen.MousePointer = vbDefault

    'exit
    Exit Sub

LoadError:
    'change the mouse
    Screen.MousePointer = vbDefault

    'show error
    MsgBox Error$

    Resume Next
End Sub
```

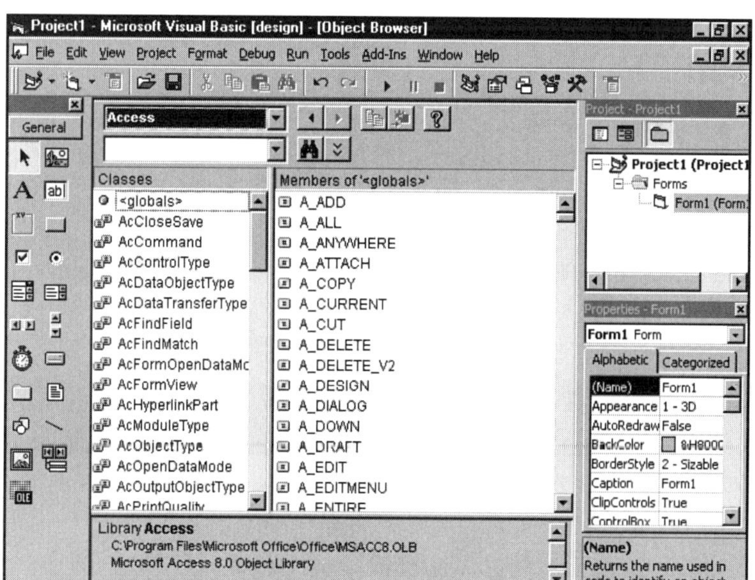

FIGURE 31.23.
The Object Browser with the Access library selected.

The first step is to create a new Access application. This is done with the following line of code:

```
Dim objAccess As New access.Application
```

Next, the database is opened with this line of code:

```
objAccess.OpenCurrentDatabase ("TIME AND BILLING.MDB")
```

This database is also in the `\Office\Access` subdirectory on the CD-ROM. Then, after the database is opened, Access is maximized with this line:

```
objAccess.DoCmd.Maximize
```

Now, here is the single line of code that does all the work in this routine:

```
objAccess.DoCmd.OpenReport "Client Listing", acViewPreview
```

This line of code runs an existing report named Client Listing. The intrinsic constant, `acViewPreview`, is passed as an argument that specifies that you want to preview the report. If this argument were omitted, the report would be printed to the printer.

Next, the report is restored with this line:

```
objAccess.DoCmd.Restore
```

Finally, the last significant line of code maximizes the previewed report:

```
objAccess.DoCmd.Maximize
```

You should be able to take the example presented here, along with the Object Browser references, and create your own solutions.

Summary

There are many new features in Access 97. One of them is the capability to run a report created in Access from Visual Basic. This chapter showed you how to run these Access reports. It also described how to use the wizards to create a fully normalized database.

You can expand on the topics discussed in this chapter to build your own Access 97 databases and use the new features of Access 97 to create a fully interactive database. You could use the techniques described here to create an exciting application, such as a report server.

32

Visual Basic's Role in Client/Server Computing

Client/server technology is important for building robust applications suitable for corporate solutions and multiple users. However, for client/server technology to work, you do need both pieces: the client and the server. In the context of this book, the client application will be developed with Visual Basic. The database (also referred to as the back end) must be designed to be a client/server database. Such databases include Microsoft SQL Server, Oracle, and Sybase. The examples shown in this chapter may be accurate for multiple database systems, but are geared toward Microsoft SQL Server.

NOTE

This chapter gives a brief overview of client/server technology. It is not intended as a complete reference. There are many Sams books that cover client/server topics, such as *Client/Server Computing, Second Edition.*

Introduction to Client/Server Technology

Client/server technology has long been a promising alternative to mainframe computing—primarily because the cost of the machines needed to run a client/server database is significantly less than a mainframe. The hardware existed, but the software has been a long time coming. While waiting for the software to come of age, the hardware has gotten significantly more powerful, reliable, and cheaper.

Even the way client/server was defined a few years ago has changed. In the past, the concept behind client/server technology was simple. You want to let the client do some of the work and the server do some of the work. This means that, for example, you don't want to have the server return data and have the client do 100 percent of the data manipulation. Instead, the client should request the data from the server, and the server processes the data and returns only the data needed. This makes sure that network traffic is kept to a minimum. In a client/server environment, each piece does what it does best. The client does a minimal amount of processing. It simply requests the data and handles user interaction. The server, on the other hand, processes all data. If designed correctly, the server should also incorporate stored procedures, which free the client of doing some work. For more information about stored procedures, refer to the section titled "Stored Procedures," later in this chapter.

So far, I've described the concept of a two-tiered client/server model. If anything in this model changes, it could potentially impact the users in a significant way. More and more companies are moving toward a three-tiered (or *n*-tiered) approach, where *n* is a variable number of tiers.

Typically, in a three-tiered architecture you have these three tiers:

- The user interface (UI) tier
- The business interface tier
- The database abstraction tier

The first tier is actually the application. The third tier is the client/server database. The middle tier is one or more objects that house all of the business rules and functionality. Theoretically, this middle tier can be used by any application in the enterprise.

Distributed Client/Server

Distributed client/server technology was not introduced in Microsoft SQL Server until version 6.0, and then was extended in version 6.5. The distributed client/server model allows for the database abstraction tier (or third tier) to be distributed across multiple servers for the sake of performance.

It could be that server A houses all of the client information and server B houses all of the order information. This is a design issue. Perhaps server A also does some intensive computing so that marketing can be done to a specific group of clients based on certain criteria. This has nothing to do with taking orders on a daily basis. Therefore, this scenario might be advisable. There are some issues with doing this, however. The system must be secure enough and reliable enough to maintain and guarantee transaction integrity and recoverability.

This is guaranteed through a two-phase commit approach. A two-phase commit ensures that all servers that are part of a transaction must complete the transaction in its entirety, or they all must roll the transaction back. This guarantees referential integrity.

The distributed computing world has made great advances. Because distributed computing promised to make servers and environments work together in a seamless fashion, expectations were high. It wasn't until recently that this became a reality. SQL Server 6.0 and 6.5 made great strides in this direction. It has become an industry standard in downsizing large mainframe systems (and resources) to more localized, distributed client/server systems that offer great performance.

The distributed client/server environment is not without its problems, however. The technology and tools are not widely known, but within a few years this will be overcome. Another problem is the number of human resources necessary to get the job done. Many people specialize in different areas because the technology is becoming complicated. For example, the following resources are required:

- System architects
- Visual Basic developers (for front end, Tier 1)
- Visual Basic developers (for business layers, Tier 2 and *n*-tiers)

- Business systems analysts
- Database administrators (DBAs)
- Testers (Quality Assurance)
- Project managers
- Technical writers

In addition to these types of human resources, more time is often necessary to develop the total distributed applications. This is true, in part, because of the complexity of some of the systems and tools required, but also because technology is changing so rapidly—you don't want to design obsolescence into your distributed environment.

Visual Basic's Role

Visual Basic is perfectly suited to be used in developing client applications. Despite much criticism in its early stages, Visual Basic has become widely accepted in the business community as being well adapted for developing client applications. Some criticism included the fact that Visual Basic is not compiled into machine-level code, like C or C++. Instead, it is compiled into P-Code, which needs a runtime interpreter, `VBRUN500.DLL`. Now that you can truly compile your Visual Basic applications, in my opinion, Visual Basic is the best language on the market for developing very rapid stand-alone or client applications.

A lot of planning is involved on both the client and server ends when you design a client/server application. You must decide how much of the work the client will do and how much the server will do. You must also decide how to abstract your business services into objects. This goes hand-in-hand with how many tiers you need to develop. You must also optimize your queries. Optimizing queries is *very* important because this ensures that the server will have to do minimal work in order to get the job done.

For more information about optimizing queries, refer to the section titled "Optimizing Queries and Indexes," later in this chapter.

Visual Basic plays an important part in the first tier and *n*-tiers. The first tier is the application itself. The application is created in Visual Basic and is what the user actually sees. The middle tier (or *n*-tier) is one or more objects that can also be created in Visual Basic.

CROSS REFERENCE

For more information about designing and coding middle-tier objects, refer to Chapter 19, "Components and Objects."

Stored Procedures

The *stored procedure* is an important part of client/server architecture. A stored procedure is a series of one or more SQL queries (statements) designed for a special purpose. The term *query* here refers to much more than a `SELECT` statement. It can be any valid SQL statement or even a database-specific statement used for a specific purpose. Such a purpose could be initiating an e-mail message. However, the query is constructed on the server instead of in Visual Basic. This query is then precompiled on the server. This allows for much faster operation. The SQL Server optimizer already knows its plan of execution. There are two types of stored procedures: user-defined and system. The following sections describe each.

User-Defined Stored Procedures

A user-defined stored procedure is a procedure that you create. It is compiled and sitting on the server, ready to be executed. Stored procedures can accept arguments. They are used in a way that is very similar to the way a function or subroutine is used in Visual Basic. To create a stored procedure, you must use an editor that enables you to connect to SQL Server. ISQL/w is one such editor, and it comes with SQL Server.

You instruct Microsoft SQL Server to create a new stored procedure by using the `CREATE PROCEDURE` or `CREATE PROC` keywords. For example, suppose you wanted to select all records from a table, named Sales, where the company name is SoftHouse. In Visual Basic, you could do this:

```
Dim x$
Dim cmd$
x$ = "SoftHouse"
cmd$ = "SELECT * FROM Sales "
cmd$ = cmd$ + "WHERE company = '" + x$ + "'"
```

CROSS REFERENCE

For more information about constructing SQL statements, refer to Chapter 29, "Structured Query Language (SQL)."

To create a stored procedure to perform the same function, you can use this syntax:

```
CREATE PROCEDURE SalesProcedure (@Company varchar(30))
AS
SELECT * FROM Sales1
WHERE company = @Company
```

This will actually create and compile the stored procedure on the server. Then, every time you want to access this stored procedure, you would simply use the following syntax, supplying a company name:

```
SalesProcedure "SoftHouse"
```

System Stored Procedures

A system stored procedure is a procedure that has already been created on the server and is available for you to execute out of the box as long as you have the correct authority to do so. System stored procedures are usually created to help an administrator manage SQL Server.

For example, suppose that you wanted to find out who is logged into a particular server. Instead of creating a user-defined stored procedure that does multiple joins with system tables, you can use the system stored procedure `sp_who`.

> **NOTE**
>
> All system procedures begin with the `sp_` prefix.

You would execute the procedure just as you would if you had created it. The only difference is that you must know which parameters it expects. For example, to execute the `sp_who` stored procedure, you would use this syntax:

```
sp_who (@loginame varchar (30)=null)
```

What this syntax means is that the `sp_who` system stored procedure accepts one argument: `@loginame`. By default, this parameter is `null`. This in effect makes the parameter not required, because a default value has been supplied. However, you can supply a name, with up to 30 characters. You supply a value like this:

```
sp_who ATM
```

Figure 32.1 shows what the results look like after executing this statement.

You can also omit a value and simply execute the `sp_who` system stored procedure, like this:

```
sp_who
```

Figure 32.2 shows what the results look like after executing this statement.

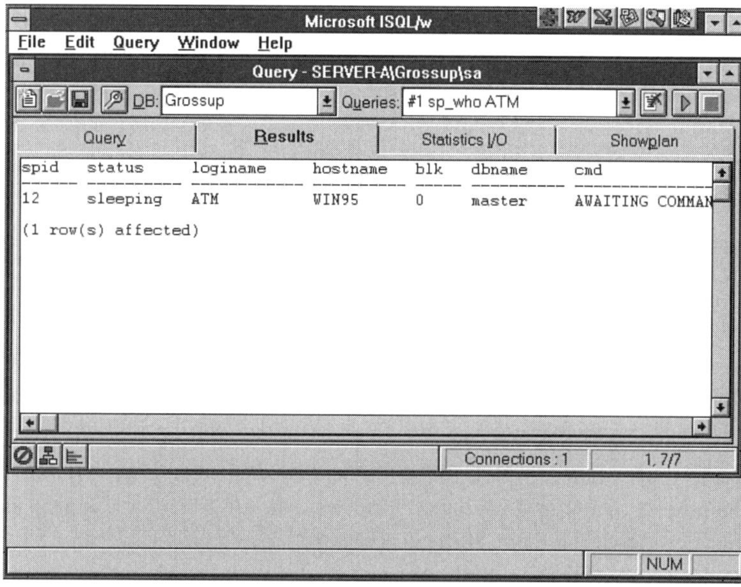

FIGURE 32.1.
The sp_who *results with a parameter given.*

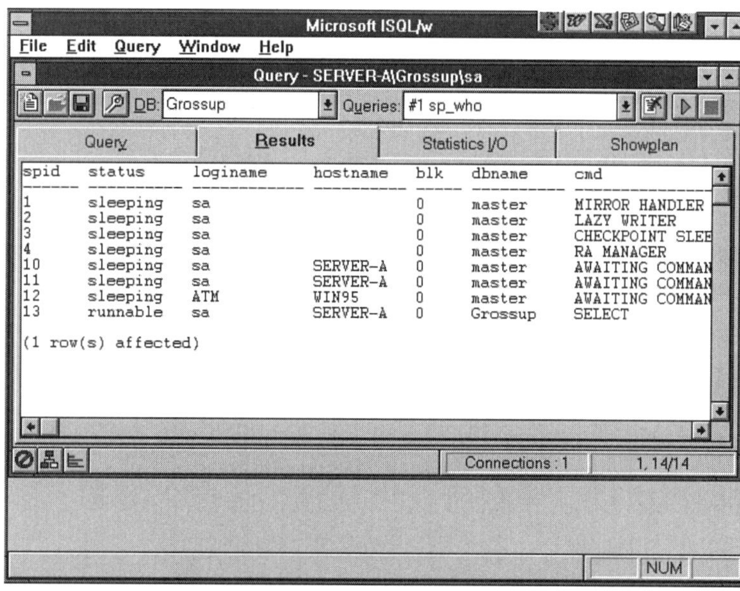

FIGURE 32.2.
The sp_who *results with no parameter given.*

NOTE

Please note that the results shown in the two figures will differ from the results you see. The concept is the same, but the login IDs shown will be different.

Microsoft also provides extended stored procedures. They are really system stored procedures that extend the basic system stored procedure functionality. They are executed the same way as `sp_` system procedures, but they begin with the prefix `xp_`.

Datatypes

Just as with Visual Basic, SQL Server also provides datatypes. There are some that are completely compatible with Visual Basic, and some that are not.

Selecting the correct datatype is very important. Perhaps, this is more important than when selecting a Visual Basic datatype. This is because, for example, in Visual Basic, if you choose a fixed-length string of 10 bytes, but use only 2 bytes, there are 8 bytes wasted. If the variable is a modular or local variable, it will be destroyed when the module or procedure is exited.

On the other hand, in SQL Server, if you choose a `char(10)` variable, but store only 2 bytes, the other 8 bytes are also wasted. However, these 8 bytes will be propagated for every column in every row of the table. If there are 10,000 rows in the table, and 8 bytes wasted in this particular column, that's 80,000 bytes just taking up space, but not being used. This would be very wasteful!

Instead, if you know that you will be storing only 2 bytes of data (such as the two digits for a state abbreviation), you could have declared the datatype as `char(2)`, or possibly even `varchar(10)`. The latter would give you a variable-length character field, with a maximum of 10 characters.

Similarly, suppose you wanted to store two dollar amounts. If you knew that the dollar amount would never be over $100,000, for example, you would use the `smallmoney` datatype. If you used the `money` datatype, you would actually be wasting 4 bytes of data for each row in the table. If there are 10,000 rows, you would waste 40,000 bytes for that column only.

Rules

A *rule* is a database object that specifies the acceptable values that can be inserted or updated in a column or user-defined datatype. These rules help to enforce data integrity. They make it impossible to store a value in a field (column) that is not allowed.

NOTE

A column or user-defined datatype can have only one rule associated with it.

To create a rule, you use the `CREATE RULE` statement, which has the following syntax:

```
CREATE RULE [owner.]rule_name
AS condition_expression
```

where *rule_name* is the name of the new rule and *condition_expression* specifies the conditions that define the new rule.

Suppose that you wanted to create a rule that states that a column can contain only the character values `"0"` through `"9"`. You create the rule like this:

```
CREATE RULE TestRule
AS
@Prefix >= "0" AND @Prefix <= "9"
```

Now that the rule is created, you must assign, or bind, the rule to a column in a database (or user-defined type). Suppose you wanted to bind this rule to a column named Prefix, in a table called UserCode. You bind the rule to the column with the following statement, using a system stored procedure:

```
sp_bindrule "TestRule","UserCode.prefix"
```

This system stored procedure assigned the `TestRule` rule defined earlier to the column Prefix in the table UserCode. You can assign this rule to any number of columns in any number of tables. You can, however, assign only one rule to one column. Now, every time a row is inserted or updated in the table, the value assigned to the Prefix column is checked. It is checked to make sure that the value conforms to the specification of the rule. In this case, a value of `"0"` through `"9"` is allowed. If, for example, you attempted to insert a value `"x"`, it would be disallowed.

NOTE

Note that the values being tested in this example are characters, not integers. Therefore, the arithmetic comparison is not the same as if it were an integer.

If you wanted to remove the rule, you must make sure to unbind the rule from the column first. If you do not unbind the rule from all columns associated with it, you will receive this message:

```
The rule 'TestRule' cannot be dropped because it is bound to one or more columns.
```

Therefore, to unbind the rule from the table column, you use the `sp_unbindrule` system stored procedure. Using the earlier example, you would unbind the rule like this:

```
sp_unbindrule "UserCode.prefix"
```

Then, you can remove the rule by using the following statement:

```
DROP RULE TestRule
```

Defaults

A *default* is a database object that will supply a value to a column, by default, if no value is specified when an SQL statement inserts data into a column. As with rules, you must create the default and then bind it to a column or user-defined type.

> **NOTE**
>
> It is preferable to create defaults when you are creating tables using the `CREATE TABLE` statement, while creating the initial table. It is easier to create defaults this way because it can save many steps.

To create a default, you use the `CREATE DEFAULT` statement. Suppose you wanted to create a default value of `"None"`. You would do that with this code:

```
CREATE DEFAULT TestDefault
AS "None"
```

Now that the default name has been created, you must bind it to a column of a table or a user-defined type by using the `sp_bindefault` system stored procedure. Suppose you wanted to bind this default to a column named City in a table named Address. You would use this code to bind the column:

```
sp_bindefault "TestDefault","address.city"
```

Now every time a row is inserted into table Address, if there is no value provided for the column City, the value `"None"` will automatically be inserted.

To remove the default, you must first unbind it from the column name. If you attempt to drop a default that is still bound to a column, you will receive the following message:

```
The default "TestDefault" cannot be dropped because it is bound to one or more
➥columns.
```

To unbind the default, you use the system stored procedure `sp_unbindefault`. Use this syntax:

```
sp_unbindefault "address.city"
```

Next, you can remove the default by using the `DROP DEFAULT` statement. You can do that like this:

```
DROP DEFAULT TestDefault
```

Triggers

Triggers are stored procedures that are automatically executed in one of three conditions: update, insert, and delete. A trigger is used to perform some action—usually to provide data integrity. If you define a trigger for update, it will automatically be executed when a row is updated in the table. Likewise, the same is true for insert or delete triggers.

You define a trigger with the syntax

```
CREATE TRIGGER [owner.]trigger_name
ON [owner.]table_name
FOR {INSERT,UPDATE,DELETE}
[WITH ENCRYPTION}
AS sql_statements
```

where:

> `trigger_name` is the name of the new trigger.
>
> `table_name` is the name of the table that will have the trigger attached to it.
>
> `INSERT,UPDATE,DELETE` provides the type of trigger. You can use any number of combinations of these in a single trigger.
>
> `WITH ENCRYPTION` encrypts the text of the trigger after creation.
>
> `sql_statements` is the list of one or more SQL statements.

Suppose that you wanted to make sure that every time a record was deleted, a check was made for duplicate values. If any are found, then a message is returned indicating that there are duplicates. For example, suppose you were inserting records into a table of ZIP codes. If you wanted to check duplicates every time you entered a city name, you could create an `INSERT,UPDATE` trigger that checks for duplicates, as follows:

```
CREATE TRIGGER TestTrigger
ON ZipCode
FOR INSERT,UPDATE
AS
IF (SELECT Count(City)
FROM ZipCode
WHERE City IN
(SELECT City FROM ZipCode
GROUP BY City
HAVING Count(*) > 1 )) > 0
RAISERROR ("There are duplicates!",0,1)
```

This trigger will automatically be executed whenever an insert or update occurs on the ZipCode table. It checks to see whether there is a duplicate city name. If there is, an error will be raised (generated).

Views

A *view* is an alternative look at one or more tables. It is also referred to as a *virtual table*. A view cannot be updated. For example, suppose you don't want to perform joins every time some tables are accessed, but you still want to keep the tables normalized. For example, suppose that you have two tables:

- User (with two columns: UserID and Name)
- Address (with three columns: UserID, City, and State)

If you want to provide the city and state every time you do a lookup in the User table, you must join the two tables together. If you want to look for the name "Anthony T. Mann," you could do so like this:

```
SELECT A.City,A.State
FROM User U,Address A
WHERE A.UserID = U.UserID
AND U.Name = "Anthony T. Mann"
```

However, if you knew that you wanted to do this join every time you queried a user, you could create a view of the tables. It, in effect, looks just like any other table, but it would be defined by the preceding SQL statement.

You create a view by using the `CREATE VIEW` statement. The syntax is

```
CREATE VIEW [owner.]view_name
[(column_name[,column_name]...)]
[WITH ENCRYPTION]
AS select_statement [WITH CHECK OPTION]
```

where:

> `view_name` is the name of the view.
>
> `column_name` is the name of the column that will be seen through the view. It is not the name of the column in the underlying tables.
>
> `WITH_ENCRYPTION` encrypts the text of the view after creation.
>
> `select_statement` is the SQL `Select` statement used to create the joins.
>
> `WITH CHECK OPTION` enables the data to remain visible even after a row in the underlying table(s) in the view is modified.

NOTE

Note that there are a few restrictions on using the `SELECT` keyword in a view. You cannot reference a temporary table. You cannot use the `INTO`, `ORDER BY`, `COMPUTE`, or `COMPUTE BY` clauses and keywords.

If you wanted to create a view using the example stated earlier, you would use these statements:

```
CREATE VIEW TestView
(JoinCity,JoinState)
AS
SELECT A.City,A.State
FROM User U,Address A
WHERE A.UserID = U.UserID
AND U.Name = "Anthony T. Mann"
```

Now that the view is created, you can use this SQL statement to execute the view:

```
Select * from TestView
```

This will return two columns from the join and label them JoinCity and JoinState.

Cursors

A *cursor* enables you to perform operations on an individual row or just a specific set of data. This has been available in SQL Server only since version 6.0. Before this version, cursors were available only in a DB-Library, which had to be purchased separately, or through ODBC cursor API functions. Unlike a view, a cursor can be updated.

To use cursors, you must first define the cursor, open the declared cursor, fetch desired rows, close the cursor, and then deallocate the cursor. These actions are performed by using the following statements:

- `DECLARE CURSOR`
- `OPEN`
- `FETCH`
- `CLOSE`
- `DEALLOCATE`

To define a cursor, you must use the `DECLARE CURSOR` statement, which has the following syntax:

```
DECLARE cursor_name [INTENSIVE][SCROLL]CURSOR
FOR select_statement
[FOR {READ ONLY¦UPDATE[OF column_list]}]
```

where:

> `cursor_name` is the name of the cursor to define.
>
> `INTENSIVE` specifies that a copy of the data is to be made in a temporary table, and all cursor operations will result from that table.
>
> `SCROLL` ensures that the cursor reflects current data, even if other users make changes to the data.

`select_statement` is the `Select` statement used to create the cursor.

`READ ONLY` ensures that updates cannot be performed on the cursor.

`UPDATE [OF column_list]` defines the columns that are updateable in the cursor.

You can declare a cursor for the ZipCode table listed earlier by using this SQL statement:

```
DECLARE TestCursor SCROLL CURSOR
FOR SELECT City,State,Zip
FROM ZipCode
```

After the cursor is declared, it must be opened to be able to use it. A cursor can be opened with the `OPEN` keyword. It uses the following very simple syntax, where *`cursor_name`* is the name of the cursor defined in the earlier step:

```
OPEN cursor_name
```

You can open the cursor defined previously, like this:

```
OPEN TestCursor
```

After the cursor is opened, you can start manipulating rows of data. The manipulation of data rows is very similar to the `MoveFirst`, `MovePrevious`, `MoveNext`, and `MoveLast` data access functions.

CROSS REFERENCE

For more information about data access, refer to Chapter 28, "Database Concepts."

You manipulate the cursor data by using the `FETCH` statement. This statement has the following syntax:

```
FETCH [[NEXT¦PRIOR¦FIRST¦LAST¦ABSOLUTE n¦RELATIVE n] FROM]cursor_name
[INTO @@variable_name1,@@variable_name2,...]
```

where:

`NEXT` returns the next row in the cursor (unless there have been no cursor functions executed, in which case it will return the first row in the cursor).

`PRIOR` returns the previous cursor row.

`LAST` returns the last cursor row.

`ABSOLUTE n` returns the *n*th cursor row.

`RELATIVE n` returns the *n*th row after the current fetched row.

`cursor_name` is the name of the cursor defined and opened.

`@@variable_name1...` enables returned data to be placed into a variable.

You can move through the rows in a cursor automatically by doing the following:

```
/* Fetch first row */
FETCH FIRST FROM TestCursor
/* Loop while there are rows left */
WHILE @@fetch_status <> -1
BEGIN
    FETCH NEXT FROM TestCursor
END
```

This will return rows to the screen. Suppose that you want to assign the results to variables. You must first declare the variables and then assign them to the results of the cursors. You would do that like this:

```
/* Declare variables */
DECLARE @City Varchar(30)
DECLARE @State Char(2)
/* Fetch first row */
FETCH FIRST FROM TestCursor
INTO @City,@State
/* Loop while there are rows left */
WHILE @@fetch_status <> -1
BEGIN
    FETCH NEXT FROM TestCursor
    INTO @City,@State
END
```

You can update a cursor by using the `UPDATE` keyword or delete it by using the `DELETE` keyword. This will update or delete the underlying data in the table with which it is associated. The update or delete action performed will affect only the current cursor row. The update and delete syntax is very similar to that of the table `UPDATE` and `DELETE` keywords; however, it is slightly different. The `UPDATE` syntax for cursors is

```
UPDATE table_name
SET column_name1 = {expression1¦NULL¦(select_statement)}
[,column_name2 = {expression1¦NULL¦(select_statement)}...]
WHERE CURRENT OF cursor_name
```

where:

`table_name` is the name of the table to update.

`column_name` is the name of the column in the table to update.

`select_statement` is the SQL `SELECT` statement that produces a resultset to update in *`table_name`*.

`cursor_name` is the name of the cursor in question.

If you wanted to update the current cursor row to the city of Denver and the state of CO, you would do that like this:

```
UPDATE ZipCode
SET City = 'Denver', State = 'CO'
WHERE CURRENT OF TestCursor
```

To delete the current row of cursor data, you would use the DELETE statement syntax, where *table_name* is the name of the table to delete data from, and *cursor_name* is the name of the cursor in question.

```
DELETE FROM table_name
WHERE CURRENT OF cursor_name
```

If you wanted to delete the current row of data in the underlying table, you would do so like this:

```
DELETE FROM ZipCode
WHERE CURRENT OF TestCursor
```

It is a good idea to close the cursor when you are finished using it. This saves resources. To close an open cursor, use the CLOSE keyword with the following syntax, where *cursor_name* is the name of the cursor to close:

```
CLOSE cursor_name
```

You would close the cursor previously opened like this:

```
CLOSE TestCursor
```

To undefine a cursor, you use the DEALLOCATE statement. This releases all data structures associated with the cursor. The DEALLOCATE statement uses the following syntax, where *cursor_name* is the name of the cursor to undefine:

```
DEALLOCATE cursor_name
```

You can undefine the TestCursor cursor by using this statement:

```
DEALLOCATE TestCursor
```

Optimizing Queries and Indexes

Making sure that your queries are optimized is very important. This makes SQL Server more efficient. It also ensures that the user is not waiting longer than necessary for the results of a query. You might not notice that a query is not efficient unless there are many rows in the table.

SQL Server includes a very intelligent optimizer. The optimizer is a part of SQL Server that determines the most efficient way to execute a query, including which index to use. The primary focus of how the optimizer determines how to execute the query is based on the SQL statement's WHERE clause.

The first area of making sure that the query is optimized is to restrict the number of results returned by a query. You do this by including a `WHERE` clause in the query. The query

```
SELECT *
FROM ZipCode
```

is less efficient than this query:

```
SELECT *
FROM ZipCode
WHERE City = 'Denver'
```

The second area is that when you are constructing a query, you must consider which columns have indexes on them. Some database developers have created indexes on all columns in a table, which is not the correct way to create indexes. You create an index on a column based on how the table will be used. If you have a table named ZipCode, and you always will be accessing the table for lookup by Zip code only, you would create an index on the column Zip. In this case, you have determined that the table will be accessed like this:

```
SELECT *
FROM ZipCode
WHERE Zip = '80206'
```

Because the Zip column has an index on it, and the Zip column is in the `WHERE` clause, the optimizer will most likely choose to use the index on this column. If you wanted the optimizer to be forced to use the index, even if the optimizer calculates that it should not use the index, you can still do so. Suppose you had an index on the Zip column, named `ZipIndex`. You could force the optimizer to use the index by using this code:

```
SELECT *
FROM ZipCode (INDEX = ZipIndex)
WHERE Zip = '80206'
```

To verify how efficient a query is, SQL Server provides a tool called ISQL/w, which has an icon in the SQL Server group. This tool provides two features, Showplan and Statistics I/O. These features existed in previous versions, but they were not in a graphical, easy-to-use format. Suppose you executed this SQL statement:

```
SELECT * FROM ZipCode
WHERE State = 'CO'
ORDER BY Zip
```

Figure 32.3 shows a tab in the ISQL/w tool labeled Statistics I/O after executing this query. This tab is used to show a graphical representation of how efficient the query is.

Figure 32.4 shows the Showplan tab in ISQL/w. This shows a graphical representation of which indexes have been chosen (or forced) by the optimizer.

FIGURE 32.3.

The Statistics I/O tab in ISQL/w, using the optimizer plan.

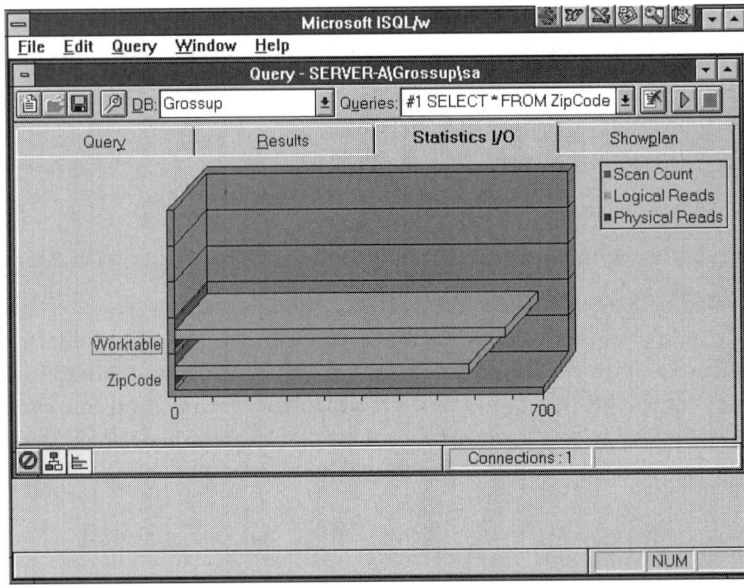

FIGURE 32.4.

The Showplan tab in ISQL/w, using the optimizer plan.

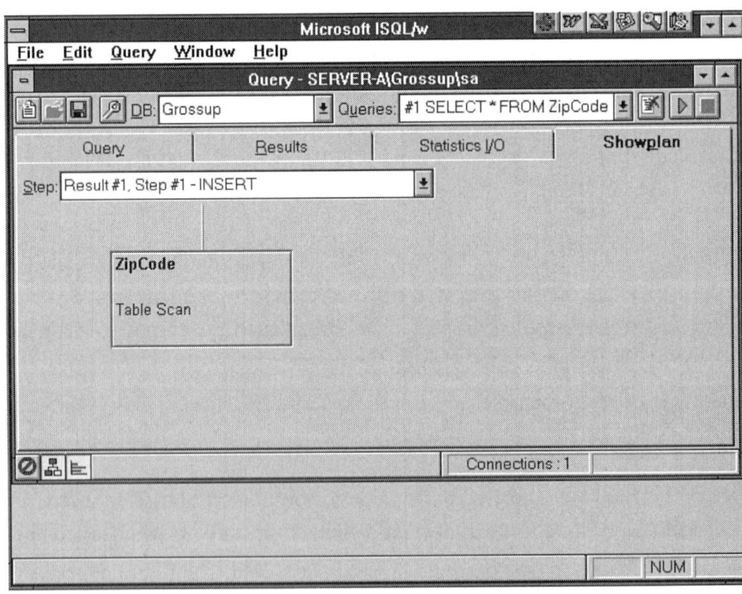

Because there is no index on the State column, the optimizer will do a table scan. If you force the optimizer to use an index, which is not part of the WHERE clause, the query will be less efficient than if it did a table scan. For example, if you forced an index, like this:

```
SELECT *
FROM ZipCode (Index = ZipIndex)
WHERE State = 'CO'
ORDER BY Zip
```

the query can take up to 20 percent longer. Therefore, it is a good rule of thumb that the optimizer is usually right. Figure 32.5 shows a tab in the ISQL/w tool labeled Statistics I/O after forcing the use of a specific index.

FIGURE 32.5.
The Statistics I/O tab in ISQL/w, forcing the index.

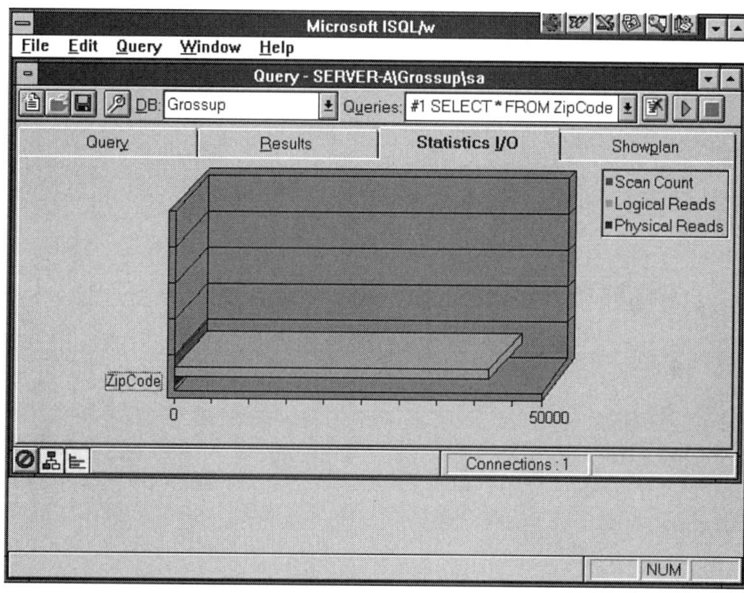

Figure 32.6 shows the Showplan tab in ISQL/w, which shows a graphical representation of which indexes have been chosen (or forced) by the optimizer.

NOTE

Depending on the version of ISQL/w you are using, you might not see the Showplan tab. The plan of execution in this case would be shown under the Results tab.

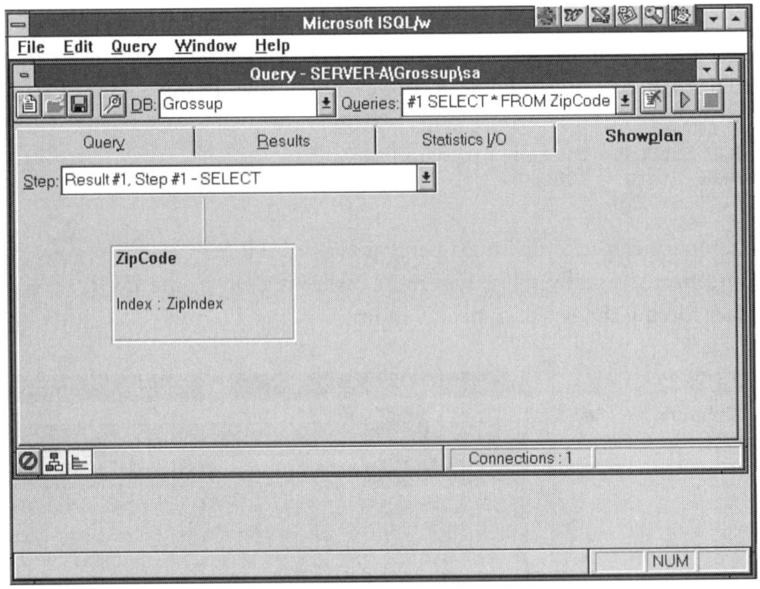

FIGURE 32.6.
The Showplan tab in ISQL/w, forcing the index.

Summary

Visual Basic plays an important role in client/server computing. You can use it to develop the front-end application or first tier. You also can use it to develop the middle tier, which encapsulates the business rules for one or more applications. You generate the back-end database or third tier with tools provided with SQL Server. This chapter defined and described how these tiers are important. Refer to this chapter to help you understand where Visual Basic fits into the client/server world.

33

SQL Server 6.5 Features

SQL Server is an incredibly robust, easy-to-use, and scaleable relational client/server database. SQL Server is fully integrated with Windows NT, and therefore can take advantage of many of its features. This includes Internet/intranet access, security, and other NT-based applications.

Many new features have been added to SQL Server version 6.5. This chapter is dedicated to outlining these features.

Internet and Intranet

SQL Server 6.5 is fully integrated with the Internet Information Server (IIS) 3.0 and has a built-in Internet Database Connector (IDC). Because IIS 3.0 supports Active Server Pages (ASP), you can use dynamic queries to build dynamic HTML using database information and passing it to the client browser. This makes for a fully dynamic database solution over the Internet and an intranet.

A new Web Assistant has been added to SQL Server 6.5 to make it easy to define a stored procedure or query to be merged into an HTML document. This HTML document can be merged to the Web server (IIS) immediately, when the data changes, or at a scheduled time.

The Web Assistant is available from the SQL Server 6.5 Start menu group when you install SQL Server. Selecting it will bring up the Login dialog box, as shown in Figure 33.1.

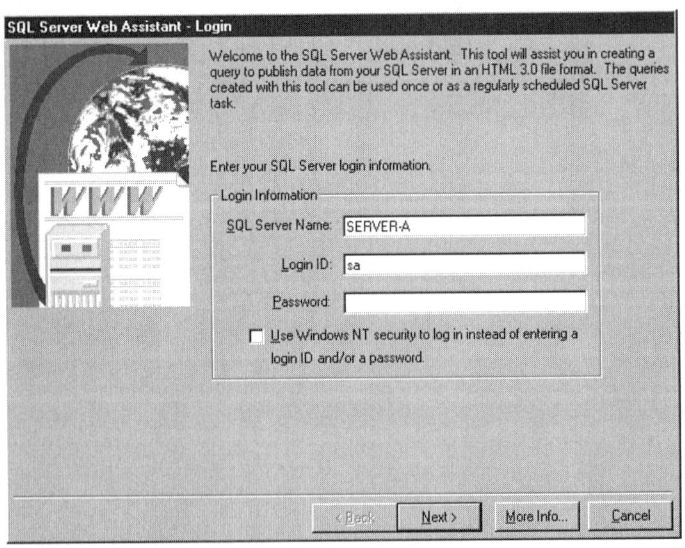

FIGURE 33.1.
The SQL Server 6.5 Web Assistant - Login dialog box.

You must enter the name of the SQL Server from which the data will come. Then, enter the ID and password to log in to SQL Server. Optionally, you can use NT security to log in with your current ID and password instead of typing them in.

Click the Next button to select the data source for the Web page. Figure 33.2 shows this step.

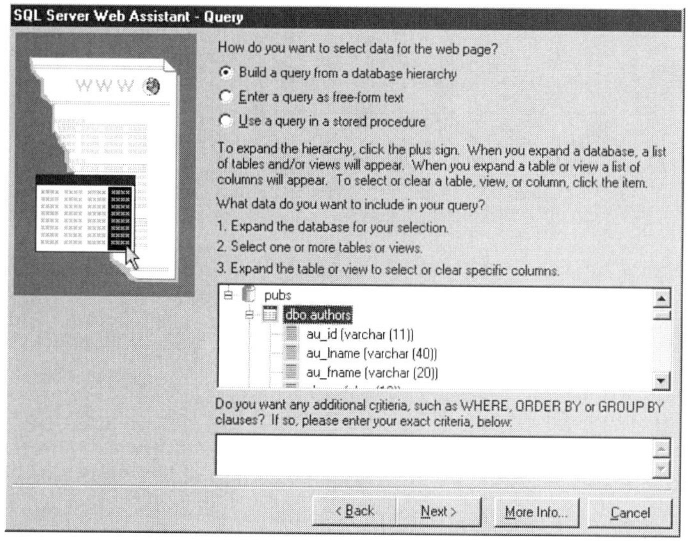

FIGURE 33.2.
Using the SQL Server 6.5 Web Assistant to select a data source.

You have these three options:

- Build a query from a database hierarchy
- Enter a query as free-form text
- Use a query in a stored procedure

For this example, simply accept the default option: Build a query from a database hierarchy. Next, expand the desired database to select from the tables in the database. You can either select an entire table or any of the columns in that table. If you want to select from multiple tables, you'll need to build a query and use that as your basis for selection. A selected column in a table appears with a green icon to the left of the table name. Click the Next button to select when you would like the Web page to be created. Figure 33.3 shows this scheduling step.

You have these five choices for scheduling:

- Now
- Later
- When Data Changes
- On Certain Days of the Week
- On a Regular Basis

FIGURE 33.3.
The SQL Server 6.5 Web Assistant's scheduling step.

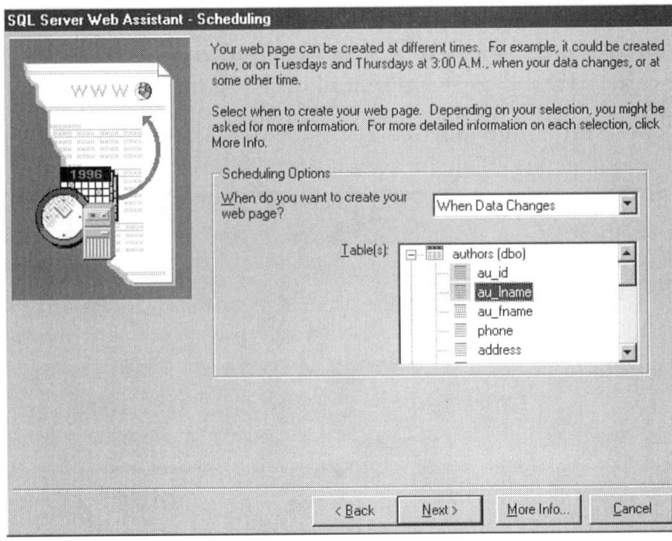

If you choose an option other than Now, you will be prompted for the appropriate information. For example, if you choose Later, you are prompted for the date and time to create the page. For this example, select When Data Changes. This automatically creates a trigger that generates the Web page when the data changes. You can select more than one column to trigger the generation of the Web page. Click the Next button to assign options to the creation of the page. Figure 33.4 shows these options.

FIGURE 33.4.
The SQL Server 6.5. Web Assistant options.

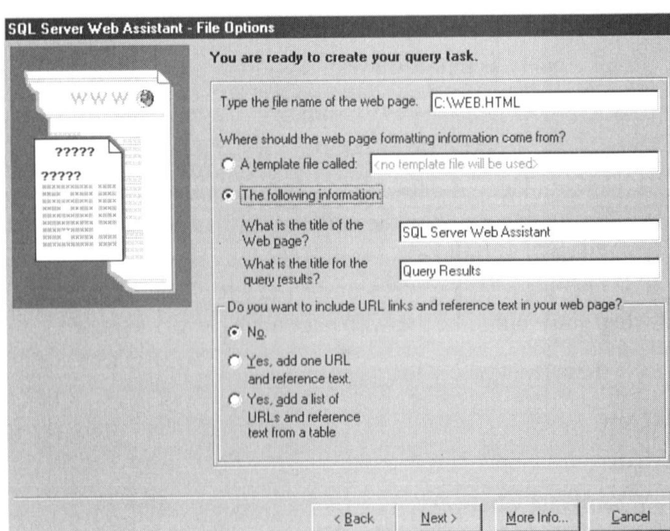

Using the options on this page, you can specify the following information:

- The filename for the Web page.
- A template for the wizard to use to format the page. Or, you can specify the titles for the page and query results.
- Whether you want to include URL information.

Click the Next button and you will be presented with the last option, which specifies formatting of the page. Figure 33.5 shows this page.

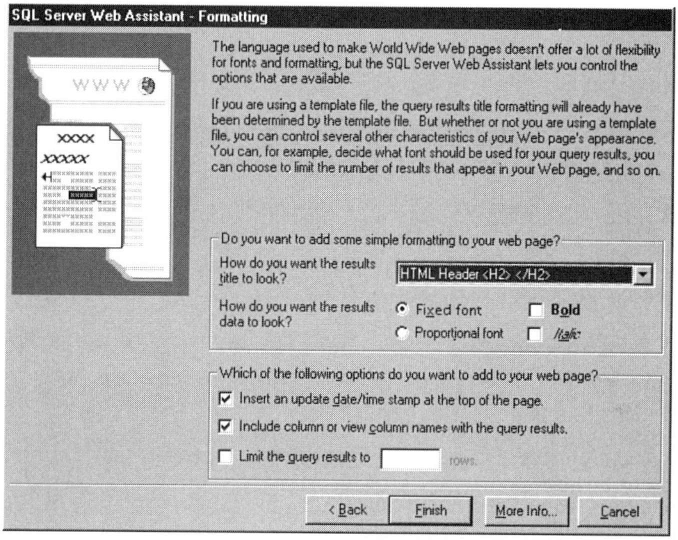

FIGURE 33.5.
The SQL Server 6.5 Web Assistant's formatting options.

First, you can choose the HTML style for the heading. You can choose from the following tags:

- `<H1> </H1>`
- `<H2> </H2>`
- `<H3> </H3>`
- `<H4> </H4>`
- `<H5> </H5>`
- `<H6> </H6>`

CROSS REFERENCE

For more information about these tags, refer to Chapter 25, "HTML Primer."

You also can choose the type of font. Your choices are as follows:

- Fixed font
- Proportional font
- Bold
- Italic

Finally, you have three options that affect the formatting of your page:

- Insert an update date/time stamp at the top of the page
- Include a column or view column names with the query results
- Limit the query results to a specific number of rows

Click Finish to either create your page or schedule the creation of the page, based on the criteria chosen in the scheduling step.

Because the option was chosen to create the Web page when the data changed, the wizard created a trigger on the `au_id` and `au_lastname` columns in the pubs database. The trigger generated looks like this:

```
if exists (select * from sysobjects where id = object_id('dbo.Web_16003088_1')
➥and sysstat & 0xf = 8)
    drop trigger dbo.Web_16003088_1
GO
CREATE TRIGGER Web_16003088_1 ON dbo.authors FOR INSERT AS IF UPDATE (au_lname)
begin
   exec sp_makewebtask @outputfile='C:\WEB.HTML',@query='select a.* from
   ➥pubs.dbo.authors a',@fixedfont=1,@bold=0,@italic=0,@colheaders=1,
   ➥@lastupdated=1,@HTMLheader=2,@username='dbo',@dbname='pubs',
   ➥@webpagetitle='SQL Server Web Assistant',@resultstitle='Query Results',
   ➥@maketask=0,@rowcnt=0
end
GO
```

Therefore, when the data changes, a Web page will be generated, as shown using the Internet Explorer in Figure 33.6.

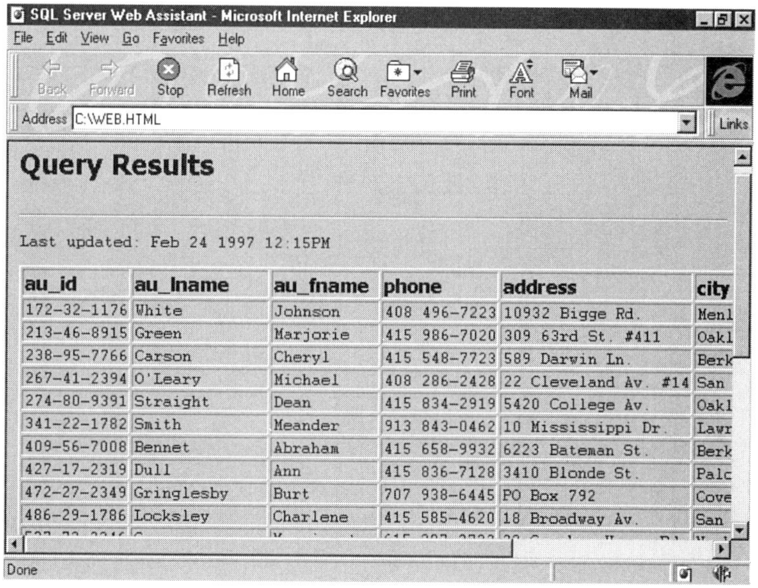

FIGURE 33.6.
SQL Server 6.5 automatically creates a Web page using data in a database.

Mail Integration

Mail integration has made SQL Server incredibly powerful. It is a great way for mail to be automatically generated for users or groups of users when data changes in a database. For example, suppose you wanted to generate a report every week that listed the names of the authors from the authors table in the pubs database.

To schedule this process, open the SQL Enterprise Manager in SQL Server 6.5. Expand the icon for the database and server you want. You'll notice an item called SQL Mail. If this icon is red, then it is not configured correctly. Right-click and select the Configure option. Type the name of a valid profile for this machine. Then right-click again and select Start. The icon should appear as shown in Figure 33.7.

After SQL Mail is running, you can schedule processes using the SQL Executive. SQL Executive is a Windows NT service installed automatically with SQL Server. Make sure the SQL Executive service is running in the Control Panel. Ensure the service is running as shown in Figure 33.8.

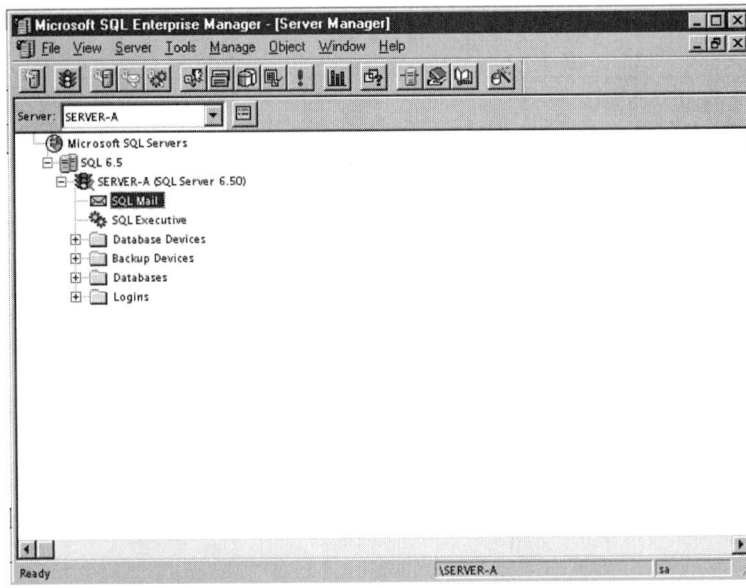

FIGURE 33.7.
SQL Server 6.5 SQL Mail.

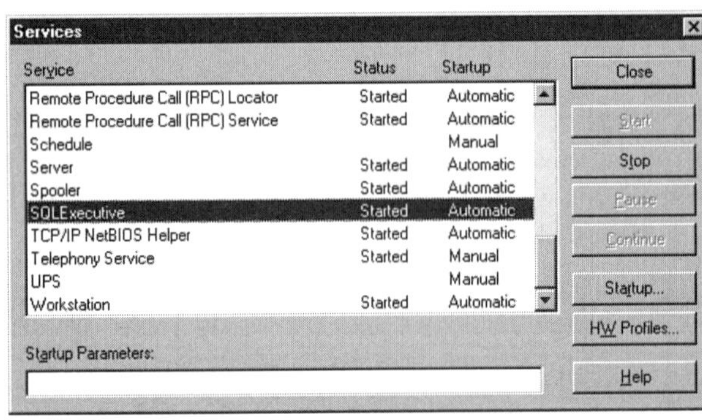

FIGURE 33.8.
The Control Panel showing SQL Executive service running.

Double-click SQL Executive in the Enterprise Manager. This brings up the Manage Scheduled Tasks dialog box shown in Figure 33.9, which displays a list of all the tasks to be performed by the SQL Executive, if there are any.

To start a new task, select the icon on the far left. This brings up the New Task dialog box in which you can assign a new task. You have the following options to configure in this dialog box:

- Name of the task
- Type of task
- Database

- Command
- Scheduling options

FIGURE 33.9.
Manage Scheduled Tasks, Task List tab.

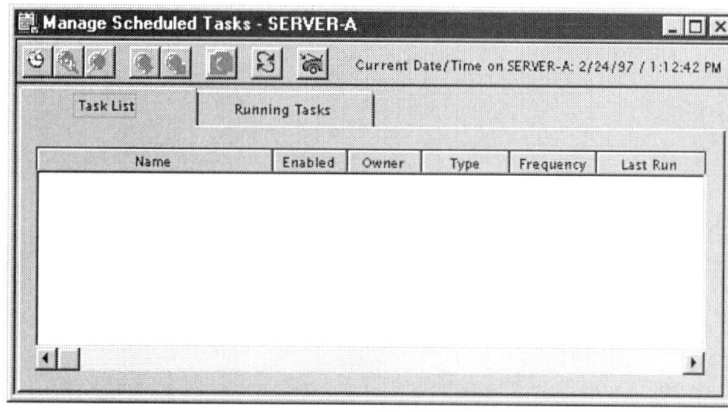

The scheduling options allow for e-mail to be generated at a specific interval. The most common interval is to generate e-mail every Sunday morning at 12:00 a.m. This way, e-mail is waiting for users on Monday morning. Figure 33.10 shows the New Task screen.

FIGURE 33.10.
Using the SQL Executive to schedule new tasks.

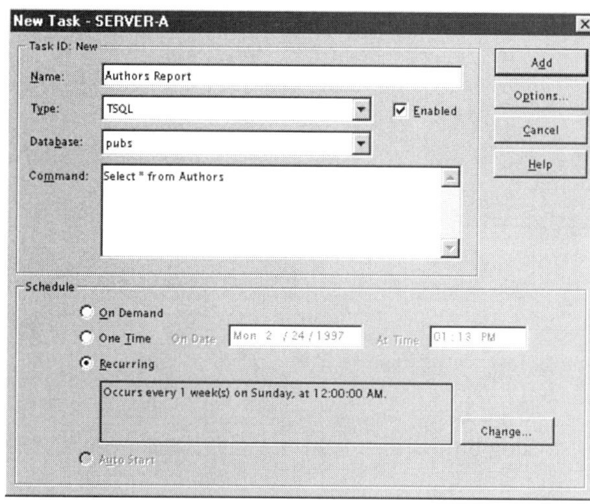

Selecting the Options button enables you to specify to whom to send mail regarding the command to be executed in this step. Figure 33.11 shows the screen that enables you to select these options.

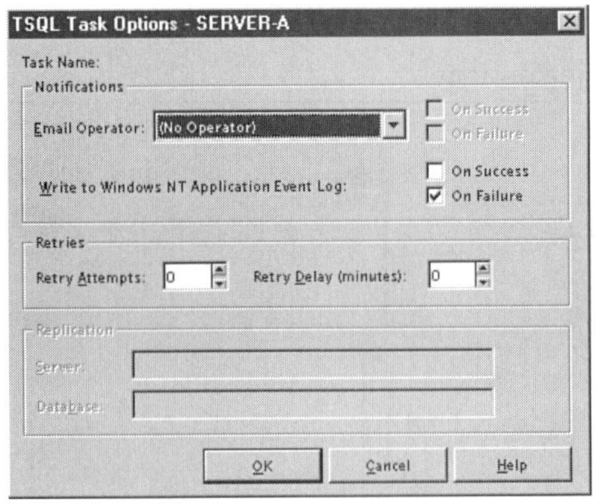

FIGURE 33.11.
Task options for SQL Executive.

To select a new operator, select the New Operator value in the Email Operator drop-down list. This, in turn, brings up another dialog box for you to select the new operator. Figure 33.12 shows the New Operator dialog box.

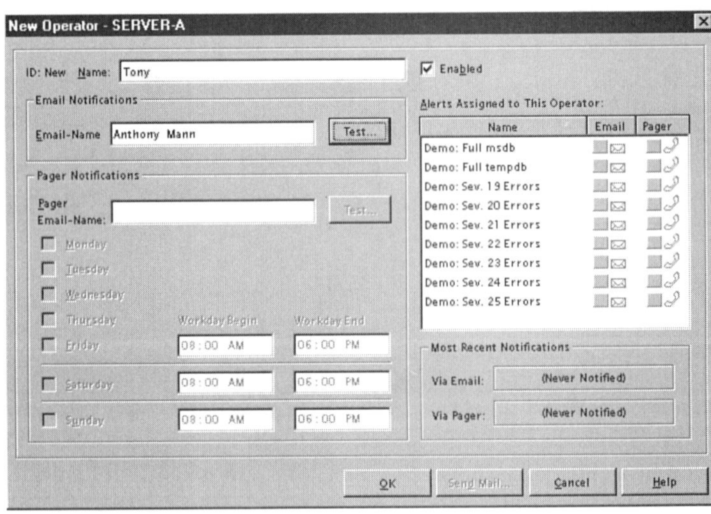

FIGURE 33.12.
The new operator options for SQL Executive.

Testing the e-mail operator you entered is a good idea. To do this, select the Test button. Upon successful completion, a test message will be placed in the inbox of the e-mail operator's messaging system. Figure 33.13 shows Word 97 with the e-mail test message in the inbox.

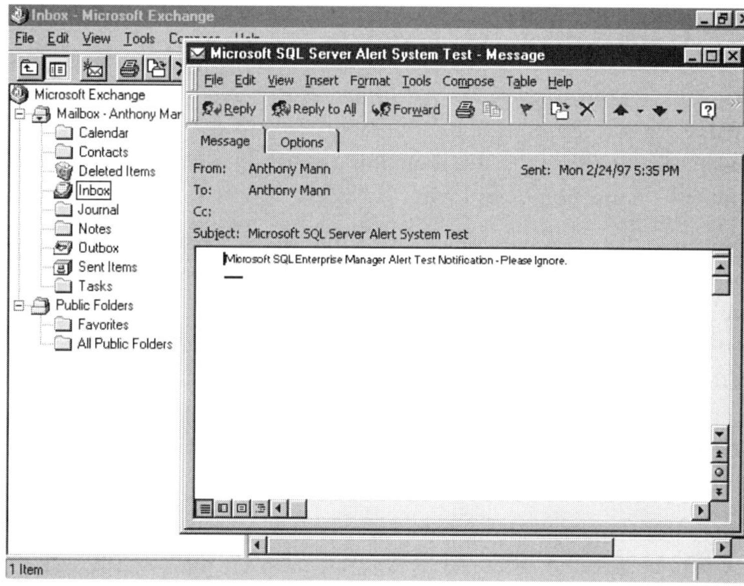

FIGURE 33.13.
A test message in the inbox of Microsoft Exchange.

You'll probably want to notify the operator upon success or failure of the task. If so, select the appropriate option, and then select the Add button to add the operator. The new task is shown in Figure 33.14. To test the task, right-click on the specific task and choose the Run option.

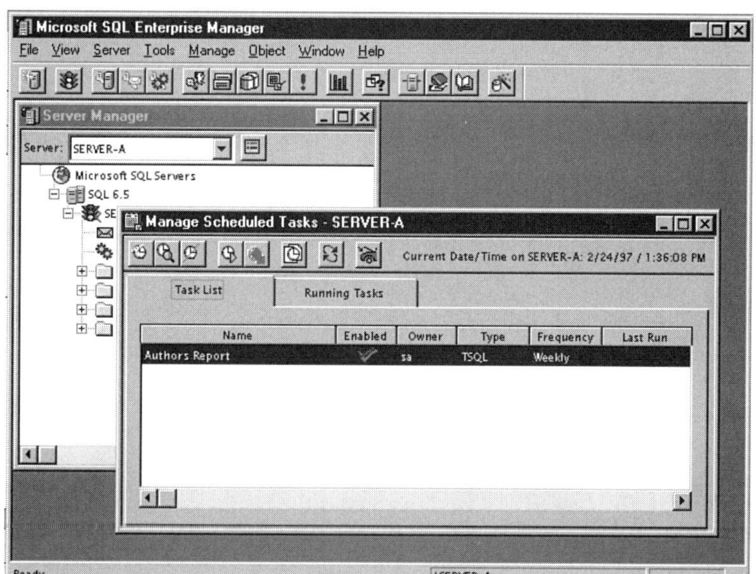

FIGURE 33.14.
The scheduled task.

Distributed Processing

Distributed processing was introduced in SQL Server 6.0. Version 6.5 makes creating distributed client/server applications and databases very easy. All transactions across multiple SQL Servers are handled so that transaction integrity is maintained. This is done through the Distributed Transaction Coordinator (DTC).

Distributed Management Objects (DMOs) make performing many actions easy. Such objects include bulk copy, registered servers, and server groups. All of these items are for use with multiple SQL Servers. These objects are available so that you can write your own Visual Basic programs that perform any of the administrative functions the SQL Enterprise Manager would perform.

Data-Related Features

Many data-related features have been added or enhanced in SQL Server 6.5. These data-related features give SQL Server 6.5 features that rival some of the features in competitive products. This makes SQL Server a viable, low-cost alternative to other client/server databases. The data-related features include the following:

- *Dynamic locking* is a feature that locks records at the page level or record level. This reduces contention between multiple users attempting to access the record at the same time.
- *Host connectivity* enables you to share data with your mainframe and other databases seamlessly. This alone is a great reason for moving to SQL Server 6.5 for enterprise-wide data access.
- *VLDB* (Very Large Database) features have been enhanced to allow for the management of databases greater than 100GB. SQL Server 6.5 allows for the dumping and loading of individual tables and indexes, just as with smaller databases. You do not need to drop and re-create the tables and indexes.
- *Data warehousing* has been optimized. This allows for the retrieval of information from multiple sources and aggregated within SQL Server tables. Support for OLAP has been enhanced with query extensions.
- *Data replication* has been improved. Data replication is almost real-time copying (replication) of data to ensure that if something goes wrong, you will have a backup of the data.
- The *INSERT EXEC* option enables the results of a remote or extended procedure (XP) to be stored in a table.
- *Columns* now have an identity property. This property can be used as a counter to uniquely identify rows in a table.

Miscellaneous Features

Support for the PowerPC has been added to SQL Server 6.5. Now SQL Server 6.5 runs identically on all supported platforms (Intel, Alpha, and MIPS). Also, SQL Server 6.5 supports single and multiple processors. This makes SQL Server an extremely scaleable solution.

The following additional miscellaneous features have been added or improved in SQL Server version 6.5:

- A cost-based optimizer
- Improved checkpointing (thus, response time is greater)
- Parallel access to multiple disks
- "Point-In-Time" recovery to restore a database (or transaction logs) to a specific point in time
- Faults can now be isolated to a single user thread
- DDL statements can now be added within transactions
- All major networks are now supported (TCP/IP, IPX/SPX, Named Pipes, Banyan Vines, AppleTalk, and DECnet)

Summary

SQL Server 6.5 has many important new features that make it a viable alternative to other client/server databases which, in the past, had more distributed-related features. It is important to place this chapter in a book dedicated mostly to Visual Basic because of the relative nature of Visual Basic and SQL Server. The products go hand-in-hand when you are developing a Microsoft-centric client/server database application. This chapter discussed the major features of SQL Server 6.5 and related them to your Visual Basic applications.

34

Crystal Reports

Crystal Reports is an easy-to-use report writer that comes with the Professional edition of Visual Basic. If you own the standard version, you can purchase Crystal Reports from Crystal Services. The topics in this chapter cover Crystal Reports version 4.6. However, most of the general topics discussed in this chapter also apply to Crystal Reports version 3.0, which is the version that comes with Visual Basic version 4.0, Professional and Enterprise editions.

The Development Cycle of Crystal Reports

It's important to understand the development cycle of a Crystal report. It is designed in two steps:

1. Design the report layout in the Crystal Reports design environment.
2. Write code in your Visual Basic application that runs the report designed in the previous step.

To access the design environment—from now on called the Integrated Design Environment (IDE)—simply click the Add-ins | Report Designer menu option. This brings up Crystal Reports. Depending on the speed of your machine and the amount of memory it has, this could take a little bit of time. The executable size is over 3MB. This runs a program called `CRW32.EXE` from the `REPORT` subdirectory of wherever you installed Visual Basic. However, this program cannot be run outside of Visual Basic. In other words, you cannot double-click on the `CRW32.EXE` program and have it run unless Visual Basic is already running. Follow the steps listed in the rest of this chapter to help develop your Crystal Reports.

If you haven't registered your copy of Crystal Reports, you are constantly reminded of this fact every time you run it. Therefore, I recommend registering the copy you have as soon as possible. The reminder screen asks you two pages of questions. The first is shown in Figure 34.1 and the second in Figure 34.2.

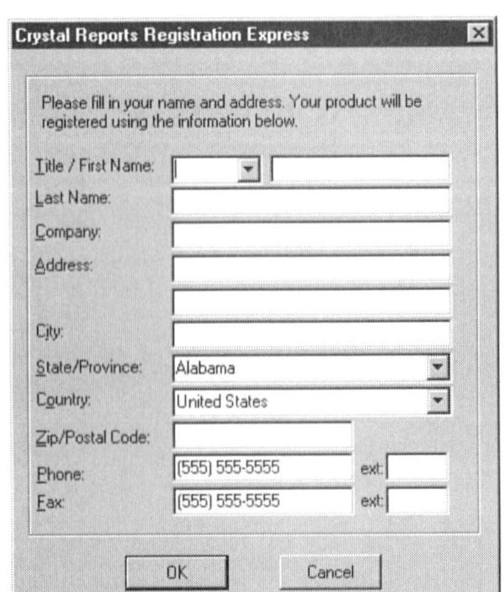

FIGURE 34.1.
The first Crystal Reports Registration reminder screen.

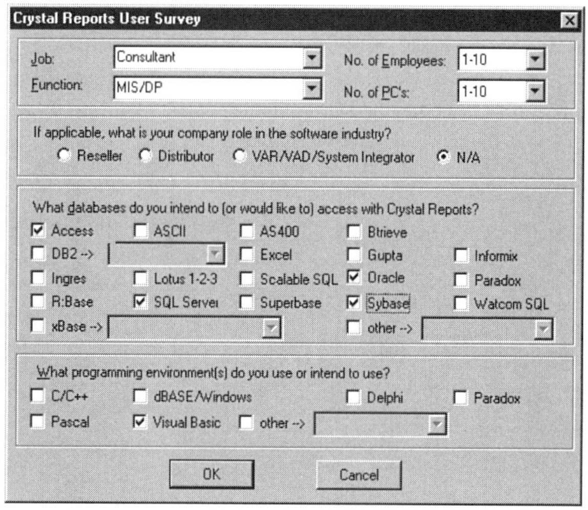

FIGURE 34.2.
The second Crystal Reports Registration reminder screen.

After both pages have been filled in, you can either mail or fax the information to Seagate Software, or you can register via modem. These options can be accomplished through the screen shown in Figure 34.3.

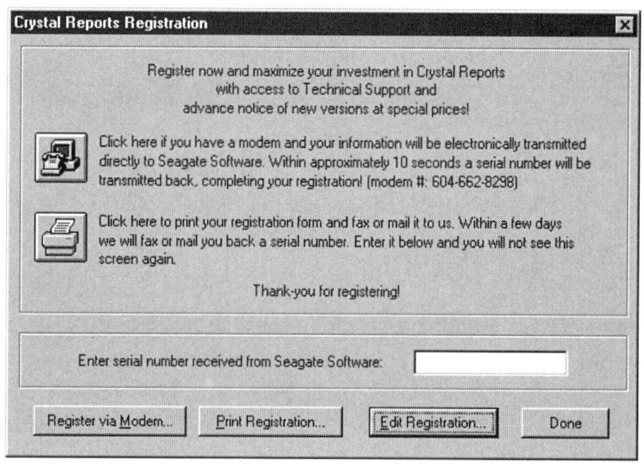

FIGURE 34.3.
The Crystal Reports Registration screen.

When registration is complete, you can begin. Figure 34.4 shows what the Crystal Reports design environment looks like after you have registered. Each of the Crystal Reports icons is listed in Figure 34.4.

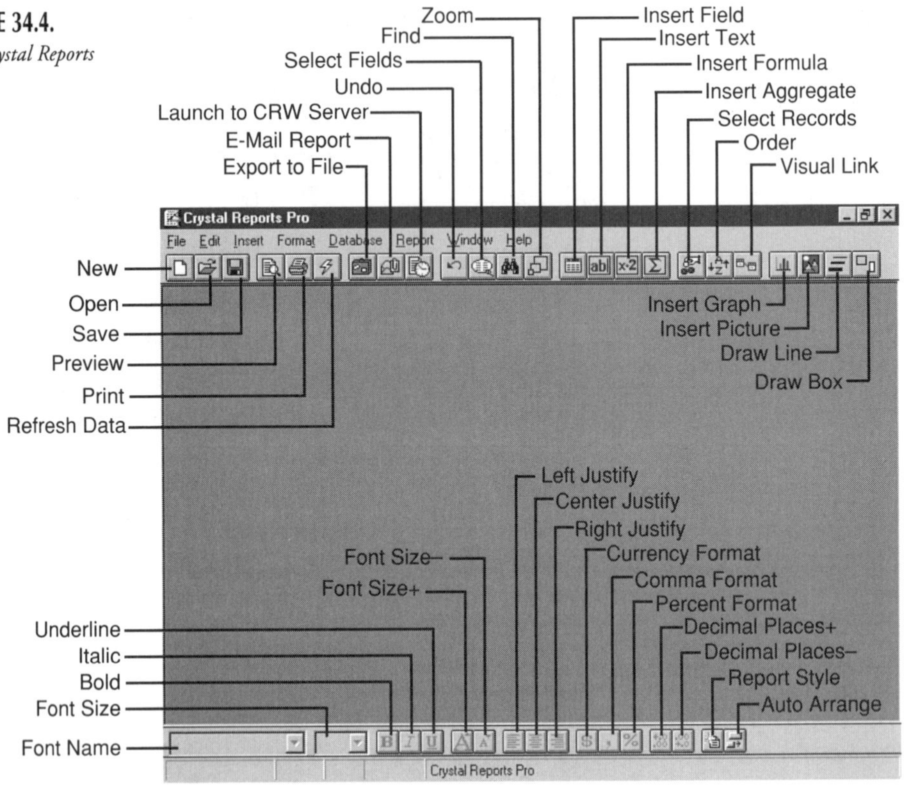

FIGURE 34.4.
The Crystal Reports IDE.

The Concept of a Report Writer Used with Visual Basic

A report writer is designed to greatly simplify the report designing process. A report writer is used, among other things, to perform the following functions:

- Design how the report looks
- Add groupings that break every time the data in this group is changed
- Add subtotals based on these groupings, if desired

For example, if you want to show a list of sales and you don't add a grouping, you can see only a list of all sales. You see one line of "Details" for every sale. For example, you cannot show a subtotal for each region. If you want to see a report based on each region individually, you must group by the field `Region`.

If, in each region, you want to see a detailed list of sales of each product, you need to add a second "level" of groupings. This grouping is based on the `Product` field.

The preceding is basically the concept of how you define your report. Despite all my efforts over the years to convince Seagate Software (formerly Crystal Services) to change its product, you cannot dynamically add a grouping from Visual Basic. Therefore, if you want to show a report grouped by region and sometimes by region and product, you must create two separate reports. Crystal Reports refers to these groupings as *group sections.*

After you define the report, you should make sure it works correctly in the IDE. The next step is to save the file. Save the file with an `*.RPT` file extension. Finally, in Visual Basic, you must include the `CRYSTL32.OCX` custom control in your project. You do this by selecting the Project | Components menu option in Visual Basic. Figure 34.5 shows the dialog box presented when you add a new custom control with the Crystal Reports 4.6 control selected.

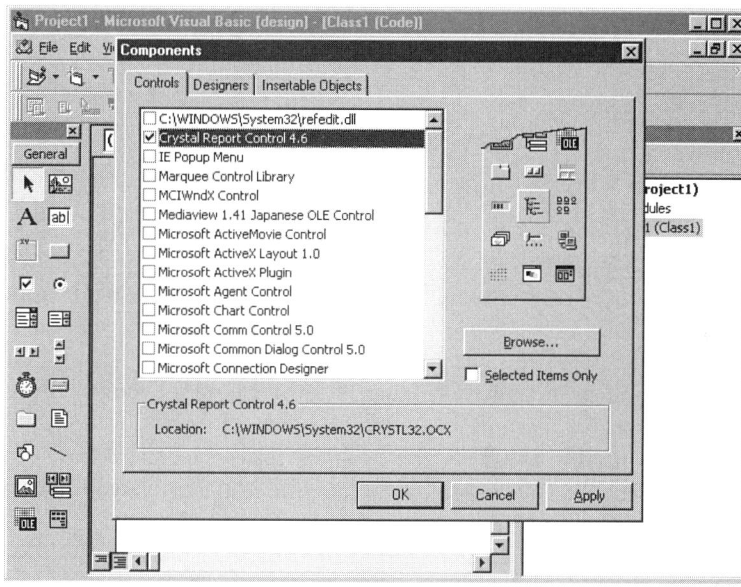

FIGURE 34.5.
Selecting the Crystal Reports custom control.

Using this ActiveX control enables you to access properties that directly use the Crystal Reports print engine. This print engine defines how Crystal Reports works and is in a file named `CRPE32.DLL`. You access properties of this ActiveX control in order to control certain parameters of your report, one of which is the actual report to run. Programming the Visual Basic code is covered later in this chapter, in the section "The Visual Basic Interface."

NOTE

A possibly confusing term that Crystal Reports uses is *printing*. Whether a report goes to the printer, screen, or to a file, it is referred to as "printing" a report. It can be confusing if you think of printing to a screen. You might tend to think of only a BASIC language printing to a screen, not a commercial product.

Creating a New Report

There are many types of reports you can create with Crystal Reports. When you are creating a new report, you are presented with all of these options. To create a new report, select the File | New menu option, or click the New report icon on the toolbar (refer to Figure 34.4). You are presented with a dialog box that contains all different types of reports to create. There is even a Custom button to enable you to customize these standard reports even further. Figure 34.6 shows the Create New Report dialog box after the Custom button is clicked.

FIGURE 34.6.
Creating a new report.

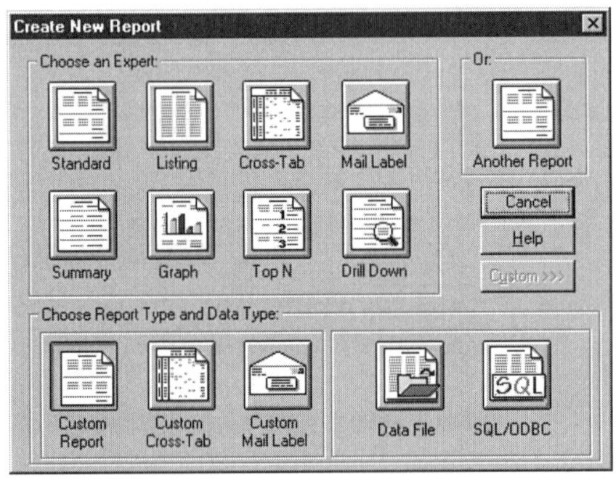

There are 11 reports shown in Figure 34.6 that can speed your report creation process by providing experts (or "wizards" as Microsoft users call them) to step you through the process. If you do not want to use the experts, you can select the Data File or SQL/ODBC option buttons. This enables you to select your data source and create your own reports manually. The following sections describe how to use the experts.

Using the Experts

There are eight experts you can use to speed up the report-creating process. Here's a list of these experts:

- Standard
- Listing
- Cross-Tab
- Mail Label
- Summary
- Graph
- Top N
- Drill Down

Each of these reports presents you with a different number of steps for creating a Crystal Report. These are described next.

The Standard Expert

The Standard Expert presents you with a series of six successive steps that guide you through the process of creating the report.

You use Step 1 to select the tables in the specific database on which you will be reporting. There are two options for the source of the data. The first is a data file, such as Access, Paradox, or xBase files. Each of these database types is stored in one physical file. The other choice is an ODBC data source, which could be one of the previously mentioned database files, or, more commonly, a client/server database, such as SQL Server, Sybase, or Oracle. Figure 34.7 shows the Tables tab.

FIGURE 34.7.
The Tables tab of the Standard Expert.

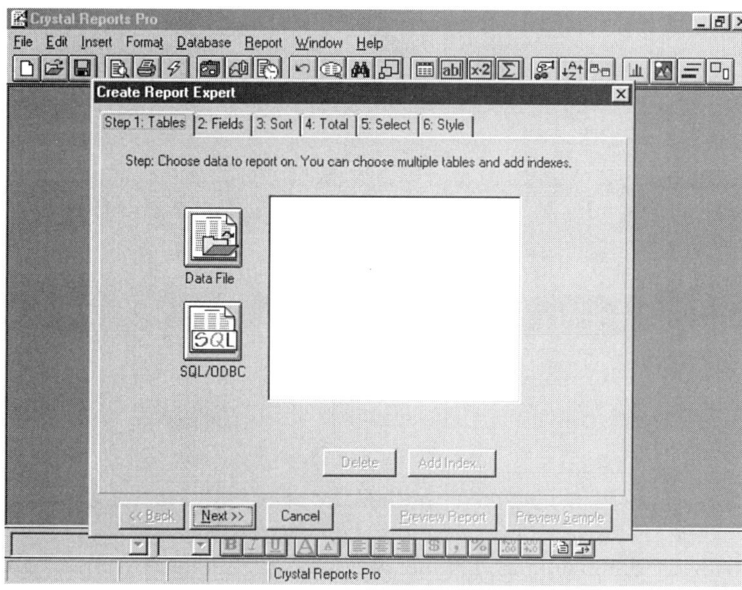

After you select the data source, you must select one or more tables on which to report. For example, if you chose to log into SQL Server to use the Pubs database, you would be presented the Choose SQL Table screen like the one in Figure 34.8.

Suppose you wanted to select the Authors and Publishers tables. You simply highlight the appropriate table and click the Add button. When you are finished, click Done. This automatically puts you into Step 2 of 7, the Links tab.

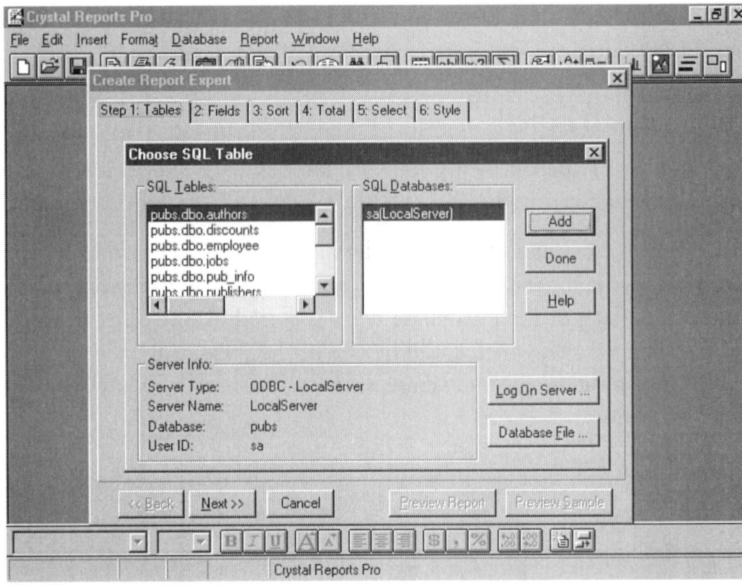

FIGURE 34.8.
The Choose SQL Table screen of the Standard Expert.

You use Step 2 to link columns within the tables. This is also known as "join" information. If you were to write an SQL statement containing joins, most likely you would do this in the `WHERE` clause.

CROSS REFERENCE

For more information about SQL, refer to Chapter 29, "Structured Query Language (SQL)."

Notice from Figure 34.9 that the links are automatically created for you. This is called "smart linking." However, sometimes the links are wrong, as shown in this figure. (I sometimes refer to this as "dumb linking.") Notice that the City field in the Authors table is linked to the City field in the Publishers table. The same is true for State. This is absolutely wrong. The only thing they have in common is the name. The City and State fields have no bearing or relationship with each other. If there were a table with all of the states in it, that might be linked to Authors and Publishers tables, but certainly not to each other.

Often, the links presented are incorrect. Therefore, you need to remove the links by clicking in the center of the link (illustrated by a line) and then pressing the Delete key.

The fact is that these tables don't link at all. You would need to add the Titles and Titleauthor tables. Figure 34.10 shows how you link these tables to relate them correctly. You can create a link between two tables simply by clicking a field in one table and dragging and dropping it on a field in another table.

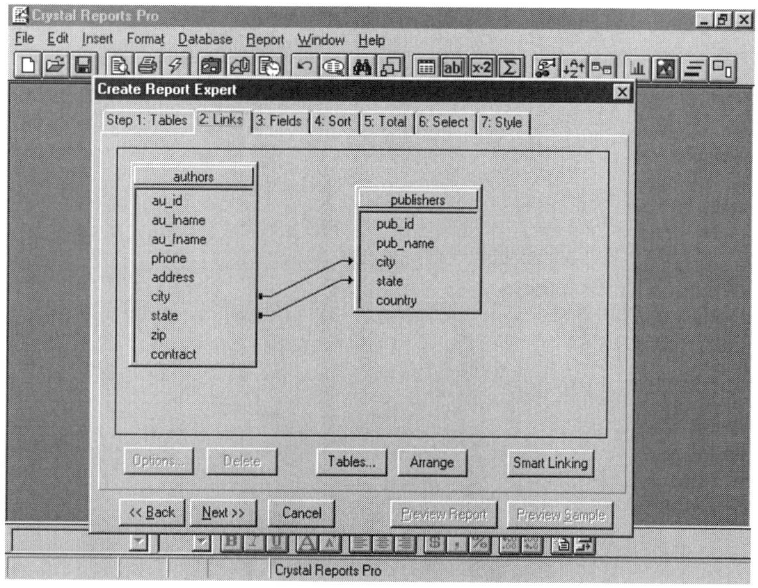

FIGURE 34.9.
Links tab of the Standard Expert.

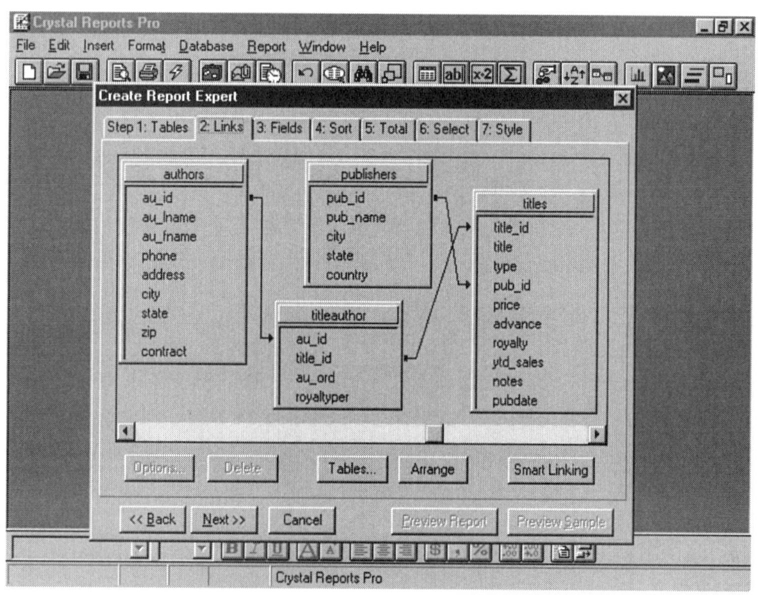

FIGURE 34.10.
The Links tab of the Standard Expert, showing correct links.

The Fields tab enables you to select the fields from the tables chosen earlier to display on the report. Suppose you wanted to see a list of all titles, with the respective authors and publishers. Because the data is not stored in one table, you must provide the links correctly on the Links tab. To select the fields, again, highlight them and click the Add button. Select the following fields:

- `authors.au_lname`
- `authors.au_fname`
- `publishers.pub_name`
- `titles.title`

Figure 34.11 shows what this step looks like after the fields have been selected.

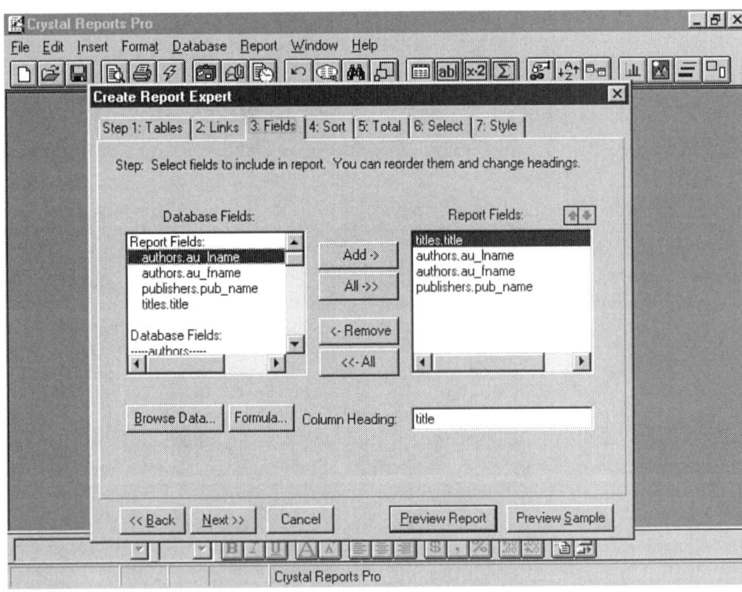

FIGURE 34.11.
The Fields tab of the Standard Expert.

The Sort tab enables you to define how you will sort your data. You can choose from the fields selected on the Fields tab or from other fields. You may choose to sort on a field that is not shown. To choose sorting, highlight the field and click Add. You can change the level of sorting by using the up and down arrows. Figure 34.12 shows this step.

Suppose you wanted to sort by title of the book, then by author last name, and then author first name. You would need to ensure that the fields are shown in that order, as they are in Figure 34.12.

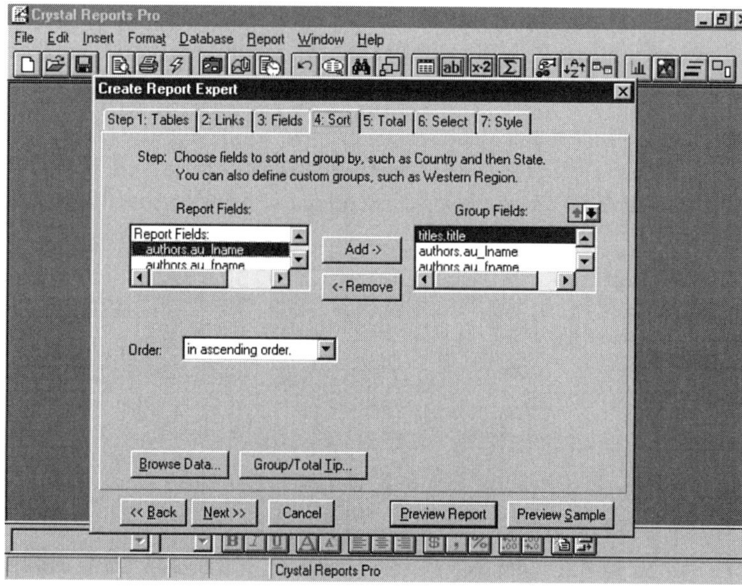

FIGURE 34.12.
The Sort tab of the Standard Expert.

The Total tab defines the types of aggregates you would like on your report. Aggregates are mathematical summing functions, such as `SUM`, `COUNT`, `MIN`, `MAX`, or `AVERAGE`. An aggregate in SQL is typically defined in the `GROUP BY` clause. In this step, you'll see a tab for each of the fields you have defined to view on your report. This enables you to select the field that is used as an aggregate. For example, you might want a count to appear in the Subtotal section in the publisher column, but the system needs to know what to count. Therefore, the tabs at the top represent which column the aggregate appears in, and the fields that you select in this step define what the aggregate will be performed on. Most likely, this is the same field.

CROSS REFERENCE

For more information about aggregates, refer to Chapter 29, "Structured Query Language (SQL)."

In this step, select the title field for the title tab. Next, you must select the type of aggregate. Because this is not a numeric or currency field, you cannot select Sum. You can only select the following:

- Count
- Distinct Count
- Maximum
- Minimum

A Distinct Count greatly differs from a Count. Suppose you had five rows in a table. The values in a column are 1, 2, 1, 3, and 4. A Count would yield the number 5. A Distinct Count would yield the number 4 because the number 1 was repeated. You want a count only of the distinct values.

The check box at the bottom of the screen, labeled Add Grand Totals, is selected by default. It includes a Grand Total section at the end of the report automatically. Figure 34.13 shows this step.

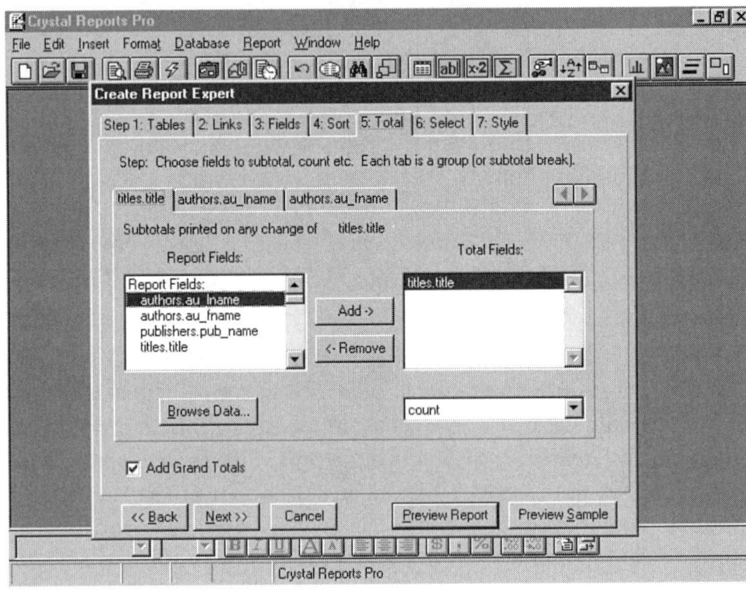

FIGURE 34.13.
The Total tab of the Standard Expert.

The Select tab is a very important step. It enables you to limit the records returned from the database. Up until now, the defined report returns every record in the database. That includes all titles, authors, and publishers. Suppose you wanted to return only the records for a given author—you would do that in this step. To select a specific author, select the au_lname column and click the Add button. Now that you've selected the column, you must compare it to some value. A text field, such as au_lname, can have the following comparisons made:

- Any value
- Equal to
- One of
- Less than
- Greater than
- Between
- Starting with

- Like
- Formula

One nice feature of this screen is that you are able to browse the data and select the value to compare with. For example, choose the "equal to" operator and choose an author. Figure 34.14 shows this step.

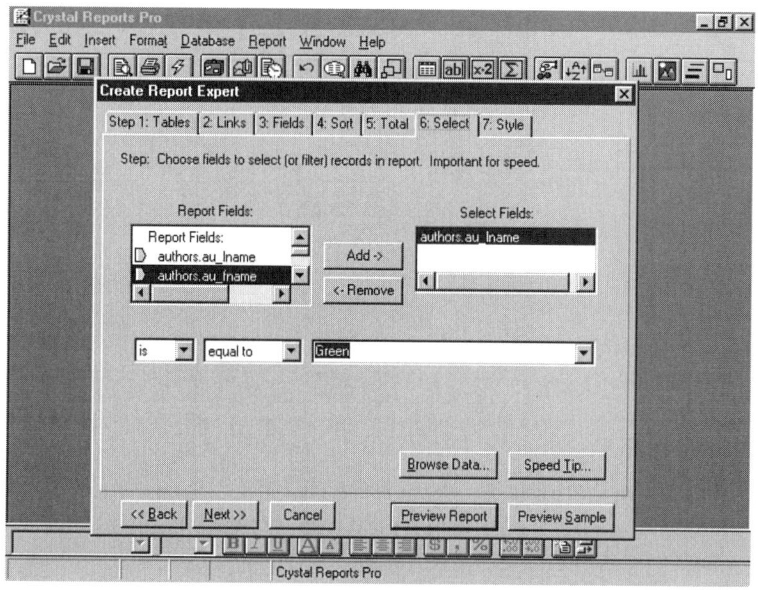

FIGURE 34.14.
The Select tab of the Standard Expert.

The Style tab enables you to pick the style of the report and to specify a title. It also enables you to include a picture, if you want to. The following styles provide a report print preview to show you how the style will affect the report:

- Standard
- Leading Break
- Trailing Break
- Table
- Drop Table
- Executive, Leading Break
- Executive, Trailing Break
- Shading
- Red/Blue Border
- Maroon/Teal Box

Figure 34.15 shows this step.

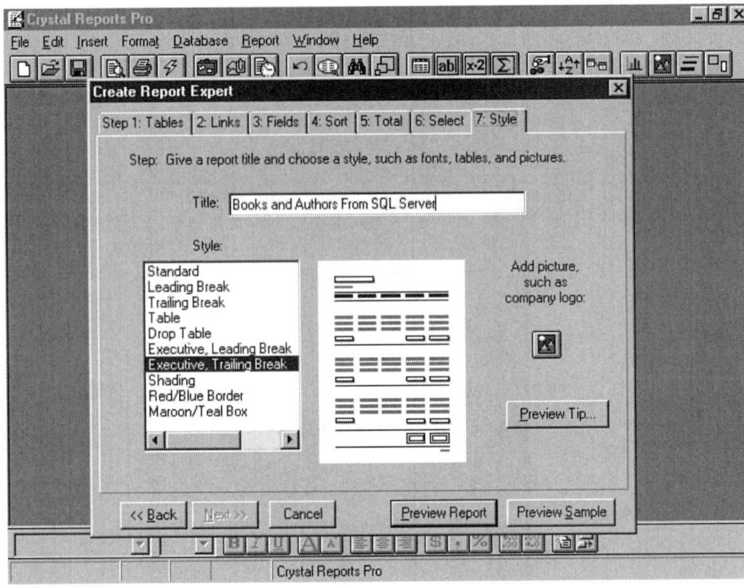

FIGURE 34.15.
The Style tab of the Standard Expert.

Now that you are finished with the steps, click the Preview Report button to create the report. Figure 34.16 shows the finished report. Even though you might want to change some features on the report, this is a good starting place. It definitely saves time in the process of creating the report. This concludes using an expert to create reports. To manually create a report, follow the steps outlined in the section "Creating Reports Manually," later in this chapter.

Notice that if you choose the Database | Show SQL Query menu option, you can view the SQL used to create the report. Listing 34.1 shows the SQL for the report we've defined.

Listing 34.1. SQL for Standard Expert selections.

```
SELECT
    authors."au_lname", authors."au_fname",
    titles."title"
FROM
    "pubs"."dbo"."authors" authors,
    "pubs"."dbo"."titleauthor" titleauthor,
    "pubs"."dbo"."titles" titles
WHERE
    authors."au_id" = titleauthor."au_id" AND
    titleauthor."title_id" = titles."title_id" AND
    authors."au_lname" = 'Green'
ORDER BY
    authors."au_lname" ASC
```

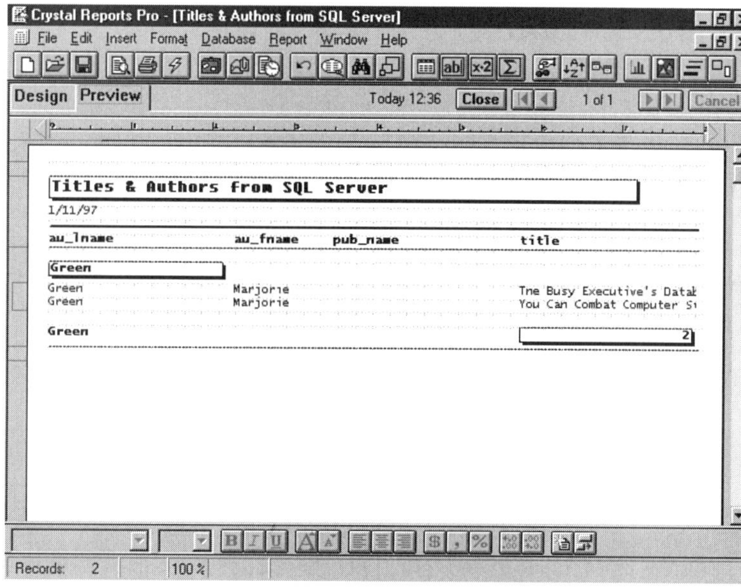

FIGURE 34.16.
The Standard Expert after all the steps are completed.

The Listing Expert

The Listing Expert presents you with a series of four successive steps that guide you through the process of creating the report. These steps are exactly the same as the first four steps in the Standard Expert; the only difference is the type of report produced. Figure 34.17 shows how the report looks when the steps are completed.

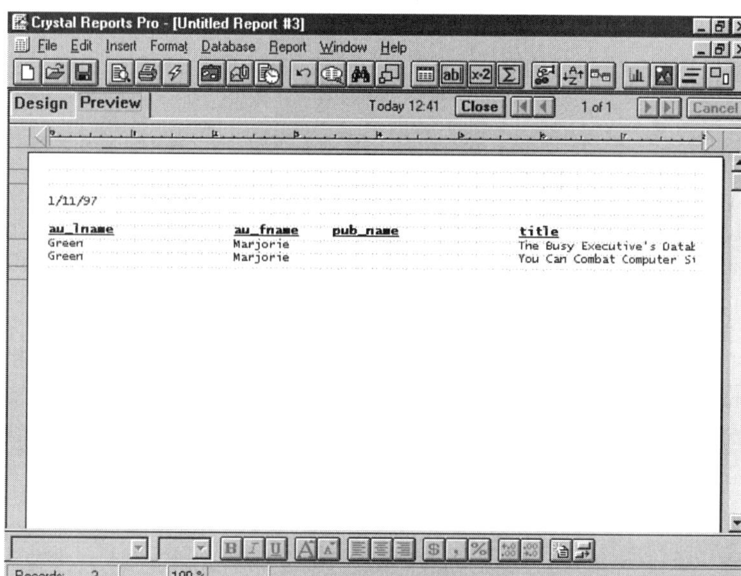

FIGURE 34.17.
The Listing Expert after all the steps are completed.

The Cross-Tab Expert

The Cross-Tab Expert presents you with a series of four successive steps that guides you through the process of creating the report. All except the third step, the CrossTab step, are the same as the steps in the Standard Expert. The CrossTab step is used to define the cross tab. A cross-tab report is a spreadsheet-style report that enables you to compare columns versus rows of data that you specify. This is a valuable report because you do not have to know how many data items are to appear on the x-axis before the report is run. Normally, in a Crystal Report, you define the number of fields to appear on the x-axis, and they cannot be moved or changed at runtime. Figure 34.18 shows what the CrossTab step looks like.

FIGURE 34.18.
The CrossTab tab of the Cross-Tab Expert.

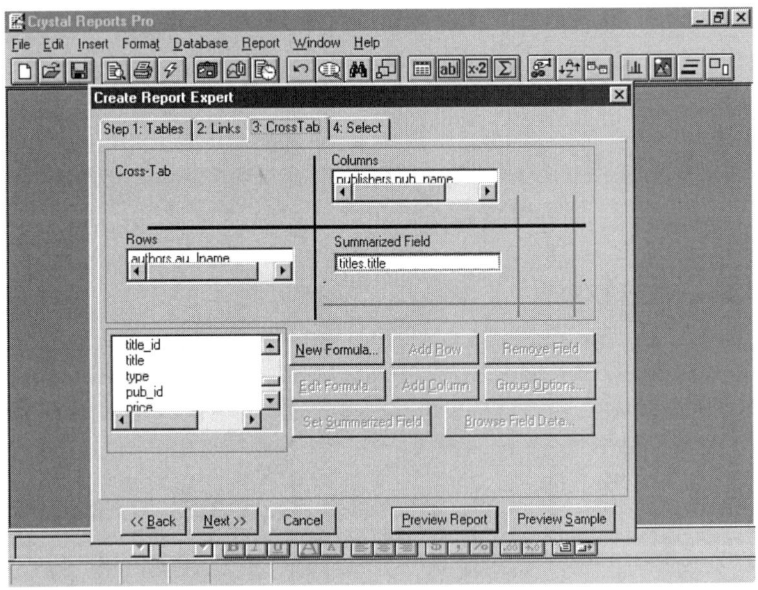

Notice that there are fields that have not been shown before. They are to define what appears on the x and y axes. Suppose you wanted to see the number of titles for each author for each publisher. You could put the publishers on the y-axis (going down) and the author on the x-axis (going across). You would do this by selecting the fields as shown in Figure 34.18. You can simply select the field from the list and drag and drop it in the appropriate axis. One final thing to do is to select the summary field that will appear in the center data section on the report. This could be the count of the number of titles for each author for each publisher. Therefore, drag and drop the title field to the summary field. In this case, do not select a limit in the last tab. Figure 34.19 shows how the report looks when the steps are completed.

FIGURE 34.19.
The Cross-Tab Expert after all the steps are completed.

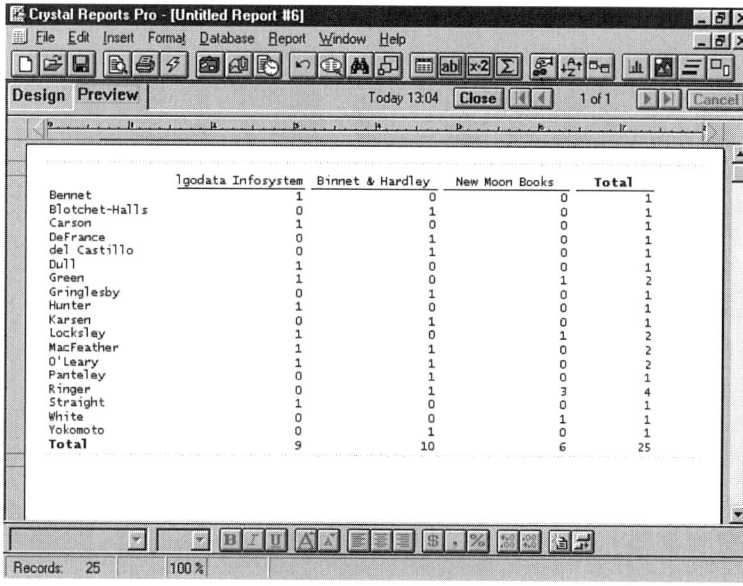

Notice that there are only so many items that can be displayed on the x-axis. Therefore, you might need to adjust the size of each column at design time. You might also want to display on the x-axis a field that you know will be limited in the number of values displayed. Otherwise, you can print a letter or legal-sized, landscape-oriented report. You can change this by selecting the File | Printer Setup menu option and changing settings where desired.

The Mail Label Expert

The Mail Label Expert presents you with a series of five successive steps that guide you through the process of creating mailing labels. All steps, except the fourth step, are the same as the steps in the Standard Expert. The fourth step, the Label tab, is used to define where the labels physically appear on the page. Figure 34.20 shows what the Label tab looks like.

You can choose from many different types of Avery standard labels, or you can define your own. Defining your own requires tedious measurement. Therefore, it is advisable to use the Avery labels. Here are the possibilities:

- User-Defined
- Return Address (Avery 5267)
- Address (Avery 5160, 5260, 5161, 5261, 5162, and 5262)
- Address/Shipping (Avery 5163 and 51964)
- Clear Address (Avery 5660, 5662, and 5663)
- Full Sheet (Avery 5165)

- File Folder (Avery 5266)
- 3.5 Diskette (Avery 5196, 5096, and 5896)
- 5.25 Diskette (Avery 5197, 5097, and 5897)
- Audio Cassette (Avery 5198)
- Video Cassette (Avery 5199)
- Video Cassette Spine
- Name Badge (Avery 5095, 5395, and 5895)
- Name Tag (Avery 5383, 5384, and 5883)
- Rotary Index Cards (Avery 5385 and 5386)
- Index Cards (Avery 5388)
- Index/Post Cards (Avery 5389)
- Round (Avery 5294)

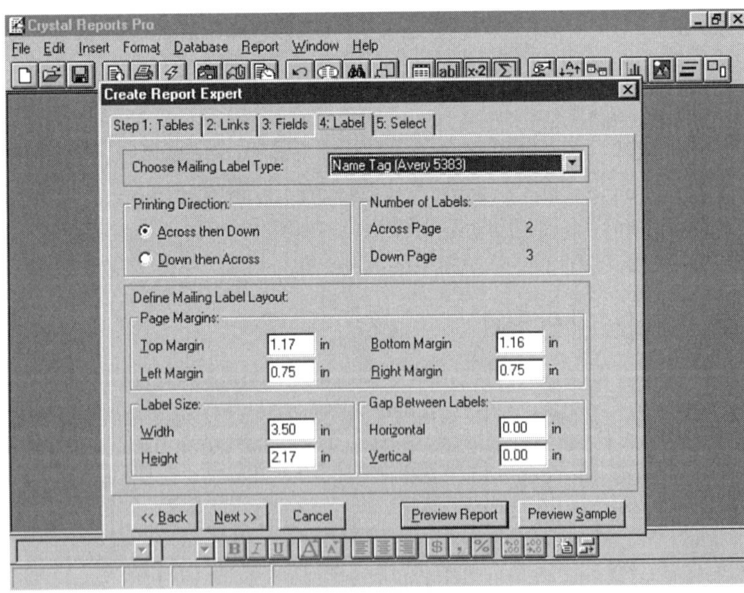

FIGURE 34.20.
The Label tab of the Mail Label Expert.

Figure 34.21 shows the finished mailing label after you select only authors' names and cities for a name tag.

The Summary Expert

The Summary Expert presents you with a series of eight successive steps that guide you through the process of creating a summary report. All steps, except for the sixth step, are the same as the steps in the Standard Expert. The sixth step, the Summary & DrillDown tab, is used to define how to summarize and drill down on detail, based on groupings you've selected in the previous steps. Therefore, you can choose whether or not to show these sections. Figure 34.22 shows what the Summary & DrillDown tab looks like.

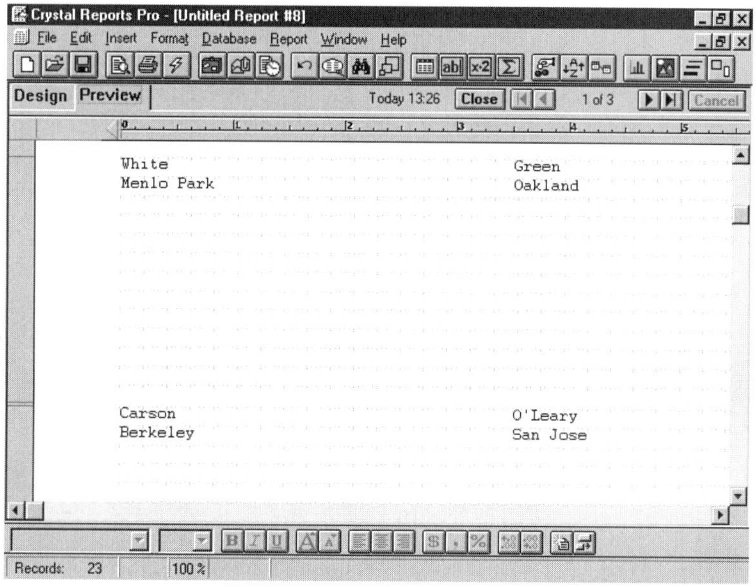

FIGURE 34.21.
The Mail Label Expert after all the steps are completed.

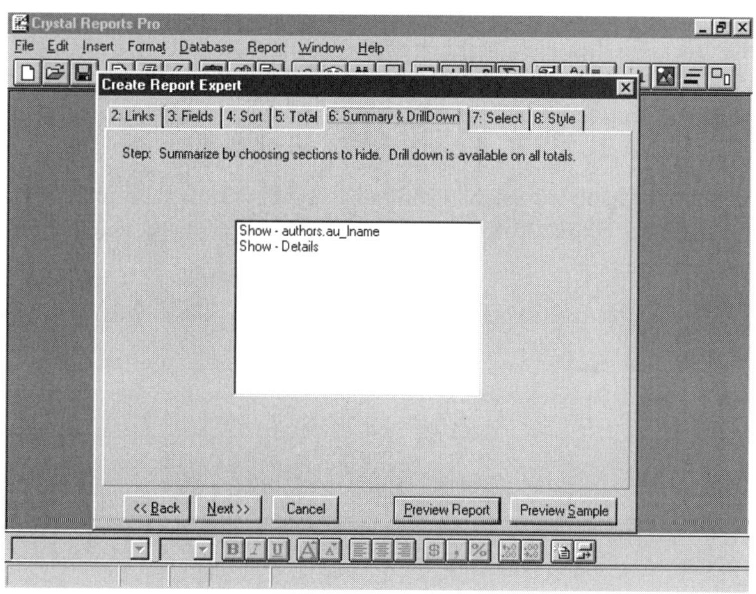

FIGURE 34.22.
The Summary & DrillDown tab of the Summary Expert.

Figure 34.23 shows what the finished report looks like.

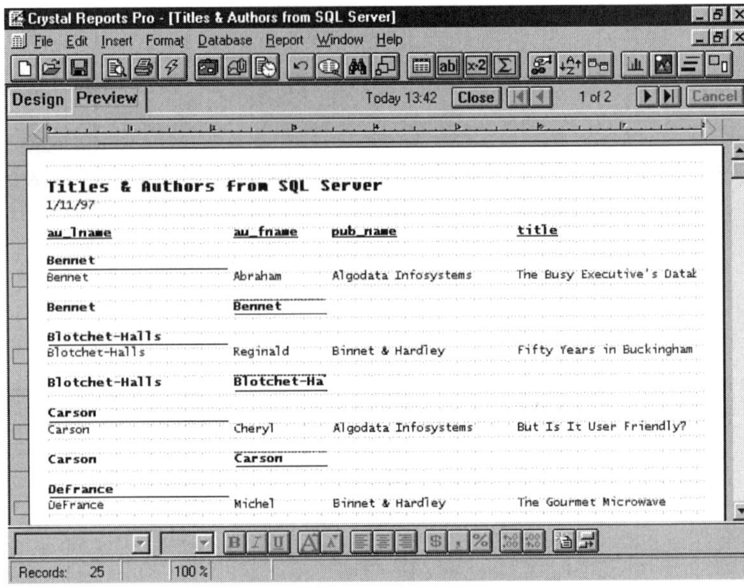

FIGURE 34.23.
The Summary Expert after all the steps are completed.

The Graph Expert

The Graph Expert presents you with a series of nine successive steps that guide you through the process of creating a graph report. All steps, except for Steps 6 and 7, are the same as the steps in the Standard Expert. Step 6, the TopN tab, is used to define how the report will select totals. You can select the top *n* number of records, where you specify the value for *n*. You can instead select the sort of all the totals. Figure 34.24 shows the TopN tab.

Step 7, the Graph tab, enables you to select the type of graph to place on the report and to set the attributes. These attributes are set in four separate tabs, which are shown in Figures 34.25 through 34.28.

The Type tab enables you to specify the type of the graph (see Figure 34.25).

The Data tab enables you to specify the data for the graph (see Figure 34.26).

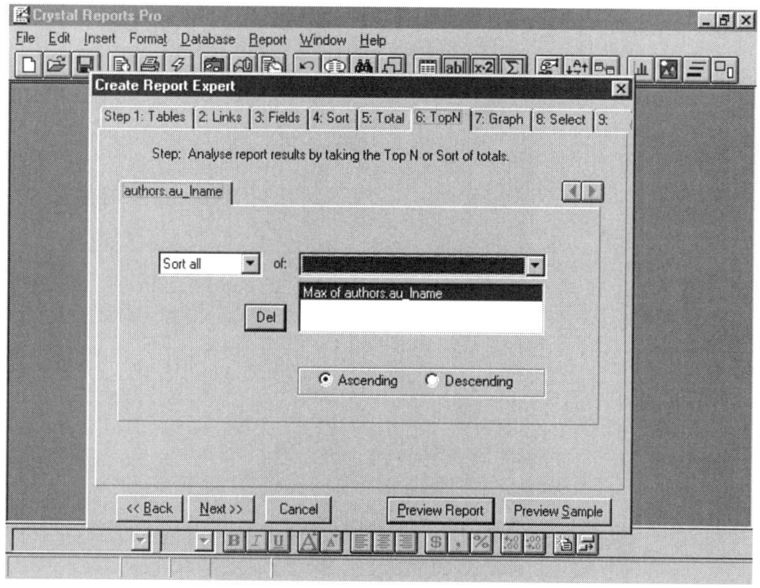

FIGURE 34.24.
The TopN tab of the Graph Expert.

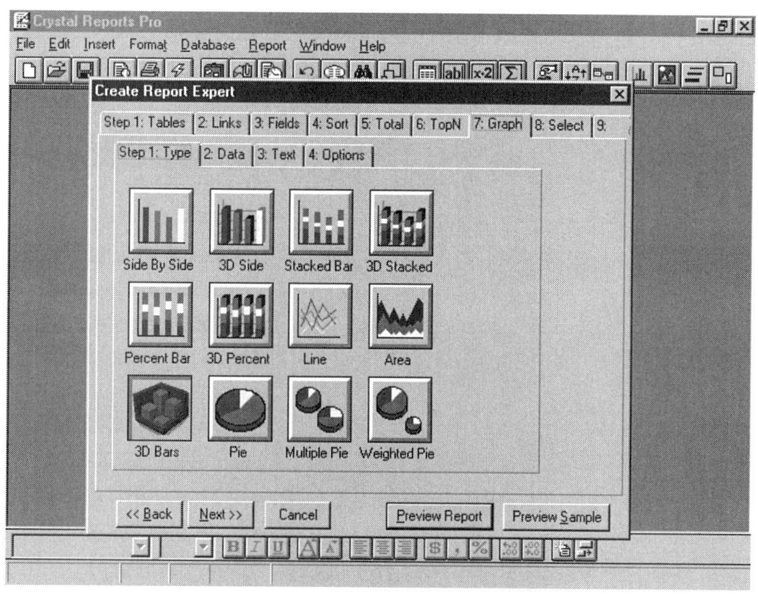

FIGURE 34.25.
The Type tab of the Graph Expert.

FIGURE 34.26.
The Data tab of the Graph Expert.

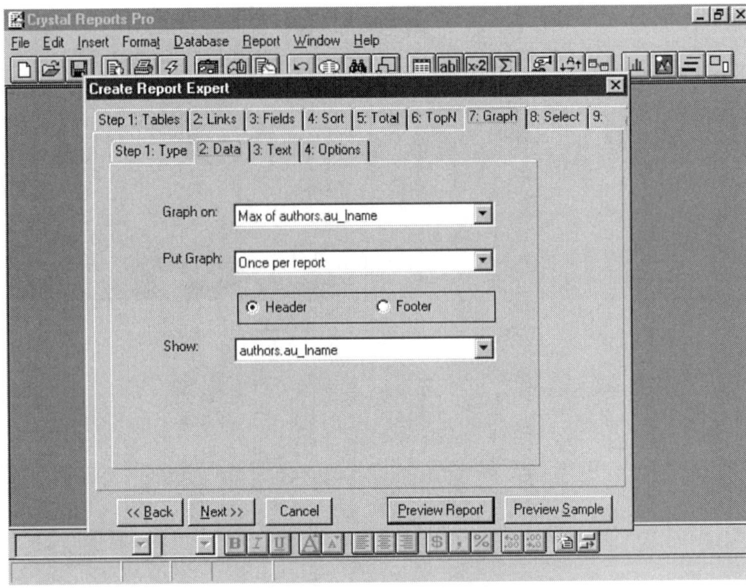

The Text tab enables you to specify the labels for the graph (see Figure 34.27).

FIGURE 34.27.
The Text tab of the Graph Expert.

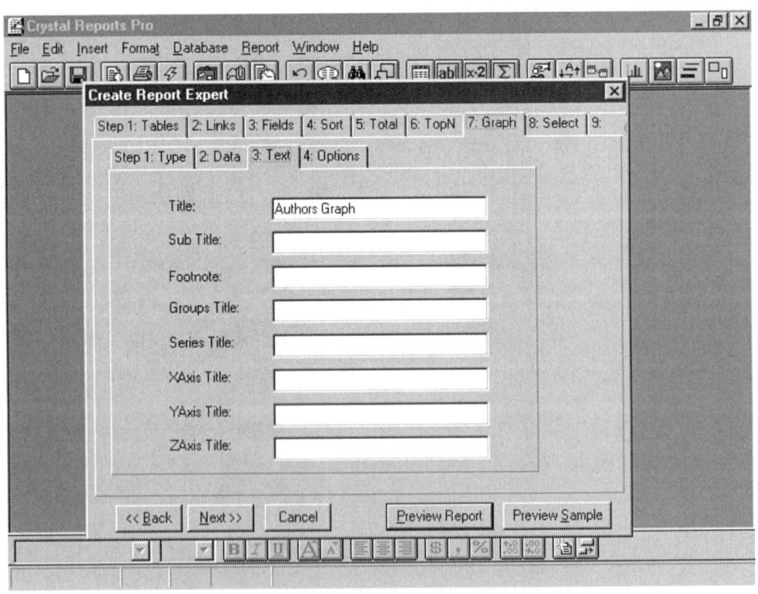

The Options tab enables you to specify miscellaneous attributes of the graph (see Figure 34.28).

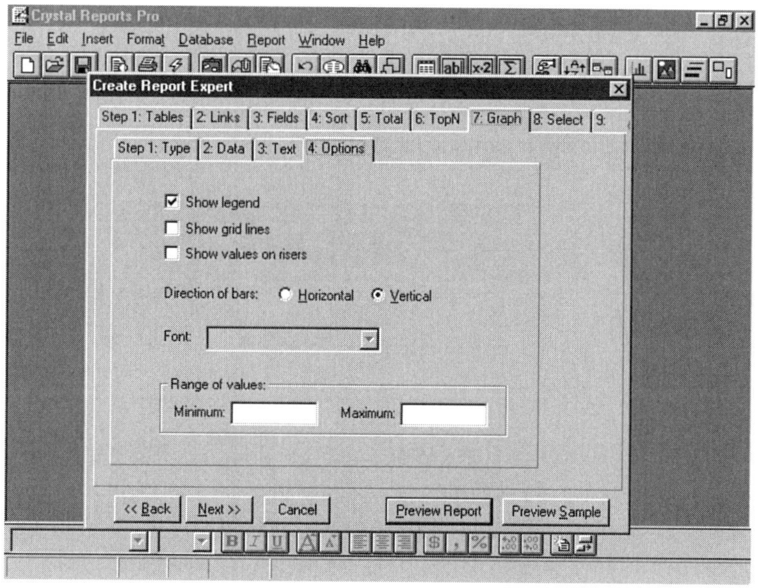

FIGURE 34.28.
The Options tab of the Graph Expert.

When you have finished, the expert will produce a report similar to the one in Figure 34.29.

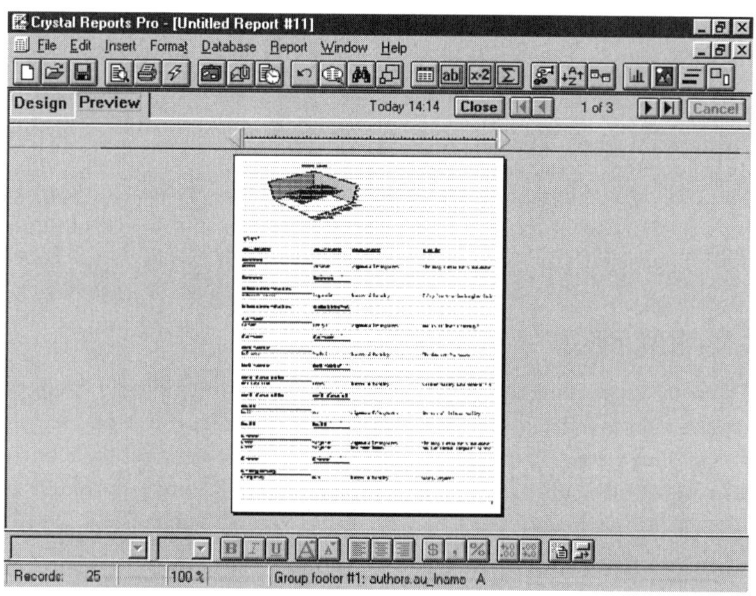

FIGURE 34.29.
The Graph Expert after all the steps are completed.

The Top N Expert

The Top N Expert presents you with a series of eight successive steps that guide you through the process of creating a hierarchical, detail-oriented report. All steps are the same as the steps described for the other experts. Figure 34.30 shows what the finished report looks like.

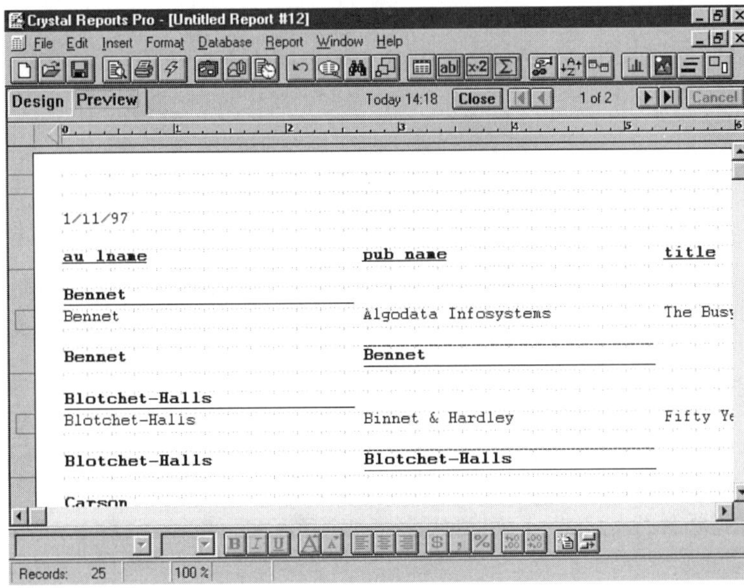

FIGURE 34.30.
The Top N Expert after all the steps are completed.

The Drill Down Expert

The Drill Down Expert presents you with a series of eight successive steps. It is essentially the same as the Top N Expert, except that you can choose which grouping sections to show or hide. The output can look exactly like the report shown in Figure 34.30.

Creating Reports Manually

To create a report manually, you can either create it completely from scratch or use one of the experts mentioned earlier in this chapter and then alter the report manually. When you are in design-time view, you can begin manipulating the objects on the report. The report is waiting for you to add fields from the database to it or to modify it in some way.

Adding Group Sections

The next step is to add the group sections of your report. It's a good idea to perform this step now because you cannot add a field to a section that doesn't yet exist. To add a group section, select the Insert | Group Section menu option. This action invokes the Select Field dialog box that prompts you to select a field on which the group section is to be based.

Add sections by planning carefully how you want your report to look. Use the scenario suggested in the "The Concept of a Report Writer Used with Visual Basic" section in this chapter for clarification. Figure 34.31 shows the Insert Group Section dialog box presented after selecting Insert | Group Section option.

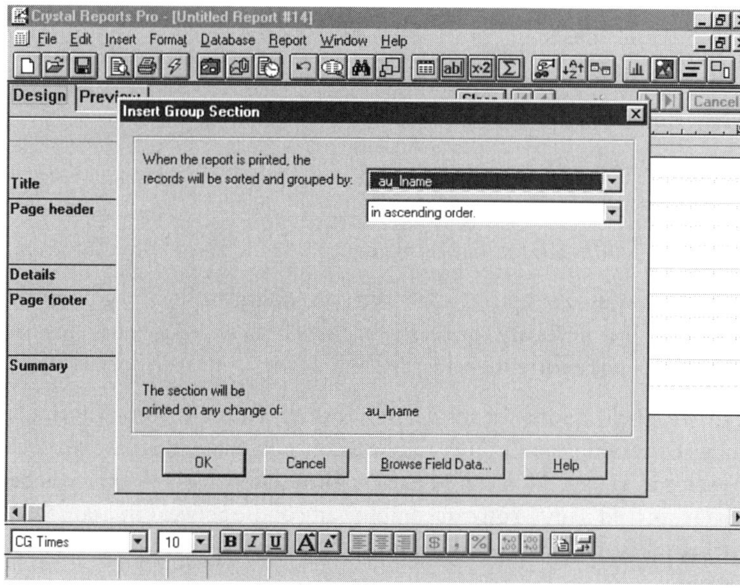

FIGURE 34.31.
The Crystal Reports Insert Group Section dialog box.

You use group sections to determine on which fields the report breaks, but they do not have to be shown when the report prints. This effectively lets you sort the report in any way you want. For example, using the previous scenario, if you want to display a tabular format report (all fields, each on every line), you can add Region and Product in the Details section, along with Sale Price. However, to ensure that the report is sorted based first on Region and then on Product, you must still have these two groupings in this order, but you must hide them. This ensures that the report is sorted correctly, but that only the desired fields are displayed.

To hide a section, click the right mouse button while the mouse cursor is in the left margin of the section. If the section currently is hidden, the option available is Show. If the section is shown, the option available is Hide. Simply click the option to perform the desired function.

NOTE

Every section except the Details section actually hides (by collapsing in size) in the Crystal Reports IDE. This is a design-time visual representation that shows that the section will not be printed. Any fields placed in the Details section are grayed and do not actually collapse.

Adding Fields to a New Report

You can add seven different types of fields to a report:

- Database fields
- Text fields
- Formula fields
- Special fields
- Subtotal/grand total fields
- Graphic fields
- Object fields

A *database* field is a field that prints data that is retrieved directly from a database.

A *text* field is used simply as a label. It can identify a field, region of the report, title, or anything else. It is necessary for these purposes because you would not use a database field and, most likely, not a formula field.

A *formula* field inserts the results of a formula into a report. A formula can be virtually anything. For example, a formula can be a constant value, such as `"WELCOME"`, which is effectively the same as a text field; it can be a static formula, such as `5 * 10`; it can be a date or time or even a database field name. You can combine any of the above. For example, you can multiply a sale price database field by a sales tax rate to determine sales tax. The possibilities for a formula field are endless.

A *special* field cannot be defined by the user. These fields are predefined in Crystal Reports. Here's a list of them:

- Print Date field
- Page Number field
- Record Number field
- Group Number field

The meanings of these fields are self-explanatory.

A *subtotal* field or a *grand total* field very often is used to insert a subtotal or a grand total at a logical break in your report. For example, suppose that you want to print a report of data, grouped by company. After the company is printed, you want to have a subtotal on each company. You do that by selecting the Insert | Subtotal Crystal Reports menu option. Then you might want to insert a grand total at the end of the report. You do this by selecting the Insert | Grand Total Crystal Reports menu option. The nice thing about these fields is that Crystal Reports keeps track of running totals internally. You do not need to create a formula or keep track of them yourself.

Database Fields

To add a new database field to the report, you need to make sure that the Insert Database Field dialog box is open. If it is not, you can invoke it by clicking the icon on the toolbar or by selecting the Insert | Database Field menu option. After the dialog box appears, you can simply double-click on the field you want. You'll see that the icon has changed, indicating that you have selected a certain field. You can then drag and drop the field to wherever you want it to appear on the report.

You must keep in mind how the report is going to work. If you put the field in the Header section, the field prints at the top of the page every time a new page prints. Similarly, if you place the field in the Footer section, it prints at the bottom of the page every time a new page prints.

Therefore, using the scenario described earlier in the "The Concept of a Report Writer Used with Visual Basic" section, if the field you're trying to place on the report is the Region, you want it to be in the first section called Region. If the first section doesn't exist, you must add it. Refer to the section "Adding Group Sections," earlier in the chapter. If you put the field in the Details section, the field prints every time a new line of detail is encountered. You don't necessarily need to see the region for every line of sales. It's generally sufficient to see a heading, such as Region, at the top of the section.

If you are trying to place a field such as Sale Price on your report, you must place it in the Details section because it's what you're trying to see at a detail level.

Text Fields

To insert a text field, select the Insert Text icon on the toolbar or the Insert | Text Field menu option (refer to Figure 34.4 for icon names). You are prompted for the text of the field to place on the report.

Formula Fields

To insert a formula field, select the icon on the toolbar or the Insert | Formula Field menu option. You are prompted for the name of the formula. Every formula must have a name. Choose something that is germane to its usage. After you choose a name and click OK, the Edit Formula dialog box appears. Figure 34.32 shows what this dialog box looks like.

This dialog box is really a "formula expert" because it enables you to point and click fields, functions, and operators to build your formula. You can, however, enter the formula text yourself. For example, if you want to use this formula field as a text field displaying the text `WELCOME`, simply type `"WELCOME"` in quotes (because it is a string literal).

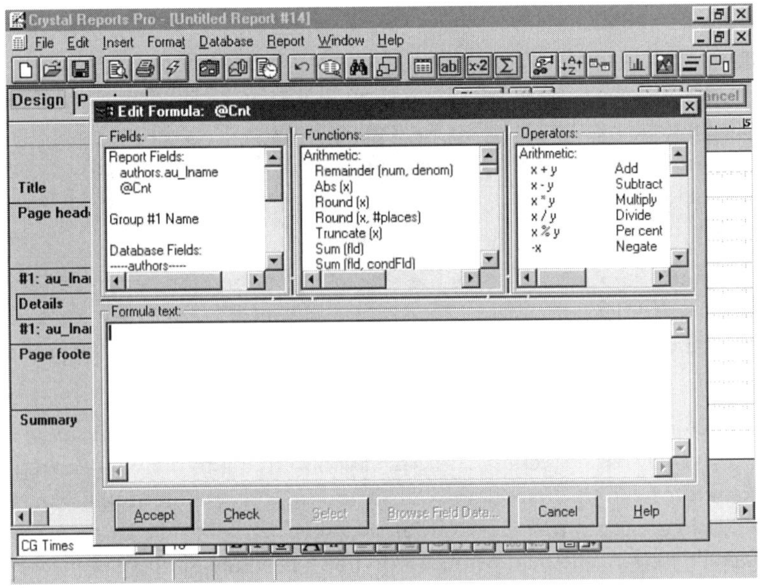

FIGURE 34.32.
The Crystal Reports Edit Formula dialog box.

This chapter cannot cover all of the possible functions and operators, but the basic rule of thumb is to double-click on the field, function, and operator you want to use. If a function requires three arguments, for example, it leaves commas showing that it expects three arguments in the formula text area. You can then place the cursor where the argument is expected and double-click again on any field, function, or operator to fill the argument required.

Use the Check command button to check the syntax of your formula. You receive an error if there are any problems. For example, if you're trying to compare or assign a string field to an integer, you receive an error. As with any programming language, if you want to compare or assign different data types, they must be converted first. There are some converting functions in the Functions section of the Edit Formula dialog box.

Clicking the Accept command button is just like clicking an OK button. This action closes the dialog box but first performs the same function as clicking the Check command button.

Graphic Fields

To insert a graphic field, select one of the appropriate icons on the toolbar or specify one of the following options:

- Insert | Line menu option
- Insert | Box menu option
- Insert | Picture menu option
- Insert | Graph/Chart Expert menu option

The first three options are self-explanatory. The fourth option presents you with four tabs from which the graph will be generated. These tabs are shown in Figures 34.25 through 34.28.

Object Fields

To insert an Object field, select the icon on the toolbar or the Insert | Object menu option. You are prompted for the type of OLE object you would like to insert. This list is generated from the Registry on your system.

Modifying or Deleting Fields on a Report

To modify many fields and areas on the report, you can click the field or area with the right mouse button. This action invokes a pop-up menu that shows options you can select. Notice that for a database field, you cannot change the column name to which the field points. To change this, you must actually delete the field and insert a new one, using the desired database field.

To delete a field or area on the report, you can use the right mouse button to click on the field or area and select the Delete option. You also can choose the Edit | Clear menu option or press the Delete key.

Limiting Records

Your report does not have to display all data items in a database. Using the scenario presented earlier, suppose that you want to see only the records for author Green. You can limit the display by selecting the Report | Select Records Expert menu option. To limit the records to authors with the last name of Green, you simply choose the field, au_lname, and click OK. This brings up a dialog box that enables you to easily select the records. Figure 34.33 shows the Select Records Expert dialog box.

Establishing Links

Very often, having the data you need in one table is not sufficient. You need to look up data in one table based on a field in another table. This is called a *join* or *link*. You can set up a link with a table in the database that is already being used (because it was selected when creating the report) or another database. If you want to link to a field in another database, you must add the database to the report first. To do this, select the Database | Add Database To Report menu option, and select the database file you want to add. If the table is in the same database, you don't need to add the same database file again.

If you want to view which links are present, select the Database | Visual Linking Expert. Using this expert is discussed under the section titled "The Standard Expert."

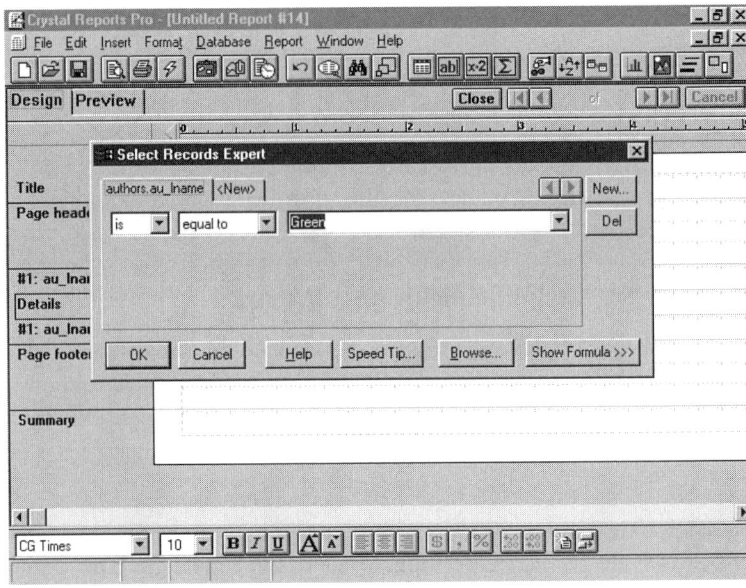

FIGURE 34.33.
Crystal Reports Select Records Expert dialog box.

File Locations and Aliases

When you add a database file to the report, you select the location of the file, which is stored internally with the report. But what happens if you move the location of the database? There is a menu option called Database | Set Location that enables you to reassign where the database is located. A dialog box appears so you can select the appropriate location.

An alias is necessary if you have two tables to add to a report that use the same name. For example, if you need to link two tables called CUSTOMER, you can alias one table as NEWCUSTOMER. An alias is almost never needed because most databases are designed so that this is not necessary. There are times, however, when situations arise that you didn't anticipate and you find yourself needing an alias for a table. If you alias a table, the name of the table inside Crystal Reports will be that alias, not the original table name.

To assign an alias, select the Database | Set Alias menu option. The Set Alias dialog box appears for you to enter the name of the alias.

Miscellaneous Topics

The following miscellaneous topics are not significant enough to be listed under their own headings but are featured in Crystal Reports.

You can format fields just as you do in most other programs, such as font, size, color, and so on. You can click the field with the right mouse button and select the Change Font, Change Format, or Change Border and Colors menu options. For a text field, you have an additional option to change the text of the field. For a formula field, you have an additional option to change the formula in the field. You can also select any of these options under the Format menu option.

It's important that you test the report before you write your Visual Basic code. You can test the report by printing it to the screen, printer, or file. To use any of these options, you can click the appropriate icon on the toolbar. Another good way to test the report is to select the File | Print Preview menu option. This prints the report to a window exactly as it will look on paper. This is similar to the way any other Microsoft print preview window looks and functions.

The Visual Basic Interface

All topics previously discussed cover creating the report in the Crystal Reports IDE environment. What about how to use the report that was created externally, inside Visual Basic?

The answer to this is that you must add to your Visual Basic project the Crystal custom control that comes with Crystal Reports. You do this by selecting the Tools | Custom Controls Visual Basic menu option. You then add the control to your form. You access properties of the custom control to change the parameters of the report. For example, this is where you enter the name of the report file you've just created. You also can specify many different parameters not available in the Crystal Reports IDE.

For the properties that are indexed, you can pass multiple values (arrays) to the Crystal Reports Print Engine (CRPE) through the control. For example, if you want to pass five formulas to the CRPE, you don't have five `Formulas` properties. You specify the five formulas with five different indexes for the `Formulas` property, starting with zero.

To see how to use the Crystal custom control, consider the application in Chapter 42, "A Client/Server Application." It uses the Crystal custom control to run reports designed in the Crystal Reports IDE.

Summary

Crystal Reports is a wonderful tool used to design and incorporate graphical reports in your Visual Basic applications. Many of the new experts speed the creation of reports. Using the reports within Visual Basic is quite simple—you use the ActiveX control. Simply setting properties and calling methods activates the reports created in the Crystal Reports IDE. This chapter outlined how to create the reports and use the ActiveX control.

VII

Rapid Application Development

35

Developing a CD Player Application

The CD player application enables you to play audio compact discs. It determines the number of tracks, the current track, the track time, and the total time. This is made possible by the `MCI32.OCX` control that comes with Visual Basic. Using this control with an audio CD requires some special consideration because of the format in which some of the properties are stored. This chapter shows you how to do this in detail. The key behind how the MCI control reports time is based on the `TimeFormat` property. For this application, the `TimeFormat` property is set to `10`, or you can use the `mciFormatTmsf` constant, which specifies that the least significant byte is tracks, the second is minutes, and the third is seconds. The fourth, frames, is not used in this application. The fourth byte is also called the most significant byte. The data is returned in a set of four bytes. The least significant byte indicates the byte with the lowest value, and the most significant byte indicates the byte with the highest value.

Figure 35.1 shows the main screen (`MAIN.FRM`) at runtime.

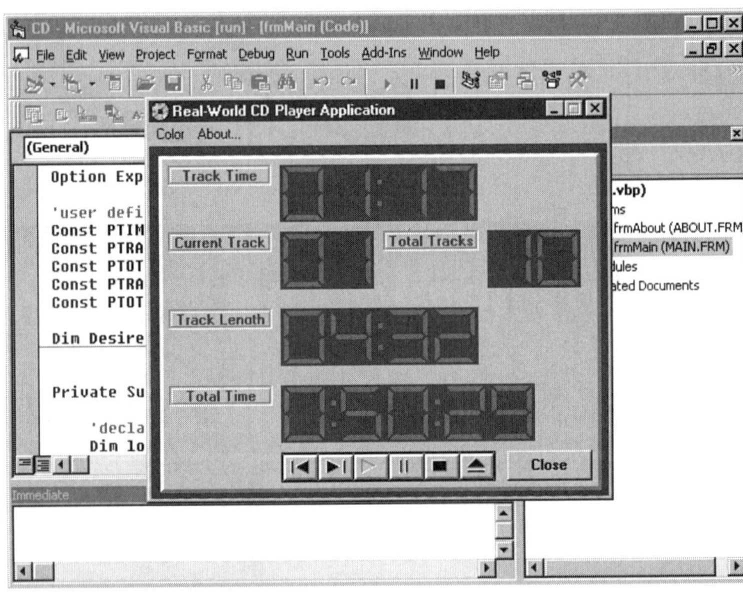

FIGURE 35.1.
The CD player at runtime.

To use the application, click the VCR-like command buttons. All displays will be updated automatically. If the time displays are blank and the multimedia control is disabled, the control has not registered the disc, or a disc is not in the drive. Try the following:

1. Eject the disc.
2. Close the `CD.EXE` program.
3. Insert the disc, making sure it is an *audio* disc.
4. Run the `CD.EXE` program.

CROSS REFERENCE

The CD player application demonstrates techniques used in Chapter 8, "Graphics," Chapter 10, "Writing Resource Files," and Chapter 11, "Multimedia."

Code Listings

The CD Player application contains the following files and listings:

- CD.VBP
- MAIN.FRM
- ABOUT.FRM
- CD.BAS
- BITMAP.RES
- CD.ICO
- CD1.ICO
- CD2.ICO
- CD.EXE

The CD.VBP File

CD.VBP is the project file for the CD player application, CD.EXE. It contains a listing of all the files necessary to load the project into Visual Basic. The CD.VBP file is contained on the CD-ROM accompanying this book in the \CD subdirectory. The file listing is shown in Listing 35.1.

Listing 35.1. CD.VBP.

```
Type=Exe
Form=MAIN.FRM
Object={C1A8AF28-1257-101B-8FB0-0020AF039CA3}#1.1#0; MCI32.OCX
Object={0BA686C6-F7D3-101A-993E-0000C0EF6F5E}#1.0#0; THREED32.ocx
Module=Module1; CD.BAS
Form=ABOUT.FRM
ResFile32="bitmap.res"
IconForm="frmMain"
Startup="frmMain"
HelpFile=""
Title="CD Player"
ExeName32="CD.exe"
Command32=""
Name="CD"
```

continues

Listing 35.1. continued

```
HelpContextID="0"
CompatibleMode="0"
MajorVer=1
MinorVer=0
RevisionVer=0
AutoIncrementVer=0
ServerSupportFiles=0
VersionCompanyName="SoftHouse"
VersionFileDescription="CD Player Application"
CompilationType=0
OptimizationType=0
FavorPentiumPro(tm)=0
CodeViewDebugInfo=0
NoAliasing=0
BoundsCheck=0
OverflowCheck=0
FlPointCheck=0
FDIVCheck=0
UnroundedFP=0
StartMode=0
Unattended=0
ThreadPerObject=0
MaxNumberOfThreads=1
```

NOTE

Please note that the way this file looks might be different on your system. This file was generated on the machine that was used to create the applications in this book. Therefore, it shows the file paths that are on that machine. Your paths can differ slightly. The important concept is that it shows the filenames of the required files for this project.

The `MAIN.FRM` File

`MAIN.FRM` is one of two forms in this application. Figure 35.1 presented the form as it appears at runtime. Figure 35.2 presents the form at design time.

Table 35.1 lists all the relevant properties of each control on the form that have been changed from their standard default values. The `MAIN.FRM` file is contained on the CD-ROM accompanying this book in the `\CD` subdirectory.

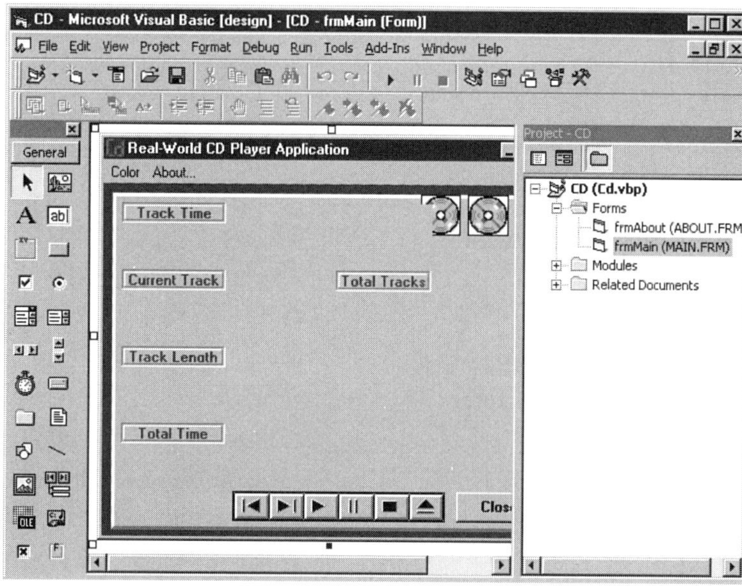

FIGURE 35.2.
The CD player at design time.

Table 35.1. Properties of each control on `MAIN.FRM`.

Object	*Control Type*	*Property*	*Value*
`frmMain`	Form	`BackColor`	&H00404000&
		`Caption`	CD Player Application
		`Height`	4815
		`Icon`	CD.ICO
		`Left`	990
		`MaxButton`	False
		`Top`	1125
		`Width`	5985
`pictIcon`	PictureBox	`AutoSize`	True
		`Height`	510
		`Index`	0, 1*
		`Left`	3960, 4560*
		`Picture`	CD1.BMP, CD2.BMP*

continues

Table 35.1. continued

Object	*Control Type*	*Property*	*Value*
		`Top`	0
		`Visible`	False
		`Width`	510
`tmrIcon`	Timer	`Enabled`	False
		`Interval`	1000
		`Left`	5280
		`Top`	0
`pictTime`	PictureBox	`AutoSize`	True
		`BackColor`	&H00C0C0C0&
		`BorderStyle`	None
		`Height`	750
		`Index`	0, 1, 2, 3*
		`Left`	1560, 2160, 2880, 3480*
		`Top`	120
		`Width`	630
`pictColon`	PictureBox	`AutoSize`	True
		`BackColor`	&H00C0C0C0&
		`BorderStyle`	None
		`Height`	750
		`Index`	0, 1, 2, 3*
		`Left`	2760, 2760, 4080, 2760*
		`Top`	1920, 2880, 2880, 120*
		`Width`	150
`pictLength`	Picture Box	`AutoSize`	True
		`BackColor`	&H00C0C0C0&
		`BorderStyle`	None
		`Height`	750
		`Index`	0, 1, 2, 3*
		`Left`	3480, 2880, 2160, 1560*
		`Top`	1920
		`Width`	630

Object	Control Type	Property	Value
pictTotal	PictureBox	AutoSize	True
		BackColor	&H00C0C0C0&
		BorderStyle	None
		Height	750
		Index	0, 1, 2, 3, 4, 5*
		Left	4800, 4200, 3480, 2880, 2160, 1560*
		Top	2880
		Width	630
pictTotalTrack	PictureBox	AutoSize	True
		BackColor	&H00C0C0C0&
		BorderStyle	None
		Height	750
		Index	0, 1*
		Left	4800, 4200*
		Top	960
		Width	630
pictTrack	PictureBox	AutoSize	True
		BackColor	&H00C0C0C0&
		BorderStyle	None
		Height	750
		Index	0, 1*
		Left	2160, 1560*
		Top	960
		Width	630
mmControl	MMControl	BackVisible	False
		DeviceType	CDAUDIO
		EjectEnabled	True
		Height	370
		Left	1200
		NextEnabled	True
		PauseEnabled	True

continues

Table 35.1. continued

Object	*Control Type*	*Property*	*Value*
		`PlayEnabled`	True
		`PrevEnabled`	True
		`RecordVisible`	False
		`StepVisible`	False
		`StopEnabled`	True
		`Top`	3720
		`Width`	2730
`cmdClose`	CommandButton	`Caption`	Close
		`Height`	375
		`Left`	4440
		`Top`	3720
		`Width`	1095
`Panel3D1`	SSPanel	`BevelWidth`	3
		`Height`	4215
		`Left`	120
		`Top`	120
		`Width`	5655
`Panel3D2`	SSPanel	`BevelInner`	2
		`BevelOuter`	1
		`BorderWidth`	1
		`Caption`	Track Time
		`ForeColor`	&H00FF0000&
		`Height`	255
		`Left`	120
		`Top`	120
		`Width`	1335
`Panel3D3`	SSPanel	`BevelInner`	2
		`BevelOuter`	1
		`BorderWidth`	1
		`Caption`	Current Track
		`ForeColor`	&H00FF0000&
		`Height`	255

Object	*Control Type*	*Property*	*Value*
		`Left`	120
		`Top`	960
		`Width`	1335
`Panel3D4`	SSPanel	`BevelInner`	2
		`BevelOuter`	1
		`BorderWidth`	1
		`Caption`	Total Tracks
		`ForeColor`	&H00FF0000&
		`Height`	255
		`Left`	2880
		`Top`	960
		`Width`	630
`Panel3D5`	SSPanel	`BevelInner`	2
		`BevelOuter`	1
		`BorderWidth`	1
		`Caption`	Track Length
		`ForeColor`	&H00FF0000&
		`Height`	255
		`Left`	120
		`Top`	1920
		`Width`	1335
`Panel3D6`	SSPanel	`BevelInner`	2
		`BevelOuter`	1
		`BorderWidth`	1
		`Caption`	Total Time
		`ForeColor`	&H00FF0000&
		`Height`	255
		`Left`	120
		`Top`	2880
		`Width`	1335
`menu_about`	Menu	`Caption`	"About..."

*This control is a control array, and these are the only properties that vary within the control. To save space, they were not listed separately.

Function, Subroutine, and Event Procedures

There are several event procedures of code for each object (control) that comprises this form. Each is listed in the following sections.

The `(general)` Object

The `(general)` object contains declarations and event procedures at the form level. Here are the event procedures for the `(general)` object:

- `(declarations)`
- `ClearAll()`
- `FindCorrectBitmap()`
- `PopulateDisplay()`

The `(declarations)` Procedure

The `(declarations)` procedure contains variable declarations used in the form `MAIN.FRM`. Listing 35.2 contains a listing of the `(declarations)` event procedure.

Listing 35.2. `MAIN.FRM, (general) (declarations)`.

```
Option Explicit

'user defined constants
Const PTIME = 1          'indicates which function to perform in populate display
Const PTRACK = 2         'indicates which function to perform in populate display
Const PTOTALTRACK = 3    'indicates which function to perform in populate display
Const PTRACKLENGTH = 4   'indicates which function to perform in populate display
Const PTOTALLENGTH = 5   'indicates which function to perform in populate display

Dim DesiredColor&         'holds current color of display
```

The `ClearAll()` Event Procedure

The `ClearAll()` event procedure clears all displays when the disc is ejected. This ensures that erroneous numbers won't be displayed. You clear the displays by assigning the picture `pictBlank.picture` to each of the displays. Listing 35.3 contains a listing of the `ClearAll()` event procedure.

Listing 35.3. `MAIN.FRM, ClearAll()`.

```
Private Sub ClearAll()

    'declare variables
    Dim loopcount%  'loop counting variable

    'clear current track time
```

```
    For loopcount% = 0 To 3
        pictTime(loopcount%).picture = LoadResPicture(FindCorrectBitmap
        ➥(BLANK), 0)
    Next loopcount%

    'clear current track
    For loopcount% = 0 To 1
        pictTrack(loopcount%).picture = LoadResPicture(FindCorrectBitmap
        ➥(BLANK), 0)
    Next loopcount%

    'clear total tracks
    For loopcount% = 0 To 1
        pictTotalTrack(loopcount%).picture = LoadResPicture(FindCorrectBitmap
        ➥(BLANK), 0)
    Next loopcount%

    'clear track length
    For loopcount% = 0 To 3
        pictLength(loopcount%).picture = LoadResPicture(FindCorrectBitmap
        ➥(BLANK), 0)
    Next loopcount%

    'clear total
    For loopcount% = 0 To 4
        pictTotal(loopcount%).picture = LoadResPicture(FindCorrectBitmap
        ➥(BLANK), 0)
    Next loopcount%

End Sub()
```

The `FindCorrectBitmap()` Event Procedure

The `FindCorrectBitmap()`event procedure determines which resource ID to use in the resource file, depending on the number to be displayed and the color in which it should be displayed. The `ConvertToMMSS()` event procedure accepts one argument, `Digit%`, which is the digit that must be displayed. The color is a global variable, `DesiredColor&`. Listing 35.4 contains a listing of the `FindCorrectBitmap()` event procedure.

Listing 35.4. MAIN.FRM, FindCorrectBitmap().

```
Private Function FindCorrectBitmap(Digit%) As Integer

    'calculate the correct bitmap to display. These integer references
    'are determined by the RESOURCE.H header file.
    If DesiredColor& = vbGreen Then
        FindCorrectBitmap = 100 + Digit%
    ElseIf DesiredColor& = vbRed Then
        FindCorrectBitmap = 200 + Digit%
    ElseIf DesiredColor& = vbYellow Then
        FindCorrectBitmap = 300 + Digit%
    End If

End Function
```

The `PopulateDisplay()` Event Procedure

The `PopulateDisplay()` event procedure is used to populate the different areas of the display, such as track time and current track to visually represent CD activity. Population is performed by assigning appropriate picture bitmaps from a resource file that is included in the `CD.VBP` project. The `PopulateDisplay()` event procedure accepts two arguments that determine what to display: `WhichArray` and the actual text to display, `texttodisplay$`. Listing 35.5 contains a listing of the `PopulateDisplay()` event procedure.

Listing 35.5. `MAIN.FRM`, `PopulateDisplay()`.

```
Private Sub PopulateDisplay(WhichArray As Integer, texttodisplay$)

    'declare variables
    Dim FirstDigit%     'first integer converted from packed integer(LSB)
    Dim SecondDigit%    'second integer converted from packed integer
    Dim ThirdDigit%     'third integer converted from packed integer
    Dim FourthDigit%    'fourth integer converted from packed integer
    Dim FifthDigit%     'fifth integer converted from packed integer

    If WhichArray = PTIME Then
        'CURRENT RUNNING TIME
        FirstDigit% = Val(Mid$(texttodisplay$, 4, 1))
        pictTime(0).picture = LoadResPicture(FindCorrectBitmap
        ➥(FirstDigit%), 0)

        SecondDigit% = Val(Mid$(texttodisplay$, 3, 1))
        pictTime(1).picture = LoadResPicture(FindCorrectBitmap
        ➥(SecondDigit%), 0)

        ThirdDigit% = Val(Mid$(texttodisplay$, 2, 1))
        pictTime(2).picture = LoadResPicture(FindCorrectBitmap
        ➥(ThirdDigit%), 0)

        FourthDigit% = Val(Mid$(texttodisplay$, 1, 1))
        pictTime(3).picture = LoadResPicture(FindCorrectBitmap
        ➥(FourthDigit%), 0)
    ElseIf WhichArray = PTRACK Then
        'CURRENT TRACK
        FirstDigit% = Val(Mid$(texttodisplay$, 2, 1))
        pictTrack(0).picture = LoadResPicture(FindCorrectBitmap
        ➥(FirstDigit%), 0)

        SecondDigit% = Val(Mid$(texttodisplay$, 1, 1))
        pictTrack(1).picture = LoadResPicture(FindCorrectBitmap
        ➥(SecondDigit%), 0)
    ElseIf WhichArray = PTOTALTRACK Then
        'TOTAL TRACKS
        FirstDigit% = Val(Mid$(texttodisplay$, 2, 1))
        pictTotalTrack(0).picture = LoadResPicture(FindCorrectBitmap
        ➥(FirstDigit%), 0)

        SecondDigit% = Val(Mid$(texttodisplay$, 1, 1))
        pictTotalTrack(1).picture = LoadResPicture(FindCorrectBitmap
        ➥(SecondDigit%), 0)
```

```
    ElseIf WhichArray = PTRACKLENGTH Then
        'TRACK LENGTH
        FirstDigit% = Val(Mid$(texttodisplay$, 4, 1))
        pictLength(0).picture = LoadResPicture(FindCorrectBitmap
        ➥(FirstDigit%), 0)

        SecondDigit% = Val(Mid$(texttodisplay$, 3, 1))
        pictLength(1).picture = LoadResPicture(FindCorrectBitmap
        ➥(SecondDigit%), 0)

        ThirdDigit% = Val(Mid$(texttodisplay$, 2, 1))
        pictLength(2).picture = LoadResPicture(FindCorrectBitmap
        ➥(ThirdDigit%), 0)

        FourthDigit% = Val(Mid$(texttodisplay$, 1, 1))
        pictLength(3).picture = LoadResPicture(FindCorrectBitmap
        ➥(FourthDigit%), 0)
    ElseIf WhichArray = PTOTALLENGTH Then
        'TOTAL LENGTH OF ALL TRACKS
        FirstDigit% = Val(Mid$(texttodisplay$, 5, 1))
        pictTotal(0).picture = LoadResPicture(FindCorrectBitmap
        ➥(FirstDigit%), 0)

        SecondDigit% = Val(Mid$(texttodisplay$, 4, 1))
        pictTotal(1).picture = LoadResPicture(FindCorrectBitmap
        ➥(SecondDigit%), 0)

        ThirdDigit% = Val(Mid$(texttodisplay$, 3, 1))
        pictTotal(2).picture = LoadResPicture(FindCorrectBitmap
        ➥(ThirdDigit%), 0)

        FourthDigit% = Val(Mid$(texttodisplay$, 2, 1))
        pictTotal(3).picture = LoadResPicture(FindCorrectBitmap
        ➥(FourthDigit%), 0)

        FifthDigit% = Val(Mid$(texttodisplay$, 1, 1))
        pictTotal(4).picture = LoadResPicture(FindCorrectBitmap
        ➥(FifthDigit%), 0)
    End If

End Sub
```

For the preceding code, the `FirstDigit%` is the rightmost digit and `FifthDigit%` if the leftmost. From this, the time is separated into as many picture boxes as those shown. For example, if there are four text boxes, the format is MM:SS. If there are five text boxes, the format is H:MM:SS.

The `cmdClose` Control

`cmdClose` is the name of the command button control that, when clicked, closes the application. The `cmdClose` control has code in only one event procedure: `cmdClose_Click()`.

The `cmdClose_Click()` Event Procedure

The `cmdClose_Click()` event procedure unloads the form, invoking the `Form_Unload()` event. Listing 35.6 contains a listing of the `cmdClose_Click()` event procedure.

Listing 35.6. MAIN.FRM, cmdClose_Click().

```
Private Sub cmdClose_Click()

    'start unloading
    Unload frmMain

End Sub
```

The `Form` Object

The `Form` object has code in three event procedures:

- `Form_Load()`
- `Form_Resize()`
- `Form_Unload()`

The `Form_Load()` Event Procedure

The `Form_Load()` event procedure opens the CD player, initializes the controls, and loads the form. Listing 35.7 contains a listing of the `Form_Load()` event procedure.

Listing 35.7. MAIN.FRM, Form_Load().

```
Private Sub Form_Load()

    'declare variables
    Dim loopcount%  'loop counting variable

    'handle errors
    On Error GoTo loaderror

    'change cursor
    Screen.MousePointer = vbHourglass

    'center the form
    Call CenterForm(Me)

    'open the device
    MMControl.Notify = False
    MMControl.Wait = True
    MMControl.Shareable = False
    MMControl.DeviceType = "CDAudio"
    MMControl.Command = "Open"
    MMControl.TimeFormat = mciFormatTmsf
```

```
    'set default color to green
    DesiredColor& = vbGreen
    menu_green.Checked = True

    Call ClearAll

    'assign new icon to form
    frmMain.Icon = pictIcon(0).picture

    'change cursor
    Screen.MousePointer = vbDefault

    'exit
    Exit Sub

loaderror:
    Resume Next

End Sub
```

The `Form_Resize()` Event Procedure

The `Form_Resize()` event procedure simply starts the timer to animate the icons, if the form is minimized. Listing 35.8 contains a listing of the `Form_Resize()` event procedure.

Listing 35.8. MAIN.FRM, Form_Resize().

```
Private Sub Form_Resize ()
    'if form is minimized-start timer,otherwise stop timer
    If frmMain.WindowState = 1 Then
        tmrIcon.Enabled = True
    Else
        tmrIcon.Enabled = False
    End If
End Sub
```

The `Form_Unload()` Event Procedure

The `Form_Unload()` event procedure prompts the user to confirm ending the program. It also enables the user to keep the CD running, if it is currently playing. Listing 35.9 contains a listing of the `Form_Unload()` event procedure.

Listing 35.9. MAIN.FRM, Form_Unload().

```
Private Sub Form_Unload(Cancel As Integer)

    'declare variables
    Dim m$      'message constructor
    Dim res%    'holds results
```

continues

Listing 35.9. continued

```
    m$ = "Confirm Close!"
    res% = MsgBox(m$, 292, "Warning")
    If res% = vbNo Then
        Cancel = True
        Exit Sub
    End If

    'ask about keeping CD running, if currently playing
    If MMControl.Mode = mciModePlay Then
        m$ = "Keep CD running?"
        res% = MsgBox(m$, 292)
        If res% = vbNo Then
            'stop CD
            MMControl.Command = "Stop"
        End If
    End If

    'close device
    MMControl.Command = "Close"

    'end program
    End

End Sub
```

The menu Object

You create the `menu` object by using Visual Basic's built-in menu editor. It has code associated with four `Click()` event procedures:

- `menu_about()`
- `menu_green()`
- `menu_red()`
- `menu_yellow()`

The menu_about_Click() Event Procedure

The `menu_about_Click()` event procedure simply shows the About form for program information. Listing 35.10 contains a listing of the `menu_about_Click()` event procedure.

Listing 35.10. MAIN.FRM, menu_about_Click().

```
Private Sub menu_about_Click()

    'show about form modally
    frmAbout.Show vbModal

End Sub
```

The menu_green_Click() Event Procedure

The menu_green_Click() event procedure selects the color green for the display. Listing 35.11 contains a listing of the menu_green_Click() event procedure.

Listing 35.11. MAIN.FRM, menu_green_Click().

```
Private Sub menu_green_Click()

    'flag this color as being changed
    DesiredColor& = vbGreen

    'check appropriate menu items
    menu_green.Checked = True
    menu_red.Checked = False
    menu_yellow.Checked = False

End Sub
```

The menu_red_Click() Event Procedure

The menu_red_Click() event procedure selects the color red for the display. Listing 35.12 contains a listing of the menu_red_Click() event procedure.

Listing 35.12. MAIN.FRM, menu_red_Click().

```
Private Sub menu_red_Click()

    'flag this color as being changed
    DesiredColor& = vbRed

    'check appropriate menu items
    menu_green.Checked = False
    menu_red.Checked = True
    menu_yellow.Checked = False

End Sub
```

The menu_yellow_Click() Event Procedure

The menu yellow Click() event procedure selects the color yellow for the display. Listing 35.13 contains a listing of the menu_yellow_Click() event procedure.

Listing 35.13. MAIN.FRM, menu_yellow_Click().

```
Private Sub menu_yellow_Click()

    'flag this color as being changed
    DesiredColor& = vbYellow
```

continues

Listing 35.13. continued

```
    'check appropriate menu items
    menu_green.Checked = False
    menu_red.Checked = False
    menu_yellow.Checked = True

End Sub
```

The MMControl Control

MMControl is the name of the actual multimedia MCI control, which is the heart of this application. It handles all communication to and from the CD player. The MMControl control has code in three event procedures:

- `MMControl_EjectCompleted()`
- `MMControl_StatusUpdate()`
- `MMControl_StopClick()`

The `MMControl_EjectCompleted()` Event Procedure

The `MMControl_EjectCompleted()` event procedure clears all displays when the CD is ejected. Listing 35.14 contains a listing of the `MMControl_EjectCompleted()`event procedure.

Listing 35.14. `MAIN.FRM`, `MMControl_EjectCompleted()`.

```
Private Sub MMControl_EjectCompleted(ErrorCode As Long)

    'make sure all displays are blank
    Call ClearAll

End Sub
```

The `MMControl_StatusUpdate()` Event Procedure

The `MMControl_StatusUpdate()` event procedure is invoked every second automatically. This procedure updates the displays during this time. The `StatusUpdate()` event procedure is the key to updating the displays on the form. This event is used to populate the displays individually. Refer to the comments in the following code for a complete description. Listing 35.15 contains a listing of the `MMControl_StatusUpdate()` event procedure.

Listing 35.15. `MAIN.FRM`, `MMControl_StatusUpdate()`.

```
Private Sub MMControl_StatusUpdate()

    'declare variables
    Dim loopcount%  'loop counting variable
    Dim x%          'most significant byte
```

```
    Dim x1%         'next significant byte
    Dim x2%         'least significant byte

    'if there is no disk, then clear all displays
    If MMControl.Mode = mciModeReady Then
        Call ClearAll
        Exit Sub
    End If

    'populate current track time
    x% = ((MMControl.Position) And &HFF00&) \ &H100
    x1% = ((MMControl.Position) And &HFF0000) \ &H10000
    PopulateDisplay PTIME, Format$(x%, "00") + Format$(x1%, "00")
    DoEvents
    DoEvents

    'populate current track
    x% = (MMControl.Position) And 255
    PopulateDisplay PTRACK, Format$(x%, "00")
    'force track property so that correct time is calculated
    MMControl.Track = x%
    DoEvents
    DoEvents

    'populate current track length
    x% = ((MMControl.TrackLength) And 255)
    x1% = ((MMControl.TrackLength) And &HFF00&) \ &H100
    PopulateDisplay PTRACKLENGTH, Format$(x%, "00") + Format$(x1%, "00")
    DoEvents
    DoEvents

    'populate colons
    For loopcount% = 0 To 3
        pictColon(loopcount%).picture = LoadResPicture(FindCorrectBitmap
        ➥(COLON), 0)
    Next loopcount%
    DoEvents
    DoEvents

    'populate total number of tracks
    PopulateDisplay PTOTALTRACK, Format$(MMControl.Tracks, "00")
    DoEvents
    DoEvents

    'populate total length of disk
    x% = (MMControl.Length) And 255
    x1% = ((MMControl.Length) And &HFF00&) \ &H100
    x2% = Int(x% / 60)
    PopulateDisplay PTOTALLENGTH, Format$(x2%, "0") + Format$(x% Mod 60,
    ➥ "00") + Format$(x1%, "00")
    DoEvents
    DoEvents

End Sub
```

The `MMControl_StopClick()` Event Procedure

The `MMControl_StopClick()` event procedure resets the MCI control to the beginning of the track. Listing 35.16 contains a listing of the `MMControl_StopClick()` event procedure.

Listing 35.16. `MAIN.FRM`, `MMControl_StopClick()`.

```
Private Sub MMControl_StopClick(Cancel As Integer)

    'make sure track resets to the beginning of track
    MMControl.Command = "Prev"

End Sub
```

The `tmrIcon` Control

`tmrIcon` is the name of the timer control that, when enabled, enables the minimized icon to appear animated. The `tmrIcon` control has code in only one event procedure, `tmrIcon_Timer()`.

The `tmrIcon_Timer()` Event Procedure

The `tmrIcon_Timer()` event procedure is invoked every second automatically. The event will be generated (by setting the `tmrIcon.enabled` property to `True`) only when the form is minimized. This procedure toggles the icon between two static icons loaded at design time so that it appears animated. Listing 35.17 contains a listing of the `tmrIcon_Timer()` event procedure.

Listing 35.17. `MAIN.FRM`, `tmrIcon_Timer()`.

```
Private Sub tmrIcon_Timer()

    'toggle icon picture
    If frmMain.Icon <> pictIcon(0).picture Then
        frmMain.Icon = pictIcon(0).picture
    Else
        frmMain.Icon = pictIcon(1).picture
    End If

End Sub
```

CROSS REFERENCE

For more information on animating icons, refer to Chapter 8, "Graphics."

The ABOUT.FRM File

`ABOUT.FRM` is the other form in this application. Figure 35.3 presents the form as it appears at runtime.

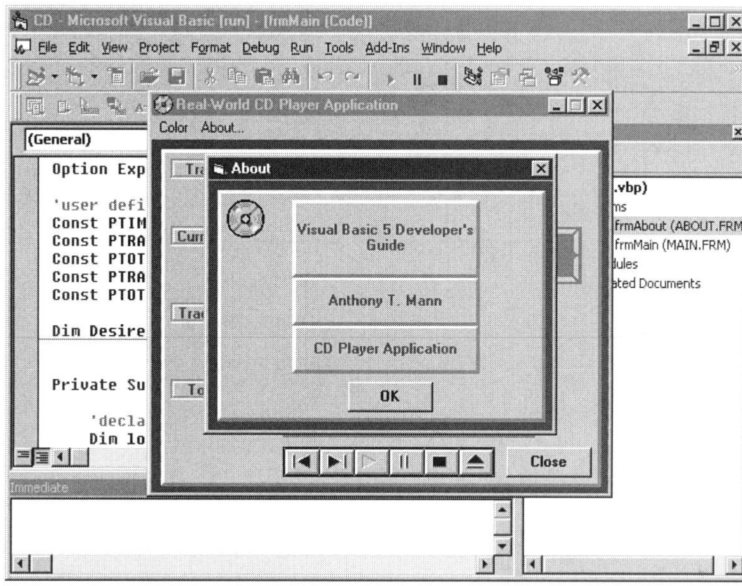

FIGURE 35.3.
The CD player About form at runtime.

Fundamentally, there is no difference in the form at design time, so it is not presented. Table 35.2 lists all the relevant properties of each control on the form that have been changed from their standard default values. The `ABOUT.FRM` file is contained on the CD-ROM accompanying this book in the `\CD` subdirectory.

Table 35.2. Properties of each control on ABOUT.FRM.

Object	*Control Type*	*Property*	*Value*
`frmAbout`	Form	`BackColor`	&H00404000&
		`Caption`	About
		`Height`	3525
		`Left`	1035
		`MaxButton`	False
		`MinButton`	Falsc

continues

Table 35.2. continued

Object	*Control Type*	*Property*	*Value*
		`Top`	1140
		`Width`	4545
`pnlMain`	SSPanel	`BackColor`	&H00C0C0C0&
		`BevelWidth`	3
		`Caption`	
		`Font3D`	None
		`ForeColor`	&H00C0C0C0&
		`Height`	2895
		`Left`	120
		`RoundedCorners`	False
		`ShadowColor`	Black
		`Top`	120
		`Width`	4215
`pnl1`	SSPanel	`BackColor`	&H00C0C0C0&
		`BevelWidth`	3
		`Caption`	Visual Basic 5 Developer's Guide
		`Font3D`	None
		`ForeColor`	&H00FF0000&
		`Height`	975
		`Left`	960
		`RoundedCorners`	False
		`ShadowColor`	Black
		`Top`	120
		`Width`	2415
`pnl2`	SSPanel	`BackColor`	&H00C0C0C0&
		`BevelWidth`	3
		`Caption`	Anthony T. Mann
		`Font3D`	None
		`ForeColor`	&H00FF0000&
		`Height`	615

Object	*Control Type*	*Property*	*Value*
		`Left`	960
		`RoundedCorners`	False
		`ShadowColor`	Black
		`Top`	1080
		`Width`	2415
`pnl3`	SSPanel	`BackColor`	&H00C0C0C0&
		`BevelWidth`	3
		`Caption`	CD Player Application
		`Font3D`	None
		`ForeColor`	&H00FF0000&
		`Height`	615
		`Left`	960
		`RoundedCorners`	False
		`ShadowColor`	Black
		`Top`	1680
		`Width`	2415
`cmdOK`	CommandButton	`Caption`	OK
		`Height`	375
		`Left`	1680
		`Top`	2400
		`Width`	1095
`pictAbout`	PictureBox	`Autosize`	True
		`BackColor`	&H00C0C0C0&
		`BorderStyle`	None
		`Height`	615
		`Left`	120
		`Top`	120
		`Width`	735

Function, Subroutine, and Event Procedures

There are several procedures of code for the objects (controls) that comprise this form. Each is listed in the following sections.

The (general) Object

The (general) object contains no event procedures. Here is the declarations procedure for the (general) object:

- (declarations)

The (declarations) Procedure

The (declarations) procedure contains only one line of declarations used in the form ABOUT.FRM. It is only used to allow for variable syntax checking and forcing the declaration of variables in each event procedure. Listing 35.18 contains a listing of the (declarations) event procedure.

Listing 35.18. ABOUT.FRM, (general) (declarations).

```
Option Explicit
```

The cmdOK Control

cmdOK is the name of the command button control that, when clicked, closes the frmAbout form. The cmdOK control has code in only one event procedure, cmdOK_Click().

The cmdOK_Click() Event Procedure

The cmdOK_Click()event procedure simply unloads the form. Listing 35.19 contains a listing of the cmdOK_Click() event procedure.

Listing 35.19. ABOUT.FRM, cmdOK_Click().

```
Private Sub cmdOK_Click ()

    'unload
    Unload frmAbout

End Sub
```

The Form Object

The Form object has code in only one event procedure, Form_Load().

The Form_Load() Event Procedure

The Form_Load() event procedure centers the form and assigns an icon to the pictAbout control. Listing 35.20 contains a listing of the Form_Load() event procedure:

Listing 35.20. ABOUT.FRM, Form_Load().

```
Private Sub Form_Load ()

    'center form
    CenterForm Me

    'load icon
    pictAbout.Picture = frmMain.Icon

End Sub
```

The CD.BAS File

This file contains the declarations and procedures that are available at a global level. The CD.BAS file is contained on the CD-ROM accompanying this book in the \CD subdirectory.

Function, Subroutine, and Event Procedures

There are several event procedures of code for the objects (controls) that comprise this module. Each is listed in the following sections.

The (general) Object

The (general) object contains declarations and one procedure at the module (global) level. Here are the event procedures for the (general) object:

- (declarations)
- CenterForm()

The (declarations) Procedure

The (declarations) procedure contains variable declarations used in the module CD.BAS. Listing 35.21 contains a listing of the (declarations) procedure.

Listing 35.21. CD.BAS, (general) (declarations).

```
Option Explicit

'declare constants used by resource file
Public Const G = 101
Public Const G0 = 102
Public Const G1 = 103
Public Const G2 = 104
Public Const G3 = 105
Public Const G4 = 106
Public Const G5 = 107
```

continues

Listing 35.21. continued

```
Public Const G6 = 108
Public Const G7 = 109
Public Const G8 = 110
Public Const G9 = 111
Public Const R = 112
Public Const R9 = 113
Public Const R8 = 114
Public Const R7 = 115
Public Const R6 = 116
Public Const R5 = 117
Public Const R4 = 118
Public Const R3 = 119
Public Const R2 = 120
Public Const R1 = 121
Public Const R0 = 122
Public Const Y9 = 123
Public Const Y8 = 124
Public Const Y7 = 125
Public Const Y6 = 126
Public Const Y5 = 127
Public Const Y4 = 128
Public Const Y3 = 129
Public Const Y2 = 130
Public Const Y1 = 131
Public Const Y0 = 132
Public Const Y = 133
Public Const COLON = 11
Public Const BLANK = 10
```

The `CenterForm()` Procedure

The `CenterForm()` procedure is used to center a form in the screen client area. It accepts one variable, `F`, which is a form object. Listing 35.22 contains a listing of the `CenterForm()` procedure.

Listing 35.22. `CD.BAS`, `CenterForm()`.

```
Public Sub CenterForm(F As Form)

    'center the form
    F.Move (Screen.Width - F.Width) / 2, (Screen.Height - F.Height) / 2

End Sub
```

The `BITMAP.RES` File

This file is a resource file that has been compiled by Visual C++ version 2.0 to provide the bitmap resources used in the CD player application. The source files are available on the CD-ROM accompanying this book in the `\CD` subdirectory.

CROSS REFERENCE

For more information about creating resource files, refer to Chapter 10, "Writing Resource Files."

The CD.ICO File

This file contains the icon that has been attached to the form at design time (see Figure 35.4). It is only used so that this icon is displayed in Windows Explorer. When the form is minimized, the `CD1.ICO` and `CD2.ICO` files are used. The `CD.ICO` file is contained on the CD-ROM accompanying this book in the `\CD` subdirectory.

FIGURE 35.4.
The CD player Windows Explorer icon.

The CD1.ICO File

This file contains one of the icons used to simulate animation of the icons when the form is minimized. `CD2.ICO` is the other icon file used in the animation process (see Figure 35.5). The `CD1.ICO` file is contained on the CD-ROM accompanying this book in the `\CD` subdirectory.

FIGURE 35.5.
One of the icons used for animation.

The CD2.ICO File

This file contains one of the icons used to simulate animation of the icons when the form is minimized. CD1.ICO is the other icon file used in the animation process (see Figure 35.6). The CD2.ICO file is contained on the CD-ROM accompanying this book in the \CD subdirectory.

FIGURE 35.6.
One of the icons used for animation.

The CD.EXE file and source files are contained on the CD-ROM accompanying this book in the \CD subdirectory.

Relating the CD Player Application to Your Application

The CD player application shows how to create a basic CD player by using the MCI control. You could possibly create a more "realistic" CD player using a bitmap of an actual CD player and creating hotspots for the controls. In this case, you would need to have the MCI control hidden, and send commands to the control as the hotspots were clicked.

CROSS REFERENCE

For more information about hotspots, see Chapter 8, "Graphics."

You can enhance the CD player as it is right now by adding a database so that the program appears to automatically detect which CD is in the player. Programs usually do this by calculating an algorithm by using the number of tracks, the total disc time, and other disc information.

One final suggestion is possibly to create a user control to encapsulate the functionality of the CD player to distribute a total solution to other Visual Basic apps, or possibly even the Web.

CROSS REFERENCE

For more information about user controls, see Chapter 20, "ActiveX Controls." For more information about the Web, refer to Part V, "Communications, Internet, and Intranet Building."

Summary

Using the MCI ActiveX control makes it easy to create a CD player application because all the communication with the underlying CD hardware is handled by the ActiveX control and the operating system. By setting properties, accessing methods, and responding to events of the ActiveX control, you too can create a CD player application. You could also create any type of multimedia application that the MCI control supports. This chapter showed how to use the MCI control in depth.

36

Developing a MAPI/ Microsoft Exchange Application

MAPI, which stands for Messaging Application Programming Interface, is the key component to making Microsoft Exchange work. Microsoft Exchange is used for many types of applications that deal with messaging. The most common types of messaging are Internet messages and internal corporate messages. Both of these types of messages are referred to as *e-mail.* E-mail capabilities can be extended greatly to enable you to store information in a message store without you even knowing it was e-mail. This is done primarily through forms. The rest of this chapter is dedicated to discussing MAPI and forms for use with Microsoft Exchange.

E-Forms

Exchange forms (or E-Forms) come as part of the setup with Microsoft Exchange. Typically, these are installed either on the server (NT Server) or an administrator's client machine. Figure 36.1 shows the Windows NT 4.0 group with E-Forms installed.

FIGURE 36.1.
The Exchange Forms Designer icon.

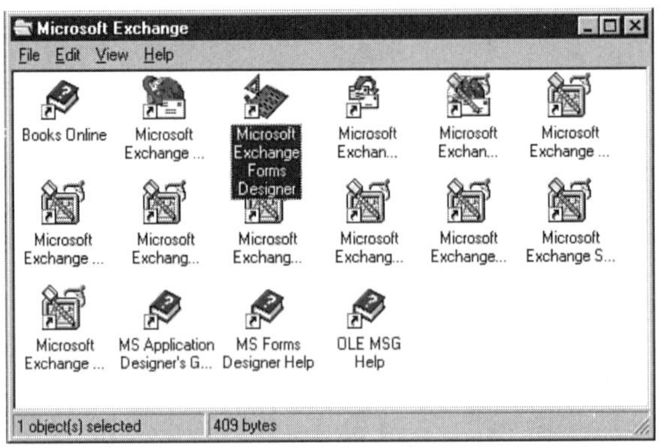

Designing Exchange forms is very similar to designing Visual Basic forms. The major difference is that the design-time environment (IDE) for E-Forms is targeted more toward forms for Exchange rather than Visual Basic. Just as you would not open Visual Basic and start coding without first designing the form, the same is true for the E-Forms IDE. Therefore, you must have a set purpose in mind before you begin coding.

You must design your form to track the data elements you want. You also need to design the "database," which is actually a message store contained in an Exchange folder. This is the easy part because no database code is needed. Next, you must design the actual form. After you have done this, you can alter it further to provide more flexibility inside Visual Basic. Finally, you can distribute the form. This chapter takes you through the following steps:

1. Planning your application
2. Designing the folder
3. Designing the form

4. Altering the form in Visual Basic
5. Distributing the form

Step 1: Planning the Application

Planning the application is very important. You must know how you will write the application and what its purpose is. Let's use an example. Suppose you wanted to track time spent on projects. Most likely, you would need to track

- The task
- The starting time
- The ending time
- Hours worked
- Comments

These items should appear in an aesthetically pleasing way on your form. The form also should include a Send button to effect saving or sending your data to the database. In this case, the database is actually the folder used to store the messages.

Step 2: Designing the Folder

Designing the folder is really quite simple. The folder is the public folder used to store message contents. Before you design the folder, consider how a Microsoft Exchange client looks (see Figure 36.2).

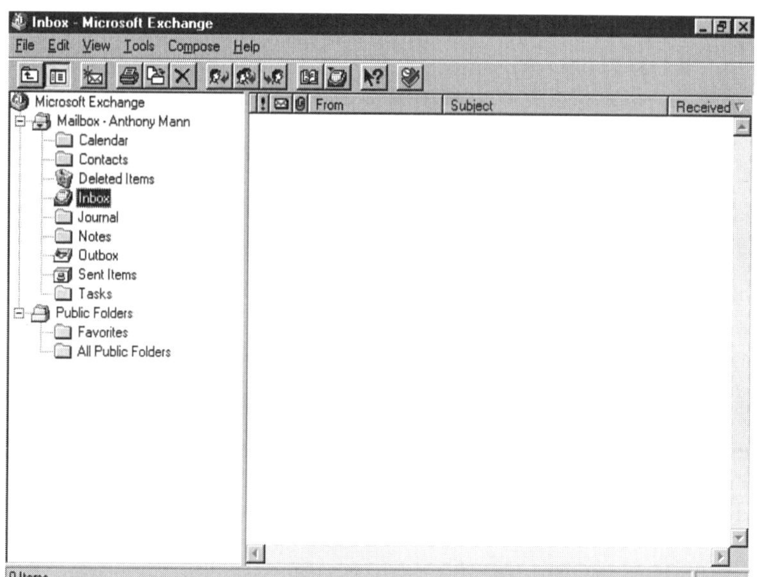

FIGURE 36.2.
The Exchange client before designing the folder.

The contents of the folder will be filled in automatically by the application, but you do need to consider who can see the folder. If you place the data in a public folder, it will be available to everyone.

On the other hand, you can define permissions for the folder either in the Exchange Server Administrator or in the Control Panel.

Step 3: Designing the Form

Start the E-Forms designer by double-clicking its icon (refer to Figure 36.1). This brings up a dialog box that asks you what type of form to design. If you select the first option, Form Template Wizard, a wizard will guide you through the creation of the form. This dialog box is shown in Figure 36.3.

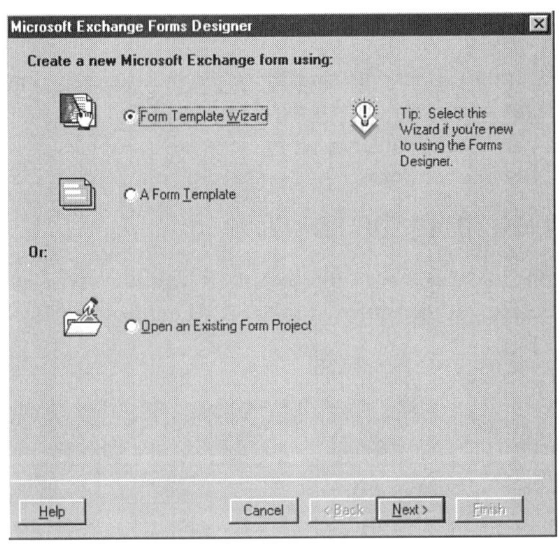

FIGURE 36.3.
The Microsoft Exchange Forms Designer screen.

Select the first option (which is the default option) and click Next. This guides you step-by-step through creating the type of E-Form you want.

Step 2 asks who the recipient of the message is. Will it be a user (mailbox) or an information store (folder)? In this case, it's a folder, so select the To a public folder (Post) option, and then click Next. Figure 36.4 shows this step.

The next step inquires how the form will be used. There are two options: To Post new information or To Post a Response. Because we do not necessarily want a response but do want to post new information, select the option labeled To Post new information, and then click Next. Figure 36.5 shows this step.

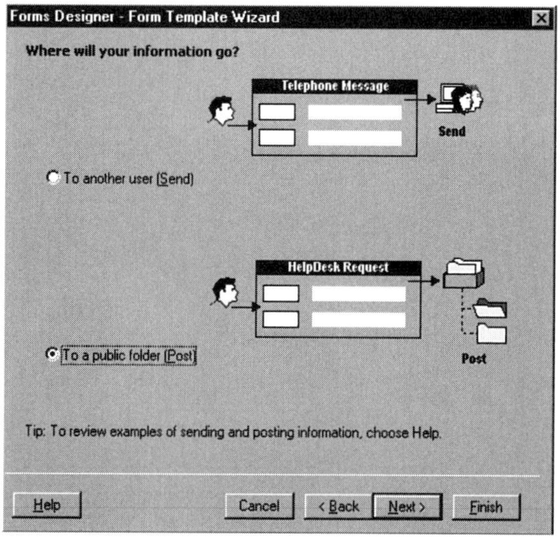

FIGURE 36.4.
Forms Designer of the Form Template Wizard.

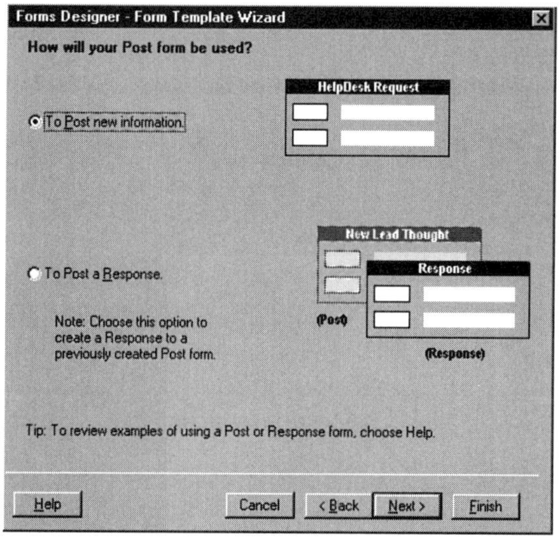

FIGURE 36.5.
The Forms Designer of the Form Template Wizard, selecting how the Post form will be used.

The next step asks how many windows will be used, one or two. If you use one window, the compose and read part of the message will be on one form. If you select two windows, each of these parts will be in separate windows. For this example, choose one. Now click the Next button. Figure 36.6 shows this step.

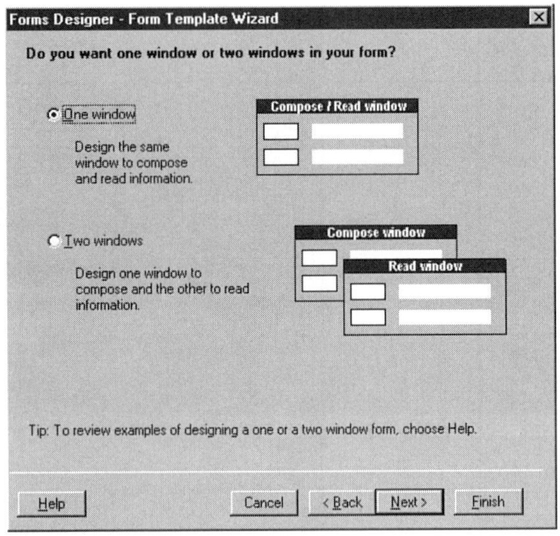

FIGURE 36.6.
The Forms Designer of the Form Template Wizard, selecting how many windows will be shown on your form.

The next step is used for setting titles and descriptions. Select a title for the form and enter an appropriate description. These are very useful when you are distributing forms throughout your organization. Complete this step and click Next. Figure 36.7 shows this step.

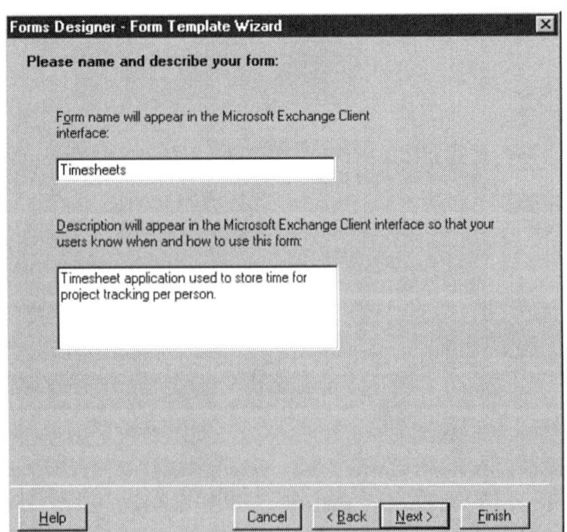

FIGURE 36.7.
The Forms Designer of the Form Template Wizard, naming and describing your form.

The final step summarizes what is necessary at this point and enables you to create the blank template, based on how you answered the questions. Figure 36.8 shows this final step. Click the Finish button to create the blank template.

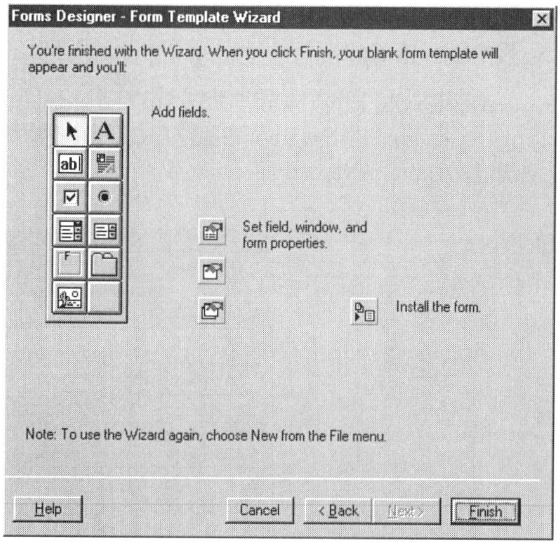

FIGURE 36.8.
The final step in the E-Forms Designer.

After the blank template is created, it should look like the one shown in Figure 36.9. It is now ready for you to place controls on it. You can see that it looks similar to the IDE in Visual Basic, and it is basically used the same way.

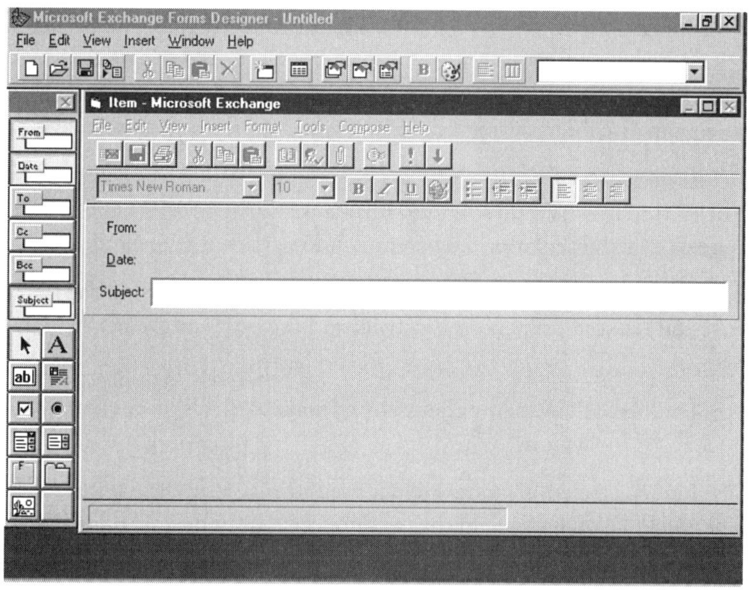

FIGURE 36.9.
The E-Forms Designer after the blank template has been created.

The sending and receiving of messages is handled automatically by the MAPI controls placed on the form. The form is ready for you to manipulate its properties, methods, and events.

There are properties for the window and the form. To view the window properties, select View | Window Properties. This brings up a dialog box with three tabs, as shown in Figure 36.10. The General tab is visible by default.

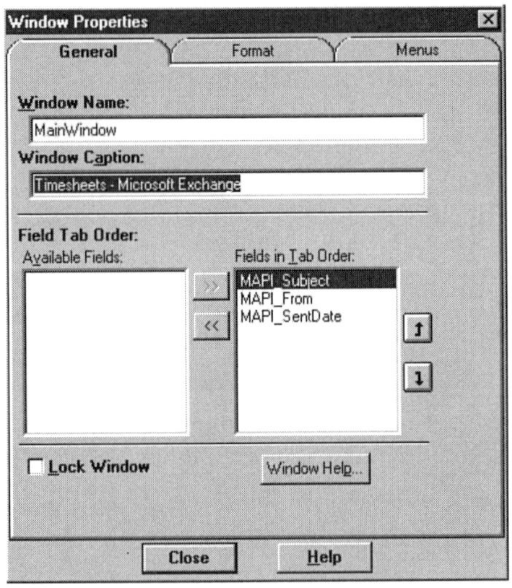

FIGURE 36.10.
The General tab of the Window Properties dialog box.

The first item is Window Name. This name uniquely identifies the window to Visual Basic when you distribute the application, so you want to use a name that is germane to the application.

The next item is Window Caption. Because this is an MDI application, the window caption appears in the title bar of the parent window when it is maximized.

Next is a section for determining tab stop order. The items on the right side of the screen will have the `TabStop` property set to `True`, and the order of the tabs will be as shown from top to bottom.

You use the Lock Window check box to make all fields on the form read-only. Therefore, it is unchecked by default.

The button labeled Window Help is used to enable you to create user help in the application. Therefore, if you had a field that was not obvious in meaning, you could click this button and define the Help window. Clicking this button brings up a Window Help for Users dialog box like the one shown in Figure 36.11. Simply type the text for your Help message and click OK.

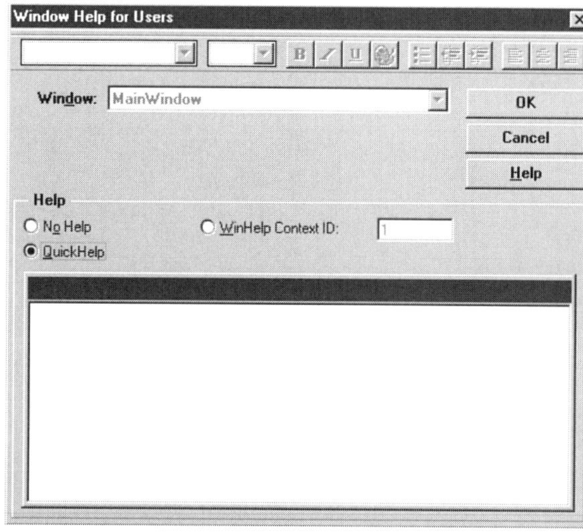

FIGURE 36.11.
Defining Help in the General tab of the Window Properties dialog box.

You use the Format tab to define the format on your window. You can choose from the following options:

Maximize button
Minimize button
Initial view options
Window icons
Background colors
Window sizing options

Figure 36.12 shows the Format tab. Choose the appropriate options for your form, and then click the Menus tab.

You use the Menus tab to define menus within your application (see Figure 36.13). This is a fairly busy screen. However, it is used only to display a hierarchical relationship of the parent menu option displayed under the Menu: keyword. The child menus are listed under the Commands: keyword. You can define the parent-level menu caption as well as the child-level caption. Furthermore, you can define the action and Help for the commands.

If you want to define Help, click the Command Help button, which brings up the screen shown in Figure 36.14.

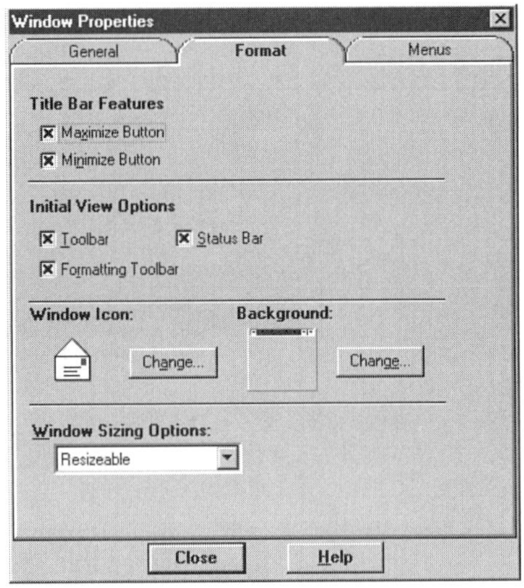

FIGURE 36.12.
The Format tab of the Window Properties dialog box.

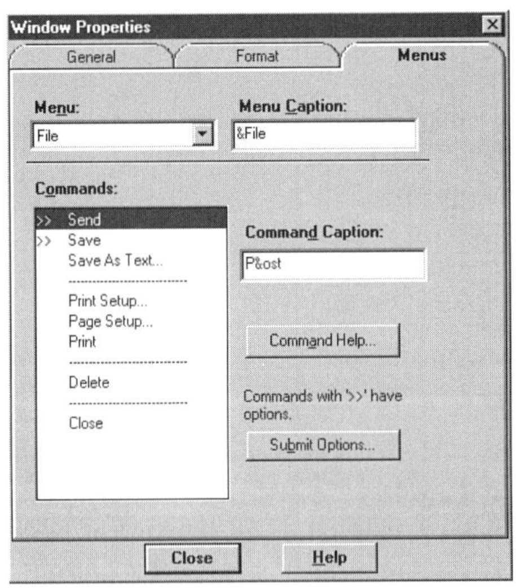

FIGURE 36.13.
The Menus tab of the Window Properties dialog box.

This screen enables you to define Help and tooltips for the menu options. Enter the appropriate Help and close the screen. If you notice a >> symbol next to a command, this means that there are options available for that command. Click the Options button to change options for that command.

There are also form properties. To select these, choose View | Form Properties. This brings up the General tab of the Form Properties dialog box, which is shown in Figure 36.15.

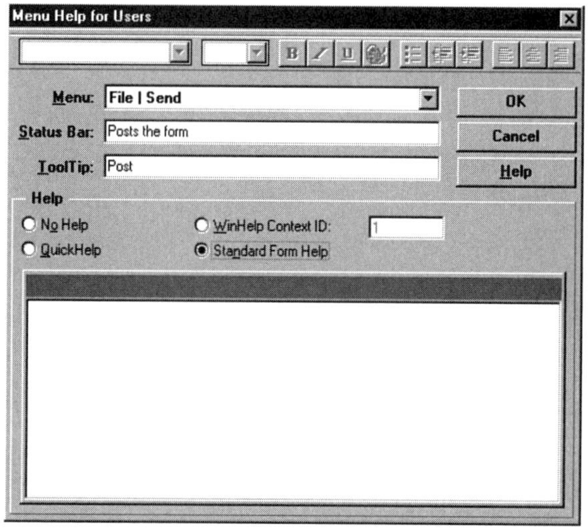

FIGURE 36.14.
The Menu Help for Users screen for the Window Properties dialog box.

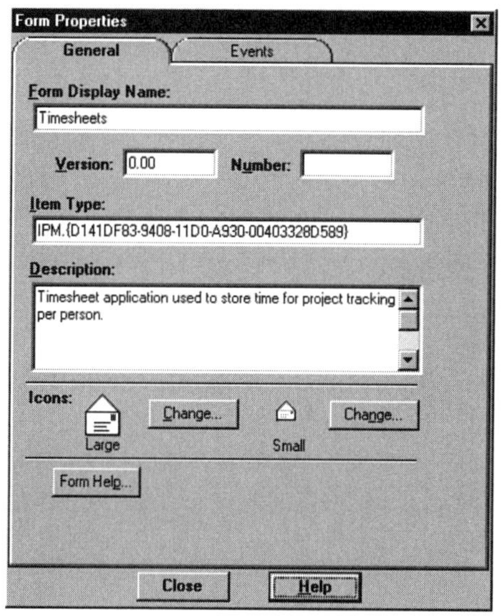

FIGURE 36.15.
The General tab of the Form Properties dialog box.

This tab enables you to define how the form looks to Exchange. It also enables you to control versioning and to change icons for the form. The next tab, Events, is shown in Figure 36.16. You use the Events tab to enable the form to respond to different types of events.

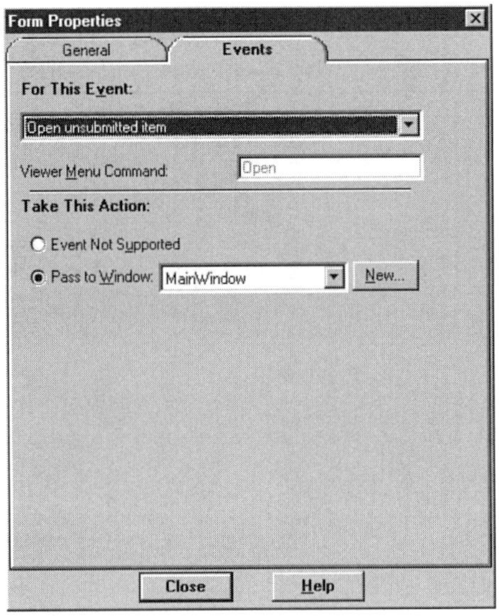

FIGURE 36.16.
The Events tab of the Form Properties dialog box.

Here's a list of the possible events:

- Create new item
- Open unsubmitted item
- Open submitted item
- Print unsubmitted item
- Print submitted item
- Save unsubmitted item as text
- Save submitted item as text
- Reply
- Reply to all
- Reply to folder
- Forward
- Custom response 1
- Custom response 2
- Custom response 3
- Custom response 4
- Custom response 5

By choosing the options on this form, you can define what happens when a user chooses a specific menu option.

You are now ready to begin placing the custom fields on the form. Place a combo box on the form. This will be used to display a predefined list of tasks. The other items are merely text boxes. Therefore, place the items on the form as you would in Visual Basic. Continue until the form looks like the one shown in Figure 36.17.

FIGURE 36.17.
The E-Form after the fields are placed.

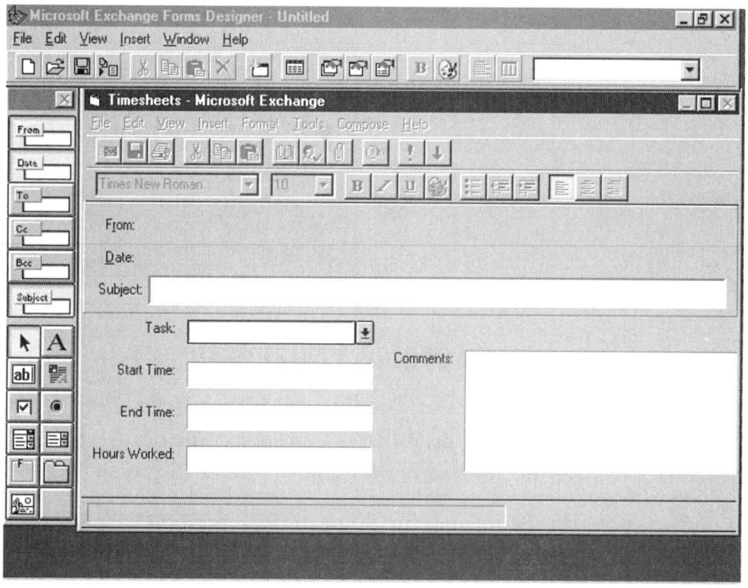

Now it is time to change the properties of the controls on the form. Be sure to name them as you would any Visual Basic control, using the conventions set forth by your IS department. For example, use prefix `lst` for a list box, and so on.

The drop-down list needs to be a required field. Therefore, bring up the Field Properties window by selecting the F4 key. In the General tab, select the Required check box. This is shown in Figure 36.18.

Continue editing the field properties. The Hours Worked text box should also be required. This way, a user cannot send the form until the task and hours are filled in. Furthermore, the hours should be read-only because they are calculated. Therefore, if you have entered a beginning and ending time, the hours will be calculated and the required field will be satisfied implicitly. This calculation is shown under the section "Step 4: Altering the Form in Visual Basic."

FIGURE 36.18.
The Field Properties' General tab.

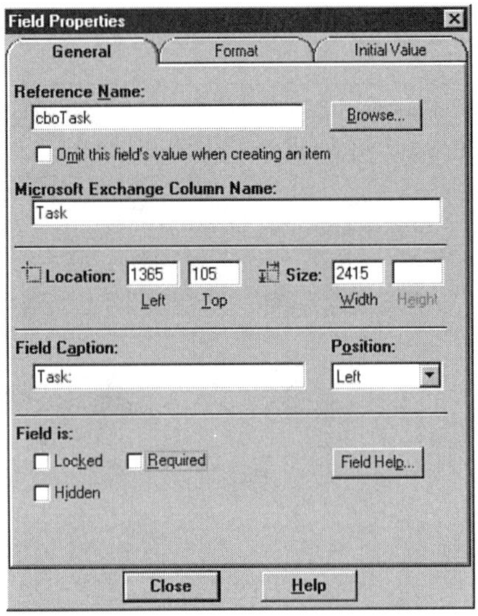

Step 4: Altering the Form in Visual Basic

If you want to alter the form in Visual Basic, you must generate the source code. You do this by selecting File | Install. (This is discussed more in the next section.) After the source code is generated, you are free to modify the code.

If you want to edit the form again, you can open the `*.EFP` file in the directory in which you saved it. The `*.EFP` file is used to re-create the form in the E-Forms Designer. However, if you modify the code in Visual Basic, you might not be able to open it in the E-Forms Designer again. This is not really a big deal because the Visual Basic code will be generated automatically.

Quite a large number of forms and modules are generated automatically. These forms and modules are used in the communication with Exchange Server. Listing 36.1 shows the `TIME.VBP` project file automatically generated from the simple example being built in all steps throughout this chapter.

Listing 36.1. The source code that is automatically generated for the `TIME.VBP` file.

```
Module=Module1; VAR.BAS
VBX=C:\WINDOWS\system\MSRICHED.VBX
Class=ChildWindow; CHILDWIN.CLS
Module=Commands; COMMANDS.BAS
Module=Constants; CONSTANT.BAS
Module=Global; GLOBAL.BAS
Module=Lang; LANG.BAS
Module=Rendering; RENDER.BAS
Module=Richedit; RE_CONST.BAS
Module=Toolbar; TOOLBAR.BAS
Module=Types; TYPES.BAS
```

```
Module=WinAPIs; WINAPIS.BAS
VBX=C:\WINDOWS\system\MAPIFORM.VBX
Form=MAINWIND.FRM
Form=ABORTFOR.FRM
Form=TOOLTIP.FRM
Form=FRMADMIN.FRM
Form=FRMPAGES.FRM
Form=FRMQHELP.FRM
Object={0BA686C6-F7D3-101A-993E-0000C0EF6F5E}#1.0#0; THREED16.OCX
Object={F9043C88-F6F2-101A-A3C9-08002B2F49FB}#1.0#0; COMDLG16.OCX
Reference=*\G{BEF6E001-A874-101A-8BBA-00AA00300CAB}#1.0#0#C:\WINDOWS\SYSTEM\
➥oc25.dll#Standard OLE Types
ProjWinSize=7,404,248,468
ProjWinShow=2
IconForm="frmAdmin"
ResFile16="INVAR.RES"
Title="Timesheets"
ExeName="AVPRQY$K.EXE"
Name="Project1"
HelpContextID="0"
StartMode=0
Description="Timesheet application used to store time for project tracking
➥ per person."
VersionCompatible="0"
MajorVer=4
MinorVer=993
RevisionVer=2
AutoIncrementVer=0
ServerSupportFiles=0
VersionCompanyName="Microsoft"
VersionProductName="Timesheets 0.00 "
```

Now you can alter the form. For example, suppose you want to calculate the number of hours based on the beginning and ending times. You could calculate it by creating this subroutine:

```
Sub Calculate()
    If Trim$(txtEnd_Ctrl.Text) <> "" And Trim$(txtStart_Ctrl.Text) <> "" Then
        txtHours_Ctrl.Text = Trim$(str$(Val(txtEnd_Ctrl.Text) -
        ➥Val(txtStart_Ctrl.Text)))
    Else
        txtHours_Ctrl.Text = ""
    End If
End Sub
```

It will calculate the time only if there is a beginning and ending time present in the text boxes. Next, you must call the subroutine from the `Change` events of the respective text boxes.

NOTE

Notice that each of the controls you named using the E-Forms Designer has `_Ctrl` appended to the name of the control. This is done automatically when the code is generated.

After you make any necessary changes, you must compile the application and then install it. The installation procedure is described in the next section.

Step 5: Distributing the Form

There are two ways to distribute the form. The first is through the E-Forms Designer. To do this, simply select File | Install. This actually generates Visual Basic 16-bit source code, using Visual Basic 4.0. Then, a special version of Visual Basic, called Visual Basic For Exchange, is invoked to compile the forms generated by the E-Forms Designer. You will be prompted for the folder into which to place the form. Then, when you are finished, save the form to a directory of your choosing. This example was saved in the `\Exchange\Time.VB` subdirectory on the CD-ROM accompanying this book. This works only if you do not modify the automatically generated source code.

A problem arises if you want to edit the Visual Basic source code, because you cannot bring the modified code into the E-Forms Designer. However, this really is not a big deal because the code has already been generated. If there is anything at this point that needs to be changed, there is no reason to have to go back to the E-Forms Designer.

After you have generated the executable, you must install the form by managing the form within the Microsoft Exchange client, itself. From the Exchange client, select Tools | Options, and then select the Exchange Server tab. This brings up the dialog box shown in Figure 36.19.

FIGURE 36.19.
The Microsoft Exchange client Options dialog box.

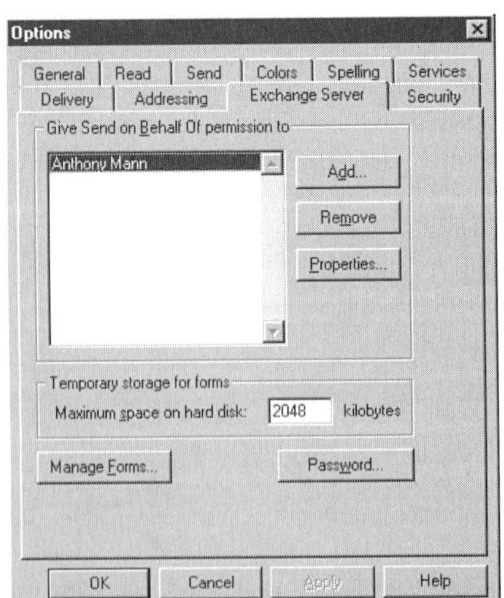

Next, select the Manage Forms button. This brings up a dialog box for managing forms, as shown in Figure 36.20.

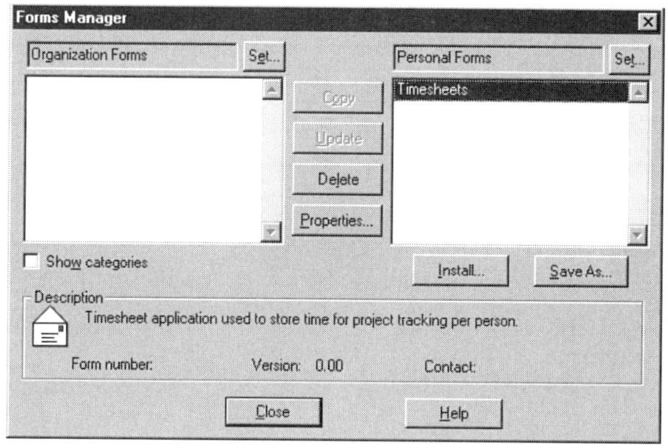

FIGURE 36.20.
The Forms Manager dialog box.

Notice that there is a Timesheets option under the Personal Forms section. This was placed there by the E-Forms Designer. Select the Install button to install a new copy of the form. You will be prompted to select a `*.CFG` file (a configuration file). The file was automatically generated by the E-Forms Designer. Listing 36.2 shows its contents.

Listing 36.2. The `TIME.CFG` form configuration file.

```
[Description]
ComposeCommand=
MessageClass=IPM.{D141DF83-9408-11D0-A930-00403328D589}
Clsid={D141DF83-9408-11D0-A930-00403328D589}
DisplayName=Timesheets
Comment=Timesheet application used to store time for project tracking
➥ per person.
Version=0.00
Locale=enu
DesignerTool=Microsoft Exchange Forms Designer 4.0
SmallIcon=dws9.ico
LargeIcon=dws11.ico
ComposeInFolder=1
[Extensions]
Extension1=Extension1
[Extension.Extension1]
Type=30
NmidPropset={00020D0C-0000-0000-C000-000000000046}
NmidInteger=1
Value=111211111
[Platforms]
Platform1=Platform1
Platform2=Platform2
Platform3=Platform3
Platform4=Platform4
Platform5=Platform5
Platform6=Platform6
Platform7=Platform7
```

continues

Listing 36.2. continued

```
Platform8=Platform8
Platform9=Platform9
Platform10=Platform10
[Platform.Platform1]
CPU=ix86
OSVersion=Win3.1
Registry1=LocalServer=%d\AVPRQY$K.EXE
File1=AVPRQY$K.EXE
[Platform.Platform2]
CPU=ix86
OSVersion=WinNT3.5
LinkTo=Platform1
[Platform.Platform3]
CPU=ix86
OSVersion=Win95
LinkTo=Platform1
[Platform.Platform4]
CPU=MIPS
OSVersion=WinNT3.5
LinkTo=Platform1
[Platform.Platform5]
CPU=AXP
OSVersion=WinNT3.5
LinkTo=Platform1
[Platform.Platform6]
CPU=PPC
OSVersion=WinNT3.5
LinkTo=Platform1
[Platform.Platform7]
CPU=ix86
OSVersion=WinNT4.0
LinkTo=Platform1
[Platform.Platform8]
CPU=MIPS
OSVersion=WinNT4.0
LinkTo=Platform1
[Platform.Platform9]
CPU=AXP
OSVersion=WinNT4.0
LinkTo=Platform1
[Platform.Platform10]
CPU=PPC
OSVersion=WinNT4.0
LinkTo=Platform1
[Property.Property1]
SpecialType=1
Enum1=cboTask_Enum
Type=30
NmidString=cboTask
DisplayName=Task
[Enum1.cboTask_Enum]
NmidString=cboTask
Val.1.Display=Design
Val.1.Index=1
Val.2.Display=Document
Val.2.Index=2
```

```
Val.3.Display=Code
Val.3.Index=3
Val.4.Display=Test
Val.4.Index=4
EnumCount=4
[Properties]
Property1=Property1
Property2=Property2
Property3=Property3
Property4=Property4
Property5=Property5
[Property.Property2]
Type=30
NmidString=txtStart
DisplayName=Start Time
[Property.Property3]
Type=30
NmidString=txtEnd
DisplayName=End Time
[Property.Property4]
Type=30
NmidString=txtHours
DisplayName=Hours Worked
[Property.Property5]
Type=30
NmidString=txtComments
DisplayName=Comments
```

After you select the appropriate `*.CFG` file, you can change the properties of the form. Figure 36.21 shows the dialog box in which you can change the properties.

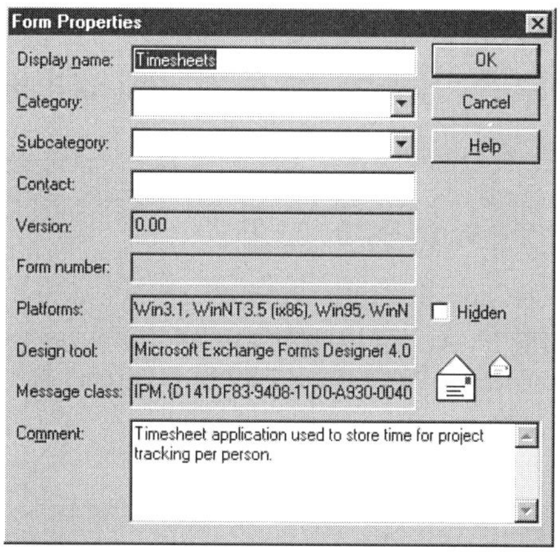

FIGURE 36.21.
The Form Properties dialog box.

You can select from categories and subcategories (if they have been set up in Exchange Server). Click OK. You'll be prompted to overwrite the existing form, as shown in Figure 36.22. Go ahead and select the Yes button.

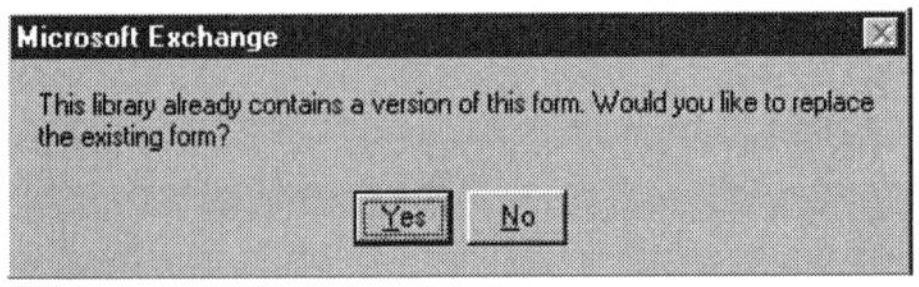

FIGURE 36.22.
Overwriting existing forms.

After the form is overwritten, you can click Close and then OK on the Options screen. The form is now installed.

To test the new form, select Compose | New Form. You'll be presented with all of the forms from which to choose. These forms are presented in the dialog box shown in Figure 36.23.

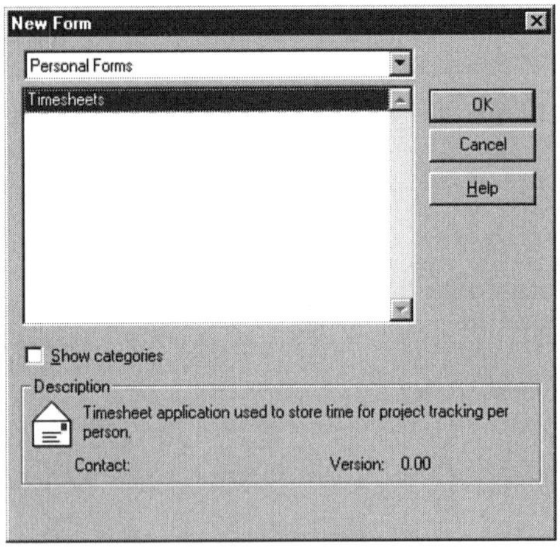

FIGURE 36.23.
Composing a message in the New Form dialog box.

Select OK to create the new form. You can then fill it out, as shown in Figure 36.24.

When you are finished, click the large post button on the right side of the screen. This sends the message through the Exchange Server. After the message is sent, it will be received in the public folder, as shown in Figure 36.25.

As you can see, creating an Exchange application is very easy. The example shown in this chapter is simplistic; however, you can create high-powered applications that you can tie to databases or the Internet, or you can add other features.

FIGURE 36.24.
Using the new form.

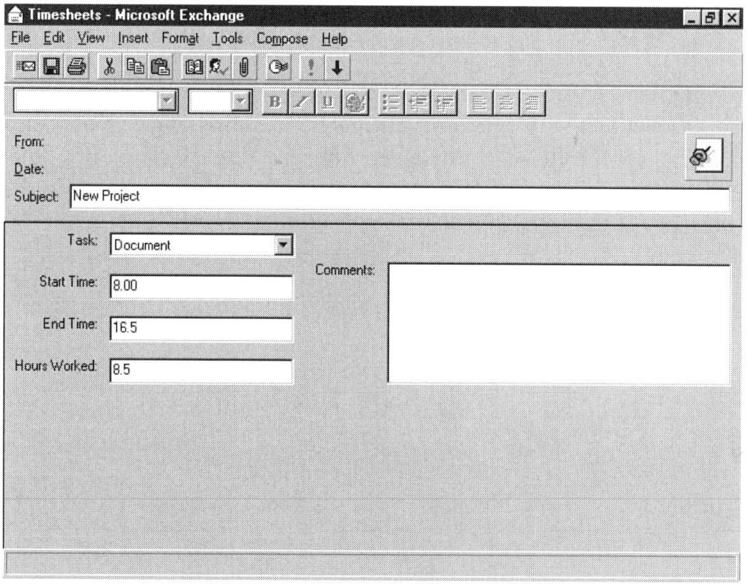

FIGURE 36.25.
Receiving the new message.

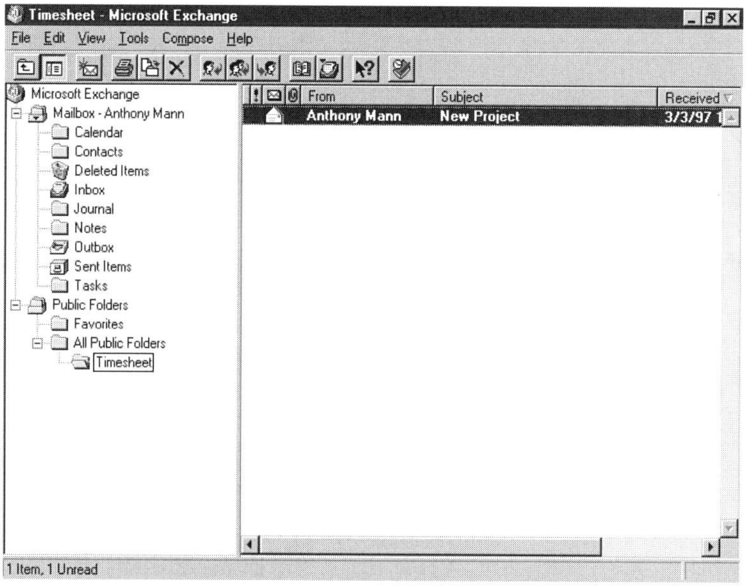

Summary

Developing a MAPI/Exchange application is quite simple with the Exchange Forms Designer. This tool comes with Microsoft Exchange. It is used to generate a Visual Basic template, reflecting forms created in the designer. After the Visual Basic code is generated, you can modify it in any way you want. This chapter walked you through creating these forms and how to generate the Visual Basic code.

37

Developing a TAPI Application

TAPI stands for Telephony Application Programming Interface, which is a set of functions for incorporating telephony into your Visual Basic applications.

CROSS REFERENCE

For more information about TAPI, refer to Chapter 27, "TAPI."

The application shown in this chapter builds upon some of the techniques in the SAPI application in Chapter 40, "Developing a SAPI Application," and adds telephone dialing capabilities. It takes the application shown in Chapter 40 one step further and allows the telephone numbers to be populated from a database. Therefore, to use this application, you must have set up your computer for speech. You might need to refer to Chapter 40 first.

This application enables a user to speak into a microphone using the techniques shown in Chapter 40 and dial a specific phone number as shown in this chapter. Therefore, there will be some overlap between the two chapters.

Using the Application

The application is very easy to use. It populates the names of everyone in the database into a list box. Then, when the speech recognition engine recognizes a name, the name is highlighted and the number is dialed. You also can use the application to add and remove items from the database .

CROSS REFERENCE

For more information about speech and SAPI, refer to Chapter 40, "Developing a SAPI Application."

The application uses an Access 97 database that contains only one table called Phone. Inside the table, there are only two fields, Name and Number. Figure 37.1 shows the Access table structure with sample data (the data is not significant). Phone numbers have been masked with 5551212. The application at runtime is shown in Figure 37.2.

This application is considered to be *assisted TAPI* because it does only part of the work: It dials the phone. You still need to pick up the receiver to talk to the person.

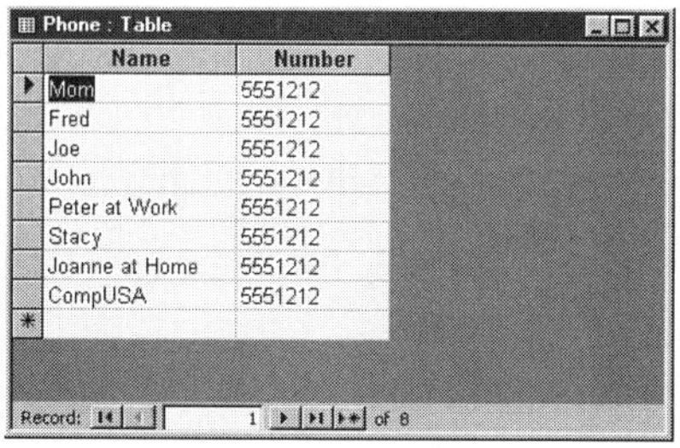

Phone : Table

Name	Number
Mom	5551212
Fred	5551212
Joe	5551212
John	5551212
Peter at Work	5551212
Stacy	5551212
Joanne at Home	5551212
CompUSA	5551212

Record: 1 of 8

FIGURE 37.1.
The Access table structure and data.

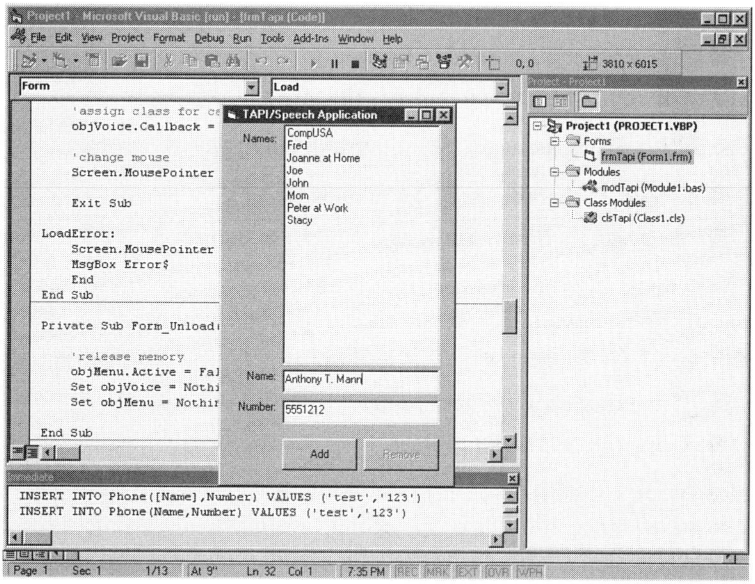

FIGURE 37.2.
The TAPI application at runtime.

Application Theory

The theory behind the application is that the code (shown in the section, "Constructing the Application") will create two objects, `VCmdAuto` and `IVMenuAuto`, in the `Speech.VoiceCommand` library. Each object has its own specific methods, properties, and events.

The `VCmdAuto` object is used as the voice command object. It actually processes spoken words and sends them to the speech engine. The following are its available methods:

- `MenuCreate`: Creates a reference to a list of commands
- `Register`: Registers the object with the speech engine

The following are the available properties of the `VCmdAuto` object:

- `Awake`: Turns the speech engine on or off
- `Callback`: Specifies the class that contains code which responds to commands
- `CommandSpoken`: Receives the menu element of the item spoken, but requires constant polling

The `IVMenuAuto` object internally stores a list of all commands to be recognized in speech. It is not truly a menu on the screen. The following are its available methods:

- `Add`: Adds an item to the menu of commands
- `ListSet`: Sets a list item in a menu
- `Remove`: Removes an item from the menu of commands

The following are the available properties of the `IVMenuAuto` object:

- `Active`: Makes the list of commands active
- `hWndMenu`: Gets the handle of the menu of commands

By manipulating these properties and methods, you can make the speech engine recognize commands from your application. It is important to understand how your code can respond to a recognized word. There are actually two ways for your code to respond:

- Using the `CommandSpoken` property
- Using the `Callback` property

If you want to use the `CommandSpoken` property, you must include a timer on your form, and set it to an im"mrval of 500 (or 1/2 second) or so. When the timer fires, check the value of the `CommandSpoken` property. If the property is null, then a word was not recognized by the speech engine. If it is not null, then this command can be processed because it was recognized. This method is not very efficient because it relies on the timer control.

The other way to respond to a recognized word is by using the `Callback` property. The string value that is placed in this property is the name of the class module that contains code procedures (subroutines) with the specific names of

- `CommandRecognize()`
- `CommandOther()`

When a command is recognized, the speech engine fires the `CommandRecognize()` subroutine, passing in the command recognized. If a command is heard but not recognized, the `CommandOther()` subroutine is fired. This enables you to respond without having to use a timer control, which is much more reliable.

Constructing the Application

The application is made up of one form, one code module, and one class module. The form is used to control the user interface. The code module is used to contain the starting point of the ActiveX EXE project, called `Sub Main()`. The class module is used to handle the callback events. All of the code shown in this application is contained on the CD accompanying this book in the `\TAPISAPI` subdirectory.

Constructing the Form

The form contains a visual interface (controls) and code. The following controls are placed on the form:

- Two text boxes
- Two command buttons
- One list box
- Three labels

The two text boxes each have had two properties changed from their default values. The properties are the name and the text. The name properties have been changed to `txtName` and `txtNumber`. The captions have been changed to "". These text boxes are used to enter a new name and telephone number into the database. The `txtName` control has code in only one event procedure. This event procedure is called `Change()`, which is shown in Listing 37.1. The `txtNumber` control has code in two events: `Change()` and `KeyPress()`. Listings 37.2 and 37.3 show the code for this control.

The code in Listing 37.1 first deselects the items in the list box and then enables the Add button if there is text in both of the text boxes.

Listing 37.1. The `txtName_Change()` event.

```
Private Sub txtName_Change()
    Call ClearList
    Call EnableButtons
End Sub
```

The code in the procedure in Listing 37.2 is exactly the same as the `txtName_Change()` event. It is used to enable the Add button if there is text in both of the text boxes.

Listing 37.2. The `txtNumber_Change()` event.

```
Private Sub txtNumber_Change()
    Call ClearList
    Call EnableButtons
End Sub
```

The code in Listing 37.3 makes sure that the user types only numeric keys. If the ASCII equivalent of the key pressed is not `0` or `9`, the `KeyAscii` code is set to zero. This negates the key press.

Listing 37.3. The `txtNumber_KeyPress()` event.

```
Private Sub txtNumber_KeyPress(KeyAscii As Integer)
    If KeyAscii < Asc("0") Or KeyAscii > Asc("9") Then
        'don't allow this character
        KeyAscii = 0
    End If
End Sub
```

The command buttons are used to add and remove names and phone numbers from the database and the list box. Each command button has code only in the `Click()` event. Each is shown in Listings 37.4 and 37.5.

The code in Listing 37.4 simply adds the data to the database and to the menu command object. This allows it to be available for voice commands. Then the list box is populated.

Listing 37.4. The `cmdAdd_Click()` event.

```
Private Sub cmdAdd_Click()
    'declare variables
    Dim sCmd As String

    'handle errors
    On Error GoTo AddError

    'insert new values
    sCmd = "INSERT INTO Phone([Name],[Number]) "
    sCmd = sCmd & "VALUES ('" & txtName.Text & "','" & txtNumber.Text & "')"
    dbPhone.Execute sCmd

    'add item to command list
    objMenu.Add txtName.Text, lstCommand.List(lstCommand.ListCount),
    ➥"Command List", ""

    'populate new values
    Call Populate

    'clear text boxes
    txtName.Text = ""
    txtNumber.Text = ""
```

```
    Exit Sub
AddError:
    MsgBox Error$

End Sub
```

The code in Listing 37.5 finds out which item is selected, and then removes it from the list and the menu option. It also deletes it from the database so that it is not populated again.

Listing 37.5. The `cmdRemove_Click()` event.

```
Private Sub cmdRemove_Click()
    'declare variables
    Dim nLoopCount As Integer
    Dim nSelect As Integer
    Dim sCmd As String
    Dim sName As String

    'initialize
    nSelect = -1

    'find out which item is selected
    For nLoopCount = 0 To lstCommand.ListCount - 1
        If lstCommand.Selected(nLoopCount) = True Then
            nSelect = nLoopCount + 1
            sName = lstCommand.List(nLoopCount)
            Exit For
        End If
    Next nLoopCount

    If nSelect >= 0 Then
        'remove the selected item from the listbox
        lstCommand.RemoveItem nSelect - 1

        'remove the selected item from the command list
        objMenu.Remove nSelect

        'also remove from the database
        sCmd = "DELETE FROM Phone "
        sCmd = sCmd & "WHERE [Name] = '" & sName & "'"
        dbPhone.Execute sCmd

        'populate new values
        Call Populate

    End If
End Sub
```

The list box has code in only one event, the `Click()` event. This is used only to enable the Remove button through the `EnableButtons()` procedure. It is shown in Listing 37.6.

Listing 37.6. The `lstCommand_Click()` event.

```
Private Sub lstCommand_Click()
    Call EnableButtons
End Sub
```

The label has no code. It simply contains the list of commands accepted by the engine.

The form contains two module-level procedures. The first is called `EnableButtons()` and is used to enable and disable the command buttons. The second is called `Populate()` and is used to populate the list box with values of names from the database. These are shown in Listings 37.7 and 37.8.

Listing 37.7. The `EnableButtons()` procedure.

```
Public Sub EnableButtons()

    'add button
    If Trim$(txtName.Text) = "" And Trim$(txtNumber.Text) = "" Then
        cmdAdd.Enabled = False
    Else
        cmdAdd.Enabled = True
    End If

    'remove button
    If lstCommand.SelCount > 0 Then
        cmdRemove.Enabled = True
    Else
        cmdRemove.Enabled = False
    End If
End Sub
```

The code in Listing 37.7 simply enables the Add button if there is a name and number entered. It also enables the Remove button if there are any items selected in the list box.

Listing 37.8. The `Populate()` procedure.

```
Public Sub Populate()
    'declare variables
    Dim sCmd As String
    Dim rsPhone As Recordset

    'clear list box
    lstCommand.Clear

    'build string
    sCmd = "SELECT [Name],[Number] "
    sCmd = sCmd & "FROM Phone "
    sCmd = sCmd & "ORDER BY Name "
    Set rsPhone = dbPhone.OpenRecordset(sCmd, dbOpenSnapshot)
```

```
    If Not rsPhone.EOF Then
        rsPhone.MoveFirst
        Do While Not rsPhone.EOF
            lstCommand.AddItem rsPhone.Fields(0)
            rsPhone.MoveNext
        Loop
    End If

End Sub
```

The code in Listing 37.8 simply clears the list box and populates it with the values from the database using SQL statements to retrieve the values.

The form also contains a `(general)(declarations)` section that declares two object variables for use throughout the form. It is shown in Listing 37.9.

Listing 37.9. The `(general)(declarations)` section.

```
Option Explicit

'declare object variables
Dim objVoice As Object
Dim objMenu As Object
```

The form also contains code in two events, `Form_Load()` and `Form_Unload()`. The `Form_Load()` event instantiates the speech engine and adds all default values to the list box. The `Form_Load()` event is shown in Listing 37.10.

Listing 37.10. The `Form_Load()` event.

```
Private Sub Form_Load()
    'declare variables
    Dim nLoopCount As Integer

    'change mouse
    Screen.MousePointer = vbHourglass

    'handle errors
    On Error GoTo LoadError

    'create voice object
    Set objVoice = CreateCbject("Speech.VoiceCommand")

    'register voice object
    objVoice.Register ""

    'open the database
    Set dbPhone = Workspaces(0).OpenDatabase(App.Path & "\PHONE.MDB")
```

continues

Listing 37.10. continued

```
    'populate phone numbers
    Call Populate

    Call EnableButtons

    'set value
    objVoice.Awake = True

    'create menu object to hold voice commands
    Set objMenu = objVoice.MenuCreate(App.EXEName, (Me.Caption), 1033, "",
    ➥vcmdmc_OPEN_ALWAYS)

    DoEvents
    DoEvents
    DoEvents

    'add all items in listbox to menu
    For nLoopCount = 0 To lstCommand.ListCount - 1
        objMenu.Add nLoopCount + 1, lstCommand.List(nLoopCount),
        ➥"Command List", ""
        DoEvents
        DoEvents
        DoEvents
    Next nLoopCount

    'make menu active
    objMenu.Active = True
    DoEvents
    DoEvents
    DoEvents

    'assign class for callback function
    objVoice.Callback = "Project1.clsTapi"

    'change mouse
    Screen.MousePointer = vbDefault

    Exit Sub

LoadError:
    Screen.MousePointer = vbDefault
    MsgBox Error$
    End
End Sub
```

It is important to note that after the object is created, it must be registered with the speech engine. The quotes are used to register it with the default values.

The `Form_Unload()` event is used to destroy the objects and reclaim memory. It is shown in Listing 37.11.

Listing 37.11. The `Form_Unload()` event.

```
Private Sub Form_Unload(Cancel As Integer)

    'release memory
    objMenu.Active = False
    Set objVoice = Nothing
    Set objMenu = Nothing

End Sub
```

Constructing the Module

The module is used mainly to house the `Sub Main()` procedure so that the application has a starting point. However, there are several procedures housed within this module to make them available throughout the application. The `Sub_Main()` procedure simply loads the form, as shown in Listing 37.12.

Listing 37.12. The `Sub_Main()` procedure.

```
Public Sub Main()
    'project starting point
    frmTAPI.Show
End Sub
```

The second procedure in the module is called `ClearList()`. It is placed in the module because it needs to be available to the form and the class module. It simply deselects all items in the list box. This procedure is shown in Listing 37.13.

Listing 37.13. The `ClearList()` procedure.

```
Public Sub ClearList()
    'Unselect all items in the list
    Dim nLoopCount As Integer

    'find out which item is selected
    For nLoopCount = 0 To frmTapi.lstCommand.ListCount - 1
        frmTapi.lstCommand.Selected(nLoopCount) = False
    Next nLoopCount

End Sub
```

The third procedure in the module is called `Dial()`. It is responsible for making the TAPI call to dial the number selected (or spoken). This procedure is shown in Listing 37.14.

Listing 37.14. The `Dial()` procedure.

```
Public Sub Dial()

    'dial the selected number

    'declare variables
    Dim sCmd As String
    Dim sName As String
    Dim rsNumber As Recordset
    Dim nLoopCount As Integer
    Dim sNumber As String
    Dim lRes As Long

    'find out which item is selected
    sName = ""
    For nLoopCount = 0 To frmTapi.lstCommand.ListCount - 1
        If frmTapi.lstCommand.Selected(nLoopCount) = True Then
            sName = frmTapi.lstCommand.List(nLoopCount)
            Exit For
        End If
    Next nLoopCount

    'display message if there's no person selected (spoken)
    If sName = "" Then
        MsgBox "There is no person selected"
        Exit Sub
    End If

    'find out number to dial
    sCmd = "SELECT Number "
    sCmd = sCmd & "FROM Phone "
    sCmd = sCmd & "WHERE Name = '" & sName & "' "
    Set rsNumber = dbPhone.OpenRecordset(sCmd, dbOpenSnapshot)
    If Not rsNumber.EOF Then
        sNumber = rsNumber.Fields(0)
    End If

    'display message if there's no number
    If sNumber = "" Then
        MsgBox "Cannot find Telephone Number"
        Exit Sub
    End If

    lRes = tapiRequestMakeCall(sNumber, "", "", "")

    'display message if dialing failed
    If lRes < 0 Then
        MsgBox "Error Dialing"
    End If

End Sub
```

The procedure loops through the list box to determine which item is selected. Then it calls the TAPI function `tapiRequestMakeCall()` to perform the dialing.

There are also declarations for use throughout the application. They are shown in Listing 37.15.

Listing 37.15. The `(general)(declarations)` section.

```
Option Explicit
Public dbPhone As Database
Declare Function tapiRequestMakeCall Lib "tapi32.dll" (ByVal stNumber As
➥String, ByVal stDummy1 As String, ByVal stDummy2 As String,
➥ByVal stDummy3 As String) As Long
```

Notice the last declaration. It is the TAPI call that will actually perform the dialing function and needs only one argument passed, the number to be dialed. If it returns a number less than zero, the dialing failed.

Constructing the Class

The class is used to store the code for the events that are fired by the speech engine. This enables your code to respond to spoken words. The procedures in this class must be named `CommandRecognize()` and `CommandOther()`. Also, the `Instancing` property must be set to `5 - Multiuse`. This allows the application to create multiple instances of the class.

The `CommandRecognize()` procedure is fired when a recognized command is received. It is shown in Listing 37.16.

Listing 37.16. The `CommandRecognize()` procedure.

```
Public Sub CommandRecognize(szCommand As String, dwID As Long)
    'this command was recognized

    'declare variables
    Dim nRes As Integer

    'handle errors
    On Error GoTo RecognizeError

    'unselect all
    Call ClearList

    'select detected word
    If dwID > 0 Then
        frmTapi.lstCommand.Selected(dwID - 1) = True
    End If

    'change mouse
    Screen.MousePointer = vbHourglass

    'dial the selected item
    Call Dial
```

continues

Listing 37.16. continued

```
    'change mouse
    Screen.MousePointer = vbDefault

    Exit Sub
RecognizeError:
    'change mouse
    Screen.MousePointer = vbDefault
    MsgBox Error$

End Sub
```

Notice in Listing 37.16 that the index of the menu command received is used to highlight the item in the list box to show that it is received. The `Dial()` procedure in the module will look for this highlighted item so that it knows to go out to the database and get the number for the selected person.

The `CommandOther()` procedure is fired when an unrecognized command is received. It is shown in Listing 37.17.

Listing 37.17. The `CommandOther()` procedure.

```
Public Sub CommandOther(szCommand As String, szApp As String,
➥szState As String)
    'this command was not recognized

    'unselect to show unrecognized command
    Call ClearList

End Sub
```

The code will simply deselect all items in the list box if a command was unrecognized.

Summary

Building upon the knowledge obtained from Chapter 40, "Developing a SAPI Application," this chapter showed you how to use voice recognition to dial telephone numbers stored in a database. It showed how you can literally speak the name of the person to dial. Then it uses the `tapiRequestMakeCall()` TAPI function to perform the actual dialing. You can incorporate this and other TAPI functions discussed in Chapter 27, "TAPI," to build complex telephony applications.

38

Data Sharing with Microsoft Office

Data is shared with Microsoft Office through OLE Automation. Microsoft Office applications expose certain properties, methods, and events for use by other applications. Your applications can take advantage of the functionality of the Microsoft Office products.

This chapter shows you how to create an application, called Office Interface, using basic functionality from Microsoft Excel and Microsoft Word. This application takes data from an ODBC data source based on a query that you construct. It then ports the data to either an Excel spreadsheet or a Word document.

NOTE

It is important to note that this application uses Remote Data Objects (RDO). Therefore, if you are not using the Enterprise edition of Visual Basic, you will not be able to use the application, but you will be able to follow the Excel and Word interface code herein.

CROSS REFERENCE

For more information about OLE Automation, refer to Chapter 21, "OLE and OLE Automation." For more information about RDO, refer to Chapter 16, "Remote Data Objects (RDO)."

This application has only one screen and very little code. The screen is shown at runtime in Figure 38.1.

FIGURE 38.1.
Data sharing with a Microsoft Office application.

Using the Application

Using the Office Interface application is quite simple. It is located on the CD accompanying this book in the `\OFFICEAP` subdirectory and is called `PROJECT1.VBP`. There are two separate frames on the screen that divide the screen into different functional areas:

- Remote Data Login
- Result Set

The Remote Data Login frame contains text box controls used to identify the necessary data to log in to a remote ODBC data source through RDO.

CROSS REFERENCE

For more information about RDO, refer to Chapter 16, "Remote Data Objects (RDO)."

If you are not using the Enterprise version of Visual Basic, this will not work for you. Refer to Figure 38.1 to see what the application looks like by default. The application assumes the following parameters:

- Database Name (where the query will be executed) is Pubs.
- DSN is LocalServer.
- Login ID is sa.
- You have no password for this login.

You can change these parameters if they do not work for your computer. If you do not have access to your server, the login will fail and the process will not work.

Next, type your SQL statement. This statement will be used to execute a query in the database that is entered in the Database Name text box, earlier.

CROSS REFERENCE

For more information about SQL, refer to Chapter 29, "Structured Query Language (SQL)."

When you are finished, you can click either the Send to Excel or Send to Word command button. This application is designed to work with Excel 97 and Word 97. However, if you are using an earlier version of Excel or Word, the application might not work exactly as shown in this chapter.

Clicking the Send to Excel button will open the RDO connection and change to the specified database. Then, the query you entered is executed. The results are populated into Excel, starting from cell A1. If you click the Include Field Names check box, the first row of data in Excel will be the field names. Figure 38.2 shows what the export to Excel looks like.

FIGURE 38.2.
Exporting to Excel.

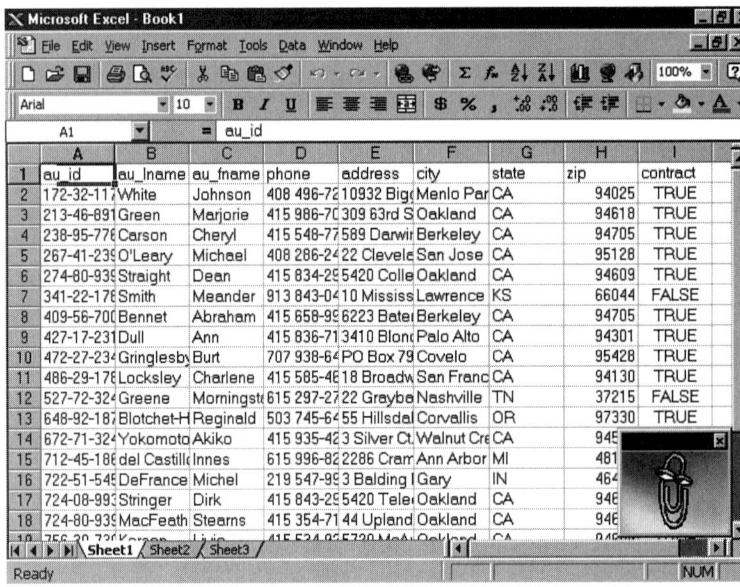

Clicking the Send to Word button will open the RDO connection and change to the specified database. Then, the query you entered is executed. The results are populated into Word, one row at a time. The fields are separated by commas. At the end of each line, a carriage return/ line feed (CR/LF) is added so that the next line starts at the beginning. If you click the Include Field Names check box, the first row of data in Word will be the field names. Figure 38.3 shows what the export to Word looks like.

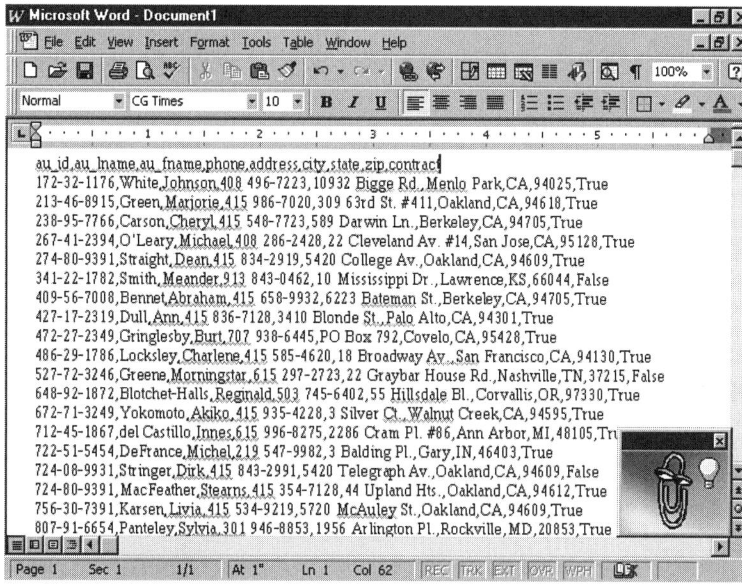

FIGURE 38.3.
Exporting to Word.

Constructing the Application

Constructing the application is actually quite simple. Many beginning developers do not interface with any of the Office products because they think it will be very difficult. You'll see in the next few sections that this is not the case.

Graphical Interface

The GUI part of this application contains only one form, which contains all of the code necessary to interface with Excel or Word. The following objects are placed on the form:

- Two frames
- Five labels
- Five text boxes
- One check box
- Two command buttons

The two frames are used simply to house the different controls. The only properties that will be changed from their default values are the `Caption` properties. They are changed to Remote Data Login and Result Set, respectively. The `Name` properties have not been changed because they are not even referred to in code.

The five labels identify the five adjacent text boxes. Again, only the `Caption` properties of the labels will be changed from their default values. Change them to this:

- Database Name:
- DSN:
- Login ID:
- Password:
- SQL Statement:

The five text boxes enable the user to enter data that will be used to connect to the server and execute a query. The text boxes have only the `Name` and `Text` properties changed from their default values. The names all begin with the prefix `txt`, followed by a name that is germane to the text boxes' usage. Change the text boxes' `Name` properties to the following:

- `txtDB`
- `txtDSN`
- `txtUID`
- `txtPWD`
- `txtSQL`

Change the `Text` properties to the following:

- `Pubs`
- `LocalServer`
- `sa`
- blank
- `Select * from Authors`

In addition, the `txtSQL` text box has one other property that needs to be changed. Change the `Multiline` property to `True`. This allows for multiple lines of SQL statements.

The only check box on the form has three properties changed from their default values:

- `Caption`
- `Name`
- `Value`

The `Caption` property is changed to `Include Field Names`. The `Name` property is changed to `chkName`. Finally, the `Value` is set to `True`. This allows for the displaying of field names by default.

There are two command buttons, and each has its `Caption` and `Name` properties changed. Change the `Caption` properties to the following:

- `Send to Excel...`
- `Send to Word...`

The `Name` properties both begin with the prefix `cmd`. Change them to the following:

- `cmdExcel`
- `cmdWord`

Code

Only three procedures have code attached to them in this application because the majority of the code is handled in the `Click` event of each of the command buttons. The following sections outline and explain the code in this application.

Module-Level Procedures

There is only one procedure at the module level in this application: the `FillDataArray()` function.

The `FillDataArray()` Function

The `FillDataArray()` function is used solely to fill an array with data retrieved from a resultset. This function is called only when you export to Excel. This is necessary because you only pass the array of data to Excel; you don't send the actual data for each cell individually. Passing the array is much more efficient. The function accepts two arguments. The first is the array to fill with data, and the second is the resultset to use when filling the array with data. The function returns an integer, which is the number of rows in the resultset. Listing 38.1 shows this function.

Listing 38.1. The `FillDataArray()` function.

```
Public Function FillDataArray(asArray(), rsRecord As rdoResultset) As Long

    'declare variables
    Dim nRow As Integer
    Dim nCol As Integer

    'handle errors
    On Error GoTo FillError

    'redim the array
    ReDim asArray(5000, rsRecord.rdoColumns.Count)
```

continues

Listing 38.1. continued

```
    nRow = 0
    If Form1.chkName.Value = 1 Then
        'loop through field names
        For nCol = 0 To rsRecord.rdoColumns.Count - 1
            asArray(nRow, nCol) = rsRecord.rdoColumns(nCol).Name
        Next nCol

        'increment row
        nRow = 1
    End If

    'loop through records
    Do While Not rsRecord.EOF
        'loop through fields
        For nCol = 0 To rsRecord.rdoColumns.Count - 1
            asArray(nRow, nCol) = rsRecord.rdoColumns(nCol).Value
        Next nCol

        'move to the next record
        rsRecord.MoveNext
        nRow = nRow + 1
    Loop

    'return the number of records
    FillDataArray = nRow
    Exit Function

FillError:
    'display error
    MsgBox Error$
    Exit Function
    Resume
End Function
```

Notice the following line of code:

```
ReDim asArray(5000, rsRecord.rdoColumns.Count)
```

This is dimmed with a dimension of `5000` because it is used as an arbitrary value. The `RowCount` property is not used because, depending on the ODBC driver you're using, the `RowCount` will sometimes be set to a value of `-1`. This indicates that the driver cannot return the number of rows. This way, it will work for all drivers, but only up to 5,000 rows of data.

There are two main loops within the function. The first is called only if you have checked the Include Field Names check box. It loops through all columns and places the field names in the first "row" of data in the array. The second loop works like the first, but it places the actual values into the array.

The cmdExcel Control

The `cmdExcel` command button is clicked when the user wants to export data to Excel. The `cmdExcel` command button has code in only one event: the `Click` event. Listing 38.2 shows the code for this event.

Listing 38.2. The cmdExcel_Click() event.

```
Private Sub cmdExcel_Click()
    'declare variables
    Dim objExcel As Object
    Dim objRange As Excel.Range
    Dim sCmd As String
    Dim asTempArray()
    Dim lNumRows As Long
    Const CLASSOBJECT = "Excel.Application"
    Dim rdoCn As New rdoConnection
    Dim rdoEn As rdoEnvironment
    Dim rdoQuery As New rdoQuery
    Dim rdoRS As rdoResultset

    'change mouse
    Screen.MousePointer = vbHourglass

    'handle errors
    On Error GoTo ExcelError

    'open Environment
    Set rdoEn = rdoEnvironments(0)

    'establish RDO Connection
    With rdoCn
        .Connect = "UID=" & txtUID.Text & ";PWD=" & txtPWD.Text & ";Database=
        ➥Master;DSN=" & txtDSN.Text & ";Database=" & txtDB.Text & ";"
        .EstablishConnection rdDriverNoPrompt, True
        rdoEn.rdoConnections.Add rdoCn
    End With

    'change databases
    rdoCn.Execute ("Use " & txtDB.Text)

    'create query
    With rdoQuery
        Set .ActiveConnection = rdoCn
        .Sql = txtSQL.Text
        .LockType = rdConcurReadOnly
        .RowsetSize = 1
        .CursorType = rdUseServer
    End With

    'open resultset for query
    Set rdoRS = rdoQuery.OpenResultset(rdOpenStatic)
```

continues

Listing 38.2. continued

```
    If Not rdoRS.EOF Then
        'first attempt to get the object if it is running
        Set objExcel = GetObject(CLASSOBJECT)

        If objExcel Is Nothing Then
            Set objExcel = CreateObject(CLASSOBJECT)
        End If

        'add a new workbook
        objExcel.Workbooks.Add

        'fill the range with the array
        lNumRows = FillDataArray(asTempArray, rdoRS)

        'set a range for the array to be placed
        Set objRange = objExcel.Range(objExcel.Cells(1, 1), objExcel.Cells
        ➥(lNumRows, rdoRS.rdoColumns.Count))

        objRange.Value = asTempArray

        'make excel visible
        objExcel.Visible = True
    End If

    'close the connection
    rdoCn.Close

    'change mouse
    Screen.MousePointer = vbDefault

    'exit - all was successful
    Exit Sub

ExcelError:
    If Err <> 432 And Err > 0 Then
        'change mouse
        Screen.MousePointer = vbDefault

        'display error
        MsgBox Error$

        'reclaim memory from object
        Set objExcel = Nothing

        'exit
        Exit Sub
    Else
        'class was not found, attempt to create it
        Resume Next
    End If

End Sub
```

The first thing that happens in this code is that the necessary variables are declared. Next, the RDO environment is established and the appropriate variables are assigned to establish a connection to the RDO data source.

After the connection is established, use the `Execute` method to switch to the specified database. If this is not done, the query might not be executed in that database, and therefore might reference objects that do not exist in that database. After the database is changed, the query is executed and assigned to a `ResultSet` object.

Next, a reference to an existing `Excel.Application` object is attempted. If Excel is not loaded, an error is produced. However, the error handler will simply `Resume Next` if this happens. This allows for the object to be created. After the object is created, a new workbook is added.

Then, the array `asTempArray()` is filled with the data from the `ResultSet` object. It does not matter that the first element of the array is dimensioned as `5000` because the next line of code sets the range for the data passed. This range is a block of cells. It is set by using the `Range` method for the `Excel.Application`. Because the `Range` method expects cell locations like A1 or C22, the `Cells` method is used to convert array coordinates to the expected syntax.

After the range is set, the data is sent to Excel with the following line of code:

```
objRange.Value = asTempArray
```

This line of code uses the `Value` property and assigns it to the whole array. After the data is sent to Excel, the worksheet is made visible and the RDO connection is closed.

The cmdWord Control

The `cmdWord` command button is clicked when the user wants to export data to Word. The `cmdWord` command button has code in only one event: the `Click` event. Listing 38.3 shows the code for this event.

Listing 38.3. The `cmdWord_Click()` event.

```
Private Sub cmdWord_Click()
    Dim objWord As New Word.Application
    Dim nLoopCount As Integer
    Dim sLine As String
    Const CLASSOBJECT = "Word.Basic"
    Dim rdoCn As New rdoConnection
    Dim rdoEn As rdoEnvironment
    Dim rdoQuery As New rdoQuery
    Dim rdoRS As rdoResultset

    'change mouse
    Screen.MousePointer = vbHourglass
```

continues

Listing 38.3. continued

```
'handle errors
On Error GoTo WordError

'open Environment
Set rdoEn = rdoEnvironments(0)

'establish RDO Connection
With rdoCn
    .Connect = "UID=" & txtUID.Text & ";PWD=" & txtPWD.Text & ";Database=
    ➥Master;DSN=" & txtDSN.Text & ";Database=" & txtDB.Text & ";"
    .EstablishConnection rdDriverNoPrompt, True
    rdoEn.rdoConnections.Add rdoCn
End With

'change databases
rdoCn.Execute ("Use " & txtDB.Text)

'create query
With rdoQuery
    Set .ActiveConnection = rdoCn
    .Sql = txtSQL.Text
    .LockType = rdConcurReadOnly
    .RowsetSize = 1
    .CursorType = rdUseServer
End With

'open resultset for query
Set rdoRS = rdoQuery.OpenResultset(rdOpenStatic)

'first attempt to get the object if it is running
Set objWord = GetObject(CLASSOBJECT)

If objWord Is Nothing Then
    Set objWord = CreateObject(CLASSOBJECT)
End If

'add a new document
objWord.Documents.Add

'loop through names, if selected
If chkName.Value = 1 Then
    'initialize
    sLine = ""

    'loop through all columns, building line
    For nLoopCount = 0 To rdoRS.rdoColumns.Count - 1
        sLine = sLine & rdoRS.rdoColumns(nLoopCount).Name & ","
    Next nLoopCount

    'remove trailing comma
    sLine = Left$(sLine, Len(sLine) - 1)

    'insert text
    objWord.ActiveDocument.Content.InsertAfter (sLine & Chr$(13) & Chr$(10))

End If
```

```
    'loop through all rows in resultset
    Do While Not rdoRS.EOF
        'initialize
        sLine = ""

        'loop through all columns, building line
        For nLoopCount = 0 To rdoRS.rdoColumns.Count - 1
            sLine = sLine & rdoRS.rdoColumns(nLoopCount).Value & ","
        Next nLoopCount

        'remove trailing comma
        sLine = Left$(sLine, Len(sLine) - 1)

        'insert text
        objWord.ActiveDocument.Content.InsertAfter (sLine & Chr$(13) & Chr$(10))

        'move to the next record
        rdoRS.MoveNext
    Loop

    'make visible
    objWord.Visible = True

    'close the connection
    rdoCn.Close

    'change mouse
    Screen.MousePointer = vbDefault

    'exit - all was successful
    Exit Sub

WordError:
    If Err <> 432 And Err > 0 Then
        'change mouse
        Screen.MousePointer = vbDefault

        'display error
        MsgBox Error$

        'reclaim memory from object
        Set objWord = Nothing

        'exit
        Exit Sub
    Else
        'class was not found, attempt to create it
        Resume Next
    End If

End Sub
```

The first thing that happens in this code is that the necessary variables are declared. Notice that the `objWord` object is not declared as a generic object. It is explicitly declared like this:

```
Dim objWord As New Word.Application
```

This is to show that you can declare objects with late binding, such as in the cmdExcel_Click event, or early binding, as shown here. Next, the RDO environment is established, and the appropriate variables are assigned to establish a connection to the RDO data source.

After the connection is established, the Execute method is used to switch to the specified database. If this is not done, the query might not be executed in that database, and therefore might reference objects that do not exist in that database. After the database is changed, the query is executed and assigned to a ResultSet object.

Next, a reference to an existing Word.Basic object is attempted. If Word is not loaded, an error is produced. However, the error handler will simply Resume Next if this happens. This allows for the object to be created. After the object is created, a new document is added.

Then, if the Include Field Names check box is checked, the code loops through all columns in the ResultSet object and constructs one line of text containing these names, separated by commas. When finished, the trailing comma is removed. Next, the line is inserted with the OLE Automation method InsertAfter, like this:

```
objWord.ActiveDocument.Content.InsertAfter (sLine & Chr$(13) & Chr$(10))
```

Notice that there are carriage return and line feed characters appended to the end of the line.

Next, there is a loop within a loop, which is used to cycle through all of the rows in the ResultSet object. Within each row, the data for a column is concatenated to the line variable sLine. After all of the data is added, it is inserted with the OLE Automation method InsertAfter.

When all of the looping is finished, the Word document is made visible and the RDO connection is closed.

Summary

The application presented in this chapter showed how you can share data dynamically with Microsoft Excel and Microsoft Word. Microsoft makes this process very simple through OLE Automation. Each of these products exposes properties and methods that are callable in Visual Basic.

One of the most common ways to share data with Office is to export data from your application to Excel. Many users want this capability so that they can manipulate and view the data in a way which your application might not provide. This chapter showed you how to do this. In your applications, you could even take this one step further. You could give formatting options of which cells the data is to be placed. You could also give options for automatic subtotaling and formatting options. Because Office 97 exports nearly all of its functionality through OLE Automation, virtually anything that can be done in the Office products directly can be done via Visual Basic.

You could also enhance the functionality shown in the Word portion of the application by allowing for the automatic generation of letters or forms. Additionally, you could provide an interface for users to specify how those letters will be formatted. The main purpose of presenting the data in a common delimited format is to show how simple it is to "dump" data into Word. This could be useful in generating ASCII files of data.

Use this application as a basis for your own applications. You will find that most of the functionality in this application is common to many Office applications.

39

Creating a Wizard Add-In

Creating a wizard add-in (or wizard) is very easy in Visual Basic 5.0. The system guides you through the steps via the Wizard Manager. The Wizard Manager is not the only way to create a wizard, but it definitely is the easiest. This chapter focuses on using the Wizard Manager.

The Wizard Manager does not create any code other than the code necessary to create the add-in itself. In other words, the Wizard Manager will manage all code needed to select your wizard, but it will not create the code needed for the actual steps in the wizard.

The Wizard Manager itself is an add-in, and therefore is available only if you have selected it for use by using the Add-In Manager. To select it for use, start a new project, and choose Add-Ins | Add-In Manager. This brings up a dialog box that contains the list of add-ins available for selection. Click the VB Wizard Manager menu option, shown in Figure 39.1.

FIGURE 39.1.
Selecting the Wizard Manager.

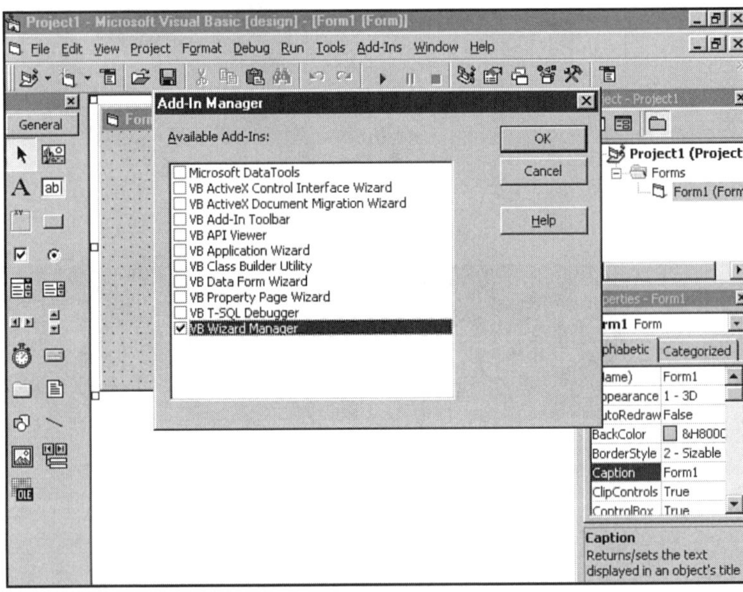

Click OK. This makes the add-in available in the Add-Ins menu. To activate the Wizard Manager, choose Add-Ins | Wizard Manager. The Wizard Manager is shown in Figure 39.2.

If this is the first time you are running the Wizard Manager for this project, you will be asked if you want to create a new wizard project. Choose Yes. This just means that the project must have a form named `frmWizard`. If a form with this name does not exist in the project, the Wizard Manager does not consider the project to be a "wizard" project. Figure 39.3 shows what this message box looks like.

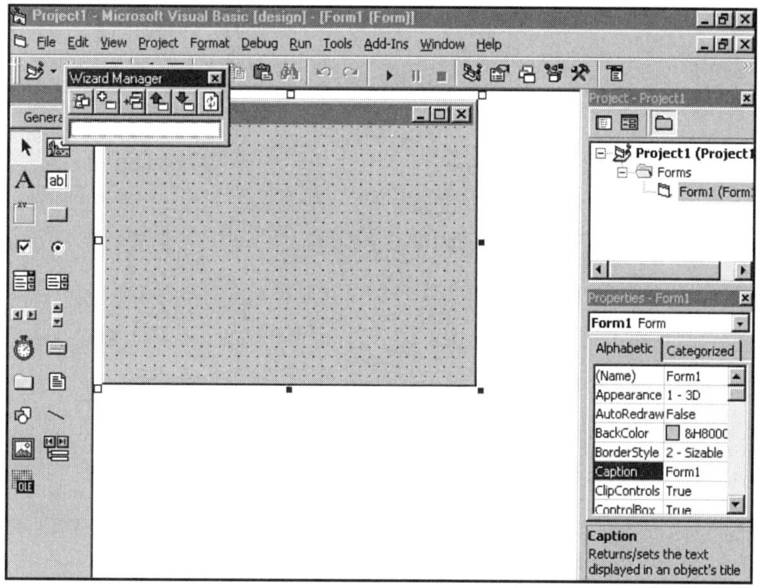

FIGURE 39.2.
The Wizard Manager.

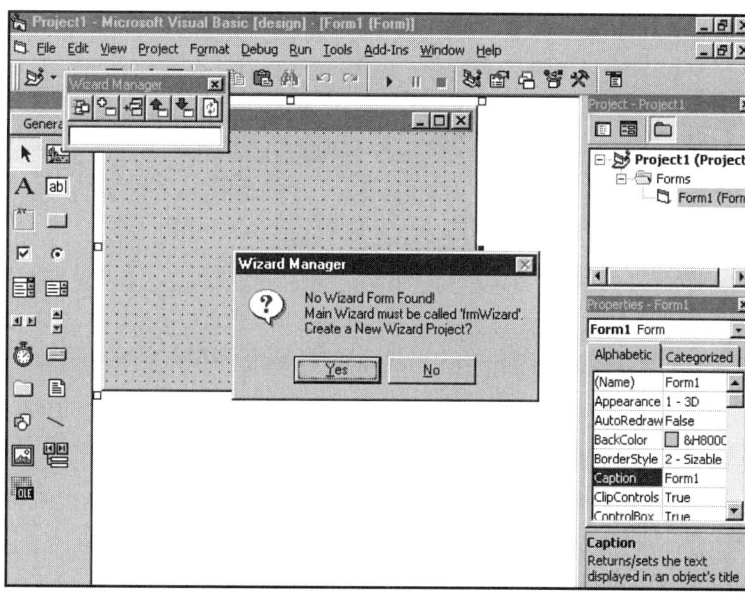

FIGURE 39.3.
Creating a wizard project.

Next, you will be prompted to save your project. The project shown in this chapter is on the CD-ROM accompanying this book in the `\Wizard` subdirectory.

After you have saved your project, a template for your wizard will be created. This wizard is initially created with four steps. Figure 39.4 shows these steps.

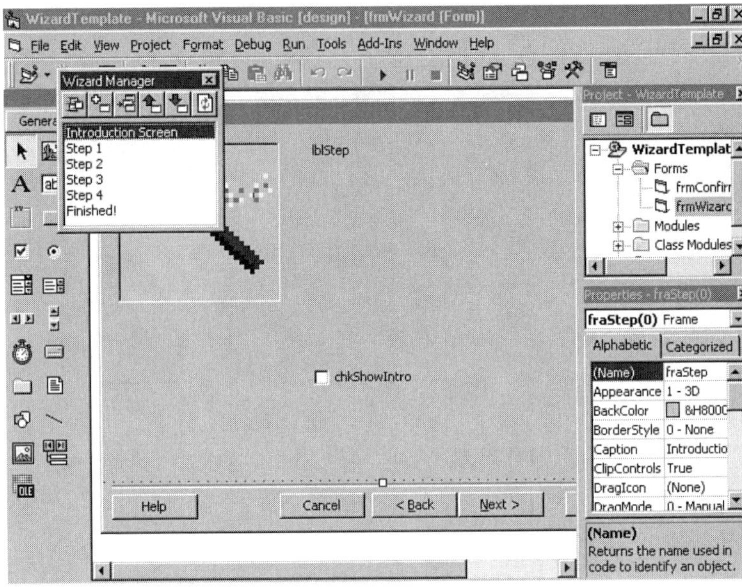

FIGURE 39.4.
Wizard blank template.

Not only did the wizard create the GUI for four steps, but it automatically created quite a bit of code, which is used to manage the add-in.

CROSS REFERENCE

For more information about add-ins, refer to Chapter 4, "Add-Ins."

The Wizard Manager created the following project components:

- `CONFIRM.FRM` (`frmConfirm`)
- `WIZARD.FRM` (`frmWizard`)
- `WIZARD.BAS` (`modWizard`)
- `WIZARD.CLS` (Wizard)
- `WIZARD.RES` (Wizard)

The `CONFIRM.FRM` file is used to confirm creation of the wizard when you click the Finish button (see Figure 39.5).

In addition to the form shown in Figure 39.5, Listing 39.1 shows the code automatically generated.

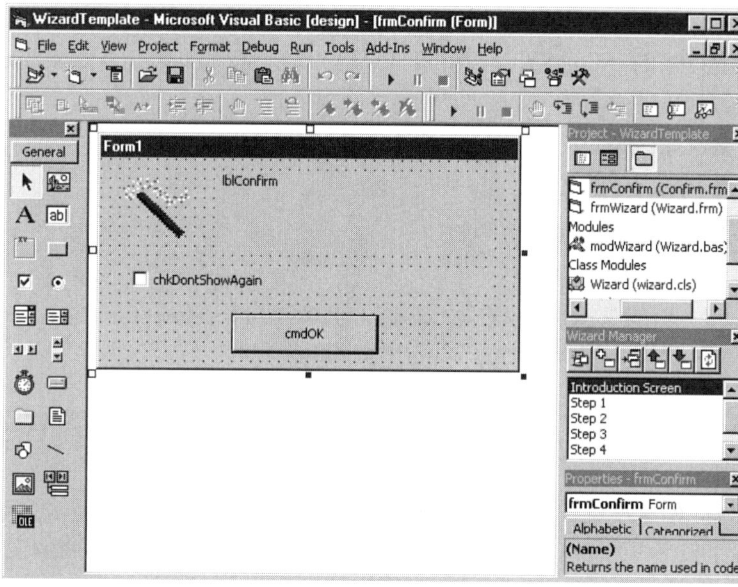

FIGURE 39.5.
The CONFIRM.FRM *file, showing the confirmation step of your wizard.*

Listing 39.1. Code that is automatically generated for CONFIRM.FRM.

```
Option Explicit

Const RES_CONFIRM_DLG = 2000

Dim msForm As String

Public Sub SetFormName(sData As String)
    msForm = sData
End Sub

Private Sub chkDontShowAgain_Click()
    On Error Resume Next

    If chkDontShowAgain.Value = vbChecked Then
        SaveSetting APP_CATEGORY, WIZARD_NAME, CONFIRM_KEY, DONTSHOW_CONFIRM
    Else
        SaveSetting APP_CATEGORY, WIZARD_NAME, CONFIRM_KEY, vbNullString
    End If

End Sub

Private Sub cmdOK_Click()
    Unload Me
End Sub

Private Sub Form_Load()
    LoadResStrings Me
    lblConfirm.Caption = ReplaceTopicTokens(LoadResString(RES_CONFIRM_DLG + 1),
    ➥ msForm, vbNullString)
End Sub
```

The `WIZARD.FRM` file is used to house the graphical interface for your wizard steps. It is, by default, comprised of the following controls:

- One image
- One line
- One label
- Five command buttons
- One check box

Each control is a control array used for all steps. Therefore, for all steps in your wizard, there is only one form. This form is shown in Figure 39.6.

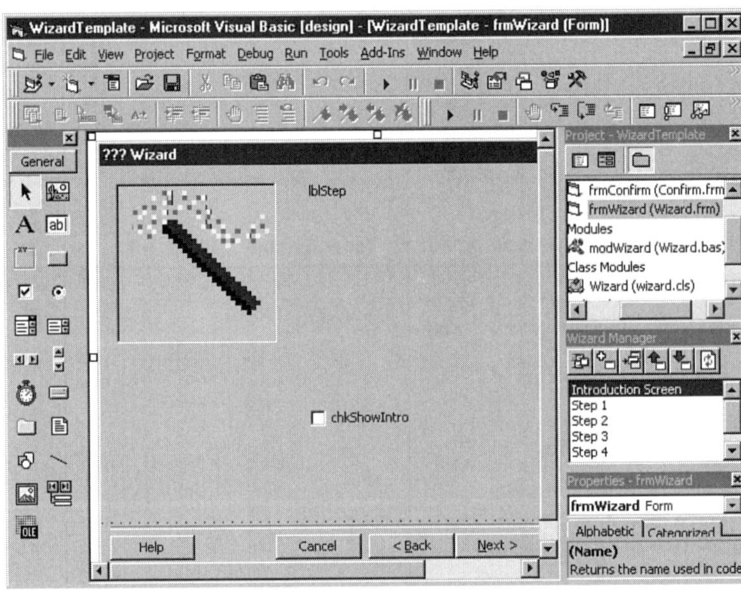

FIGURE 39.6.
The `WIZARD.FRM` *file, showing the form used for all wizard steps.*

In addition to the form shown in Figure 39.6, Listing 39.2 shows the code that is automatically generated.

Listing 39.2. Code that is automatically generated for `WIZARD.FRM`.

```
Option Explicit

Const NUM_STEPS = 6

Const RES_ERROR_MSG = 30000

'BASE VALUE FOR HELP FILE FOR THIS WIZARD:
Const HELP_BASE = 1000
Const HELP_FILE = "MYWIZARD.HLP"
```

```
Const BTN_HELP = 0
Const BTN_CANCEL = 1
Const BTN_BACK = 2
Const BTN_NEXT = 3
Const BTN_FINISH = 4

Const STEP_INTRO = 0
Const STEP_1 = 1
Const STEP_2 = 2
Const STEP_3 = 3
Const STEP_4 = 4
Const STEP_FINISH = 5

Const DIR_NONE = 0
Const DIR_BACK = 1
Const DIR_NEXT = 2

Const FRM_TITLE = "Blank Wizard"
Const INTRO_KEY = "IntroductionScreen"
Const SHOW_INTRO = "ShowIntro"
Const TOPIC_TEXT = "<TOPIC_TEXT>"

'module level vars
Dim mnCurStep       As Integer
Dim mbHelpStarted   As Boolean

Public VBInst       As VBIDE.VBE
Dim mbFinishOK      As Boolean

Private Sub chkShowIntro_Click()
    If chkShowIntro.Value Then
        SaveSetting APP_CATEGORY, WIZARD_NAME, INTRO_KEY, SHOW_INTRO
    Else
        SaveSetting APP_CATEGORY, WIZARD_NAME, INTRO_KEY, vbNullString
    End If
End Sub

Private Sub cmdNav_Click(Index As Integer)
    Dim nAltStep As Integer
    Dim lHelpTopic As Long
    Dim rc As Long

    Select Case Index
        Case BTN_HELP
            mbHelpStarted = True
            lHelpTopic = HELP_BASE + 10 * (1 + mnCurStep)
            rc = WinHelp(Me.hwnd, HELP_FILE, HELP_CONTEXT, lHelpTopic)

        Case BTN_CANCEL
            Unload Me

        Case BTN_BACK
            'place special cases here to jump
            'to alternate steps
            nAltStep = mnCurStep - 1
            SetStep nAltStep, DIR_BACK
```

continues

Listing 39.2. continued

```
        Case BTN_NEXT
            'place special cases here to jump
            'to alternate steps
            nAltStep = mnCurStep + 1
            SetStep nAltStep, DIR_NEXT

        Case BTN_FINISH
            'wizard creation code goes here

            Unload Me

            If GetSetting(APP_CATEGORY, WIZARD_NAME, CONFIRM_KEY, vbNullString)
            ➥ = vbNullString Then
                frmConfirm.Show vbModal
            End If

    End Select
End Sub

Private Sub Form_KeyDown(KeyCode As Integer, Shift As Integer)
    If KeyCode = vbKeyF1 Then
        cmdNav_Click BTN_HELP
    End If
End Sub

Private Sub Form_Load()
    Dim i As Integer
    'init all vars
    mbFinishOK = False

    For i = 0 To NUM_STEPS - 1
      fraStep(i).Left = -10000
    Next

    'Load All string info for Form
    LoadResStrings Me

    'Determine 1st Step:
    If GetSetting(APP_CATEGORY, WIZARD_NAME, INTRO_KEY, vbNullString) =
    ➥SHOW_INTRO Then
        chkShowIntro.Value = vbChecked
        SetStep 1, DIR_NEXT
    Else
        SetStep 0, DIR_NONE
    End If
End Sub

Private Sub SetStep(nStep As Integer, nDirection As Integer)

    Select Case nStep
        Case STEP_INTRO

        Case STEP_1

        Case STEP_2
```

```
        Case STEP_3

        Case STEP_4
            mbFinishOK = False

        Case STEP_FINISH
            mbFinishOK = True

    End Select

    'move to new step
    fraStep(mnCurStep).Enabled = False
    fraStep(nStep).Left = 0
    If nStep <> mnCurStep Then
        fraStep(mnCurStep).Left = -10000
    End If
    fraStep(nStep).Enabled = True

    SetCaption nStep
    SetNavBtns nStep

End Sub

Private Sub SetNavBtns(nStep As Integer)
    mnCurStep = nStep

    If mnCurStep = 0 Then
        cmdNav(BTN_BACK).Enabled = False
        cmdNav(BTN_NEXT).Enabled = True
    ElseIf mnCurStep = NUM_STEPS - 1 Then
        cmdNav(BTN_NEXT).Enabled = False
        cmdNav(BTN_BACK).Enabled = True
    Else
        cmdNav(BTN_BACK).Enabled = True
        cmdNav(BTN_NEXT).Enabled = True
    End If

    If mbFinishOK Then
        cmdNav(BTN_FINISH).Enabled = True
    Else
        cmdNav(BTN_FINISH).Enabled = False
    End If
End Sub

Private Sub SetCaption(nStep As Integer)
    On Error Resume Next

    Me.Caption = FRM_TITLE & " - " & LoadResString(fraStep(nStep).Tag)

End Sub

'=========================================================
'this sub displays an error message when the user has
'not entered enough data to continue
'=========================================================
Sub IncompleteData(nIndex As Integer)
    On Error Resume Next
```

continues

Listing 39.2. continued

```
    Dim sTmp As String

    'get the base error message
    sTmp = LoadResString(RES_ERROR_MSG)
    'get the specific message
    sTmp = sTmp & vbCrLf & LoadResString(RES_ERROR_MSG + nIndex)
    Beep
    MsgBox sTmp, vbInformation
End Sub

Private Sub Form_Unload(Cancel As Integer)
    On Error Resume Next
    Dim rc As Long
    'see if we need to save the settings
    If chkSaveSettings.Value = vbChecked Then

'        SaveSetting APP_CATEGORY, WIZARD_NAME, "OptionName", Option Value

    End If

    If mbHelpStarted Then rc = WinHelp(Me.hwnd, HELP_FILE, HELP_QUIT, 0)
End Sub
```

The `WIZARD.BAS` file is used to hold public (global) declarations and functions that the wizard needs. Listing 39.3 shows the code that is automatically generated for `WIZARD.BAS`.

Listing 39.3. Code that is automatically generated for `WIZARD.BAS`.

```
Option Explicit

Global Const WIZARD_NAME = "WizardTemplate"

Declare Function WritePrivateProfileString& Lib "Kernel32" Alias
➥"WritePrivateProfileStringA" (ByVal AppName$, ByVal KeyName$,
➥ByVal keydefault$, ByVal FileName$)

'WinHelp Commands
Declare Function WinHelp Lib "user32" Alias "WinHelpA" (ByVal hwnd As Long,
➥ByVal lpHelpFile As String, ByVal wCommand As Long,
➥ByVal dwData As Long) As Long
Public Const HELP_QUIT = &H2                  '  Terminate help
Public Const HELP_CONTENTS = &H3&             '  Display index/contents
Public Const HELP_CONTEXT = &H1               '  Display topic in ulTopic
Public Const HELP_INDEX = &H3                 '  Display index

Global Const APP_CATEGORY = "Wizards"

Global Const CONFIRM_KEY = "ConfirmScreen"
Global Const DONTSHOW_CONFIRM = "DontShow"
```

```
'-----------------------------------------------------------------------
'this sub must be executed from the  immediate window
'it will add the entry to VBADDIN.INI if it doesn't already exist
'so that the add-in is on available next time VB is loaded
'-----------------------------------------------------------------------
Sub AddToINI()
    Debug.Print WritePrivateProfileString("Add-Ins32", WIZARD_NAME & ".Wizard",
    ➥ "0", "VBADDIN.INI")
End Sub

Function GetResString(nRes As Integer) As String
    Dim sTmp As String
    Dim sRetStr As String

    Do
        sTmp = LoadResString(nRes)
        If Right(sTmp, 1) = "_" Then
            sRetStr = sRetStr + VBA.Left(sTmp, Len(sTmp) - 1)
        Else
            sRetStr = sRetStr + sTmp
        End If
        nRes = nRes + 1
    Loop Until Right(sTmp, 1) <> "_"
    GetResString = sRetStr

End Function

Function GetField(sBuffer As String, sSep As String) As String
    Dim p As Integer

    p = InStr(sBuffer & sSep, sSep)
    GetField = VBA.Left(sBuffer, p - 1)
    sBuffer = Mid(sBuffer, p + Len(sSep))

End Function

Sub LoadResStrings(frm As Form)
    On Error Resume Next

    Dim ctl As Control
    Dim obj As Object

    'set the form's caption
    If IsNumeric(frm.Tag) Then
        frm.Caption = LoadResString(CInt(frm.Tag))
    End If

    'set the controls' captions using the caption
    'property for menu items and the Tag property
    'for all other controls
    For Each ctl In frm.Controls
        If TypeName(ctl) = "Menu" Then
            If IsNumeric(ctl.Caption) Then
                If Err = 0 Then
                    ctl.Caption = LoadResString(CInt(ctl.Caption))
                Else
```

continues

Listing 39.3. continued

```
                Err = 0
            End If
        End If
    ElseIf TypeName(ctl) = "TabStrip" Then
        For Each obj In ctl.Tabs
            If IsNumeric(obj.Tag) Then
                obj.Caption = LoadResString(CInt(obj.Tag))
            End If
            'check for a tooltip
            If IsNumeric(obj.ToolTipText) Then
                If Err = 0 Then
                    obj.ToolTipText = LoadResString(CInt(obj.ToolTipText))
                Else
                    Err = 0
                End If
            End If
        Next
    ElseIf TypeName(ctl) = "Toolbar" Then
        For Each obj In ctl.Buttons
            If IsNumeric(obj.Tag) Then
                obj.ToolTipText = LoadResString(CInt(obj.Tag))
            End If
        Next
    ElseIf TypeName(ctl) = "ListView" Then
        For Each obj In ctl.ColumnHeaders
            If IsNumeric(obj.Tag) Then
                obj.Text = LoadResString(CInt(obj.Tag))
            End If
        Next
    Else
        If IsNumeric(ctl.Tag) Then
            If Err = 0 Then
                ctl.Caption = LoadResString(CInt(ctl.Tag))
            Else
                Err = 0
            End If
        End If
        'check for a tooltip
        If IsNumeric(ctl.ToolTipText) Then
            If Err = 0 Then
                ctl.ToolTipText = LoadResString(CInt(ctl.ToolTipText))
            Else
                Err = 0
            End If
        End If
    End If
Next

End Sub

'=======================================================
'Purpose: Replace the <TOPIC_TEXT> string(s) in
'         res file string for correct placement
'         of localized tokens
'
```

```
'Inputs:  sString = String to search and replace in
'         sReplacement = String to replace token with
'         sReplacement2 = 2nd String to replace token with
'
'Outputs: New string with token replaced throughout
'==================================================
Function ReplaceTopicTokens(sString As String, _
                            sReplacement As String, _
                            sReplacement2 As String) As String
    On Error Resume Next

    Dim p As Integer
    Dim sTmp As String

    Const TOPIC_TEXT = "<TOPIC_TEXT>"
    Const TOPIC_TEXT2 = "<TOPIC_TEXT2>"

    sTmp = sString
    Do
        p = InStr(sTmp, TOPIC_TEXT)
        If p Then
            sTmp = VBA.Left(sTmp, p - 1) + sReplacement + Mid(sTmp, p +
            ➥Len(TOPIC_TEXT))
        End If
    Loop While p

    If Len(sReplacement2) > 0 Then
        Do
            p = InStr(sTmp, TOPIC_TEXT2)
            If p Then
                sTmp = VBA.Left(sTmp, p - 1) + sReplacement2 +
                ➥Mid(sTmp, p + Len(TOPIC_TEXT2))
            End If
        Loop While p
    End If

    ReplaceTopicTokens = sTmp

End Function

Public Function GetResData(sResName As String, sResType As String) As String
    Dim sTemp As String
    Dim p As Integer

    sTemp = StrConv(LoadResData(sResName, sResType), vbUnicode)
    p = InStr(sTemp, vbNullChar)
    If p Then sTemp = VBA.Left$(sTemp, p - 1)
    GetResData = sTemp
End Function

Function AddToAddInCommandBar(VBInst As Object, sCaption As String,
➥oBitmap As Object) As Object   'Office.CommandBarControl
    On Error GoTo AddToAddInCommandBarErr

    Dim c As Integer
    Dim cbMenuCommandBar As Object 'command bar object
    Dim cbMenu As Object
```

continues

Listing 39.3 continued

```
    'see if we can find the Add-Ins menu
    Set cbMenu = VBInst.CommandBars(1).Controls(9)
    If cbMenu Is Nothing Then
        'not available so we fail
        Exit Function
    End If

    'add it to the command bar
    Set cbMenuCommandBar = cbMenu.CommandBar.Controls.Add(1)
    c = cbMenu.CommandBar.Controls.Count - 1
    If cbMenu.CommandBar.Controls(c).BeginGroup And _
        Not cbMenu.CommandBar.Controls(c - 1).BeginGroup Then
        'this s the first addin being added so it needs a separator
        cbMenuCommandBar.BeginGroup = True
    End If
    'set the caption
    cbMenuCommandBar.Caption = sCaption
    'undone:set the onaction (required at this point)
    cbMenuCommandBar.OnAction = "hello"
    'copy the icon to the clipboard
    Clipboard.SetData oBitmap
    'set the icon for the button
    cbMenuCommandBar.PasteFace

    Set AddToAddInCommandBar = cbMenuCommandBar

    Exit Function
AddToAddInCommandBarErr:

End Function
```

The `WIZARD.CLS` file is the class module used as the wizard itself. It is instantiated when the wizard is selected in the Add-In menu. Listing 39.4 shows the code that is automatically generated for `WIZARD.CLS`.

Listing 39.4. Code that is automatically generated for `WIZARD.CLS`.

```
Option Explicit

Implements IDTExtensibility

Dim mcbMenuCommandBar         As Office.CommandBarControl  'command bar object
Public WithEvents MenuHandler As CommandBarEvents  'command bar event handler
Dim mfrmWizard As frmWizard
Dim VBInstance As VBIDE.VBE


'------------------------------------------------------
'this method adds the Add-In to the VB menu
'it is called by the VB addin manager
'------------------------------------------------------
```

```
Private Sub IDTExtensibility_OnConnection(ByVal VBInst As Object,
➥ByVal LoadMode As vbext_ConnectMode, ByVal AddInInst As VBIDE.AddIn,
➥custom() As Variant)
   On Error GoTo error_handler

   Set VBInstance = VBInst

   If LoadMode = vbext_cm_External Then
       'Used by the wizard toolbar to start this wizard
       LoadMe
   Else
       Set mcbMenuCommandBar = AddToAddInCommandBar(VBInst, LoadResString(15),
       ➥ LoadResPicture(5000, 0))
       'sink the event
       Set Me.MenuHandler = VBInst.Events.CommandBarEvents(mcbMenuCommandBar)
   End If

   Exit Sub

error_handler:
   MsgBox Err.Description
End Sub

'------------------------------------------------------
'this method removes the Add-In from the VB menu
'it is called by the VB addin manager
'------------------------------------------------------
Private Sub IDTExtensibility_OnDisconnection(ByVal RemoveMode As
➥vbext_DisconnectMode, custom() As Variant)
    'delete the command bar entry
    mcbMenuCommandBar.Delete
End Sub

Private Sub IDTExtensibility_OnStartupComplete(custom() As Variant)
  'stub needed
End Sub

Private Sub IDTExtensibility_OnAddInsUpdate(custom() As Variant)
  'stub needed
End Sub

'this event fires when the menu is clicked in the IDE
Private Sub MenuHandler_Click(ByVal CommandBarControl As Object,
➥handled As Boolean, CancelDefault As Boolean)
    LoadMe
End Sub

Private Sub LoadMe()
    Set mfrmWizard = New frmWizard
    'pass the vb instance to the wizard module
    Set mfrmWizard.VBInst = VBInstance
    'load and show the form
    mfrmWizard.Show vbModal
    Set mfrmWizard = Nothing
End Sub
```

The code in Listing 39.4 uses a class module to handle the events contained within the add-in. When the user checks the add-in from the Add-In manager, the `On_Connection()` event is automatically fired. This is where any initialization code is placed. When the user unchecks the add-in from the Add-In Manager, the `On_Disconnection()` event is automatically fired. This allows for any clean up of variables. The `Click()` event for the menu handler is automatically fired when the user clicks the desired add-in.

CROSS REFERENCE

For more information about these events, refer to Chapter 4, "Add-Ins."

The `WIZARD.RES` file is compiled from the `WIZARD.RC` file. The `WIZARD.RC` file is used as the "source code" for the resource compiler. Listing 39.5 shows the source code automatically generated for the `WIZARD.RC` file. Next, this file needs to be compiled into the `WIZARD.RES` file for inclusion into the Visual Basic project. The `WIZARD.RC` file can be compiled using the resource compiler built into Visual C++ or the resource compiler that comes with Visual Basic. The resource compiler, `RC.EXE`, is placed by default in the `C:\Program Files\DevStudio\VB\Wizards` subdirectory upon setup of Visual Basic.

Listing 39.5. Source code that is automatically generated for `WIZARD.RC`.

```
STRINGTABLE DISCARDABLE
BEGIN
        //Wizard Caption
        10          "Wizard Template"
        15          "Wizard Template..."

        //Button Captions for Navigation Control:
        100         "Help"
        101         "Cancel"
        102         "< &Back"
        103         "&Next >"
        104         "&Finish"

        //Intro Info:
        1000        "Introduction"
        1001        "The ??? Wizard will help you ..."
        1002        "&Skip this screen in the future."

        //Other Step Control Captions:
        2000        "Step 1"
        2001        "Instructions for this step."
        2002        "Step 2"
        2003        "Instructions for this step."
        2004        "Step 3"
        2005        "Instructions for this step."
        2006        "Step 4"
        2007        "Instructions for this step."
```

```
        //Finish Step:
        3000        "Finished!"
        3001        "The ??? Wizard is finished collecting information.\r\n\r\n_"
        3002        "To build your ???, press Finish!"
        3003        "Save current settings as default"

        //Confirmation dialog
        10000       "??? Created"
        10001       "The ??? has been created."
        10002       "Don't show this dialog in the future."
        10003       "OK"

        //Misc strings:
        20000       "(None)"

        //Error messages:
        30000       "Incomplete Data."
        30001       "You must ... before you can continue."

         5000    BITMAP     wizmenu.bmp
END
```

The resource compiler is a DOS-based program that compiles the `WIZARD.RC` file into the `WIZARD.RES` file. To use it, go to the DOS prompt and change the directory to the one that contains `RC.EXE`. Then type

```
RC path\WIZARD.RC
```

where *`path`* is the path that contains the `WIZARD.RC` file.

The `RC.EXE` program can also accept other command-line arguments. These arguments can be obtained by typing `RC/?` at the command prompt (see Figure 39.7).

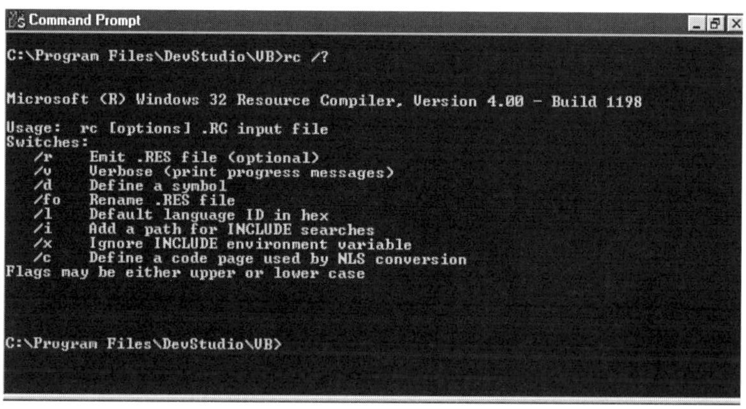

FIGURE 39.7.
Resource compiler arguments.

When you are finished compiling the `WIZARD.RES` file, it will contain a default string table used to display errors and the strings for your wizard steps. Placing the strings in a string table makes it possible to localize your application. This means that you can change the strings for different languages. It also contains a default bitmap used for your steps.

Customizing the Wizard

Now that you have created the wizard template, it is time to customize the wizard. You need to know what you want the wizard to do. For example, suppose the forms in all of your applications have the same look and feel (as they should). However, you know that your organization will use only certain fonts, sizes for command buttons, and so on. You could design a wizard so that other developers have to answer only a few questions when they create new forms.

For the rest of this wizard example, the ultimate goal is to create a form that looks like the one in Figure 39.8 and to mimic the functionality of the Data Form Designer. This way you can customize it to suit your organization's needs and use its standards.

FIGURE 39.8.
The goal of the wizard.

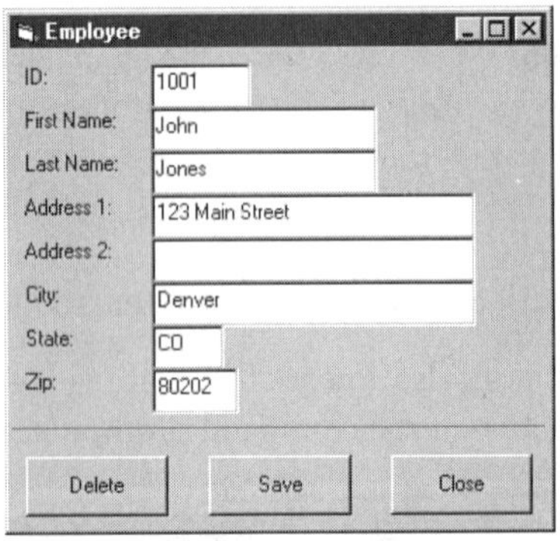

Now let's create the wizard. First, you need to think of the wizard in logical steps. You can do this by thinking about the items that the developer can change. In our example, the steps will be as follows:

- Introduction. (This step is not considered the "first" step.)
- Step 1: Database Selection.
- Step 2: Field Selection.
- Finish. (This step is not considered "Step 3.")

The following sections show how you can create such a wizard. Most of the steps are divided into two sections:

- GUI design
- Code

You might want to test each step. To test each step, follow the instructions in the next section.

Testing Each Step

To test each step, you must follow these steps:

1. Compile the resource file, if anything was changed.
2. Run the project.
3. Register the wizard in the `VBADDIN.INI` file.
4. Start another instance of Visual Basic.
5. Select the add-in for use in the Add-In Manager.
6. Choose the add-in itself.

To compile the resource file, use the `RC.EXE` program, as described earlier. Next, run the project. You will see no visible interface because there is no starting form or `Sub Main()` as the startup form. If this is the first time you are running the wizard, you must register it in the `VBADDIN.INI` file to make it available for testing by selecting it in the Add-In Manager. The code for registering it is built into the project. You can run it from the Debug window. First, you must put Visual Basic into pause mode by selecting the pause icon or by selecting the Ctrl+Break key combination. Then, in the debug window, type `AddToINI`.

This routine has already been placed in the `WIZARD.BAS` file. When the add-in is registered, start another instance of Visual Basic. Then, select Add-Ins | Add-In Manager to bring up a list of available add-ins. These add-ins are either registered in the Registry or are currently running. Choose the Wizard Template option, which is the name of the wizard automatically generated by the Wizard Manager. Figure 39.9 shows what the Add-In Manager looks like, with the wizard selected.

Next, choose Add-Ins | Wizard Template. This will start the wizard. Use this technique to test each step below. If you recompile the `WIZARD.RES` file, you do not need to reload your wizard project. It will automatically be used.

There are times when you have a lot of code to test and it is too lengthy a process to perform all the steps listed. In this case, you can change the project type to a standard EXE. Do this by selecting Project | Properties. Next, select the startup form as `frmWizard`, and then you simply run and test your project.

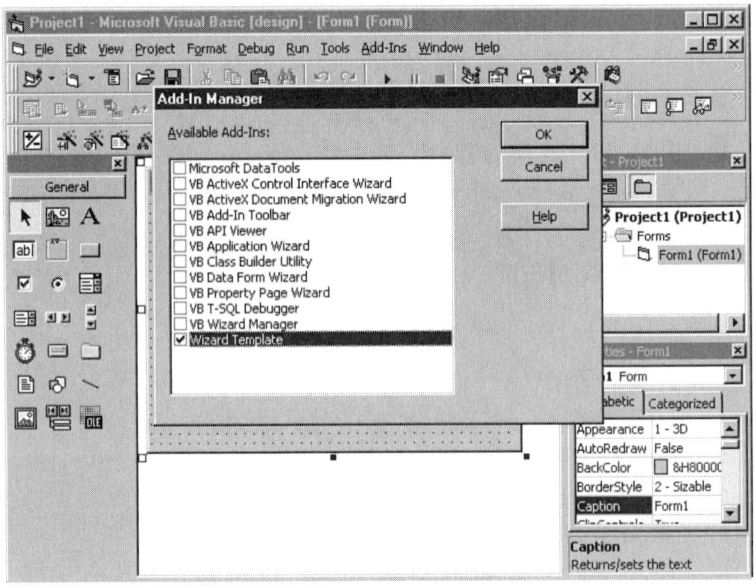

FIGURE 39.9.
Selecting the wizard using the Add-In Manager.

Introduction

This step simply indicates what the wizard will do. This step is basically created automatically by the Wizard Manager. Please note that this step is not actually called "Step 1" because the user can option not to show this step again in the future. If the user does this and it is called Step 1, then next time the wizard would start at Step 2. This would be misleading. Therefore, the introduction is not considered to be Step 1, but rather the "Introduction" step. To view this step, click the Introduction list box item in the Wizard Manager.

GUI Design

To design the GUI, you really need to change only the bitmap, if you want. For the sake of example, leave the bitmap. You can change it in your application if you want. Therefore, the only visual component that must change is the caption of the label control. The caption is stored in the `WIZARD.RC` file. Change the caption from Listing 39.5 to this:

```
1001       "The Form Wizard will help you to design forms, based on the
➥corporate standard."
```

Test this string by following the steps outlined in the section "Testing Each Step," earlier in the chapter. Figure 39.10 shows the results of customizing this step.

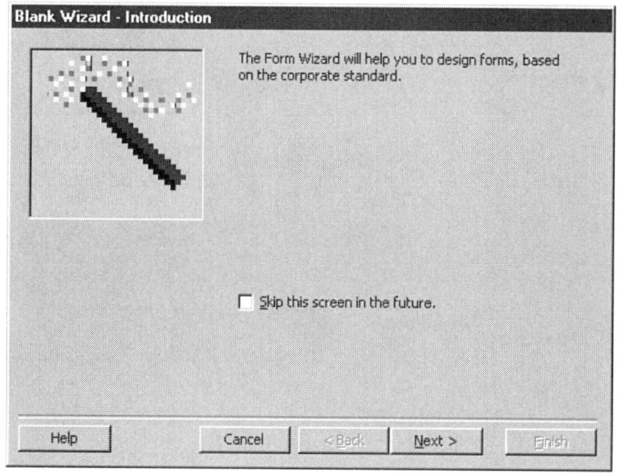

FIGURE 39.10.
The results of customizing the Introduction step.

Step 1: Selecting the Database

This step is used to select a database and table from which you will build the form. To view this step, click the Step 1 list box item in the Wizard Manager.

GUI Design

The GUI design of this step needs to include these four items:

- A label showing the name of the selected database (`lblDB`)
- A common dialog box to select a database (`dlgCommon`)
- A command button to invoke a common dialog box (`cmdSelect`)
- A list box to choose the tables from the database (`lstTable`)

Rename all controls to the names shown in parentheses. Then, make sure the `Caption` property of the label control is blank. Also, change the command button caption to "cmdSelect...". Then, change the `Custom` property of the common dialog box to assign the properties as shown in Figure 39.11.

You also need to change the string resource table in the `WIZARD.RC` file to add an appropriate description of the step:

```
2001       "Open an Access Database and select a table from which a form will
➥be built."
```

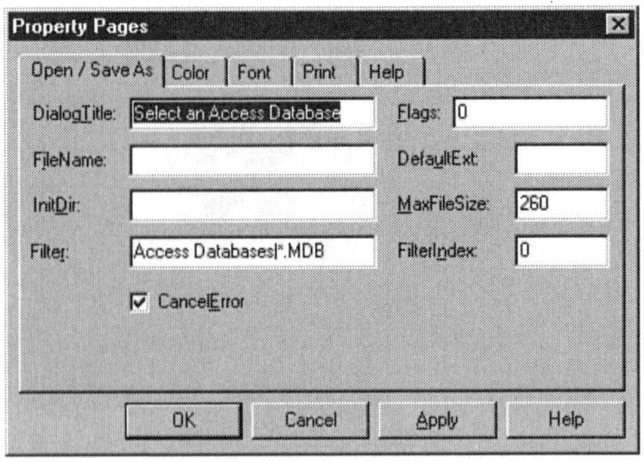

FIGURE 39.11.
The common dialog box `Custom` *settings.*

Code

The code for this step is quite easy. It incorporates techniques discussed throughout this book. The first thing to do is to declare a global database variable to enable users to access the database opened in this step. Place this line of code in the BAS module:

```
Global gdbDatabase As Database
```

Now, it is time to code the events associated with the controls placed on the form at design time. Most of the code is placed in the `Click` event of the cmdSelect command button. Listing 39.6 shows the code for this event.

Listing 39.6. The `cmdSelect_Click()` event code.

```
Private Sub cmdSelect_Click()

    'declare variables
    Dim nLoopCount As Integer

    'handle errors
    On Error GoTo dlgError

    'open common dialog
    dlgCommon.ShowOpen

    'display database
    lblDB.Caption = dlgCommon.FileName

    'open database
    Set gdbDatabase = Workspaces(0).OpenDatabase(dlgCommon.FileName)

    'initialize
    lstTable.Clear
    cmdNav(BTN_NEXT).Enabled = False

    'populate tables
    For nLoopCount = 0 To gdbDatabase.TableDefs.Count - 1
        If gdbDatabase.TableDefs(nLoopCount).Attributes = 0 Then
            'this is not a system table
```

```
            lstTable.AddItem gdbDatabase.TableDefs(nLoopCount).Name
        End If
    Next nLoopCount

    Exit Sub

dlgError:

    'blank out displays
    lblDB.Caption = ""
    lstTable.Clear

    If Err = cdlCancel Then
        'user cancelled
        Exit Sub
    Else
        MsgBox Error$
    End If
End Sub
```

This code shows a common dialog box being called that is used to open the database in the following line. When the database is opened, the list box is populated with a list of tables from that database. Note that only user-added tables are populated. No system tables are populated.

Only when a table is selected in the list box will the Next button become enabled. Here is the code for the `lstTable` list box `Click` event:

```
cmdNav(BTN_NEXT).Enabled = True
lblTable.Caption = "Selected Table: " & lstTable.Text
```

The second line of code enables the next step (shown later) to display the table selected when the fields for that table are listed.

There is one final bit of code: The wizard will automatically call a subroutine called `SetNavBtns` when a step is entered. It passes in one argument, `(nStep As Integer)`, which is the step currently being entered. This way you can initialize the step before it is shown. In this step, it is important not to enable the Next button until the table is selected. Listing 39.7 shows the code required for this. Note the branch for `mnCurStep = 1`.

Listing 39.7. The code for `SetNavButtons`.

```
If mnCurStep = 0 Then
    cmdNav(BTN_BACK).Enabled = False
    cmdNav(BTN_NEXT).Enabled = True
ElseIf mnCurStep = 1 Then
    cmdNav(BTN_BACK).Enabled = True
    If lstTable.SelCount = 0 Then
        cmdNav(BTN_NEXT).Enabled = False
    Else
        cmdNav(BTN_NEXT).Enabled = True
    End If
```

continues

Listing 39.7. continued

```
ElseIf mnCurStep = NUM_STEPS - 1 Then
    cmdNav(BTN_NEXT).Enabled = False
    cmdNav(BTN_BACK).Enabled = True
Else
    cmdNav(BTN_BACK).Enabled = True
    cmdNav(BTN_NEXT).Enabled = True
End If
```

Figure 39.12 shows the results, at runtime, after customizing Step 1.

FIGURE 39.12.

The results of customizing Step 1: Selecting the Database.

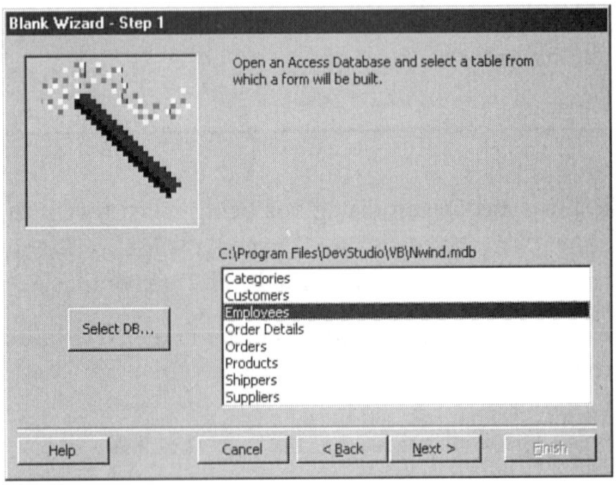

Step 2: Selecting the Fields

This step is used to select the fields from the table in the previous step from which to create the form. To view this step, click the Step 2 list box item in the Wizard Manager.

GUI Design

The GUI design of this step needs to include these two items:

- A label showing the name of the selected table (`lblTable`)
- A list box to choose the fields from the table (`lstField`)

Rename both of the controls so that they have the names shown in parentheses. Then, make sure the `Caption` property of the label control is blank. If you want to be able to select multiple fields, you need to change the `MultiSelect` property of the list box to "2 - Extended."

You also need to change the string resource table in the `WIZARD.RC` file to add an appropriate description of the step:

```
2003       "Select the field(s) you wish to display on the form."
```

Code

Very little code is required in this step. The code basically needs to populate the list of available fields within the table selected in the earlier step. First, it populates the fields when the user clicks the Next button from Step 1. This is done in the `SetNavBtns` subroutine. This could have been done in the previous step when the user clicks the table itself, but then, if the user clicks a different table, he or she has to wait until the fields populate. It is better to populate the fields only when they are needed. Therefore, you need to add a branch in the `SetNavBtns` subroutine for Step 2, as shown in Listing 39.8.

Listing 39.8. `SetNavButtons` code.

```
ElseIf mnCurStep = 2 Then
    'change mouse
    Screen.MousePointer = vbHourglass

    'populate fields for database
    lstField.Clear

    For nLoopCount = 0 To gdbDatabase.TableDefs(lstTable.Text).Fields.Count - 1
        lstField.AddItem gdbDatabase.TableDefs(lstTable.Text).Fields
        ➥(nLoopCount).Name
    Next nLoopCount

    cmdNav(BTN_NEXT).Enabled = False

    'change mouse
    Screen.MousePointer = vbDefault
```

Also, you need to take care of enabling the Next button. You do so in the `Click()` event for the `lstField` list box. Listing 39.9 shows what this event code looks like.

Listing 39.9. Code for `lstField_Click()`.

```
Private Sub lstField_Click()
    If lstField.SelCount > 0 Then
        cmdNav(BTN_NEXT).Enabled = True
    Else
        cmdNav(BTN_NEXT).Enabled = False
    End If
End Sub
```

Figure 39.13 shows the results, at runtime, after customizing Step 2.

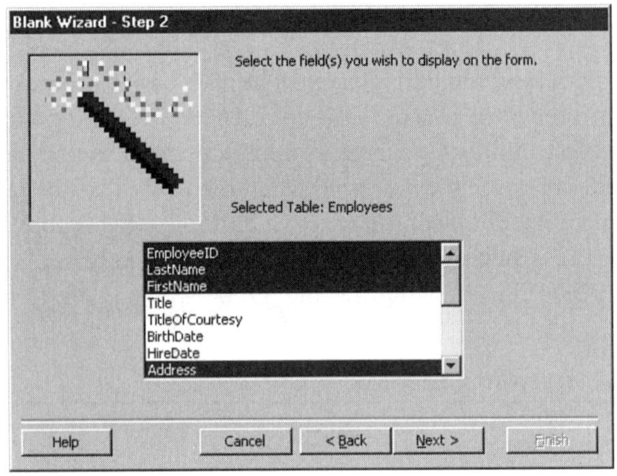

FIGURE 39.13.
The results of customizing Step 2: Selecting the Fields.

Finish Step

The finish step is used to display summary information and to enable the Finish button. The wizard actually performs the appropriate action when the Finish button is pressed because all appropriate information has been collected by this time. To view this step, click the Finished! list box item in the Wizard Manager.

GUI Design

In this example, nothing needs to be placed on the form. However, you will need to change the string resource table in the `WIZARD.RC` file to add an appropriate description of the step:

```
3001        "The Form Wizard is finished collecting information.\r\n\r\n_"
3002        "To build your Form, press Finish!"
```

The other thing you might want to do is remove Steps 3 and 4. You do this by selecting the appropriate step in the Wizard Manager and clicking the right mouse button. Now, select the Delete option. This will remove the step.

Code

Because you removed the code in the prior step, you need to remove references to the removed steps. Otherwise, the steps will not behave as you expect. You need to change the code in the `(general)(declarations)` section of the `WIZARD.FRM` from this:

```
Const STEP_INTRO = 0
Const STEP_1 = 1
Const STEP_2 = 2
Const STEP_3 = 3
Const STEP_4 = 4
Const STEP_FINISH = 5
```

to this:

```
Const STEP_INTRO = 0
Const STEP_1 = 1
Const STEP_2 = 2
Const STEP_FINISH = 3
```

You also need to change the reference to these steps in the `SetStep` subroutine in the `WIZARD.FRM` form from this:

```
Select Case nStep
        Case STEP_INTRO

        Case STEP_1

        Case STEP_2

        Case STEP_3

        Case STEP_4
            mbFinishOK = False

        Case STEP_FINISH
            mbFinishOK = True

    End Select
```

to this:

```
Select Case nStep
        Case STEP_INTRO

        Case STEP_1

        Case STEP_2
            mbFinishOK = False

        Case STEP_FINISH
            mbFinishOK = True

    End Select
```

The majority of the code required in this step is needed to create the form. Therefore, you need to build a subroutine called `BuildForm()`. This subroutine is called from the `cmdNav_Click()` event when the Finish button is clicked. The section of code for the Finish button in the `cmdNav_Click()` event is shown in Listing 39.10.

Listing 39.10. The `cmdNav_Click()` event code—Finish button case.

```
Case BTN_FINISH
            'wizard creation code goes here

            'Change Mouse
            Screen.MousePointer = vbHourglass
```

continues

Listing 39.10. continued

```
            Call BuildForm

            Unload Me

            'Change Mouse
            Screen.MousePointer = vbDefault

            If GetSetting(APP_CATEGORY, WIZARD_NAME, CONFIRM_KEY, vbNullString)
            ➥ = vbNullString Then
                frmConfirm.Show
            End If
```

Next, you need to create the `BuildForm()` routine. This routine uses the extensibility model to create the form and place the fields on the form according to the questions answered. For this to work, you need to reference the Extensibility library. To do this, select the Project | References menu option, and then select the Microsoft Visual Basic 5.0 Extensibility item. The Extensibility reference is an object library installed automatically when you set up Visual Basic. The Extensibility library, often called the Extensibility model, is a model that gives an add-in the capability to extend Visual Basic. Listing 39.11 shows the `BuildForm()` routine.

Listing 39.11. The code for `BuildForm()`.

```
Public Sub BuildForm()

    'this routine builds the form according to the

    'declare variables
    Dim objForm As VBComponent
    Dim nLoopCount As Integer
    Dim nFound As Integer
    Dim vbf As VBForm
    Dim nTop As Integer
    Dim nStartLeft As Integer
    Const HORFACTOR = 300
    Const VERTFACTOR = 100
    Const NUMBUTTONS = 2
    Const BUTTONWIDTH = 1260

    'add a new form
    VBInstance.ActiveVBProject.VBComponents.Add (vbext_ct_VBForm)

    'set a reference to the new form
    Set objForm = VBInstance.ActiveVBProject.VBComponents(VBInstance.
    ➥ActiveVBProject.VBComponents.Count)

    'set properties of the form
    For nLoopCount = 1 To VBInstance.ActiveVBProject.VBComponents.Count
        If VBInstance.ActiveVBProject.VBComponents(nLoopCount).Name =
        ➥"AutomaticForm" Then
            nFound = True
            Exit For
        End If
```

```
 Next nLoopCount

 If nFound = False Then
     'this form was not found, rename it
     objForm.Name = "AutomaticForm"
     objForm.Properties("Caption") = "Automatically Generated Form"
 Else
     'activate the form
     Set objForm = VBInstance.ActiveVBProject.VBComponents("AutomaticForm")
 End If

 'set designer
 Set vbf = objForm.Designer

'define default form size
objForm.Properties("Width") = 4000
objForm.Properties("Height") = 7000

'initialize
nTop = 300

 'add the fields to the form
 For nLoopCount = 0 To mfrmWizard.lstField.ListCount - 1
     If mfrmWizard.lstField.Selected(nLoopCount) = True Then
          'this field is used

          If objForm.Type = vbext_ct_VBForm Then

               'add the Label
               vbf.VBControls.Add ("Label")

               'change the caption of the label
               vbf.VBControls.Item(vbf.VBControls.Count).Properties("Caption")
               ➥= mfrmWizard.lstField.List(nLoopCount)

               'change the position of the label
               vbf.VBControls.Item(vbf.VBControls.Count).
               ➥Properties("Left") = 120
               vbf.VBControls.Item(vbf.VBControls.Count).
               ➥Properties("Top") = nTop

               'add the Text box
               vbf.VBControls.Add ("TextBox")

               'change the text of the textbox
               vbf.VBControls.Item(vbf.VBControls.Count).
               ➥Properties("Text") = ""

               'change the position of the textbox
               vbf.VBControls.Item(vbf.VBControls.Count).
               ➥Properties("Left") = 1560
               vbf.VBControls.Item(vbf.VBControls.Count).
               ➥Properties("Top") = nTop
               nTop = nTop + 500
          End If
     End If
```

continues

Listing 39.11. continued

```
    Next nLoopCount

   'compute nStartLeft
   nStartLeft = (objForm.Properties("ScaleWidth") - ((NUMBUTTONS * BUTTONWIDTH)
   ➥+ ((NUMBUTTONS - 1) * HORFACTOR))) / 2

   'add command buttons
    vbf.VBControls.Add ("CommandButton")
    vbf.VBControls.Item(vbf.VBControls.Count).Properties("Caption") = "&Save"
    vbf.VBControls.Item(vbf.VBControls.Count).Properties("Top") = objForm.
    ➥Properties("ScaleHeight") - vbf.VBControls.Item(vbf.VBControls.
    ➥Count).Properties("Height") - VERTFACTOR
    vbf.VBControls.Item(vbf.VBControls.Count).Properties("Width") = BUTTONWIDTH
    vbf.VBControls.Item(vbf.VBControls.Count).Properties("Left") = nStartLeft

    vbf.VBControls.Add ("CommandButton")
    vbf.VBControls.Item(vbf.VBControls.Count).Properties("Caption") = "&Close"
    vbf.VBControls.Item(vbf.VBControls.Count).Properties("Top") = objForm.
    ➥Properties("ScaleHeight") - vbf.VBControls.
    ➥Item(vbf.VBControls.Count).Properties("Height") - VERTFACTOR
    vbf.VBControls.Item(vbf.VBControls.Count).Properties("Width") = BUTTONWIDTH
    vbf.VBControls.Item(vbf.VBControls.Count).Properties("Left") =
    ➥nStartLeft + BUTTONWIDTH + HORFACTOR

    'insert code for close Button (Command2)
    objForm.CodeModule.InsertLines 2, ""
    objForm.CodeModule.InsertLines 3, "Private Sub Command2_Click()"
    objForm.CodeModule.InsertLines 4, "    Unload AutomaticForm"
    objForm.CodeModule.InsertLines 5, "End Sub"

End Sub
```

To follow the code, it is a good idea to look at the object model diagram in Chapter 4. The first thing that is done is that a new form is added. This is made possible because of the `VBInstance` variable. This is set automatically when the add-in is connected, via the `OnConnection` event. Then a reference, `objForm`, is assigned to the new form.

After a reference is added, the code loops through all available forms in the project to see if one is named AutomaticForm. If there is not one with this name, then the name and caption are changed. If it does exist, a new reference to `objForm` is set to the existing form. Now you can start manipulating the controls on the form.

To start adding controls to the form, it is necessary to invoke the `Designer` method for the form. When this is done, the `Add` method can be used to add controls of a certain class type. The form itself is then resized.

For this add-in to add controls to the form, it needs to query the result of what the user chose for tables in the prior wizard step. Therefore, the list of items in the list box is traversed, and, if a selected item is found, a label and a text box are created for that item. A starting point, `nTop`, is initialized and recomputed in every loop. That enables you to use the `Properties` property to assign the Top, Left, Name, and Caption properties for a label. You assign the Top, Left, Name, and Text properties for a text box. Each has its Left property set in a predetermined place.

After that, command buttons need to be placed at the bottom of the form. Two command buttons have been predetermined to appear on this form: Save and Close. Therefore, nStartLeft is computed, based on the spacing between the buttons and the number of buttons. Each of these numbers is declared as a constant at the beginning of the procedure. nStartLeft is computed so that there is a starting point for the Save command button. Then, more buttons can be added based on the previous button's Left and Width properties as well as the HORFACTOR spacing between buttons. The Top property of the command buttons is computed by taking the ScaleHeight of the form less the Height of the command button less a factor of VERTFACTOR.

Finally, it is time to add some code. This example does not code an entire application, but it does show how you can add code with the new VBIDE extensibility model. To do this, you simply add the code with the InsertLines method for the CodeModule object. This object is a sub-object of the VBComponent object. It accepts two arguments: The first is the line number in which to place the code, and the second is the string containing the code to add. The reason the code in Listing 39.11 starts at Line 2 is that the Option Explicit statement will already be added in the code module.

Figure 39.14 shows the results, at runtime, after customizing the Finish step.

FIGURE 39.14.
The results of customizing the Finish step.

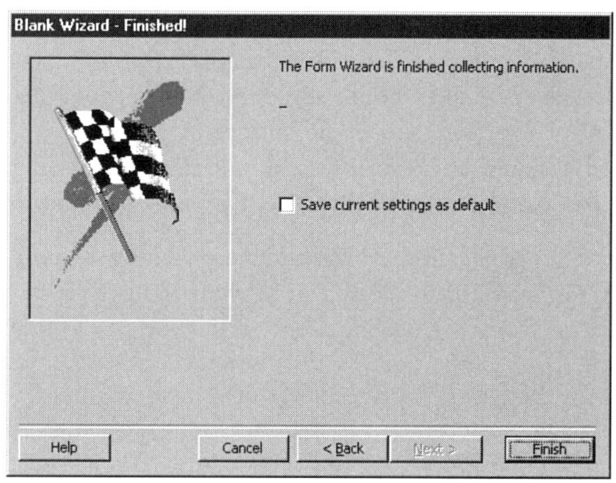

After the wizard is run, a form is created. This is shown in Figure 39.15.

If you have changed the project type to make it easy to debug, don't forget to change it back to an ActiveX DLL. Finally, you deploy the wizard as you would any other add-in. For more information about this, refer to Chapter 4.

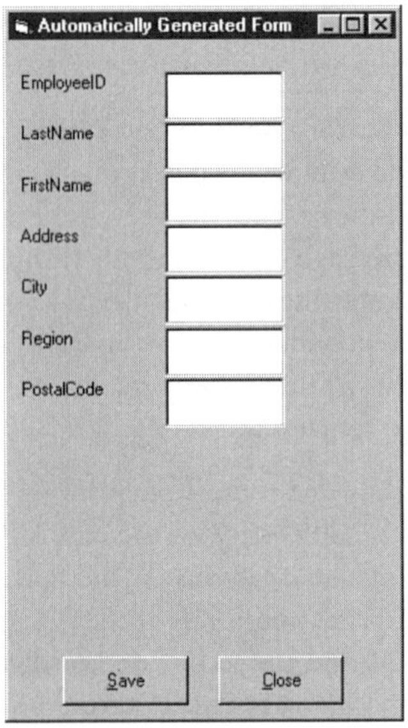

FIGURE 39.15.
The form created by using the new wizard.

Summary

Visual Basic 5.0 has made it very easy to create wizards by using the Wizard Manager. The Wizard Manager creates a Visual Basic template, including code, for a given number of steps in your wizards. It enables you to add or remove steps at will. Therefore, you do not need to explicitly plan every possible step of your wizard in advance. This chapter showed how to use the Wizard Manager to create a wizard that places fields on a form and repositions them so that they are lined up horizontally. Also, Save and Close buttons are placed onto the form.

You can use this application as a basis to build your own wizards. Reference the code shown in this chapter to manipulate the objects on your form when the user clicks the available add-in in the Add-Ins menu.

40

Developing a SAPI Application

SAPI, which stands for Speech Application Programming Interface, is a set of functions you use to incorporate two types of speech into your applications:

- Text-To-Speech
- Voice recognition

Text-To-Speech is a technology that enables a document to be spoken through a sound card. Voice recognition is a technology whereby voice commands spoken through a microphone can make your computer respond in some way. This can be as simple as activating a macro or as complex as speaking into your computer to construct a letter. In either case, the API alone does not perform all necessary functions. The API must respond through a speech engine. There are many speech engines on the market. You can find an up-to-date list on the Microsoft Web site at the following address:

`http://www.microsoft.com/msdn/library/technote/speech.htm`

You can download the Microsoft Whisper Command & Control engine, as well as the API (known as the Speech SDK), from the Microsoft Web site at the following address:

`http://research.microsoft.com/research/srg/`

Developing a SAPI Text-To-Speech Application

Developing a SAPI Text-To-Speech (TTS) application is easier than you might expect, primarily because the API has been encapsulated into a set of Visual Basic objects available through a type library. The type library for SAPI TTS is the file `VTXTAUTO.TLB`, which is installed when you install the Speech SDK from Microsoft. The voice recognition library is the file `VCAUTO.TLB`. Each of these files is placed, by default, in the `\WINDOWS\SPEECH` subdirectory. The rest of this chapter is dedicated to showing how to incorporate voice recognition into your programs.

Preparation

The first thing to do is to attempt to use one of the applications that comes with the Speech SDK. First, it is a good idea to take a look at the applications and utilities that come with the SDK. Figure 40.1 shows a folder that contains all of these applications and utilities.

Run the Feedback Test application. It enables you to train your computer to recognize speech. If you cannot run the Feedback Test application, you will not be able to run the Visual Basic application, either. If you have any trouble running the Feedback Test application, try reinstalling the speech engine. Figure 40.2 shows the main dialog box that appears when you run this application.

FIGURE 40.1.
Speech SDK applications and utilities.

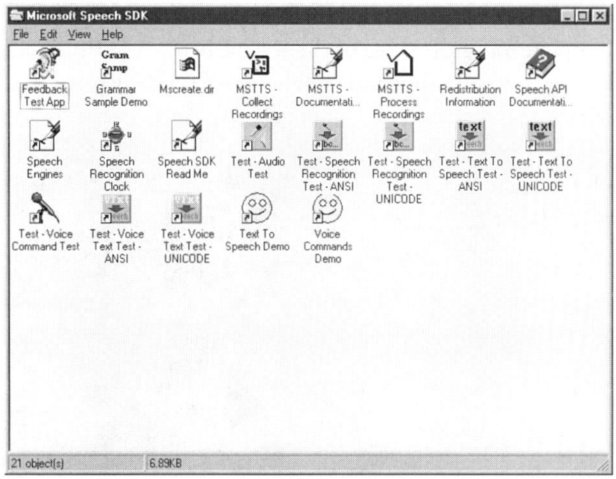

FIGURE 40.2.
The Feedback Test application.

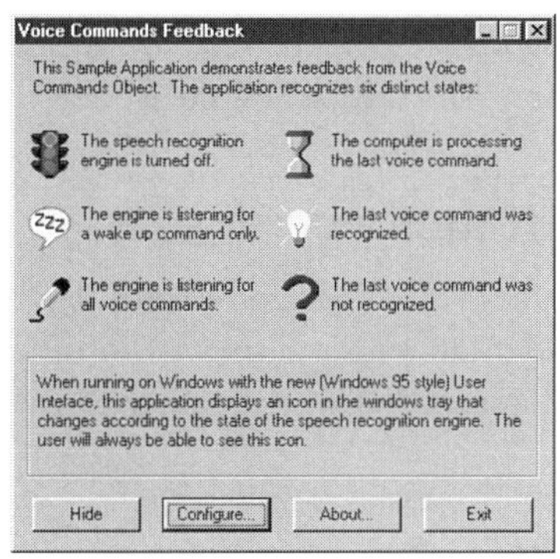

Click the Configure button to enable you to configure the speech engine. This brings up the Configuration Options dialog box shown in Figure 40.3.

FIGURE 40.3.
The Configuration Options dialog box.

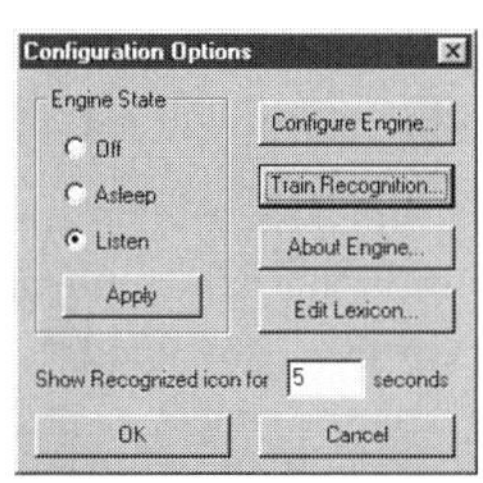

Click the Train Recognition button to begin the Training Wizard, which is shown in Figure 40.4. Complete all of the steps of the wizard before continuing. If you encounter errors while you use this wizard, the application will not work. Be sure to correct the errors according to the documentation.

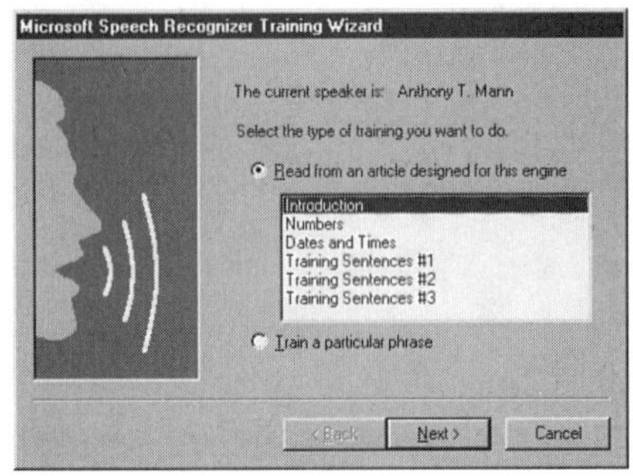

FIGURE 40.4.
The Training Wizard.

After the training is complete, make sure to exit the application completely. You will know that it is closed if there isn't a Microphone icon at the bottom-right side of the taskbar.

Using the Application

The application enables you to add commands to a list box. These commands are made up of spoken words. These commands can then perform actions in your programs. To start you out, the following four commands have been added by default:

- End
- Launch Notepad
- Launch Calculator
- Engine Off

The End command will end the application. The Launch Notepad application command will launch the `NOTEPAD.EXE` application. The Launch Calculator command will launch the `CALC.EXE` application. The Engine Off option will turn off speech recognition.

These are, of course, only a small sample of the things you can do with voice recognition. You can add your own commands that the application will respond to by highlighting the command when it is spoken. However, you need to modify the application to perform some action in code. To remove a command, simply click the appropriate command, and then click the Remove button. The application is shown at runtime in Figure 40.5.

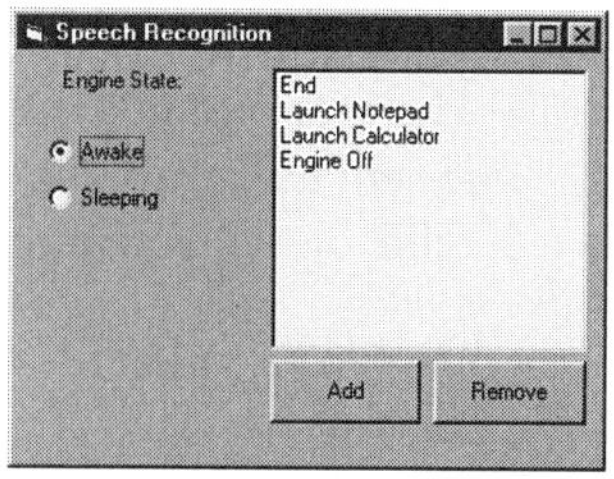

FIGURE 40.5.
Speech recognition program at runtime.

Application Theory

The theory behind the application is that the code (shown in the section "Constructing the Application") will create two objects in the `Speech.VoiceCommand` library: the `VCmdAuto` and `IVMenuAuto` objects. Each has its own specific methods, properties, and events.

The `VCmdAuto` object is used as the voice command object. It actually processes spoken words and sends them to the speech engine. Here are the available methods:

- `MenuCreate` creates a reference to a list of commands.
- `Register` registers the object with the speech engine.

Here are the available properties:

- `Awake` turns the speech engine on or off.
- `Callback` specifies the class containing code to respond to commands.
- `CommandSpoken` receives the menu element of the item spoken, but requires constant polling.

The `IVMenuAuto` object internally stores a list of all commands to be recognized in speech. It is not truly a menu on the screen. Here are the available methods:

- `Add` adds an item to the menu of commands.
- `ListSet` sets a list item in a menu.
- `Remove` removes an item from the menu of commands.

Here are the available properties:

- `Active` makes the list of commands active.
- `hWndMenu` gets the handle of the menu of commands.

By manipulating these properties and methods, you can have the speech engine recognize commands from your application. It is important to understand how you can respond to a recognized word. There are actually two properties you can use to do this:

- `CommandSpoken` property
- `Callback` property

If you want to use the `CommandSpoken` property, you must include a timer on your form. Then, set it to an interval of 500 (a half second) or so. When the timer fires, check the value of the `CommandSpoken` property. If it is not null, then this command can be processed. This method is not very efficient because it relies on the timer control.

The other method is to use the `Callback` property. The string value that is placed in this property is the name of the class module, which contains code procedures (subroutines) with the following specific names:

- `CommandRecognize()`
- `CommandOther()`

When a command is recognized, the speech engine fires the `CommandRecognize()` subroutine, passing in the command recognized. If a command is heard but not recognized, the `CommandOther()` subroutine is fired. This enables you to respond without having to use a timer control, and is much more reliable.

Constructing the Application

The application is made up of one form, one code module, and one class module. The form is used to control the user interface. The code module is used to contain the starting point of the ActiveX EXE project, called `Sub Main()`. The class module is used to handle the callback events. All of the code shown in this application is contained on the CD accompanying this book in the `\SPEECH` subdirectory.

Constructing the Form

The form contains a visual interface (controls) and code. The following controls are placed on the form:

- Two option buttons
- Two command buttons
- One list box
- One label

The two option buttons each have two properties that must be changed from their default values. The properties are `Name` and `Caption`. The `Name` properties should be changed to `optAwake` and `optSleep`, respectively, and the `Caption` properties should be changed to `Awake` and `Sleeping`. These are used to turn the speech engine on and off. Listings 40.1 and 40.2 show the code for each of these option buttons.

Listing 40.1. The `optAwake_Click()` event.

```
Private Sub optAwake_Click()
    'declare variables
    Dim nLoopCount As Integer

    'handle errors
    On Error GoTo AwakeError

    'set value
    objVoice.Awake = True

    'display status of engine
    Call DisplayStatus

    'create menu object to hold voice commands
    Set objMenu = objVoice.MenuCreate(App.EXEName, (Me.Caption), 1033, "",
    ➥ vcmdmc_OPEN_ALWAYS)

    DoEvents
    DoEvents
    DoEvents

    'add all items in listbox to menu
    For nLoopCount = 0 To lstCommand.ListCount - 1
        objMenu.Add nLoopCount + 1, lstCommand.List(nLoopCount),
        ➥"Command List", ""
        DoEvents
        DoEvents
        DoEvents
    Next nLoopCount

    'make menu active
    objMenu.Active = True
    DoEvents
    DoEvents
    DoEvents

    'assign class for callback function
    objVoice.Callback = "Project1.clsSpeech"

    Exit Sub
AwakeError:
    MsgBox Error$
    Exit Sub
End Sub
```

This code first turns on the speech engine with the `Awake` property being set to `True`. Then, a menu object is created. Notice the `1033` number. It is used to indicate the language as U.S. English. This menu option is used to maintain an internal list of menu commands to be recognized. Next, a list of commands is added with a unique number identifying the menu item. It also specifies a category of "Command List." The following quote is used for a description, but is optional. Finally, the menu is made active.

Listing 40.2. The `optSleep_Click()` event.

```
Private Sub optSleep_Click()

    'set value
    objVoice.Awake = False

    'display status of engine
    Call DisplayStatus
End Sub
```

The two command buttons each have two properties that need to be changed from their default values. The properties are `Name` and `Caption`. The `Name` properties should be changed to `cmdAdd` and `cmdRemove`, respectively, and the `Caption` properties should be changed to `Add` and `Remove`. These are used to add and remove menu commands from the menu object. Listings 40.3 and 40.4 show the code for each of these option buttons.

Listing 40.3. The `cmdAdd_Click()` event.

```
Private Sub cmdAdd_Click()
    'declare variables
    Dim sResult As String

    'add a new command to the list
    sResult = InputBox("Enter the Command to Add", "Speech Recognition")

    If Trim$(sResult) <> "" Then
        'add item to listbox
        lstCommand.AddItem sResult

        'add item to command list
        objMenu.Add lstCommand.ListCount, lstCommand.List
        ➥ (lstCommand.ListCount - 1), "Command List", ""
    End If

End Sub
```

This code provides an input box to let the user enter a new command to be recognized. After it is entered, the item is added to the list box and to the menu object for recognition.

Listing 40.4. The `cmdRemove_Click()` event.

```
Private Sub cmdRemove_Click()
    'declare variables
    Dim nLoopCount As Integer
    Dim nSelect As Integer

    'initialize
    nSelect = -1
```

```
    'find out which item is selected
    For nLoopCount = 0 To lstCommand.ListCount - 1
        If lstCommand.Selected(nLoopCount) = True Then
            nSelect = nLoopCount + 1
            Exit For
        End If
    Next nLoopCount

    If nSelect >= 0 Then
        'remove the selected item from the listbox
        lstCommand.RemoveItem nSelect - 1

        'remove the selected item from the command list
        objMenu.Remove nSelect
    End If
End Sub
```

Neither the list box nor the label have code. The name of the list box has been changed to `lstCommand`. It simply contains the list of commands accepted by the engine.

The form contains one module-level procedure, called `DisplayStatus()`. It simply queries the `Awake` property and displays the status of the speech engine, as reflected in the option buttons. It is shown in Listing 40.5.

Listing 40.5. The `DisplayStatus()` procedure.

```
Public Sub DisplayStatus()
    'query value and display status of engine
    If objVoice.Awake = True Then
        optAwake.Enabled = True
    Else
        optSleep.Enabled = True
    End If

End Sub
```

The form also contains a `(general)(declarations)` section. It declares two object variables for use throughout the form, and is shown in Listing 40.6.

Listing 40.6. The `(general)(declarations)` section.

```
Option Explicit

'declare object variables
Dim objVoice As Object
Dim objMenu As Object
```

The form also contains code in two events: `Form_Load()` and `Form_Unload()`. The `Form_Load()` event handles the instantiation of the speech engine and adds all default values to the list box. The `Form_Load()` event is shown in Listing 40.7.

Listing 40.7. The `Form_Load()` event.

```
Private Sub Form_Load()

    'change mouse
    Screen.MousePointer = vbHourglass

    'handle errors
    On Error GoTo LoadError

    'create voice object
    Set objVoice = CreateObject("Speech.VoiceCommand")

    'register voice object
    objVoice.Register ""

    'display status of engine
    Call DisplayStatus

    'add default display items
    lstCommand.AddItem "End"
    lstCommand.AddItem "Launch Notepad"
    lstCommand.AddItem "Launch Calculator"
    lstCommand.AddItem "Engine Off"

    'change mouse
    Screen.MousePointer = vbDefault

    Exit Sub

LoadError:
    Screen.MousePointer = vbDefault
    MsgBox Error$
    End
End Sub
```

It is important to note that after the object is created, it must be registered with the speech engine. The quotes are used to register it with the default values.

The `Form_Unload()` event is used to destroy the objects and reclaim memory. It is shown in Listing 40.8.

Listing 40.8. The `Form_Unload()` event.

```
Private Sub Form_Unload(Cancel As Integer)

    'release memory
    objMenu.Active = False
```

```
    Set objVoice = Nothing
    Set objMenu = Nothing

End Sub
```

Constructing the Module

The module is used mainly to house the `Sub Main()` procedure so that there is a starting point of the application. It simply loads the form, as shown in Listing 40.9.

Listing 40.9. The `Sub Main()` procedure.

```
Public Sub Main()
    'project starting point
    frmSpeech.Show
End Sub
```

The other procedure in the module is called `ClearList()`. This procedure is placed in the module because it needs to be available to the form and the class module. It simply deselects all items in the list box. This procedure is shown in Listing 40.10.

Listing 40.10. The `ClearList()` procedure.

```
Public Sub ClearList()
    'Unselect all items in the list
    Dim nLoopCount As Integer

    'find out which item is selected
    For nLoopCount = 0 To frmSpeech.lstCommand.ListCount - 1
        frmSpeech.lstCommand.Selected(nLoopCount) = False
    Next nLoopCount

End Sub
```

Constructing the Class

The class is used to store the code for the events that are fired by the speech engine. This enables your code to respond to spoken words. The procedures in this class must be named `CommandRecognize()` and `CommandOther()`. Also, the `Instancing` property must be set to 5 - Multiuse. This allows the application to create multiple instances of the class.

The `CommandRecognize()` procedure is fired when a recognized command is received. This procedure is shown in Listing 40.11.

Listing 40.11. The `CommandRecognize()` procedure.

```
Public Sub CommandRecognize(szCommand As String, dwID As Long)
    'this command was recognized

    'declare variables
    Dim nRes As Integer

    'handle errors
    On Error GoTo RecognizeError

    'unselect all
    Call ClearList

    'select detected word
    If dwID > 0 Then
        frmSpeech.lstCommand.Selected(dwID - 1) = True
    End If

    'handle these specific commands
    Select Case (szCommand)
        Case "End":
            Unload frmSpeech
        Case "Launch Notepad":
            nRes = Shell("C:\WINDOWS\NOTEPAD.EXE", 1)
        Case "Launch Calculator":
            nRes = Shell("C:\WINDOWS\CALC.EXE", 1)
        Case "Engine Off":
            frmSpeech.optSleep = True
    End Select

    Exit Sub
RecognizeError:
    If Err <> 6 Then    'not an Overflow error
        MsgBox Error$
    End If
    Exit Sub

End Sub
```

Notice in this code that the index of the menu command received is used to highlight the item in the list box to show that it is received. In addition, if the command is any of the four default commands, the appropriate action is taken. The "Launch" commands use the `Shell` function to run the application. Sometimes an overflow error occurs when the `Shell` command is used, even though there was no overflow. Therefore, the command is trapped and thrown away.

The `CommandOther()` procedure is fired when a command that is not recognized is received. This procedure is shown in Listing 40.12.

Listing 40.12. The `CommandOther()` procedure.

```
Public Sub CommandOther(szCommand As String, szApp As String, szState As String)
    'this command was not recognized

    'unselect to show unrecognized command
    Call ClearList

End Sub
```

The code simply deselects all items in the list box if a command was unrecognized.

Summary

Used in conjunction with a speech engine, the Speech Application Programming Interface, or SAPI, can enable you to write very interactive speech programs. Speech recognition is very reliable if you train the speech engine well. This chapter showed how to write a basic speech recognition program in Visual Basic. This program will respond to voice commands and launch programs. This type of application can be very useful in a timesaving capacity. You can use the code in this application as a basis for your own applications.

41

Developing an Access-to-SQL Server Upsizing Application

Although Microsoft provides an upsizing wizard to take the structure and data of an Access database and port it to an SQL Server database, understanding how this is done is a good idea. The application presented in this chapter does not provide the exact same level of functionality as the Microsoft Upsizing Wizard; instead, it's intended to get you to think about the procedures that must be in place to perform such functionality. This is a great exercise in using SQL, Access, and SQL Server.

CROSS REFERENCE

For more information about SQL, refer to Chapter 29, "Structured Query Language (SQL)." For more information about Access, refer to Chapter 28, "Database Concepts," and Chapter 31, "Database Applications with Access 97." For more information about SQL Server, refer to Chapter 32, "Visual Basic's Role in Client/Server Computing," and Chapter 33, "SQL Server 6.5 Features."

The application source code is contained on the CD-ROM accompanying this book in the `\UPSIZE` subdirectory. You can use the code, modify it, or do with it as you see fit. Here's a list of some of the things that the application will not do:

- Support every datatype (only the most common ones are supported)
- Upsize relationships
- Enable you to span multiple devices for a database

All of these things (and more) can be done, and it makes for a very sophisticated application. The purpose of this application is to teach the technique, not create the "perfect" application.

The theory behind creating this application is that you open an Access database, choose one or more tables, and cycle through all fields and indexes in those tables. You need to dynamically build the SQL statements to create the structure. In addition, you need to provide a way to take the data and import it into SQL Server. One other feature is the capability to create a new database, if you want. Consider how the application looks at runtime (see Figure 41.1).

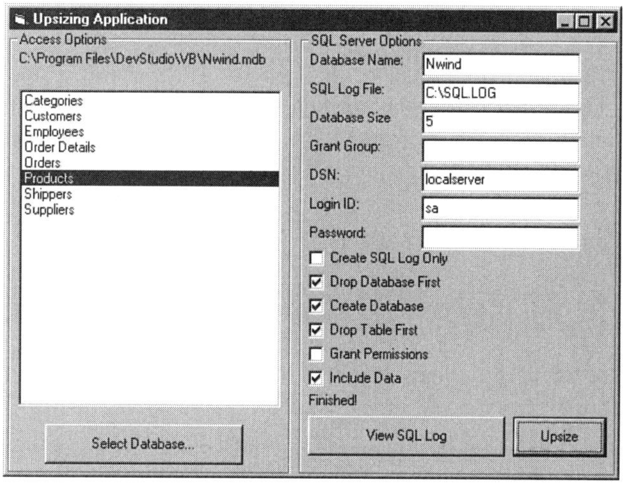

FIGURE 41.1.
The Upsizing application at runtime.

Using the Application

Using the SQL Server Upsizing application is very simple, but you need to know what each control on the form is doing. The first step is to open the Access database by selecting the Select Database command button. This invokes the common dialog box control to enable you to select a database.

After you have selected the database, it is opened and the tables contained within the database are populated in the list box. You can choose multiple tables in the list box. After you choose one or more tables, it is time to choose the SQL Server options.

The database name is computed based on the name of the Access database. This name can be overwritten in the text box. The default log file is called `C:\SQL.LOG`. It is used to generate the SQL statements so that they can be executed again later.

The database size specified by this application, by default, is 5MB. You can change the size by typing in the appropriate value. The database size value is only used when you select the option to create a database.

You use the Grant Group text box to grant permissions on a newly created table to a specific group, but only if the Grant Permissions check box is checked.

For the Upsizing application to work, it needs to establish a connection with the remote (ODBC) data source. This connection is an RDO connection. Using the application requires a data source name as well as the login ID and password. These are used to build the connect string for the RDO connection. The database used for this application is Master. Therefore, you need to have rights to this database as well as the one you are creating or using.

CROSS REFERENCE

For more information about RDO, refer to Chapter 16, "Remote Data Objects (RDO)."

There are six check box options on the Upsizing Wizard main screen. The first is called Create SQL Log Only. If this is checked, the SQL log file will be generated and the commands will not be sent to the database. (You can do this at a later time.)

If the Drop Database First option is checked, it will drop the database shown under Database Name before any other operation is invoked. Therefore, if you do not check the Create Database option (shown next), the database will not exist by the time all operations are complete.

The Create Database option creates the database using the name shown in the Database Name text box. This option creates the database using the Default segment and the size that is indicated in the Database Size text box. (The size is 5MB by default.) A *segment* is a term describing where the new database will be physically stored on one or more hard disks. You can leave this option blank, and the = clause will be left out of the DDL generated for building the database.

The Drop Table First option ensures that the appropriate table is dropped before being created. This ensures that if the table already exists, the SQL statement to create the table will not fail. In this application, all tables highlighted in the list box are created. You could modify the application to give a choice for this.

You use the Grant Permissions option to grant permissions to the table based on the group listed in the Grant Group text box. Permissions are granted after the table is created.

The Include Data option will take the data in the appropriate table and port it to SQL Server, one row at a time. This option takes into account most data types. It is not the perfect import feature, but it can be modified to include all data types.

Using the application will create the log shown in the SQL Log File text box. The log file shows all errors and successfully completed statements (unless you have the Create SQL Log Only option checked). If the Create SQL Log Only option is checked, the statements will be generated but errors are not shown because they cannot be reported if they are not executed.

Listing 41.1 shows a sample log file after creating and including data for the Products table in the Nwind database, which comes with Access. This listing has been truncated so that not every row of data is shown; however, they will be shown in the actual log.

Listing 41.1. The log file after upsizing the Products table.

```
/* Log File Created 03/09/97  11:50 AM*/


/*Table - Products*/
DROP TABLE Nwind..Products
GO

CREATE TABLE Nwind..Products ( ProductID INT IDENTITY,
➥ProductName VARCHAR (40) , SupplierID INT  NULL, CategoryID INT  NULL,
➥QuantityPerUnit VARCHAR (20)  NULL, UnitPrice DECIMAL(10,2) NULL,
➥UnitsInStock SMALLINT  NULL, UnitsOnOrder SMALLINT  NULL,
➥ReorderLevel SMALLINT  NULL, Discontinued BIT )
GO


/*Indexes for Table - Products*/
CREATE INDEX Products0 ON Nwind..Products(CategoryID)
GO

ALTER TABLE Nwind..Products ADD CONSTRAINT PrimaryKey PRIMARY KEY (ProductID)
GO

CREATE INDEX Products3 ON Nwind..Products(ProductName)
GO

CREATE INDEX Products4 ON Nwind..Products(SupplierID)
GO

CREATE INDEX Products5 ON Nwind..Products(SupplierID)
GO

SET IDENTITY_INSERT Nwind..Products ON
GO

INSERT INTO Nwind..Products ( ProductID ,ProductName ,SupplierID ,CategoryID ,
➥QuantityPerUnit ,UnitPrice ,UnitsInStock ,UnitsOnOrder ,ReorderLevel ,
➥Discontinued ) VALUES (1,'Chai',1,1,'10 boxes x 20 bags',18,39,0,10,0)
GO

INSERT INTO Nwind..Products ( ProductID ,ProductName ,SupplierID ,CategoryID ,
➥QuantityPerUnit ,UnitPrice ,UnitsInStock ,UnitsOnOrder ,ReorderLevel ,
➥Discontinued ) VALUES (2,'Chang',1,1,'24 - 12 oz bottles',19,17,40,25,0)
GO
```

continues

Listing 41.1. continued

```
INSERT INTO Nwind..Products ( ProductID ,ProductName ,SupplierID ,CategoryID ,
➥QuantityPerUnit ,UnitPrice ,UnitsInStock ,UnitsOnOrder ,ReorderLevel ,
➥Discontinued ) VALUES (3,'Aniseed Syrup',1,2,'12 - 550 ml bottles',
➥10,13,70,25,0)
GO

SET IDENTITY_INSERT Nwind..Products OFF
GO
```

Constructing the Application

Constructing the application requires knowledge of SQL. Here are the two types of SQL that will be generated:

- DDL: DDL stands for Dynamic Data Language. It is used to construct databases, tables, indexes, constraints, and so on. It does not deal with any data at all.
- `INSERT` statements: `INSERT` statements will be used to actually insert rows of data into SQL Server from Access.

CROSS REFERENCE

For more information about SQL, refer to Chapter 29, "Structured Query Language (SQL)."

Probably the most difficult concept in this application is that of Identity columns. An Identity column is to SQL Server what a Counter column is to Access. Therefore, you need to be very careful when you deal with these columns. Because an Identity column is used to automatically insert a value into the column as the row is inserted, you need to be able to insert your own values into this table because the Upsizing application is used to mimic the data. You do not want the new values for the columns to be automatically generated. This would violate the referential integrity in the Access table. The proper way to maintain the referential integrity would be to use a special statement in SQL Server 6.5:

```
SET IDENTITY_INSERT table value
```

Here, *`table`* is the name of the table that contains the Identity column, and *`value`* is either `ON` or `OFF`.

If the value is set to `ON`, then you can insert values into this table. If the value is set to `OFF`, then you cannot. Therefore, this application sets the value to `ON`, but only for tables that contain an Identity column. If you set the value on a table that does not contain an Identity column, an error occurs.

Graphical Interface

The GUI part of this application consists of only one form, which contains all of the code necessary to upsize an Access database. The following objects are placed on the form:

- Two frames
- Nine labels
- One list box
- Three command buttons
- Six check boxes
- Seven text boxes
- One common dialog control

The frames serve only as containers for other controls. The names have not even been changed from their default values.

Seven of the labels serve only as static labels. The other two labels are dynamic. One label, named `lblDB`, is used to display the full path of the Access database name. The other, named `lblStatus`, is used to display the status of the current operation as the code cycles through the selected items in the list box.

The only list box in the application, named `lstTable`, is used to house all of the tables within the Access database chosen. This list box is used within the main loop of the application. The list box has had only one property changed from its default value: the `MultiSelect` property. The value has been set to "2 - Extended" to allow for multiple table selections.

All three command buttons are very useful in the application—each starts an important process. The first, named `cmdDataBase`, is used to open the common dialog box to select the database to open. After it is selected, the appropriate database is opened. The second, named `cmdView`, is used to view the SQL log file. It invokes `NOTEPAD.EXE` to show the results stored in the SQL log file. The third, named `cmdUpsize`, performs the main functionality of the application. It is used to start the upsize process, taking into account the values in the other controls in the application.

The six check boxes on the form actually are control arrays. These arrays are referenced with constant values declared in the `(general)(declarations)` section of the form. All of these text boxes are named `chkOption`, with indexes from top to bottom ranging from 0 to 5. Only three of the check boxes have had properties changed from their default values. They are Drop Database First, Create Database, and Drop Table First. The `Value` properties for these controls (indexes 1, 2, and 3) have been changed to `True` so that they are selected automatically when the application is run.

The seven text boxes on the form are used to collect data for the creation of tables, databases, and the ODBC connection itself. The first text box, named `txtDB`, shows the database name.

The name is calculated from the name of the database opened in Access. The second, named `txtSQLLog`, shows what the DOS log file is called. This log file stores the results of all SQL statements generated, as well as errors. The default `Text` property value for this control is `C:\SQL.LOG`. The third, named `txtSize`, is used only to specify the size of the database, if you have opted to create one. The default `Text` property value for this control is `5`. The fourth text box, named `txtGrant`, is used to store the name of the group to grant permissions to for a given table. The fifth, named `txtDSN`, is an integral part of connecting to the ODBC data source. It is the data source name, as registered in your ODBC Control Panel applet. The sixth, named `txtUID`, is the user ID for building the connect string. The default `Text` property value for this control is sa. The seventh, and final, text box control on this form, named `txtPWD`, is the password used to build the connect string. The only property value for this control that was changed from its default value is the `PasswordChar` property. It has been changed to `*` to mask the password entered into the text box.

The only common dialog box control in the application, named `dlgCommon`, is used to handle the selecting of the Access database file to open. It has two properties changed from their default values. Selecting the Custom property will bring up the Property Pages dialog box. The Property Pages dialog box is shown in Figure 41.2. The `Filter` value needs to be changed to Access Databases|*.MDB. This will filter out all file extensions except for `*.MDB` file extensions. The CancelError check box needs to be checked. This will allow an error to occur when the user cancels out of the common dialog box at runtime.

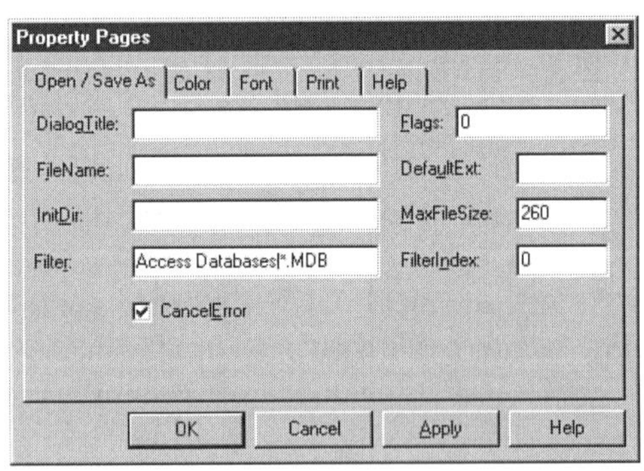

FIGURE 41.2.
The common dialog box custom properties.

Code

There are only a few procedures that have code attached to them in this application because the majority of the code is handled in the `cmdUpsize_Click()` event. The following sections outline and explain the code in this application.

Declarations

There are very few declarations. Listing 41.2 shows the `(general)(declarations)` section in the application.

Listing 41.2. The code in the `(general)(declarations)` section.

```
Option Explicit

'constants for option buttons
Const LOGONLY = 0
Const DROPDB = 1
Const CREATEDB = 2
Const DROPTABLE = 3
Const GRANT = 4
Const DATA = 5

'global variables
Public gdbDatabase As Database
```

The constants are used to identify a specific item in the `chkOption` control array. The database object variable is used to hold the open Access database.

Module-Level Procedures

There are five module-level procedures (subroutines and functions) that perform various tasks for this application. They are shown in the next five sections.

The `CheckApostrophe()` Function

The `CheckApostrophe()` function is used to determine whether there is an apostrophe (`'`) within the text. If there is, for SQL Server to consider it to be as such instead of a quote, it has to have another apostrophe directly following it. Therefore, this function will accept a string to check. Then, it returns a string with the appropriate apostrophe in place. Listing 41.3 shows the `CheckApostrophe()` function.

Listing 41.3. The `CheckApostrophe()` function.

```
Private Function CheckApostrophe(ByVal sTemp As String) As String
   'this function checks to see if there are any unmatched quotes (apostrophes)
   'if there is, it will append another one to the string so that SQL Server
   'doesn't fail

   Dim sFinal As String
   Dim nLoopCount As Integer
```

continues

Listing 41.3. continued

```
    For nLoopCount = 1 To Len(sTemp)
        If Mid$(sTemp, nLoopCount, 1) = "'" Then
            'there is a quote, see if there is another just after
            If nLoopCount <> Len(sTemp) Then
                'this is not the last character

                If Mid$(sTemp, nLoopCount + 1, 1) = "'" Then
                    'there is another apostrophe, go ahead and use it
                    sFinal = sFinal & Mid$(sTemp, nLoopCount, 1)
                Else
                    'there is no second apostrophe
                    sFinal = sFinal & Mid$(sTemp, nLoopCount, 1) & "'"
                End If
            Else
                'this is the last character
                sFinal = sFinal & Mid$(sTemp, nLoopCount, 1) & "'"
            End If
        Else
            'no apostrophe, use character
            sFinal = sFinal & Mid$(sTemp, nLoopCount, 1)
        End If
    Next nLoopCount

    'return the new string

    CheckApostrophe = sFinal
End Function
```

The `EnableDisable()` Subroutine

The `EnableDisable()` subroutine is used to enable any text boxes appropriate to a specific option. This subroutine shows only one option, `txtGrant`, being enabled and disabled. However, if you want to enhance this application, you can expand this routine. Listing 41.4 shows the `EnableDisable()` subroutine.

Listing 41.4. The `EnableDisable()` subroutine.

```
Private Sub EnableDisable()
    'this routine will enable or disable text boxes, as appropriate

    If chkOption(GRANT).Value = 1 Then
        txtGrant.Enabled = True
    Else
        txtGrant.Enabled = False
    End If
End Sub
```

The FindFields() Function

The FindFields() function builds a list of fields, based on the index being returned from Access. An index is returned in this form, which indicates an index on two columns in the table:

```
+OrderID;+ProductID
```

Listing 41.5 shows the FindFields() function.

Listing 41.5. The FindFields() function.

```
Private Function FindFields(ByVal sFields As String) As String

    Dim nPos As Integer
    Dim sTempString As String
    Dim nLoopCount As Integer
    Dim sFieldName As String
    Dim sFinalString As String
    Dim nCurrPos As Integer
    Dim sUltimateString As String

    sTempString = ""
    sFinalString = ""

    'this procedure finds fields in the string being passed in
    For nLoopCount = 1 To Len(sFields)
        Select Case UCase$(Mid$(sFields, nLoopCount, 1))
            Case "+":
                'ignore
                sFinalString = sFinalString & sTempString
                sTempString = ""
            Case ";":
                sTempString = sTempString & ","
            Case Else:
                sTempString = sTempString & Mid$(sFields, nLoopCount, 1)
        End Select
    Next nLoopCount


    If Len(sTempString) > 0 Then
        If Right$(sTempString, 1) = ";" Then
            sTempString = Left$(sTempString, Len(sTempString) - 1)
        End If
        sFinalString = sFinalString & sTempString
    End If

    'at this point, there is one string for this index, each field
    'separated by commas.  Now loop through each field

    'initialize
    nPos = 1
```

continues

Listing 41.5. continued

```
    nCurrPos = 1
    sUltimateString = ""
    Do Until nPos = 0
        nPos = InStr(nCurrPos, sFinalString, ",")
        If nPos > 0 Then
            'there was a comma
            sUltimateString = sUltimateString & Trim$(Mid$(sFinalString,
            ➥nCurrPos, nPos - nCurrPos)) & ","
            nCurrPos = nPos + 1
        Else
            'either there were no commas, or we are at the end of the string
            sUltimateString = sUltimateString & Trim$(Mid$(sFinalString,
            ➥nCurrPos, Len(sFinalString) - nCurrPos + 1))
            nCurrPos = nPos + 1
        End If
    Loop


    'remove trailing comma, if it exists
    If Right$(sUltimateString, 1) = "," Then
        sUltimateString = Left$(sUltimateString, Len(sUltimateString) - 1)
    End If

    FindFields = sUltimateString

End Function
```

The `IsFieldInPrimaryKey()` Function

The `IsFieldInPrimaryKey()` function returns a Boolean representing whether a field is a primary key field within a `TableDef` object. Listing 41.6 shows the `IsFieldInPrimaryKey()` function.

Listing 41.6. The `IsFieldInPrimaryKey()` function.

```
Private Function IsFieldInPrimaryKey(TableDef As TableDef,
➥sFieldName As String) As Integer
'Determine if field is part of primary key in Access DB tabledef
'Field names are stored in then Fields property of an index object,
➥delimited by a semicolon

    Dim nLoopCount As Integer
    Dim sFieldList As String
    Dim sCurrentField As String
    Dim nParsePosition As Integer

    For nLoopCount = 0 To TableDef.Indexes.Count - 1
        If TableDef.Indexes(nLoopCount).Primary Then
            sFieldList = TableDef.Indexes(nLoopCount).Fields
```

```
            Do
                If Left(sFieldList, 1) = "+" Then sFieldList =
                ➥Right(sFieldList, Len(sFieldList) - 1)
                nParsePosition = InStr(sFieldList, ";")
                If nParsePosition > 0 Then
                    sCurrentField = Left(sFieldList, nParsePosition - 1)
                    sFieldList = Right(sFieldList, Len(sFieldList) -
                    ➥nParsePosition)
                Else
                    sCurrentField = sFieldList
                    sFieldList = ""
                End If
                If sCurrentField = sFieldName Then
                    IsFieldInPrimaryKey = True
                    Exit Function
                End If
            Loop Until Len(sFieldList) = 0
            Exit For
        End If
    Next nLoopCount

    IsFieldInPrimaryKey = False

End Function
```

The `StripSpace()` Function

The `StripSpace()` function cycles through a string and strips out all spaces. It then returns the string. The reason for this is that some Access tables have spaces in their names, but SQL Server will not accept them. Listing 41.7 shows the `StripSpace()` function.

Listing 41.7. The `StripSpace()` function.

```
Private Function StripSpace(ByVal sTemp As String) As String

    'this function strips out all spaces in the string passed in as sTemp

    'declare variables
    Dim nLoopCount As Integer
    Dim sFinal As String

    'loop through string
    For nLoopCount = 1 To Len(sTemp)
        If Mid$(sTemp, nLoopCount, 1) <> " " Then
            'build final string without spaces
            sFinal = sFinal & Mid$(sTemp, nLoopCount, 1)
        End If
    Next nLoopCount

    StripSpace = sFinal
End Function
```

The chkOption Control

The `chkOption` control is a control array that is used to identify the specific options chosen. However, the options are queried when the upsizing starts. Therefore, the only code in an event procedure for this control is in the `Click()` event. This event simply calls the `EnableDisable()` subroutine to enable and disable where appropriate. Listing 41.8 shows the `chkOption_Click()` event procedure in the application.

Listing 41.8. The `chkOption_Click()` event.

```
Private Sub chkOption_Click(Index As Integer)
    Call EnableDisable
End Sub
```

The cmdDatabase Control

The `cmdDatabase` control is a command button that opens a common dialog box control for the selection of an Access database. Then, when the database is selected, it is also opened. Listing 41.9 shows the `cmdDatabase_Click()` event procedure in the application.

Listing 41.9. The `cmdDatabase_Click()` event.

```
Private Sub cmdDatabase_Click()
    'declare variables
    Dim nLoopCount As Integer
    Dim nPos As Integer
    Dim sTemp As String
    Dim sFinal As String

    'change mouse
    Screen.MousePointer = vbHourglass

    'handle errors
    On Error GoTo dlgError

    'open common dialog
    dlgCommon.ShowOpen

    'change mouse
    Screen.MousePointer = vbHourglass

    'display database
    lblDB.Caption = dlgCommon.filename

    'open database
    Set gdbDatabase = Workspaces(0).OpenDatabase(dlgCommon.filename)

    'initialize
    lstTable.Clear
```

```
    'populate tables
    For nLoopCount = 0 To gdbDatabase.TableDefs.Count - 1
        If gdbDatabase.TableDefs(nLoopCount).Attributes = 0 Then
            'this is not a system table
            lstTable.AddItem gdbDatabase.TableDefs(nLoopCount).Name
        End If
    Next nLoopCount

    'assign sTemp
    sTemp = lblDB.Caption

    'determine default SQL Server database name
    nPos = InStr(sTemp, ".")

    'extract name of database, without the ".MDB"
    If nPos > 0 Then
        For nLoopCount = nPos To 1 Step -1
            If Mid$(sTemp, nLoopCount, 1) = "\" Then
                sFinal = Mid$(sTemp, nLoopCount + 1, nPos - nLoopCount - 1)
                Exit For
            End If
        Next nLoopCount
    End If

    'assign default database
    If sTemp <> "" Then
        txtDB.Text = sFinal
    Else
        txtDB.Text = ""
    End If

    'change mouse
    Screen.MousePointer = vbDefault

    Exit Sub

dlgError:

    'blank out displays
    lblDB.Caption = ""
    lstTable.Clear

    If Err = cdlCancel Then
        'user cancelled

        'change mouse
        Screen.MousePointer = vbDefault

        Exit Sub
    Else
        MsgBox Error$
        Resume
    End If

End Sub
```

The cmdUpsize Control

The cmdUpsize control is a command button that handles the majority of the code in this application. It actually performs the upsizing. Listing 41.10 shows the cmdUpsize_Click() event procedure in the application.

Listing 41.10. The cmdUpsize_Click() event.

```
Private Sub cmdUpsize_Click()
    Dim sGO  As String
    Dim nLogFile As Integer
    Dim sCmd As String
    Dim nLoopCount As Integer
    Dim nLoopCount2 As Integer
    Dim sTable As String
    Dim sColumn As String
    Dim nIsIdentity As Integer
    Dim sSize  As String
    Dim sIndexName As String
    Dim sIndexFields As String
    Dim nPrimary As Integer
    Dim nUnique As Integer
    Dim sIndexColumns As String
    Dim sFieldName As String
    Dim nResult As Integer
    Dim rdoCn As New rdoConnection
    Dim rdoEn As rdoEnvironment
    Dim rsTemp As Recordset
    Dim nTableColumns As Integer
    Dim nContainsIdentity As Integer

    'change mouse
    Screen.MousePointer = vbHourglass

    'handle errors
    On Error GoTo SQLUpsizeError

    'open SQL Log file
    nLogFile = FreeFile
    Open txtSQLLog.Text For Output As #nLogFile

    Print #nLogFile, "/* Log File Created " & Format$(Now, "MM/DD/YY  HH:MM
    ➥AM/PM") & "*/" & Chr$(13) & Chr$(10)

    If chkOption(LOGONLY).Value = False Then
        'open Environment
        Set rdoEn = rdoEnvironments(0)

        'open Connection
        lblStatus.Caption = "Opening Connection With ODBC DataSource"
        DoEvents
        DoEvents
        With rdoCn
            .Connect = "UID=" & txtUID.Text & ";PWD=" & txtPWD.Text & ";
            ➥Database=Master;DSN=" & txtDSN.Text & ";"
```

```
            .EstablishConnection rdDriverNoPrompt, True
            rdoEn.rdoConnections.Add rdoCn
        End With
    End If

    'create separator between statements
    sGO = Chr(13) & Chr(10) & "GO" & Chr(13) & Chr(10)

    'Drop database
    If chkOption(DROPDB).Value = 1 Then
        sCmd = "USE master " & Chr(13) & Chr(10) & "DROP DATABASE " & txtDB.Text
        Print #nLogFile, sCmd & sGO
        If chkOption(LOGONLY).Value = False Then
            lblStatus.Caption = "Dropping Database"
            DoEvents
            DoEvents
            rdoCn.Execute sCmd, dbSQLPassThrough
        End If
    End If

    'Create database
    If chkOption(CREATEDB).Value = 1 Then
        sCmd = "USE master " & Chr(13) & Chr(10) & "CREATE DATABASE " &
        ➥txtDB.Text
        sCmd = sCmd & " ON DEFAULT "
        If txtSize.Text <> "" Then
            sCmd = sCmd & " = " & txtSize.Text
        End If
        Print #nLogFile, sCmd & sGO
        If chkOption(LOGONLY).Value = False Then
            lblStatus.Caption = "Creating Database"
            DoEvents
            DoEvents
            rdoCn.Execute sCmd, dbSQLPassThrough
        End If
    End If

    'loop through list box and create tables for selected items
    For nLoopCount = 0 To lstTable.ListCount - 1
        If lstTable.Selected(nLoopCount) = True Then
            'initialize
            nContainsIdentity = False

            sTable = StripSpace(lstTable.List(nLoopCount))
            Print #nLogFile, Chr$(13) & Chr$(10) & "/*Table - " & sTable & "*/"

            'drop table, if selected
            If chkOption(DROPTABLE).Value = 1 Then
                sCmd = "DROP TABLE " & txtDB.Text & ".." & sTable
                Print #nLogFile, sCmd & sGO
                If chkOption(LOGONLY).Value = False Then
                    lblStatus.Caption = "Dropping Table " & sTable
                    DoEvents
                    DoEvents
                    rdoCn.Execute sCmd, dbSQLPassThrough
                End If
```

continues

Listing 41.10. continued

```
            End If


            'create this table
            lblStatus.Caption = "Creating Table: " & sTable
            DoEvents
            DoEvents

            sCmd = "CREATE TABLE " & txtDB.Text & ".." & sTable & " ( "

            For nLoopCount2 = 0 To gdbDatabase.TableDefs(lstTable.List
            ➥(nLoopCount)).Fields.Count - 1
                sFieldName = gdbDatabase.TableDefs(lstTable.List
                ➥ (nLoopCount)).Fields(nLoopCount2).Name
                sColumn = StripSpace(gdbDatabase.TableDefs(lstTable.List
                ➥(nLoopCount)).Fields(nLoopCount2).Name)
                nIsIdentity = (gdbDatabase.TableDefs(lstTable.List
                ➥(nLoopCount)).Fields(nLoopCount2).Attributes And 16) = 16

                'flag identity for this table
                If nIsIdentity = True Then
                    nContainsIdentity = True
                End If

                Select Case gdbDatabase.TableDefs(lstTable.List
                ➥(nLoopCount)).Fields(nLoopCount2).Type
                   Case dbText:
                        sSize = Trim$(Str$(gdbDatabase.TableDefs(lstTable.
                        ➥List(nLoopCount)).Fields(nLoopCount2).Size))
                        sCmd = sCmd & sColumn & " VARCHAR (" & sSize & ") "
                    Case dbMemo:
                        sCmd = sCmd & sColumn & " TEXT "
                    Case dbDate:
                        sCmd = sCmd & sColumn & " DATETIME "
                    Case dbSingle:
                        sCmd = sCmd & sColumn & " REAL "
                    Case dbDouble:
                        sCmd = sCmd & sColumn & " FLOAT"
                    Case dbCurrency:
                        sCmd = sCmd & sColumn & " DECIMAL(10,2)"
                    Case dbLong:
                        If nIsIdentity = True Then
                            'this is an Access COUNTER datatype
                            sCmd = sCmd & sColumn & " INT IDENTITY"
                        Else
                            'this is a real LONG datatype
                            sCmd = sCmd & sColumn & " INT "
                        End If
                    Case dbInteger:
                        sCmd = sCmd & sColumn & " SMALLINT "
                    Case dbByte:
                        sCmd = sCmd & sColumn & " TINYINT "
                    Case dbBoolean:
                        'this is a Yes/No Field
                        sCmd = sCmd & sColumn & " BIT "
```

```
                Case Else:
                    'send command to server
                    Print #nLogFile, "Unsupported Datatype" &
                    ➥Trim$(Str$(gdbDatabase.TableDefs(lstTable.List
                    ➥(nLoopCount)).Fields(nLoopCount2).Type))
                    MsgBox "Unsupported datatype"
            End Select

            If Not nIsIdentity And Not IsFieldInPrimaryKey
➥(gdbDatabase.TableDefs(lstTable.List(nLoopCount)), sFieldName) And
➥(gdbDatabase.TableDefs(lstTable.List(nLoopCount)).Fields(nLoopCount2).
➥Required = False) And (gdbDatabase.TableDefs(lstTable.List(nLoopCount)).
➥Fields(nLoopCount2).Type <> dbBoolean) Then
                sCmd = sCmd & " NULL"
            End If
            sCmd = sCmd & ", "
        Next nLoopCount2

        sCmd = Trim$(sCmd)
        If Right$(sCmd, 1) = "," Then
            sCmd = Left$(sCmd, Len(sCmd) - 1)
        End If
        sCmd = sCmd & ") "
        'send command to server
        Print #nLogFile, sCmd & sGO
        If chkOption(LOGONLY).Value = False Then
            lblStatus.Caption = "Creating Table " & sTable
            DoEvents
            DoEvents
            rdoCn.Execute sCmd, dbSQLPassThrough
        End If

        'Create indexes for table
        Print #nLogFile, Chr$(13) & Chr$(10) & "/*Indexes for Table - " &
        ➥ sTable & "*/"
        For nLoopCount2 = 0 To gdbDatabase.TableDefs(lstTable.List
        ➥(nLoopCount)).Indexes.Count - 1
            sIndexName = gdbDatabase.TableDefs(lstTable.List
            ➥(nLoopCount)).Indexes(nLoopCount2).Name
            sIndexFields = gdbDatabase.TableDefs(lstTable.List
            ➥(nLoopCount)).Indexes(nLoopCount2).Fields
            nPrimary = gdbDatabase.TableDefs(lstTable.List
            ➥(nLoopCount)).Indexes(nLoopCount2).Primary
            nUnique = gdbDatabase.TableDefs(lstTable.List
            ➥(nLoopCount)).Indexes(nLoopCount2).Unique
            If nPrimary = True Then
               If FindFields(sIndexFields) <> sIndexColumns Then
                    'add primary key index

                    sCmd = "ALTER TABLE " & txtDB.Text & ".." & sTable &
                    ➥" ADD CONSTRAINT " & sIndexName &
                    ➥" PRIMARY KEY (" & FindFields(sIndexFields) & ") "

                    Print #nLogFile, sCmd & sGO
                    If chkOption(LOGONLY).Value = False Then
                        lblStatus.Caption = "Creating Indexes"
```

continues

Listing 41.10. continued

```
                    DoEvents
                    DoEvents
                    rdoCn.Execute sCmd, dbSQLPassThrough
                End If
                If sIndexColumns = "" Then
                    sIndexColumns = FindFields(sIndexFields)
                End If
            Else
                sIndexColumns = ""
            End If
        Else
            'just add the index
            If FindFields(sIndexFields) <> sIndexColumns Then
                If nUnique = True Then
                    sCmd = "CREATE UNIQUE INDEX " & sTable &
                    ➥Trim$(Str$(nLoopCount2)) & " ON " &
                    ➥txtDB.Text & ".." & sTable & "(" &
                    ➥FindFields(sIndexFields) & ") "
                Else
                    sCmd = "CREATE INDEX " & sTable &
                    ➥Trim$(Str$(nLoopCount2)) & " ON " &
                    ➥txtDB.Text & ".." & sTable & "(" &
                    ➥FindFields(sIndexFields) & ") "
                End If
                Print #nLogFile, sCmd & sGO
                If chkOption(LOGONLY).Value = False Then
                    lblStatus.Caption = "Creating Indexes"
                    DoEvents
                    DoEvents
                    rdoCn.Execute sCmd, dbSQLPassThrough
                End If
                If sIndexColumns = "" Then
                    sIndexColumns = FindFields(sIndexFields)
                End If
            Else
                sIndexColumns = ""
            End If
        End If
    Next nLoopCount2

    If nLoopCount2 = 0 Then
        Print #nLogFile, "/*NO INDEXES*/"
    End If

    'Grant permissions for table
    If chkOption(GRANT).Value = 1 Then
        sCmd = "GRANT ALL ON " & txtDB.Text & ".." & sTable &
        ➥" TO " & txtGrant.Text
        'send command to server and file
        Print #nLogFile, sCmd & sGO
        If chkOption(LOGONLY).Value = False Then
            lblStatus.Caption = "Granting Permission"
            DoEvents
            DoEvents
            rdoCn.Execute sCmd, dbSQLPassThrough
        End If
```

```
End If

'import data
If chkOption(DATA).Value = 1 Then
    sCmd = "SELECT * FROM [" & lstTable.List(nLoopCount) & "]"
    Set rsTemp = gdbDatabase.OpenRecordset(sCmd, dbOpenSnapshot)
    If Not rsTemp.EOF Then
        lblStatus.Caption = "Importing Table " & sTable
        rsTemp.MoveFirst
    Else
        lblStatus.Caption = "Table: " & sTable & "    No Records"
        DoEvents
        DoEvents
    End If

    'allow inserts for an identity column
    If nContainsIdentity = True Then
        sCmd = "SET IDENTITY_INSERT "
        sCmd = sCmd & txtDB.Text & ".." & sTable & " ON "
        Print #nLogFile, sCmd & sGO
        If chkOption(LOGONLY).Value = False Then
            rdoCn.Execute sCmd, dbSQLPassThrough
        End If
    End If
    'loop through each field to build insert statement
    While Not rsTemp.EOF
        sCmd = "INSERT INTO "
        sCmd = sCmd & txtDB.Text & ".." & sTable & " ( "

        nTableColumns = rsTemp.Fields.Count

        'build list of column names in table
        For nLoopCount2 = 0 To nTableColumns - 1
            sCmd = sCmd & gdbDatabase.TableDefs("[" & lstTable.List
            ➥ (nLoopCount) & "]").Fields(nLoopCount2).Name &
            ➥" " & ","
        Next nLoopCount2

        'remove the trailing comma
        sCmd = Left$(sCmd, Len(sCmd) - 1) & ") "
        sCmd = sCmd & "VALUES ("

        'build list of column values in table
        For nLoopCount2 = 0 To nTableColumns - 1
            Select Case rsTemp.Fields(nLoopCount2).Type
                Case dbSingle, dbDouble, dbCurrency, dbLong,
                ➥dbInteger, dbByte
                   If IsNull(rsTemp.Fields(nLoopCount2)) Or
                   ➥rsTemp.Fields(nLoopCount2) = "" Then
                        sCmd = sCmd & "Null,"
                    Else
                        sCmd = sCmd & Trim$(Str$(rsTemp.Fields
                        ➥ (nLoopCount2))) & ","
                    End If
                Case dbText, dbMemo
                    If Not IsNull(rsTemp.Fields(nLoopCount2)) And
                    ➥rsTemp.Fields(nLoopCount2) <> "" Then
```

continues

Listing 41.10. continued

```
                            sCmd = sCmd & "'" & CheckApostrophe(Trim$
                            ➥ (rsTemp.Fields(nLoopCount2))) & "',"
                        Else
                            sCmd = sCmd & "Null,"
                        End If
                    Case dbDate
                        sCmd = sCmd & "'" & Trim$(Str$(rsTemp.Fields
                        ➥ (nLoopCount2))) & "',"
                    Case dbBoolean
                        If Not IsNull(rsTemp.Fields(nLoopCount2)) Then
                            If rsTemp.Fields(nLoopCount2) = False Then
                                sCmd = sCmd & "0,"
                            Else
                                sCmd = sCmd & "-1,"
                            End If
                        Else
                            sCmd = sCmd & "Null,"
                        End If
                    Case Else:
                        'send command to server
                        Print #nLogFile, "Unsupported Datatype" &
                        Trim$(Str$(gdbDatabase.TableDefs(lstTable.
                        ➥List(nLoopCount)).Fields
                        ➥(nLoopCount2).Type))
                        MsgBox "Unsupported datatype"
                End Select
            Next nLoopCount2
            'remove the trailing comma
            sCmd = Left$(sCmd, Len(sCmd) - 1) & ") "

            'insert into database
            Print #nLogFile, sCmd & sGO
            If chkOption(LOGONLY).Value = False Then
                rdoCn.Execute sCmd, dbSQLPassThrough
            End If

AfterStringSpace:
            rsTemp.MoveNext
            DoEvents
            DoEvents
        Wend

        'turn off inserts for an identity column
        If nContainsIdentity = True Then
            sCmd = "SET IDENTITY_INSERT "
            sCmd = sCmd & txtDB.Text & ".." & sTable & " OFF "
            Print #nLogFile, sCmd & sGO
            If chkOption(LOGONLY).Value = False Then
                rdoCn.Execute sCmd, dbSQLPassThrough
            End If
        End If
    End If

  End If
Next nLoopCount
```

```
    lblStatus.Caption = "Finished!"

    Close #nLogFile

    'change mouse
    Screen.MousePointer = vbDefault

    Exit Sub

SQLUpsizeError:
    Screen.MousePointer = vbDefault
    Print #nLogFile, "/*" & Error$ & "*/"
    If Err = 14 Then
        'out of string space
        MsgBox "There is no more string space!  Upsizing cannot take place on
        ➥table " & sTable & "."
        Resume AfterStringSpace
    Else
        nResult = MsgBox(Error$, 1)
        If nResult = vbCancel Then
            lblStatus.Caption = ""
            DoEvents
            DoEvents

            Print #nLogFile, "/* Upsizing Cancelled by user - NOT COMPLETE! */"
            Close #nLogFile
            Exit Sub
        End If
    End If

    'change mouse
    Screen.MousePointer = vbHourglass

    'resume the next line
    Resume Next

End Sub
```

Although there is a lot of code in this listing, it is not difficult to follow. The specific options chosen on the screen are each handled in a different way. If you were to expand upon this application, you probably would want to break this up into smaller procedures. For the sake of example, however, I think it is easier to follow in one procedure.

The first thing that happens is that the log file is opened. The current date and time is written to the file. Then, as long as the Log File Only check box is not checked, an RDO connection is opened. This option indicates that you will not be executing the SQL at this time.

If you have selected to drop the database, this is done next, followed by the creation of the database. When all of that is finished, the list box is traversed to determine which tables have been selected.

For each selected table, the table is dropped (if that option was chosen). Then, the table is created. The creation of the table needs to have an inner loop to cycle through each field in the table and determine its datatype. Then, if the datatype is not the same as it is in Access, it is changed. If there is an Access Counter datatype, it is changed to an Identity datatype in SQL Server.

Next, a loop is created for the indexes in the table. Each of the indexes is then created in the SQL Server table. After all the indexes are created, permissions are granted to the group specified (if that option was chosen).

Finally, if you choose to include data, the system will loop through all columns in the table and build the SQL `INSERT` string. The system actually will loop through twice. The first time is to build a list of columns and the second is to build the data. The datatype is checked to make sure that the data is formatted correctly.

The `cmdView` Control

The `cmdView` control is a command button that simply enables you to view the text file stored in the SQL Log File text box. It does this by shelling the `NOTEPAD.EXE` program and passing the name of this file. Listing 41.11 shows the `cmdView_Click()` event procedure in the application.

Listing 41.11. The `cmdView_Click()` event.

```
Private Sub cmdView_click()
    Dim X As Integer
    Dim lLength As Long
    Dim sTemp As String

    sTemp = txtSQLLog.Text

    If sTemp = "" Then Exit Sub

    'change mouse
    Screen.MousePointer = vbHourglass

    On Error GoTo ViewError

    lLength = FileLen(sTemp)

    X = Shell("NOTEPAD.EXE " & sTemp, 3)

    'change mouse
    Screen.MousePointer = vbDefault

    Exit Sub
ViewError:
    'change mouse
    Screen.MousePointer = vbDefault
    If Err = 53 Then 'file not found
        MsgBox "File " & sTemp & " not found."
```

```
    ElseIf Err = 6 Then 'overflow
        Resume Next
    Else
        MsgBox Error
    End If
    Exit Sub
End Sub
```

Summary

Although you can use the Upsizing Wizard from Microsoft to take the structure of an Access database and port it to SQL Server, you will have many more capabilities if you write one yourself. This chapter showed how to do just that. It showed the complexities of creating tables and indexes and the issues that can arise with using Identity columns in SQL Server.

This chapter is a great exercise to understand SQL and the differences between Access and SQL Server. You can expand on this application to allow upsizing to other databases, such as Oracle and Informix. You also could make this application a wizard by using the Wizard Manager. A detailed discussion of the Wizard Manager is in Chapter 39, "Creating a Wizard Add-In."

42

A Client/Server Application

The client/server application shown in this chapter is a fairly simple example of the structure of a three-tier client/server application. This application uses the pubs database and SQL Server as the database engine. Because the third tier (the database tier) is already created, this application focuses on only the first (front-end application) and second (database abstraction) tiers. The same concepts discussed in this chapter apply to *n*-tier client/server applications, where *n* is any number of middle tiers.

This chapter shows you how to create both the Tier 1 and Tier 2 applications. First comes Tier 1, simply called Test, because it simply calls one of four methods in Tier 2. Here are the methods:

- `Lookup`
- `Add`
- `Delete`
- `Update`

One of the major advantages of three-tier architecture is that the programmer of Tier 1 does not need to know the complexities of Tier 2. Also, he or she does not need to even know how the data is stored in Tier 3.

CROSS REFERENCE

For more information about three-tier and *n*-tier architecture, refer to Chapter 19, "Components and Objects," as well as Chapter 32, "Visual Basic's Role in Client/Server Computing."

The Test application has only one screen and very little code. The code for this application is on the CD accompanying this book in the `\CS` subdirectory. The only screen in the Test application is shown at runtime in Figure 42.1.

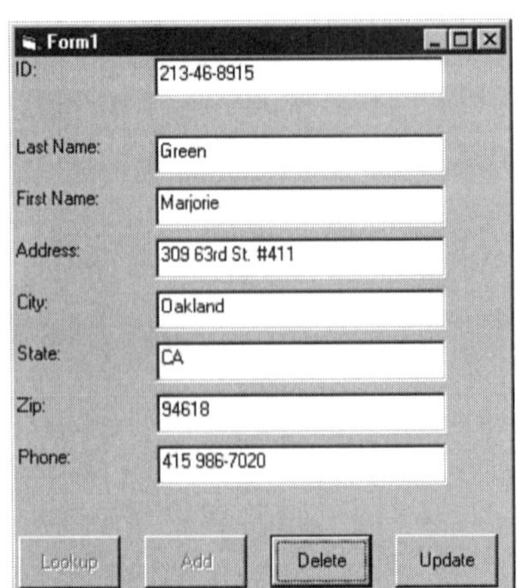

FIGURE 42.1.
The client/server application.

Using the Application

Using the application is quite simple. However, before you continue, refer to Figure 42.2, which shows a screen of data coming from the authors table in the pubs database with the ISQL/w utility. The ISQL/w (Interactive SQL for Windows) utility comes with SQL Server. It is used to send and receive SQL to and from SQL Server. The pubs database is installed automatically when SQL Server is set up. Knowing what this data looks like will help when you test the application shown in this chapter. In addition, you need to make sure that the Tier 2 application is registered on your system or the Tier 1 application won't be able to create the `Author` object necessary for this to run. To do this, make sure the `TIER2.DLL` file is copied onto your hard drive. The installation program should do this for you. Then, register the DLL with the Windows program, `REGSVR32.EXE`. Select Start | Run and type

```
REGSVR32 TIER2.DLL
```

This will register the `Author` object contained within the `TIER2.DLL` file. Constructing this DLL is discussed under the section, "Constructing the Tier 2 Application," later in this chapter.

FIGURE 42.2.
The authors table in the pubs database as shown with ISQL/w.

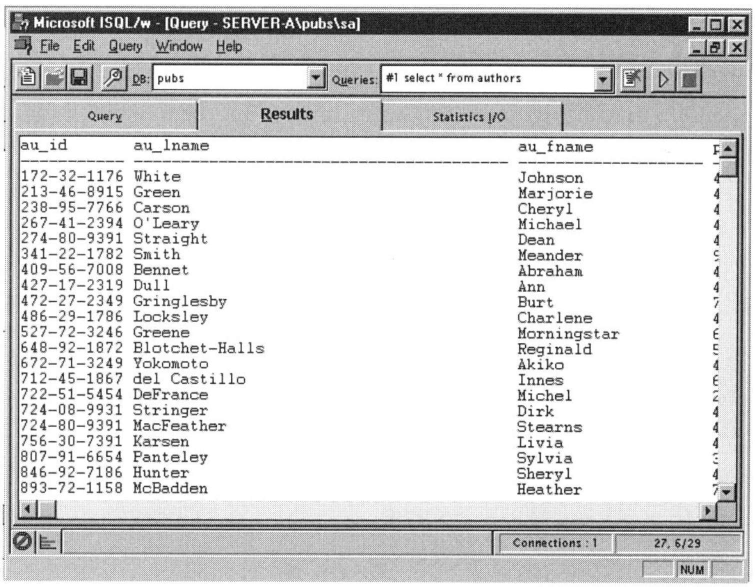

To use the application, simply type a Social Security number that exists in the authors table. It will be formatted by the `LostFocus` event, so explicitly placing the dashes in the text box is not necessary.

As you type in the ID field, the Lookup, Add, and Delete buttons become enabled, and the Update button is disabled. As you type in any other fields, the Lookup and Add buttons become disabled, and the Delete and Update buttons become enabled.

If you want to look up an ID, click the Lookup button. The application calls the `Lookup` method of the Tier 2 object and places the results in the text boxes.

If you want to add a new ID, you must type all the data in the text boxes and then click Add. All the data is inserted in the database at once. Because the table is keyed on the ID field, the operation will fail if you click the Add button for an ID that already exists.

If you want to delete an ID, simply type the ID and click Delete. The ID and all of its data will be deleted.

If you want to update an ID, change the data where appropriate and click Update. If you change the ID, the Update button will become disabled because a new ID must be added.

Constructing the Tier 1 Application

Constructing the Tier 1 application is extremely simple. The purpose of Tier1 in a three-tiered client/server application is so that the application is isolated. This way, the complexities of the database queries are isolated from the Tier 1 application.

Graphical Interface

The GUI part of this application contains only one form, which contains all of the code necessary to call the Tier 2 application and to handle all database activity. The following objects are placed on the form:

- Eight labels
- Eight text boxes
- Four command buttons

The eight labels used are to identify the eight adjacent text boxes. Only one property of the labels has been changed from its default value: the `Caption` property. Change the respective `Caption` properties to the following:

- `ID:`
- `Last Name:`
- `First Name:`
- `Address:`
- `City:`
- `State:`
- `Zip:`
- `Phone:`

The eight text boxes enable the user to enter data that will be used to transmit data to the database. The text boxes must have the `Name` and `Text` properties changed from their default values. All the names begin with the prefix `txt`, followed by a name that is germane to the objects' usage. Change the respective `Name` properties to the following:

- `txtID`
- `txtLastName`
- `txtFirstName`
- `txtAddress`
- `txtCity`
- `txtState`
- `txtZip`
- `txtPhone`

The `Text` properties should be changed in all cases to blank.

There are four command buttons. Each has two properties to change. The first is the `Caption` property. Change the respective `Caption` properties to the following:

- `Lookup`
- `Add`
- `Delete`
- `Update`

The second is the `Name` property. All names begin with the prefix `cmd`. Change the respective `Name` properties to the following:

- `cmdLookup`
- `cmdAdd`
- `cmdDelete`
- `cmdUpdate`

Code

There are only a few procedures that have code that make this application work. The following sections outline and explain the code in the Tier 1 application.

Module-Level Procedures

There is only one declaration in the `(general)(declarations)` section. The rest of the code is placed in two procedures at the module level in this application. They are shown in the following sections.

The `(general)(declarations)` Section

The `(general)(declarations)` section contains two lines of code, shown in Listing 42.1. This code is used to declare the event procedure for use with the Tier 2 object.

Listing 42.1. The `(general)(declarations)` section.

```
Option Explicit
Private WithEvents objAuthor As Author
```

The `objAuthor_Operation()` Subroutine

The `objAuthor_Operation()` subroutine is the code for the `Operation` event declared when the Tier 2 application was designed. It passes in one argument, `nStatus`, as an integer. This is used to determine whether there are any errors that occur during the desired operation. Listing 42.2 shows this subroutine.

Listing 42.2. The `objAuthor_Operation()` subroutine.

```
Private Sub objAuthor_Operation(ByVal nStatus As Integer)
    'handle event
    Select Case (nStatus)
        Case 0:
            'all is OK, do nothing
        Case -1:
            'general error
            MsgBox "General Error"
        Case -2:
            'no results
            MsgBox "No Results"
    End Select
End Sub
```

This event is fired automatically by the Tier 2 application. It is not "called" within the Tier 1 application.

The `EnableDisable()` Subroutine

The `EnableDisable()` subroutine is used as a centralized routine that enables and disables all command buttons. It passes in one argument, `nIDField`, which is used to indicate whether the changed field is the ID field or not. If the value is `True`, this is the ID field. Listing 42.3 shows this subroutine.

Listing 42.3. The `EnableDisable()` subroutine.

```
Public Sub EnableDisable(ByVal nIDField As Integer)
    If nIDField = True Then
        'this is the ID field
        cmdLookup.Enabled = True
        cmdAdd.Enabled = True
        cmdDelete.Enabled = True
        cmdUpdate.Enabled = False
    Else
        'this is NOT the ID field
        cmdLookup.Enabled = False
        cmdAdd.Enabled = False
        cmdDelete.Enabled = True
        cmdUpdate.Enabled = True
    End If

End Sub
```

The `cmdLookup` Command Button

The user clicks the `cmdLookup` command button when he or she wants to look up the data from the database, based on the ID entered in the `txtID` text box. It has code in only one event, the `Click()` event. Listing 42.4 shows the code for this event.

Listing 42.4. The `cmdLookup_Click()` event.

```
Private Sub cmdLookup_Click()
    'specify an ID
    objAuthor.AuthorID = txtID.Text

    'Lookup
    objAuthor.Lookup

    'fill in text boxes
    txtLastName.Text = objAuthor.LastName
    txtFirstName.Text = objAuthor.FirstName
    txtAddress.Text = objAuthor.Address
    txtCity.Text = objAuthor.City
    txtState.Text = objAuthor.State
    txtZip.Text = objAuthor.Zip
    txtPhone.Text = objAuthor.Phone
End Sub
```

The first thing that happens in this code is that the value of the `txtID` text box is assigned to the `AuthorID` property of the `objAuthor` object. This allows for the `Lookup` method to have a basis to look up the data. That is done next. The Tier 2 application fills the other properties with the values of the lookup, so each needs to be assigned to its corresponding text box.

The cmdAdd Command Button

The user clicks the cmdAdd command button when he or she wants to add data to the database, based on the ID entered in the txtID text box. It has code in only one event, the Click() event. Listing 42.5 shows the code for this event.

Listing 42.5. The cmdAdd_Click() event.

```
Private Sub cmdAdd_Click()

    'specify an ID
    objAuthor.AuthorID = txtID.Text

    'assign values
    objAuthor.LastName = txtLastName.Text
    objAuthor.FirstName = txtFirstName.Text
    objAuthor.Address = txtAddress.Text
    objAuthor.City = txtCity.Text
    objAuthor.State = txtState.Text
    objAuthor.Zip = txtZip.Text
    objAuthor.Phone = txtPhone.Text

    'Add
    objAuthor.Add

End Sub
```

The first thing that happens in this code is that the value of the txtID text box is assigned to the AuthorID property of the objAuthor object. This allows for the Add method to have a basis to add the data. Next, each of the properties of the objAuthor object is also assigned to the values of their corresponding text boxes. Finally, the Add method is invoked to actually add the data.

The cmdDelete Command Button

The user clicks the cmdDelete command button when he or she wants to delete data from the database, based on the ID entered in the txtID text box. It has code in only one event, the Click() event. Listing 42.6 shows the code for this event.

Listing 42.6. The cmdDelete_Click() event.

```
Private Sub cmdDelete_Click()

    Dim nRes As Integer

    nRes = MsgBox("Are you sure you want to Delete " & txtID.Text &
    ➥"?", vbYesNo)
```

```
    If nRes = vbNo Then
        Exit Sub
    End If
    'specify an ID
    objAuthor.AuthorID = txtID.Text

    'Delete
    objAuthor.Delete

    'clear text boxes
    txtID.Text = ""
    txtLastName.Text = ""
    txtFirstName.Text = ""
    txtAddress.Text = ""
    txtCity.Text = ""
    txtState.Text = ""
    txtZip.Text = ""
    txtPhone.Text = ""

    'display message
    MsgBox "Record Deleted"

    'change buttons
    cmdAdd.Enabled = False
    cmdDelete.Enabled = False
End Sub
```

The first thing that happens in this code is that the user is prompted to confirm if he really wants to delete this ID. If so, the code continues. If not, the code exits.

Next, the value of the `txtID` text box is assigned to the `AuthorID` property of the `objAuthor` object. This allows for the `Delete` method to have a basis to delete the data. It is not necessary to assign the other properties because the deletion is done based on the ID because it is the key to the field. When the deletion is finished, all text boxes are cleared to reflect the change.

The `cmdUpdate` Command Button

The user clicks the `cmdUpdate` command button when he or she wants to update data from the database, based on the ID entered in the `txtID` text box. It has code in only one event, the `Click()` event. Listing 42.7 shows the code for this event.

Listing 42.7. The `cmdUpdate_Click()` event.

```
Private Sub cmdUpdate_Click()
    'specify an ID
    objAuthor.AuthorID = txtID.Text

    'assign values
    objAuthor.LastName = txtLastName.Text
```

continues

Listing 42.7. continued

```
    objAuthor.FirstName = txtFirstName.Text
    objAuthor.Address = txtAddress.Text
    objAuthor.City = txtCity.Text
    objAuthor.State = txtState.Text
    objAuthor.Zip = txtZip.Text
    objAuthor.Phone = txtPhone.Text

    'Update
    objAuthor.Update

    'display message
    MsgBox "Record Updated"

    'change buttons
    cmdAdd.Enabled = False
    cmdDelete.Enabled = False

End Sub
```

The first thing that happens in this code is that the value of the `txtID` text box is assigned to the `AuthorID` property of the `objAuthor` object. This allows for the `Update` method to have a basis to update the data. Next, all of the properties of the `objAuthor` object are also assigned to the values of their corresponding text boxes. Finally, the `Update` method is invoked to actually update the data.

The `Form` Object

The `Form` object has code in only one event, the `Load()` event. It is used to initialize the application. Listing 42.8 shows the code for this event.

Listing 42.8. The `Form_Load()` event.

```
Private Sub Form_Load()
    'initialize buttons
    cmdLookup.Enabled = False
    cmdAdd.Enabled = False
    cmdDelete.Enabled = False
    cmdUpdate.Enabled = False

    'instantiate object
    Set objAuthor = New Author

End Sub
```

First, all of the command buttons are disabled because the `EnableDisable()` subroutine handles all of this functionality. Then, a new object of type `Author` is instantiated. This is what allows the application to function. The `Author` object is the Tier 2 application. After it is instantiated, it is used throughout the application.

The `txtID` Text Box

The `txtID` text box has code in two events, `Change()` and `LostFocus()`. Listings 42.9 and 42.10 show the code for these events.

Listing 42.9. The `txtID_Change()` event.

```
Private Sub txtID_Change()
    Call EnableDisable(True)
End Sub
```

This code simply calls the `EnableDisable()` subroutine, passing a value of `True`, indicating that the `txtID` text box is the ID field.

Listing 42.10. The `txtID_LostFocus()` event.

```
Private Sub txtID_LostFocus()
    txtID.Text = Format$(txtID.Text, "###-##-####")
End Sub
```

This event is used to format the text as a Social Security number.

The `txtLastName` Text Box

The `txtLastName` text box has code in only one event, the `Change()` event. Listing 42.11 shows the code for this event.

Listing 42.11. The `txtLastName_Change()` event.

```
Private Sub txtLastName_Change()
    Call EnableDisable(False)

End Sub
```

The code simply calls the `EnableDisable` routine, passing a value of `False`, indicating that the `txtLastName` text box is not the ID field.

The `txtPhone` Text Box

The `txtPhone` text box has code in only one event, the `Change()` event. Listing 42.12 shows the code for this event.

Listing 42.12. The `txtPhone_Change()` event.

```
Private Sub txtPhone_Change()
    Call EnableDisable(False)

End Sub
```

This code simply calls the `EnableDisable` routine, passing a value of `False`, indicating that the `txtPhone` text box is not the ID field.

The `txtState` Text Box

The `txtState` text box has code in only one event, the `Change()` event. Listing 42.13 shows the code for this event.

Listing 42.13. The `txtState_Change()` event.

```
Private Sub txtState_Change()
    Call EnableDisable(False)

End Sub
```

This code simply calls the `EnableDisable` routine, passing a value of `False`, indicating that the `txtState` text box is not the ID field.

The `txtZip` Text Box

The `txtZip` text box has code in only one event, the `Change()` event. Listing 42.14 shows the code for this event.

Listing 42.14. The `txtZip_Change()` event.

```
Private Sub txtZip_Change()
    Call EnableDisable(False)

End Sub
```

This code simply calls the `EnableDisable` routine, passing a value of `False`, indicating that the `txtZip` text box is not the ID field.

The `txtAddress` Text Box

The `txtAddress` text box has code in only one event, the `Change()` event. Listing 42.15 shows the code for this event.

Listing 42.15. The `txtAddress_Change()` event.

```
Private Sub txtAddress_Change()
    Call EnableDisable(False)

End Sub
```

This code simply calls the `EnableDisable` routine, passing a value of `False`, indicating that the `txtAddress` text box is not the ID field.

The `txtCity` Text Box

The `txtCity` text box has code in only one event, the `Change()` event. Listing 42.16 shows the code for this event.

Listing 42.16. The `txtCity_Change()` event.

```
Private Sub txtCity_Change()
    Call EnableDisable(False)

End Sub
```

This code simply calls the `EnableDisable` routine, passing a value of `False`, indicating that the `txtCity` text box is not the ID field.

The `txtFirstName` Text Box

The `txtFirstName` text box has code in only one event, the `Change()` event. Listing 42.17 shows the code for this event.

Listing 42.17. The `txtFirstName_Change()` event.

```
Private Sub txtFirstName_Change()
    Call EnableDisable(False)

End Sub
```

This code simply calls the `EnableDisable` routine, passing a value of `False`, indicating that the `txtFirstName` text box is not the ID field.

Constructing the Tier 2 Application

Constructing the Tier 2 application is a little more complex than creating the Tier 1 application because it has no visual interface. It is actually compiled into a DLL and distributed throughout all machines needing this functionality. The Tier 2 application has code in numerous procedures that are described throughout the rest of this chapter. The code for this application, called TIER2, is located on the CD accompanying this book in the `\TIER2` subdirectory.

Graphical Interface

Again, there is no graphical interface—there is only code running in the background. Therefore, if you run this application through Visual Basic, you will see nothing (except the debug window).

Code

The code for this Tier 2 application is encapsulated into a class module. As you might expect, the name of the class module is `Author`.

Class-Level Procedures

There are many class-level procedures needed to make up the properties, methods, and events in this application. They are shown in the following sections.

The `(general)(declarations)` Section

The `(general)(declarations)` section is used to declare class-level variables necessary to make the class work. Listing 42.18 shows this code.

Listing 42.18. The `(general)(declarations)` section.

```
Option Explicit

'SQL Server variables
Private rdoCn As New rdo.rdoConnection
Private rdoEn As rdo.rdoEnvironment

'local variable(s) to hold property value(s)
Private mvarAuthorID As String 'local copy
Private mvarLastName As String 'local copy
Private mvarFirstName As String 'local copy
Private mvarPhone As String 'local copy
Private mvarAddress As String 'local copy
Private mvarCity As String 'local copy
Private mvarState As String 'local copy
Private mvarZip As String 'local copy

'To fire this event, use RaiseEvent with the following syntax:
'RaiseEvent Operation[(arg1, arg2, ... , argn)]
Public Event Operation(ByVal Status As Integer)
```

The majority of the code is used to store a local copy of the value of each of the properties. The beginning of the declarations are used for RDO connections. They are private to the class.

The `Class` Declarations

The `Class` declarations are used to handle events generated by the class. There are two events that require code, `Class_Initialize()` and `Class_Terminate()`. They are shown in Listings 42.19 and 42.20.

Listing 42.19. The `Class_Initialize()` event.

```
Private Sub Class_Initialize()

    'Connect to SQL Server

    Set rdoEn = rdoEnvironments(0)
    With rdoCn
        .Connect = "UID=sa;PWD=;Database=Pubs;DSN=LocalServer;"
        .EstablishConnection rdDriverNoPrompt, True
        rdoEn.rdoConnections.Add rdoCn
    End With

End Sub
```

The `Initialize` event automatically fires when the class is instantiated. This is a great place to establish the RDO connections. This application connects to a specific database, but you might want to provide a way for the user to choose a database.

CROSS REFERENCE

For more information about RDO, refer to Chapter 16, "Remote Data Objects (RDO)."

Listing 42.20. The `Class_Terminate()` event.

```
Private Sub Class_Terminate()

    'close the active connection
    rdoCn.Close

End Sub
```

The `Terminate` event needs to handle the closing of the RDO connection. This is fired when the instance of the class is destroyed.

Property Procedures

There are eight properties in this class:

- Address
- AuthorID
- City
- FirstName
- LastName
- Phone
- State
- Zip

Each of these properties has a `Property Let` and a `Property Get` procedure. A `Property Let` procedure is called when the value of a property is set or assigned by the calling application. A `Property Get` procedure is called when the calling application requests the value of a property.

There are many class-level procedures needed to make up the properties, methods, and events in this application. They are shown in the following sections. Each was created with the Class Builder Utility. The Class Builder Utility saves much time when creating properties, methods, and events in classes.

CROSS REFERENCE

For more information about the Class Builder Utility, refer to Chapter 3, "Classes."

The `Address` Properties

The `Address` properties are used to set and retrieve values from the `Address` property in the class. Listings 42.21 and 42.22 show this code.

Listing 42.21. The `Property Get Address` subroutine.

```
Public Property Get Address() As String
'used when retrieving value of a property, on the right side of an
'assignment.  Syntax: Debug.Print X.Address
    Address = mvarAddress
End Property
```

Listing 42.22. The `Property Let Address` subroutine.

```
Public Property Let Address(ByVal vData As String)
'used when assigning a value to the property, on the left side of an
'assignment.  Syntax: X.Address = 5
    mvarAddress = vData
End Property
```

The `AuthorID` Properties

The `AuthorID` properties are used to set and retrieve values from the `AuthorID` property in the class. Listings 42.23 and 42.24 show this code.

Listing 42.23. The `Property Get AuthorID` subroutine.

```
Public Property Get AuthorID() As String
'used when retrieving value of a property, on the right side of an
'assignment.  Syntax: Debug.Print X.AuthorID
    AuthorID = mvarAuthorID
End Property
```

Listing 42.24. The `Property Let AuthorID` subroutine.

```
Public Property Let AuthorID(ByVal vData As String)
'used when assigning a value to the property, on the left side of an
'assignment.  Syntax: X.AuthorID = 5
    mvarAuthorID = vData
End Property
```

The `City` Properties

The `City` properties are used to set and retrieve values from the `City` property in the class. Listings 42.25 and 42.26 show this code.

Listing 42.25. The `Property Get City` subroutine.

```
Public Property Get City() As String
'used when retrieving value of a property, on the right side of an
'assignment.  Syntax: Debug.Print X.City
    City = mvarCity
End Property
```

Listing 42.26. The `Property Let City` subroutine.

```
Public Property Let City(ByVal vData As String)
'used when assigning a value to the property, on the left side of an
'assignment.  Syntax: X.City = 5
    mvarCity = vData
End Property
```

The `FirstName` Properties

The `FirstName` properties are used to set and retrieve values from the `FirstName` property in the class. Listings 42.27 and 42.28 show this code.

Listing 42.27. The `Property Get FirstName` subroutine.

```
Public Property Get FirstName() As String
'used when retrieving value of a property, on the right side of an
'assignment.  Syntax: Debug.Print X.FirstName
    FirstName = mvarFirstName
End Property
```

Listing 42.28. The `Property Let FirstName` subroutine.

```
Public Property Let FirstName(ByVal vData As String)
'used when assigning a value to the property, on the left side of an
'assignment.  Syntax: X.FirstName = 5
    mvarFirstName = vData
End Property
```

The `LastName` Properties

The `LastName` properties are used to set and retrieve values from the `LastName` property in the class. Listings 42.29 and 42.30 show this code.

Listing 42.29. The `Property Get LastName` subroutine.

```
Public Property Get LastName() As String
'used when retrieving value of a property, on the right side of an
'assignment.  Syntax: Debug.Print X.LastName
    LastName = mvarLastName
End Property
```

Listing 42.30. The `Property Let LastName` subroutine.

```
Public Property Let LastName(ByVal vData As String)
'used when assigning a value to the property, on the left side of an
'assignment.  Syntax: X.LastName = 5
    mvarLastName = vData
End Property
```

The Phone Properties

The `Phone` properties are used to set and retrieve values from the `Phone` property in the class. Listings 42.31 and 42.32 show this code.

Listing 42.31. The `Property Get Phone` subroutine.

```
Public Property Get Phone() As String
'used when retrieving value of a property, on the right side of an
'assignment.  Syntax: Debug.Print X.Phone
    Phone = mvarPhone
End Property
```

Listing 42.32. The `Property Let Phone` subroutine.

```
Public Property Let Phone(ByVal vData As String)
'used when assigning a value to the property, on the left side of an
'assignment.  Syntax: X.Phone = 5
    mvarPhone = vData
End Property
```

The State Properties

The `State` properties are used to set and retrieve values from the `State` property in the class. Listings 42.33 and 42.34 show this code.

Listing 42.33. The `Property Get State` subroutine.

```
Public Property Get State() As String
'used when retrieving value of a property, on the right side of an
'assignment.  Syntax: Debug.Print X.State
    State = mvarState
End Property
```

Listing 42.34. The `Property Let State` subroutine.

```
Public Property Let State(ByVal vData As String)
'used when assigning a value to the property, on the left side of an
'assignment.  Syntax: X.State = 5
    mvarState = vData
End Property
```

The `Zip` Properties

The `Zip` properties are used to set and retrieve values from the `Zip` property in the class. Listings 42.35 and 42.36 show this code.

Listing 42.35. The `Property Get Zip` subroutine.

```
Public Property Get Zip() As String
'used when retrieving value of a property, on the right side of an
'assignment.  Syntax: Debug.Print X.Zip
    Zip = mvarZip
End Property
```

Listing 42.36. The `Property Let Zip` subroutine.

```
Public Property Let Zip(ByVal vData As String)
'used when assigning a value to the property, on the left side of an
'assignment.  Syntax: X.Zip = 5
    mvarZip = vData
End Property
```

Method Procedures

There are four methods in this class:

- `Add`
- `Delete`
- `Lookup`
- `Update`

The code in each of these methods performs the actions needed to manipulate the database. Each is described throughout the next few sections.

The `Add` Method

The `Add` method adds data to the database by using the `INSERT` SQL statement. Listing 42.37 shows the code for this method.

Listing 42.37. The Add method.

```
Public Sub Add()
    'declare variables
    Dim sCmd As String

    'clear errors
    rdo.rdoEngine.rdoErrors.Clear

    'construct SQL statement
    sCmd = "INSERT INTO Authors(au_id,au_lname,au_fname,phone,address,city,
➥state,zip,contract) "
    sCmd = sCmd & "VALUES ('" & AuthorID & "','"
    sCmd = sCmd & LastName & "','"
    sCmd = sCmd & FirstName & "','"
    sCmd = sCmd & Phone & "','"
    sCmd = sCmd & Address & "','"
    sCmd = sCmd & City & "','"
    sCmd = sCmd & State & "','"
    sCmd = sCmd & Zip & "',"
    sCmd = sCmd & "0)"
    rdoCn.Execute (sCmd)

    'respond
    If rdo.rdoEngine.rdoErrors.Count > 0 Then
        'there was an error
        RaiseEvent Operation(-1)
    Else
        'all was OK

        'raise the event that everything is ok
        RaiseEvent Operation(0)
    End If
End Sub
```

This code is easy to follow. First, all RDO errors are cleared. Then, an SQL statement is built based on the values in each of the properties and is inserted into the database. The `Execute` method is used to issue the statement. Then, the `Operation` event is raised, passing the error status. Zero is passed if there are no errors.

The `Delete` Method

The `Delete` method deletes data from the database by using the `DELETE` SQL statement. Listing 42.38 shows the code for this method.

Listing 42.38. The Delete method.

```
Public Sub Delete()
    'declare variables
    Dim sCmd As String
```

continues

Listing 42.38. continued

```
    'clear errors
    rdo.rdoEngine.rdoErrors.Clear

    'construct SQL statement
    sCmd = "DELETE FROM Authors "
    sCmd = sCmd & "WHERE au_id = '" & AuthorID & "' "
    rdoCn.Execute (sCmd)
    'respond
    If rdo.rdoEngine.rdoErrors.Count > 0 Then
        'there was an error
        RaiseEvent Operation(-1)
    Else
        'all was OK
        'Clear all
        AuthorID = ""
        LastName = ""
        FirstName = ""
        Phone = ""
        Address = ""
        City = ""
        State = ""
        Zip = ""

        'raise the event that everything is ok
        RaiseEvent Operation(0)
    End If
End Sub
```

This code is also easy to follow. First, all RDO errors are cleared. Then, an SQL statement is built based on the value in the `AuthorID` property. The `Execute` method is used to issue the statement. Then, the `Operation` event is raised, passing the error status. Zero is passed if there are no errors. Each of the other property values are cleared to reflect the deletion of the author.

The `Lookup` Method

The `Lookup` method looks up data from the database by using the `SELECT` SQL statement. Listing 42.39 shows the code for this method.

Listing 42.39. The `Lookup` method.

```
Public Sub Lookup()
    'declare variables
    Dim sCmd As String
    Dim rdoRs As rdoResultset

    'clear errors
    rdo.rdoEngine.rdoErrors.Clear
```

```
    'construct SQL statement
    sCmd = "SELECT * FROM Authors "
    sCmd = sCmd & "WHERE au_id = '" & AuthorID & "' "
    Set rdoRs = rdoCn.OpenResultset(sCmd)

    'respond
    If rdo.rdoEngine.rdoErrors.Count > 0 Then
        'there was an error
        RaiseEvent Operation(-1)
    ElseIf rdoCn.rdoResultsets(0).EOF = True Then
        'no results
        RaiseEvent Operation(-2)
    Else
        'all was OK

        'First, Clear all except ID
        LastName = ""
        FirstName = ""
        Phone = ""
        Address = ""
        City = ""
        State = ""
        Zip = ""

        'populate with results
        LastName = rdoCn.rdoResultsets(0).rdoColumns("au_lname").Value
        FirstName = rdoCn.rdoResultsets(0).rdoColumns("au_fname").Value
        Phone = rdoCn.rdoResultsets(0).rdoColumns("phone").Value
        Address = rdoCn.rdoResultsets(0).rdoColumns("address").Value
        City = rdoCn.rdoResultsets(0).rdoColumns("city").Value
        State = rdoCn.rdoResultsets(0).rdoColumns("state").Value
        Zip = rdoCn.rdoResultsets(0).rdoColumns("zip").Value

        'raise the event that everything is ok
        RaiseEvent Operation(0)
    End If

End Sub
```

This code is also easy to follow. First, all RDO errors are cleared. Then, an SQL statement is built based on the value in the `AuthorID` property. A `ResultSet` is opened to assign the values of the lookup to the properties in the `Author` class. Then, the `Operation` event is raised, passing the error status. Zero is passed if there are no errors. If there is no data, an error of `-2` is passed to the `Operation` event.

The `Update` Method

The `Update` method is used to update data in the database by using the `UPDATE` SQL statement. Listing 42.40 shows the code for this method.

Listing 42.40. The `Update` method.

```
Public Sub Update()
    'declare variables
    Dim sCmd As String

    'clear errors
    rdo.rdoEngine.rdoErrors.Clear

    'construct SQL statement
    sCmd = "UPDATE Authors "
    sCmd = sCmd & "SET au_lname = '" & LastName & " ',"
    sCmd = sCmd & "au_fname = '" & FirstName & " ',"
    sCmd = sCmd & "phone = '" & Phone & "',"
    sCmd = sCmd & "address = '" & Address & "',"
    sCmd = sCmd & "city = '" & City & "',"
    sCmd = sCmd & "state = '" & State & "',"
    sCmd = sCmd & "Zip = '" & Zip & "',"
    sCmd = sCmd & "contract = 0 "
    sCmd = sCmd & "WHERE au_id = '" & AuthorID & "' "
    rdoCn.Execute (sCmd)

    'respond
    If rdo.rdoEngine.rdoErrors.Count > 0 Then
        'there was an error
        RaiseEvent Operation(-1)
    Else
        'all was OK

        'raise the event that everything is ok
        RaiseEvent Operation(0)
    End If
End Sub
```

This code is also easy to follow. First, all RDO errors are cleared. Then, an SQL statement is built based on the values in each of the properties and updated in the database. The `Execute` method is used to issue the statement. Then, the `Operation` event is raised, passing the error status. Zero is passed if there are no errors.

Summary

Many Visual Basic developers have not yet delved into three-tier or *n*-tier client/server architecture. These developers will find that they will receive more requests for this architecture. This chapter showed how to create not only the client application (Tier 1), but the business layer (Tier 2 or middle tier) as well.

Using the Class Builder Utility, you can quickly create your classes, which are the basis of the middle tier. Then, using the properties and methods exposed from these classes, the Tier 1 application can use those properties and methods.

Use this chapter as a basis for your three-tier or *n*-tier applications. You can expand on the topics discussed here to let the application obtain data from other data sources, such as Access. You can even use the concepts in this chapter to build a three-tier application that does not even communicate with a database at all. It can perform business calculations or even show multimedia presentations. The possibilities are endless.

43

Creating an Electronic Commerce Internet Application

This shopping cart application enables your customers to shop over the Internet by browsing through your virtual store, selecting items for purchase, reviewing them, and then paying for them. This is made possible with the Microsoft Merchant Server, which is the focus of this chapter. There are other servers that will perform similar operations, however. Refer to ICat Corporation's ICat Electronic Commerce Suite in Appendix A, "Third-Party Vendors," for more information.

In addition to simply seeing products displayed on the Web, more and more customers are demanding that their transactions be secure. This means that personal information is encoded so that, for example, credit card information is not transmitted over the Internet in a pure text form.

This chapter assumes that you have installed not only the Merchant Server BackOffice product from Microsoft, but the Clock Peddler sample application as well. The code for this chapter is on the CD-ROM accompanying this book in the `\MERCHANT` subdirectory.

The merchant server can (and should) get its product information from a database, such as SQL Server. This information can include the following:

- Products
- Pricing
- Tax rates
- Promotions

CROSS REFERENCE

This chapter illustrates many topics discussed throughout this book. These topics are from the following chapters:

- Chapter 6, "The Registry"
- Chapter 16, "Remote Data Objects (RDO)"
- Chapter 20, "ActiveX Controls"
- Chapter 23, "The Internet"
- Chapter 25, "HTML Primer"
- Chapter 28, "Database Concepts"
- Chapter 29, "Structured Query Language (SQL)"

Setting Up a New Store

To set up a new store, you first need to understand the directory structure. It is a good idea to set up many directories on the server for different purposes; you'll also need to control security to these directories. Suppose you wanted to set up a simple store to sell books online. This example uses my company, SoftHouse (or SH for short), as the vendor name.

NOTE

All of the directory structures shown in this chapter are samples. Your directory structure might be slightly different. It is possible that the only difference in your directory structures is that the `SH` subdirectory will be substituted for the name of your Internet store.

The directory structure would look like this:

- `\STORES\SH`—The store's parent directory
- `\STORES\SH\ADMIN\ELEMENTS`—Common elements to be used on the administrator's templates
- `\STORES\SH\ADMIN\TEMPLATES`—HTML templates used by the administrator for adding, deleting, and updating products
- `\STORES\SH\ASSETS\IMAGES`—Site-related images
- `\STORES\SH\ASSETS\PRODIMG`—Product images
- `\STORES\SH\LOGIN\TEMPLATES`—All login-related HTML pages
- `\STORES\SH\SHOP\ELEMENTS`—Common elements (such as headers and footers)
- `\STORES\SH\SHOP\TEMPLATES`—HTML pages relating to the shopping experience
- `\STORES\SH\SQL\SQLSVR`—All SQL related to creating and populating the database

Again, these files are all stored on the CD-ROM accompanying this book in the `\MERCHANT` subdirectory. Because the only thing in this subdirectory is the code necessary for the SH store, the `\STORES\SH` subdirectories are omitted on the CD-ROM. For example, the `\STORES\SH\ADMIN\ELEMENTS` subdirectory within Merchant Server is placed in the `\MERCHANT\ADMIN\ELEMENTS` subdirectory on the CD.

Creating the Database Schema

The schema of the database needs to be set up in SQL Server. It's a good idea to create your database, not in the SQL Enterprise Manager, but in the ISQL/w utility instead. This way the DDL (Data Definition Language) statement can be saved, in case you have to re-create your database.

Let's define the structure of the database. There will be five tables. Each is created with a Data Definition Language, or DDL, statement. All of these DDL statements are stored in `\STORES\SH\SQL\SQLSVR\SCHEMA.SQL`. Each of these DDL statements must be run in the Microsoft Merchant database, which was automatically set up when you installed Merchant Server. For this application, the database is called MSMerchant. The first three tables are mandatory to all Microsoft Merchant stores:

- *prefix*_sql stores SQL statements used within the store.
- *prefix*_shopper stores information about individual shoppers.
- *prefix*_basket stores temporary information about items placed in a shopper's basket.

Here, *prefix* is some prefix identifying your store. For example, sh_sql is the name of the table identifying all of the SQL statements used for SoftHouse.

sh_sql is the first table. It is defined in Listing 43.1.

Listing 43.1. sh_sql definition.

```
/* sql table */
create table sh_sql (
name varchar(40) unique,
sql_text text)
```

This table simply stores SQL statements for later execution. The next table is sh_shopper. It is defined in Listing 43.2.

Listing 43.2. sh_shopper definition.

```
/* Shopper table */
create table sh_shopper (
shopper_id varchar(32) unique,
created datetime,
address1 varchar(50) NULL,
address2 varchar(50) NULL,
city varchar(30) NULL,
state char(2) NULL,
country varchar(10) NULL,
zip varchar(10) NULL,
phone varchar(20) NULL,
fax varchar(20) NULL,
email varchar(50) NULL)
```

The system will create a 32-byte representation of a shopper ID. That's why the `shopper_id` field is of type `Varchar(32)`. This is a mandatory field, along with the `created` field, which is the system-generated date/time for when the ID was created. All of the other fields have been added to this table. They are not mandatory, but they are useful for tracking purposes.

The next table, sh_basket, is another mandatory table used to track the contents of a shopper's basket before checkout. This table is defined in Listing 43.3.

Listing 43.3. sh_basket definition.

```
/* Basket Table */
create table sh_basket (
shopper_id varchar(32) unique,
date_changed datetime,
marshalled_order image)
```

All three columns in this table are mandatory. Each is tracked and handled automatically by Merchant Server.

The next two tables are not mandatory, but they are very useful for storing the products, themselves. The first table, sh_product, is used to simply store product information. It is defined in Listing 43.4.

Listing 43.4. sh_product definition.

```
/* Product table */
create table sh_product (
sku varchar(30) unique,
name varchar(50),
cat_id int,
description text,
list_price int,
image_file varchar(20) NULL,
image_width int NULL,
image_height int NULL)
```

This table stores SKU numbers (unique identifiers for each product), product names, category IDs (used to join with the next table), ad descriptions, pricing, and image information.

The last table, sh_category, is used to identify the categories stored in the sh_product table, under the cat_id column. This table is defined in Listing 43.5.

Listing 43.5. sh_category definition.

```
/* Category table */
create table sh_category(
cat_id int,
cat_name varchar(50),
cat_description varchar(200) NULL)
```

This table simply stores the ID, a name, and a description (which can be `NULL`).

After you have set up your tables, Merchant Server needs to know where these tables are located. For this store, they are listed in the Registry under the following keys:

```
HKEY_LOCAL_MACHINE\SOFTWARE\Microsoft\MerchantServer\Stores\sh\Database\
➥db_table_sql=sh_sql
HKEY_LOCAL_MACHINE\SOFTWARE\Microsoft\MerchantServer\Stores\sh\Database\
➥db_table_order=sh_basket
HKEY_LOCAL_MACHINE\SOFTWARE\Microsoft\MerchantServer\Stores\sh\Database\
➥db_table_shopper=sh_shopper
```

You must substitute `sh` for the name of your store, where appropriate, as well as the name of your table to reference.

An easy way to create the appropriate Registry entries is to use the Administrator utility that comes with Merchant Server. To use this utility, select Start | Programs | Microsoft Merchant Server | Merchant Server Administrator. This will bring up a utility with five tabs. Select the last tab, Add Store, which is shown in Figure 43.1.

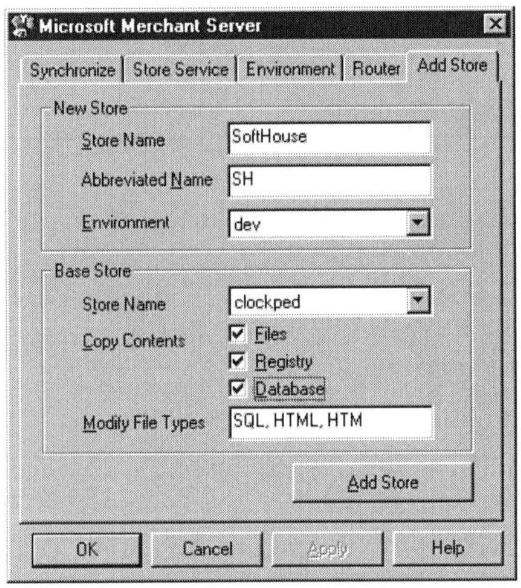

FIGURE 43.1.
Adding a Merchant Server store.

The easiest way to create a new store is to base it on an existing store and then make changes where appropriate. There are two sections on the Add Store tab. The first section is called New Store. This tab contains the following three entries:

- Store Name
- Abbreviated Name
- Environment

The Store Name is the full name of your new store to be created. The Abbreviated Name will wind up being the abbreviated name of your directories and Registry entries. The Environment is the type of environment desired. There are three possible choices:

- Dev (development environment)
- Prd (production environment)
- State (staging environment between development and production)

The next section is Base Store, and it also contains three entry fields. The first is the store name upon which to base the new store. Select from one of the existing stores that most closely matches your new store so that you do not have to change too much. The second section, Copy Contents, contains three check boxes:

- Files
- Registry
- Database

Each of these types, if checked, will be copied to the new store. It is a good idea to copy all of these because you will be changing them where appropriate. The third section is Modify File Types. This is a text box containing the list of file extensions to modify in the new store from the old store. By default, there are three types of files:

- Files
- Registry
- Database

When you have selected the desired entries, click the Add Store command button to create a new store.

Inserting the Database Data

If you have chosen to copy your store from the Clockped store, then there will be three additional SQL files for creating data in tables:

- `data.dept.sql`
- `data.product.sql`
- `data.queries.sql`

The first step is to rename the first item. The sh database does not use departments but rather categories for the products. Rename `data.dept.sql` as `data.cat.sql`. Open the `data.cat.sql` script and do a search and replace for all occurrences of `dept` and change them to `category`. Next, add categories for products into your SQL `INSERT` statements. The SoftHouse store categories are shown in Listing 43.6.

Listing 43.6. The `data.cat.sql` file.

```
/************************************************************************
 *                                                                      *
 *   DATA.CAT.SQL                                                      *
 ************************************************************************/

/* - data.cat.sql for sh */

/*-------------------------------
** Delete all the old data
*/
truncate table sh_category
go

/*-------------------------------
** Insert some categories
*/

insert into sh_category values(
1,
'Software',
'X-10 Software')
go

insert into sh_category values(
2,
'Books',
'Visual Basic Books')
go

insert into sh_category values(
3,
'Literature',
'Information Requests')
go
```

The next step is to change the data related to the sh_products table. Open the `data.product.sql` script. Then, add products that relate to your store. The SoftHouse store products are shown in Listing 43.7.

Listing 43.7. The `data.product.sql` file.

```
/************************************************************************
 *                                                                      *
 *   DATA.PRODUCT.SQL                                                  *
 ************************************************************************/

/* data.product.sql for sh
**
**  Inserts data into the product table
*/

/*-------------------------------
** Delete all the old data
```

```
*/
truncate table sh_product
go

/*------------------------------
** Insert the products
*/
/*
** Product 1
*/
insert into sh_product values(
'VBX10HS',
'VBX-10 Hardware/Software Kit',
1,
    '<UL><li>3-Piece serial port hardware<li>16-bit VBX for use with Visual
    ➥Basic 3 or Visual Basic 4 (16-bit)<li>Sample Application</UL>',
15995,
NULL,
NULL,
NULL)
go

/*
** Product 2
*/
insert into sh_product values(
'VBX10S',
'VBX-10 Software Only',
1,
    '<UL><li>16-bit VBX for use with Visual Basic 3 or Visual Basic 4 (16-bit)
    ➥<li>Sample Application</UL>',
12995,
NULL,
NULL,
NULL)
go

/*
** Product 3
*/
insert into sh_product values(
'VBX10H',
'VBX-10 Hardware Only',
1,
'<UL><li>3-Piece serial port hardware</UL>',
5995,
NULL,
NULL,
NULL)
go

/*
** Product 4
*/
insert into sh_product values(
'OCX10HS',
'OCX-10 Hardware/Software Kit',
```

continues

Listing 43.7. continued

```
1,
    '<UL><li>3-Piece serial port hardware<li>32-bit OCX for use with Visual
    ➥Basic 4 (32-bit) or Visual Basic 5<li>Sample Application</UL>',
17995,
NULL,
NULL,
NULL)
go

/*
** Product 5
*/
insert into sh_product values(
'OCX10S',
'OCX-10 Software Only',
1,
    '<UL><li>32-bit OCX for use with Visual Basic 4 (32-bit) or Visual Basic
    ➥5<li>Sample Application</UL>',
14995,
NULL,
NULL,
NULL)
go

/*
** Product 6
*/
insert into sh_product values(
'OCX10H',
'OCX-10 Hardware Only',
1,
'<UL><li>3-Piece serial port hardware</UL>',
5995,
NULL,
NULL,
NULL)
go

/*
** Product 7
*/
insert into sh_product values(
'UPGRADE',
'VBX-10 to OCX-10 Software Upgrade',
1,
    '<UL><li>32-bit OCX for use with Visual Basic 4 (32-bit) or Visual Basic
    ➥5<li>Sample Application</UL>',
4995,
NULL,
NULL,
NULL)
go

/*
** Product 8
*/
insert into sh_product values(
```

```
'RWPROGVB',
'Real-World Programming With Visual Basic Book',
2,
'<UL><li>884 page book for Visual Basic 3<li>32 Chapters<li>CD-ROM
➥Included</UL>',
3600,
NULL,
NULL,
NULL)
go

/*
** Product 9
*/
insert into sh_product values(
'RWPROGVB4',
'Real-World Programming With Visual Basic 4 Book',
2,
'<UL><li>1154 page book for Visual Basic 4<li>42 Chapters<li>CD-ROM
➥Included</UL>',
4000,
NULL,
NULL,
NULL)
go

/*
** Product 10
*/
insert into sh_product values(
'VB4DEVGUIDE',
'Visual Basic 4 Developer''s Guide',
2,
'<UL><li>997 page book for Visual Basic 4<li>35 Chapters<li>CD-ROM
➥Included</UL>',
4400,
NULL,
NULL,
NULL)
go

/*
** Product 11
*/
insert into sh_product values(
'VB5DEVGUIDE',
'Visual Basic 5 Developer''s Guide',
2,
'<UL><li>To Be Announced<li>43 Chapters<li>CD-ROM Included</UL>',
4800,
NULL,
NULL,
NULL)
go

/*
** Product 12
```

continues

Listing 43.7. continued

```
*/
insert into sh_product values(
'BROCHURE',
'Home Automation Brochure',
3,
'<UL><li>About X-10 Technolgy<li>SoftHouse Software</UL>',
000,
NULL,
NULL,
NULL)
go
```

Notice on Product 11, the word `Developer''s` has two apostrophes. This is because if there were only one apostrophe, SQL Server would consider this an unmatched quotation mark, and the `INSERT` statement would fail.

In all of these examples, there are no images to load. There is only text. To add images to your database, you don't actually add images to the database, per se. You are including the GIF filename of the image, itself. This goes where the first `NULL` is on each product. The second `NULL` is where you would enter the width of the image, and the third `NULL` is where you would enter the height of the image.

The next step is to change the data related to the sh_sql table. Open the `data.queries.sql` script. Although you might need additional queries in the future, the only thing to do at this point is to perform a search and replace. Search for instances of `dept_id` and replace them with `cat_id`. Then, search for instances of `sh_dept` and replace them with `sh_category`. The SoftHouse store's queries are shown in Listing 43.8.

Listing 43.8. The `data.queries.sql` file.

```
/*****************************************************************************
 *                                                                           *
 *   DATA.QUERIES.SQL                                                        *
 *****************************************************************************/

/* - data.queries.sql for sh
**
**  Creates all the queries necessary to run the store.
*/


truncate table sh_sql
go


/*
**   ----------------------------------------------
**   -- Queries for the Admin pages:
**   ----------------------------------------------
```

```
*/

insert into sh_sql
values (
'query-by-name',
'select * from sh_sql where name = :1'
)
go


/*
**  -----------------------------------------------
**  -- Queries for the Store pages:
**  -----------------------------------------------
*/
insert into sh_sql
values (
'products-by-cat',
'select * from sh_product where cat_id = convert(numeric,:1)'
)
go

insert into sh_sql
values (
'category',
'select * from sh_category where cat_id = convert(numeric,:1)'
)
go

insert into sh_sql
values (
'product',
'select * from sh_product where sku = :1'
)
go
```

Changing the HTML Pages

Because much of the text is on the HTML pages, they need to be modified. Probably the easiest way to change the pages is to attempt to run them through the application and see where they need to be edited.

To run the application, a specific syntax is required. You would think that you could simply click the HTML filename in the Windows Explorer and everything will work great. However, this is not so. You need to follow this syntax:

`http://`*`ComputerName`*`/`*`env.s`*`/pgen/`*`Store`*`/`*`x`*`L/welcome.html`

where:

> *`ComputerName`* is the name of the server that contains Merchant Server.
>
> *`env`* is the environment. (`dev` is for development and `prd` is for production.)

`s` is the security level. (`i` is for insecure and `s` for secure.)

`Store` is the name of your store.

`x` is the number of the level you want to attempt to log in to. The possibilities are `0` for a new shopper and `1` for an administrator.

If you log in as an administrator, you'll be required to enter a user name and password. These are both stored in the Registry under the `HKEY_LOCAL_MACHINE\SOFTWARE\Microsoft\MerchantServer\Stores\DesiredStore\Admin` key where `DesiredStore` is the name of your store.

Therefore, for this example, to try to log in to the SERVER-A server as a new shopper, type this address:

```
http://server-a/dev.i/pgen/sh/0L/welcome.html
```

This brings up the store shown in Figure 43.2.

FIGURE 43.2.

The store after it has been copied from the clock peddler store.

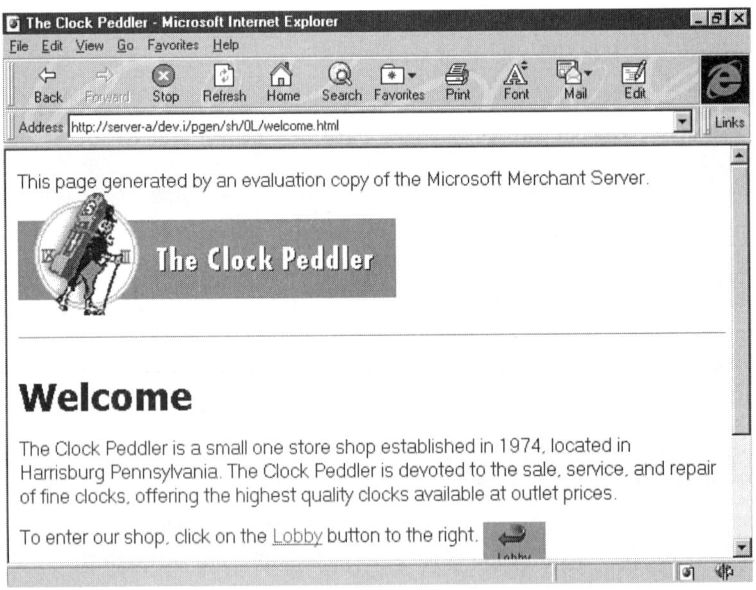

Obviously, this page needs to be edited because it relates to the Clockped store, not the store you are trying to create. To do this, you need knowledge of HTML.

CROSS REFERENCE

For more information about HTML, refer to Chapter 25, "HTML Primer."

The HTML for WELCOME.HTML is edited as shown in Listing 43.9.

Listing 43.9. The newly edited WELCOME.HTML page.

```
<!--
[# ########################################################################]
[#   WELCOME.HTML                                                         #]
[# ########################################################################]
-->

<HTML>
<HEAD>
<TITLE>SoftHouse</TITLE>
<META HTTP-EQUIV charset=iso-ir-100>
</HEAD>
<BODY BGCOLOR="#FFFFC0" LINK=[value const.color_red] VLINK=[value
➥const.color_firebrick]>

<IMG SRC="[img]images/softhse.gif" WIDTH=310 HEIGHT=60 BORDER=0
➥ALT="SoftHouse">
<HR>

<H1>Welcome</H1>

SoftHouse is a small company specializing in X-10 technology.  This allows
➥you to control lights, appliances, and other electrical devices from
➥your computer.
<P>
To enter our shop, click on the [xlink shopper.guest]Lobby[/xlink] button to
➥the right.
[xlink shopper.guest]<IMG SRC="[simg]navbar/btnmenu.gif" WIDTH=53 HEIGHT=41
➥BORDER=0 ALT="Lobby" ALIGN=TOP>[/xlink]

<P>
<HR>
&copy; 1997 SoftHouse. All rights reserved.
<BR>

</BODY>
</HTML>
```

This HTML is reflected in the browser when you click the Refresh button. This is shown in Figure 43.3.

Clicking the Lobby area brings up the MAIN.HTML page. Figure 43.4 shows this page. Again, it needs to be edited.

The MAIN.HTML page refers to a DEPT.HTML page. Therefore, DEPT.HTML needs to be edited first as well as renamed to CAT.HTML. Listing 43.10 shows the edited CAT.HTML page.

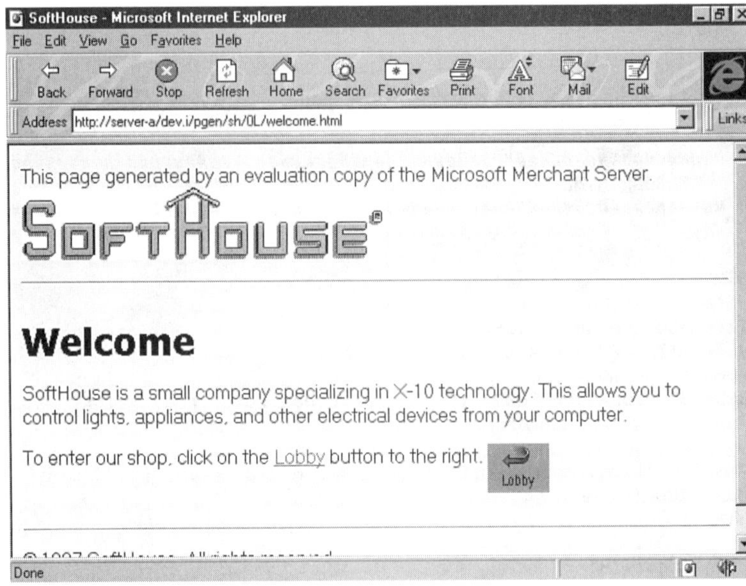

FIGURE 43.3.
`WELCOME.HTML` *after it is edited.*

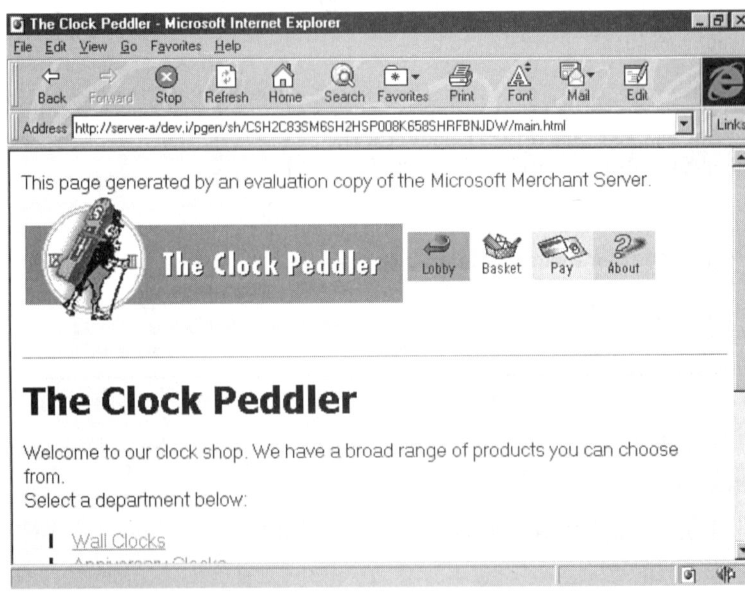

FIGURE 43.4.
`MAIN.HTML` *before it is edited.*

Listing 43.10. The newly edited `CAT.HTML` page.

```
<!--
[# ##########################################################################]
[#   CAT.HTML                                                              #]
[# ##########################################################################]
```

```
-->

<HTML>

<HEAD>
    <TITLE>Category Page </TITLE>
    <META HTTP-EQUIV charset=iso-ir-100>
</HEAD>

[include "header.html"]

[fetchrows catinfo "category" args.cat_id]

<H1>[value catinfo.cat_name]</H1>
[value catinfo.cat_description]

<BR>
Select a product from the list below.

[fetchrows catproducts "products-by-cat" args.cat_id]

<UL>
    [eachrow catproducts]
        <LI>[link "product.html" sku=catproducts.sku]
       ➥[value catproducts.name][/link]
    [/eachrow]
</UL>

[include "footer.html"]

</HTML>
```

Next, you need to edit `MAIN.HTML` as well. Listing 43.11 shows the edited `MAIN.HTML` page.

Listing 43.11. The newly edited `MAIN.HTML` page.

```
<!--
[# ##########################################################################]
[#   MAIN.HTML                                                              #]
[# ##########################################################################]
-->

<HTML>

<HEAD>
    <TITLE>SoftHouse</TITLE>
    <META HTTP-EQUIV charset=iso-ir-100>
</HEAD>

[include "header.html"]

<H1>SoftHouse</H1>

Welcome to SoftHouse. We have many X-10 products you can choose from,
➥as well as Visual Basic books sold well below retail prices.
```

continues

Listing 43.11. continued

```
<BR>
Select a category below:

<UL>
[tfetchrows cats "sh_category" "cat_id"]

[eachrow cats]
    <LI>[link "cat.html" cat_id=cats.cat_id][value cats.cat_name][/link]
[/eachrow]

</UL>

[include "footer.html"]

</HTML>
```

Notice that each of the pages references `"header.html"` and `"footer.html"`. Each of these references is used to convey a consistent look and feel to the header and footer of each page. First, edit the `HEADER.HTML` page. Listing 43.12 shows the edited `HEADER.HTML` page.

Listing 43.12. The newly edited `HEADER.HTML` page.

```
<!--
[# ##########################################################################]
[#   HEADER.HTML                                                            #]
[# ##########################################################################]
-->

<BODY BGCOLOR=[value const.color_clockpedbg] LINK=[value const.color_red]
➥ VLINK=[value const.color_firebrick]>

<TABLE BORDER=0>
    <TR ALIGN=LEFT>
        <TD>
        <IMG SRC="[img]images/softhse.gif" WIDTH=310 HEIGHT=60 BORDER=0
        ➥ALT="SoftHouse">
        </TD>
        <TD ALIGN=RIGHT ALIGN=TOP>
            [link "main.html"]<IMG SRC="[simg]navbar/btnmenu.gif" WIDTH=53
            ➥HEIGHT=41 BORDER=0 ALT="Lobby" ALIGN=TOP>[/link]
            [link "basket.html"]<IMG SRC="[simg]navbar/btnbskt.gif" WIDTH=53
            ➥HEIGHT=41 BORDER=0 ALT="Basket" ALIGN=TOP>[/link]
            [link "orderform.html"]<IMG SRC="[simg]navbar/btnpay.gif"
            ➥WIDTH=53 HEIGHT=41 BORDER=0 ALT="Pay" ALIGN=TOP>[/link]
            [link "about.html"]<IMG SRC="[simg]navbar/btnabout.gif" WIDTH=53
            ➥HEIGHT=41 BORDER=0 ALT="About" ALIGN=TOP>[/link]
        </TD>
    </TR>
</TABLE>
<P>
<HR>
```

Next, edit the `FOOTER.HTML` page. Listing 43.13 shows the edited `FOOTER.HTML` page.

Listing 43.13. The newly edited `FOOTER.HTML` page.

```
<!--
[# ###########################################################################]
[#   FOOTER.HTML                                                             #]
[# ###########################################################################]
-->

<BR>
&copy; 1997 SoftHouse. All rights reserved.

</BODY>
```

This page simply shows copyright information. Now, the following files have been edited:

- `FOOTER.HTML`
- `HEADER.HTML`
- `MAIN.HTML`
- `WELCOME.HTML`
- `CAT.HTML`

The following figures represent the results of the editing you've done to this point. Figure 43.5 shows the `MAIN.HTML` screen, and Figure 43.6 shows the `CAT.HTML` screen. Each screen shows the edited header and footer.

FIGURE 43.5.
`MAIN.HTML` *after it has been edited.*

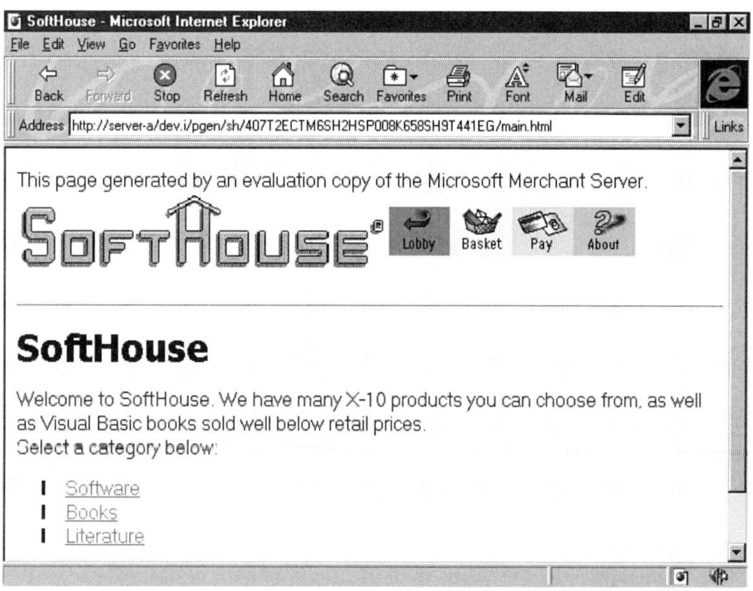

FIGURE 43.6.
`CAT.HTML` *after it has been edited.*

When you click one of the products within a category, the `PRODUCT.HTML` form is shown. (See Figure 43.7.)

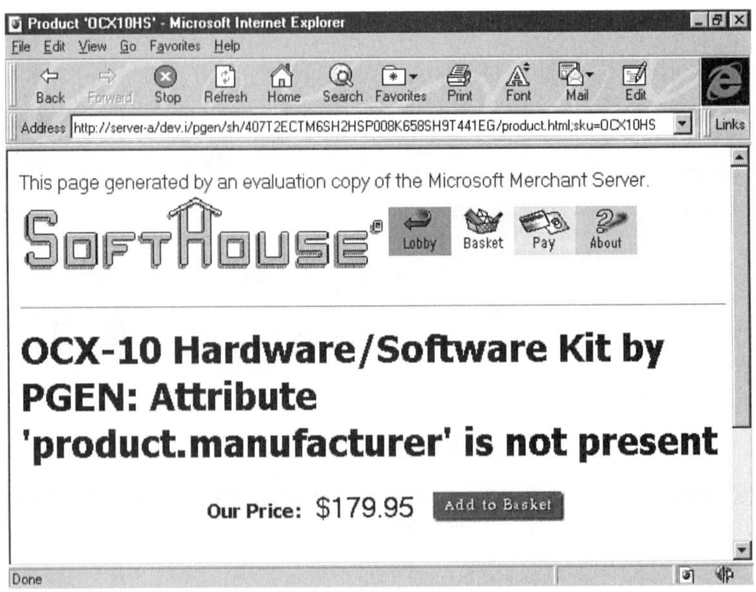

FIGURE 43.7.
`PRODUCT.HTML` *before it has been edited.*

This screen "almost" works. Because there are no manufacturers, you must edit the `PRODUCT.HTML` script. Listing 43.14 shows the edited `PRODUCT.HTML` script.

Listing 43.14. The newly edited `PRODUCT.HTML` page.

```
<!--
[# ##########################################################################]
[#   PRODUCT.HTML                                                          #]
[# ##########################################################################]
-->

<HTML>

<HEAD>
    <TITLE>Product '[value args.sku]'</TITLE>
    <META HTTP-EQUIV charset=iso-ir-100>
</HEAD>

[include "header.html"]

[fetchrows product "product" args.sku]

[if product.count > 0]
    <H1>[value product.name] </H1>
    <TABLE CELLPADDING=5>
        <TR>
            <TD>
                [if product.image_file != ""]
                    <IMG SRC="[img]prodimg/[value product.image_file]"
                    ➥WIDTH=[value product.image_width]
                    ➥HEIGHT=[value product.image_height]>
                [else]
                    Image not available
                [/if]
            </TD>
            <TD VALIGN=TOP WIDTH=400>
                <STRONG>Our Price:</STRONG>   <FONT SIZE="+2">
                ➥[money product.list_price]</FONT>
                   [xlink order.additem sku=product.sku]
                ➥<IMG SRC="[simg]buttons/btnaddbskt1.gif" WIDTH=112
                ➥HEIGHT=24 BORDER=0 ALT="Add to Basket"
                ➥ALIGN=MIDDLE>[/xlink]
                <P>
                [html product.description]
                </TD></TR>
            </TD>
        </TR>
    </TABLE>
[else]
    Product not available
[/if]

<P>

[include "footer.html"]

</HTML>
```

Figure 43.8 shows how the PRODUCT.HTML page looks after it has been edited.

FIGURE 43.8.
PRODUCT.HTML *after it has been edited.*

Clicking the Add to Basket picture will add the product to the basket. Because the sh_basket table was not changed, this works exactly as described. The BASKET.HTML script does not need to be edited. It is shown in Listing 43.15.

Listing 43.15. The BASKET.HTML page.

```
<!--
[# ##########################################################################]
[#   BASKET.HTML                                                            #]
[# ##########################################################################]
-->

<HTML>

<HEAD>
    <TITLE>Shopping Basket</TITLE>
    <META HTTP-EQUIV charset=iso-ir-100>
[nocache]
</HEAD>

[include "header.html"]

<H1>Shopping Basket</H1>

[if order._error_shopper_change != ""]
    <UL>
        [html order._error_shopper_change]
    </UL>
```

```
[/if]

[fetchitems orderitem order.items]

[if orderitem.count > 0]
    You have [value orderitem.count] item[if orderitem.count > 1]s[/if]
    ➥in your shopping basket:
    [xform order.editquantities]
        <TABLE BORDER=0>
            <TR>
                <TH ALIGN=LEFT>Label</TH>
                <TH ALIGN=LEFT>Qty</TH>
                <TH ALIGN=LEFT>Description</TH>
                <TH ALIGN=CENTER>Unit Price</TH>
                <TH ALIGN=CENTER>Total Price</TH>
                <TH></TH>
            </TR>
            [eachrow orderitem]
                <TR>
                    <TD>
                        [value orderitem.sku]
                    </TD>
                    <TD>
                        <INPUT TYPE="Text"
                               NAME="[value orderitem.rowidx]"
                               SIZE=3,1
                               VALUE="[value orderitem.quantity]">
                    </TD>
                    <TD>
                        [value orderitem._product_name]
                    </TD>
                    <TD ALIGN=RIGHT>
                        [money orderitem._product_list_price]
                    </TD>
                    <TD ALIGN=RIGHT>
                        [money orderitem._oadjust_adjustedprice]
                    </TD>
                    <TD>
                        [xlink order.delitem index=orderitem.rowidx]
                        ➥<IMG SRC="[simg]buttons/btnremove1.gif"
                        ➥BORDER=0 ALT="Delete item">[/xlink]
                    </TD>
                </TR>
            [/eachrow]

            [# show subtotal: ]
            <TR>
                <TD COLSPAN=4 ALIGN=RIGHT> <STRONG>Subtotal: </STRONG></TD>
                <TD ALIGN=RIGHT> [money order._oadjust_subtotal] </TD>
            </TR>
        </TABLE>

      <P>
      To change an item's quantity, edit the number and press "Update Basket".
      <P>

   <TABLE>
```

continues

Listing 43.15. continued

```
        <TR>
        <TD>
        <INPUT TYPE="Image"
               VALUE="Update Order"
               SRC="[simg]buttons/btnupdatebskt1.gif"
               WIDTH=116
               HEIGHT=25
               BORDER=0
               ALT="Update Basket">
        [/xform]
        </TD>

        <TD>
      [xform order.clearitems]
        <INPUT TYPE="Image"
               VALUE="Clear Order"
               SRC="[simg]buttons/btnempty1.gif"
               WIDTH=116
               HEIGHT=25
               BORDER=0
               ALT="Clear Basket">
        [/xform]
        </TD>

        <TD>
        [form "orderform.html"]
        <INPUT TYPE="Image"
               VALUE="Purchase"
               SRC="[simg]buttons/btnpurchase1.gif"
               WIDTH=116
               HEIGHT=25
               BORDER=0
               ALT="Purchase">
        [/form]
        </TD>

        </TR>
       </TABLE>
[/if]

[if orderitem.count == 0]
    <BLOCKQUOTE>
        <STRONG>Your basket is empty.</STRONG>
    </BLOCKQUOTE>
[/if]

<P>
[include "footer.html"]

</HTML>
```

Figure 43.9 shows the BASKET.HTML page.

FIGURE 43.9.
The BASKET.HTML *page.*

Clicking either the Pay icon at the top of the page or the Purchase icon at the bottom of the page invokes the ORDERFORM.HTML page. This works exactly as expected without modification. The ORDERFORM.HTML script does not need to be edited. It is shown in Listing 43.16.

Listing 43.16. The ORDERFORM.HTML page.

```
<!--
[# ###########################################################################]
[#   ORDERFORM.HTML                                                          #]
[# ###########################################################################]
-->

<HTML>
<HEAD>
    <TITLE>Order Form</TITLE>
    <META HTTP-EQUIV charset=iso-ir-100>
[nocache]
</HEAD>

[include "header.html"]

<H1>Address Form</H1>
<BR>
[fetchitems orderitem order.items]
[if orderitem.count == 0]
    <BLOCKQUOTE>
        <STRONG>Your basket is empty.</STRONG>
    </BLOCKQUOTE>
[else]
```

continues

Listing 43.16. continued

```
<TABLE WIDTH=500>
    <TR>
        <TD>
            If you need to change any items, please go to the
            [link "basket.html"]shopping basket[/link] to correct them.
            <P>
            If the order is correct, then please fill out the shipping
            instructions below and press the "Total" button.  This will
            show you what your total cost (including tax and shipping)
            will be.  If the total is satisfactory, then you'll be able
            to complete the purchase.
        </TD>
    </TR>
</TABLE>

<P>

[xform order.plan]

<INPUT TYPE="HIDDEN" NAME="bill_to_country" VALUE="USA">
<INPUT TYPE="HIDDEN" NAME="ship_to_country" VALUE="USA">

<P>

<TABLE BORDER=0 COLS=4>
    [# ship-to: ]
    <TR>
        <TD></TD>
        <TD ALIGN=CENTER COLSPAN=3>
            <FONT SIZE="+1"><STRONG>Shipping Address</STRONG></FONT>
        </TD>
    </TR>
    <TR>
        <TD ALIGN=RIGHT>
            <B>Name:</B>
        </TD>
        <TD COLSPAN=3>
            <INPUT TYPE="text"
                   NAME="ship_to_name"
                   SIZE=54,1
                   VALUE="[value order.ship_to_name]">
        </TD>
    </TR>
    <TR>
        <TD ALIGN=RIGHT>
            <B>Street Address:</B>
        </TD>
        <TD COLSPAN=3>
            <INPUT TYPE="text"
                   NAME="ship_to_street"
                   SIZE=54,1
                   VALUE="[value order.ship_to_street]">
        </TD>
    </TR>
    <TR>
        <TD ALIGN=RIGHT>
```

```
            <B>City:</B>
        </TD>
        <TD COLSPAN=3>
            <INPUT TYPE="text"
                   NAME="ship_to_city"
                   SIZE=54,1
                   VALUE="[value order.ship_to_city]">
        </TD>
    </TR>
    <TR>
        <TD ALIGN=RIGHT>
            <B>State:</B>
        </TD>
        <TD>
            <INPUT TYPE="text"
                   NAME="ship_to_state"
                   SIZE=5,1
                   VALUE="[value order.ship_to_state]"> 
        </TD>
        <TD ALIGN=RIGHT>
            <B>Zip:</B>
        </TD>
        <TD>
            <INPUT TYPE="text"
                   NAME="ship_to_zip"
                   SIZE=10,1
                   VALUE="[value order.ship_to_zip]"> 
        </TD>
    </TR>
    <TR>
        <TD ALIGN=RIGHT>
            <B>Phone:</B>
        </TD>
        <TD COLSPAN=3>
            <INPUT TYPE="text"
                   NAME="ship_to_phone"
                   SIZE=54,1
                   VALUE="[value order.ship_to_phone]">
        </TD>
    </TR>

    <TR>
        <TD>
             
        </TD>
    </TR>

    [# bill-to: ]
    <TR>
        <TD></TD>
        <TD ALIGN=CENTER COLSPAN=3>
            <FONT SIZE="+1"><STRONG>Billing Address</STRONG></FONT>
        </TD>
    <TR>
        <TD>
        </TD>
        <TD COLSPAN=3>
```

continues

Listing 43.16. continued

```
            <INPUT TYPE=CHECKBOX NAME="_bill_to_copy">Same as
            ➥Shipping Address
        </TD>
    </TR>
    <TR>
        <TD ALIGN=RIGHT>
            <B>Name:</B>
        </TD>
        <TD COLSPAN=3>
            <INPUT TYPE="text"
                    NAME="bill_to_name"
                    SIZE=54,1
                    VALUE="[value order.bill_to_name]">
        </TD>
    </TR>
    <TR>
        <TD ALIGN=RIGHT>
            <B>Street Address:</B>
        </TD>
        <TD COLSPAN=3>
            <INPUT TYPE="text"
                    NAME="bill_to_street"
                    SIZE=54,1
                    VALUE="[value order.bill_to_street]">
        </TD>
    </TR>
    <TR>
        <TD ALIGN=RIGHT>
            <B>City:</B>
        </TD>
        <TD COLSPAN=3>
            <INPUT TYPE="text"
                    NAME="bill_to_city"
                    SIZE=54,1
                    VALUE="[value order.bill_to_city]">
        </TD>
    </TR>
    <TR>
        <TD ALIGN=RIGHT>
            <B>State:</B>
        </TD>
        <TD>
            <INPUT TYPE="text"
                    NAME="bill_to_state"
                    SIZE=5,1
                    VALUE="[value order.bill_to_state]">  
        </TD>
        <TD ALIGN=RIGHT>
            <B>Zip:</B>
        </TD>
        <TD>
            <INPUT TYPE="text"
                    NAME="bill_to_zip"
                    SIZE=10,1
                    VALUE="[value order.bill_to_zip]"> 
        </TD>
```

```
        </TR>
        <TR>
            <TD ALIGN=RIGHT>
                <B>Phone:</B>
            </TD>
            <TD COLSPAN=3>
                <INPUT TYPE="text"
                       NAME="bill_to_phone"
                       SIZE=54,1
                       VALUE="[value order.bill_to_phone]">
            </TD>
        </TR>

        <TR>
            <TD>
                 
            </TD>
        </TR>

        <TR>
            <TD></TD>
            <TD ALIGN=CENTER COLSPAN=1>
                <INPUT TYPE="Image"
                       VALUE="Total"
                       SRC="[simg]buttons/btntotal1.gif"
                       WIDTH=116
                       HEIGHT=25
                       BORDER=0
                       ALT="Total">
            </TD>
            <TD ALIGN=CENTER COLSPAN=2>
                <INPUT TYPE="reset"
                       VALUE="Reset">
            </TD>
        </TR>
    </TABLE>
     <P>

    [/xform]
[/if]

[include "footer.html"]

</HTML>
```

Figure 43.10 shows the ORDERFORM.HTML page.

Clicking the Total picture allows the user to check out. This brings up the PURCHASE.HTML page, which is used to begin the credit card payment process. The PURCHASE.HTML script does not need to be edited. It is shown in Listing 43.17.

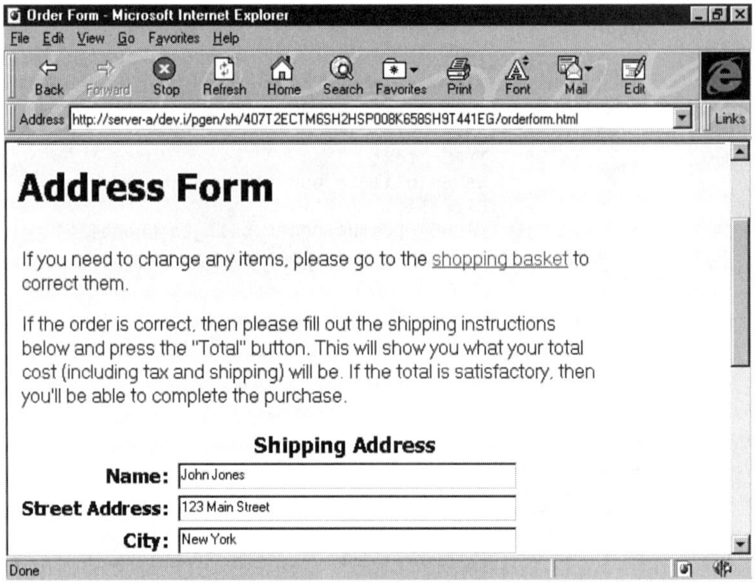

FIGURE 43.10.
The ORDERFORM.HTML *page.*

Listing 43.17. The PURCHASE.HTML page.

```
<!--
[# ########################################################################]
[#   PURCHASE.HTML                                                        #]
[# ########################################################################]
-->

<HTML>
<HEAD>
    <TITLE>Purchase Verification</TITLE>
    <META HTTP-EQUIV charset=iso-ir-100>
[nocache]
</HEAD>

[include "header.html"]

<TABLE WIDTH=500>
    <TR>
        <TD>
            Your purchase will cost [money order._total_total].
            ➥Please enter your credit card information and press the
            ➥"Purchase" button
            below.
        </TD>
    </TR>
</TABLE>
<P>

<TABLE BORDER=0>
    <TR>
        <TD ALIGN=RIGHT WIDTH=100>
```

```
            <B>Subtotal:</B>
        </TD>
        <TD ALIGN=RIGHT>
            [money order._oadjust_subtotal]
        </TD>
    </TR>
    <TR>
        <TD ALIGN=RIGHT>
            <B>Tax:</B>
        </TD>
        <TD ALIGN=RIGHT>
            [money order._tax_total]
        </TD>
    </TR>
    <TR>
        <TD Align=RIGHT>
            <B>Shipping:</B>
        </TD>
        <TD ALIGN=RIGHT>
            [money order._shipping_total]
        </TD>
    </TR>
    <TR>
        <TD ALIGN=RIGHT>
            <B>TOTAL:</B>
        </TD>
        <TD ALIGN=RIGHT>
            [money order._total_total]
        </TD>
    </TR>
</TABLE>
<P>

[sxform order.purchase]
[verifywith "_total_total" "ship_to_zip" "_tax_total"]

    <TABLE>
        <TR>
            <TD></TD>
            <TD ALIGN=CENTER COLSPAN=4>
                <FONT SIZE="+1"><STRONG>Credit Card Information</STRONG></FONT>
            </TD>
        </TR>
        <TR>
            <TD ALIGN=RIGHT>
                <B>Name on card:</B>
            </TD>
            <TD COLSPAN=4>
                <INPUT TYPE="text"
                       NAME="cc_name"
                       SIZE=70,1>
            </TD>
        </TR>
        <TR>
            <TD ALIGN=RIGHT>
                <B>Card Number:</B>
            </TD>
```

continues

Listing 43.17. continued

```
        <TD COLSPAN=4>
            <INPUT TYPE="text"
                   NAME="_cc_number"
                   SIZE=70,1>
        </TD>
    </TR>
    <TR>
        <TD ALIGN=RIGHT>
            <B>Type:</B>
        </TD>
        <TD>
            <SELECT NAME="cc_type">
                <OPTION VALUE="Visa"> VISA
                <OPTION VALUE="Mastercard"> MasterCard
            </SELECT>
        </TD>

        <TD ALIGN=RIGHT>
            <B>Expiration Date:</B>
        </TD>
        <TD>
            <SELECT NAME="_cc_expmonth">
                <OPTION VALUE=1> Jan
                <OPTION VALUE=2> Feb
                <OPTION VALUE=3> Mar
                <OPTION VALUE=4> Apr
                <OPTION VALUE=5> May
                <OPTION VALUE=6> Jun
                <OPTION VALUE=7> Jul
                <OPTION VALUE=8> Aug
                <OPTION VALUE=9> Sep
                <OPTION VALUE=10> Oct
                <OPTION VALUE=11> Nov
                <OPTION VALUE=12> Dec
            </SELECT>
        </TD>
        <TD>
            <SELECT NAME="_cc_expyear">
                <OPTION VALUE=1996> 1996
                <OPTION VALUE=1997> 1997
                <OPTION VALUE=1998> 1998
                <OPTION VALUE=1999> 1999
                <OPTION VALUE=2000> 2000
                <OPTION VALUE=2001> 2001
                <OPTION VALUE=2002> 2002
                <OPTION VALUE=2003> 2003
            </SELECT>
        </TD>
    </TR>
    <TR>
        <TD></TD>
        <TD COLSPAN=4>
            <INPUT TYPE="Image"
                   VALUE="Purchase"
                   SRC="[simg]buttons/btnpurchase1.gif"
                   WIDTH=116
                   HEIGHT=25
```

```
                        BORDER=0
                        ALT="Purchase">
            </TD>
        </TR>
        </TABLE>
[/sxform]

[include "footer.html"]

</HTML>
```

Figure 43.11 shows the PURCHASE.HTML page.

FIGURE 43.11.
The PURCHASE.HTML *page.*

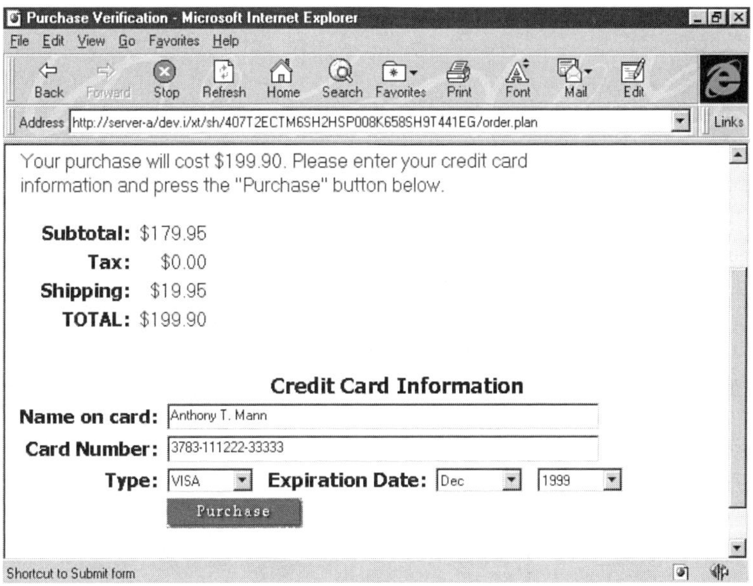

When the Purchase picture is clicked, an attempt is made to authorize the transaction. This is done by using the vPOS software. If there are no errors, the CONFIRMED.HTML page is displayed. This script requires slight modification because it references the Clock Peddler store. Therefore, to edit it, you must replace instances of "Clock Peddler" with the name of your store. Listing 43.18 shows the modified CONFIRMED.HTML page.

Listing 43.18. The CONFIRMED.HTML page after it has been edited.

```
<!--
[# ########################################################################]
[#   CONFIRMED.HTML                                                       #]
[# ########################################################################]
-->
```

continues

Listing 43.18. continued

```
<HTML>
<HEAD>
<TITLE>Purchase Confirmation</TITLE>
<META HTTP-EQUIV charset=iso-ir-100>
</HEAD>

[include "header.html"]

<H1>Purchase Confirmed</H1>

Your order number is <STRONG>[value args.order_id]</STRONG>.
➥Please record it for referencing your order.
<P>
Thank you for your shopping at SoftHouse.
<P>
If you want to continue shopping, simply return to the [link "main.html"]
➥lobby[/link].

[include "footer.html"]

</HTML>
```

Figure 43.12 shows the `CONFIRMED.HTML` page after it has been edited.

FIGURE 43.12.
The `CONFIRMED.HTML` *page after it has been edited.*

If there are errors during processing, the `ERROR.HTML` script will be run. The `ERROR.HTML` script does not need to be edited. It is shown in Listing 43.19.

Listing 43.19. The `ERROR.HTML` page.

```
<!--
[# ##########################################################################]
[#   ERROR.HTML                                                             #]
[# ##########################################################################]
-->

[nocache]

<HTML>
<HEAD>
<TITLE>Error</TITLE>
<META HTTP-EQUIV charset=iso-ir-100>

</HEAD>

[include "header.html"]

We are sorry, but we are unable to process your request:<br>
<UL>
    [html args.error]
</UL>
Please go back and correct the error and try again.

[include "footer.html"]

</HTML>
```

Figure 43.13 shows the `ERROR.HTML` page.

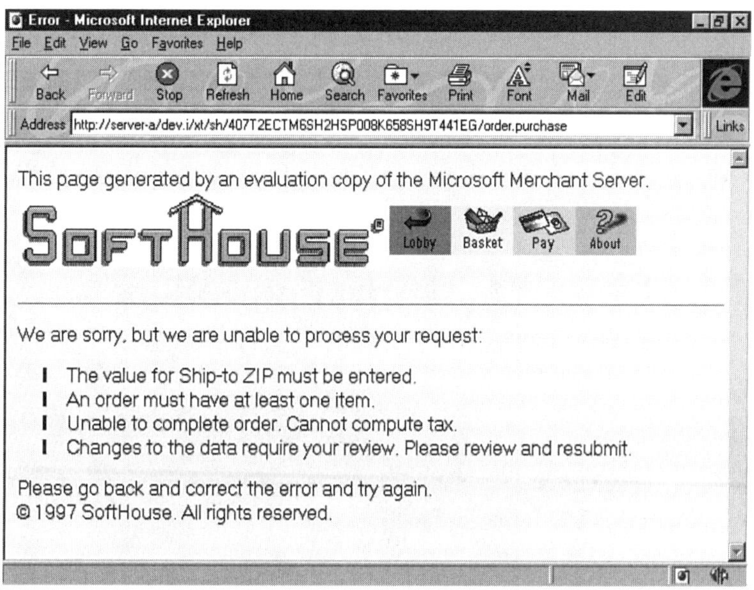

FIGURE 43.13.
The ERROR.HTML *page.*

If there is an authorization failure, the `AUTHFAILURE.HTML` page is run. It requires only slight modification. The copyright notice is for a Microsoft copyright. Change it to your company. Also, change the e-mail address in the text of the message. Listing 43.20 shows the `AUTHFAILURE.HTML` script after it has been edited.

Listing 43.20. The `AUTHFAILURE.HTML` page after it has been edited.

```
<!--
[# ##########################################################################]
[#   AUTHFAILURE.HTML                                                       #]
[# ##########################################################################]
-->

<HTML>
<HEAD>
<TITLE>Authorization Failure</TITLE>
<META HTTP-EQUIV charset=iso-ir-100>
</HEAD>
<BODY>
<H1>Authorization Failure</H1>

We are sorry, but we cannot fulfill that request for you.  If you are
having problems, then please contact our support at tmann@vbasic.com.
<P>
&copy; 1997 SoftHouse.  All rights reserved

</BODY>
</HTML>
```

Figure 43.14 shows the edited `AUTHFAILURE.HTML` page.

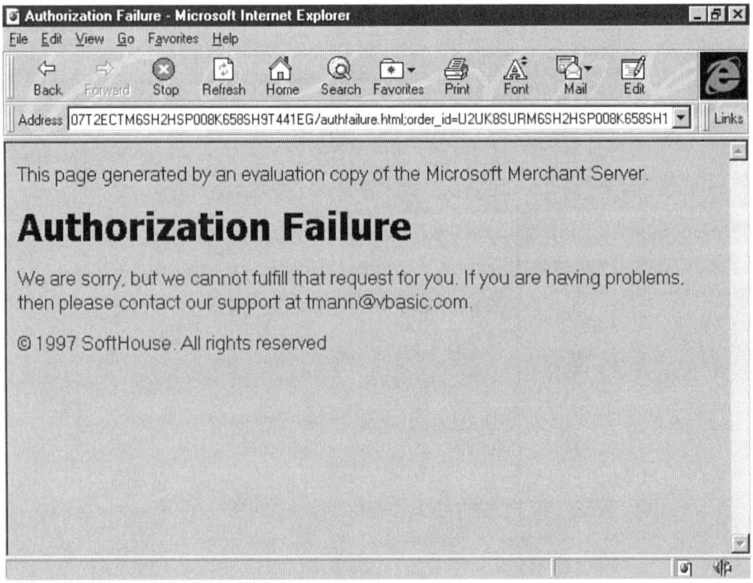

FIGURE 43.14.
The edited `AUTHFAILURE.HTML` *page.*

One final HTML page, ABOUT.HTML, needs to be edited. This page tells a little bit about the company and its products. You can access ABOUT.HTML from the header on any page by clicking the About icon. Listing 43.21 shows the ABOUT.HTML script after it has been edited.

Listing 43.21. The ABOUT.HTML page after it has been edited.

```
<!--
[# ##########################################################################]
[#   ABOUT.HTML                                                             #]
[# ##########################################################################]
-->

<HTML>
<HEAD>
<TITLE>About SoftHouse</TITLE>
<META HTTP-EQUIV charset=iso-ir-100>
</HEAD>

[include "header.html"]

<TABLE WIDTH=500><TR><TD>

<H1>About SoftHouse</H1>

SoftHouse is a small company which specializes in home automation (X-10 based)
➥ controls for Visual Basic.
<P>
SoftHouse also specializes in Visual Basic books.
<P>
Please browse through the catalog to see the services we offer.
<P>
All products are shipped UPS Ground. Please allow up to 2 weeks for delivery.
<P>
A 7.3% sales tax for all Colorado residents will be computed in your bill.
<P>
A shipping charge of $5.95 per order will be added to your bill.

[# "WLStdOrder.FixedShipping @ 1000" in sh registration area sets up $10
➥charge for shipping]

<P>

</TABLE>

<P>

[include "footer.html"]

</HTML>
```

Figure 43.15 shows the ABOUT.HTML page after it has been edited.

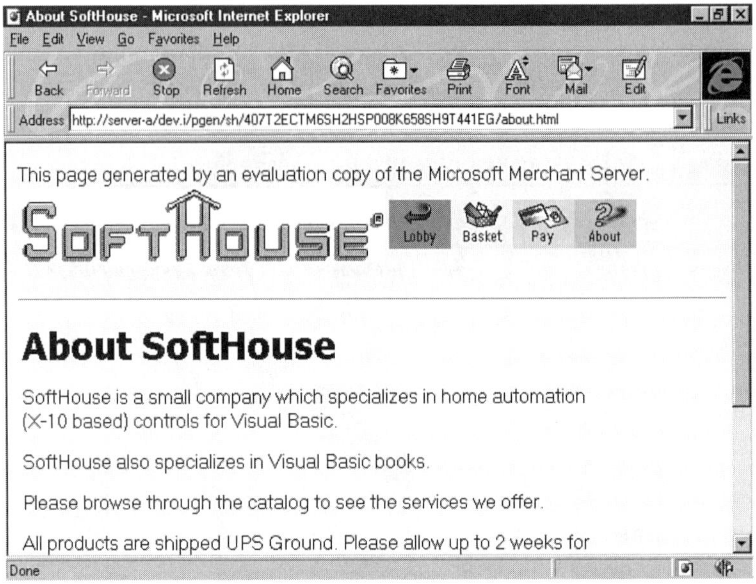

FIGURE 43.15.
The edited ABOUT.HTML *page.*

Summary

Creating an Electronic Commerce Internet Application is very easy with Microsoft Merchant Server. This chapter walked you through copying one of the sample applications that comes with Merchant Server and modifying it. Modifying the sample application is the fastest way for you to create your Electronic Commerce applications, called stores. Use this chapter as a reference for creating your stores.

VIII

Appendixes

A

Third-Party Vendors

This appendix lists data about specific third-party vendors who are listed in consideration for their help or demos. All pricing is in retail U.S. dollars, and prices are subject to change. Demos of these products are included on the CD-ROM that accompanies this book in the directories specified. If there is no directory listed, then there is no demo available. Not all information was available for all companies at the time of publication. I have made every attempt to make sure that all information is accurate and up-to-date. I disclaim any responsibility for inaccuracies within this information, because it is provided by the vendors themselves. The vendors are in no particular order.

SoftHouse

Web: `www.vbasic.com`
Contact: Anthony T. Mann
E-mail: `tmann@vbasic.com`

OCX-10 Home/Office Automation Custom Control ($179)

There are no demos on the CD-ROM accompanying this book. For current information about X-10 products and demos, refer to the SoftHouse Web site.

Create custom X-10–based automation applications with Visual Basic. X-10 applications use industry standard hardware available from Radio Shack and mail order companies to customize a security system, as well as to time many types of X-10 devices. Such devices include lamp modules, appliance modules, relays, sensors, motors, and many others.

This is a very low-cost solution for effective custom X-10–based applications. Developed by the author of this book, you can be assured of great quality at a low price. Visit the SoftHouse Web site for more information.

Great Lakes Business Solutions

Address: 2200 N Canton Center Road
Suite 220
Canton, MI
48187
Telephone: (313) 981-4970
Fax: (313) 981-9746
Sales: (800) 554-8565
Web: `www.glbs.com`
Contact: Andy Vernier
E-mail: `sales@glbs.com`

Wise Installation System ($199)

CD-ROM demo directory: `\DEMOS\GLBS\WISEINST`

Create your installations via drag and drop without writing a single line of code. WISE scans your programs for the VBXs or DLLs they reference, so you will never forget to include the proper files again, and it automatically compresses and splits your files across multiple floppy disks. It includes true multiple-language support; a single installation script can contain up to 15 languages. The latest version contains both a 16-bit and 32-bit edition of the WISE integrated development environment (IDE). The installations created under either environment will support both 16-bit and 32-bit destination platforms. WISE can create a single EXE file, perfect for online or e-mail distribution.

Here are just some of the new features in 5.0:

- Windows 95 wizard look and feel: Create complete wizard installations with a click of the mouse.
- Multilingual wizard installs/uninstalls created automatically: The wizard now ships with German, French, Italian, and Spanish dialog boxes.
- Easy-to-use installation expert: The Installation Expert now includes graphics, components, file associations, INI files, Registry editing, capability to add devices and services, and editing `Autoexec.bat` and `Config.sys`.
- Customizable progress bar: Sample source code is included to create your own progress bar.
- Customizable wizard dialog boxes: Use the standard Windows 95 look and feel, or create the installation to match your application.
- Text-based script files: Cut and paste using your favorite editor.
- Customizable uninstall process: Fully customize the uninstall process, including language and background properties. Also, remove files and Registry keys created by your program after the install. Execute external programs during the uninstall.
- Compiler variables for conditional compilations: Design a single script that can be used to create installations for multiple versions of your software. Pass the version in as a command-line parameter when compiling.
- Customizable exit/cancel events: You can add code that executes when the user exits, or cancel your installation to perform a cleanup or some other task.
- Create service during install: You can add a service (background process) to an NT system.
- Enhanced search for file capability: Now you can search local drivers only, network drives only, or all drives defined on the user's system.
- Read/update text files: Read each line of a text file and perform string manipulation before writing it back out.

- Self-register OCXs/DLLs: Enables you to register files that are already installed on the workstation or server.
- Windows NT 4.0 support: Compliant with Microsoft's Windows NT 4.0 installation requirements.
- SMS/MIF support: Create a MIF file for use with an SMS-type distribution system.

To use the demo on the CD-ROM, you will need the following password:

```
mwv5LJA42
```

SmartPatch ($169)

The SmartPatch add-in works with the Wise Installation System to create installations that will enable you to upgrade previous versions of your software or data files without having to ship an entire new copy of the software. Instead of shipping the entire file, you can ship only the differences between the older versions of your files and the latest version. This can greatly reduce the size of the resulting installation. You can use the SmartPatch add-in to create installations that can upgrade files from a set of possible previous versions. In addition, because the upgrade can be performed only on a valid previous version of your software, SmartPatch can be used to provide freely distributed updates. Only valid owners of a previous version of your software will be able to install the upgrade. This can make it much easier to post upgrades via online services or Web pages.

The SmartPatch add-in runs under the Win32 edition of the Wise Installation System. You must be running the Win32 IDE to compile installation scripts that contain SmartPatches. You can edit scripts that contain SmartPatch entries using either the Win16 or Win32 IDE. The installations that contain SmartPatches can run under Win16 or Win32 (for example, Windows 3.1*x*, WFWG, Windows 95, or Windows NT).

The SmartPatch add-in is a separately purchased product that integrates into the Wise Installation System IDE. You must own the Wise Installation System 4.0 and be running Wise 4.0g or higher to use the SmartPatch add-in. You can order the SmartPatch add-in by calling 800-554-8565 or 313-981-4970.

System Requirements

- Windows 95 or Windows NT
- Intel 386 or higher (Pentium recommended)
- At least 8MB of memory
- 4MB free disk space
- Wise Installation System 4.0g or higher

Distinct Software

Web: `www.distinct.com`
Contact: Rachelle Arcayena
E-mail: `rachelle@distinct.com`

Distinct TCP/IP Software Development Toolkit ($295/$545 with Subscription)

CD-ROM demo directory: `\DEMOS\DISTINCT\TCPIP`

Since the 1980s, Distinct has led the marketplace in providing the developer community with top-quality development tools to build TCP/IP-based applications for intranets and the Internet. Distinct's toolkits today are used worldwide both in corporate and commercial application development. The Distinct toolkits have won several editor's and readers' choice awards. Today, Distinct provides the widest range of Internet and intranet protocols for developers to incorporate into their own applications. The following provides a summary of some of the ActiveX components in the Distinct Visual Internet Toolkit:

- Firewall: The Distinct Firewall component enables developers to write applications that securely traverse a network firewall. This component currently supports SOCKS 5. Firewall support is also built into the FTP Client, NNTP, POP, SMTP, Telnet, and Windows Sockets components.
- FTP Client: The File Transfer Protocol (FTP) is the standard protocol for copying files to and from remote machines. With the Distinct FTP client component, developers can quickly and securely incorporate automated, timed file transfers, or transfer on demand into any application. Firewall proxy (SOCKS 5) support is embedded.
- FTP Server: The Distinct FTP Server component enables developers to integrate custom FTP server functionality into their own applications, turning the PCs that are running their applications into FTP servers. A customized FTP server could be focused toward enabling fast, convenient, and easy file transfer within the company or making updates available to customers.
- MIME: Multipurpose Internet Mail Extensions (MIME) is the Internet standard for sending e-mail messages that contain non-US-ASCII character sets, enriched text, GIF images, and other types of files such as multimedia, including audio and video. The Distinct MIME component enables developers to easily build applications that have MIME encoding and decoding.
- NNTP: News Network Transfer Protocol (NNTP) is used to build Usenet, a public discussion forum made up of various newsgroups. The Distinct NNTP component enables the developer to integrate the functionality of reading, posting, or listing news items into any application. Firewall proxy support is embedded.

- POP: The Post Office Protocol (POP) provides a way for a server machine to store and serve mail for various client machines that are not continuously connected to the Internet or are behind a company's firewall. E-mail is held in the POP server until you log in and retrieve it using a POP client. The Distinct POP client component enables developers to integrate POP capabilities into their applications.
- RCP: The Distinct Remote Copy (RCP) component enables developers to integrate remote copy operations into their applications.
- RLIB, REXEC, RSHELL, RLOGIN: The Distinct Remote Execution component enables developers to integrate remote shell (rsh), remote login (rlogin), and remote execution (rexec) into their applications. rsh passes a command to a remote host for execution. Both the standard output and errors from that execution are returned to the local host. rlogin provides interactive access to remote hosts in a similar way that Telnet does. rexec is similar in function to rsh but requires a user login and password to be sent to the remote host for verification.
- SMTP: The Simple Mail Transfer Protocol (SMTP) delivers mail. The Distinct SMTP component enables developers to add the capability to send e-mail from within any application. Combined with the MIME component, developers can automate the encoding of e-mail attachments. The SMTP component provides an interface to the mail delivery service, including the option to connect via a firewall proxy server. An application can use SMTP to send notification, such as a report detailing logins to a secure system or information about hits on the company's Web site, to a user via e-mail.
- TCP Server: The Distinct TCP Server component enables developers to build robust server functionality to serve multiple TCP clients on the network. It enables any workstation to act as a server—to listen for connection requests and process client queries.
- Telnet: The Distinct Telnet component enables developers to integrate Telnet-based login capabilities into their applications.
- TFTP Client: The Distinct TFTP component enables developers to integrate TFTP-based file transfer into their applications.
- VT220: The Distinct VT220 component enables developers to integrate VT220 emulation and optional login capabilities into their applications. This component supports full emulation and includes keyboard mapping.
- Windows Sockets: The Distinct Windows Sockets component gives your application a fast, robust, secure interface for sending and receiving data between computers. You can create Windows Sockets applications that run over TCP without making a single socket call.
- HTTPS: The HyperText Transfer Protocol (HTTP) is an application-level protocol for distributed, collaborative, hypermedia information systems. This control implements HTTP version 1.1. The Distinct HTTP control implements the Secure Sockets

Layer (SSL) and user authentication, providing a secure way to transfer files over LANs and WANs using standard encryption methods.

- Finger: This component can be used to monitor users logged into a remote system by getting information about the users based on their user names and tracking the amount of time they have been logged on.
- WHOIS: The Distinct WhoIs component enables developers to integrate WhoIs search capabilities into their applications.

Pepperwhite

Address: PO Box 1084
Medford, NJ
08055-1084
Telephone: (609) 983-2884
Web: `www.pepperwhite.com`
Contact: Tony Sammartino
E-mail: `sales@pepperwhite.com`

pepperwhite street ($495 + $15 Shipping)

CD-ROM demo directory: `\DEMOS\PEPPER\STREET`

pepperwhite street is a fast and very easy-to-use custom control that adds mapping and powerful geographic query capabilities to your applications developed for Windows 3.1, Windows 95, and Windows NT.

What makes them different:

- *pepperwhite street* is the fastest mapping component on the market.
- *pepperwhite street* includes the most complete and compact U.S. street map data on the market.
- Pepperwhite has developed many applications using component software and knows first-hand what makes a great control and what doesn't.

Features include

- Ready-to-go right out of the box. You won't spend time or money purchasing, downloading, or translating the TIGER data that our competitors force you to acquire separately.
- Royalty free map data for all 50 states (over 3,100 counties). Everything from state outlines to side streets with structure numbers is included on a single CD.
- Royalty free VBX16 and OCX32 (ActiveX) versions of custom control included.

- Royalty free sample applications source code.
- Online and printed documentation.
- Free, fast response online technical support.
- 30-day, 100% money-back guarantee.
- All orders are shipped FedEx overnight.

Designed for software developers:

- *pepperwhite street* was designed from the beginning to be a component as easy to use as a text box or pushbutton. It's not a "library" or DLL with interface or stack size issues. It's not a legacy desktop mapping product with a cloaking wrapper around it.
- No prior experience with Geographic Information System (GIS) technology is required to add feature-rich map graphics and impressive query capabilities to your applications.

Easy to use:

- *pepperwhite street* enables you to get started quickly.
- Drop a map box on your form, just as you would a text box, stretch it out to the desired size, and run your application! Many features don't require any code!

Power without code:

- Straight out of the box, *pepperwhite street* can perform the following functions without coding: zoom; pan and scroll seamlessly across the entire country; render multicolor labeled maps; offer and respond to rendering customization options; manage mouse events to drill down from a map of the entire United States to a few blocks, delineate areas for querying and for zooming, look up addresses anywhere in the United States, copy a map to the Clipboard, and print the currently viewed map.
- *pepperwhite street* also automatically detects and adjusts to any screen resolution, responds to changes in window size, and preserves aspect ratios when moving from screen to printer to plotter.

More power with just a little code. Cut and paste code from over a dozen included sample applications that clearly demonstrate how to do the following:

- Look up addresses from your forms or databases and display them on the map.
- Determine the nearest store/doctor/service facility to a customer.
- Create thematic maps that shade states or counties to represent database information graphically.
- Retrieve database information by clicking a point on the map.
- Locate all database items that are within a given radius of a clicked map position or within a rubber-banded area.

- Add your own points, lines, and areas to the map.
- Use the map with a global positioning system (GPS) receiver to track vehicles and equipment.
- Compute distances, bearings, and other mapping/GIS math functions.
- Much, much more.

Clear documentation:

- Both the manual and the online help file assume that your expertise is in an area other than mapping.
- The manual introduces you to the benefits of GIS, focusing on practical business applications. Topics are logically arranged and reference the included sample programs to illustrate the techniques.
- The developer's online help file provides all of the details that you'll need on the properties, methods, and events along with cut-and-paste sample code.

Included Map Data CD:

- All of the United States map data needed for typical business applications is included on a single CD provided with the control. The royalty free data can be installed in whole or in part on a local hard drive as well as on network drives. The control is also capable of running directly against the CD.
- If your application doesn't require the detail data for Wolverine Drive in Dogpatch, Alaska, you can use an included utility program to select only the data that you want to distribute. Should you need the complete detail for the entire country, the total database size is only 500MB. (That's an average of a mere 10MB per state.)

Included Map Topographic Layers. The database consists of over 181 million latitude and longitude samples that describe the following:

- Geopolitical boundaries (50 states, all 3100+ counties)
- 5-digit ZIP codes and 3-digit SCF's
- Complete list of 131,729 cities, towns, villages, and so on
- Limited access highways (U.S. Geological Survey Class [USGS] 1)
- Highways (USGS 2)
- Main roads (USGS 3)
- Side streets (USGS 4)
- Water features (coastlines to creeks)
- Landmarks (such as airport runways and tarmac outlines)
- Railroads (main track, spurs, tunnels, overpasses)
- Power and pipelines

Included control types:

- 16-bit VBX and 32-bit OCX (ActiveX) versions included.

Compatibility:

- Any programming platform that accepts VBX or OCX (ActiveX) controls. Developers are currently using *pepperwhite street* with Visual Basic V2.0, V3.0, V4.0-16, V4.0-32, Delphi V1.0, V2.0, Visual C++ V4.0+, Access, Visual FoxPro, and Clarion for Windows 2.001.

Seagate Software

Address:	1095 West Pender Street 4th Floor Vancouver, BC, Canada V6E 2M6
Telephone:	(604) 681-3435
Fax:	(604) 681-5147
Sales:	(800) 877-2340
Web:	`img.seagatesoftware.com`
E-mail:	`tsmisc@img.seagatesoftware.com`

Crystal Reports Professional 5.0

CD-ROM demo directory: `\DEMOS\SEAGATE\CRYSTAL`

Crystal Reports is the world's leading client/server report writer that lets you design unlimited types of presentation-quality reports and integrate them into database applications. Report from all popular PC and SQL databases and distribute reports through popular communication infrastructures including the Internet, cc:mail, Microsoft Mail, Lotus Notes, Microsoft Exchange, and more.

Use Crystal Reports Professional 5.0 to publish reports to the Web!

New HTML publishing capabilities instantly turn reports into presentation-quality, information-rich documents for the World Wide Web. Instantly distribute business-critical information from databases, database applications, and data warehouse solutions, complete with summarizing, grouping, and graphing, to a broad audience via internal or external Web servers. No manual HTML editing is required! This information enhances decision-making capabilities and on-the-spot business analysis for customers, suppliers, and employees. Industry leaders Microsoft, Netscape, and Oracle are including or supporting Crystal Web technology in their products.

Crystal Reports Professional 5.0 gives you reporting the way you want it.

Use new Crystal Report Experts to create unlimited types of reports such as the following:

- Subreports. Replace several reports with one main report that contains embedded reports.
- Conditional reports. Use new tools such as Multiple Detail Sections and Text Objects to product different report results depending on data conditions.
- Form-style reports. Easily output database information onto forms.
- Multiple summary cross-tab reports. Present summary information clearly and replace numerous columnar reports.
- BackOffice reports. Turn your BackOffice systems data into decision-making information.

Powerful reporting options include grouping, custom grouping, Top N, Bottom N, drilldown, and integrated graphing.

Other cool 5.0 features include new desktop publishing-style Report Designer and object technology, which places report elements exactly where you want them. Plus, there is a new query tool with comprehensive SQL editing, expanded database support, and much more.

Seamlessly integrate reports into applications using the full-featured ActiveX control (OCX), VBX, VCL, and MFC. FREE runtime. Supports a Windows platform including Windows 95, NT, and 3.1 or Windows for Workgroups. Available in both 16- and 32-bit versions.

KL Group, Inc.

Address:	260 King Street East Toronto, Ontario, Canada M5A 1K3
Telephone:	(416) 594-1026
Fax:	(416) 594-1919
Sales:	(800) 709-2947
Web:	`www.klg.com`
Contact:	April Dunford
E-mail:	`april@klg.com`

Olectra Chart, Version 5.0

CD-ROM demo directory: `\DEMOS\KLGROUP\OLECTRA`

Olectra Chart combines high-performance graphing power with the freedom to easily create and customize virtually any type of chart. Olectra Chart provides hundreds of properties and methods to create an unlimited variety of charts with endless variations of color, style annotations, and perspectives.

Optimized for performance, Olectra Chart is fast enough for real-time scrolling strip charts such as scientific and financial charts. With new code-free data binding, charts created with Olectra Chart can easily be bound to any data source to create dynamic data-driven charts. Loaded with demos and sample code, Olectra Chart helps developers get started quickly and easily and also includes full printed and online documentation.

Olectra Chart 5.0 provides unrivaled features, including the following:

- Numerous chart types, including bar (horizontal or vertical), stacking bar, 100% stacking bar, floating bar, pie, area, line, surface, polar, radar, filled radar, HiLo, HiLoOpenClose, candlestick, scrolling time charts, logarithmic charts, and many more
- Data binding to any data source without writing a single line of code
- Built-in zooming, scaling, and rotation
- Interactive interfaces such as drill-downs with hit detection
- Annotations anywhere with unlimited labels
- High-performance real-time charting with fast update methods
- Dynamic date and time axis on any plot
- Dual Y axis and logarithmic axes supported
- Axis annotation options, including scientific, accounting, currency, fraction, and percent
- Custom zone and contour styles
- Flexible data layout supporting regular or irregular data structures
- Support for missing values (holes)
- Intuitive grid-style data editor
- Support for background pictures (bitmap or `.wmf` format)
- 16-bit and 32-bit versions included
- Object-based C API, MFC, and OWL wrappers
- More than 60 demos with source code and 30 sample code files included
- Printed and online documentation included
- Royalty free runtime distribution
- 30-day money-back guarantee
- Free 30-day technical support

Add Sizzle to Your Web Pages with Olectra Chart 5.0

Display stunning charts on your Web pages quickly and easily with Olectra Chart 5.0. Chart specifications and data can be loaded from any URL for easy modification and updating. Users can interact with charts displayed on Web pages and can customize chart properties using Olectra Chart's built-in property pages. Olectra Chart's controls have been signed with a VeriSign Digital ID, which ensures that the control has not been altered or damaged before it is downloaded.

Visual Basic, Visual C++, and Beyond!

Olectra Chart's ActiveX/OCX interfaces can be used with Visual Basic 4 or Visual Basic 5 as well as Visual C++ 4.0 and above, Delphi 2.01 and above, PowerBuilder 5.0 and above, Optima++, or any other development environment that supports ActiveX or OCX controls. C developers using Visual C++ 1.5 or higher or Borland C++ 4.5 and above can access the DLL through a fully documented object-based C API, MFC, and OWL wrapper. Both 16-bit and 32-bit versions are included.

Unrivaled Performance

If performance is important for your application, Olectra Chart is your obvious choice. Create real-time scrolling strip charts for network monitoring, scientific data plots, financial charts, and more. With performance that is more than four times faster than the competition, you can't beat Olectra Chart. Charts created with Olectra Chart can be bound to any data source without writing a single line of code. Using Data Binding, data can be plotted "live" in dynamic data-driven charts.

Get Started Fast—It's Easy With Olectra Chart!

Olectra Chart comes loaded with more than 60 full-featured demo programs with source code to help you get started quickly. Also included are more than 30 sample code files illustrating a wide variety of chart types, over 800 pages of printed documentation, and comprehensive online help. Olectra Chart's handy object hierarchy reference poster is not only functional but also looks great on your wall.

Vision Software

Address:	2101 Webster St. 8th Floor Oakland, CA 94612
Telephone:	(510) 238-4100
Fax:	(510) 238-4118
Sales:	(800) 984-SOFT
Web:	`www.vision-soft.com`

Vision StoryBoard

CD-ROM demo directory: `\DEMOS\VISION\STORY`

Every Visual Basic professional agrees that writing an application is what makes them tick. It's writing about the application that is painful. But in today's corporate development environment, timely documentation and project presentation not only are required, they're usually critical to bringing the project to completion in time and under budget.

Vision StoryBoard Professional Edition is a Microsoft Visual Basic add-in giving you the ability to quickly and easily annotate and present all facets of your project to all of the people involved—from your fellow coders, to tech writers, to test engineers, even to the users themselves. Quickly jot down notes during requirements gathering and development phases while you're working in VB. StoryBoard is right there to capture your ideas. Need a quick presentation for a UI review? StoryBoard will build you an annotated side show in HTML format for intranet-ready viewing. Leverage your notes later on in the project to produce online help. You can even output your code files in Help format for instant cross-referencing and API documentation.

Robust and comprehensive documentation at your fingertips! Isn't it time you stopped spending your time writing all of those crummy specs and started StoryBoarding today?

New & Improved UI—Document Explorer gives you a hierarchical overview of your project. Now you've got complete control over grouping forms together and manipulating the order in which they show up in your output. Doc Explorer enables you to comment objects without having them open, giving you even more flexibility in the way you use StoryBoard PRO.

New Feature—Document Explorer makes it easy to organize even the most complex projects in a familiar Windows Explorer-like interface.

New Feature—Capture and document different views of complex forms with multiple panels or during runtime.

New Feature—API Help Generator compiles an online help file for your classes and OLE Servers describing the methods and parameters.

New Feature—Code Analyzer puts key information about your VB code at your fingertips: cross-references, statistics, last-changed files—all in standard `.RTF` or `.HLP` format.

New Feature—After you've created project documentation you can save your configuration as a template for future use.

New Feature—HTML SlideShow lets you present your application over the intranet in a Web browser.

Enhanced—SpecMaker has been cleaned up and simplified for easier use.

Enhanced—SlideShow builds annotated slides of your project for pre-prototyping and early feedback.

Enhanced—The SlideShow designer is easier to use: add color, new comments, backgrounds, even incremental slides.

Enhanced—Wizards help you output your comments, screen shots, even your code in a robust `.RTF` file ready for use in MS-Word or any other Windows word processor

Enhanced—On-line Help generator takes your notes and creates fully context-sensitive and indexed help for your project—fully contained and directly usable.

Enhanced—Team Development support for MS SourceSafe and other third-party source code control systems. New reports for exceptions to naming standards.

VideoSoft

Address:	5900 Hollis Street Suite T Emeryville, CA 94608
Telephone:	(510) 595-2400
Fax:	(510) 595-2424
Sales:	1-888-ACTIVE-X
Web:	`www.videosoft.com`

VideoSoft VS-OCX

CD-ROM demo directory: `\DEMOS\VIDSOFT\VSOCX`

Using VideoSoft VS-OCX means no more resizing code! Just add a single Elastic control to your existing form, set a few properties, and voila! Your forms become resolution independent. Even if the user switches screen resolutions between EGA, VGA, or SVGA, the Elastic control automatically will resize all controls on the form. Use the Elastic control to implement splitter bars to create a standard user interface for your forms. Your users will be able to customize the size of controls. The "no-label" feature of the Elastic control makes it possible to create multiline captions, 3D gauges, or both simultaneously on a single Elastic.

No more switching between forms! Let the IndexTab control present several screens worth of data in the space of one by using notebook-style tabs like those in Microsoft Word or Excel. Resize the form and watch the contents of each tab resize automatically.

No more slow code to parse strings and read files! Let VSAwk slice and dice strings automatically. VSAwk even includes an expression evaluator that supports variables. Simply plug in your formula or expression and VSAwk will summon your code at runtime, retrieve the value, and return the expression's results. What could be easier?

No more tedious work! Let these three controls do the work for you.

VideoSoft VS-OCX highlights:

- Includes VBX, 16- and 32-bit ActiveX controls
- Creates forms that are resolution independent
- Automatically resizes all controls on your form
- Implements splitter bars between controls
- Saves resources by eliminating the need for labels
- Creates notebook-style tabs in multiple styles
- Adds wizards to your apps
- Parses and scans files automatically

To order, call 1-888-ActiveX (228-4839).

VideoSoft VSVIEW

CD-ROM demo directory: `\DEMOS\VIDSOFT\VSVIEW`

VideoSoft VSVIEW makes printing intuitive. It uses a familiar word processing metaphor to create documents. VideoSoft VSView enables you to create output in the form of words, lines, paragraphs, tables, or columns, and the text will wrap automatically. You can easily combine paragraphs, graphs, graphics, tables, and columns anywhere on a page.

VideoSoft VSView makes printing easy. It contains a rich set of formatting options such as headers, footers, text alignment, text angle, indentation, borders, and margins.

VideoSoft VSView also delivers Print Preview. The printer becomes a visible object on the screen. You can use the same code to print and preview multipage documents. Simply drag your text file to the visual printer and preview it on the screen at different zoom levels.

VideoSoft VSView includes a drawing control, a ViewPort, and a control that makes other controls look and behave like forms. VideoSoft VSView provides a revolutionary step in printing.

VideoSoft VSVIEW highlights:

- Includes VBX, 16- and 32-bit ActiveX controls
- 27 new properties, four new events, 15 new methods, and 12 new settings
- Saves your report to a file
- Rich Text Format (RTF) support
- Automatic zooming, scrolling, and panning
- Enhanced tables: vertical and bottom alignment, optical word wrap on columns, automatic shading, spill tables (when too wide), and automatic cell headers on next page
- Allows independent customization of headers and footers

To order, call 1-888-ActiveX (228-4839).

VideoSoft VSFLEX

CD-ROM demo directory: `\DEMOS\VIDSOFT\VSFLEX`

VideoSoft VSFLEX is a powerful set of ActiveX controls that enable you to add decision support to your applications. One of the controls is a flexible data-bound grid control. This control is fast and very light in system resources.

Impress your users! Give your applications a professional look and feel. Using VideoSoft VSFLEX's unique cell-merging capabilities, adjacent cells containing the same information can be merged to create one larger cell.

Empower your users! Allow them to visually pivot the columns or rows to arrange and rearrange the information in the control. You can configure the control to perform automatic subtotaling and outlining, delivering a pivoting outline with dynamic data in your application. VideoSoft VSFlex also supports in-cell editing and is backward compatible with the grid included with Visual Basic.

So why wait? Get your copy today!

VideoSoft VSFLEX highlights:

- Advanced data binding
- In-cell editing with optional drop-downs
- Automatic groups and subtotals
- Outline views "like Explorer"
- Virtual loading of data
- Automatic statistics such as average, percent, minimum, and maximum
- International support for sorting and dates
- Plus 35 new features and settings

To order, call 1-888-ActiveX (228-4839).

VideoSoft VSDATA

CD-ROM demo directory: `\DEMOS\VIDSOFT\VSDATA`

VideoSoft VSDATA is a complete database engine in one ActiveX control. This powerful control gives applications faster access to data. Due to its small footprint, VideoSoft VSData is the ideal database system for your Internet or multimedia applications. You can easily create multiuser/network ready databases with variable length fields and records. Just drop a VideoSoft VSData control on your form, set a couple of properties, and you're ready! Your application can access a fully functional database system that is 20 times faster than Microsoft Access.

VideoSoft VSData gives you full control of your data access by supporting record locking and multifield indexing. You can get multiple VideoSoft VSData controls working together in any ActiveX container including Microsoft Visual Basic and Visual C++.

VideoSoft VSData is also multimedia aware. Store your video and sound files into native database fields. Then, use any of the built-in playback methods to give life to your applications with sound or video. There's more! VSData is Internet aware and supports hyperlinks as a native datatype, too.

VideoSoft VSData includes conversion utilities that enable you to migrate to and from other existing databases such as Microsoft Access and dBASE.

VideoSoft VSDATA highlights:

- OCX: Same interface from any language
- Less than 200KB
- 20 times faster than the leading database, Microsoft Access
- Exceptional Data Manager embedded in the control
- Multimedia aware—supports audio, video fields, and Internet
- Multiuser
- Variable-length records
- Record and field locking
- Multiple index types including single, multikey, and 3D
- Numerous field types including number, string, currency, picture, sound, video, data, and Internet

To order, call 1-888-ActiveX (228-4839).

VideoSoft VSREPORTS

CD-ROM demo directory: `\DEMOS\VIDSOFT\VSREPORT`

VideoSoft VSREPORTS is the reporting tool that lets you print Microsoft Access–created reports without having Access installed on the user's machine. This ActiveX control permits you to use the industry-leading report designer, Access, to create your reports and then print them using Visual Basic or any ActiveX container.

VideoSoft VSReports enables you to print reports created in Microsoft Access without having to distribute any Access runtime DLLs. Now you can print them in Visual Basic using VSReports. Place a VSReports ActiveX control on your form, set a few properties, and presto, your Access report is ready to be printed.

VideoSoft VSReports re-creates Access reports reproducing the exact positioning of fields and page breaks, fonts, colors, sorting, and filtering into groups and sections, just as in the original report. VideoSoft VSReports automatically supports all Access Report Writer features, including the following:

- Visual Basic for Applications (VBA) expressions, aggregated fields, and watermarks. Multicolumn and parameterized reports are supported as well. You can even output them to an HTML file to be published on the Web.
- VideoSoft VSReports dynamically reads the data at runtime from Access or any ODBC database such as Oracle, Sybase, or VSData.

VideoSoft VSREPORTS highlights:

- OCX: Same interface from any language
- Compact: Less than 200KB
- Use Access to create your reports and Visual Basic to print them
- Reports can be printed to file as HTML

To order, call 1-888-ActiveX (228-4839).

Logic Works, Inc.

Address:	111 Campus Drive Princeton, NJ 08540
Telephone:	(609) 514-1177
Fax:	(609) 514-1175
Sales:	(800) 78-ERWIN [783-7946]
Web:	`www.logicworks.com`

There are no demos on the CD-ROM accompanying this book. For a guided tour of these products, refer to Logic Works' Web site.

Logic Works ER*win*/ERX

Logic Works ER*win*/ERX is a powerful, easy-to-use data modeling tool that lets you design and generate databases for client/server, Web/intranet, and data warehouse applications. Use ER*win* to create an Entity-Relationship (E-R) diagram, or logical model of your database. The data model automatically generates the database and provides a solid foundation for application development.

Featuring forward and reverse engineering, ER*win* provides a direct connection to your system catalog, creating a data model straight from your database tables. Changes to the data model can be forward engineered to update the current database or used to create a new one in over 20 supported DBMSs. Tables, indexes, referential integrity (primary key, foreign key), defaults, domain/column constraints, and thousands of lines of stored procedure and trigger code are all generated automatically, providing a solid foundation for new development.

ER*win*'s powerful Complete-Compare feature lets you compare a data model with the physical database, SQL schema, or another ER*win* model. The model can be selectively synchronized with changes in the target database. Incremental changes to a data model can be forward engineered, keeping your model aligned with your physical database.

Approximately 85,000 IS professionals who plan, build, and deploy today's client/server and Internet/intranet applications voted ER*win* the Best CASE/Modeling tool for five consecutive years in the *DBMS Magazine* Reader's Choice Awards poll.

Logic Works ER*win*/OPEN

Logic Works ER*win*/OPEN is a powerful version of Logic Works award-winning data modeling tool that combines back-end database design and front-end application development in one unified environment. Featuring seamless multiclient support, ER*win*/OPEN generates Visual Basic data-entry forms, PowerBuilder DataWindows, and PROGESS SmartObjects from the same data model, making corporate application developers highly productive in three of today's leading database development environments.

ER*win*/OPEN also provides a bidirectional link to the Designer/2000 repository, enabling you to use ER*win*'s state-of-the-art data modeling features to design applications stored in the Designer/2000 repository.

Logic Works Enterprise Developer's Suite for Visual Basic

Logic Works Enterprise Developer's Suite for Visual Basic is a set of tightly integrated design tools that dramatically enhance Visual Basic's capability to build high-performance client/server and intranet database applications. Enterprise Developer's Suite for Visual Basic adds powerful data management features to Visual Basic, so corporate development teams can build enterprise-level database applications faster than ever before.

Logic Works ER*win* Modeling

Using ER*win's* integrated client/server modeling capabilities, you can create a graphical data model and quickly design an efficient SQL database. You can specify Visual Basic client properties such as edit styles, display formats, and default values directly in the ER*win* model. When the model is complete, ER*win* automatically generates the schema on all major SQL and desktop databases.

Logic Works DataBOT Application Development

After generating the database, DataBOT uses the ER*win* model information to speed form construction and to manage data access. Because DataBOT stores both database schema information and front-end client properties, it makes Visual Basic a more data-aware environment and automatically generates optimized data access code.

Template Graphics Software, Inc.

Address: 9920 Pacific Heights Blvd.
Suite 200
San Diego, CA
92121
Telephone: (619) 457-5359
Fax: (619) 452-2547
Web: `www.tgs.com`
E-mail: `info@tgs.com`

Visual 3Space Control

CD-ROM demo directory: `\DEMOS\TGS\3SPACE`

Visual 3Space Control is a complete 3D/VRML ActiveX control used to add 3D functionality to Excel, Microsoft Visual C++, Visual Basic, Internet Explorer, and other ActiveX platforms. Delivering over 400 property and method settings, Visual 3Space Control supports both intranet- and Internet-capable 3D applications, DXF, VRML, and Open Inventor.

Combine the power of interactive 3D graphics and Visual Basic using the Visual 3Space Control. A native 32-bit ActiveX control, Visual 3Space Control delivers over 30 properties and 400 methods to manipulate and control geometry, lights, and cameras. It supports DXF, VRML 2.0, and Open Inventor 2.*x* file formats, as well as e-mail and the WWW through both the x-world/x-vrml and application/x-inventor MIME types. Examples of application uses are 3D interactive user interfaces, 3D models integrated with technical documentation, online training manuals, interactive 3D clip art for Microsoft Office products, architectural walk throughs, virtual representation of remote events, and data visualization.

Other features of the Visual 3Space Control include support for linking 3D content to text, video, audio, or other 3D graphics data into Word, PowerPoint, and Internet Explorer plus compatibility with 3D modeling applications such as Autodesk 3D Studio, Yonowat Amapi, CAD/CAM applications including PTC Pro/Engineer, EDS Unigraphics, and SDRC Ideas. The control also supports VBScript and JavaScript.

Users of Microsoft Word, PowerPoint, and other popular ActiveX container applications can view thousands of 3D files on the Internet with the Visual 3Space Control. A custom application can be generated in minutes in Visual Basic. An example would be a representation of a warehouse in which Microsoft Access database entries are retrieved and displayed in an adjoining control, when a scene is touched. Clicking 3D objects in the warehouse can cause AVI files to be downloaded from the Internet and played using a separate AVI control. Example uses of the product range from 3D user interfaces for client-server applications to interactive 3D training and help facilities.

LEAD Technologies, Inc.

Address:	900 Baxter Street Charlotte, NC 28204
Telephone:	(704) 332-5532
Fax:	(704) 372-8161
Sales:	(800) 637-4699
Web:	`www.leadtools.com`
E-mail:	`sales@leadtools.com`

LEADTOOLS ActiveX (OCX) 16 PRO (No Demo)

Integrate black-and-white, grayscale, and color images into any 16-bit ActiveX (OCX) compliant application. The toolkit contains a Win 16 OLE control, providing 150 methods and properties. Capabilities include importing and exporting of 40 file formats, image processing with region of interest, color conversion, image compression, displaying (with scrolling, zooming, and dithering), printing, scanning, and data binding. Includes sample applications for Visual Basic and Access 2.0. Supports Access 2.0, ActiveX, Visual Basic 4.0, and Visual C++.

LEADTOOLS ActiveX (OCX) 16/32 PRO (No Demo)

Two programming libraries in one toolkit, LEADTOOLS ActiveX 16 and LEADTOOLS ActiveX 32 Pro, are bundled together in one package. Develop one application for two platforms, Win 16 and Win 32. Includes everything you need to support raster images with 150+ functions in eight imaging categories: importing/exporting 40+ file formats, optimal compression, rich image processing with region of interest, color conversion, annotation, displaying, printing, and scanning. Supports Access 2.0 and 7.0, ActiveX, Visual Basic 4.0, Visual C++, Java 32-bit, and Visual FoxPro 32-bit.

LEADTOOLS ActiveX (OCX) 32 PRO

CD-ROM demo directory: `\DEMOS\LEADTOOL\IMAGE`

Integrate black-and-white, grayscale, and color images into any 32-bit ActiveX (OCX) compliant application. The toolkit contains a Win 16 OLE control, providing 150 methods and properties. Capabilities include importing and exporting of 40 file formats, image processing with region of interest, color conversion, image compression, displaying (with scrolling, zooming, and dithering), printing, scanning, and data binding. Includes sample applications for Visual Basic and Delphi, Visual FoxPro, and Access 7.0. Supports Access 7.0, ActiveX, Visual Basic 4.0, Visual C++, Java, and Visual FoxPro.

LEADTOOLS Pro Express (No Demo)

The Pro Express version is for programmers who are looking for faster code or document imaging capabilities. Includes all of the features of the LEADTOOLS Win 16/Win32 Pro bundle, with enhanced speed performance, refined bitonal imaging support, and annotations. CCITT G3 and G4, CMP, and JPEG compression techniques have been hand optimized. Develop one application for both Win 16 and Win 32. Includes sample applications with source code for C/C++, MFC, Visual Basic, Visual Fox, Access 2.0, Access 7.0, and Delphi. Supports Access, ActiveX, Visual Basic 4.0, Visual C++, Java 32-bit, and Visual FoxPro 32-bit.

LEADTOOLS Win 16 Pro (No Demo)

This toolkit contains a DLL, ActiveX (OCX), and VBX, providing 150 functions. Capabilities include importing and exporting of 40+ file formats, image processing with region of interest, color conversion, image compression, printing, scanning, and data binding. Provides high-level and low-level functions and applications with source code for C/C++, MFC, Visual Basic, Access 2.0, and Delphi. Supports Access 2.0, ActiveX, Visual Basic 3.0 and 4.0 16-bit, and Visual C++.

LEADTOOLS VBX Pro (No Demo)

Integrate black-and-white, grayscale, and color images into any VBX-compliant application. The toolkit contains a Win 16 custom control, providing 150 properties. Capabilities include importing and exporting of 40+ file formats, image processing with region of interest, color conversion, image compression, displaying (with scrolling, zooming, and dithering), printing, scanning, and data binding. Provides high-level and low-level functions and applications with source code for Visual Basic and Delphi. Supports Visual Basic 3.0 and Visual C++ 1.5.

LEADTOOLS Win 16/32 Pro (No Demo)

Five programming libraries in one toolkit, LEADTOOLS Win 16 Pro and LEADTOOLS Win 32 Pro are bundled together in one package. You can develop one application for two platforms, Win 16 and Win 32. The toolkit contains a VBX, ActiveX (OCX) 16 and 32, and DLLs for Win 16 and 32. Ships with source code for C/C++, MFC, Visual Basic, Delphi, Access 2.0 and 7.0, and Visual FoxPro. Supports Access 2.0 and 7.0, ActiveX, Visual Basic 4.0, Visual C++, Java 32-bit, and Visual FoxPro.

LEADTOOLS Win 32 PRO (No Demo)

Two programming libraries in one toolkit. Integrate black-and-white, grayscale, and color images into any Win 32 application. The toolkit contains a DLL, ActiveX (OCX), and VBX, providing 150 functions. Capabilities include importing and exporting of 40 file formats, image processing with region of interest, color conversion, image compression, displaying (with scrolling, zooming, and dithering), printing, scanning, and data binding. Provides high-level and low-level functions and applications for C/C++, MFC, Visual Basic, Visual FoxPro, and Access 7.0. Supports Access 7.0, ActiveX, Visual Basic 4.0, Visual C++, Java, and Visual FoxPro.

Sylvain Faust, Inc. (SFI)

Address:	SFI Building 880 Boulevard de la Carriere Suite 130 Hull, Quebec, Canada J8Y 6T5
Telephone:	(819) 778-5045
Fax:	(819) 778-7943
Web:	`www.sfi-software.com`
Contact:	Karen Pallister
E-mail:	`info@sfi-software.com`

SQL-Sombrero/OCX for DB-Library (6.*x*) ($479 US)

CD-ROM demo directory: `\DEMOS\SYLVAIN\DBLIB326`

The DB-Library (6.*x*)/OCX is an ActiveX control that provides access to the DB-Library (6.*x*) API. The DB-Library (6.*x*) programming interface provides native API access to Microsoft SQL Server (6.*x*). Access to this API provides the most direct and efficient method of connecting to SQL Server and accessing the data on SQL Server. The ActiveX control is provided in both 16- and 32-bit versions. The code for both 16- and 32-bit is identical, so porting an application from 16- to 32-bit is easy.

ActiveX terminology might seem frightening for programmers who have never embarked down the OLE development path. SQL-Sombrero simply is an object within your application that contains a set of methods which map to the native server API. SQL-Sombrero is a non-visual control. Simply drop one of these controls on a form and an object is established in your application. This object exposes a set of methods, variables, and events that are straightforward and familiar to any Visual Basic/SQL Server developer.

SQL-Sombrero has its own installation procedure, which creates the required Registry entries and installs many samples. These samples provide VB projects with code illustrating the use of DB-Library to access Microsoft SQL Servers. There are samples showing how to maintain a table, execute stored procedures, store and retrieve data (including text and images), and use the BCP methods. There also is an example of using SQL-Sombrero with Excel to populate a spreadsheet. Remember that as an ActiveX control SQL-Sombrero allows any OLE Automation-enabled applications to use the DB-Library API directly from that application.

SQL-Sombrero becomes part of the Visual Basic language. Use the Visual Basic browser facility to access methods and constants. Take advantage of the online help facility to gain direct context-sensitive help about SQL-Sombrero/OCX functions.

SQL-Sombrero provides access to the full DB-Library (6.*x*) command interface. There are methods to create connections to SQL Server and then send commands to be executed by SQL Server. There are methods that can be used to retrieve the results of executed commands including the retrieval of data from the SQL Server. There is a full API to allow access to the DB-Library Bulk Copy functionality.

SQL-Sombrero provides an Event CallBack capability. DB-Library provides callbacks for error/message notification. SQL-Sombrero maps those callbacks to Visual Basic events.

SQL-Sombrero/OCX for DB-Library (4.*x*) ($479 US)

CD-ROM demo directory: `\DEMOS\SYLVAIN\DBLIB324`

The DB-Library (4.*x*)/OCX is an ActiveX control that provides access to the DB-Library API. The DB-Library (4.*x*) programming interface provides native API access to both Microsoft and Sybase SQL Server. Access to this API provides the most direct and efficient method of connecting to SQL Server and accessing the data on SQL Server. The 4.*x* level of DB-Library supports both Microsoft and Sybase SQL Server with an identical API. SQL-Sombrero takes care of any differences in the DB-Library provided by either server so that all code is identical for each server. The ActiveX control is provided in both 16- and 32-bit versions. The code for both 16- and 32-bit is identical, so porting an application from 16 to 32 bit is easy.

ActiveX terminology might seem frightening to programmers who have never embarked down the OLE development path. SQL-Sombrero simply is an object within your application that contains a set of methods which map to the native server API. SQL-Sombrero is a non-visual control. Simply drop one of these controls on a form and an object is established in your application. This object exposes a set of methods, variables, and events that are straightforward and familiar to any Visual Basic/SQL Server developer.

SQL-Sombrero has its own installation procedure, which creates the required Registry entries and installs many samples. These samples provide VB projects with code illustrating the use of DB-Library to access Microsoft and Sybase SQL Servers. There are samples showing how to maintain a table, execute stored procedures, store and retrieve data (including text and image), and use the BCP methods. There is also an example of using SQL-Sombrero with Excel to populate a spreadsheet. Remember that as an ActiveX control SQL-Sombrero allows any OLE Automation-enabled applications to use the DB-Library API directly from that application.

SQL-Sombrero becomes part of the Visual Basic language. Use the Visual Basic browser facility to access methods and constants. Take advantage of the online help facility to gain direct context-sensitive help on SQL-Sombrero/OCX functions.

SQL-Sombrero provides access to the full DB-Library (4.*x*) command interface, with the exception of the cursor methods, which are client-side cursors and very slow to execute. There are methods to create connections to SQL Server and then send commands to be executed by SQL Server. There are methods that can be used to retrieve the results of executed commands, including the retrieval of data from the SQL Server. There is a full API to allow access to the DB-Library Bulk Copy functionality.

SQL-Sombrero provides an Event CallBack capability. DB-Library provides callbacks for error/message notification. SQL-Sombrero maps those callbacks to Visual Basic events.

SQL-Sombrero/OCX for Oracle Call Interface (OCI) ($479 US)

CD-ROM demo directory: `\DEMOS\SYLVAIN\OCI32`

The SQL-Sombrero OCI/OCX is an ActiveX control that provides access to the Oracle Call Interface (OCI). The OCI programming interface provides native API access to Oracle servers. Access to this API provides the most direct and efficient method of connecting to the database server and accessing the data on that server. The ActiveX control is provided in both 16- and 32-bit versions. The code for both 16 and 32 bit is identical, so porting an application from 16 to 32 bit is easy.

ActiveX terminology might seem frightening to programmers who have never embarked down the OLE development path. SQL-Sombrero simply is an object within your application that contains a set of methods which map to the native server API. SQL-Sombrero is a non-visual control. Simply drop one of these controls on a form and an object is established in your application. This object exposes a set of methods, variables, and events that are straightforward and familiar to any Visual Basic/SQL Server developer.

SQL-Sombrero has its own installation procedure, which creates the required Registry entries and installs many samples. These samples provides both a 16 and 32 VB project with code illustrating the use of SQL-Sombrero/OCX for OCI. There is sample code showing how to fetch data from an Oracle server (including long and long raw data), use placeholders to input parameters to SQL statements, and execute procedures.

SQL-Sombrero becomes part of the Visual Basic language. Use the Visual Basic browser facility to access methods and constants. Take advantage of the online help facility to gain direct context-sensitive help about SQL-Sombrero/OCX functions.

SQL-Sombrero provides access to the full OCI command interface. There are methods to create connections to an Oracle server and then send commands to be executed by the server.

There are methods that can be used to retrieve the results of executed commands including the retrieval of data from the Oracle server.

SQL-Sombrero using objects to bind data to SQL statements allows the execution of SQL statements and the subsequent retrieval of the data from the bound objects.

SQL-Sombrero/OCX for CT-Library ($479 US)

CD-ROM demo directory: `\DEMOS\SYLVAIN\CTLIB32`

The CT-Library/OCX is an ActiveX control that provides access to the Open Client API, also known as CT-Library. The Open Client programming interface provides native API access to Sybase SQL Server. Access to this API provides the most direct and efficient method of connecting to Sybase SQL Server and accessing the data on Sybase SQL Server. The ActiveX control is provided in both 16- and 32-bit versions. The code for both 16 and 32 bit is identical, so porting an application from 16 to 32 bit is easy.

ActiveX terminology might seem frightening to programmers who have never embarked down the OLE development path. SQL-Sombrero simply is an object within your application that contains a set of methods which map to the native server API. SQL-Sombrero is a non-visual control. Simply drop one of these controls on a form and an object is established in your application. This object exposes a set of methods, variables, and events that are straightforward and familiar to any Visual Basic/SQL Server developer.

SQL-Sombrero has its own installation procedure, which creates the required Registry entries and installs many samples. These samples provide VB projects with code illustrating the use of Open Client (CT-Library) to access Sybase SQL Server. There are samples showing how to maintain a table, execute stored procedures, store and retrieve data (including text and image), and use the BCP methods. There is also an example of using SQL-Sombrero with Excel to populate a spreadsheet. Remember that as an ActiveX control SQL-Sombrero allows any OLE Automation–enabled application to use the Open Client API directly from that application.

SQL-Sombrero becomes part of the Visual Basic language. Use the Visual Basic browser facility to access methods and constants. Take advantage of the online help facility to gain direct context-sensitive help on SQL-Sombrero/OCX functions.

SQL-Sombrero provides access to the full Open Client (CT-Library) command interface. There are methods to create connections to SQL Server and then send commands to be executed by SQL Server. There are methods that can be used to retrieve the results of executed commands including the retrieval of data from the SQL Server.

SQL-Sombrero provides an Event CallBack capability. Open Client provides callbacks for error/message notification and function completion. SQL-Sombrero maps those callbacks to Visual Basic events. Using this capability allows the developer to do asynchronous processing using those Visual Basic events.

Level Five Research

Address: 1335 Gateway Drive
Suite 2005
Melbourne, FL
32901
Telephone: (407) 729-6004
Fax: (407) 727-7615
Sales: (800) 444-4303
Web: WWW.L5R.COM
Contact: Doug Taylor
E-mail: doug@L5R.com

LEVEL\5 Quest ($129 Desktop, $499 Server)

CD-ROM demo directory: `\DEMOS\LEVEL5\QUEST`

LEVEL\5 Quest is a simple but powerful database search and publishing tool that enables users to always find "best fit" results from their Web databases. Quest's Intelligent technology ranks and grades query results by how closely they match the user's ideal preferences.

Quest is a breakthrough Intelligent technology that always finds "best fit" results in a database—ranked and graded by how closely they match a user's ideal preferences. Quest is available as a desktop data mining workstation, as an Internet DBMS server to quickly and easily put a "searchable" database on the World Wide Web. Quest data search-and-discovery technology components can be integrated into large-scale custom applications.

Quest's unique combination of fuzzy logic, semantic concept maps, proximity search, relative importance, and relevance ranking completely eliminates "no records found" problems by always returning answers that are near, similar, or most representative of the users' criteria. Quest's "best of" solutions let you create online comparison shopping systems, performance appraisals, and compare and contrast decision support applications; solve complex requirements matching and trade-off analysis problems; quickly perform multidimensional analysis of financial information.

APEX Software Corporation

Address: 4516 Henry Street
Pittsburgh, PA
15213
Telephone: (412) 681-4343
Fax: (412) 681-4384
Sales: (800) 858-2739
Web: `www.apexsc.com`
E-mail: `sales@apexsc.com`

MyData Control ($149.95) (No Demo)

MyData Control lets you use all data-bound controls with any data source or DBMS accessible in Visual Basic.

There are three ways to use MyData Control with your data source:

- Special Visual Basic Events: Unlike the Visual Basic built-in data control, which retrieves data from the Jet Engine, MyData Control fires special Visual Basic events that let you provide your own data. Program the events once with your data source, and then use them over and over in all your projects.

  MyData Control ships with source code (for the special events) for Visual Basic array and ODBC 2.0 data sources. More sample source code will be available from the APEX Web site.
- XArray ActiveX Object: For small databases, the easiest way to use MyData Control is with the XArray ActiveX object that ships with the product. Using the XArray object, you do not need to code any special event handlers. Fill the XArray with your data as you would a Visual Basic array, and MyData Control will handle the rest. You gain instant access to the world of data-aware controls with unprecedented speed and performance.
- C++ Internal Interfaces: MyData Control also has internal C++ interfaces that can connect directly to your data source to create a custom Data Source Control for your data source or proprietary databases. The internal interface is available to DBMS or data source vendors through a special licensing agreement with APEX. Please call APEX at 412-681-4343 or e-mail `mydata@apexsc.com` for detailed licensing information.

  MyData Control lets you use all data-bound controls with any data or DBMS accessible in Visual Basic: Q+E Database Library, Successware Database Engine (xBase files), CodeBase Database Engine, Smithware (Btrieve files), Lotus Notes files, Excel and other spreadsheet files, delimited text files, Visual Basic arrays, and much more.

True DBGrid ($199.95) (No Demo)

APEX was chosen to develop the MSDBGrid for Visual Basic 5.0 because of its commitment to quality and innovative technology. As the developer of MSDBGrid, APEX knows how to enhance and improve its powerful and time-saving features. This is why True DBGrid is the only enhanced data grid of choice.

True DBGrid is widely recognized as the most efficient grid on the market. Most notable are True DBGrid's speed and abundant features. When you use True DBGrid, you know you will automatically satisfy all software standards set by Microsoft, and you will benefit from the latest ActiveX/OCX and database technologies built into all Microsoft development systems.

APEX will be releasing a new version of True DBGrid called True DBGrid Pro 5.0 Q2 of 1997. It will have the same functionality as True DBGrid, with many additional features (some of which are listed next). Both products are compatible with VB 4.0 and 5.0.

The APEX Web site contains maintenance upgrades, samples, a technical support FAQ list, and additional documentation for True DBGrid. Stop by to download the free VBA Companion OCX Edition, enter a drawing for free APEX products, and test the ActiveX ToolboX demo. Product order forms are also available on the APEX Web site.

Features:

- Microsoft Excel and Word-like styles
- Microsoft Excel-like splits
- Per-cell color and font control
- Multiple row/column selection
- Interactive visual editing capabilities
- Display format mask
- Flexible unbound modes
- Fixed, non-scrolling columns
- In-cell graphics, combo box, check box, and radio buttons
- Unbound columns
- Features to drag and drop cell contents
- Automatic data translation (for example, display 0/1 as No/Yes, without writing a single line of code)
- Pop up any control from a cell
- Multiple lines per record
- Multiple column, built-in drop-down data-aware list box
- Array-based unbound mode
- Reusable grid layouts

- Input masking
- Celltips to aid grid end users
- Properties and methods to manipulate a recordset
- Add-in grid design utility
- Per-row color and font control using RowStyle
- Free runtime distribution
- The most responsive technical support in the industry
- Much more

iCat Corporation

Address: 1420 Fifth Ave.
Suite 1800
Seattle, WA
98101
Telephone: (206) 505-8800
Web: `www.icat.com`

iCat Electronic Commerce Suite (No Demo)

iCat was founded by Craig Danuloff in1993 to develop software for building interactive multimedia catalogs. In the beginning, interactive catalogs were limited to CD-ROM implementation. However, when the Internet emerged as a viable delivery mechanism for information, the iCat technologies were expanded to create the first and most complete solution for developing order-enabled Internet and intranet catalogs. Unlike many other catalog solutions, which are add-ons to existing database or Internet technologies, iCat Electronic Commerce Suite represents the only complete solution developed solely for the purpose of creating dynamic, interactive catalogs complete with secure transaction processing.

A privately owned company, iCat has grown rapidly to meet the increasing demands of the market and currently employs 125 people on three continents. The company's goal is to deliver products, technologies, and services that provide everything needed to create, manage, and deliver sophisticated Internet catalogs and process secure transactions.

The iCat Business Partner program is an international network of more than 250 companies throughout 25 countries that use iCat Electronic Commerce Suite to develop, deliver, and host interactive catalogs for their customers. These include value-added resellers, systems integrators, Web developers, advertising agencies, marketing firms, and Internet service providers.

In addition, iCat has developed joint marketing and technology development agreements with key strategic partners to add further value to its software. For example, an agreement with First Virtual, a company specializing in electronic payment processing, provides merchants with secure online transactions and real-time credit card processing for Internet shoppers. More than 25 best-of-breed technology partners are using iCat Carbo technology to create extensions to iCat software. These include companies such as EDS, UPS, LitleNet, Intermind, PaylinX Corporation, TAXWARE, Tan Data Corporation, CyberCash, and Open Market.

Desaware

Address:	1100 E. Hamilton Ave Suite 4 Campbell, CA 95008
Telephone:	(408) 377-4770
Fax:	(408) 371-3530
Web:	`www.desaware.com`
E-mail:	`support@desaware.com`

SpyWorks

CD-ROM demo directory: `\DEMOS\DESAWARE\SPYWORKS`

If you think Visual Basic 5.0 has made SpyWorks obsolete, think again. New ActiveX extension and OLE Hook technology lets you override the default behavior of standard interfaces and add new interfaces to your classes and controls—even those not compatible with Visual Basic. New Dynamic Export Technology lets you export functions from your Visual Basic ActiveX DLLs. Create Control Panel applets, export function libraries, ISAPI filters, and true NT services.

SpyWorks continues to be the ultimate low-level toolkit for thousands of Visual Basic programmers worldwide. It includes the most advanced subclassing and hook controls available for intercepting Windows messages or keystrokes to any window in the system. And now that Visual Basic supports in-process subclassing, count on us to show you how to do it right with a new set of low-level tools written in Visual Basic with full source code. With extensive sample code, debugging tools, and the Desaware API Class Library, you will be able to perform virtually any task that Windows is capable of doing. Available in VBX or ACTIVEX (16- and 32-bit) editions ($129 each) or a professional subscription-based edition with both and three updates for $249 plus shipping and handling. Detailed information and demos can be found at the Desaware Web site at `http://www.desaware.com`.

VersionStamper

CD-ROM demo directory: `\DEMOS\DESAWARE\VSTAMPER`

An end user or customer calls. Your program is behaving strangely or no longer loads. Did another program install an older DLL, VBX, or ActiveX on their system? Or maybe a later, but incompatible, version? Is there some other version conflict? If only your program could tell you what has gone wrong. Now it can, with VersionStamper.

VersionStamper enables you to embed into your Visual Basic executable information about all of the dynamic link libraries and custom controls used by that application, along with required current versions, file date and time, and your choice of warning conditions. The VersionStamper custom control can use this information to check the versions of the actual modules that are available on the target system. Incompatibilities are instantly detected.

VersionStamper and the Internet

VersionStamper 5 adds new support for the Internet and corporate intranets. Now you can keep an updated list of file dependencies on your Web or FTP site that your application can be programmed to check. If it finds a problem or updated file, it can notify the user, send e-mail back to your company, or even have VersionStamper automatically download the correct components from your Web or FTP site. It is also useful for corporate IS departments who can now be sure that their clients really do have the right components on their system, before tying up the service desk for hours.

VersionStamper includes 16- and 32-bit ActiveX controls for VB 4.0 and 5.0 and other OLE containers. It also includes VB 3.0 VBX version, which can embed true version resources into your VB executables. The price is $149 plus shipping and handling. Detailed information and demos can be found at our Web site at `http://www.desaware.com`.

StorageTools

CD-ROM demo directory: `\DEMOS\DESAWARE\STOOLS`

StorageTools is your key to the OLE 2.0 Structured Storage Technology. Structured Storage enables you to create files that organize complex data easily in a hierarchical system. It is like having an entire file system in each file. OLE 2.0 takes care of allocating and freeing space within a file, so just as you need not concern yourself with the physical placement of files on disk, you also can disregard the actual location of data in the file. Additionally, with its support for transactioning, you can easily implement undo operations and incremental saves in your application. StorageTools enables you to take advantage of the same file storage system used by Microsoft's own applications. In fact, it includes programs (with Visual Basic source code) that let you examine the structure of any OLE 2.0–based file so that you can see exactly how they do it.

StorageTools includes documentation and controls to make it easy to work with the registration database under Windows 3.1, Windows NT, and Windows 95. For Visual Basic 4 and 5. It also includes a simple resource compiler (with Visual Basic source code) so that you can create your own `.RES` files for use with Visual Basic.

StorageTools includes 16- and 32-bit ActiveX controls, extensive documentation, and sample code. Only $129 plus shipping and handling. Detailed information and demos can be found at our Web site at `http://www.desaware.com`.

The Custom Control Factory (No Demo)

The Custom Control Factory is a powerful tool for creating your own animated buttons, multiple state buttons, toolbars, and enhanced button style controls in Visual Basic and other OLE control clients, without programming. Comes with 256- and 24-bit color support, automatic 3D backgrounds, image compression, over 50 sample controls, and more, plus MList2, an enhanced list box control. 16- and 32-bit ActiveX controls and 16-bit VBXs are included. Only $48 plus shipping and handling. Detailed information and demos can be found at our Web site at `http://www.desaware.com`.

Griffin Technologies, Inc.

Address:	1617 St. Andrews Drive Lawrence, KS 66047
Telephone:	(913) 832-2070
Fax:	(913) 832-8787
Sales:	(800) 986-6578
Web:	`WWW.GRIFTECH.COM`
E-mail:	`angela@griftech.com`

Products

TX Text Control OCX, TopMagic, DocKit_GT

ProtoView

Address: 2540 Route 130
Cranbury, NJ
08512
Telephone: (404) 467-8086
Fax: (404) 467-8082
Sales: (800) 231-8588
Web: `www.protoview.com`
Contact: Karen Miller
E-mail: `karenm@protoview.com`

Products

CD-ROM demo directory: **`\DEMOS\PROTVIEW\DATATABL`**

Data Table

CD-ROM demo directory: **`\DEMOS\PROTVIEW\DATAEXPL`**

Data Explorer

CD-ROM demo directory: **`\DEMOS\PROTVIEW\WINX`**

WinX Component Library

CD-ROM demo directory: **`\DEMOS\PROTVIEW\INTERACT`**

Interact

Sax Software

Products

Webster Control, Setup Wizard, Basic Engine

Mabry Software

Products

Mega Pack 2, Internet Pack, MIDI Pack

B

Error Tables

Visual Basic errors are not included in this listing for two reasons. First, they are easily available online. Second, there are over 800 errors in Visual Basic. Therefore, for the sake of saving paper, they are not listed.

ODBC Errors

SQLSTATE	*Error*
01000	General warning
01001	Cursor operation conflict
01002	Disconnect error
01003	Null value eliminated in set function
01004	String data, right truncated
01006	Privilege not revoked
01007	Privilege not granted
01S00	Invalid connection string attribute
01S01	Error in row
01S02	Option value changed
01S06	Attempt to fetch before the resultset returned the first rowset
01S07	Fractional truncation
01S08	Error saving File DSN
01S09	Invalid keyword
07002	COUNT field incorrect
07005	Prepared statement not a cursor specification
07006	Restricted datatype attribute violation
07009	Invalid descriptor index
07S01	Invalid use of default parameter
08001	Client unable to establish connection
08002	Connection name in use
08003	Connection does not exist
08004	Server rejected the connection
08007	Connection failure during transaction
08S01	Communication link failure
21S01	Insert value list does not match column list
21S02	Degree of derived table does not match column list

SQLSTATE	*Error*
22001	String data, right truncated
22002	Indicator variable required but not supplied
22003	Numeric value out of range
22007	Invalid datetime format
22008	Datetime field overflow
22012	Division by zero
22015	Interval field overflow
22018	Invalid character value for cast specification
22019	Invalid escape character
22025	Invalid escape sequence
22026	String data, length mismatch
23000	Integrity constraint violation
24000	Invalid cursor state
25000	Invalid transaction state
25S01	Transaction state
25S02	Transaction is still active
25S03	Transaction is rolled back
28000	Invalid authorization specification
34000	Invalid cursor name
3C000	Duplicate cursor name
3D000	Invalid catalog name
3F000	Invalid schema name
40001	Serialization failure
40003	Statement completion unknown
42000	Syntax error or access violation
42S01	Base table or view already exists
42S02	Base table or view not found
42S11	Index already exists
42S12	Index not found
42S21	Column already exists
42S22	Column not found

continues

SQLSTATE	*Error*
44000	WITH CHECK OPTION violation
HY000	General error
HY001	Memory allocation error
HY003	Invalid application buffer type
HY004	Invalid SQL datatype
HY007	Associated statement is not prepared
HY008	Operation canceled
HY009	Invalid use of null pointer
HY010	Function sequence error
HY011	Attribute cannot be set now
HY012	Invalid transaction operation code
HY013	Memory management error
HY014	Limit on the number of handles exceeded
HY015	No cursor name available
HY016	Cannot modify an implementation row descriptor
HY017	Invalid use of an automatically allocated descriptor handle
HY018	Server declined cancel request
HY019	Non-character and non-binary data sent in pieces
HY020	Attempt to concatenate a null value
HY021	Inconsistent descriptor information
HY024	Invalid attribute value
HY090	Invalid string or buffer length
HY091	Invalid descriptor field identifier
HY092	Invalid attribute/option identifier
HY093	Invalid parameter number
HY095	Function type out of range
HY096	Invalid information type
HY097	Column type out of range
HY098	Scope type out of range
HY099	Nullable type out of range

SQLSTATE	*Error*
HY100	Uniqueness option type out of range
HY101	Accuracy option type out of range
HY103	Invalid retrieval code
HY104	Invalid precision or scale value
HY105	Invalid parameter type
HY106	Fetch type out of range
HY107	Row value out of range
HY109	Invalid cursor position
HY110	Invalid driver completion
HY111	Invalid bookmark value
HYC00	Optional feature not implemented
HYT00	Timeout expired
HYT01	Connection timeout expired
IM001	Driver does not support this function
IM002	Data source name not found and no default driver specified
IM003	Specified driver could not be loaded
IM004	Driver's `SQLAllocHandle` on `SQL_HANDLE_ENV` failed
IM005	Driver's `SQLAllocHandle` on `SQL_HANDLE_DBC` failed
IM006	Driver's `SQLSetConnectAttr` failed
IM007	No data source or driver specified; dialog prohibited
IM008	Dialog failed
IM009	Unable to load translation DLL
IM010	Data source name too long
IM011	Driver name too long
IM012	`DRIVER` keyword syntax error
IM013	Trace file error
IM014	Invalid name of File DSN
IM015	Corrupt file data source

MAPI Errors

Error Constant	*Error*	*Description*
`mapSuccessSuccess`	32000	Action returned successfully.
`mapUserAbort`	32001	The current action was not completed because the user canceled the process.
`mapFailure`	32002	An unspecified error occurred during the current action. For example, the action was unable to delete or address mail correctly.
`mapLoginFail`	32003	Login has failed. There was no default logon, and the user failed to log on correctly.
`mapDiskFull`	32004	The disk is full. The current action could not create a disk file.
`mapInsufficientMem`	32005	There is insufficient memory to proceed with the current action.
`mapAccessDenied`	32006	Access denied.
`mapGeneralFailure`	32007	General failure. This is an unspecified error.
`mapTooManySessions`	32008	The user has too many sessions open at once.
`mapTooManyFiles`	32009	Too many file attachments are contained in the message. The mail wasn't sent or read.
`mapTooManyRecipients`	32010	There are too many message recipients specified. Mail wasn't sent or read.
`mapAttachmentNotFound`	32011	The specified attachment wasn't found, and mail wasn't sent.
`mapAttachmentOpenFailure`	32012	The attachment couldn't be located. Mail wasn't sent. Verify that the `AttachmentPathName` property is valid.
`mapAttachmentWriteFailure`	32013	An attachment could not be written to a temporary file. Check directory permissions.
`mapUnknownRecipient`	32014	The recipient doesn't appear in the address list. Mail wasn't sent.
`mapBadRecipType`	32015	The type of recipient was incorrect. Valid type values are 1 (primary recipient), 2 (copy recipient), and 3 (blind copy recipient).

Error Constant	*Error*	*Description*
`mapNoMessages`	32016	Unable to find the next message.
`mapInvalidMessage`	32017	An invalid message ID was used. The current action was not completed.
`mapTextTooLarge`	32018	The text in the message was too large to send, and the mail wasn't sent. Text is limited to 32KB.
`mapInvalidSession`	32019	An invalid session ID was used. To associate the MAPI messages control with a valid messaging session, set the `SessionID` property to the MAPI session control's `SessionID`.
`mapTypeNotSupported`	32020	Type not supported
`mapAmbiguousRecipient`	32021	One or more recipient addresses are invalid. Make sure the addresses for the `RecipAddress` property are valid.
`mapMessageInUse`	32022	Message in use.
`mapNetworkFailure`	32023	Network failure.
`mapInvalidEditFields`	32024	The value of the `AddressEditFieldCount` property is invalid. Valid values are from 0 to 4.
`mapInvalidRecips`	32025	One or more recipient addresses are invalid. Make sure the addresses for the `RecipAddress` property are valid.
`mapNotSupported`	32026	The current action is not supported by the underlying mail system.
`mapSessionExist`	32050	The MAPI messages control is already using a valid session ID.
`mapInvalidBuffer`	32051	Property is read only when not using Compose Buffer. Set `MsgIndex` equal to 1.
`mapInvalidReadBufferAction`	32052	Action only valid for Compose Buffer. Set `MsgIndex` equal to 1.
`mapNoSession`	32053	The MAPI messages control does not have a valid session handle from the MAPI session control.

continues

Error Constant	*Error*	*Description*
`mapInvalidRecipient`	32054	No originator in the Compose Buffer. You cannot see message originator information while in the Compose Buffer (`MsgIndex` set to 1).
`mapInvalidComposeBufferAction`	32055	Action not valid for Compose Buffer. The attempted action is not valid in the Compose Buffer (`MsgIndex` set to 1).
`mapControlFailure`	32056	Cannot perform action, no messages in list.
`mapNoRecipients`	32057	Cannot perform action, no recipients.
`mapNoAttachment`	32058	Cannot perform action, no attachments.

Tab Strip, Toolbar, Status Bar, Progress Bar, Tree View, List View, Image List, and Slider Errors

Error Constant	*Error*	*Description*
`ccInvalidProcedureCall`	5	Invalid procedure call.
`ccOutofMemory`	7	Out of memory.
`ccTypeMismatch`	13	Type mismatch.
`ccInvalidPropertyValue`	380	Invalid property value.
`ccSetNotSupportedAtRuntime`	382	Property cannot be set at runtime.
`ccSetNotSupported`	383	Property is read-only.
`ccSetNotPermitted`	387	Property can't be set on this control.
`ccGetNotSupported`	394	Property is write-only.
`ccInvalidClipboardFormat`	460	Invalid Clipboard format.
`ccInvalidObjectUse`	425	Invalid object use.
`ccDataObjectLocked`	672	DataObject formats list may not be cleared or expanded outside of the `OLEStartDrag` event.

Error Constant	*Error*	*Description*
`ccExpectedAnArgument`	673	Expected at least one argument.
`ccRecursiveOleDrag`	674	Illegal recursive invocation of OLE drag and drop.
`ccIndexOutOfBounds`	35600	Index out of bounds.
`ccElemNotFound`	35601	Element not found.
`ccNonUniqueKey`	35602	Key is not unique in collection.
`ccInvalidKey`	35603	Invalid key.
`ccCol1MustBeLeftAligned`	35604	When the `ListView` control's `View` property is set to `3` (Report), the left column (column 1) can only be left aligned. Any attempt to set the alignment to another value will result in this error.
`ccElemNotPartOfCollection`	35605	This item's control has been deleted.
`ccCollectionChangedDuringEnum`	35606	Control's collection has been modified.
`ccMissingRequiredArg`	35607	The required argument is missing.
`ccBadObjectReference`	35610	Invalid object.
`ccReadOnlyIfHasImages`	35611	Property is read-only if image list contains images.
`ccImageListMustBeInitialized`	35613	Image list must be initialized before it can be used.
`ccWouldIntroduceCycle`	35614	This would introduce a cycle.
`ccNotSameSize`	35615	All images in list must be same size.
`ccMaxPanelsExceeded`	35616	Maximum panels exceeded.
`ccImageListLocked`	35617	Image list cannot be modified while another control is bound to it.
`ccMaxButtonsExceeded`	35619	Maximum buttons exceeded.
`ccCircularReference`	35700	Circular object referencing is not allowed.

UpDown and Animation Controls

Error Constant	*Error*	*Description*
`cc2InvalidProcedureCall`	5	Invalid procedure call
`cc2BadFileNameOrNumber`	52	Bad filename or number
`cc2FileNotFound`	53	File not found
`cc2InvalidPropertyValue`	380	Invalid property value
`cc2SetNotSupportedAtRuntime`	382	Property cannot be set at runtime
`cc2SetNotSupported`	383	Property is read-only
`cc2InvalidObjectUse`	425	Invalid object use
`cc2InvalidClipboardFormat`	460	Invalid Clipboard format
`cc2DataObjectLocked`	672	DataObject formats list may not be cleared or expanded outside of the `OLEStartDrag` event
`cc2ExpectedAnArgument`	673	Expected at least one argument
`cc2InconsistentObject`	35750	Internal state of the control has become corrupted
`cc2ErrorDuringSet`	35751	Unable to set property
`cc2ErrorOpeningVideo`	35752	Unable to open AVI file
`cc2ErrorPlayingVideo`	35753	Unable to play AVI file
`cc2NoValidBuddyCtl`	35754	`BuddyControl` property must be set first
`cc2VideoNotOpen`	35755	Must open AVI file first
`cc2AutoBuddyNotSet`	35756	`AutoBuddy` not set, no potential buddy controls found
`cc2ErrorStoppingVideo`	35757	Error trying to stop playing video file
`cc2ErrorClosingVideo`	35758	Error closing open video file
`cc2CantStopAutoPlay`	35759	Stop method does not affect `AutoPlay` property
`cc2BuddyNotASibling`	35760	`BuddyControl` must be a separate control within the same container
`cc2NoUpDownAsBuddy`	35761	An `UpDown` control cannot be buddied with another `UpDown` control

Rich Text Box Control

Error Constant	*Error*	*Description*
`rtfInvalidProcedureCall`	5	Invalid procedure call
`rtfOutOfMemory`	7	Out of memory
`rtfPathFileAccessError`	75	The specified path/filename cannot be accessed or is invalid
`rtfInvalidFileFormat`	321	Invalid file format
`rtfInvalidPropertyValue`	380	Invalid property value
`rtfInvalidPropertyArrayIndex`	381	Invalid property array index
`rtfSetNotSupported`	383	Property is read-only
`rtfSetNotPermitted`	387	Property cannot be set
`rtfGetNotSupported`	394	Property is write-only
`rtfInvalidObjectUse`	425	Invalid object use
`rtfDataObjectLocked`	672	DataObject formats list may not be cleared or expanded outside of the `OLEStartDrag` event
`rtfExpectedAnArgument`	673	Expected at least one argument
`rtfInvalidCharPosition`	32000	Invalid character position
`rtfInvalidHdc`	32001	Invalid HDC
`rtfCannotLoadFile`	32002	Unable to load specified file
`rtfInvalidKeyName`	32005	Invalid or missing key name
`rtfInvalidClassName`	32006	Invalid or missing OLE class name
`rtfKeyNotFound`	32007	Key does not exist
`rtfOLESourceRquired`	32008	Required source document or class name is missing
`rtfNonUniqueKey`	32009	Key is not unique in collection
`rtfInvalidObject`	32010	Invalid object
`rtfProtected`	32011	The operation cannot be performed on protected text
`rtfOleCreate`	32012	Unable to create object
`rtfOleServer`	32013	Unable to start server application

I

Index

Symbols

A

E

I

J-K

L

M

N

Q

R

S

V

X-Y-Z

Visual Basic for Applications Unleashed

—Paul McFedries

Combining both power and ease of use, Visual Basic for Applications (VBA) is the common language for developing macros and applications across all Microsoft Office components. Using the format of the best-selling *Unleashed* series, users will master the intricacies of this popular language and exploit the full power of VBA. The book covers user interface design, database programming, network programming, Internet programming, and stand-alone application creation.

The CD-ROM is packed with the author's sample code, sample spreadsheets, databases, projects, templates, utilities, and evaluation copies of third-party tools and applications.

Price: $49.99 USA/$70.95 CDN *User Level: Accomplished–Expert*
ISBN: 0-672-31046-5 *800 pages*

VBScript Unleashed

—Brian Johnson

In *VBScript Unleashed*, Web programming techniques are presented in a logical and easy-to-follow sequence that helps readers understand the principles involved in developing programs. The reader begins by learning the basics and writing a first program and then builds on that to add interactivity, multimedia, and more to Web page designs. This book gives the reader a thorough understanding of the VBScript language and teaches communication across the Internet, safety, security, CGI, and more.

Price: $39.99 USA/$56.95 CDN *User Level: Casual–Accomplished–Expert*
ISBN: 1-57521-124-6 *650 pages*

Sams' Teach Yourself Database Programming with Visual Basic 5 in 21 Days, Second Edition

—Michael Amundsen and Curtis Smith

Programmers use Visual Basic, the 32-bit programming language from Microsoft, to create Windows and Windows 95 applications. It can also be used to program applications for the Web. This book shows you how to design, develop, and deploy Visual Basic applications for the World Wide Web. Written by a Microsoft-certified Visual Basic professional, the lessons are presented in a daily format, with each week focusing on a different area of database development.

Price: $45.00 USA/$63.95 CAN *User Level: New–Casual–Accomplished*
ISBN: 0-672-31018-X *1,000 pages*

World Wide Web Database Developer's Guide with Visual Basic 5

—Mark Swank, Drew Kittel and Mark Spenik

Written by developers for developers, this advanced guide shows users how to design, develop, and deploy secure client/server databases on the Internet and intranet Web sites using the latest version of Microsoft Visual Basic. It includes real-world examples and applications throughout the book for users to implement on their sites.

Price: $59.99 USA/$83.95 CAN *User Level: Accomplished–Expert*
ISBN: 1-57521-276-5 *900 pages*

Book ISBN 0-672-31048-1

Installation Instructions

Windows 95/NT 4

1. Insert the CD-ROM into your CD-ROM drive.
2. From the Windows desktop, double-click the My Computer icon.
3. Double-click the icon representing your CD-ROM drive.
4. Double-click the icon titled SETUP.EXE to run the installation program.
5. Installation creates a program group with the book's title as the group name. This group will contain icons to browse the CD-ROM.

Note that if Windows 95/NT 4.0 is installed on your computer and you have the AutoPlay feature enabled, the SETUP.EXE program starts automatically whenever you insert the disc into your CD-ROM drive.

System Requirements

The CD-ROM contains the Microsoft Visual Basic Control Creation Edition. Some of the features of Visual Basic 5 discussed in this book might not be possible with the use of the Control Creation Edition. The Control Creation Edition is provided to enable you to become familiar with the Visual Basic environment and to create your own ActiveX controls.

The following are the minimum system requirements for the Visual Basic Control Creation Edition:

- A personal computer with a 486 or higher processor.
- Microsoft Windows 95 or Windows NT Workstation 4.0 or later.
- 8MB of memory (12MB recommended) if you are running Windows NT Workstation.
- Hard-disk space:

  Typical installation: 20MB

  Minimum installation: 14MB

  CD-ROM installation (tools run from the CD-ROM): 14MB
- A CD-ROM drive.
- VGA or higher resolution monitor (SVGA recommended).

LIMITED WARRANTY

NO WARRANTIES. Microsoft expressly disclaims any warranty for the SOFTWARE PRODUCT. The SOFTWARE PRODUCT and any related documentation is provided "as is" without warranty of any kind, either express or implied, including, without limitation, the implied warranties or merchantability, fitness for a particular purpose, or noninfringement. The entire risk arising out of use or performance of the SOFTWARE PRODUCT remains with you.

NO LIABILITY FOR DAMAGES. In no event shall Microsoft or its suppliers be liable for any damages whatsoever (including, without limitation, damages for loss of business profits, business interruption, loss of business information, or any other pecuniary loss) arising out of the use of or inability to use this Microsoft product, even if Microsoft has been advised of the possibility of such damages. Because some states/jurisdictions do not allow the exclusion or limitation of liability for consequential or incidental damages, the above limitation may not apply to you.

install the SOFTWARE PRODUCT on a single computer provided you keep the original solely for backup or archival purposes. You may not copy the printed materials accompanying the SOFTWARE PRODUCT.

5. **DUAL-MEDIA SOFTWARE.** You may receive the SOFTWARE PRODUCT in more than one medium. Regardless of the type or size of medium you receive, you may use only one medium that is appropriate for your single computer. You may not use or install the other medium on another computer. You may not loan, rent, lease, or otherwise transfer the other medium to another user, except as part of the permanent transfer (as provided above) of the SOFTWARE PRODUCT.
6. **U.S. GOVERNMENT RESTRICTED RIGHTS.** The SOFTWARE PRODUCT and documentation are provided with RESTRICTED RIGHTS. Use, duplication, or disclosure by the Government is subject to restrictions as set forth in subparagraph (c)(1)(ii) of the Rights in Technical Data and Computer Software clause at DFARS 252.227-7013 or subparagraphs (c)(1) and (2) of the Commercial Computer Software—Restricted Rights at 48 CFR 52.227-19, as applicable. Manufacturer is Microsoft Corporation, One Microsoft Way, Redmond, WA 98052-6399.
7. **EXPORT RESTRICTIONS.** You agree that neither you nor your customers intend to or will, directly or indirectly, export or transmit (i) the SOFTWARE or related documentation and technical data or (ii) your software product as described in Section 1(b) of this License (or any part thereof), or process, or service that is the direct product of the SOFTWARE, to any country to which such export or transmission is restricted by any applicable U.S. regulation or statute, without the prior written consent, if required, of the Bureau of Export Administration of the U.S. Department of Commerce, or such other governmental entity as may have jurisdiction over such export or transmission.

MISCELLANEOUS

If you acquired this product in the United States, this EULA is governed by the laws of the State of Washington.

If you acquired this product in Canada, this EULA is governed by the laws of the Province of Ontario, Canada. Each of the parties hereto irrevocably attorns to the jurisdiction of the courts of the Province of Ontario and further agrees to commence any litigation which may arise hereunder in the courts located in the Judicial District of York, Province of Ontario.

If this product was acquired outside the United States, then local law may apply.

Should you have any questions concerning this EULA, or if you desire to contact Microsoft for any reason, please contact the Microsoft subsidiary serving your country, or write: Microsoft Sales Information Center, One Microsoft Way, Redmond, WA 98052-6399.

c. Separation of Components. The SOFTWARE PRODUCT is licensed as a single product. Its component parts may not be separated for use by more than one user.

d. Rental. You may not rent, lease, or lend the SOFTWARE PRODUCT.

e. Support Services. Microsoft may provide you with support services related to the SOFTWARE PRODUCT ("Support Services"). Use of Support Services is governed by the Microsoft policies and programs described in the user manual, in "online" documentation, and/or in other Microsoft-provided materials. Any supplemental software code provided to you as part of the Support Services shall be considered part of the SOFTWARE PRODUCT and subject to the terms and conditions of this EULA. With respect to technical information you provide to Microsoft as part of the Support Services, Microsoft may use such information for its business purposes, including for product support and development. Microsoft will not utilize such technical information in a form that personally identifies you.

f. Software Transfer. You may permanently transfer all of your rights under this EULA, provided you retain no copies, you transfer all of the SOFTWARE PRODUCT (including all component parts, the media and printed materials, any upgrades, this EULA, and, if applicable, the Certificate of Authenticity), **and** the recipient agrees to the terms of this EULA. If the SOFTWARE PRODUCT is an upgrade, any transfer must include all prior versions of the SOFTWARE PRODUCT.

g. Termination. Without prejudice to any other rights, Microsoft may terminate this EULA if you fail to comply with the terms and conditions of this EULA. In such event, you must destroy all copies of the SOFTWARE PRODUCT and all of its component parts.

3. **UPGRADES.** If the SOFTWARE PRODUCT is labeled as an upgrade, you must be properly licensed to use a product identified by Microsoft as being eligible for the upgrade in order to use the SOFTWARE PRODUCT. A SOFTWARE PRODUCT labeled as an upgrade replaces and/or supplements the product that formed the basis for your eligibility for the upgrade. You may use the resulting upgraded product only in accordance with the terms of this EULA. If the SOFTWARE PRODUCT is an upgrade of a component of a package of software programs that you licensed as a single product, the SOFTWARE PRODUCT may be used and transferred only as part of that single product package and may not be separated for use on more than one computer.

4. **COPYRIGHT.** All title and copyrights in and to the SOFTWARE PRODUCT (including but not limited to any images, photographs, animations, video, audio, music, text, and "applets" incorporated into the SOFTWARE PRODUCT), the accompanying printed materials, and any copies of the SOFTWARE PRODUCT are owned by Microsoft or its suppliers. The SOFTWARE PRODUCT is protected by copyright laws and international treaty provisions. Therefore, you must treat the SOFTWARE PRODUCT like any other copyrighted material except that you may

c. Redistributable Components.

(i) Sample Code. In addition to the rights granted in Section 1, Microsoft grants you the right to use and modify the source code version of those portions of the SOFTWARE designated as "Sample Code" ("SAMPLE CODE") for the sole purposes of designing, developing, and testing your software product(s), and to reproduce and distribute the SAMPLE CODE, along with any modifications thereof, only in object code form provided that you comply with Section c(iii), below.

(ii) Redistributable Components. In addition to the rights granted in Section 1, Microsoft grants you a nonexclusive royalty-free right to reproduce and distribute the object code version of any portion of the SOFTWARE listed in the SOFTWARE file `REDIST.TXT` ("REDISTRIBUTABLE SOFTWARE"), provided you comply with Section c(iii), below.

(iii) Redistribution Requirements. If you redistribute the SAMPLE CODE or REDISTRIBUTABLE SOFTWARE (collectively, "REDISTRIBUTABLES"), you agree to: (A) distribute the REDISTRIBUTABLES in object code only in conjunction with and as a part of a software application product developed by you that adds significant and primary functionality to the SOFTWARE and that is developed to operate on the Windows or Windows NT environment ("Application"); (B) not use Microsoft's name, logo, or trademarks to market your software application product; (C) include a valid copyright notice on your software product; (D) indemnify, hold harmless, and defend Microsoft from and against any claims or lawsuits, including attorney's fees, that arise or result from the use or distribution of your software application product; (E) not permit further distribution of the REDISTRIBUTABLES by your end user. The following **exceptions** apply to subsection (iii)(E), above: (1) you may permit further redistribution of the REDISTRIBUTABLES by your distributors to your end-user customers if your distributors only distribute the REDISTRIBUTABLES in conjunction with, and as part of, your Application and you and your distributors comply with all other terms of this EULA; and (2) you may permit your end users to reproduce and distribute the object code version of the files designated by ".ocx" file extensions ("Controls") only in conjunction with and as a part of an Application and/or Web page that adds significant and primary functionality to the Controls, and such end user complies with all other terms of this EULA.

2. **DESCRIPTION OF OTHER RIGHTS AND LIMITATIONS.**

   a. Not for Resale Software. If the SOFTWARE PRODUCT is labeled "Not for Resale" or "NFR," then, notwithstanding other sections of this EULA, you may not resell, or otherwise transfer for value, the SOFTWARE PRODUCT.

   b. Limitations on Reverse Engineering, Decompilation, and Disassembly. You may not reverse engineer, decompile, or disassemble the SOFTWARE PRODUCT, except and only to the extent that such activity is expressly permitted by applicable law notwithstanding this limitation.

END-USER LICENSE AGREEMENT FOR MICROSOFT SOFTWARE

Microsoft Visual Basic, Control Creation Edition

IMPORTANT—READ CAREFULLY: This Microsoft End-User License Agreement ("EULA") is a legal agreement between you (either an individual or a single entity) and Microsoft Corporation for the Microsoft software product identified above, which includes computer software and may include associated media, printed materials, and "online" or electronic documentation ("SOFTWARE PRODUCT"). By installing, copying, or otherwise using the SOFTWARE PRODUCT, you agree to be bound by the terms of this EULA. If you do not agree to the terms of this EULA, do not install or use the SOFTWARE PRODUCT; you may, however, return it to your place of purchase for a full refund.

SOFTWARE PRODUCT LICENSE

The SOFTWARE PRODUCT is protected by copyright laws and international copyright treaties, as well as other intellectual property laws and treaties. The SOFTWARE PRODUCT is licensed, not sold.

1. **GRANT OF LICENSE.** This EULA grants you the following rights:

   a. Software Product. Microsoft grants to you as an individual, a personal, nonexclusive license to make and use copies of the SOFTWARE for the sole purposes of designing, developing, and testing your software product(s) that is designed to operate in conjunction with any Microsoft operating system product. You may install copies of the SOFTWARE on an unlimited number of computers provided that you are the only individual using the SOFTWARE. If you are an entity, Microsoft grants you the right to designate one individual within your organization to have the right to use the SOFTWARE in the manner provided above.

   b. Electronic Documents. Solely with respect to electronic documents included with the SOFTWARE, you may make an unlimited number of copies (either in hardcopy or electronic form), provided that such copies shall be used only for internal purposes and are not republished or distributed to any third party.